INSIDE
TEXAS POLITICS

INSIDE
TEXAS POLITICS

POWER, POLICY, AND PERSONALITY
OF THE LONE STAR STATE

Brandon Rottinghaus

University of Houston

NEW YORK OXFORD
OXFORD UNIVERSITY PRESS

Oxford University Press is a department of the University of Oxford. It furthers the University's objective of excellence in research, scholarship, and education by publishing worldwide. Oxford is a registered trade mark of Oxford University Press in the UK and certain other countries.

Published in the United States of America by Oxford University Press
198 Madison Avenue, New York, NY 10016, United States of America.

© [2018] by Oxford University Press

For titles covered by Section 112 of the US Higher Education Opportunity Act, please visit www.oup.com/us/he for the latest information about pricing and alternate formats.

Library of Congress Cataloging-in-Publication Data

CIP data is on file at the Library of Congress
9780190299514

9 8 7 6 5 4 3 2 1
Printed by LSC Kendallville

To Tracy, this one is for you.

BRIEF CONTENTS

CONTENTS

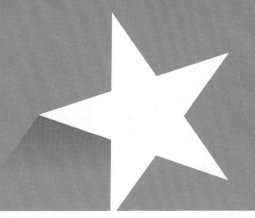

Chapter 3   Federalism   66

Chapter 4   Voting and Elections   96

Chapter 5	Political Parties: Texas in Blue and Red 132

Chapter 8	Governors of Texas 232

Chapter 9	The Plural Executive and the Bureaucracy 266

Chapter 10   The Texas Judiciary   302

Chapter 13   Budget, Finances, and Policy   402

ABOUT THE AUTHOR

BRANDON ROTTINGHAUS is a Professor of Political Science at the University of Houston. He is a Dallas native who has published research and taught American and Texas government for more than 15 years, but has also worked in Texas politics at every level. Dr. Rottinghaus regularly provides commentary on national and Texas politics in hundreds of media outlets.

His research interests include Texas politics, executive and legislative politics, and research methods. His work on these subjects has appeared in dozens of academic journals and multiple edited volumes. He is also the author of three other books: *The Provisional Pulpit: Modern Conditional Presidential Leadership of Public Opinion* (Texas A&M University Press, 2010), *The Institutional Effects of Executive Scandal* (Cambridge University Press, 2015), and *The Dual Executive: Unilateral Orders in Separated and Shared Powers System* (Stanford University Press, 2017).

The author frequently partners with *Houston Public Media* (Houston's PBS) to produce relevant and topical coverage of public affairs, and is a regular guest on *Houston Matters*, the station's daily news discussion program. Dr. Rottinghaus also co-hosts *Political Perspectives*, a digital series on current events, and a podcast on national and state politics. He is also the creator and weekly contributor to *Monday Morning Politics* on Houston's Fox 26 that reviews the political events of the past week and previews the week to come.

His commentary on national and Texas politics has also appeared in the *Texas Tribune*, the *Houston Chronicle*, the *Dallas Morning News*, the *Austin-American Statesman*, the *Corpus Christi Caller*, the *Lubbock Avalanche Journal*, the *McAllen Monitor*, the *San Antonio Express-News*, the *El Paso Times*, CNN, The Texas Standard, National Public Radio, the *Guardian,* the *Washington Post*, and the *New York Times*.

PREFACE

THE LATE MOLLY IVINS once wrote, "Good thing we've got politics in Texas—finest form of free entertainment ever invented." Or, as she put it later in her career, "If Texas were a sane place, it wouldn't be nearly as much fun."

The characters in Texas politics are among the most interesting and influential in all levels of government. Three of the last nine presidents hailed from Texas. Incensed by a federal ban on Mirax, a Texas exterminator became US House majority leader, determined to exact revenge on the Environmental Protection Agency. State officials frequently come to blows over education, taxation, and smaller issues like whether teachers should be allowed to shoot students on school buses in self-defense. The state legislature tries to ban cities from offering sanctuary to undocumented immigrants while cities go to battle against state agencies that plan to store nuclear waste in their backyards.

Teaching Texas government and politics is exciting because the history of the state is rich with these stories of political struggles, and speculation about the future of Texas politics provides for intriguing learning opportunities.

THEME

True to the title—*Inside Texas Politics*—the book takes a unique tactic to describing and analyzing Texas politics from an insider's perspective. I wrote the text to make the material on Texas government and politics accessible and memorable for today's students, and to provide an insider's perspective on how power struggles have shaped Texas institutions and political processes. My goal is to bring Texas government to life by recounting how colorful characters and Texans from all walks of life have both influenced and been influenced by the governing process. The chapters are rich with historical accounts, engaging recent examples, and relevant (but accessible) statistical data.

The Texas Higher Education Coordinating Board (THECB) requirements have recently added additional fundamental component areas for social and personal responsibility, where students are asked to understand knowledge of civic responsibility, community engagement, and connecting actions and consequences to ethical decision making. The theme and data presentation developed in this text lends itself well to executing and assessing these requirements. Marginal questions query students to consider concepts from a social and personal responsibility perspective. Questions below every figure and table ask students to practice analyzing the data, to think critically about it, to evaluate trends, and to communicate them.

This book exploits use of original data (collected for this project by the author) and institutional data (from official government sources) to provide a whole picture of government and politics in Texas. Data literacy is a major component of how material is presented and students will be able to build skills to serve as a foundation for future learning.

FEATURES

The book is rich in features that draw students in and explore the important features and events from Texas politics from an insider's perspective. Opening vignettes explore a particular political struggle and how Texans shape and are shaped by government. A concluding section of each chapter, "The Insider View," provides a summary of the chapter's theme, emphasizing how the institutions and processes discussed in the chapter are evolving. In addition, each chapter has four boxed features.

Insider Interviews. Following the theme of an inside look at politics in Texas, each chapter has an "Insider Interview" with an individual who is a practitioner in the subject of the chapter. For example, in Chapter 8 former Texas governor Mark White discusses the challenges he faced as governor and his insights on the office.

Great Texas Political Debates. These features tell the story behind a current event or issue, such as texting-while-driving legislation and the 2014 lawsuit against Governor Perry. These features are organized around concepts, such as political culture and the formal powers of the Texas governor. After reading the context, students assess two or more perspectives.

Is it Bigger in Texas? Each chapter contains at least one "Is it Bigger in Texas?" boxed features that compares Texas with other states in the union. Like the figures and tables, each feature presents a question related to THECB goals and provides bulleted observations for students to consider.

Angles of Power. This feature investigates political and personal interactions between the politics or personality of individuals and groups and how this shapes state politics or policy. The feature then asks students to explain or analyze the situation.

ENSURING STUDENT SUCCESS

Oxford University Press offers instructors and students a comprehensive ancillary package for qualified adopters of *Inside Texas Politics*.

Ancillary Resource Center (ARC): This convenient, instructor-focused website provides access to all of the up-to-date teaching resources for this text while guaranteeing the security of grade-significant resources. In addition, it allows Oxford University Press to keep instructors informed when new content becomes available. Register for access and create your individual user account by visiting **www.oup.com/us/Rottinghaus**.

The following items are available on the ARC:

- **Instructor's Manual and Test Bank:** includes chapter objectives, detailed chapter outlines, lecture suggestions and activities, discussion questions, and video and Web resources. The test bank includes multiple-choice, short answer, and essay questions.

- **Computerized Test Bank:** utilizes Diploma, a test authoring and management tool. Diploma is designed for both novice and advanced users and enables instructors to create and edit questions, compose randomized quizzes and test with an intuitive drag-and-drop tool, post quizzes and tests to online courses, and print quizzes and tests for paper-based assessments.

- **Downloadable and customizable PowerPoint slides:** including one set for in-class presentations and the other for text images

- **Access to fifteen CNN videos** correlated to the chapter topics of the text. Each clip is approximately five to ten minutes long, offering a great way to launch your lecture

Companion website at www.oup.com/us/Rottinghaus. This open access companion website includes a number of learning tools to help students study and review key concepts presented in the text including learning objectives, key-concept summaries, quizzes, essay questions, Web activities, and Web links.

Dashboard (www.oup.com/us/dashboard). Oxford University Press's nationally hosted learning management system. Designed to offer students and instructors maximum flexibility, numerous assessment options, a variety of interactive content organized by chapter, and adaptive learning tools, this learning management system offers best in class, cutting edge functionality.

- **Numerous Assessment Options:** Every chapter has many chapter-level tests to help your students learn—and not memorize—important concepts.

- **Available Anytime/Anywhere:** Everything is in one place, and is accessible from any device, anywhere students can get connected.

- **Interactive Content:** Students have access to fifteen CNN videos, as well as others, Interactive Graphics, and Key Terms Flashcards.

For more information about Dashboard, and ordering information, contact your Oxford University Press Representative or call 800.280.0280

Course Cartridges containing student and instructor resources are available through Angel, Blackboard, Canvas, D2L, Moodle, Respondus, or whatever course management system you prefer.

Format Choices. Oxford University Press offers cost-saving alternatives to meet the needs of all students. This text offered in a Loose Leaf format at a 30 percent discount off the list price of the text; and in an eBook format, through CourseSmart for a 50 percent discount. You can also customize our textbooks to create the course material you want for your class. For more information, please contact your Oxford University Press sales representative at 800.280.0280, or visit us online at www.oup.com/us/morone.

PACKAGING OPTIONS

Adopters of *Inside Texas Politics* can package *any* Oxford University Press book with the text for a 20 percent savings off the total package price. See our many trade and scholarly offerings at www.oup.com, then contact your local OUP sales representative to request a package ISBN.

ACKNOWLEDGMENTS

John Graves wrote in *Goodbye to a River*, "Mankind is one thing; a man's self is another. What that self is tangles itself knottily with what his people were, and what they came out of. Mine came out of Texas, as did I. If those were louts, they were my own louts." Writing a book is a self-reflective undertaking, but no book is written from one perspective alone.

Special thanks to friends and colleagues in politics and journalism who kindly shared insights or observations about Texas politics, each shaping the content or coverage here in subtle or major ways, including Rebecca Acuna, John Austin, Jordan Berry, Bobby Blanchard, Scott Braddock, Bobby Cervantes, Craig Cohen, Kiah Collier, Kevin Diaz, Rebecca Elliott, Peggy Fikac, Joe Holley, Jay Leeson, Katie Leslie, Enrique Rangel, Marty Schalden, Andrew Schneider, Patrick Svitek, Anna Tinsley, and Mike Ward.

Enormous thanks are due to those interviewed for the "Insider Interview" feature. Generous with their time and insightful in their comments, each was too modest to call himself or herself an "insider," but each has clearly left a mark on the state and indelibly on this book.

It is genuinely hard to imagine a better team to work with than Oxford University Press. Jen Carpenter, Executive Editor, was the architect of the project and encouraging from start to finish. Tony Mathias gave great advice on framing and big picture presentation. Naomi Friedman, Senior Development Editor, deserves her own section in the acknowledgements for all the time she took to bring this project to life. No one has helped to bring the ideas in my head to fruition like Naomi and she shares incomparably in whatever success this book finds. Research assistants Philip Waggoner, Leonardo Antenangeli, and Sarah Scott ably helped collect data for the book.

BJ and Benjamin, the two best top hands a dad could ask for, were patient longer than kids should be for this book to be finished. I'm looking forward to returning to our travels around the Lone Star State, deadline free. Finally, this book is dedicated to Tracy, whose heart is as big as Dallas and whose mind is as big as all Texas.

MANUSCRIPT REVIEWERS

We are greatly indebted to the many talented scholars and instructors who reviewed the manuscript of *Inside Texas Government*. Their insight and suggestions helped shape the work.

Kevin Bailey
Houston Community College

Michelle Belco
Houston University

Madelyn Bowman
Tarrant County College

Rachel Bzostek
Collin College

Philip Crosby
Central Texas College

Heidi Galito
Houston Community College

Mary M. Louis
Houston Community College

Michael McConachie
Collin College

Sharon Navarro
University of Texas at San Antonio

William Parent
San Jacinto College

Raymond Sandoval
Richland College

Tom Miles
University of North Texas

Maribel Santoyo
El Paso Community College

Lanny S. Lambert
North East Lakeview College

Patrizio Amezcua
San Jacinto College

Tiffany Cartwright
Collin College

Fiona Ross
Lone Star College–Montgomery

Mark A. Cichock
University of Texas at Arlington

John Carnes
Lone Star College–Kingwood

Gabriel Ume
Palo Alto College

Lisa Perez
Austin Community College

Lydia Andrade
University of Incarnate Word

Sara Price
Odessa College and Portland Community College

Drew Landry
South Plains College

Brian Bearry
University of Texas at Dallas

Sonia Iwanek
Collin College

Patrick Moore
Richland College

Corena White
Tarrant County College

Jennifer Danley-Scott
Texas Women's University

Jose Gutierrez
University of Texas at Arlington

1

THE STRUGGLE FOR TEXAS: DEMOGRAPHICS, CULTURE, AND POLITICAL POWER

Although government may seem like a remote concept, Texans don't even have to leave their homes to feel the life-changing consequences of government policies. In 2015 in Pecos, Texas, a pit bull attacked and killed an eighty-three-year-old man, Noberto Legardo, who was sitting outside in his daughter's backyard. Legardo was one of 232 Americans killed by pit bulls between 2005 and 2015—one death every seventeen days. A friend of Legardo, speaking to reporters, urged officials to do something about these attacks so that this never happens again.[1] In Texas, the state legislature has tried and failed to ban pit bulls. Some city governments have prohibited ownership of this breed—although not Pecos.

In 2016, most of the residents of Nordheim, Texas (population 316), descended on Austin, wearing yellow "Concerned About Pollution" t-shirts, to protest the state's decision to locate a 143-acre waste material facility in their community. Texas Railroad Commission experts had decided that the facility would not pollute the town's groundwater, but exasperated eighty-year-old resident Kermit Koehler told reporters, "that's what you call a little town getting sh&% on."[2]

Texas's energy industry employs tens of thousands of workers, some undocumented. Undocumented workers are more vulnerable to wage fraud, but when forty-one-year-old Guillermo Perez's boss told him that he didn't have the $1,200 to pay him, Perez took action: "I told him that I'm going to the Texas Workforce Commission, which I did. Then after that, he came back two weeks later and paid me."[3]

LEARNING OBJECTIVES

1.1 Describe the settlement history of Texas.

1.2 Assess the impact industries have made to the Texas economy from 1860 to today.

1.3 Analyze how the changing demographics of the state affect government.

1.4 Examine the source and impact of political culture in Texas.

● Historian T.R. Fehrenbach wrote that the Texas mystique was created by the "chemistry of the frontier in the crucible of history." Sam Houston put his affection for the Lone Star State more bluntly: "Texas is the finest portion of the globe that has ever blessed my vision."

The stories of Legardo, Perez, and the residents of Nordheim show us how ordinary Texans, as individuals and as groups, have reacted to and shaped Texas politics. Their values, visions, and goals, however, often clash, and so Texas public policies—and even the structure of our institutions and the way they operate—are often the outcome of conflict.

In this chapter, we explore the interactions among the communities of natives, settlers, and immigrants. We discover who wins—and who loses. We examine how the booms and busts in the Texas economy and the shifting demographics impact the politics of who gets what, when, and how. Finally, we examine political culture to see how Texans relate to government and politics. In doing so, we will witness the great battles that sculpted the face of Texas today.

THE ORIGINS OF TEXAS

1.1 Describe the settlement history of Texas.

Power in Texas politics is shaped by the people who have settled and inhabited the state. Immigration is not a new political issue in Texas. Conflicts over territory and resources have transformed Texas for millennia. So, it is to this topic that we turn first.

NATIVE AMERICANS

Native Americans occupied the lands of Texas more than 10,000 years before the arrival of Europeans in the early sixteenth century.[4] Tribes in North America competed for land, pushing each other into new territory and eventually settling in lands throughout Texas (see Figure 1.1). The Caddo and Apache Indians, descendants of the first people to walk into North America, arrived early on. The Caddo enjoyed a more sedentary life because the region they lived in had plentiful game and favorable conditions for growing crops. The settlements of Caddo Indians extended from the Trinity River to the Red River and as far east as Mississippi. The Apache, splintered by pressure from other tribes, pushed farther south and west into the area around Big Bend. Almost exclusively nomadic, they lived completely off the roaming buffalo. The Karankawa and Coahuiltecan people settled along the coast and the coastal prairies of South Texas beginning around the seventeenth century.[5]

Disease and conflict with the newly arriving Spanish and French settlers greatly diminished their numbers of Native Americans by the 1860s.

FIGURE 1.1   **Ethnolinguistic Distribution of Major Native American Tribes in Texas in 1776**

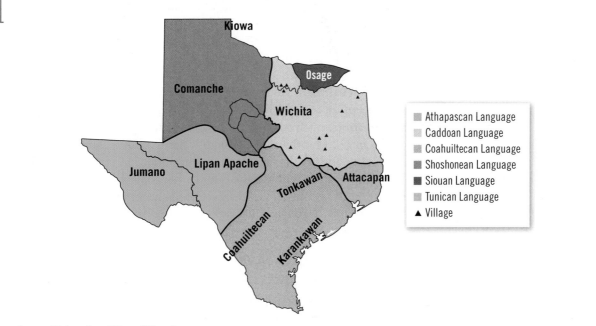

Source: University of Texas Libraries

 COMMUNICATION:

Where did the Native American tribes settle in Texas?

- The multiple tribes that settled Texas between 1500 and 1776 arrived in Texas from the northern plains states.
- The Comanche and Apache resided in the north and west. Tonkawa, Caddo, and Wichita settled in the northeast and east. Karankawa and Coahuiltecan resided along the coast.

 CRITICAL THINKING:

What factors explain the settlement pattern?

- Some tribes settled in locations that suited their methods of sustaining themselves. For instance, Comanche and Apache settled in drier areas where they hunted on horseback. The Karankawan Indians settled along the marshy coast and their food supply was primarily connected to coastal cuisine. The Caddo Indians farmed, living off staples such as corn and squash in East Texas.
- Intertribal conflict also assisted in settlement patterns. Pressure from Comanche Indians pushed the Apaches farther to the south and west.

The Comanche, Wichita, and Kiowa Indians migrated from the western United States on horseback in the eighteenth century, fleeing other warring groups and tracking bison herds.

The name *Texas* derives from a Spanish word that means "friendly" or "ally"—the term attributed to native populations by Spanish explorers. However, many native tribes resisted Spanish attempts to integrate them into Spanish missions and convert them to Christianity. The Caddo, for example, preferred to live in small clusters along fertile river valleys. They resented the unwillingness of the Spanish to supply them with firearms and the outrages committed by Spanish soldiers, including the molestation of Caddo women.[6]

Conflicts erupted when Anglos, white settlers from the United States, streamed into Texas. Sam Houston, nicknamed "Big Drunk" by the leaders of the Cherokee Indian tribe he lived with as a young man, tried to make peace and prevent Europeans from encroaching on Indian lands.[7] Houston negotiated a treaty in 1836 for the recognition of Cherokee land claims in exchange for a pledge of neutrality during the Texas revolution. In the early days of the Republic, however, President Mirabeau B. Lamar relocated Native Americans to reservations. Today only three reservations remain in Texas, home to the Alabama-Coushatta, Tigua, and Kickapoo.

SPANISH SETTLERS

Searching for treasure, the legendary Fountain of Youth, and the fabled land of warlike Amazon women, Spanish explorers pursued romantic dreams in America. In the 1530s and 1540s, Cabeza de Vaca, Francisco Vasquez de Coronado, and Luis de Moscoso Alvarado first penetrated coastal, North, and East Texas.[8] Over the next two centuries, the Spanish established missions and military outposts. The mission system in Texas operated as the political arm of "New Spain" that occupied what is now Mexico and southern Texas.[9] The expansion into Texas allowed for protection of the interior of New Spain against the French settlers in Louisiana. "Glory, God, and Gold" was the phrase that summarized the Spanish colonists' approach to settlement, who established more than fifty missions and presidios (garrisons to guard the missions) in the area between 1680 and 1740.

Burdened with rising debts from wars in Europe and South America and an economic downturn, Spain increased taxes and cut expenses in its colonies. Autocratic Spanish rule and resentment of rigid class distinctions and slavery prompted a revolutionary movement in New Spain. After a series of small revolts, New Spain—now known as United Mexican States or Mexico—won her independence in 1821.

Tejanos: Mexican Texans during the time of the Texas revolution

see for yourself 1.1

Explore how Tejano music, food, and culture have shaped the state.

TEJANOS

In 1821, most **Tejanos** (Mexican Texans) were more than happy to throw off the yoke of Spanish rule. Tejanos primarily worked in and around the ranching communities of the region that had sprung up near military outposts along the northern frontier of Mexico.[10] Tejanos occupied much of what is now South Texas. Like the Anglos who were immigrating to Texas during this time, Tejanos resisted centralized authority and embraced *ayuntamiento*, a form of local, self-government.

ANGLOS

After gaining independence, Mexico sought to use the land that made up Texas as a buffer from the natives to the north and as source of economic revenue, charging taxes on land. Rapid westward expansion of the land-hungry United States in the early 1800s also threatened Spanish control over Texas. By the 1820s, however, the Mexican government aggressively promoted Anglo settlement of Texas, as we will see in Chapter 2, to promote commerce, spread religion, and as a buffer against attacks by hostile Native Americans. Mexico inked deals with *empresarios*—individuals granted the right to help settle a new land and recruit new settlers—who orchestrated the settlement of American citizens in Texas. Some settlers were fugitives on the run or wandering adventurers, although most were subsistence farmers moving to Texas for cheap land and abundant space to support themselves and their families.

Anglo settlers, first coming from neighboring southern states in the 1830s and 1840s, often cut "Gone to Texas" (or "GTT" in haste) into wooden doors in their old homesteads. The phrase evoked hope for a better life that might be achieved through grit and toil. Today, the Texas flag has become a symbol of the rugged individualism these settlers brought with them.

Tejanos first viewed Anglo immigrants with hostility—as competitors for land and valuable resources. Friction between Anglo settlers and Tejanos erupted almost immediately. Cultured, Mexican aristocrats, like Martin DeLeon, were openly scornful of the Anglo riff-raff streaming in. Anglo empresarios, like Green DeWitt from Victoria, often turned a blind eye when Anglos in their settlements smuggled in contraband tobacco and guns, or stole livestock from Tejano ranchers. DeLeon traveled to Victoria swearing to "return with DeWitt's head."[11] Stephen F. Austin quietly intervened and averted armed conflict, but ethnic tensions remained.

Laws decreed in 1830 to stop further immigration into Texas (and declaring empresario contracts void) spurred Anglo illegal immigration. Rising tariff rates fanned the flames of rebellion, and eventually both Anglos and Tejanos demanded independence for Texas (which was then part of the Mexican state of Coahuila y Tejas). Following the Texas revolution, however, relations between Anglos and Tejanos soured as Anglos—now in the majority—seized land from Tejano ranchers. War heroes from the revolution and many of the original empresarios took the reins of power, leaving the Tejanos without direct representation in the newly formed Texas government.

AFRICAN AMERICANS

By 1823, Mexico had banned slavery, but beginning in 1829, Anglo settlers brought African American slaves with them under the guise of "contract labor." At the time of the revolution in 1836, about 5,000 African Americans resided in

Texas.[12] By 1847, after Texas gained her independence and subsequently joined the United States, the number had risen to 38,753. The expansion of agriculture as an economic force prompted many settlers to import or purchase slaves.

In the years before the Civil War, African Americans faced harsh slave codes that severely restricted their education, travel, public meetings, and possession of weapons. The Civil War and Reconstruction brought the promise of freedom that was soon snatched away with a series of "Black Codes" passed by the legislature and several cities that restricted access to public facilities and largely relegated African Americans to rural areas as agricultural laborers.

Economic crises following the Civil War did little to provide independence to emancipated slaves. Policies of land redistribution, often referred to as "forty acres and a mule," initially offered African Americans economic opportunity, but by the 1890s most African Americans worked as tenant farmers on former plantations. During this period, many African Americans moved from the state's rural areas to major urban areas, such as Dallas, Austin, Houston, and San Antonio. On the outskirts of cities, they established "freedmantowns" which became (and often continue to be) the heart of the African American community. City schools, public transportation, and other facilities remained segregated for over a century after the war.[13]

⭐ TEXAS TAKEAWAYS

1 Who settled Texas and why?

2 Why did the Texans rebel against Mexico?

🤠 CONTINUITY AND CHANGE IN THE TEXAS ECONOMY

1.2 Assess the impact various industries have made to the Texas economy from 1860 to today.

If Texas were an independent nation, its economy would be ranked twelfth in the world. Texas is home to six of the top fifty companies on the Fortune 500 list. Its 2015 gross state product (the sum of all goods and service produced in a state) topped $1.5 trillion, the second highest in the United States. Although natural resources and energy production are still a major economic resource, a balanced Texas economy has sustained stable growth for a decade. A diverse set of industries—including real estate, manufacturing, and technology—has contributed to Texas's economic success.

Until the 1980s, the Texas economy was heavily dependent on natural resources, especially oil and gas and agriculture. Many Texans got so rich so quickly in the oil boom of the 1980s that they were called the "Big Rich." "Better nouveau than never" was their rallying cry as they donned lynx fur coats and seventeen-carat diamonds to arrive at the grocery in white Rolls-Royces.[14] However, when the price of oil dropped 24 percent between 1981 and 1986, personal bankruptcies, large oil manufacturing layoffs, and bank foreclosures rippled through the teetering Texas economy.

Texas responded by promoting economic diversity. The Texas economy today relies on a mix of agriculture and ranching, oil and natural gas, military and defense, information technology, electric power, and manufacturing (see Figure 1.2). It is balanced so that souring in one sector of the economy, like a drastic drop in oil prices, will not topple the whole economy.

FOOD AND FIBER

In Antebellum Texas, three-quarters of all families drew their living from the state's plentiful farmland. Agriculture interests dominated the politics of the day. Settlers spread across Texas, planting new crops: corn in the east, sorghum in the west, wheat in the northern high plains, citrus in South Texas, and rice in coastal prairies. However, "King Cotton" was the most prominent crop. Slave owning planters produced 90 percent of all the cotton grown in the state. Since the early 1900s, Texas has been the leading cotton-producing state in the nation, and today Texas accounts for 25 percent of the entire US crop.[15]

Timber production, located in the dense forests of East Texas, also played a major role in the state's economy between 1880 and 1910. Lumber production peaked in 1907, following demand for Texas pine after depletions in the Midwest, when a record 2.1 billion board feet were logged.[16] As surplus stacked up in the 1920s, the prices fell dramatically, hurting many Texas farm families and putting the lumber industry on tenterhooks. The Great Depression sent timber prices tumbling. The industry didn't recover until World War II, as wartime demand forced prices higher and mechanization made farming more productive.

After World War II, large commercial farms eclipsed small family homesteads. The farm population dropped from 1.52 million to about 245,000 between 1945 and 1990.[17] Today, Texas leads the nation in the production of several agricultural staples, generates more than $100 billion annually, and ranks sixth overall in the value of agricultural exports.

FUEL

"It roared, I'm tellin' you, it roared. . ." exclaimed a Beaumont resident upon hearing a particularly massive oil gusher in Southeast Texas.[18] The discovery of a major oil deposit beneath the marshy soil at Spindletop Hill in Beaumont, Texas, in 1901 ushered in a new economic era and one that continues to drive the state's financial booms and busts, despite the state's more balanced economy. In the late 1910s and early 1920s, the industry served as the state's main source of tax revenue.[19] By 1940, Texas was the leading oil-producing state in the United States and central to the war effort.

FIGURE 1.2   **Booms in the Texas Economy**

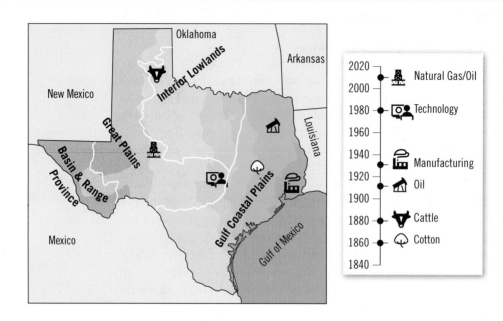

 COMMUNICATION:

What industries have spurred the Texas economy?

- Texas has had six major economic booms: cotton, beginning in the 1860s; cattle, beginning in about the 1880s; oil in the 1910s; manufacturing in the 1930s; high tech in the 1990s; and oil and natural gas from about 2005.

 CRITICAL THINKING:

Why have these industries grown?

- The state's abundant natural resources provide opportunity to meet national and international demand for these products.

- Hard work and luck are required to make these phases of the economy grow.

- Government matters, too: both by staying out of the way in some instances and offering incentives to invest in others.

The new industry also expanded state government. The discovery of the East Texas field by Columbus Marion "Dad" Joiner in 1930 near Kilgore prompted the then recently created Texas Railroad Commission to limit pumping and production. The commission continues to regulate the industry today.

Today Texas's energy industry is not just a leader in the state but in the world. Texas is currently home to several major energy companies—ConocoPhilips, Marathon Oil, ExxonMobil, Tesoro, Valero, Total, and Shell—as well as 5,000 other energy-related companies. Energy firms in the state also lead in alternative energy sources, including wind, solar, and biomass (animal and vegetable material converted to energy). Despite falling prices at the pump, oil and gas revenues accounted to 14 percent of all state revenue in 2015 (down from 28 percent in 1981).[20]

KING CATTLE (AND OTHER FOUR-LEGGED FRIENDS)

As the nation gained an appetite for Texas beef in the 1860s, Texas cowboys began driving their herds north to reach market hubs in Kansas and Colorado. Cattle ranches, both enormous and modest, sprung up all over Texas in the 1870s. Barbed wire, once called the "devil's hatband," brought controversy, bloodshed, and (ultimately) civilization to the harsh Texas frontier.[21] Cheap to produce and easy to string, the wire was used by ranchers to fence their property and the open range was gone. Barbed wire, a shift to corporate ownership tendencies (like paying ranch hands in wages instead of cattle), drought, and better access to rail lines by 1890 ended cattle drives but not the ranching industry in Texas. Although cattle no longer roam freely, today Texas leads the nation in the production of cattle, sheep, and goats, which generates cash receipts of more than $10 billion.[22]

MANUFACTURING

After World War II, Texas experienced rapid industrial growth, doubling the number of manufacturing facilities in the period from 1930 to 1947. Wartime industries ballooned throughout Texas: steel mills in Houston; tin smelting in Texas City; aircraft factories in Garland, Grand Prairie, and Fort Worth; shipyards along the coast; and revitalized paper and wood pulp in East Texas.[23] Manufacturing today amounts to approximately 15 percent of the state's gross domestic product and the number of manufacturing jobs in Texas ranks second only to California.[24]

MILITARY AND DEFENSE INDUSTRIES

Texas has been home to an active military presence since World War II when it served as the largest training ground in the world for soldiers and sailors.[25] Texas is currently home to fifteen military bases, with all branches of the armed services represented except the Marines and Coast Guard. These posts are spread across the state but concentrated in and around San Antonio (see Figure 1.3).

Defense contracting, a business that provides products or services to the military, is also a major part of the economy in the state, especially as a significant employer. Major corporations like Lockheed Martin, Boeing, KBR (formerly Kellogg Brown & Root, a Halliburton subsidiary), EDS and Perot Systems, and many others, furnish aircraft, weapons, and technical know-how to support the US military.

HIGH TECH

As early as the mid-nineteenth century, technology has sparked economic growth in Texas. H. Ross Perot left IBM in 1962 to form Electronic Data

FIGURE 1.3   **Texas Military Installations**

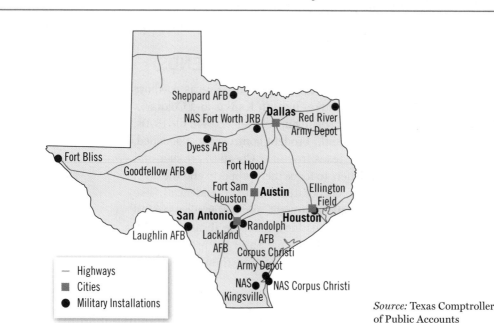

Source: Texas Comptroller of Public Accounts

COMMUNICATION:

How big is the US military presence in Texas?

- Texas is currently home to fifteen military bases, if we count the San Antonio joint base as three separate bases. These bases are primarily located in or outside of urban areas, especially around San Antonio and El Paso.

- The total military personnel stationed in Texas is approximately 195,000.

CRITICAL THINKING:

Why is the military presence so great in Texas?

- Texas has historically been an outpost for western expansion and many of the military bases remain from the states' frontier days.

- Texas has a vast supply of cheap land and diverse geography for bases on both sea and land.

- Texas politicians have fought to keep these bases open, as bases bring in tens of thousands of jobs and millions of dollars in revenue.

Systems, which designed computer systems for Medicare and Medicaid. Technology went from rich to "big rich" in the 1980s when Rod Canion formed Compaq and "technobrat" Michael Dell founded Dell Computers—at age twenty-three in his dorm room at the University of Texas.[26] The tech boom, which extends to information technology, financial services, health care technology, and aeronautics, continues today. Several major national corporations are headquartered in Texas, including Dell, Texas Instruments, Perot Systems, and Hewlett-Packard.

In addition, thousands of smaller, start-up technology companies have sprouted in Texas, many in the "Silicon Hills" in and around Austin.

HEALTH CARE

The health care industry is among the fastest growing industries in the state, and Texas boasts some of the largest hospitals and health systems in the country. The Texas Medical Center in Houston is the largest medical center in the world. The industry not only has a significant economic impact, but also brings in millions of dollars in grants for medical innovation.

RECREATION AND RETIREMENT

Stroll along the river walk in San Antonio or the beaches of South Padre Island. Hike in Big Bend National Park. Gaze at the incredible art in Houston's many museums. The state is teeming with recreational and entertainment options and tourists flock to the state for leisure activities. Although many rural Texas counties have lost mainstay industries, such as oil and gas production and agriculture, many still find they are positioned for growth in recreation and as retirement havens. Among these local recourses are tourism, hunting and fishing, birding, and retirement communities. Travel spending in Texas tops $70 billion and supports almost 630,000 jobs.[27]

ASSESSING THE "TEXAS MIRACLE"

Boom and bust cycles aside, the Texas economy was in tall cotton from 2000 to 2011 and successfully weathered national economic downturns in 2001 and

GREAT TEXAS POLITICAL DEBATES
Raising the Minimum Wage

In 2015, the Texas legislature rejected a proposal to submit to voters a plan to raise the minimum wage from the federally mandated $7.25 to $10.10 an hour. The measure was voted down on party lines (all Republicans voting no, and all Democrats voting yes). Worries about the "working poor" (those employed but below the poverty line) prompted the effort—the number of individuals working minimum wage jobs quadrupled between 2008 and 2013.

 PERSONAL RESPONSIBILITY: **Should Texas increase its minimum wage?**

NO: Small businesses cannot afford a higher minimum wage. They would have to cut the number of hours and employees. The importance of a low minimum wage is to produce more of those jobs that are an entry point into the workforce.

YES: Giving Texans adequate wages for their work reinforces the Texan ideal of hard work and self-sufficiency. Paying workers a living wage gives them stability. Further, studies show that income inequality, exacerbated by great differences in pay, may slow future economic growth by decreasing state sales tax revenue.[32]

Texas is famous for its extremes of weather. It is also known for extremes of wealth and poverty.

PERSONAL RESPONSIBILITY: **Has the state left behind its most economically vulnerable populations at the expense of a strong statewide economy?**

Texas Miracle: economic good fortune the state experienced from 2001 to 2008

2008. Many refer to the state's economic good fortune during this time as the **"Texas Miracle."** The number of jobs grew by two million from 2000 to 2015 and the state gross domestic product grew from $730 billion to over $1 trillion.[28] Since the financial crisis in 2008, Texas has added 1.1 million jobs—which compares favorably to the 3.3 million added by the rest of the country.[29] Every industry grew while the cost of living remained low: something that costs $1 on average in the rest of the country costs just 96.5 cents in Texas—this is like getting 3.5 percent off everything you buy in Texas.[30] Texas's proximity to the border also encourages trade, immigration to fuel population growth, and job creation. In fact, border protection itself has been a boon to the Rio Grande Valley in terms of jobs, investment in infrastructure, and sales tax revenue.[31]

But, the news is not all rosy. Some sectors, such as oil and gas, were propping up the Texas Miracle more than others. Once oil prices fell in 2016, state unemployment jumped, commercial real estate vacancies spiked, and the economic strain was felt from chain restaurants to airlines.[33]

Moreover, the "miracle" has not blessed all groups equally. The number of minimum wage and low-pay, low-skilled positions has exploded, prompting some to claim that the job growth in Texas is all low-paying "McJobs."[34] Median family income has not increased much.[35] This is in part because population growth has provided a steady supply of workers to keep salaries low.

Critics also complain about chronically underfunded public schools, lack of access to health care for rural and poor Texans, and underinvestment in transportation infrastructure. Because of low wages, a large share of Texans live below the poverty line. Although the number of uninsured Texans has been falling in recent years, 32 percent of Hispanics and 18 percent of women still lack health care coverage.[36]

Texas ranks fifth from the top nationally in income inequality. The gap between the rich and poor is huge—the richest 5 percent of households earned on average $317,661 per year while the poorest 20 percent earned on average $11,296.[37] Urban areas have particularly high rates of inequality. Race is a factor too—poverty rates for African Americans and Hispanics are three times as high for Anglos, and Hispanics earn approximately 75 percent of what Anglos make. So, while the Texas Miracle has consecrated the fortunes of many, it has left others behind.

★▬ **TEXAS TAKEAWAYS**

3 How large is the Texas economy? How does it compare to other states?

4 What Texas industries have experienced economic booms and in what sequence?

5 What is the "Texas Miracle"?

🤠 CONTINUITY AND CHANGE IN THE TEXAS DEMOGRAPHICS

Power and politics in Texas hug the arc of demographic shifts. As the state has become more urban and industrialized, citizens have required additional government services—driver's licenses, garbage pick-up, and water and sewer systems. As foreign-born populations grow, the state confronts new demands for social services and access to schools. As the state ages, new debates erupt about health care and pensions. Political power, meanwhile, has shifted from rural to urban to new suburban communities with the movement of high-income echelons of Texas society to these areas. These demographic shifts have repercussions for Texas politics.

> **1.3** Analyze how the changing demographics of the state affect government.

STATE POPULATION GROWTH

Since achieving statehood, Texas has grown rapidly. Once a lonely, inhospitable frontier land fraught with danger, Texas has emerged as a major population center. The state's population was a mere 212,592 in 1850 but ballooned to twenty-seven million by 2016. In every census taken since 1850, Texas has grown faster than the United States as a whole. Population growth and economic expansion have often gone hand in hand in Texas as first land, then oil, and finally industry drew newcomers.

Texas today is the fastest growing of the largest states in the United States (see Figure 1.4). "Sunbelt" states, such as Texas, are growing rapidly as baby boomers retire and as jobs move from the industrial northeast and Midwest to the South. With population growth comes greater sway in the presidential elections, more seats in Congress, and thus more power on the national level.

Urbanization.   The population has not increased uniformly across the state. Much of the growth has occurred in major urban areas. In 1890, Texas had no

IS IT BIGGER IN TEXAS?

FIGURE 1.4   **US States with the Largest Population Increases, 2000–2010**

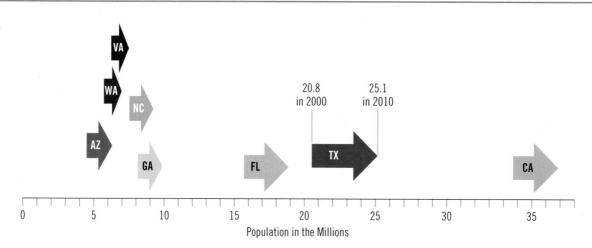

Source: US Census Bureau. The arrows show population growth of each state. The numeric growth shows the total increase in the number of individuals living in Texas.

 COMMUNICATION:

How does Texas population growth compare to other large states?

- Texas had the largest increase in population growth between 2000 and 2010.

 CRITICAL THINKING:

Why has Texas grown so quickly?

- Hispanic population growth (both in terms of births and migration) has driven Texas population growth.
- Economic expansion has brought many companies and thousands of jobs to the state, boosting the population.
- Affordable real estate has made the state attractive for first-time home buyers and retirees, especially in urban and suburban areas.

urban areas with a population larger than 40,000, but by 1920, four cities—Dallas, Fort Worth, Houston, and San Antonio—boasted more than 100,000 residents each.[38] *Texas Monthly's* Paul Burka described modern Texas as an "urban state with a rural soul." Rural population has declined and urban (especially suburban) populations have skyrocketed. The mechanization of farm labor and job opportunities in urban areas led people to flock to cities between 1900 and 1920. This migration continues today and has amplified in

TABLE 1.1   Population by County Type, 1960–2010

COUNTY TYPE	1960	1990	2010
Big Six (Harris, Dallas, Tarrant, Bexar, Travis, El Paso)	41.2%	48.2%	47.0%
Suburban	8.8%	14.1%	20.7%
Other Metro	23.4%	19.4%	18.1%
Small Town	26.6%	18.3%	14.2%

Source: Red State, Wayne Thornburn (2014).

 COMMUNICATION:

How have the populations of where Texans live changed over time?

- The "Big Six" counties account for almost half of the population of the state in both 1990 and 2010. The population trend, however, is flat in the past decade.
- While only 8 percent of the state lived in suburbs in 1960, by 2010 21 percent did.
- Rural areas have seen the largest population percentage drop.

 CRITICAL THINKING:

Why are some areas growing and others not?

- Suburban areas grew because of "white flight," where Anglo residents of urban areas moved to areas that were cheaper, had better public schools, and were perceived to be safer.
- As urban and suburban areas expanded, rural areas began to shrink, seeing economic opportunities move to more populated areas. Agriculture declined as a family run business.

recent years (see Table 1.1). About 75 percent of the population of Texas lives in the "urban triangle" between Houston, Dallas, and San Antonio.

Suburbanization.   The most significant growth over time has been a **surbanization** of the state, a process in which the population shifts from the urban and rural areas to suburban areas adjacent to major cities. While the smaller metro cities in the state have lost population and small towns have been drained of population, the suburbs in the state have swelled with new residents.

Implications of Population Shifts.   Population shifts explain how and why political power in Texas has shifted from rural to urban to suburban centers. State policy priorities follow growing populations and wealthier citizens. As political power moves geographically, the institutions of Texas government— the legislature, the bureaucracy, the courts—shift to address urban and suburban problems and may focus less on rural issues. As the population rises in the cities and suburbs, so do the number of representatives in the Texas legislature. Consequently, greater resources and funding are streaming to these areas as

suburbanization:
population shifts from the urban and rural areas to suburban areas adjacent to major cities

see for yourself 1.2

Find out how urbanization is encroaching on a staple of rural traditions, the honky-tonk.

state legislators bring projects and funds back to their electoral districts in the form of newer schools, highway funds, and other infrastructure projects. In addition, as like-minded individuals settled into neatly urban and suburban pockets, political divisions have begun to develop between the conservative suburbs and the more liberal urban areas.

CHALLENGES OF POPULATION GROWTH

The state's population is expected to double by 2050 to 54.4 million people. The urbanization and suburbanization of Texas is likely to continue through the middle of the century. Let's take a look at how these trends are impacting and will continue to impact our lives in the coming decades.

Infrastructure. As the state grows, so do the demands on roads and other transportation systems. The state's transportation system is funded by state fuel taxes, vehicle registration fees, toll road revenues, bond proceeds, and federal transportation aid. As the state grows in population, some of this revenue will expand and some will not. The Texas Department of Transportation (TxDOT) estimates that road use in the state will grow 214 percent by 2033 and road capacity will grow by only 6 percent.

Water Use. The Texas Water Development Board annual surveys show that the average residence consumes eighty-six gallons of water per day. Without planning for expected population increases, a drought in 2060 could mean that 85 percent of Texans would not have enough water to sustain their current levels of use.[39] An extended drought creates water shortages, makes agricultural irrigation (and therefore food) more expensive, and makes the state susceptible to wildfires.

Health Care. The number of Texans without health insurance was 17 percent in 2015, which amounts to about 5.5 million Texans who did not have medical coverage.[40] Under federal law, hospitals must treat patients who show up in emergency rooms regardless of their ability to pay, placing a serious burden on hospitals that are not reimbursed for these costs. More residents, especially more residents without health insurance, could stifle the already overburdened health care system.

Energy Use. In 2014, Texas ranked sixth in the nation in per capita energy consumption, significantly above the national average in the United States. As the population surges, so will the demand for energy. The state has access to enough coal and natural gas to meet demands through 2030, but the state has been turning to alternative sources of energy (such as wind and nuclear energy) to meet growing market demand.

RACIAL AND ETHNIC TRENDS IN TEXAS

As impactful as *where* people live is *who* lives there. The distribution of resources reflect the struggle for political power among both residential and demographic

TABLE 1.2	Ethnic and Racial Changes in Texas, 1980–2014		
	POPULATION		PERCENT CHANGE
	1980	2014	1980–2014
Anglo	9,350,297	11,458,442	22%
Black	1,692,542	3,110,393	84%
Hispanic	2,985,824	10,680,414	257%
Other	200,528	1,707,710	751%

Source: US Census Bureau, QuickFacts. Texas Demographic Center.

 COMMUNICATION:

How have ethnic and racial populations changed in Texas?

- In 1980, Anglos accounted for more than nine million of the state's fourteen million population (66 percent of the state's population) while Hispanics accounted for almost three million (21 percent).
- By 2014, the change in Anglo population was modest (22 percent greater) while the change in Hispanic population was incredible (257 percent).

 CRITICAL THINKING:

Why have some groups grown and others not?

- Hispanic families on average have more children than either Anglos or African Americans, increasing the group's population.
- Asian (included in "other") groups have exploded in population due primarily to immigration.
- Immigration trends continue to flow new residents to Texas, in search of jobs or reuniting with family.

groups. Although Anglos (whites) were a clear supermajority in the 1980s in Texas, the rapid rise of the Hispanic (sometimes called Latino) population since then has altered the social and political shape of the state (see Table 1.2). Texas is one of a few states where Hispanic residents are over one million—other such states include California, Florida, and New York.[41] Asian, Native Hawaiian, Pacific Islander, American Indian, and Alaska Native populations (which the census labels "other") have also experienced significant growth. The Census Bureau's estimates suggest this trend is part of a long-term development in the United States for the population to become less white, older, and more Hispanic.

Residential **segregation** is prevalent in Texas: most Anglos live in the suburbs, most African Americans live in urban areas, and most Hispanics live in smaller metropolitan areas. Hispanics make up a larger portion of the urban workforce in Texas than any other group, and they are moving into the state's fast growing suburbs to find affordable housing.[42]

segregation: enforced or de facto separation of different racial groups

Why does diversity matter to policymaking in Texas? Demographic groups have different needs that governments must respond to. For example, Latinos have higher poverty rates and greater health challenges than Anglos.[43] As a result, twice as many Texas Hispanics obtain health insurance through the Affordable Care Act (ACA) than whites.[44]

Driving some of the growth of the Hispanic population in the state is the foreign-born population. Foreign-born populations spike in areas with other population increases because they are often following employment opportunities. How does the influx of foreign-born populations alter politics in the state? This trend impacts both the economy and government of Texas. The supply of labor will be high so wages are likely to stay low, allowing Texas businesses to stay competitive by having cheap and plentiful labor. Immigrants also pay taxes, which promotes economic stability, and their unique cultures contributes to educational diversity. Yet, if certain areas of the state are more populated with those born in other countries, demand for public services and political representation will increase. Long-time residents may grow frustrated with an influx of newcomers and may press authorities to restrict immigration and the delivery of social services to immigrants.

CHALLENGES OF SHIFTING RACIAL AND ETHNIC TRENDS

As we have seen, Texas is a growing state. This increase is and will likely continue to be fueled largely by the growth in Hispanic residents (see Figure 1.5). What opportunities and challenges does this pose of Texans?

"Juan Crow" laws that enforced discrimination against Latinos mirrored "Jim Crow" laws and used some of the same tactics. Signs reading "No Spanish or Mexicans" were common across Texas restaurants and other public accommodations.

SOCIAL RESPONSIBILITY: **Should Texas take governmental action to achieve ethnically and racially balanced residential areas and school systems? How?**

Education.   Texas has more public school students than twenty-eight states have residents. Texas public schools serve more than five million students, and that population is diversifying.[45] Racial and ethnic segregation has been a point of tension since the days Texas was part of Spain and Mexico. This is most apparent in public schools. In the 1950s, 90 percent of schools in South Texas were segregated and separate schools for Texans of Mexican descent existed in at least 122 school districts.[46] Thousands of public schools are still as segregated now as they were sixty years ago: half of Texas students attend a school that is 80 percent of one race or ethnicity.[47] Inequality in educational access remains an issue. Texas has an overall graduation rate of 88 percent, but Anglos graduate at a rate of 93 percent, Hispanics at 84 percent, and African Americans at 84 percent.[48] Sixty-seven percent of Anglos received a college degree within six years of graduation compared to 51 percent of Hispanics and 41 percent of African Americans.[49]

Pressure on public schools to educate more students, especially more diverse students, will put stress on the primary and secondary education system in the state as teacher training and educational materials will need to be adapted to be inclusive of this diversity. In Chapter 13, we will explore what Texas is doing to meet the challenges of a growing and increasingly diverse student body.

FIGURE 1.5 **Projected Race Population Changes in Texas, 2015–2050**

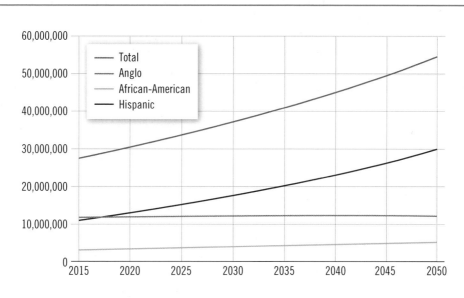

Source: Office of the State Demographer, Population Projections.

 COMMUNICATION:

What will the state look like racially and ethnically in forty years?

- The number of African Americans is projected to remain steady and the number of Anglo citizens is predicted to decline.
- The number of Hispanic citizens is expected to rise from ten million to almost sixteen million by 2050.

 CRITICAL THINKING:

Why are some groups increasing but not others?

- Population replacement for African Americans and Anglos is only average: birth rates are low and migration from other states or nations is modest.
- Most of the growth from Hispanic families stems from high birth rates to families living in Texas.
- A healthy economy drew more immigrants from Latin American countries and kept many recent immigrants and their subsequent generations in Texas.

Housing. Racial segregation in housing is still a major issue in Texas. Government-assisted housing may be located in areas that are not ethnically or racially diverse, perpetuating similar living conditions. Vouchers for public housing may also encourage residents to live in areas that are less racially or ethnically diverse. Individual preferences play a role too: Some groups, like Anglos and Asians, respond in surveys that they would be less likely to buy a home in a neighborhood made up significantly of a different racial or ethnic group.[50]

The US Supreme Court ruled in 2015 that the Texas Department of Housing and Community Affairs, the agency which administers federally backed housing subsidies for low incoming housing, had from 1990 to 2011 illegally distributed these credits in neighborhoods of mostly poor blacks and Hispanics. In effect, the department enforced racial segregation by subsidizing construction of apartments in non-white neighborhoods (about three-quarters of the credits) instead of in white suburbs.[51] Today San Antonio and Dallas top the charts for the highest rates of residential segregation.[52]

AN AGING STATE

Texas is aging. Texas currently has three million residents age sixty-five and older. Baby boomers, those born after World War II (1946 to 1964), constitute the nation's largest generation in the twentieth century and are now rapidly aging. By 2050, the number of citizens aged sixty-five years and older is expected to reach about 6.5 million. The growth of younger Texans is not significant enough to replace those aging. The number of total projected population growth of individuals under the age of eighteen remains constant between now and 2050. Much of the increase in young residents comes from Hispanics while most of the older group is due to expected aging of Anglo residents.

CHALLENGES OF AN AGING TEXAS

As the baby boomer generation retires, there will be added pressure on the resources of the state.

Income Security.   Poverty rates among elderly citizens in Texas are greater than 11 percent, making Texas one of fifteen states with a significant rate of poverty among older Americans.[53] Income insecurity may be particularly acute among Hispanics who have a higher life expectancy than non-Hispanics and are less economically secure in their old age compared to other groups. Because only 31 percent of non-Hispanics and only 8 percent of Hispanics have investment income, it is particularly important that both the US and Texas governments keep Social Security solvent.[54]

Medicaid.   Medicaid is an entitlement program through which qualified low-income individuals can receive medical care. Many elderly Texans qualify for access to Medicaid services, but budget cuts have restricted this access. Texas cut spending to Medicaid by $350 million in 2015, potentially reducing the ability of elderly Texans on fixed incomes to receive ongoing medical care.[55]

Safety.   Many elderly citizens are vulnerable to unscrupulous individuals or outright criminals. Elder abuse in nursing homes and assisted living facilities must continue to be monitored by the Texas Adult Protective Services. The Texas Attorney General's office runs programs to protect senior consumers against retirement planning or medical service scams.

★▬ TEXAS TAKEAWAYS

6 How does Texas's population growth compare to other states?

7 How would you characterize the demographics of the recent population growth in Texas?

8 What challenges does the state face due to population growth?

🤠 CONTINUITY AND CHANGE IN TEXAS POLITICAL CULTURE

Texas is a "state of mind," writes American author John Steinbeck, and "a nation in every sense of the word." The early pioneers infused Texas with a spirit of rugged individualism and a strong sense of fair play that continues to permeate the political environment today. Texans have always had an expansive and grandiose vision of the state. President Mirabeau B. Lamar, who succeeded Sam Houston as the Republic's second president, envisioned a Texas nation that was large and powerful enough to rival the United States.

> **1.4** Examine the source and impact of political culture in Texas.

Although the issues may change and party labels may shift, Texans have retained core political values. **Political culture** is a set of shared values and practices held by people that informs their expectations of government and their vision of a just society. These sentiments give order and meaning to the political process and explain behavior.[56]

> **political culture:** a set of shared values and practices held by people that informs their expectations of government and their vision of a just society

INSIDER INTERVIEW

Joe Holley, Houston Chronicle Writer

How would you describe the personality of Texas politics?

The dominant Texas political personality is conservative and suspicious of government intrusion into the lives of individuals. This political personality is the result of the state's origins. The Texas ethos is that of Scots-Irish borderlanders who migrated down from the Appalachians, people who brought with them a fierce independence, a suspicion of outsiders, and a willingness to resort to violence when provoked. Southerners who also settled Texas had similar characteristics.

🦫 PERSONAL RESPONSIBILITY: **In what ways do you represent or not represent this description of Texas's political culture? How is your impression of Texas political culture similar or different?**

Why does a state's political culture matter? Political culture defines the relationship between a government and its people. Our political culture influences how we feel about the rights and responsibilities of citizens, the limits on government intervention in people's lives, and the obligations of government to the people. Do you expect government to solve problems or do you want government to leave them alone? Do you expect to have constant input in making policy judgments or should the elected officials make decisions on their own?

Your answers to these questions—and the answers of other Texans—determine the types of actions government takes, including what policies the legislature enacts, the types of executive actions governors take, how agencies in Austin enforce laws, how judges rule on cases, and how much power local governments have. Such cultural patterns are reinforced by a collective ethos about what makes us Texans and the embrace of iconic images and figures that are passed from generation to generation—the ubiquitous Texas flag, reverence to Texas music, celebrity icons, and larger-than-life historical figures.

Political scientist Daniel Elazar developed a classification of political culture by states. He argued that political cultures in the states vary in beliefs and values about the appropriate goals of the political system, the activities of citizens, and the relationship of government to the people.[57] Elazar identified three basic political cultures that he argues all states can fit into: individualistic, traditionalistic, and moralistic (see Table 1.3).

Elazar placed Texas at the intersection of individualistic and traditionalistic political cultures. Those who settled Texas infused the state with the political cultures they brought with them. Texas shows elements of individualistic political culture through support for free enterprise, fierce opposition to big government (especially the federal government), and entrepreneurship. Traditionalistic political culture in Texas is seen in characteristics like low voter

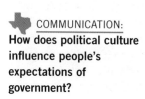

COMMUNICATION:
How does political culture influence people's expectations of government?

TABLE 1.3   Elazar's Classification of Political Culture

INDIVIDUALISTIC	TRADITIONALISTIC	MORALISTIC
The political arena is a clearinghouse for ideas. Government's role is limited. Government exists for utilitarian reasons only. Private concerns are more important than public concerns.	The goal of the political system is to maintain order. Political elites largely determine public policy. Government is a hierarchy, with a few elites in charge. Citizen participation is low.	The goal of the political system is to achieve the broadest good for the community. Government is a positive force designed to activate the public will and citizens participate strenuously in government. Party competition is strong but not completely controlled by political elites.

participation, one-party dominance (first Democrats, then Republicans), and conservative social values as informed by strict religious beliefs.

INDIVIDUALISTIC POLITICAL CULTURE

Texans embrace an **individualistic political culture** that emphasizes personal achievement, individual freedoms, individual enterprise, and loyalty to self instead of others. Individuals retain specific rights and government does not alter or abridge those rights except in extreme circumstances. Individuals hold government accountable for protection of basic rights and little else. You're on your own in Texas, to sink or swim, and Texans like it that way. As famed Texas folklorist and historian Frank Dobie wrote affectionately, an idealized Texan citizen was called a "Texan out of an Old Rock," a model of self-sufficiency and ingenuity.

Consider how these values spill over into state politics. People who embrace an individualistic political culture prefer **minimal government.** They believe governments should only provide minimal services. Government should only protect individuals from grave harm, maintain a functioning free market, provide a consistent legal system, and ensure contracts are fairly upheld. They believe that the government should not interfere with free transactions among individuals or institutions.

This attitude shapes Texans's stance on a range of policy issues, such as health insurance, taxes, business regulation, and social welfare. Take, for example, the question of whether or not the government has an obligation to provide assistance to low-income individuals. Most Texans responded that the poor should be responsible for their own situation, rather than government helping them (see Table 1.4).

Texans are also protective of individual rights, and prefer that government not meddle in their private lives. Texans generally oppose gun control believing those rights are protected under the Second Amendment, but do support background checks for those purchasing guns. Voters in Texas also approve of

individualistic political culture: emphasizes personal achievement, individual freedoms, individual enterprise, and loyalty to self instead of others

minimal government: a government that provides minimal services and interferes as little as possible in the transactions of individuals and institutions

TABLE 1.4 Opinions on the Role of Government in Social Welfare

	Percent of Texans that Strongly or Mildly Agree
Government should take a more active role in helping low-income individuals.	29%
Individuals should be responsible for improving their own situation.	52%
No strong opinion on whether governments or individuals should take a more active role.	16%

Source: Texas Politics Project / University of Texas Poll, June 2009.

SOCIAL RESPONSIBILITY: **Does government have an obligation to help those in need or are government's only obligations to maintain a level playing field and basic security?**

ANGLES OF POWER
Individual Rights, Equality, and Religious Freedom

Texans do support some limits on individual rights, particularly when they conflict with other dominant values. In the wake of the Supreme Court's 2015 decision to allow same-sex couples to marry, Texas Attorney General Ken Paxton issued a ruling indicating that county clerks (who are in charge of distributing marriage licenses) could deny same-sex couples licenses based upon their religious objections. The attorney general also argued that justices of the peace and judges could refuse to perform wedding ceremonies that violated their religious objections.[58] Opponents argued that issuing marriage licenses is not a religious act and state employees take an oath to serve all Texans equally. Opponents also claim this is discrimination, whether based on religious principles or not.

PERSONAL RESPONSIBILITY: **Where do you draw the line between individual liberty and religious liberty?**

doctor-assisted suicide for terminally ill patients, allowing for individuals to choose to end their lives with dignity.

Distrust of Government. Texans are generally distrustful of government at most levels. Only 58 percent of Texans believe that the state government in Austin can be trusted to do what is right some or none of the time.[59] Texans also prefer politicians who are from "outside" politics, even over politicians who have tangible experience in their fields. Fifty percent feel that the state "needs leaders from outside politics" compared to the 19 percent who noted that the state needs "leaders with experience in politics."[60]

Trust in the Free Market. Texans tend to believe that businesses should be allowed to run without—or with minimal—government interference. The role of government should be to support economic growth by building infrastructure and a business-friendly environment.

TRADITIONALISTIC POLITICAL CULTURE

traditionalistic political culture: the goal of the political system is to maintain order and a hierarchical set of political elites largely determine public policy

People who espouse **traditionalistic political culture** expect government to maintain the existing social order. Consider how traditionalistic political culture shapes state policies on law and order and social policies, such as abortion.

law and order: a dimension of Texas political culture that demands a strict adherence to a fair and adequate criminal justice system and swift enforcement of laws

Law and Order. Traditionalistic political culture places a priority on the strict enforcement of **law and order**. Consistent with these values, Texans support harsh punishments. Texans are strongly supportive of the application of the death penalty in appropriate cases, with almost 75 percent of Texans supporting it.[61] Individualist values may, at times, conflict with law and order concerns. Most Texans view high-tech scanners at airports, police "stop and frisk" procedures, and red light cameras at busy intersections with suspicion and must balance their desire for personal freedoms with the need for law and order.

FIGURE 1.6   **Role of Religion in Texas**

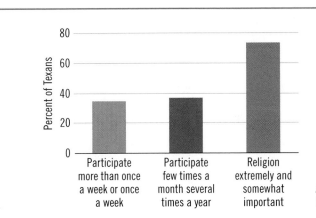

Source: Texas Politics Project / University of Texas Polls.

 COMMUNICATION:

How religious are Texans?

- Religion is a major part of the lives of most Texans. Around 74 percent of respondents indicated that religion was extremely or somewhat important in their lives in 2014.

- Many Texans (35 percent) attend religious services weekly or more than once a week and more than a third (37 percent) participate several times a year.

 CRITICAL THINKING:

Why is religion such a major part of Texans's lives?

- Fear and uncertainty of frontier life promoted religion as a civil and social organization in early Texas history.

- Two major population segments in Texas—Latinos and African Americans—are very religious, increasing Texas's religiosity.

- Texas has built several of the largest, most influential, and nationally famous congregations—televised mega churches of all denominations that are each home to more than 20,000 members.

Religion and Traditional Family Values.   The traditionalistic character of Texas's political culture emphasizes rules and values that support existing institutions, such as church and traditional family structure. Texans attend church often (see Figure 1.6), more so than other Americans. More than 13 million people signaled that they were part of an organized religion in the state.[62] **Religiosity** shapes Texans's views of political issues and thus informs policy. Governor Rick Perry, who had designs on becoming president in 2012 and 2016, embraced this religious mindset in a prayer gathering at Reliant Stadium in 2011 where "the connections between fiscal conservatism, social conservatism, and Bible-Belt religious beliefs were clearly on display."[63]

Consider for example Texans's views on abortion. Opponents of abortion often take a religious stance arguing that abortion ends human life and thus

religiosity: the belief, practice, and activity of organized religion

FIGURE 1.7   **Availability of Abortion**

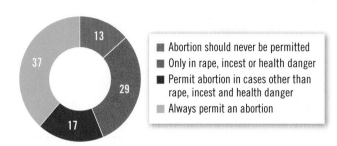

- Abortion should never be permitted
- Only in rape, incest or health danger
- Permit abortion in cases other than rape, incest and health danger
- Always permit an abortion

Source: Texas Politics Project / University of Texas Poll, February 2014.

 COMMUNICATION:

Where do Texans stand on abortion?

- A core of about 13 percent of Texans never approve of abortion in any circumstances, while about 37 percent approve of access to abortions for any reason.

- A large share of Texans are in the middle positions, approving of abortion in specific cases, such as rape, incest, or when there is a health danger to the mother (17 percent and 29 percent in 2014).

 CRITICAL THINKING:

Why?

- Abortion is legal and an established right as determined by the Supreme Court. Most Texans, even if they disagree with the procedure, desire the law to be followed.

- Abortion is both a moral and individual issue. Texans split on the rights of women in pursing an abortion: some are against the termination of a pregnancy but others approve of an individual's right to choose.

constitutes murder. Advocates of abortion rights argue that unwanted pregnancies create burdens for the health or economic welfare of women. Today, most Texans temper their religious convictions and believe it should be allowed always or in cases of rape, incest, or health risk (see Figure 1.7).

Many Texas also believe in a firm set of "family values" that include encouraging marital fidelity, protecting children, supporting family members, and acting on faith-based principles. These values are contested, especially in politics. Republicans in Texas are more likely to define family values in conservative terms, such as supporting traditional roles for women and opposition to same-sex relationships and to legalization of drugs. Democrats are more likely to consider family values in terms of protecting an extended family, including expanded health care, a living wage, and expanded social programs.

CULTURE CONFLICTS

The relationship between the people and government must adapt to shifting economic, social, and political arrangements. As Mary Lasswell writes in her book, *I'll Take Texas*, the culture of Texas is one of adaptability, especially from its frontier past where there is conflict between its "pioneer past and his urban present."[64] However, the values and modern realities of Texans often conflict. Consider how these conflicts shape Texans's view of three issues: college funding, gambling, marijuana, and home schooling.

College Funding.   Texans generally expect their government to maintain an equal playing field. College education is critical to individual advancement and to building a skilled in-state workforce, but it can be expensive. The state can help students pay for their education, but this opens up questions about who should receive these funds. When asked which individuals should receive state funds for higher education, most Texans (46 percent) respond that all groups should instead of "only the most needy Texans." Only a small segment of Texans (13 percent) favored expanding higher education funds to needy Texans. Underlying this approach is the sense that the state should not pick "winners and losers" but rather provide opportunities for all individuals.

Yet, Texans do believe in rewarding individuals for services rendered to the state. For example, most Texans do not generally support a "path to citizenship" for immigrants who come to the United States illegally. However, 57 percent of Texans support clearing a path to children of illegal immigrants who join the military—although Texas do not feel the same about a path to citizenship for those children of undocumented immigrants who go to college. Both college education and military service produce a skilled workforce that benefits the economy, but most Texans feel that only military service should be rewarded with citizenship.

Morals and Money.   Another clash occurs over the desire to keep taxes low, an individualistic value, with the belief that certain types of activities, such as gambling or use of illicit drugs, should be prohibited, a traditionalistic value often connected to religion. In response to the 2011 budget crisis, Texans were asked if they approved of specific measures to raise revenue. Legalization of marijuana ranked lower on the list than increasing taxes on alcohol or allowing gambling as a means to raise needed revenue.

The scope and scale of government ultimately reflects the state's political culture. The political and social values of Texans inform government activity. As a result the struggle between groups with different values and even the clash of different values within the same group shape both public policy and the government institutions themselves.

The Texas Supreme Court took a case in 2015 that accused a family who homeschooled their children in El Paso of failing to teach their children basic educational material since they were waiting for the rapture.* The family countered that the El Paso school district is anti-Christian and families should have the freedom to educate their children in whatever way they want.

SOCIAL RESPONSIBILITY: **In the conflict between freedom and religion in this case, where do you draw the line?**

★ TEXAS TAKEAWAYS

9 How do we classify political culture in Texas?

10 What are the values that derive from Texas's political culture?

🤠 THE INSIDER VIEW

Texas has always been a land of conflict—first with Native American tribes battling over territory, then with the Spanish settling the hostile land and converting the native tribes, followed by Mexican rule that both encouraged then discouraged settlement, and finally the Anglos who fought a revolution to achieve independence. Today, land is not the only resource Texans fight to control. Public policy in the state is contested over economic priorities as new and expanding groups seek a greater share of the public resources and established groups demand a greater share as well. Demographic shifts have reoriented the scope and direction of public policy in Texas. Through history, Texans have always embraced individual rights, minimal government interference, and law and order. Issues may change and politicians come and go, but Texas government remains committed to these core political values even as these values come into conflict and politicians make choices on difficult issues.

★ TEXAS TAKEAWAYS

1 Texas was first settled by Native Americans battling for territory and being pushed by other tribes and pulled by the roaming buffalo, then by the Spanish explorers looking for an expanded empire, then by the Mexican government anxious to provide a buffer between them and the United States.

2 Texans revolted against Mexico because of anger over halted Anglo immigration, few legal rights, higher taxation, and a general sense of self-sufficiency.

3 If Texas were an independent nation, its economy would be ranked 12th in the world. Its 2014 gross state product (the sum of all goods and service produced in a state) topped $1.7 trillion, the second highest in the United States.

4 The Texas economy has gone through several boom and bust cycles—first cotton and cattle, then energy (primarily oil), then manufacturing, then (again) energy (natural gas especially).

5 The "Texas Miracle" is what some have called the Texas economy from 2001 to 2008, which experienced a major boom: low unemployment, low inflation, and growing state coffers. The economy was not rosy for everyone, however, as many jobs were low income and many residents lacked access to health care.

6 Texas had the largest increase in population (more than 4 million people) of any state in the union. Even other large states like California and Florida did not add population as rapidly as Texas between 2000 and 2010

7 Texas's recent population growth is younger, more Hispanic, and more urban now than in the past 10 years.

8 Pressure on the state to educate a diverse population, a strain on state health funds for aging Texans, protecting equal opportunity housing, and ensuring racial tolerance are all challenges the state faces as the demographics change.

9 Political culture in Texas, according to political scientist Daniel Elazar's analysis, involves two primary value dimensions: individualistic and traditionalistic.

10 Texans are religious, favor minimal government, approve of the free market, and embrace law and order. These values shape political beliefs on several issues like abortion, state spending, and illegal drugs.

KEY TERMS

individualistic political culture
law and order
minimal government
political culture
religiosity
segregation
suburbanization
Tejanos
Texas Miracle
traditionalistic political culture

PRACTICE QUIZ

1. What did early Spanish settlers call the territory of Texas?
   a. "The New World"
   b. "New Spain"
   c. "Tenochtitlan"
   c. "The West"

2. Where would the Texas economy rank in the world if it were an independent nation?
   a. Fifth
   b. Twelfth
   c. Twenty-third
   c. Forty-fifth

3. The discovery of the East Texas oil field in 1930 near Kilgore prompted which agency to monitor pumping and production:
   a. Oil Commission
   b. Pumping and Natural Gas Commission
   c. Fracking and Heavy Machinery Commission
   d. Railroad Commission

4. What is the "Texas Miracle"?
   a. The discovery of oil.
   b. The state's good economic fortune.
   c. The lack of scandals by Texas governors.
   d. The massive size of the state, claimed after the "Great War with Mexico."

5. Today only three Native American reservations remain in Texas. Which of the following reservations is *not* included in the three currently occupied in the state?
   a. Alabama-Coushatta
   b. Tigua
   c. Cheyenne
   d. Kickapoo

6. By the 1820s, the Mexican government aggressively . . .
   a. Promoted Anglo settlement of Texas
   b. Prohibited Anglo settlement of Texas
   c. Promoted Spanish settlement of Texas
   d. Prohibited Spanish settlement of Texas

7. By 1823, Mexico _____ slavery?
   a. Permitted
   b. Promoted
   c. Turned a blind eye to
   d. Banned

8. What was the rallying cry of the "Big Rich?"
   a. "Black gold; Texas tea!"
   b. "Don't Tread on Me!"
   c. "Better nouveau than never!"
   d. "Seize the oil!"

9. What notable event kick-started the struggling Texas economy in the wake of the Great Depression?
   a. World War I
   b. World War II
   c. The Vietnam War
   d. The Iran-Contra Scandal

10. Today, the cash receipts generated by the production of cattle, sheep, and goats in Texas totals more than . . .
    a. Ten billion dollars
    b. One trillion dollars
    c. One billion dollars
    d. Fifty million dollars

[Answer Key: B, B, D, B, C, A, D, C, B, A]

2 THE TEXAS CONSTITUTION

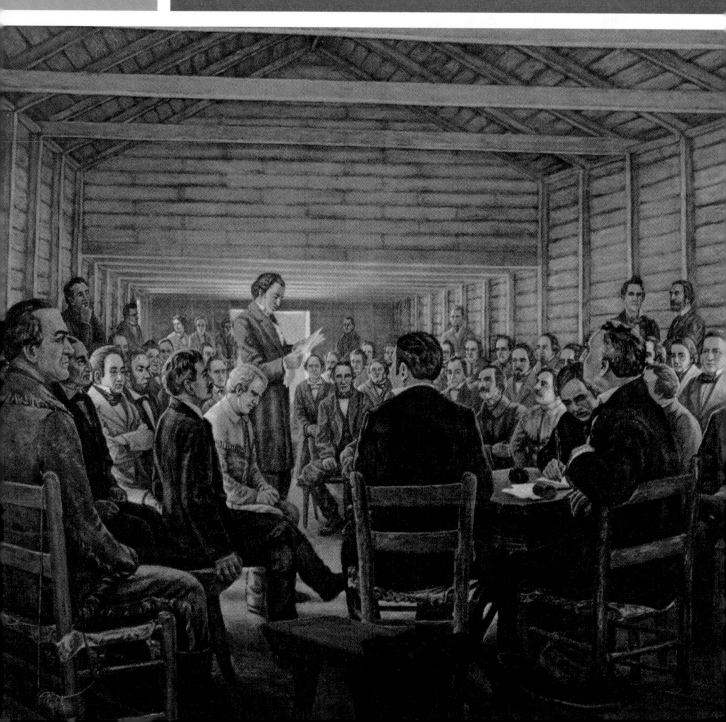

As the delegates to the young Texas government arrived in Washington-on-the-Brazos in 1836 to draft a declaration of independence and provisional constitution, they were less than inspired by their location. The town was a "disgusting place" of only "about a dozen wretched cabins or shanties" and only "one well-defined street," wrote one delegate. He concluded this was "a rare place to hold a national convention in. They will have to leave it promptly to avoid starvation."[1] As dawn broke early on March 3, 1836, the delegates confronted cold weather from a Texas norther that brought freezing rain and hail. The building where the delegates met had only one long wooden table, no doors in the doorways, and only a piece of cotton cloth stretched across the windows kept out the cold.

The delegates to the convention who had been assigned to a committee for drafting worked quickly to write a declaration of independence. The first draft was found to have so many errors that it was returned to the committee for correction. Before supper, Lieutenant Colonel's Travis's letter arrived from the Alamo pleading for reinforcements but generating optimism in the cause of the Alamo defenders. After supper, to illustrate the fate of the new nation considering the news from the Alamo, General Houston positioned two men who had too much drink and were half asleep shoulder to shoulder. He declared it was evident to all that "united they stand; divided they fall."[2]

This was the first birthday of the new Republic of Texas. Most of the delegates in that room would go on to shape the destiny of the

● The delegates of Texas efforts for independence met in Washington-on-the-Brazos in 1836 to sign a declaration of independence from Mexico and forge a constitution for the new Republic.

LEARNING OBJECTIVES

2.1 Identify the function of constitutions.

2.2 Explain the events that led to the Texas Declaration of Independence.

2.3 Relate the goals of the 1836 Constitution to its outcome and reactions to it.

2.4 Differentiate between the 1845 Constitution and prior Texas constitutions.

2.5 Analyze the goals of 1860s constitutions in the context of the political and social developments.

2.6 Describe the principles of the modern Texas Constitution.

2.7 Outline the process for amending the Texas Constitution and attempts at constitutional change.

state. The declaration of independence, although created when prospects for success seemed darkest, reflected an ardent desire for democratic self-rule.[3] The constitution drafted in that session would be the first of many for Texas, but it would also outline the core principles of liberty, popular rule, and limited government that all Texas constitutions would guarantee. The struggle to establish and maintain the Texas Constitution would test these values as new issues and challenges emerged.

In this chapter, we take a close look at the organization and disposition of the constitutions that have given Texas her basic structure. We first outline the roles of constitutional government in general and in Texas. We then examine and evaluate the causes of the Texas revolution as they relate to future constitutional considerations. We next observe the scope and functions of the constitutions from the Republic, statehood, Confederacy, Reconstruction (after the Civil War), and post-Reconstruction (modern) constitution. This final constitution (from 1876) is examined in greater detail to assess the provisions, process, and prospects of amendment.

🤠 CONSTITUTIONAL GOVERNMENT

| **2.1** | Identify the function of constitutions. |

constitution: a document that establishes principles, powers, and responsibilities of government

bill of rights: a formal declaration of the rights of the citizens within government

Constitutional government in Texas has shaped the rules and the actors in government since Texas was a province of Mexico. A **constitution** lays out the principles and responsibilities of government and specifies the powers of the branches of government and elected officials. The constitution structures the rules of the game and so shapes strategies used in political struggles. A major part of most constitutions, and all constitutions in Texas, is the **bill of rights**, a formal declaration of the rights of the citizens within government. These may be rights that the government must provide (the right to a trial by jury) or rights that the government cannot restrict (freedom of speech).

The painstaking process of wording these rights in the state's first constitution led Thomas Rusk, the President of the Convention, to exclaim in exasperation, "we shall be here six weeks yet." But Texans were determined to get the wording right. Why? The answer lies in a revolution that had begun two centuries earlier. In the seventeenth and eighteenth centuries, political thinkers had proposed the idea that the legitimacy of government rested not on a "divine right" of kings but on the consent of the governed. The governed agree to give up some of the freedoms that they possess in the "state of nature" (an anarchical society with no government) in return for the government's commitment to their physical security and safeguarding certain "natural rights." This agreement between the government and the governed is called a **social contract**, which—in republics—are often enshrined in written constitutions.

Early Anglo Texans valued rugged individualism and were not inclined to give up their freedoms to government rule lightly. The challenge in crafting a constitution for Texas, therefore, was to balance freedoms and government power. Throughout Texas history, the two themes woven into the many constitutions that have governed the Lone Star State have been a commitment to individual rights (for most) and a strict separation of powers among the three branches of government, but with a tendency toward strong legislative authority.

Constitutional government in Texas is older than the Republic itself. The story of how Texas constitutional principles were established starts when Texas was part of Mexico and has changed as the state has grown and the political environment has changed.

THE CONSTITUTION
OF THE
STATE OF TEXAS,
AS AMENDED IN 1861.
THE CONSTITUTION OF
THE CONFEDERATE STATES
OF AMERICA.
THE ORDINANCES
OF THE
TEXAS CONVENTION:
AND
AN ADDRESS TO THE PEOPLE OF TEXAS.

PRINTED BY ORDER OF THE CONVENTION AND THE SENATE.

AUSTIN:
PRINTED BY JOHN MARSHALL, STATE PRINTER,
1861.

Texas has had six constitutions that have been shaped by historical circumstances and political reactions to crises. Each version reflected the values of the time as well as a reaction to past crises.

SOCIAL RESPONSIBILITY: **What key rights should a constitution protect?**

social contract: an agreement in which the governed give up freedoms in return for government protection

---

★ TEXAS TAKEAWAYS

1 Explain what a constitution does.

2 What two themes run through the Texas Constitutions?

🤠 THE ROOTS OF REBELLION AND THE DECLARATION OF INDEPENDENCE

The spirit of Texas government was forged in direct reaction to tyranny from multiple governments and several overbearing rulers. After the death of his father, Stephen F. Austin, the "father of Texas," traveled to Mexico City to request the continuation of his father's colony in Mexico. Arriving in 1822, Austin found himself in the middle of a debate in the Mexican Congress about whether to establish

2.2 Explain the events that led to the Texas Declaration of Independence.

Stephen F. Austin was the first and most famous Texan empresario. His steady leadership helped to smooth over several delicate skirmishes between settlers and the Mexican government.

monarchy: a government run by a single individual, often a king or queen, until death or abdication

republic: a form of government in which people rule indirectly through elected representatives

sovereignty: authority over a political entity, such as a province or a state

a **monarchy** or a **republic**. It mattered little in the short term as Augustín de Iturbide, who helped Mexico gain independence from Spain, abruptly seized power himself and replaced the democratically chosen Mexican Congress with a loyal junta, a small group of leaders. In 1823, Iturbide was forced to abdicate after he lost support. Under the newly written Mexican Constitution of 1824, following the exile of Iturbide, the Mexican Congress expanded settlement of the northern Mexico territory using empresarios and established a colonization law that future settlers were to obey. Empresarios were regional land distributors, serving as the local recruiter and leader of a fixed area of land and the people who settled there. The empresarios (like Austin) would be in charge, but the Mexican government promised to protect the liberty, property, and civil rights of all "foreigners" who would in turn profess the Roman Catholic faith.

The Constitution of 1824, created by the Mexican National Congress, established a federal republic for the nation as a whole. In 1827, the Constitution of the State of Coahuila & Tejas established a separation of power system for that state within the nation with three branches of government, not unlike the United States Constitution, and provided for basic freedom of speech, although it forbade the practice of any other religion except Catholicism, limited voting rights to those who could read and had employment, and limited slavery. The Constitution of 1824 is the high point of liberty granted to the Mexican colonists, later to be a rallying cry for the restitution of rights during the Texas Revolution. Most observers believed that if Mexico had agreed to reestablish the rights of Texians under the Constitution of 1824, the Texas revolution would have lost momentum.

It didn't take long for new immigrants to Texas to populate much of the east of the province, prompting the Mexican government to dispatch a surveyor to assess the situation. The unflattering report to the Mexican president stated that the "Mexican influence is disproportionately diminished," and the "ratio of Mexicans to foreigners is one to ten."[4] After disparaging remarks against the citizens and government, the surveyor prophetically noted, "Texas could throw the whole nation into revolution." Following this assessment, the Mexican legislature passed the Law of April 6, 1830, which called for more Mexican soldiers to enforce a strict no slavery policy and, most burdensome to the colonies, a freeze on emigration of settlers from the United States.

In reaction to the new decrees, Texans met in convention in October of 1832 and April 1833 to draw up a formal petition to allow **sovereignty** and independence for the Texas state and a repeal of the Law of April 6, 1830. Stephen F. Austin was dispatched to Mexico City to deliver the petition to President Antonio Lopez de Santa Anna. In a moment of uncharacteristic impatience, Austin told Vice President Gomez Farias that if the situation were not remedied, "Texas would remedy them of themselves without waiting any longer." Gomez Farias interpreted this as a threat of rebellion and imprisoned Austin.[5]

Fanning the flames of rebellion by centralizing power in his own hands, Mexican President Santa Anna sent his vice president into exile, disbanded Congress, and dissolved the state legislatures in 1835. Santa Anna also dismissed the empresarios who organized local migration, including Stephen F. Austin. Austin declared that the Mexican government could not "legally deprive Texans of these rights without the consent of the people.[6] The stage for rebellion was set, and delegates met in March of 1836 to draft a Declaration of Independence. On March 2, 1836, the delegates approved the document that proclaimed that Mexico had abandoned the constitutional principles expressed in the Constitution of 1824 (see Table 2.1) and compromised the republican principles of self-government and representation.

Not all Texas residents embraced the cause of revolution. Benjamin Lundy, a New Jersey born Quaker, had a religious and moral objection to slavery. Mexico had outlawed slavery in Texas, although a covert slave trade market persisted. Lundy asserted in a book published at the time of the revolution that the Texas Revolution was fought to further Texas as a slave state and eventually seek entry to the United States. Although derided at the time, Lundy's contention may have influenced Americans to delay annexation of Texas into the United States because of problems balancing slave and non-slave states in the Union.[7]

TABLE 2.1 Grievances Against the Mexican Government Expressed in the Declaration of Independence

Citizens forced to alter their religion by adopting Catholicism
Incarceration with no just cause of Stephen F. Austin
Refused right to trial by jury
Failed to establish public system of education
Dissolution of Congress from Coahulia & Tejas
Commissioned foreign "desperados" for "piratical" attacks on commerce
Demanded collection of arms
Incitement of Native American attacks

Source: Texas Declaration of Independence.

SOCIAL RESPONSIBILITY: **In your opinion, are these grievances sufficient to justify rebellion? Or, are these better remedied through political means?**

Many Tejanos—Spanish-speaking Texans—were also divided between their loyalty to the young Texas government and the growing dissatisfaction with the highly centralized Mexican government. Yet many joined with the Anglos; and indeed, three Hispanics (two of them Tejanos) signed the Texas Declaration of Independence: Jose Antonio Navarro, Jose Francisco Ruiz, and Lorenzo de Zavala. During the Texas Republic, four Tejanos served in the legislature out of 44 total, all centered in San Antonio. Juan Nepomuceno Seguin fought in the battle for independence and went on to serve as mayor of his native San Antonio, but conflicts with local Anglos led to death threats and prompted his move back to Mexico.

★ TEXAS TAKEAWAYS

3 What events provoked Texans to rebel against Mexico?

4 What were the stated grievances of the Texas Declaration of Independence?

🤠 THE 1836 CONSTITUTION OF THE REPUBLIC

2.3 Relate the goals of the 1836 Constitution to its outcome and reactions to it.

Writing in haste and under fear of the approaching Mexican army, the delegates "scarcely put the finishing touches upon the Constitution" of 1836 before adjourning.[8] News of the fall of the Alamo contributed to a hastily written document.

Yet the 1836 Constitution was more than a governing document. It aggressively voiced the ideals of frontier independence that would come to dominate the future political culture of the state. The Constitution of 1836 included a Declaration of Rights, outlining several unimpeachable liberties, which "shall never be violated on any pretense whatever" and guarded "against the transgression of the high powers which we have delegated." Familiar liberties included freedom to worship; freedom of speech; freedom from unreasonable search and seizure; and the right to bear arms, bail, legal counsel, and a speedy trial.

One significant right incorporated into the 1836 Constitution not included in the US Constitution is the prohibition of monopolies for businesses. The right of free enterprise, unencumbered by government interference, was, however, paramount. This capitalistic spirit, and the power provided to the organizations that promote it, has been a central feature of Texas politics ever since.

The Constitution of 1836 also provided for a strict **separation of powers** between the legislative, executive, and judicial branches. Under this system,

separation of powers: a system that vests political, judicial, and policymaking authority across different branches of government

each branch is selected by different procedures, serves different tenures in office, and is responsible for specific obligations. Most of the authority was housed in the legislature, which had the power to collect taxes, levy tariffs, and pay debts. The executive (styled President) was the commander-in-chief of the army and navy (and militia) but was not to command the troops in the field unless ordered to by the legislature. Like the US president, the President of Texas was able to make treaties and appointments (with two-thirds of the Senate in agreement), fill vacancies, and "upon extraordinary occasions" convene the legislature.

In the Constitution of 1836, we see hints of aversion to centralized power and an extreme distrust of executive authority. The president was not eligible to run for reelection in the presidential race directly following his term. All appointed offices were subject to the approval of the senate; and, if removal was necessary, the senate had to approve that as well.

The 1836 Texas Constitution borrowed heavily from the US Constitution. However, there were additional differences with the federal constitution worth noting. First, no member of the clergy was eligible to serve in elected office in Texas, although the constitution also required at least a "belief" in a higher power. Second, to separate the funding of government from those who serve it, the constitution established that persons "holding an office of profit under the government" or holders of "public monies" were not eligible to serve in the legislature. These passages provided the first framework for ethical government within the state.

At the time the 1836 Constitution was drafted, many Texas residents presumed that the new Texas Republic would quickly join the United States. An overwhelming number of Texas citizens favored annexation only to find the United States cold to the idea. Slavery was the issue. The 1836 Constitution did not allow government to prohibit the importation of slaves into Texas. In fact, slaveholders were not allowed to emancipate slaves without immediately removing them from Texas's borders. The state eventually went so far as to establish a law that all free persons of color were required to leave the state by 1842 or be sold into slavery. The act sparked opposition among some Texas residents who petitioned the legislature to overturn the law on behalf of friends or neighbors. The strong linkage to slavery prevented Texas's immediate entrance into the United States for more than a decade after the revolution ended.

The current Texas Constitution outlaws a religious test for public office, but the constitution requires a candidate "acknowledge the existence of a Supreme Being." Several groups have challenged this provision with little success, and a past attorney general decision rendered it void, but the provision remains.

SOCIAL RESPONSIBILITY: **Should the state require candidates to recognize the existence of a supreme being?**

⭐ **TEXAS TAKEAWAYS**

5 What was the structure of government established by the 1836 Constitution?

6 What were the similarities and differences between the 1836 Constitution of the Republic and the US Constitution with respect to the power of the president and the role of free enterprise?

🤠 THE 1845 CONSTITUTION OF THE (NEW) STATE OF TEXAS

2.4 Differentiate between the 1845 Constitution and prior Texas constitutions.

Both the internal struggle between slave and non-slave states and the threat of war with Mexico if the United States annexed Texas blocked the state's entrance into the Union. But in 1844, James Polk was elected to the US presidency on a platform of Western expansion, which initiated Texas joining the Union. Because of a robust cotton trade, Texas's growing ties to Great Britain, a rival of the United States, prompted a worried United States to initiate annexation talks. Texas, suffering from a drop in cotton prices that pinched the state's major revenue stream, welcomed the invitation. Texas formally entered the Union in December of 1845.

Now a state in the union, Texas needed a new state constitution. The task of writing the new state constitution fell to an able group of individuals, including the president of the Republic, members of Congress, several convention members from the 1836 session, cabinet officers, and ministers. They modeled the document after the Louisiana Constitution, characterized by famous Senator Daniel Webster as the best of all state constitutions at the time.[9]

The Constitution of 1845 (the "statehood constitution") was remarkably similar to the Constitution of 1836 in balancing government authority between the branches and outlining fundamental rights for citizens. The framers, however, erupted into a spirited debate about whether Tejanos should be allowed to vote. Some argued that voting rights should be limited to "free white males." The attempted exclusion failed due to the efforts of delegate Jose Antonio Navarro (the only native born Texan at the convention) and President Rusk, who thought it wrong to insult the character of the state's heritage by excluding Tejanos.[10] Native Americans and African descendants were, however, excluded from voting.

At the same time, the Anglo framers introduced significant democratic reforms by extending **suffrage** to those not holding property. In the legislative branch, the doors of the building were to be physically kept open during

suffrage: the right to participate in the electoral process by voting

the session—probably welcome in the days before air conditioning—and the legislators were to be paid the meager sum of $3 each day (plus mileage), not dissimilar to the current $600 per month (or roughly $20 per day) legislators are paid.

One significant innovation in the 1845 version of the constitution was a more muscular allowance of judicial authority. The state had a growing population, and the judicial system that had been modest and ineffective under Mexican rule was expanded to provide greater access to the court system for Texans. The framers granted the Texas supreme court appellate jurisdiction on legal matters, meaning that they hear arguments from lower courts. In addition to this authority, the Texas supreme court

The first Texas capital building was built at Main Street and Texas Avenue in Houston before the capital moved to Austin in 1846. The Rice Hotel stands today where the capital building once stood. The final president of the Republic, Anson Jones, distraught over not being selected to serve as US Senator, committed suicide here.

could "enforce its own jurisdiction" and compel a judge of a lower court to proceed to trial and judgment in a case.

We also see the introduction of a lieutenant governor for the first time in Texas history in the 1845 Constitution. Although today the Texas lieutenant governor is the most powerful statewide officer alongside the governor, the lieutenant governor in this version of the constitution was selected by the governor as a "running mate" instead of elected separately as would be the case later. The lieutenant governor was to be the president of the Senate and, like the vice president of the United States, have a tiebreaking vote in the Senate.

The 1845 Constitution did not include provisions for popular election of many offices, such as judges or other executive officers—who instead were appointed by the governor. However, as a means to hold the state government accountable to the will of the people, Texans passed an amendment in 1850 to select these officials through popular election.

Two noteworthy provisions highlighted the state's concern about private property rights. The Constitution of 1845 birthed the **homestead law** in Texas, a rule that gives special protection to Texans' homes. Many of the early settlers came to Texas to flee creditors in the United States or abroad. At the time, Stephen F. Austin worried that many settlers would lose their homes or significant property if these debts were collected, and he successfully pushed the Mexican government for protection of the homestead. Although the Mexican legislature passed homestead protections during the pre-Republic days, they later repealed these laws. The threat of losing their homesteads and source of livelihood left a stamp of defiance in the minds of the ruggedly independent Texans. Subsequent constitutions broadened the exemption to limit the amount of property taxes collected on one's home and to allow local governments to give reductions to older or disabled Texans. These laws allow

homestead law: a law that prevents Texans from losing their homes in the event of bankruptcy or other financial problems

only certain creditors to force the sale of a homestead (such as a mortgage holder or the government). The 1845 Constitution was also innovative in its treatment of women's property rights. The framers extended property ownership to married women for property owned before marriage or acquired during marriage.

★ TEXAS TAKEAWAYS

7 Why did the 1845 Constitution extend popular control to state government?

8 In what ways was the 1845 Constitution different from the 1836 Constitution on property rights?

⟨🤠⟩ SECESSION, RECONSTRUCTION, AND THE CONSTITUTIONS OF 1861, 1866, AND 1869

2.5 Analyze the goals of 1860s constitutions in the context of the political and social developments.

The political battles over slavery, the turmoil of the Civil War, and the refashioning of political power in the South produced a rapid making and remaking of Texas government over the period of a decade. In the decade of the 1860s, the constitution was rewritten three times!

Largely in response to the election of Abraham Lincoln in 1860, Texas began the process of secession from the United States just 15 short years after joining. Citing failure of the federal government to protect her borders and the limitations of prosperity due to the likely abolition of slavery, anti-Union sentiment ran high. A series of mysterious fires in Denton and Dallas linked to a rumored slave rebellion fueled hysteria among Anglos. Many Texans in favor of secession also believed that the Confederacy was more likely than the Union to open the route to Westward expansion.[11]

Sam Houston, the governor at the time, was against leaving the Union and did not want to see his life's work plunged into war. The secessionist movement gained considerable strength, however, and forced Houston to call a special session of the legislature to consider the matter. In his office, Houston fumed at "the mob upstairs."[12] Ultimately, a convention in Austin issued an ordinance of secession and a declaration of secession in February of 1861, which was ratified by the majority of counties (see Figure 2.1). Sam Houston refused to sign an oath as required by the Session Convention affirming his allegiance to the Confederacy and was removed from office.

FIGURE 2.1   **1861 Texas Vote on Succeeding from the Union**

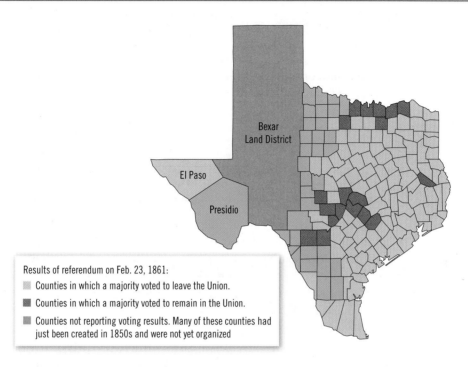

Results of referendum on Feb. 23, 1861:

Counties in which a majority voted to leave the Union.

Counties in which a majority voted to remain in the Union.

Counties not reporting voting results. Many of these counties had just been created in 1850s and were not yet organized

Source: Texas Almanac.

 COMMUNICATION:

Did most counties in Texas support secession?

- By a vote of 166 to 8, Texas declared her secession in February of 1861.
- Most counties voted to secede from the union, although others chose to remain in the union.

 CRITICAL THINKING:

Why are there such geographic differences?

- Much of North Texas and the western border of the state voted in favor of staying in the union due to safety concerns on the frontier and the fact that these settlers had migrated from neutral border states.
- Counties populated by immigrants from the southern United States voted to leave the union primarily to preserve the practice of slavery.
- German settlers in counties in central Texas were opposed to secession because many did not have slaves. Counties where they held a majority voted in favor of staying in the Union.
- Sharing an agricultural need for the continuation of slavery, much of east Texas voted to secede from the Union.

THE 1861 CONSTITUTION—"THE CONFEDERACY CONSTITUTION"

In 1861, delegates to the Secession Convention wrote a constitution that was substantially similar to the statehood constitution but certified the state's membership in the Confederate States of America. Most prominently, the first passage added a clause granting supreme sovereign rights to the state, asserting that no "government or authority" can exercise power within the state without the consent of the people. The 1861 version also protected slavery and forbid slave owners from freeing their slaves without state permission.

THE 1866 CONSTITUTION—"THE READMISSION CONSTITUTION"

After the Civil War ended, Republicans were victorious in the elections of 1866 at the national level, leading to passage of severe legislation that expanded military rule of southern states. New rules for former Confederate states required the states to write new constitutions recognizing the US Constitution and declaring allegiance to the union.

Texas faced a significant threat of federal intervention if they did not abide by the requirement to issue declarations against secession and demonstrate a "paramount allegiance" to the United States. As a result, the Constitution of 1866 showed an unusual tendency toward centralized power, especially in the governor's powers to appoint public officials, the governor's extended term in office, and the position's higher pay. These measures ensured that the state presented a pro-Union front toward the federal government even at a time when Texas was deeply divided in support for the Union.

The 1866 Constitution convention split into three factions: two aggressive factions of Unionists and Secessionists and a third group of moderate Unionists who held the balance of power. The Secessionists and moderate Unionists combined forces to elect James W. Throckmorton as president of the convention, who had been an ardent opponent of secession (the only vote against secession in the legislature in 1861) but eventually joined the Confederate service and rose to the rank of brigadier general. This alliance steered the convention toward a few select goals. The convention agreed to minimum demands for readmission to the union such as allegiance to the union, repudiation of the state's war debt, and invalidation of all laws passed by the state government during the war.

Former Secessionists hindered progress toward the extension of rights to African Americans. Other delegates, such as Governor Hamilton, the provisional governor appointed by US President Andrew Johnson, believed in giving full rights to former slaves, including voting rights and full rights to have legal testimony heard in court. The Secessionists fought against these measures. The Constitution of 1866 reached a compromise. It gave African Americans the right to purchase and sell property, to sue and be sued, and to enter into legally binding agreements, but it deprived them of the right to vote, access to public office, and jury participation. The legislature also passed "black codes" to control the labor of former slaves, a move that many Texas Republicans and Unionists saw as just another form of slavery.

THE 1869 CONSTITUTION—"THE RECONSTRUCTION CONSTITUTION"

Military rule over Texas was to continue until a "loyal sentiment" existed in at least a majority of inhabitants.[13] Racial resentment and friction with a domineering state government made this a challenge. Additional changes in the terms of Reconstruction set by the US Congress forced Texas state leaders to draft another constitution in 1869 to meet new objectives to end Reconstruction and formally return to the Union. All male citizens, regardless of race or color, were allowed to elect delegates to the convention. With several overtures to the supremacy of the Constitution of the United States, the Reconstruction Constitution was required to specify the equality of all persons before the law, ratify the 14th Amendment, and decry the "heresies" of secession.

The Constitution of 1869 established a similar state government structure as past Texas constitutions, but for the first time it began to expand the responsibilities assigned to the state government. For instance, the constitution expanded the duty of the legislature to make "suitable provisions for the support and maintenance of a system of public free schools." The constitution also outlined the power of the state to regulate the land belonging to railroads and affixed the power of the state to regulate and promote immigration.

The Reconstruction Constitution also departed from the old political tradition by extending full voting rights to African Americans, settling a longstanding dispute between confederate sympathizers and reformers looking to appeal to national interests. African Americans were a political power during this era; and one prominent African American delegate, George Thompson Ruby from Galveston, helped to foster equality in the new constitution. Between 1866 and 1896, African American politicians helped build the Republican Party in Texas, inform new voters on voting procedures, and push for issues like education and equal rights.[14] Nevertheless, the state remained highly segregated, and racial violence continued.

As soon as it was drafted, the Reconstruction Constitution of 1869 drew ire from Texans for its centralization of power, especially in the hands of what some deemed the "radical" Republicans who aligned with the national Republicans who had set Reconstruction rules. In Texas, the 1869 elections swept Republican reformer Edmund Davis into the governor's office. The powers of the governor under the Reconstruction Constitution were so far-reaching that it allowed the governor to appoint local officials such as mayors, alderman, and district attorneys. The constitution also granted the governor full control to appoint voter registrars in each county and school superintendents.

Voters were also required to register and vote at the county seats, a hardship for many. State guard units, already despised by many, kept watch over the polling places.

A crime spree between 1865 and 1868, partially initiated by the Ku Klux Klan, targeted freedmen and federal soldiers. Motivated by racism and ill feelings over the outcome of the Civil War, roving gangs of "murderers and horse thieves" preyed on Texans in areas where union sympathy was strong.[15] Governor Davis ordered state police and militia units to calm the violence and lawlessness and aggressively seek out criminals throughout the state. Families in Central Texas resisted during the "Hill County Rebellion," jailing state police officials who were tracking the criminals responsible for local violence. The governor imposed martial law in Hill, Walker, and Bastrop Counties. Accustomed to minimal government oversight, many Texans charged that the governor had become the "Dictator of Texas" who took property or life at his own will; and they called the state police the "Governor's Hounds" and derided them as "snakes, wolves, and other undesirable things." [16] Texans accused the state police of tampering in local elections and murdering prisoners as a form of harsh retribution for criminal actions.[17]

The Davis administration also contributed to rampant corruption and cronyism in state politics. Observers reacted negatively to provisions in the 1869 Constitution that allowed the governor substantial authority to appoint offices made vacant after Texas was admitted to the union until the next general election. Many Texans complained that the candidates for the governor's appointees, the "henchmen of the governor," required no qualifications, as "no recommendation seemed to be needed other than that the incumbents were Democrats and that the aspirants were Republicans."[18] These powers, combined with a short legislative session, instilled tremendous authority in the executive. These powers were contrary to Texas's political tradition, and reformers sought to return to a limited government approach.

In addition to the political problems, several social problems confronted the state at this time. The crime wave in the early 1870s had put pressure on the judicial system, and the "incompetence" of the judges appointed by Governor Davis elicited a desire for an elective judiciary with shorter terms.[19] Substantial financial relief given to railroads, in the form of state financial subsidies, threatened to bankrupt the state.

The Texas Declaration of Independence claimed that the Mexican government did not make provisions for adequate education. Subsequent state constitutions explicitly made quality public education a right for Texans.

SOCIAL RESPONSIBILITY: **Is it a basic right to have free, quality public schools? Should people who don't have children be taxed to support a public education system?**

Local citizens complained that they had no control over their education system because the governor held the power of appointment of school superintendents.

Governor Davis was defeated by 50,000 votes in 1873 but refused to leave office right away, noting that he was allowed to finish out his months as governor. The Texas Supreme Court agreed. But Democrats led by Richard Coke, the winner of the 1873 election, snuck past the guards on the first floor of the Capitol, secured keys to the second floor, and took possession. The Travis Rifle brigade, dispatched to protect Davis, refused to obey the order and instead insured the inauguration of Coke. US President Ulysses S. Grant refused to send federal troops and a compromise was reached in which Davis left office.

TEXAS TAKEAWAYS

9 What was the position of the Constitution of 1861 on states' rights?

10 What prompted the Constitution of 1866 to be written, and what unusual features did it contain as a result?

11 What are three important features of the Constitution of 1869?

THE CONSTITUTION OF 1876— THE CURRENT CONSTITUTION

Born from the Reconstruction Era resentment of the perceived overreaching power of Governor Davis, the Constitution of 1876 is still in use in Texas. In creating the constitution in 1876, factions in the state fought over the role of the federal government and their growing concerns about the fate of liberty under a centralized state government. This fever continues to fuel debates about the constitution today.

2.6 Describe the principles of the modern Texas constitution.

THE CRAFTING OF THE 1876 CONSTITUTION

The radical Republicans' rule was ending by the middle of 1870 as moderate Republicans joined the Democratic Party at the state and national levels. Under Governor Coke, Democrats began to call for a new constitution that would fix what they saw as the flaws in the Constitution of 1869: the centralized executive power, an unwieldy judiciary, and duplicative state offices. In many ways, the framers fashioned the 1876 Constitution in direct reaction to the frustration of strong, costly government imposed on Texas after the Civil War and to the governorship of Edmund Davis. Delegates relied on the Constitution of 1845 as a model and generally favored a return to limited government and frugality, even going so far as to limit their per diem for meals to $5 as opposed to the $8 received by the legislature at that time.

Future governors and current Texas Rangers were delegates, along with many farmers from the Grange Movement who exerted a significant influence on economic reform to benefit agricultural interests and limited government. Five of the fifteen Republican delegates were African American, with the Republican Party having successfully promoted the political participation of the African American community.[20]

Delegates demonstrated great enthusiasm for the new constitution. Upon final passage of the draft, one delegate voted "aye, with the Lord's blessing on it."[21] But passage by the voters proved challenging. Proponents of the new constitution argued that the proposed constitution returned too much authority to the people. Opponents of the proposed constitution took issue with the weakening role of the state in fostering immigration and consistent quality public education. After a grueling campaign, the new constitution was ratified by voters in the 1876 election, 136,606 votes to 56,652.

PRINCIPLES OF THE TEXAS CONSTITUTION

The current Texas Constitution, organized into seventeen articles (see Table 2.2), contains four key principles: popular sovereignty, limited state government through local control, separation of powers, and personal rights and liberties. These principles and their implementation within the 1876 Constitution strongly reflect Texas's political culture.

Popular Sovereignty. The 1876 Constitution recognizes the centrality of **popular sovereignty** to Texas's republican form of government: "political power is inherent in the people, and all free governments are founded on their authority, and instituted for their benefit" (Article 1, Section 2). The people rule through suffrage, the right to vote in elections, which today is extended to all citizens of the state, except those under 18 years of age, those deemed mentally incompetent, and those convicted of certain crimes (including bribery, perjury, forgery, or other "high crimes"). Because all substantial policy changes must be approved by the voters, the role of the people in governing the state is critical. One prominent constitutional restriction is on taxes on income—any attempt to establish a state income tax must be approved by a majority of voters who vote in an election.

National trends at the time of drafting that edged toward more inclusive, unrestricted suffrage for adult males also influenced the framers of the 1876 Constitution. Unlike today's version, the 1876 Constitution, however, did not immediately extend suffrage to all Texans. Women were excluded from voting. The universal sovereignty provisions also took on a racial overtone. Anglos feared that the African American majority in some counties would "put whites completely under the control of their former slaves."[22] Republicans, who developed "Union Leagues" to encourage voting, banded together to form a slate of all African American candidates to support the constitution in predominantly

see for yourself 2.1

Consider whether the 1876 Constitution gives the people too much power as you listen to senate rules expert Karina Davis explain how it limits lawmakers.

popular sovereignty: rule by the people

TABLE 2.2 Articles of the Texas Constitution

Article 1	Bill of Rights	Outlines rights and responsibilities
Articles 2-5, 9, 15, 16	Power of Government	Establishes powers of each branch of government; impeachment process
Article 6	Voting	Establishes right to vote and qualifications
Article 7	Education	Summarizes the right to education and local responsibility
Article 8, 11, 12	Taxes, Revenue, and Corporations	Enumerates the type and limits on taxes and revenue
Articles 10, 14	Public Lands, Railroads	Identifies the rights of state to control
Article 17	Amendments	Specifies how to amend the Constitution

Source: Texas Constitution.

African American counties. As a result, several newspapers in those areas demanded Anglos vote against the proposed constitution and the provisions for unrestricted suffrage. The constitution ultimately extended suffrage to all males.

The framers of the 1876 Constitution, however, appeased Anglo fears of universal male suffrage by adding a provision that voters must be taxpayers before voting on city finance elections. A poll tax of one dollar was also required to vote. Most Republican delegates in 1876 were opposed, primarily because African Americans were a major constituency and could not always afford to pay the tax. Some Democratic opposition came from the progressive Grange political movement who opposed more taxes for farmers. A temporary partnership between Republicans who relied on African American voters and farmers from the progressive Granger Movement, referred to as the "holy alliance," tried unsuccessfully to block the poll tax. The measure, in fact, remained unchallenged until the passage of the 24th Amendment in 1964 and was not removed in Texas until 1966 when the Supreme Court ruled it unconstitutional.

Limited Government. **Limited government** is another central organizing feature of the Texas Constitution. Limited government implies that the impact of government is kept as small as possible, with few laws passed and as little intervention in the lives of citizens as possible. Experiences with overreaching executive power and with the "obnoxious acts" of the Twelfth Legislature under Governor Davis caused the authors of the 1876 Constitution to restrict government's power.

First, the framers of the 1876 Constitution fragmented the power of the executive branch, creating new offices and ripping the power to appoint established offices from the governor and granting this power to the people, who now elect these officers. The powers of the executive branch of government rested not just in the governor's office but also in other important offices: the lieutenant governor, secretary of state, comptroller of public accounts, commissioner

SOCIAL RESPONSIBILITY:
What possible political issues do the articles of the Texas Constitution address? What political issues should they address, if any?

limited government: a political system in which the government's functions and powers are restricted to protect individual liberty

INSIDER INTERVIEW
Former Chief Justice Tom Phillips

As a conservative judge on the Texas Supreme Court, what do you believe are the greatest strengths of the Texas Constitution?

The greatest strengths of the Texas Constitution, in my opinion, are negative ones. The limitation on legislative sessions makes our part-time legislators more aware of the effects of their laws than federal or other large state representatives. The constitution is too detailed, but at least it's easier to amend than those in some states. The constitution doesn't permit initiative and referendum.

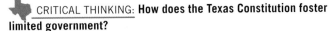

CRITICAL THINKING: **How does the Texas Constitution foster limited government?**

---

plural executive: diffusion of authority and power throughout several entities in the executive branch

of the General Land Office, and attorney general. Each office, except the secretary of state, is elected separately from the governor, diffusing the power of the executive into several offices and limiting executive authority. This structure is called a **plural executive**.

Second, the framers of the 1876 Constitution also took aim at the legislative branch. The new constitution shortened the terms of office and increased the number of representatives that had been established by previous constitutions. The Constitution of 1876 also stripped the legislature of its power to suspend laws that provide for access to courts for Texans.

The framers also sought to limit the ability of the state to encroach on the rights of local governments. The 1876 Constitution restricts the legislature from "regulating the affairs of counties, cities, towns, wards or school districts" and lists several specific things the state cannot do, including locating a county seat, laying out roads, granting divorces, and managing public schools. Whereas the legislature is required to create and fund public schools, the constitution gives full authority to local, independent school districts to use these funds. Local counties are also permitted to establish a hospital district for the purchase, construction, operation, or maintenance of a hospital system.

Over time, however, Texans have voted to amend the Constitution of 1876 to modestly expand government's authority. Several amendments have given greater authority to the legislature to manage the economic and social affairs of the state, such as regulating railroads, administering state prisons, and monitoring local banks. Other amendments have restricted government's reach, such as those that established or increased term limits for judges.

Separation of Powers. The Texas Constitution of 1876 separates powers so that the legislative, executive, and judicial branches have the power to enact laws,

FIGURE 2.2 **Separation of Powers**

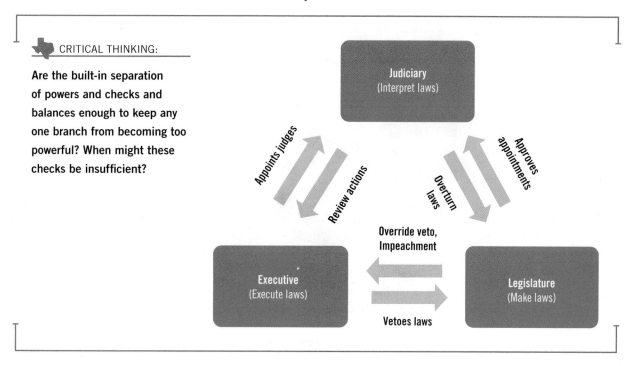

CRITICAL THINKING:

Are the built-in separation of powers and checks and balances enough to keep any one branch from becoming too powerful? When might these checks be insufficient?

implement laws, and interpret laws, respectively (see Figure 2.2). This separation of powers prevents excessive concentration of power into any one branch and promotes effective government by encouraging each branch to specialize. As with past Texas constitutions, the framers endowed the legislative branch with the greatest authority.[23]

In 1876, however, concerns about overreaching government were tempered by worry about the crime wave that afflicted the state during the early 1870s. Jails were full and thus were expensive to maintain, and thousands of undecided cases sat before the supreme court. An 1874 amendment to the 1869 Constitution to increase the number of supreme court judges from three to five had not solved the problem, and Texans bristled at the incompetence of judges appointed by Governor Davis. As a result, the framers agreed to alternative means to select judges: Texas would elect judges.

Personal Rights and Liberties. The 1876 Constitution makes use of principles of liberty, equality, and freedom to guide the Texas Bill of Rights, which are contained in Article 1 of the Texas Constitution. The rights granted in this section are inviolate, or are forever protected by the state and safe from removal by government.

The Texas Bill of Rights is similar in many respects to the US Constitution's Bill of Rights. Both contain references to equal rights, a republican form of government, freedom to worship, freedom of speech and the press, and the

SOCIAL RESPONSIBILITY:

Compare and contrast the state legislature's attempts to limit certain rights, such as those for same-sex couples and abortion, with the Constitution's requirements of individual liberty.

right to bear arms. Both Bills of Rights contain rights protecting against unreasonable searches and seizures, the rights of the accused, right to trial by jury, the right to bail, and protections against "double jeopardy" whereby a defendant cannot be tried twice for the same crime.

GREAT TEXAS POLITICAL DEBATES
Confederate Flag License Plates and the Battle over Free Speech

Texas has hundreds of specialty license plates that drivers can choose from, including "God Bless Texas," "Choose Life," and for the bold, dozens of out-of-state colleges who might be football enemies of one of Texas's universities. A major controversy erupted over the "Sons of Confederate Veterans" plate that prominently displayed the confederate flag. A coalition of conservative and liberal Texas elected officials denounced the plates and banned their use, while the ACLU defended the plates as free speech. Joining Governor Rick Perry in disapproving of the plates, Democratic State Senator Royce West asked, "Why should we as Texans want to be reminded of a legalized system of involuntary servitude, dehumanization, rape, mass murder?"[24] The Supreme Court ruled in 2015 that Texas could refuse to issue the plates, ruling that the state had a right to restrict "government speech" that expresses disagreeable opinions.

SOCIAL RESPONSIBILITY: **Should Texans be allowed to choose government approved license plates to represent their beliefs?**

YES: Texans have a right to advocate for their beliefs, and short of hurting another person, should be able to have outlets to express these positions. There is no harm to other Texans when expressing views on a license plate.

NO: Some beliefs are too repugnant to be expressed and Texas must regulate which groups are allowed to advocate on state-issued materials.

The Texas Bill of Rights has been amended to encompass newer rights that evolved later. For example, the Texas Bill of Rights now includes the rights of crime victims (Article 1, Section 30), added to the constitution in 1989, which entitles a crime victim to reasonable protection from the accused throughout the criminal justice process and provides for restitution for the crimes committed. In 2009, voters also approved unrestricted public access to public beaches (Article 1, Section 33), much to the delight of Texas spring breakers. The Texas Bill of Rights now includes a provision for equal protection under the law with respect to sex, designed to reduce discrimination, an extension of what the US Constitution does. An amendment also provides for denial of bail for individuals involved in family violence cases. As a result, the Bill of Rights of the 1876 Constitution contains many rights that the framers of the 1876 Constitution would not likely have conceived of over 140 years ago.

The Texas Constitution provides for additional rights in other articles within the constitution. Like earlier constitutions, the Texas Constitution stresses a "suitable provision" for the support and maintenance of an "efficient" system of public (K–12) free schools (Article 7). The legislature and the courts often interpret this language differently when it comes to funding, but in principle, the Texas Constitution provides for adequate and reasonably funded public schools throughout the state.

 **TEXAS TAKEAWAYS**

12 What prompted the Constitution of 1876 to be written?

13 What are the four principles guiding the Texas Constitution?

14 Describe the Texas Bill of Rights and how it has evolved over time.

🤠 AMENDING THE CONSTITUTION

Texans have rejected any major reform efforts to overhaul the 1876 Constitution, preferring incremental change through constitutional amendments. In this section, we examine how the constitution changes incrementally and why reforms to modernize the constitution have failed.

2.7 Outline the process for amending the Texas Constitution and attempts at constitutional change.

CONSTITUTIONAL AMENDMENTS

Although the basic structure of government is largely the same as the one established by the original 1876 Constitution, the document has grown significantly in length because it is frequently amended. Since 1876, the legislature has proposed 673 constitutional amendments: 670 have gone before Texas voters, and 491 have been approved (see Figure 2.3).[25] The most frequent

FIGURE 2.3   **Total Amendments Approved by Voters by Year**

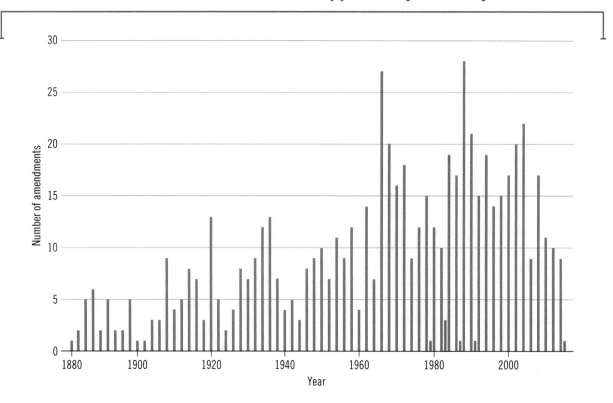

Source: Texas Legislative Council.

COMMUNICATION:

How many amendments are approved on average?

- In some years, only one proposed amendment was passed by the voters, such as in 1978, 1986, and 2014.

- In a multiple years, 20 or more amendments were approved. For instance, in 2001, 20 amendments were proposed by voters, primarily "constitutional cleanup" matters in which specific provisions are moved from one section to another more appropriate section or when outdated or unnecessary language is eliminated from the document.

CRITICAL THINKING:

Why are there so many in some years and so few in others?

- In some years, constitutional reform efforts become legislative priorities, often when the legislature faces fewer pressing policy issues.

- The legislature asks voters to approve measures that are controversial rather than create legislation and take possible blame.

- In years where major issues are on the table (tax cuts, school reform), voters often must approve of changes.

amendments proposed deal with taxation, salary increases, and policy matters such as prison, pensions, and highways.

Why are there so many amendments to the Texas Constitution? As we've seen, the 1876 Constitution limited the role of government. Any change to state government that requires expansion of state authority must be approved by a constitutional amendment. Since 1876, the state's population and economy has grown significantly—and as a result, the state government has had to take on new responsibilities. For example, amendments have allowed the expansion of the state university system and funding for public roads. Every little change in municipal taxation or local authority needs to be codified in the constitution. The frequently amended document is now thick with regulations, rules, and rights that have accrued over the decades.

The Texas Constitution can be amended through a four-step process. The process begins in the legislature, where two-thirds of both houses of the legislature propose an amendment. This does not require the governor to agree, but rather the secretary of state and the attorney general approve the proposals, and the proposals are advertised across the state. Voters have the final say in the process: a majority must approve each individual proposal in a general election or in a special election. Once the voters have spoken, the governor finalizes the new amendment by issuing a proclamation.

Since 1879, most amendments put to the voters pass—on average 74 percent. Many of these are "housekeeping" measures that concern outdated or unnecessary provisions, such as a series of deleted "deadwood amendments" in 1969 concerning prohibitions on dueling with deadly weapons and the use of manual labor as payment for those convicted of misdemeanors.

When considering constitutional amendments, voters are more willing to approve some types of amendments than others (see Figure 2.4 and Table 2.3). For example, Texans tend to favor the issuing of bonds or tax relief. Since 1879, bond extension proposals, amendments to allow for the issuance of bonds to borrow funds for specific purposes, have passed the voters' bar at a rate of 98%! When asked to cap, reduce, or eliminate several forms of taxes, voters approved of these measures on average by 84%. Voters were less willing to approve of constitutional cleanup measures, which pass by a rate of 79%. Voters have been historically very unwilling to alter the organization of a branch of government or to extend additional powers to politicians. These measures have only been approved 38% of the time by voters. Such propositions have included moving to an annual legislative session or altering the size of the Supreme Court.

The benefit of the complicated amendment process is that it often allows legislators to require the voters to decide on controversial issues. For example, in 2014, in the midst of public outcry over the deteriorating quality of roads in the state, voters were asked in Proposition 1 whether they would divert some funds from the Rainy Day Fund, the state's reserve piggy bank it uses for emergency funding matters, to pay for the cost of transportation

FIGURE 2.4   **Highest and Lowest Percent Approval Rates of Proposed Amendments**

Property tax relief

93.8%

Mobile drilling equipment

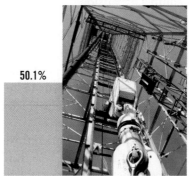

50.1%

Source: Texas Legislative Council.

 COMMUNICATION:

By how much do voters approve of amendments to the Constitution?

- At the low end, in 1987, passing with only 50.1% of the vote, voters approved an amendment that allowed the legislature to provide for property tax relief for mobile marine drilling equipment that is being stored but not in use in certain Gulf Coast counties.

- At the high end, in 1997 voters overwhelmingly approved (at 93.8%) raising the property tax homestead exemption, a major tax cut.

 CRITICAL THINKING:

Why are some proposed amendments more popular than others?

- Most amendments that pass with large margins are beneficial to voters' pocketbooks. More specific or less relatable amendments have a harder time passing.

- Amendments that overwhelmingly pass are often the subject of advertising campaigns, such as efforts in 2014 to approve new transportation funding.

improvements. The voters approved the amendment, but months passed before the funds were made available. Hence, the disadvantage of placing power more directly in the hands of voters is that lawmakers are often hamstrung by a lengthy process when they want to make substantive changes to the system or to public policy.

Moreover, an ongoing weakness of the amendment process is low citizen participation. Voter interest in constitutional change has historically been low,

| TABLE 2.3 | Proposed Amendments to the Texas Constitution |

KEY PROPOSITIONS THAT PASSED	
AMENDMENT	YEAR ENACTED
Mandatory Judicial Retirement Age	1965
Elimination of Poll Tax	1965
Authorizing Bingo Games for Charitable Purposes	1979
Denial of Bail for Family Violence Cases	2007
KEY PROPOSITIONS THAT FAILED	
AMENDMENT	YEAR FAILED
Raise per Diem and Mileage Reimbursement for Legislators	1887, 1897, 1905, 1913
Provide for Annual Legislative Sessions	1958, 1969
Increase Size of the Texas Senate	1965
Increase Length of Term for House Members	1965

Source: Texas Legislative Council.

 COMMUNICATION:

What sorts of amendments pass? What sorts fail?

- Voters generally disapprove of changes to the institutions, such as lengthening terms of Texas House members or increasing the size of the Texas Senate.

- Voters tend to vote in favor of amendments that align with ideological or moral principles. For instance, voters voted to eliminate the poll tax and extending rights to crime victims.

 CRITICAL THINKING:

Why do some pass and not others?

- Uncertainty about the impact of changes in government's design leads voters to reject institutional changes.

- Voters treat constitutional changes like a referendum on issues—voters consider the personal impacts of policy and vote accordingly.

even on important or impactful matters (see Figure 2.5). Lack of voter interest is not terribly surprising because constitutional reform is often dense and legalistic. Yet the more citizens participate, the more the outcome is representative of the interests and values of the people.

Indeed, it is hard to blame the public for their lack of interest. Voters are asked to approve or disapprove often in years without presidential elections in which high profile candidates, like presidents, are not on the ballot. The content and wording of the proposed amendments are often confusing.

FIGURE 2.5   **Numbers and Percentages Voting for Amendments**

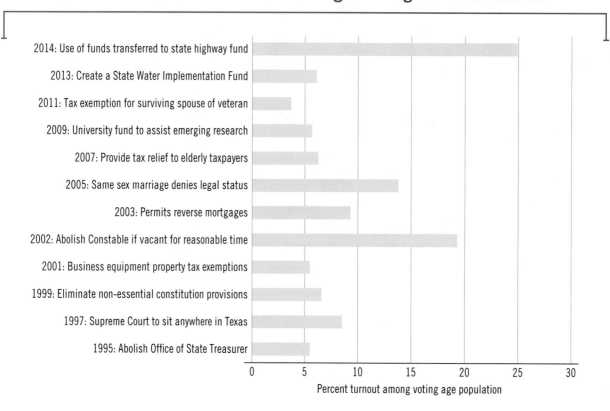

Source: Texas Secretary of State, Election Returns.

 COMMUNICATION:

For what years and what issues is voter turnout higher? Lower?

- Some issues spark voter interest and some do not. For instance, turn-out was only 3.7% in 2011 when the amendment allowed tax exemption for the surviving spouse of a veteran, whereas the 2005 amendment to change the constitution's definition of marriage to one man and one woman drew 18% of the vote.

- Turnout in amendment elections tends to be higher when they coincide with a general election but lower otherwise.

 CRITICAL THINKING:

Why does turnout vary?

- Turnout in amendment elections tends to be lower when the issues are narrow or procedural, making them difficult for most voters to understand.

- Turnout tends to be higher when the issues in the amendment are of greater social or economic importance.

- Amendment elections also have no popular candidate to back or direct party involvement and are often held at times that don't correspond to other elections.

The information about the proposals is often minimal and only habitual voters are likely to understand what the proposed amendment would do. For example, the wording for a 2015 amendment read as follows:

> The constitutional amendment increasing the amount of the residence homestead exemption from ad valorem taxation for public school purposes from $15,000 to $25,000, providing for a reduction of the limitation on the total amount of ad valorem taxes that may be imposed for those purposes on the homestead of an elderly or disabled person to reflect the increased exemption amount, authorizing the legislature to prohibit a political subdivision that has adopted an optional residence homestead exemption from ad valorem taxation from reducing the amount of or repealing the exemption, and prohibiting the enactment of a law that imposes a transfer tax on a transaction that conveys fee simple title to real property.

In layman's terms, the amendment reduces property taxes. After reading it, do you clearly understand it? Many Texans don't. In 2014, voters were asked whether they approved of Proposition 1, the language of which was confusing and convoluted. In polling from October of 2014, two weeks before the election, 17% of those responding indicated that they "didn't know" how they would vote.[26] Furthermore, the amendments are always listed last on the ballot, so voters must often pass all the way to the end of the ballot—something they often do not do.

RECENT MAJOR REFORM ATTEMPTS

Critics of the Texas Constitution often claim that the constitution is too long; that it is often redundant because there are several outdated passages; that it reads more like a legal statute than a compact with citizens; and, perhaps most important, that it hamstrings the ability of elected officials to efficiently manage public policy. The Texas Constitution's verbose 86,000 words both restrain government action but also assign additional responsibilities. Whereas the constitutions in many other states have not grown significantly, the constitution in Texas has expanded greatly over time (see Figure 2.6). One editorial in the Dallas Morning News in 1929 stated that the constitution was "like an overgrown boy in short pants."[27] Proponents for constitutional change also claim that the limitations on governmental authority are outdated and reflect a concern during the drafting in 1876 that the federal government would intervene should institutions be made too strong. Several attempts have been made to alter the document to remedy these shortcomings.

Most reform efforts have aimed to expand the tenure of elected officials, widen their political powers, or increase their pay. Voters have been less willing to allow for this expansion of authority, holding steadfast to the original, basic

IS IT BIGGER IN TEXAS?

FIGURE 2.6   **Number of Words in State Constitutions**

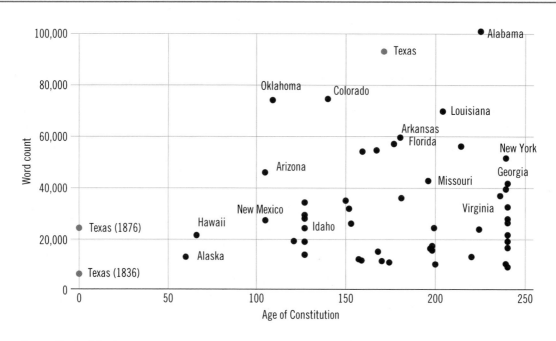

Source: Book of the States.

 COMMUNICATION:

How does the Texas Constitution compare to other state constitutions?

- Alabama's constitution is the longest because it has seen the most changes. Texas's constitution trails far behind in second place but has also had many amendments.

- Newer, western, and smaller states have shorter constitutions, such as Hawaii, New Mexico, and Alaska.

 CRITICAL THINKING:

Why is Texas's Constitution so long?

- The Texas Constitution is so restrictive that it requires amendments to deviate from limited government to allow the government to act at all. Minor issues such as tax relief by exempting manufactured aircraft parts from taxation must be changed through the amendment process. As a result, the Texas Constitution's length increases consistently.

- Southern states have larger constitutions than other states because they had to adapt restrictive constitutions after the Civil War. Alabama, Texas, Louisiana, and Virginia (and others not displayed) all have seen major changes.

- Western states, such as Hawaii, New Mexico, and Alaska, have a desire for small government; and modest population growth has kept the number of changes small.

ANGLES OF POWER
Debates About Amending the Constitution

The delegates to the 1876 Constitutional Convention spent a great deal of time on a great many issues. A critical issue about the method of amendment emerged: would the legislature or the people have final say?

As proposed, the amendment process would require two-thirds of the legislature to put an amendment to the voters; a majority of voters must approve; and the process *would end when two-thirds of the members of each house in the next legislature agreed to the final amendments*.

Delegate Judge Ballinger proposed eliminating the requirement of a legislative acceptance after the voters had voted. Ballinger and his supporters held that the legislature should not have the power to defeat the will of the people. The idea that just over 100 legislators would overturn the will of the people "was utterly at war with the whole theory of our Government."[28] Ballinger's opponents asserted that this would prevent hasty amendments and would be a safeguard against "injudicious" amendments. Delegate Judge West asserted that this prevented the constitution from being altered with "every change in the moon."[29] The Ballinger proposal passed, and the people have a final say in the amending of the constitution.

 PERSONAL RESPONSIBILITY: **Who should have the final say in the amendment process?**

design of the Constitution of 1876. The first attempt to change the constitution occurred in 1901 and was repeated almost every legislative session for two decades. We highlight three recent attempts here.

1974 Constitutional Convention. Constitutional conventions are the most thorough method of reforming the Texas Constitution. The most recent convention took place in 1974 after the Texas legislature established the Constitutional Revision Commission. The voters approved (by a margin of over half a million votes) a "limited convention" composed of members of the legislature that would not have the power to change the bill of rights. Following the recommendations from the commission, a Constitutional Convention (dubbed the "con-con") drafted a series of proposals to reform the 1876 Constitution.

As with so many legislative sessions, the focus of the convention quickly shifted to controversial issues, and reform efforts lost momentum. Two issues of great concern to powerful interest groups stalled progress: a growing religious conservative movement opposed the expansion of racetrack gambling (pari-mutuel betting), and organized labor opposed the continuation of the state as a "right to work" state that would have prohibited limited union membership and agreements between unions and labor. Partisan conflict also erupted over proposed changes to public education funding. After seven months, the convention closed without passing a slate of constitutional changes to submit to the voters.

No Proposal Alive in 1975. Disappointment over the failure of the 1974 convention to produce any serious constitutional reform laid the groundwork for

see for yourself 2.2

Listen to Former Speaker of the Texas House argue for constitutional change. Do his reasons still apply today?

ten proposals that were put to voters in 1975. The Texas Legislative Council cast the constitution as a used car that may "no longer be effectively patched and spot repaired, but must be overhauled."[30] Indeed, several of the proposals would have radically reshaped government authority across the branches. The executive branch would have established a new cabinet system of government that the governor would appoint at the beginning of their term. The legislative branch would have been subject to term limits, and a special "veto session" would have allowed the legislature to respond to any gubernatorial veto. The court system would have been consolidated into fewer courts, including combining the two courts of last resort into a single supreme court. The proposals also required that Texas students have equal opportunity to public education and that petroleum tax revenue could be spent for any purpose, not just roads or the School Fund.

Some claimed that the proposals were "not controversial"—just housekeeping changes—but the voters rejected every single one. Some of these changes were minor, technical issues of little concern to most voters, including the modernization of county government through home rule and state debt-granting authority. Other changes were more significant and would have benefited voters, such as property tax relief and exempting goods, such as medicines and food, from sales taxes. However, Texans—fearful of expanding government power—rejected the lot.

Junell–Ratliff Proposals (1999).   In the 1999 legislative session, two major power players in government—Representative Rob Junell, the Chair of the House Appropriations Committee, and Senator Bill Ratliff, the Chair of the Senate Finance Committee—proposed several new constitutional amendments involving structural adjustments to the tenure or authority of the branches of Texas government. Many of these proposals were similar to past proposals. For the legislative branch, the terms of the House and Senate members would be increased to four and six years, respectively. For the judicial branch, the court system would (again) be consolidated into fewer courts, and a merit system would replace the partisan reelection system of selecting judges. With no crisis to generate support for change, however, the proposals perished in committee and were eventually withdrawn by their supporters.

It has been difficult to convince the state's voters to significantly change the core design of the constitution, despite frequent amendment. Instead of fixing a flat tire, Texas voters have chosen not to fix it if the car can still run. Most observers agree, however, that the frequent need to change the constitution perpetuates an outdated system that better fits the small, agricultural state of the past rather than the mega-diverse and massive state Texas has become.

TEXAS TAKEAWAYS

15 Why is the Texas Constitution amended so often?

16 What reforms have critics of the Texas Constitution tried to advance? Why have they been unsuccessful?

17 What percentage of amendments is approved by voters? What types of amendments do voters support and what types do they reject?

🤠 THE INSIDER VIEW

During the state's early history, Texas created and ratified five different constitutions as it transferred sovereignty from the Texas Republic to the United States to the Confederacy and back to the United States. Each constitution was written to challenge or embrace the political forces facing Texas—the constitution of the Republic constructed a system that expanded local authority, whereas the Reconstruction Constitution centralized power at the state level and demanded loyalty to the federal government. The current Texas Constitution was forged in reaction to a domineering governor, creating a plural executive and restoring the power of the legislative branch. Today, the independent spirit of Texas lives on in the Texas Constitution— and as a result, Texans have rejected major changes. Voters have amended the constitution to reflect changing political circumstances, economic diversification, and social values. The present constitution is a lengthy document designed to limit power from amassing in any one political corridor and to promote popular control over government, in line with the political ethos of Texas.

TEXAS TAKEAWAYS

1 A constitution implements a social contract between people, spells out rights and responsibilities, and sets rules of government.

2 The two themes in each of Texas's constitutions have been a commitment to individual rights and a strict separation of powers.

3 The revoking of the Constitution of 1824, the high point of liberty granted to the colonists, became a rallying cry for the restitution of rights during the Texas Revolution.

4 The grievances contained in the Texas Declaration of Independence include forced

Catholicism, no trial by jury, no education system, collection of weapons, incitement of Native American attacks.

5 A separation of powers arranged responsibility between the legislative, executive, and judicial branches.

6 The 1836 Texas Constitution limited the role of the chief executive but enhanced the role of free enterprise.

7 The 1845 Constitution extended popular control to state government to provide more voter control over state officials.

8 The 1845 Constitution extended property rights to married women. It also included the Homestead Law.

9 The Constitution of 1861 took a strong position in favor of states' rights.

10 The Confederacy's loss in the Civil War brought federal government control, along with specific rules, to former confederate states.

11 The Reconstruction Constitution was required to specify the equality of all persons before the law, ratify the 14th Amendment, and decry the "heresies" of secession. The right to a public education was also first introduced. The right to vote was extended to African Americans.

12 Distrust over centralized government, lack of local control of government, and a crime wave promoted a rewriting of the Texas Constitution in 1876.

13 There are four key principles of the current Texas Constitution: popular sovereignty, limited state government through local control, separation of powers, and personal rights and liberties.

14 The rights granted by the Bill of Rights are inviolate and certify the rights that Texans possess under the constitution. The Bill of Rights has also expanded to include specific individual rights such as access to public lands and restitution for victims of crime.

15 The Texas Constitution is easy to amend. The Texas Constitution is frequently amended because it inherently restricts state power to those provisions outlined in the constitution.

16 Critics of the constitution argue that it is too long, reads like a legal statute, and isn't flexible in allowing local governments to act efficiently. Proponents of change have been largely unsuccessful in changing these points.

17 Voters approve 74 percent of amendments and favor those that cut taxes especially.

KEY TERMS

bill of rights
constitution
homestead law
limited government
monarchy
plural executive
popular sovereignty
republic
separation of powers
social contract
sovereignty
suffrage

PRACTICE QUIZ

1. In 1823, when Emperor Iturbide was forced to abdicate, the new Congress ratified Austin's charter but established a colonization law that future settlers must obey. Regional land distributors served as the local recruiters and leaders of a fixed area of land and the people who settled there. What was the name of these distributors?

    a. Colonizers
    b. Luchadores
    c. Empresarios
    d. Coahuilans

2. The current Texas Constitution is also known as

    a. The Constitution of 1876
    b. The Constitution of 1845
    c. The Constitution of 1869
    d. The Constitution of 1888

3. Most amendments put to Texas voters

    a. Pass
    b. Fail
    c. Are referred to a "Special Session"
    d. Are debated by the Governor and the Legislature

4. The following individual was dispatched to Mexico City to deliver the petitions, only to be imprisoned for inciting Texas to revolution by organizing a new state government without permission:

    a. Anastacio Bustamante
    b. Stephen F. Austin
    c. Sam Houston
    d. General Robert E. Lee

5. Which type of system vests political, legal, and policymaking authority across different branches of government?

    a. Gubernatorial System
    b. Constitutional Monarchy
    c. Electoral College
    d. Separation of Powers

6. In the single decade of the 1860s, how many times was the Texas Constitution rewritten?

    a. None
    b. 1
    c. 3
    d. 8

7. In terms of state authority and power, the current Texas Constitution

    a. Remained ambivalent on the matter.
    b. Called for a strong central governing body.
    c. Was severely limiting.
    d. Remained completely silent on the matter.

8. All of the following concepts guided the creation of the Texas Constitution of 1876, EXCEPT

    a. Popular sovereignty
    b. Limited government
    c. Self-government
    d. Capitalism

9. Former Chief Justice of Texas Supreme Court Tom Phillips said which of the following regarding the level of detail included in the Texas Constitution?

    a. It is too detailed.
    b. It is not detailed enough.
    c. It has just the right amount of detail.
    d. He did not remark on this element of the Texas Constitution.

10. Voters have been willing to change the structure of government by constitutional amendment.

    a. True
    b. False

[Answers: C, A, A, B, D, C, C, D, A, A]

3 FEDERALISM

In his inaugural address in 2015, newly sworn in Governor Greg Abbott charged up the crowd of 10,000 onlookers outside the Texas Capitol: "As governor, I will continue my legacy of pushing back against Washington, if they spend too much, regulate too much, or violate our state sovereignty." Referencing a famous phrase from the Texas revolution, he continued: "Any government that uses the guise of fairness to rob us of our freedom will get a uniquely Texan response: 'Come and take it.'" Governor Abbott challenged the federal government by claiming that "Texans aren't spoiling for a fight, but we won't shrink from one if the cause is right. For too long Washington has tried to remake America in its image. In Texas, we offer a different approach: We don't put our trust in government; we put our trust in the people, and I will make sure we keep it that way."[1]

The new Governor's message was more than rhetorical. As Attorney General, Abbott had spent more than $2.5 million filing 31 lawsuits against the Obama Administration. Indeed, Governor Abbott finished his inaugural address by saying, "I didn't invent that phrase, 'Don't Mess with Texas,' but I have applied it more than anyone else ever has."[2] Between 2009 and 2015, Texas has sued the Obama Administration more times than any other state. The results, however, are mixed—Texas won only a quarter of the cases, including a lawsuit to block the implementation of President Obama's executive order limiting deportation for certain classifications of immigrants. However, Texas fought to a draw on two of the biggest and most expensive cases: challenging regulations about pollution from Texas drifting into other states and defending the state's redistricting lines.[3]

LEARNING OBJECTIVES

3.1 Identify the types of governmental systems and the sources of federal and state power.

3.2 Describe the advantages of federalism.

3.3 Evaluate how Texas uses the funding received from the federal government.

3.4 Assess how elements of cooperation and coercion within the federal system have changed over time.

3.5 Analyze examples of the conflicts over federalism.

● Governor Abbott finished his inaugural address by saying, "I didn't invent that phrase, 'Don't Mess with Texas,' but I have applied it more than anyone else ever has."

Texas takes pride in its independent and ruggedly individualistic character. Politicians aggressively guard the state's rights from encroachment of the federal government. The trouble for Texas (and every other state) is that the design of the American political system allows the federal government to set rules that must be followed by the state. The federal government also makes enticing financial offers that are too good to pass up, encouraging cash-strapped states to play by federal rules. In fact, more than a third of the state's budget comes from the federal government. Even as Republican leaders in Texas vilify Washington, the relationship between the state and federal government is hopelessly intertwined, creating a constant source of friction. The tug of tension between state politics, national rules, and healthy budgets complicates power sharing between levels of government.

In this chapter, we explore the relationship between Texas and the federal government established by the US Constitution. Then we identify the alternative styles of federalism through which Texas and the federal government struggle for control on a range of public policy issues. Finally, we examine major controversies between Texas and the federal government.

ORGANIZING THE CONSTITUTIONAL SYSTEM

3.1 Identify the types of governmental systems and the sources of federal and state power.

unitary system: a central government that has complete authority over all levels of government

There are three primary types of governmental systems: unitary, confederal, and federal. Some systems create a "top-down" style of government. This type of centralized organization of government is referred to as a **unitary system**—a style of government in which a sovereign state is granted complete governing authority over the people. The central government's authority is supreme and grants specific powers to state and local governments. Many European states adopted unitary systems, as did the Republic of Texas. The republic and later state constitutions established local governments as "creatures of the state," deriving their power and authority from the Texas Constitution and the state legislature. So, for example, the Republic of Texas's Constitution in 1836 established a right to public education; and the state set aside funds for public schools beginning in the 1876 Constitution. Texas has since created specific performance standards for public schools. Local school boards must abide by these state standards.

In a **confederal system**, sovereign states or provinces delegate power to a central government for specific purposes only. The vast majority of power rests with the lower-level governments, whereas the central government has very little power. The United States experimented with a confederal system in its infancy. The Articles of Confederation was the United States' first constitution. The agreement amounted to little more than a "firm league of friendship," which limited central authority to matters of diplomacy, printing money, resolving controversies between states, coordinating any war effort, and running the post office. Within just a few years of its creation, the American confederation grew vulnerable to attack or rebellion and was on the verge of bankruptcy.

As a result, the original thirteen states ratified the US Constitution of 1787, which established a federal system. A **federal system** is a power-sharing arrangement between a central government and states or provinces. The federal government has authority over the states in some matters, the federal government and states share authority in other matters, and states have sole authority in still other matters. Let's take a look at how the Constitution lays out this power-sharing arrangement.

Law enforcement is conducted by local, state, and federal governments.

PERSONAL RESPONSIBILITY: **When you see problems around you (potholes, traffic congestion, crime), what level of government do you hold most accountable? What role should individual people or communities of interest play in addressing the problems around them?**

confederal system: a power-sharing arrangement in which a central government's authority is granted by the individual political units

federal system: a power-sharing arrangement between central governing authority and individual political units

supremacy clause: Article VI, Section 2 of the Constitution that states that the US Constitution and federal laws "shall be the supreme law of the land"

THE SUPREMACY CLAUSE

The Constitution outlines the specific provisions that establish the authority of the federal system in the United States. To assert that federal powers are superior to and above state powers, the **supremacy clause** specifies that the laws created under the authority of the United States "shall be the supreme law of the land." Every state constitution, state legislature, and state judge is bound by these determinations. Laws that are interpreted to be conflictual with the US Constitution or federal laws are void and are not enforced.

The supremacy clause puts the federal government and Texas on a collision course on several issues. Texas has a long border with Mexico. The federal government is responsible for controlling population flow across the border, but it does not always do so to the satisfaction of the state. Texas is among the top two emitters of carbon dioxide. The federal government has created clean air standards that, for example, emissions-producing refineries along the coast must maintain. In these and other cases, federal rules often conflict with state goals.

ENUMERATED AND IMPLIED POWERS

enumerated powers: powers that are expressly identified as powers that the federal government can take

How does the US Constitution share powers between the central and state governments? First, the founders expressly identified actions that the federal government can take. These **enumerated powers** (sometimes called expressed or delegated powers) are specified in writing and retained by the federal government so that Congress has exclusive province to act on them. Article I, Section 8 of the Constitution lists these powers, which range from economic to military to commerce—more than thirty in all. These include the power to collect taxes, provide for the common defense, borrow and print money, protect patents, raise and support the armed forces, and organize militia as needed. Although grand in scope, the fact that these powers are specified demonstrates a limiting feature of the federal system. Those powers not specified are reserved to other actors in government, most prominently the states.

implied powers: powers that the federal government is not expressly granted but that it is assumed to possess so that Congress can carry out its duties

However, realizing the need for flexibility in the growing nation, the framers of the Constitution also provided for **implied powers**. Implied powers are powers that the federal government could possess but that are not expressly identified. The last part of Section 8 reads as follows:

> *Congress shall have the power . . . To make all laws which shall be necessary and proper for carrying into execution the foregoing powers, and all other powers vested by this Constitution in the government of the United States, or in any department or officer thereof.*

necessary and proper clause: Article 1, Section 8 of the Constitution, which specifies that Congress is allowed to assume additional powers needed to carry out its function

Referred to as the **necessary and proper clause**, this section has been interpreted to allow for Congress to make laws to carry out the enumerated powers. Because the clause stretches the Constitution to allow for Congress to include anything implied in its text, it is often called the "elastic clause."

The federal government generally has an advantage when it comes to determining which level of government is in charge. Table 3.1 lists four key cases in which the federal government has been challenged in court by states on various issues and has won. These cases often involve either the implied powers clause, as in the case of *McCullough v. Maryland* in 1819, or the commerce clause. The **commerce clause** is one of the enumerated powers listed in the Constitution. It reads Congress shall have the power "To regulate Commerce with foreign Nations, and among the several States, and with the Indian Tribes." Courts have generally taken a broad view of Congress' ability to control, regulate, and manipulate interstate commerce. The commerce clause has been used by Congress and the Supreme Court as one of the most fundamental powers delegated to the federal government.

commerce clause: the clause in the US Constitution that gives Congress the power to regulate commerce with foreign nations and among the states

The commerce clause has also been used, ironically, to allow Congress to regulate non-commerce activities. In a case in 1942 (*Wickard v. Filburn*), the Court dramatically expanded the permissible use of the commerce clause. The case involved Roscoe Filburn, an Ohio wheat farmer who grew more wheat than was allowed by Depression-era limits to keep prices low. Filburn was ordered to pay a fine but argued that he had no intention of selling the wheat. The Court reasoned that the production of the extra wheat reduced the amount of chicken

TABLE 3.1	Key Federalism Cases Decided by the US Supreme Court

CASE (YEAR)	QUESTION	THE STATES SAY . . .	THE COURT SAYS . . .	IMPORTANCE TO FEDERALISM
McCullough v. Maryland (1819)	Can the federal government establish a national bank even though that power is not identified in Constitution?	Maryland can tax the bank.	Maryland cannot tax the bank because it is federal property.	Congress could draw on "implied powers" to operate the national bank as they wished (Maryland could not tax it).
Gibbons v. Ogden (1824)	Are states allowed to control commerce between states?	New York can set fees and regulate its own navigation privileges.	Only the US Congress can set and alter rates for interstate commerce.	Interstate commerce set by Congress includes transportation of goods to and from states.
Baker v. Carr (1962)	Can the Supreme Court overrule state-drawn legislative districts?	Tennessee can draw its own boundaries for legislative districts.	Tennessee must consider the number of individuals in each district.	State decisions, even regarding elections, can be overruled by the federal government.
Arizona v. United States (2012)	Do federal immigration laws supersede state law enforcement?	Arizona can establish laws allowing law enforcement to check citizenship status of apprehended individuals.	Arizona may not implement its own immigration rules; only Congress can do this.	States may investigate immigration status but may not use race as a factor in apprehension.

Source: Oyez Project.

 COMMUNICATION:

Do states or the federal government generally get their way in federalism cases? Explain.

- Generally, the Supreme Court has ruled that when the state and federal governments clash, the federal government's view is paramount.

 CRITICAL THINKING:

Why has the Court ruled this way?

- Most early court cases granted significant authority to the federal government.

- Recent cases, such as *Arizona v. United States*, have given states more latitude to implement policies so long as they are careful not to violate federal law.

feed on the open market, which is subject to interstate commerce. Cumulative actions by farmers across the country could have a significant impact on chicken feed and thus should be regulated by the federal government. Critics of the expansive use of the commerce clause use examples like this to claim that Congress has overstepped its authority.

The federal government's regulations have their limits. In San Antonio in 1992, a twelfth grader at Edison High School carried a concealed .38 pistol along with ammunition into his school. This violated the Gun-Free School Zone Act that Congress passed two years prior. The case made its way to the Supreme Court (in *United States v. Lopez* [*1995*]), which ruled that the federal government could not justify prohibiting firearms in state public schools based on the Commerce Clause because the possession of firearms isn't technically commerce. The federal government had the last say though. The law was rewritten to include a provision that if the firearm in question affected interstate commerce in any way, it would be illegal.

RESERVED POWERS

reserve clause: the Tenth Amendment to the US Constitution, which states that powers not delegated to the federal government are reserved for the states

The balance of power wouldn't be complete without state autonomy as well. Proponents of states' rights often point to the US Constitution's Tenth Amendment as evidence that state sovereignty should be respected. The Tenth Amendment, often called the **reserve clause**, states that the listing of the powers not delegated in the Constitution are reserved for the states (or the people)—it reads: "The powers not delegated to the United States by the Constitution, nor prohibited by it to the States, are reserved to the States respectively, or to the people." The states' reserved powers include policy matters such as public education, public health, and state elections. States have the power to protect citizens and promote safety, welfare, and morals.

CONCURRENT POWERS

concurrent powers: powers shared between the state and federal governments

Federal and state governments share **concurrent powers** over a range of policy issues that affect both. In a way, federalism is a mixed recipe of unitary and confederal systems. The federal system in the United States requires the centrality of federal control on many issues but also limits this power. The federal system in the United States also provides expressed autonomy to the states by reserving specific power to the states. Concurrent powers allow both federal and state governments to establish courts and to tax citizens. Whereas Texas relies heavily on property taxes for revenue, other states rely more heavily on income taxes (Illinois), government service fees (New York), or a combination (California).

Enforcement of laws is an example of a concurrent power. Sanctuary cities—localities that do not enforce federal immigration laws—sparked a battle in 2015 in which Texas, oddly enough, came down on the side of the federal government. Facilitating the federal government's enforcement of immigration detention policies, Governor Abbott sent a threatening letter to Dallas County Sherriff Lupe Valdez, who was releasing incarcerated immigrants earlier than

US Immigration and Customs Enforcement (ICE) regulations required. "Your refusal to fully participate in a federal law enforcement program intended to keep dangerous criminals off the streets leaves the State no choice but to take whatever actions are necessary to protect our fellow Texans," Abbott wrote.[4] The governor threatened to cut off state grant support for cities that did not honor all ICE detainment regulations for immigrants.[5] Supporters of Sherriff Valdez argued that her actions were necessary to develop trust and that the sheriff's actions were consistent with federal law.

FULL FAITH AND CREDIT

For federalism to work properly, the states must not only adhere to the federal government's policies but also respect the policies of the other states. The Constitution specifically directs that each state allow for the rights and privileges of their state to be extended in other states. The **full faith and credit clause** addresses the duties that all states have to respect "the public acts, records, and judicial proceedings of every other state" (Article 4, Section 1). Take the example of same-sex marriage. In the 1990s, same-sex marriage appeared to be on the horizon in several states, which raised the question of whether this right extended in one state must be respected in another. In this case, the US Congress passed a law called the Defense of Marriage Act, which held that states did not need to recognize same-sex marriages as valid in their states, essentially waiving the full faith and credit clause in these instances. In addition, several states, including Texas in 2005, amended their state constitutions to prohibit marriage between couples of the same gender. Other states, however, allowed these marriages to take place. The Supreme Court's 2015 ruling in *Obergefell v. Hodges*, which held that same-sex marriage cannot be banned, mooted the argument and set a national standard to which all states were required to adhere.

Sheriff Lupe Valdez of Dallas, the first openly gay female elected county sheriff, clashed with Governor Abbott over the role of local government in enforcing immigration laws.

SOCIAL RESPONSIBILITY: **Which level of government should be in charge of immigration enforcement: local, state, or national? Should state or local officials be granted flexibility to further societal goals?**

full faith and credit clause: a Constitution clause that requires that each state respect the rights and proceedings of other states

★▬ TEXAS TAKEAWAYS

1 Name the three types of constitutional systems.

2 Explain the differences between enumerated and implied powers.

3 Describe an example of concurrent powers.

🤠 ADVANTAGES OF FEDERALISM

3.2 Describe the advantages of federalism.

Both prior to and following its establishment, the federal system served as a way to balance the needs of the states and the necessary authority of at least some centralized government. Because of this, federalism has several advantages.

A STRONGER CENTRAL GOVERNMENT

The US Constitution established a federal government in large part that would create a stronger, more central government than that established originally by the Articles of Confederation. With no federal power to tax citizens or states to pay off debts, no provisions for independent leadership, and no mechanism for enforcement of laws under the Articles, the young US government faltered in the face of several challenges—perhaps the most notable of which was Shays' Rebellion in 1786 and 1787. Fueled by economic inequity over taxation in western Massachusetts, frustration over the inflation of currency, and concerns about their inability to pay debts with worthless paper money, 4,000 rebels marched east behind Daniel Shays with the intention of capturing a weapons arsenal in Springfield, Massachusetts. The United States government had to raise a private militia led by George Washington, who came out of retirement to end the rebellion but not without grave consequences. Four rebels were killed and dozens wounded in the calamity. The rebellion vividly demonstrated the young nation's need for a stronger, more central government. In addition, a weak central government also contributed to the difficulty of raising an army, as states refused to pay soldiers promised wages; and the inability to raise revenue, as miserly states refused to send funds to the capitol—both factors that weakened the government.

Citizens in Bastrop protesting the federal government's Jade Helm 15 operation.

ANGLES OF POWER
Texas, the Military, and Jade Helm

Jade Helm 15 sounds like a science fiction movie but was actually the codename for the largest military training exercise of its kind, involving about 1,200 special operations troops across several states. Concerns from all over the state poured in about the proposed operation, most stating that they "did not trust the president" on military matters, many claiming this was the beginning of psychological warfare, and a few making racist or xenophobic remarks.[6] Rumors circulated online, one suggesting Walmart locations might be turned into death camps.[7] Governor Abbott relented to public pressure. He directed the Commander of the Texas State Guard to provide updates to the Governor's Office to "ensure that Texans' safety, constitutional rights, private property rights, and civil liberties will not be infringed."[8]

SOCIAL RESPONSIBILITY: **Does the federal government have Texas' best interests at heart?**

The governor's order antagonized some, as it looked like he was giving in to conspiracy theorists. One letter writer demanded a "hand written apology for your idiotic paranoid delusion that Texas was under attack by our federal government." Another noted that this was the "stupidest thing to come out of Texas in 20 years."[9] Politicians in both parties called out the governor for "pandering" to extremists' claims.

At the heart of the debate about Jade Helm is the suspicion that many Texans have of the federal government. In polling conducted after the operation, 39% supported the governor's decision and 28% opposed (32% responded they didn't know). Almost 50% of the public believed that the federal government would send troops to Texas to impose martial law, confiscate firearms, or violate property rights.[10] These attitudes may reflect Texas' long history of conflict with the federal government dating back to the Civil War.

REPRESENTATION

Unlike a unitary system, a federal system provides responsibility at many levels of government—the local, state, and national. Any four-year-old can tell you that you can't fit a round peg into a square hole. A "one-size-fits-all" approach to creating public policy may make taxes too high in Wyoming and education underfunded in Illinois. Who better to decide where and how to spend government resources than the individual states themselves? Federalism allows states and local governments to have a major say in how these funds are spent to meet their specific needs and goals. If you summed up the number of elected public officials who represent you at various levels of government in Texas, the number is more than two dozen, including state representatives, county officials, city council members, and judges. A federal system gives the responsibility of representation to these local officials and a wealth of opportunities for lower-level governments to craft policies to match the needs of Texans.

POLICY INNOVATION

A federal system allows states to have autonomy over issues that are most critical to the people of that state and to innovate on matters of public policy. As a result, states are often called "laboratories of democracy." States experiment

FIGURE 3.1   **Percent of Texans With a Favorable View Toward Local, State, and National Government**

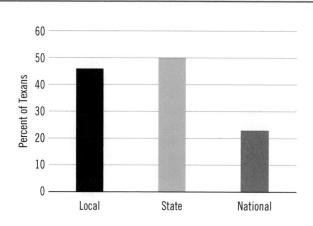

Source: Texas Tribune Poll, February 2015.

 COMMUNICATION:

Do Texans hold favorable opinions about local, state, or national government?

- Texans are more likely to favor state government than local or national government.
- A total of 50 percent of Texans favor state government followed by 45 percent for local government and only 23 percent for the national government.

 CRITICAL THINKING:

Why do Texans favor local and state government over the federal government?

- One explanation is political—most Texans are Republicans, whereas government at the local and national level are likely run by Democrats. This is especially true in large cities in the state.

with policy solutions, and if they prove to be effective, other states and the federal government often adopt them. Two examples highlight state innovation.

During the 1990s, Texas grappled with reforming an underperforming education system. Texas Governor George W. Bush promoted annual testing for students to improve school and teacher accountability. When Bush became president in 2001, he brought his solution to Washington, and Congress passed his signature education policy "No Child Left Behind" in 2001, which he had developed to provide parental choice and local spending flexibility in Texas. A modified version of the Texas program garnered bipartisan support but also significant disagreement among President Bush's own party, many of whom felt education should be left fully to the states.

In the early 2000s, California, Texas, Florida, and other states suffered from overcrowded prisons. Texas experimented with different solutions to relieve overcrowding and introduced the "Texas Model." The policy increased the

FIGURE 3.2   **Percent of Texans Who Support State and Federal Policies**

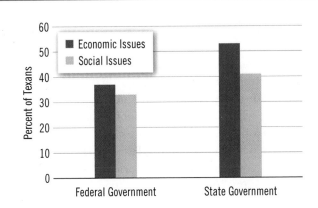

Source: Texas Tribune Polling, February 2014.

 COMMUNICATION:

On what issues do Texans trust federal or state government?

- A total of 53 percent of Texans trusted the state government to make economic policy over 37 percent who trusted the federal government's economic policy.
- Although the support Texans gave to any policy affecting social issues was lower than to policy affecting economic issues, Texans were more supportive of state government making these policies (41 percent) than the federal government (33 percent).

 CRITICAL THINKING:

Why?

- Texans feel like they have more control over economic policies at the state level.
- Texans also have a clearer sense of how state funds are used.

number of beds for outpatient substance abuse facilities for individuals on probation, increased in-prison treatment for drug abuse, and allowed for more flexibility in sentencing. The state ultimately saved money but failed to reduce the number of incarcerated individuals or decrease the racial or income disparity in prisons, calling the effectiveness of the model into question.[11]

TRUST IN LEVELS OF GOVERNMENT

Perhaps more than citizens in most states, Texans have historically been distrustful of national government. When asked about their views of the different levels of government, Texans express a much higher degree of trust in local and state government than they do of national government (Figure 3.1). In general, the American public tends to trust in lower levels of government—in governments that are geographically closer to the people. In Texas, the legacy of federal intervention following the Civil War entrenched the value of state autonomy. Hence, Texans trust state and local government more than the federal government. As a result, at least in the eyes of the citizens, the federalist system improves political efficacy such that Texans feel like they have more of a say in government.

Texans are also more likely to support the state government on economic or social policy matters than the national government. Texans don't trust any level of government on social issues but are more likely to trust the state over the federal government when it comes to economic issues (see Figure 3.2). There are several reasons for this. First, the state's approach to regulation and oversight is more in line with values of most Texans than the policies of the federal government. Texas government has historically viewed business regulation with reluctance, as many Texans see it as restricting business growth. Second, the state of Texas is perceived to provide more of the resources individuals and businesses need to succeed—in terms of fuel, food, fiber, or technology—than the federal government.

 TEXAS TAKEAWAYS

4 What are the advantages of federalism?

5 On what issues do Texans support state government over the federal government?

 # TEXAS AND FEDERAL FUNDING

3.3 Evaluate how Texas uses the funding received from the federal government.

One important way that the federal government and states share power is through budget finance. More than 500 separate federal programs provide grants and funds to the states. In the 2016–2107 budget, Texas received $68 billion from the federal government. This ranked Texas 30th among states in per capita total federal funding—Texas received about $8,800 in federal spending per capita while the national average was approximately $11,300.[12]

Texas' average would be higher, but in 2012 the state rejected federal funds for expansion of Medicaid, a health care program for low income families and individuals, under the Affordable Care Act ("Obamacare").[13] The argument from then Governor Perry was that Medicaid was a "broken program," and he didn't trust the federal government to pay the promised 90 percent expense of the expansion. The cost to Texas of the 10 percent remaining would have been $2.6 billion in the first six years, but it stood to gain $20 billion annually for agreeing.[14]

Texas relies on the federal government for just over a third of its total budget (see Figure 3.3). Texas' share of federal funds grew from 23 percent in 1989 to 35 percent in 2015. Driving the federal government's share of the

IS IT BIGGER IN TEXAS?

FIGURE 3.3   **Federal Aid as a Percentage of General Revenue**

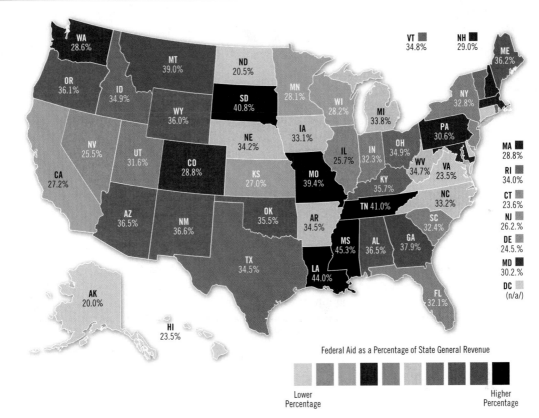

Source: U.S. Census Bureau.

 COMMUNICATION:

Which states accept more federal funding than others?

- Texas relies on the federal government for just over a third of its total budget, approximately $68 billion in 2015.[15]

- States similarly situated (a third of their budget) include Oklahoma, Arkansas, and Indiana. For comparison purposes, Mississippi relies on the federal government the most (43%), followed by Louisiana (42%), Tennessee (40%), and South Dakota (39%).

 CRITICAL THINKING:

Why do some states take more funds from the federal government than others?

- The biggest factor in a state accepting (or not) federal funds is a weak state economy, perhaps caused by falling energy prices, necessitating federal help.

- States that experience economic challenges or natural disasters, like Texas, receive more federal aid.

- States with a larger population of poor residents, like Texas and much of the south and rural states, have greater need for federal assistance.

FIGURE 3.4   **Federal Funds as a Percentage of All Texas Funds, 2014–2015 Biennium**

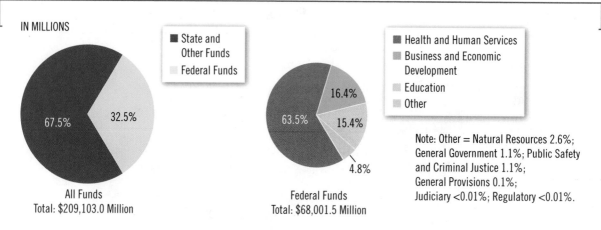

IN MILLIONS

- ■ State and Other Funds
- □ Federal Funds

67.5%   32.5%

All Funds
Total: $209,103.0 Million

- ■ Health and Human Services
- ■ Business and Economic Development
- ▨ Education
- ▥ Other

16.4%
63.5%   15.4%
4.8%

Federal Funds
Total: $68,001.5 Million

Note: Other = Natural Resources 2.6%;
General Government 1.1%; Public Safety
and Criminal Justice 1.1%;
General Provisions 0.1%;
Judiciary <0.01%; Regulatory <0.01%.

Source: Legislative Budget Board.

 COMMUNICATION:

What are federal funds used for in Texas?

- Most of the state's federal share of funds goes to agencies involved in health and human services—totaling $42.2 billion in the 2014–2015 budget—amounting to almost 62% of all federal funds allocated to the state.

- Education is the third largest category of federal funds and was appropriated $10.6 billion in federal funds in the 2014–2015 budget.

- Other pricey items include highway planning and construction, the national school lunch program, the Children's Health Insurance Program, and Temporary Assistance to Needy Families.

 CRITICAL THINKING:

Why?

- Texas has a large population and thousands of road miles, so it absorbs a significant share of federal transportation funds.

- Federal programs designed to help lower-income individuals funnel a significant amount of funds to Texas because the state has a large share of individuals who qualify.

state's budget up over this period was the American Recovery and Reinvestment Act of 2009 (also known as the "stimulus package") that increased the amount of federal money available to the states in several areas. Despite the anti-federal-government rhetoric from many politicians in Texas, the state needs federal funds to meet budget goals and maintain several policies.

How does Texas use the funds it receives from the federal government? Medicaid comprises most of the federal funds allocated to Texas (see Figure 3.4).

Both the state and federal government have an incentive to work together on Medicaid funding. The federal government has a responsibility to offer the entitlement to participants, and states have access to funding to cover needy and at-risk populations. Funds for business development is the second largest category of federal funds, whereas education falls in third place. The remaining funds include smaller funding for transportation projects and other social programs.

One major way in which the states receive funds from the federal government is through disaster relief (see Figure 3.5). The disaster process is initiated by state governors who must formally declare a disaster and request federal assistance. Governors of Texas have declared disasters over 20 times since 2001. The president, if he or she chooses, then sanctifies the governor's disaster declaration by issuing a federal disaster declaration, which allows the state to tap into federal funds to deal with the disaster. In fact, Texas relies on federal disaster funding more than any other state. Declaring a disaster costs the governor and president nothing. The costs do not come out of the state coffers, and presidents have a fund already allocated from which to draw resources. Governors and presidents can both claim credit for solving a major problem. Presidents may get a better deal than governors: research shows that presidents get a 1 percent bump in statewide votes for a single disaster declaration.[16] Disaster relief is an example of how the state and federal government can work together to achieve both practical and political goals.

States can use disaster funds to replace public infrastructure, repair damaged water facilities, establish roads, and remove debris. States cannot use these funds to create new facilities beyond repair or replacement and cannot repair private homes or businesses (although individuals can apply for these funds). However, the federal government attaches strings to these funds: states must follow procedures to allow for competitive procurement, an environmental review, payment of prevailing local wage, protection of worker civil rights, and annual audits.

Texas and the federal government also pool resources, share responsibility, and cooperate effectively on other issues. Texas and the US Department of Agriculture partner to manage conservation efforts on public lands such as the Sam Houston National Forest or the Caddo National Grasslands. After the offshore oil rig Deepwater Horizon exploded in the Gulf of Mexico in 2010, causing the largest oil spill in US waters, the federal government partnered with Texas and the other affected states to monitor the long-term environmental effects. The Texas Department of Public Safety collaborates with federal agencies to combat human trafficking, sharing information and program funding.

TEXAS TAKEAWAYS

6 How much money and what percentage of the state budget does Texas receive from the federal government?

7 What did Texas spend the federal funds on?

FIGURE 3.5   **Texas Disaster Declarations and Federal Emergency Management Administration Funds Spent**

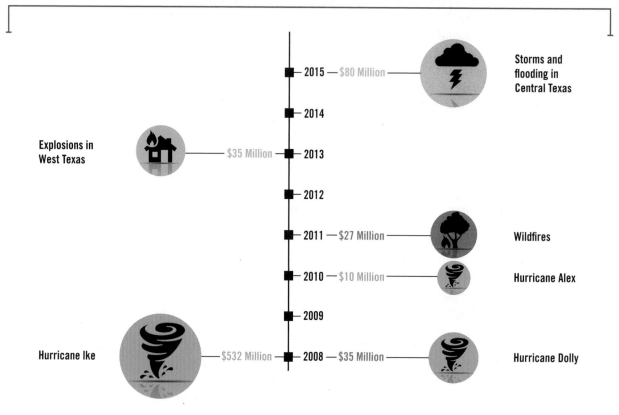

Source: Federal Emergency Management Administration.

 COMMUNICATION:

How much in disaster funds does Texas receive and for what?

- Texas has received billions of dollars from the federal government since 2001.

 CRITICAL THINKING:

Why does Texas get so much disaster funding?

- Most disaster funds comes in the wake of major hurricanes. Hurricane Rita in 2005 involved more than $2 billion in federal funds.
- Severe storms and flooding also increase the disaster tab. Storms in central Texas in 2015 topped $80 million.

 STYLES OF FEDERALISM

The division of power between the federal, state, and local governments is not static, nor are the ways in which the federal and state governments work together to achieve their goals. The allocation of authority, the channeling of funds, the implementation of programs, and the enforcement of rules is fluid and constantly changing. Let's take a look at how this cooperation and struggle for control over policy has changed over time.

3.4 Assess how elements of cooperation and coercion within the federal system have changed over time.

DUAL FEDERALISM

The simplest type of arrangement between a federal government and the individual states is referred to as **dual federalism**, whereby each branch is coequal and sovereign. Under dual federalism, the federal, state, and local government each has exclusive powers that are reserved to it alone. This is often referred to as "layer cake" federalism in which each layer of government is distinct from the others and maintains its own power and authority. In the United States, the federal government is responsible for issues of trade, foreign policy, war and diplomacy, and immigration. States implement policies in the areas of education, criminal justice (prisons), police, elections, and pensions.

dual federalism: a federalist system in which the federal, state, and local government each has exclusive powers that are reserved to it alone

Dual federalism guided federal–state relations until the middle of the twentieth century and the onset of World War II. A small pink worm illustrates the distinct, but hierarchical, levels of government under dual federalism. In 1919, the cotton crops in southern Texas were plagued by the pink bollworm, a small pest that burrows into the bolls of the cotton and feeds on the seeds. The federal government ordered Governor William P. Hobby to enact legislation to control the problem. Should Texas not act to control the infestation, the federal government would quarantine Texas cotton. This was one of the first incidents of direct intervention of the national government in internal affairs of the state since the establishment of martial law after the Civil War.[17] Agreeing to the federal government's demand, the legislature passed legislation in 1920 to continue quarantine regulations and establish a board to oversee and limit future infestations.[18]

COOPERATIVE FEDERALISM

Cooperative federalism refers to a style of federalism in which each level of government has overlapping and intertwined authority over shared issues. Instead of the layer cake served for the dual federalism arrangement, cooperative federalism is better described as a "marble cake," where the layers (government) overlap and mix with each other, and jurisdictions on policy and regulatory matters are not bound by cleanly set layers. The responsibilities of federal, state, and local governments were increasingly swirled together for issues like funding, rule-making, administration, and implementation. As the responsibilities

cooperative federalism: a federalist system in which each level of government has overlapping and intertwined authority over shared issues

of the federal government grew, so did the interaction between the federal government and the states. As the nation industrialized and the world globalized, the federal government took a larger role in the economy of the states.

The turning point that triggered this change was the economic disaster of the Great Depression, starting in 1929 when the stock market crashed. Americans were unable to find work, and states whose budgets were hit hard by the crisis were powerless to help their citizens. In Texas, farmers were particularly hard hit. Federal government efforts to funnel funds to the Reconstruction Finance Corporation aided many as crop prices fell and relief was further away. Federal efforts continued as the US Congress passed the Federal Emergency Relief Act to distribute billions of dollars to Texas and other states. Texas received more than $166 million in federal funds by August 31, 1936, putting Texans back to work.[19]

Cooperative federalism relies on grants-in-aid, payments made to state governments to implement social welfare, health care, educational, and other types of programs. **Categorical grants** are funds distributed to state or local governments for specific programs and policies that require that states meet certain conditions. States must comply with any directive from the federal government, including eligibility criteria, outcomes reporting, and adherence to rules about discrimination or promotion of diversity. Financially, these grants require that Texas has "skin in the game"—that they provide matching funds. **Matching grants** make certain that the state is committed to the project and will be thrifty with the funds.

NEW FEDERALISM

In the 1970s, President Richard Nixon introduced a new style of federalism called **new federalism**, a system that returns greater responsibilities, duties, and funding to the states and reduces the size of the federal government. This transfer of power to states is often called devolution. Nixon and modern proponents of devolution believe that states should be the most involved in the creation of their own public policy. At the center of devolution is a conservative philosophy, echoed by Republicans today, that states should have greater say in the affairs of government than the federal government. President Ronald Reagan called out what he considered federal intervention by saying "what was once a federal helping hand has become a mailed fist."[20] The Reagan Administration cemented the practice of new federalism, focusing on making the federal government smaller by returning much of the responsibility of social and

COMMUNICATION:

In a crisis, which could affect a region or the nation, where do federal powers supersede state authority? Explain why.

categorical grants: funds distributed to state or local governments for programs that require governments to meet conditions established by the federal government

matching grants: funds the state adds to supplement specific federal government programs

new federalism: a federal system that returns greater responsibilities, duties, and funding to the states

economic assistance to the states. Part of the Republican Party of Texas' 2014 platform encouraged the state to "ignore, oppose, refuse, and nullify" federal legislation that infringes on the state's Tenth Amendment rights.[21]

Greater autonomy for states in new federalism does not mean that the federal government folds up their wallet and leaves the states on their own. The difference between funding arrangements in new federalism and other styles of federalism is that the funds are delivered to the states with fewer strings attached and with more flexibility for state use. Funding is often done through **block grants**—fixed funds that are transferred to states for the application of a general issue, such as Medicaid. Medicaid in Texas covers more than 3.7 million poor, disabled, and elderly people and costs roughly $40 billion a year, of which the federal government pays 60%.[22]

block grants: fixed funds that are transferred to states for the implementation of a policy or program

The major advantage of block grants is that they provide ultimate flexibility for states seeking to address specific problems. New federalism devotee President Reagan called this a way for states to function as "laboratories of change in a creative democracy" by having the federal government cut the strings attached to funds.[23] Texas, like other states, prefers a block grant that allows the state to make state-level changes to the program without receiving direct federal approval.[24] Block grants are not strictly an endless bag of cash left by the federal government at the states' doorstep. These federal programs are often open ended in terms of projects chosen but directed to solve a specific need.

One major example in the Lone Star State is the Texas Community Development Block Grant. The program is federally funded through a block grant of $8 million to the Texas Department of Agriculture to develop viable communities, provide decent housing, and expand economic opportunity for individuals of low-to-moderate income. These projects have included drainage improvements, housing rehabilitation, accessibility to public buildings, and building community centers. Power is again distributed across state and federal activities, tilting toward states in the case of block grants because states have more flexibility in determining spending priorities.

Critics of letting the states play mad scientist in the "laboratory" contend that shifting responsibility is a veiled way to cut liberal domestic programs. States looking to save money may ignore serious social problems without any federal oversight to ensure the truly needy have adequate aid.

COERCIVE FEDERALISM

Beginning in the 1970s, states turned away from Washington, DC, for policy solutions, and economic troubles weakened the federal government's financial ability to encourage state–federal collaboration.[25] Even so, federal power was significant, as two decades of Supreme Court rulings centralized power in the federal government. In coercive federalism, the federal government began using this authority to pressure states to achieve specific policy objectives, punishing the states for not participating in its programs in a system that became known as **coercive federalism**.

coercive federalism: a system in which the federal government establishes guidelines for the states and may punish the states for not participating

INSIDER INTERVIEW

George Kelleman, President of the Texas Retailers Association

Given your 20 years of experience working with both state and federal governments, do you think states should lead on issues such as border security, racial and gender equality, and same-sex marriage?

No. We are, after all, one nation; therefore these issues should fall to the purview of the federal government. By contrast, should the federal government dictate primary and secondary education, local economic development, or basic local services such as emergency services? No. The feds should limit their tendency to over-reach into what are ultimately state and local issues. However, there are areas where common sense dictates a collaborative approach, such as infrastructure upgrades and improvements, or public health care.

SOCIAL RESPONSIBILITY: **Do you agree or disagree with this balance of state and federal responsibilities?**

The Affordable Care Act (or "Obamacare") of 2010 expanded the Medicaid program for the states to cover up to 133% of the cost of the program. The original law punished states if they did not agree to the expansion of Medicaid by depriving them of their existing Medicaid benefits. Because a quarter of all state budget funds are comprised of federal reimbursements for Medicaid, no state could afford not to join. The 2012 Supreme Court ruling found the Affordable Care Act to be constitutional but also held that coercion of the states in this manner was not permissible. Supreme Court Chief Justice Roberts said that the conditions on participation in the program would put a "gun to the head" of states and said participating in the expanded program should be voluntary.[26]

As a result of the ruling, many states chose not to participate in the program. Texas was one of those states. Most Republicans opposed the expansion of Medicaid and didn't believe the federal government would keep promises to cover the costs the state will incur if it chooses to expand the program.[27] The federal government granted a temporary Medicaid waiver to Texas through 2017, but Texas must use that time to study the impacts of not accepting the Medicaid expansion and come up with an alternative, giving the federal government leverage to encourage Texas to accept expansion of Medicaid under the Affordable Care Act. If Texas ultimately refuses the expansion, they may lose their federal matching funds for Medicaid. Matt Salo, executive director of the National Association of Medicaid Directors, put it more directly: "You want this money? You do the expansion."[28]

Unfunded Mandates.   Congress routinely passes legislation or rules are created at the federal level that require the states to implement policies without federal funding. This is an **unfunded mandate**. The federal government does

unfunded mandates: federal or state legislation that requires the states to implement policies but does not supply funding necessary for implementation

not necessarily direct the state to spend money; rather, they set rules to be followed or goals to be met that require states spend money to achieve these outcomes. In effect, states are getting a bill for a dinner they didn't order but have to eat. Often local governments pick up the tab. Because the state also passes legislation that local governments must comply with, unfunded mandates are significant "cost drivers" for Texas county government.

For example, a rite of passage for Texas school kids is a medical examination for scoliosis, an abnormal curvature of the spine that can lead to permanent disabilities. School nurses all over Texas line up pupils in the sixth and ninth grades for the process, which most kids love because it gets them out of class. The screening is medically valuable but also represents an unfunded mandate to local school districts that must foot the bill for the examinations. State-mandated assessment tests, gifted and talented programs, dropout prevention, and reporting requirements also wrench resources from local school districts. Counties must cover the cost of several social issues, including defense of indigent criminal defendants, health care in county jails, and appointments of counsel in child protective services.

preemptions: when the federal government grants states permission and funding to implement federal regulations in policy areas but only if the states comply with a host of conditions

The issue of unfunded mandates became so pronounced that in 2011, Governor Rick Perry established a bipartisan task force of local officials, mayors, city council members, judges, and school district superintendents to study the issue. The commission came up with several solutions to reduce the burden of unfunded mandates, including reducing certain state reporting requirements, exempting government-owned vehicles from inspection, allowing local regulation of swimming pool standards, and reimbursing cities for cost recovery for public information requests and management of records.[29] The governor's distaste for unfunded mandates was not absolute, especially when it came to medical care of the youngest Texans. A bill passed by the legislature in 2013 would have allowed school districts to opt out of the scoliosis screening process, but Governor Perry vetoed this measure.[30]

Preemptions. Preemptions (sometimes called "conditional preemptions") occur when the federal government grants states permission and funding to implement federal regulations in policy areas but only if the states comply with a host of conditions. If states don't comply, the federal government preempts the states' policies and implements the program themselves. Texas's long fight with the federal government over environmental regulations provides one example.

Tension between Texas and the federal government peaks when policy goals conflict. This friction is acute when the levels of government are controlled by different political parties. Governor Perry met with President Obama in 2014 on how the federal government and Texas could work together to solve collective problems.

SOCIAL RESPONSIBILITY: **How much flexibility states should be given to develop their own policies and in what areas?**

In 2010, the Environmental Protection Agency (EPA) began requiring companies that wanted to build new industrial plants to get "greenhouse gas permits" before beginning construction. When the Texas Commission on Environmental Quality (TCEQ; the Texas equivalent of the EPA) refused, the EPA took over responsibility for the permitting process, causing delays for some companies that lasted up to two years.[31] In 2013, to circumvent preemption, the Texas legislature passed a law to authorize TCEQ to have control over the rule-making process with EPA approval. The EPA turned full permitting responsibility back to TCEQ in 2014.[32]

★ TEXAS TAKEAWAYS

8 Explain "layer cake" federalism and "marble cake" federalism.

9 Describe the differences between new federalism and coercive federalism.

10 Explain what an unfunded mandate is and why it is potentially harmful to local government.

🤠 TEXAS AND CONFLICTS OVER FEDERALISM

3.5 Analyze examples of the conflicts over federalism.

Texas's distrust of the federal government, individualistic culture, and robust sense of states' sovereignty from the days of the Republic have prompted several intergovernmental squabbles over the years. These fights have been both political and substantive.

TEXAS VERSUS WASHINGTON

In recent years, a resurgent Republican Party in Texas combined with the political opportunity to challenge a Democratic presidential administration has led to conflicts between the state and the federal government. The legal system is often the arena for battle. As shown in the Table 3.2, Texas has sued the federal government most frequently over environmental issues including air quality, climate change, and natural resources. The state's win–loss record is mixed in terms of success, where the state received a favorable outcome (either a win or a dismissal of the case or withdrawal of the case that was in the state's favor) in only about a fourth of the cases. On issues related to voting rights, the state was somewhat more likely to succeed. These victories are due in part to a Supreme Court holding in *Shelby County v. Holder* (2013), which held that provisions of the Voting Rights Act of 1965 that required certain

TABLE 3.2 **The State of Texas Versus the Obama Administration**

During the Obama Administration, Texas politicians have bragged about suing the federal government 46 times between 2009 and 2016, costing taxpayers a total of $6 million. Below are a few of the issues and the outcomes.

ISSUE	CASES AND ISSUES	CASES WON BY TEXAS/ TOTAL CASES
Environment	Texas sued the Environmental Protection Agency (EPA) for rejecting rules the state instituted. Texas also sued over overall acceptable sulfur dioxide limits. The state also sued the EPA over greenhouse gas emission standards.	6/25
Business Regulations	Texas sued over reporting regulations and financial oversight. The state also sued the Equal Employment Opportunity Commission over rules stating a ban on hiring felons was discriminatory, a conflict with Texas law that bans hiring felons for state positions.	1/4
Health Care	Texas sued the Obama Administration, challenging the expansion of Medicare under the Affordable Care Act ("Obamacare"). Texas also sued to allow religious organizations to refuse to subsidize contraception services.	1/3
Voting and Elections	Texas sued the Department of Justice over requirements that election districts lines must pass "pre-approval." The state also sued over the requirements for voter identification for the same reason, winning in this case but ultimately losing later.	2/2

Sources: "Texas vs. the Feds: A Look at the Lawsuits." *Texas Tribune,* July 27, 2016. Texas Attorney General website.

 COMMUNICATION:

On which issues is Texas more successful in challenging the federal government in court?

- Texas has sued the federal government most over environmental issues (25 times) but has only won 6—a 24% win rate.
- Court cases involving health care or business regulations have been mixed for the state—only on a fourth of the cases does the state succeed.
- Texas is most effective in court against the federal government when the issue is a voting or election issue—the state is 2 for 2 (100%) in those cases in recent years. Texas withdrew the suit they filed against the federal government because the preclearance issue was rendered moot but ultimately lost on the voter identification case after the federal government successfully challenged the law in court.

 CRITICAL THINKING:

Why does Texas have a low win rate?

- The Supreme Court has been stricter in enforcing pollution emission standards.
- On the requirement that election changes be "pre-approved" by the federal government, the Court has indicated it believes that the need for such protection, a holdover from a time of significant discrimination, is no longer necessary.

southern states to obtain "preclearance" before altering voting laws or practices were unconstitutional. Preclearance was a tool the federal government used to examine and authorize any changes to voting laws from Texas or other southern states. The Court held that the provision requiring preclearance was outdated and a "drastic departure from basic principles of federalism" and that all states "enjoy equal sovereignty."

TIDELANDS CONTROVERSY

The tidelands controversy involved a question of the legal title to more than 2½ million acres of submerged land in the Gulf of Mexico off the coast of Texas. Upon entering the Union in 1845, Texas was to keep all her land, including the boundary three leagues (about 10 miles) from shore. As important as the principle of ownership was to Texas, the financial stakes were even greater. The coastal area was rich in natural resources the state used to generate major revenue.

Before Texas entered the Union, the US Supreme Court had already written two decisions holding that lands submerged under coastal waters within the boundaries of the original states "were not granted by the Constitution to the United States, but were reserved to the States respectively" and that "the new States have the same rights, sovereignty and jurisdiction over this subject as the original States."[33] The Annexation Agreement by which Texas became part of the United States March 1, 1845, sealed the state's ownership of the tidelands: "That Congress doth consent that the territory properly included within and rightfully belonging to the Republic of Texas, may be erected into a new State, to be called the State of Texas . . . and said State shall also retain all the vacant and unappropriated lands lying within its limits."

Between 1845 and 1948, Texas made use of the tidelands to execute mineral rights for the School Land Board to fund public schools, selling the lands to private organizations and setting up lighthouses and fortifications. Yet several court cases initiated by the federal government challenged Texas's rights to these lands. The Supreme Court held that although the state had owned tidelands and soil under navigable waters, because oil and other property may be necessary for national defense purposes, the federal government should be responsible for them.

Politically, the tidelands issue split the Democratic Party, which was made up of conservative and liberal Democrats. The conservative Democrats urged support of General Dwight D. Eisenhower in the 1952 election in part because he promised to restore Texas's lands. The new Congress in 1953 made the restoration of the tidelands one of their first orders of business. The legislation, coauthored by Texas Senator Price Daniel, survived what was then the longest filibuster in US Senate history (twenty-seven days) but finally won a majority in both houses of Congress.[34] The state ultimately prevailed on the issue, retaining title to its three-league sunken land boundary, generating multiple billions of dollars in leases, rentals, and royalties.

IMMIGRATION

By way of administrative rule change in 2014, President Obama allowed certain undocumented immigrants, including those who have children who are already US citizens or residents, to receive work permits to allow them to stay temporarily and work legally in the United States (if they had lived in the country for more than five years, passed a criminal background check, and paid taxes). Republican Texas State Representative Bob Goodlatte countered that the president's unilateral action "ignores the will of the American people and flouts the Constitution."[35] Texas Democratic State Representative Armando Walle disagreed: "We are talking about Texas students who know no other country but the United States, and parents of U.S. citizen children. These children pledge allegiance every day in school to the U.S. and Texas flags."[36]

Texas Governor Abbott led a 26-state charge challenging the Obama Administration's order. The suit, filed in the Southern District of Texas, argued that the president's actions were unconstitutional and that the order's impact would "exacerbate" the border crisis and force states to spend more on law enforcement, health care, and education. The governor's case was built on constitutional grounds, state sovereignty grounds, and challenged the unfunded mandate of the order that the lawsuit alleged would drive up participation in social welfare programs.[37] Texas argued that it did not support the policy and considered the unfunded mandate to be burdensome. The White House claimed that the policy was needed if the country was to live up to her status as a "nation of immigrants" and that the federal government has authority over immigration matters. In 2016, a divided Supreme Court halted the implementation of the President's order.

VOTER IDENTIFICATION AT ELECTION PLACES

Voter identification laws require some form of formal identification to be presented at the polls prior to voting in an election. Depending on the state, identification can be a phone bill, a credit card bill, a student ID, or a state-issued photo ID. Texas has long required state identification to vote, stretching back to 1971. In 2011, the state legislature limited valid identification to include only a state-issued ID card, a driver's license, a military ID, a concealed handgun license issued by the Department of Public Safety, or a passport—documents that contain a photo of the holder.[39] Since the 2011 law passed, there have been several legal challenges to it, primarily advancing the argument that the law discriminated against minority voters because they are disproportionately less likely to have the proper identification.

The first step for Texas (and other southern states) in changing any election-related policy was

The federal government challenged Texas's rigid voter identification law in court. Governor Abbott defended the law saying "they are trying to deny Texas our sovereign rights." Ever the watchdog for voting fraud, Governor Abbott referenced cases of electoral fraud as justification for the voter ID law. Opponents counter that the instances of voter fraud are extremely rare.

GREAT TEXAS POLITICAL DEBATES
Sanctuary Cities

In 2015, an illegal immigrant who had been deported several times from the United States was charged with murder in San Francisco. The murder prompted outrage and reassessment of local immigration policies, especially in what some have called "sanctuary cities." Legislation passed the US House in 2015 that punished cities for not enforcing federal immigration laws by cutting off much needed federal funding, a form of coercive federalism. The Texas legislature tried and failed to pass similar legislation in 2011 and 2015. Many Republicans support this legislation to ensure orderly adherence to state and federal laws and to promote public safety. Some business leaders, however, opposed the measure because it may stain Texas's reputation and possibly lead to boycotts. Mayors and immigrant rights groups oppose the measures because these groups advocate inclusion and fear that the legislation would lead to racial profiling.[38]

CRITICAL THINKING **Should cities be required to enforce federal immigration policy?**

YES: We elect individuals to serve our needs in the federal government and to make choices on our behalf. The federal government helps Texas and other states reach clean air standards, provide health insurance to the elderly, create jobs, fund education, and reach many important national goals. Sometimes these national goals conflict with state goals, but national interests outweigh state and local interests.

MAYBE: Texans' tax dollars pay for many of the basic services the federal government provides. Texans should expect some responsiveness from the federal government and flexibility in dealing with state issues.

NO: It is wrong for the federal government to impose rules and demand compliance when these solutions harm state interests. Texas should set its own immigration rules because it has the longest border with Mexico and bears the consequences of immigration policy—more so than any other state. Texas should not be forced to accept solutions that fit national interests but that ignore state interests.

to receive "preclearance" of the change in voting process by the Department of Justice, as required by the Voting Rights Act of 1965. However, as noted previously, in 2013 the Supreme Court struck down the automatic formula that is used to identify which state and local governments must comply with the preclearance provision in *Shelby County v. Holder*. With the need to clear Texas's voter ID law through the federal government removed, Texas implemented the voter ID law.

A federal court struck down the law in 2016 arguing that it discriminated against minority voters. Trumpeting the importance of the legislation to preserve the secrecy and safety of the ballot, Governor Greg Abbott has remained an advocate of the law. He tweeted about a voter fraud case in Fort Worth where a candidate for a Democratic precinct chair position admitted to having her son vote on behalf of his father.[40] However, between 2004 and 2013, only four cases were prosecuted by the Texas Attorney General that involved someone illegally casting a ballot at a polling place where a picture ID would have prevented the fraud. Most cases of voter fraud involve irregular mail-in ballots.[41]

COMMON CORE EDUCATION STANDARDS

One major policy arena in which states innovate is education. States are almost exclusively responsible for education policy, both establishing standards and funding. In 2010, the National Governors Association, working with organizations such as the Bill and Melinda Gates Foundation and the Council of State School Officers, developed education standards in math and literacy to prepare students for college or the work force.[42] President Obama's "Race to the Top" initiative gave states an incentive to adopt the standards. The US Department of Education dispersed $5 million to states that adopted the Common Core Standards, among other criteria such as teacher evaluations and data collection on student success.

In 2013, the Texas legislature passed a law prohibiting school districts from using Common Core in their lesson plans. Texas was not alone, although their allies were few in number. Oklahoma, Virginia, Alaska, Nebraska, North Carolina, South Carolina, and Indiana also did not adopt (or adopted and backed out of) the Common Core standards.[43] Critics of Common Core argued that it created a "one size fits all" model for education and amounts to a federal takeover of education. Common Core may also incur unfunded mandate costs such as purchasing corresponding textbooks, teacher training, testing, and assessment. Those in favor of Common Core counter that basic education standards are necessary for the states to educate kids for higher education or occupational readiness. The merits mattered little to Republican leadership in Texas. In his inaugural speech as lieutenant governor, Dan Patrick proudly supported Texas's decision to reject Common Core, insisting, "We need to keep the Federal Government out of our schools."[44]

★ TEXAS TAKEAWAYS

11 How often does Texas win in court against the federal government?

12 On what issues does Texas challenge the federal government?

13 What important Supreme Court case freed Texas from automatic federal oversight on voting and election issues?

 THE INSIDER VIEW

Principles and politics clash consistently over the practice of federalism. The Texas Constitution emphasizes the importance of preserving of "local self-government."[45] Many Texans are still suspicious of the federal government, long after the Civil War. However, politics plays a major role in structuring Texans' response to federal intervention. Liberal Democrats welcome federal policies that forward goals such as Medicaid expansion, voting laws, or adoption of Common Core standards. Conservative Republicans actively challenge federal intervention, as Greg Abbott has done both as attorney general and then as governor. Still such challenges steer attention away from the many ways in which Texas and the federal government work together, on US Army bases, in disaster relief, and in the implementation of social welfare, business growth, and other programs that impact many spheres of Texans' daily life. Relying on federal assistance to fund over one-third of the state budget, Texas is indeed thoroughly entrenched in our federalist system.

★▬ TEXAS TAKEAWAYS

1 The three types of constitutional systems are unitary, confederal, and federal.

2 Enumerated powers are specified in writing and retained by the federal government so that Congress has exclusive province to act on them. Implied powers are powers that the federal government could possess but that are not expressly identified.

3 Examples of concurrent powers include the power of taxation and enforcement of immigration laws, which are shared at the state and federal level.

4 The advantages of federalism are a stronger central government, representation of interests, policy innovation, and the ability to locate government closer to the people, which often results in a higher trust in government.

5 Texans support state government over the federal government on both economic and social issues.

6 The state received $69 billion in funding from the federal government. This amounted to 35% of the state's budget.

7 Most of the federal funds spent by the state went to social programs such as Medicare, followed by education. Other programs include transportation and other social welfare programs. Disaster funds (not regularly provided) are provided following a disaster.

8 Layer cake federalism is the model of dual federalism in which the arrangement of each layer of government is distinct from the other and each maintains its own power and authority. Marble cake federalism describes the style of cooperative federalism whereby the layers (of government) overlap and mix with each other, and jurisdictions on policy and regulatory matters are not bound by cleanly set layers.

9 New federalism gives more authority to the states, whereas coercive federalism makes demands on states to achieve specific objectives.

10 An unfunded mandate is a policy set by a higher level of government that requires spending funds but does not allocate funds for that purpose. In many cases, local governments may not have the funds to cover the policy.

11 Texas wins about 25% of the time in court against the federal government, although the number may be less important than the substance of the legal victory.

12 Texas challenges the federal government most on issues of immigration, education standards, environmental rules, administering elections, medical care coverage, and business regulations.

13 *Shelby County v. Holder* was the Supreme Court case that released Texas from automatic federal oversight on voting and election issues.

KEY TERMS

block grant
categorical grant
coercive federalism
commerce clause
concurrent powers
confederal system
cooperative federalism
dual federalism
enumerated powers
federal system
full faith and credit clause
implied powers
matching grant
necessary and proper clause
new federalism
preemptions
reserve clause
supremacy clause
unfunded mandates
unitary system

PRACTICE QUIZ

1. _____ grants are provided by the federal government to states to offer flexibility to enact policies.
   a. Block
   b. Matching
   c. Formula
   d. Project

2. The transfer of federal power to the states is often called . . .
   a. Tea Party politics
   b. Revolution
   c. Devolution
   d. Delimiting Powers

3. During President Obama's administration (2008–current), how many lawsuits and how much in taxpayer funds have Texas politicians spent on such efforts?
   a. 125 lawsuits; $1 billion in taxpayer funds
   b. 34 lawsuits; $5 million in taxpayer funds

c. 78 lawsuits; $11.5 million in taxpayer funds
d. 10 lawsuits; $1.3 million in taxpayer funds

4. What is the name of the power-sharing arrangement between a central governing authority and political units?
   a. Federalism
   b. Unionism
   c. Colonialism
   d. Texas Reunification

5. What is the current (as of 2014) portion of the Texas budget that is received from the federal government?
   a. About 1/6
   b. About 1/5
   c. About 1/4
   d. About 1/3

6. Which of the following is NOT a type of Federalism mentioned in this chapter?
   a. Cooperative Federalism
   b. Regressive Federalism
   c. Dual Federalism
   d. New Federalism

7. Dual federalism is often described as a layered cake.
   a. True
   b. False

8. Cooperative federalism is often described as a lemon cake.
   a. True
   b. False

9. Coercive federalism promotes good will between the states and the federal government.
   a. True
   b. False

10. Enumerated powers are powers that are expressly identified as powers that the government can take.
    a. True
    b. False

[Answers: A, C, B, A, D, B, A, B, B, A]

Family fights are always the ugliest, and the 2016 fight within the Republican Party to become a party nominee for the Texas legislature was as down-and-dirty as it gets. In a central Texas district, State Representative Doug Miller criticized his opponent for dressing up as "gay Hitler" and called attention to a restraining order served on his opponent during a bitter custody battle.[1] Miller won the race. In another house race east of Houston, Brisoe Cain challenged incumbent Wayne Smith for his seat. Flyers were circulated alleging that Cain "is well known to those who frequent Montrose [Houston] area night clubs and gay bars." Smith denied that his campaign had produced the flyer, but Cain won the seat in a runoff.[2] The Democrats got into the action too. Challenger for a senate seat Helen Madla ran ads using undercover video ostensibly showing incumbent Senator Carlos I. Uresti, who is married, flirting with other women.[3] Uresti won the primary and kept his seat.

Texas campaigns can get so nasty that voters actually stay away from the polls, and this makes it harder to achieve a goal that is important to most Texans: rule by the people. In this chapter, we look at how Texans vote and who votes. We explore how the struggle to broaden suffrage has changed Texas politics. We consider why voter turnout is so low, ways to improve on this, and why participation is so important. We also examine campaigns and the role of money in the electoral process. Finally, we investigate factors that help determine who will win and who will lose elections.

LEARNING OBJECTIVES

4.1 Explain the process of registering and voting in Texas.

4.2 Assess how the expansion of franchise has impacted Texas politics.

4.3 Evaluate how different factors affect voter turnout.

4.4 Describe how candidates campaign in Texas.

4.5 Analyze factors that influence election outcomes in Texas.

● There is a saying in politics that "all politics are local." This is especially true when Texans vote in community centers, grocery stores, and, as shown here, public libraries.

VOTING IN TEXAS

4.1 Explain the process of registering and voting in Texas.

If voters and nonvoters looked alike, it wouldn't really matter who voted as those who did vote would represent everyone else well. Unfortunately, this is not the case. Voters with higher education and higher income earners are significantly more likely to cast a ballot—and therefore are more likely to influence policy.[4] The bottom line is—if you want your interests and values represented in state and local policy, you have to vote.

REGISTRATION

register: sign up to vote in elections

Voters are required to **register** before the election as a way to ensure that the individual is eligible to vote in the election. In Texas, a prospective voter must register thirty days before an election, and must be a US citizen, a resident of the county where the individual intends to vote, at least eighteen years old, not legally mentally incapacitated, and not a convicted felon (or if so, must have completed the sentence, probation, and parole or have been pardoned for the crime).[5]

You can register to vote in person or by mail. You can acquire a registration form through the Texas Secretary of State's website and mail it in, or you can go in person to the county's voter registrar's office, the county clerk, or elections administrator's offices and fill out the form. Registration forms can be found in several locations, county offices, many university student centers, and in 2016, taco trucks around Houston. Are you currently registered to vote? Check out the state's online voter lookup at www.votetexas.gov—and also find out where to vote and when.

In an effort to make registration to vote easier—particularly for young people—the federal government passed the National Voter Registration Act of 1993, usually referred to as the **motor voter law**. Motor voter required state governments to provide voter registration opportunities to individuals applying for or renewing their driver's license. The motor voter policy and registration drives are shown to increase the proportion of registrants on the rolls and those individuals are more likely to vote.[6]

motor voter law: a statute mandating that state governments provide voter registration opportunities to individuals applying for or renewing their driver's license

Some states have experimented with Election Day (or "same day") registration so that voters can register and vote on the same day. Scholars have found same-day registration does increase turnout by a small amount—mostly for Republican voters.[7] A few states (five) have automatic registration, where everyone is registered to vote automatically upon turning 18. Texas does neither.

see for yourself 4.1

Learn about an obscure law that aims to get Texas high school seniors voting.

If you are a registered voter and you vote in person in Texas, you need some form of picture identification—including a driver's license, a handgun license, a US military identification, or a passport—or a sworn statement of citizenship and non-photo proof of residency like a utility bill, paystub, or bank statement, as we discuss later.

TYPES OF ELECTIONS

Once you are registered, you can vote in several different types of elections. Although the general election—the races in which nominees from different parties square off against each other—gets more media attention, the **primary election** is often more important in Texas. Before the general election, each major party holds a primary election in which voters elect the party's nominee for governor, senate, and other offices. Because Republicans currently win most of the statewide offices in Texas, the primary election often in reality decides who will be governor, lieutenant governor, comptroller, attorney general, and a range of other offices.

There are two types of primary elections: open and closed. In an **open primary**, any qualified registered voter can vote in a party's primary. In a **closed primary,** only voters registered with a party may vote in that party's primary. Registered Democrats vote in the Democratic primaries, Republicans in the Republican primaries, and independents in neither. Texas technically has closed primaries because participants declare a party affiliation before voting—but this declaration is nonbinding for future elections. So, Texas primaries resemble open primaries, which encourage crossover voting in which a voter might vote for candidates from the other party who are weaker or more ideologically extreme so that their own party's candidates have a better chance of winning. The 2008 Democratic primary turnout swelled to 2.8 million voters, more than three times the number in earlier primaries. Known as "Operation Chaos," approximately one-quarter of these voters tried to pack the Democratic primary elections with conservative nominees. They later voted Republican in the general election.[8]

In Texas, if no candidate gets a majority of the vote in the primary, a **runoff election** is held, which matches the top two vote getters against each other, normally held six weeks after the primary. Runoff elections are not held in the general elections where a plurality suffices. The state holds a **special election** to fill vacancies created by death, resignation, or removal from office. The governor calls for the special election, setting the day, which can be no later than thirty-six days before a scheduled election.

EARLY VOTING

In any election in Texas, you can vote early or on Election Day. **Early voting** starts on the Monday two weeks before the election and continues until the Friday before Election Day. Polls are normally open twelve hours on weekdays and on the weekend between the first and second weeks. You can avoid long voting lines on Election Day, and—in some counties—you can vote at any one of several locations, not just your assigned precinct.

Early voting has become very popular in Texas, increasing by 50 percent in many major counties since 2006 (see Figure 4.1). Early voting is argued to reduce the "cost" of voting because it provides flexibility to vote when convenient. In some counties, more than one-third of voters vote before Election Day. Early voters are typically older, more affluent, and long-term homeowners.

primary election: an election in which each party selects its nominees for office

open primary: an election in which any registered voter can vote for a party's candidates

closed primary: an election in which only voters registered with a party may vote for the party's candidates

runoff election: an election where, if no candidate receives a majority of the votes, the two top vote getters run again

special election: an election contest held as needed to fill vacancies created by death, resignation, or removal from office

early voting: voters are able to cast a ballot in Texas two weeks before Election Day

FIGURE 4.1   **Percent of Voters Voting Early, 2012 and 2016**

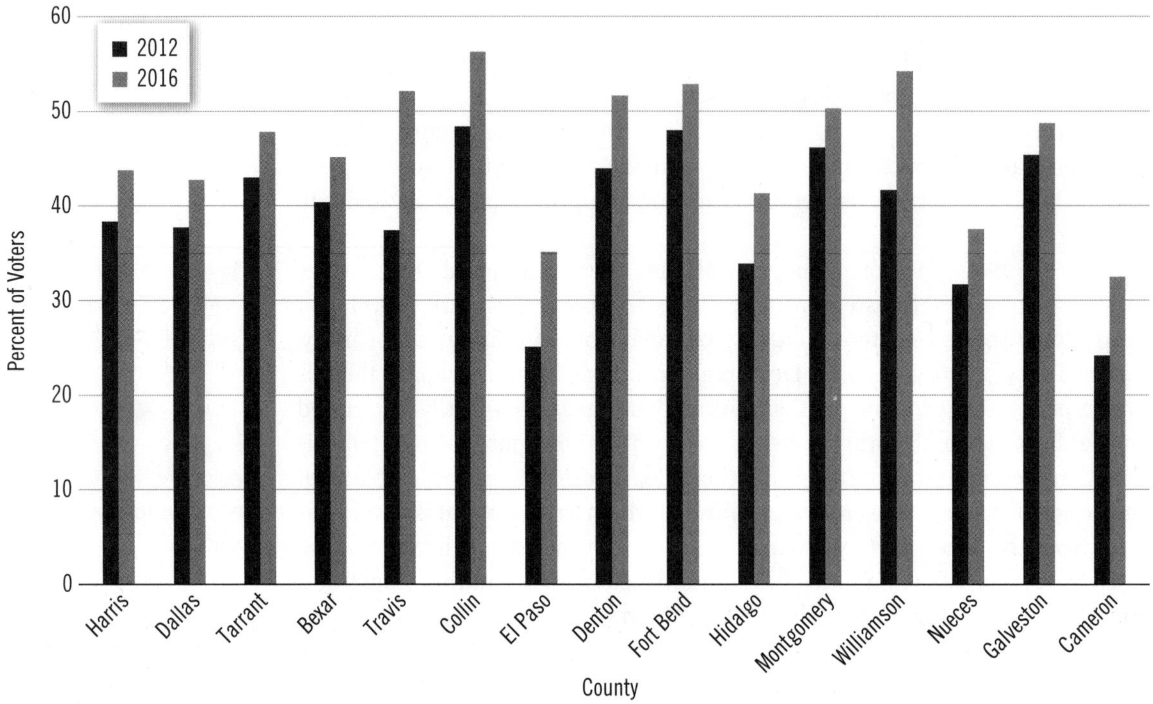

Source: Texas Secretary of State. Percentages are total voters out of total registered voters.

 COMMUNICATION:

How has early voting worked in Texas's most populous counties?

- In almost every county, the percentage of those voting early in the top ten counties has increased. The biggest jumps are in Travis County (15 percent increase), Williamson (13 percent), and El Paso (10 percent).
- Suburban counties like Collin and Denton both rose by 8 percent.

CRITICAL THINKING:

Why is there variation in early voting?

- A rise in Latino turnout in El Paso County increased early voting figures.
- Population increases in Travis and Williamson counties increased the number of voters, increasing early votes.
- Suburban areas tend to have larger turnout and active voters, as seen in Collin and Denton counties.

Political science research has found that racial minorities are less likely to vote early in part because the polling locations are difficult to reach. Early voting reinforces participation of those already active and longer-term residents who know the process.

MOBILE VOTING

Mobile voting (sometimes called "rolling voting") allows for a polling place to be moved around to different locations. These programs are popular because they enable individuals who would otherwise have difficulty getting to the polls, including rural residents, senior citizens, and the physically challenged, to vote.[9] Concerns, however, that mobile voting had been used to tip the scales in favor of one candidate or party caused lawmakers to clarify rules about the use of mobile voting. For example, an election official could harvest votes in favor of a bond proposal to raise funds for a cash-strapped school district by parking the poll outside school sporting events. The new rules require the location to be fixed for two days with extended hours.[10]

ELECTION DAY

On Election Day in most counties, Texans fill out some of the longest ballots in the nation. Confronted with this long list of names and offices, what do you do? Many voters choose to vote straight ticket. **Straight ticket voting** provides a good solution if you don't have the time or interest in researching candidates in the general election. You can just figure out which party's platform appeals most to you (see Chapter 5) and push one button or check one box—a little like one-stop shopping. If, however, you want to elect some candidates from one party and other candidates from another, you will be **split ticket voting**.

straight ticket voting: checking one box to vote for every candidate a specific party has on the ballot

split ticket voting: choosing candidates from different parties for different offices

You can also "write in" names of candidate who are not party nominees. Like candidates appearing on the ballot, these write-in candidates must officially file with the state and must have signatures of thirty-eight individuals who can serve as presidential electors, registered voters who can cast a ballot in the Electoral College. In recent presidential elections, several prominent politicians received write-in votes, in addition to Jesus Christ, Willie Nelson, Big Bird, and Chuck Norris.[11] No write-in candidate, however, has ever won in Texas.

Neighborhood Precincts.   Each county designates neighborhood polling locations, which must be located within twenty-five miles from the home of each voter in the precinct on Election Day. The neighborhood precinct must be a public place—often a school or community center, but sometimes a grocery store, flea market, or barbecue joint.

Vote Centers.   In 2005, the Texas legislature approved county-level decisions to move from traditional, neighborhood precinct polls to "vote centers." All voters in counties that allow it can vote in these centers in the general election, regardless of their address, so that they can choose the most convenient

FIGURE 4.2   **Vote Centers and Vote Change**

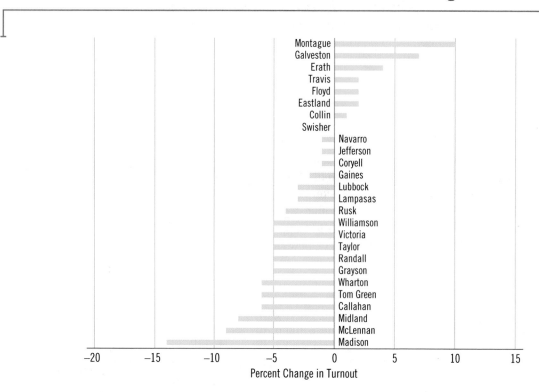

Source: Texas Secretary of State website. Counties are those that adopted a vote center voting process. Percentages indicate increase or decrease in registered voter turnout.

 COMMUNICATION:

What is the effect of vote center voting process?

- For most counties, the switch to vote centers resulted in a net negative in turnout.
- Smaller counties had better success with vote centers: Montague, Galveston, and Erath counties all had turnout change greater than 4 percent.

 CRITICAL THINKING:

Why do vote centers increase turnout in some counties but not others?

- Voter unfamiliarity with the (new) process may cause early reduction in voter turnout.
- As a new voting tradition sets in, voters may grow more comfortable with the process. This is accelerated in smaller counties because word of mouth may help neighbors understand the new process more quickly.
- In counties in which turnout is already high (such as Collin), vote centers may help increase turnout.

location and no longer need to panic at the last moment if they can't remember their assigned polling location. The hope is that vote centers might increase turnout, but research suggests community connections encourage turnout and a loss of traditional neighborhood precincts could decrease turnout (see Figure 4.2).[12]

★ TEXAS TAKEAWAYS

1 How far in advance of an election must a Texas citizen be registered to vote?

2 What sort of identification do Texas voters need at the polls?

3 What are the differences between an open and closed primary?

SUFFRAGE STRUGGLES AND THEIR CONSEQUENCES

For almost two centuries, Texans have engaged in riotous arguments about who gets to vote, how, and when. Scholar Alex Keyssar, author of *The Right to Vote*, argues that these decisions are made by those in power to maintain that power. Many practices keep the status quo firmly entrenched. Keyssar wrote, "Voting is like motherhood and apple pie, especially for 'my' people. If 'your' people want to vote, I'm not so sure."[13]

4.2 Assess how the expansion of franchise has impacted Texas politics.

There is a practical reason behind this sentiment: Election results depend on the ability of a candidate or a party to build coalitions among groups. The struggle of groups to win the right to vote, and their success, has changed the makeup of these coalitions and thus challenged the status quo. In this section, we explore the practices used to **disenfranchise** Texans, the struggle of groups to regain access to the polls, and how these groups shape election outcomes— and thus public policy by siding with one party or candidate over another.

disenfranchise: Deprive individuals of the right to vote

LITERACY TESTS

Beginning in the 1890s, southern states began to adopt literacy tests—an impromptu examination of an individual's ability to speak and pronounce specific legal passages or a short quiz pertaining to facts of state or US government. Anglos were also subject to the requirements, but the grandfather clause exempted those eligible to vote before the Civil War. Because the tests were administered locally by voter registrars, Anglo voters were also often given easier passages to read than minorities. Literacy tests were upheld by federal courts in the 1950s but abolished in the South in the landmark 1965 Voting Rights Act. Texas never directly mandated literacy tests like other southern states, but used other methods of disenfranchisement.

POLL TAX

poll tax: an unconstitutional tax that required those desiring to register to vote to pay a fee

In 1902, Texans fearful of racial minorities "flooding the polls" and outvoting Anglos passed a constitutional amendment that restricted access to the ballot by instituting a **poll tax**, which required those desiring to register to vote to pay a fee. The fee ranged from $1.50 to $2.00.[14] Although all voters would have to pay the tax, Latinos and African Americans were less likely to be able to afford the tax.[15] The poll tax was meant to discriminate against racial and ethnic minorities but also disenfranchised Anglos who could not or chose not to pay it. When the flour salesman and front man for the Light Crust Doughboys band Pappy O'Daniel ran for governor in 1938, his political rivals pointed out that he "hadn't been civic-minded" enough to pay his $1.75 poll tax. Pappy declared that "no politician in Texas is worth $1.75," and won the election.[16] Once elected, however, he did not eliminate the poll tax. The federal government outlawed the poll tax in federal elections in 1964 and the Supreme Court extended that to state elections in 1966.

WHITE PRIMARY

"I know you can't let me vote, but I've got to try." With this statement in 1924, Dr. Lawrence A. Nixon of El Paso issued the first challenge to the white primary.[17] With registration card and poll tax receipt in hand, Dr. Nixon—a charter member of the El Paso NAACP and a prominent physician—was turned away from the polling location.

Federal law prohibited discrimination in the general election, so Texas passed a law stipulating that only whites could participate in the *primary* election. In 1927, the US Supreme Court ruled in Dr. Nixon's favor finding that states could not hold white primaries. The Texas legislature then passed a law allocating responsibility for primary rules to the political parties, and the parties re-established white primaries. Democrats who controlled the state government at the time wanted to ban African Americans from voting in part because of strong racial dislike and in part because they voted Republican and had sufficient numbers to politically dominate some districts.

The white primary was like an "iron curtain," for even if African Americans became literate, acquired property, and paid their poll taxes, they could not change the color of their skin.[18] Anglo Democrats would hold a "pre-election" to nominate a candidate through a political organization called the Jaybird Democratic Association. This early vote excluded African Americans from voting and the winners of these "Jaybird primary" contests would inevitably win in the official primary. Latinos were also subject to exclusion in the white primary unless they were willing to go before an election committee and declare "I am a white person and a Democrat."[19]

Finally, in 1944, the case of Lonnie E. Smith, an African American dentist from Houston, came before the Supreme Court. In this case, *Smith v. Allwright*, the Supreme Court held that it was unconstitutional for the state to delegate all its authority to the Democratic Party to practice discriminatory voting processes because it disenfranchised African Americans. This did away with the white primary once and for all.[20] Yet minority groups still had a long struggle ahead to overcome voting barriers during the twentieth century.

HISPANICS

Exclusion, bossism, corruption, and intimidation have impacted Hispanic electoral experiences in Texas. Although Tejano settlers arrived in Texas before Anglos, the Texas Constitution of 1836 revoked citizenship from individuals who had left Texas during the revolution. This included many Tejanos who had sided with Mexico. Those who had sided with Texas were granted citizenship and voting rights. However, throughout the nineteenth century, intimidation—threats of being fired from work or physical harm—kept many from the polls. Outright bribery, like free food and alcohol on Election Day, pressured Hispanic Texans to vote in accordance with the Anglo majority.[21]

Hispanics throughout much of Texas history had an "ambiguous racial identity"—not Anglo but not African American. Hispanics were counted as "white" for purposes like school integration but not for political inclusion.[22] After the 1923 white primary law passed, Hispanics were allowed to vote

ANGLES OF POWER
Political Machines

Political machines are organizations run by local bosses that engage in graft, bribery, and electoral fraud to collect and maintain political power. They gain the loyalty of groups of voters by delivering financial help or political favors. In the early 1900s, the *patrón* system in South Texas, a boss-run system with a wealthy, powerful leader, manipulated Hispanic voters caught in a feudal agrarian system into supporting a wealthy Anglo landowner's political stranglehold. Local Hispanics, who marked their allegiances with red or blue ribbons, exchanged their vote for household necessities, jobs, and even funeral expenses.

The most notorious *patrones* were the Parr family of Duval County. In 1914 on the night before a court-ordered investigation into his family's local finances, Archie Parr set fire to the courthouse to attempt to end the investigation.[23] Archie's son, George, known as the Duke of Duval after consolidating regional political power, is widely suspected of delivering the eighty-seven infamous (some say manufactured) votes that won Lyndon Johnson a place in the US Senate in 1948.[24] The dynasty ended after the machine's primary guardian angel, Lyndon Johnson, left office and when state and federal investigators returned hundreds of indictments against machine members.[25] In 1975, Parr shot himself the day he was to be taken to prison after being convicted of income tax evasion. The boss system as a whole, however, ended gradually—not with a bang but a whimper—as bosses died or as voters organized to reject boss rule in favor of social activists or party leaders.

 SOCIAL RESPONSIBILITY: **What rules should be in place to limit voter intimidation?**

in some counties but not others, depending on the needs of "los jefes" ("the bosses"), the Anglo political power brokers. Change was slow for Hispanics, but iconic Latino figures like Henry B. Gonzales (first Latino elected to the Texas Senate) and Hector P. Garcia (founder of the American GI Forum), and other local leaders, emerged in the 1950s. Only a handful of Hispanics were elected to the legislature from 1900 to 1930, but by 1960 seven Hispanics represented their communities in the legislature.

Aggressive activism, demographic change, and the concentration of Hispanics into urban communities sparked a great political "awakening" of Hispanic voters in the late 1960s. Many Latinos in Texas embraced the civil rights movement. Several groups protested discrimination, registered voters, and organized into PASSO (the Political Association of Spanish-Speaking Organizations).[26] The "Viva Kennedy" clubs in Texas supported John F. Kennedy's bid for presidency and yielded 91 percent of the Hispanic vote in Texas. Hispanic voters began winning local elections in Crystal City and Zavala County and elsewhere across South Texas.[27] As we see in Chapter 6, after the Democratic Party fended off a challenge from the Latino political party La Raza, a faction of liberal Democrats began to fight for the inclusion of Latino voters.

In 1965, Congress passed the **Voting Rights Act,** which prohibited discrimination against racial minorities, but left the status of "language minorities" ambiguous.[28] In 1974, Willie Velasquez of San Antonio established the Southwest Voter Registration Education Project, which launched voter registration drives all over the state and became a vehicle of political influence for Latinos across the nation. The organization's efforts became synonymous with the phrase "Su voto es su voz" ("Your vote is your voice") and "lengthened the stride" of the Latino political power movement.[29] In 1975, the Voting Rights Act was finally amended to include language minorities and mandated the translation of voting materials.

Conflicts over voting power also worked their way into the court system. Supreme Court rulings in *White v. Regester* (1972) and *Graves v. Barnes* (1974) declared that several Texas cities had diluted the Latino vote. The court forced redrawing of electoral district lines, and the replacement of countywide districts with **single-member districts**, opening the door to greater representation. The Mexican American Legal Defense and Education Fund—often called the law firm of the Latino community—also helped take the door off the hinges in 1990 when a federal court ruled in *Garza v. County of Los Angeles* that the city had discriminated against Latinos by diluting their influence across districts. The impact fractured the practice of drawing district lines to benefit Anglos at the expense of Latinos. The decision forced the Texas legislature to draw districts that keep Latino communities intact.[30]

Growth and concentration of the Hispanic population in geographic areas increased representation in certain quarters of the state. The number of Hispanic elected officials exploded by 643 percent between 1975 and 1994.[31]

Voting Rights Act: a landmark piece of federal legislation that outlawed racial discrimination in voting

single-member districts: an electoral unit that elects only one member of a political body, such as a legislature, and through which smaller communities can gain representation on that bod

Victor Morales, US Senatorial Candidate in 1996, US House Candidate in 1998

What lessons about the Latino vote in Texas did you learn from your campaigns?

I knew the Latino vote could be huge. I also felt that it could be energized. With the right candidate, and I felt like I could be that, that I would get a large turnout in the Hispanic vote. There is a hunger for a leader in the Hispanic population, a pride in seeing someone that looked like them for a big role. People were always telling me that they were so excited to see someone who looked like them who could share in their culture.

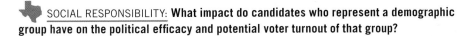 SOCIAL RESPONSIBILITY: **What impact do candidates who represent a demographic group have on the political efficacy and potential voter turnout of that group?**

By 2000, Hispanic candidates were a permanent fixture for elected office (see Figure 4.3). In 2002, the Democrats, seeking to claim some statewide offices, nominated the "Dream Team"—a Hispanic gubernatorial candidate (millionaire businessman Tony Sanchez) and an African American US Senate candidate (former Dallas Mayor Ron Kirk). The Democrats poured tremendous resources into the race, including $60 million of Sanchez's personal fortune. However, the strategy didn't work. The Democrats alienated the white vote and overestimated the strength of the Hispanic vote. Sanchez carried just seven of the counties north of Interstate 10.[32]

Today, the Hispanic vote in Texas is still smaller than in other states either because many—as noncitizens—are not eligible to vote or because a sizeable portion are either too young to vote or inattentive to politics. Yet, Hispanics do place issues of importance to the community onto the state's political agenda. Issues like sanctuary cities, halting deportations, and birth certificate denials all have the potential to ignite the Latino base. However, the Republican majority in Texas does not depend on Hispanic voters to maintain their position.[34] Even so, Republicans have expanded their political reach and have searched for ways to embrace Hispanic causes to court their votes.

AFRICAN AMERICANS

The Texas Reconstruction Constitution extended full voting rights to African Americans, harnessing the legal authority of the **Fifteenth Amendment**. During Reconstruction, African Americans flocked to the Republican Party, the party of Lincoln. However, once the Union's military rule ended, Anglos

Fifteenth Amendment: the 1870 amendment to the US Constitution, which prohibited the denial of voting rights upon the basis of race

FIGURE 4.3   **Support for Statewide Latino Candidates in Largely Hispanic Texas Counties, 2006–2012**

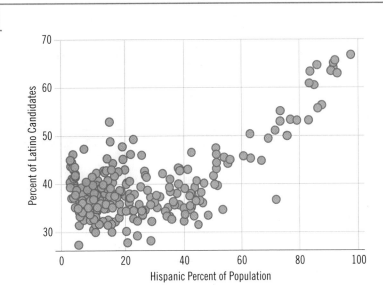

Source: Texas Secretary of State. Data include candidates of both parties for lieutenant governor, governor, and US Senate. US Census. Latino candidate percent is the percentage of the vote the Latino candidate won in the county. Hispanic percent is the percentage of total Hispanic population in the county.

 COMMUNICATION:

Do Latino candidates get more votes in counties with more Latinos?

- The scatterplot shows that candidates with Latino surnames get more votes in counties as the Latino population of the county increases.

 CRITICAL THINKING:

Why are Latino candidates overperforming in Latino-heavy counties?

- Sensing shared values and concerns, Latino voters vote for Latino candidates, regardless of their party affiliation.[33]
- Latinos who self-identify racially more strongly as Latinos are more likely to vote for Latino candidates.

were able to keep African Americans economically subservient and reinforce discriminatory voting practices through intimidation. The Republican Party in Texas, champion of African American voting rights, found itself in the minority and relatively powerless to help. Moreover, the Republican Party leadership remained almost exclusively Anglo, making little room for African American participation. African Americans were further alienated from the Republican Party in 1906, when Republican President Theodore Roosevelt dishonorably dismissed 167 African American soldiers barracked in Brownsville for killing an Anglo bartender despite evidence they were not involved. Many African Americans still voted Republican as the lesser of two evils but some moved to the Democratic Party. Unease with African Americans voting led Democrats to press for the white primary.

Following World War II, African Americans migrated to large cities in significant numbers. African American veterans from the war who had fought racism in Europe came home to find it unopposed in their own state. These veterans and other African Americans achieved a major victory in 1948 when Democratic President Truman desegregated the US military. The national and Texas branch of the National Association for the Advancement of Colored People (NAACP) continued to bring court cases that challenged discriminatory voting practices. Many conservative Democrats in Texas held strong to segregation even in the wake of Supreme Court rulings, but liberal Democrats opposed them.

Then, in 1956, African American precincts in Fort Worth voted in great enough numbers to force a runoff in the US Senate Democratic primary between liberal Ralph Yarborough and conservative Price Daniels.[35] Yarborough lost but won the seat in a special election in 1957 with similar backing from African Americans. Liberal Democrats attempted to purge the party of segregationists from the 1950s to the 1960s with limited success. Those archconservatives who left the Democratic Party found a welcome home in the Republican Party in 1960, just at the time when conservative Barry Goldwater denounced the Civil Rights Act of 1957.[36] African Americans rallied to support Democrats who took a strong stand in favor of civil rights. This support may have made a difference in the 1960 presidential election which saw Democratic candidate John F. Kennedy win Texas by a slim margin.[37]

The national struggle for civil rights prompted the passage of the Voting Rights Act (VRA) in 1965. Many voting restrictions in Texas law ran afoul of the VRA. The VRA and changes to federal law through the Supreme Court's intervention in the 1960s empowered African Americans, increasing voter turnout. Redistricting in 1970 helped elect many African Americans into office as districts were drawn with more African American communities within the boundaries, increasing the number of elected positions held in Texas from forty-five in 1971 to 472 in 1992.[38] African American elected officials worked to desegregate public housing, improve inner-city education, and expand representation.

As the conservative exodus from the Democratic Party continued, more minorities began to vote. Before the Voting Rights Act of 1965, only 29 percent of eligible African Americans in Texas registered to vote, but this number increased dramatically by the 1970s. Today, African American turnout rivals Anglo turnout (see Figure 4.4) and African Americans are a powerful component of the Democratic Party. Approximately 80 percent of African Americans support the Democratic Party, the most loyal group to the party by far.[39]

WOMEN

Women were equal partners in the settlement of Texas, but not always in politics. Politics, it was thought, would make women "coarse and crude" and their involvement would endanger the social order.[40] Through the progressive

FIGURE 4.4   **Voting Rates of Racial Groups in Texas**

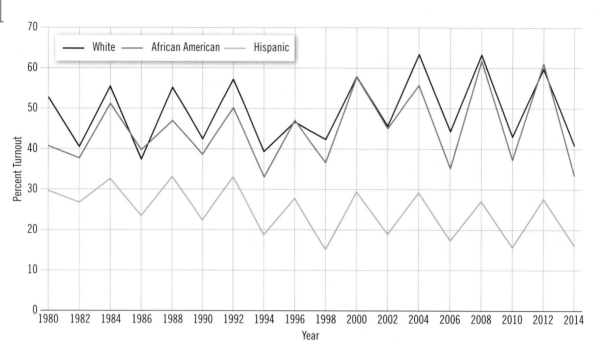

Source: US Census.

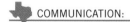 COMMUNICATION:

At what rate do racial groups turn out in Texas elections?

- The zig-zag pattern demonstrates that Texans are more likely to vote in presidential than midterm elections.

- Anglos are the most likely to vote, followed closely by African Americans. In some elections the percentage turnout of African Americans is equal to or higher than Anglos.

- Hispanics trend far behind both Anglos and African Americans in turnout, and turnout has been declining since the 1980s.

 CRITICAL THINKING:

What causes the variation in participation?

- Anglos are more likely to vote for Republicans, and Republicans have dominated state politics for more than 20 years, so Republicans have an incentive to promote the turnout of Anglo voters.

- African Americans are historically the most loyal group to the Democratic Party. These numbers spike when a presidential candidate is embraced by African Americans, like Barack Obama in 2008.

- Hispanic turnout is low because of low assimilation into the politics of Texas, eligibility concerns, and a larger population of individuals under eighteen.

movement and women's suffrage organizations, however, women won the right to vote in primary elections in 1918 and were extended full voting rights in 1920 through the ratification of the Nineteenth Amendment.

Women gradually became a force to be reckoned with, placing issues on the political agenda and serving as a catalyst during Texas's transition from a Democratic to a Republican state. In response to the New Deal, middle- and upper-class suburban women bolted from the Democratic Party out of fear of their children growing up in a "socialist nation." The "Minute Women" clubs of Houston and Dallas pledged to vote in every election, remove "every vestige of communism from federal and state governments," and focus on states' rights, fairer taxes, and the right to work.[41] Republican women's organizations sprang up all over the state from the 1950s to the 1970s, helping to elect Presidents Eisenhower (1956), Nixon (1972), and Reagan (1980) and reelect John Tower to the Senate (1966).[42] The tables have turned slightly in Texas today: women are more likely to identify with the Democratic Party (50 percent) than the Republican Party (40 percent).[43] This is slightly lower than the national figure of 52 percent who identify as Democrats.[44]

The growth of Republican politics in Texas did not guarantee an emergence of women in leadership roles—women were often relegated to "housekeeping" chores that "earned male praise but not authority in the party hierarchy."[45] This changed in recent decades as women have taken on prominent roles, particularly within conservative groups, such as the Tea Party and the Texas Eagle Forum. The number of women serving in the Texas legislature rose from two in 1967 to thirty-seven in 2015. Women have served in recent years as mayors of major cities (Anise Parker of Houston, Laura Miller of Dallas, Ivy Taylor of San Antonio) and as governor (Ann Richards). Yet, observers claim that some areas of Texas, such as the Rio Grande Valley, are still hostile to female candidates. A high-profile 2016 congressional race in South Texas featuring Latina candidate Dolly Elizando ended in her missing the runoff by 1,026 votes out of more than 50,000 cast.[46]

ASIAN AMERICANS

Asian Americans have often been treated as "outsiders" in politics.[47] The Chinese were the first Asian immigrants to arrive in Texas in the 1870s and the most numerous until an influx of Vietnamese one hundred years later.[48] In 1882 Congress passed the Chinese Exclusion Act, which restricted immigration and classified Asian immigrants as "aliens," rendering them ineligible for citizenship and unable to vote. The act was not repealed until 1943.

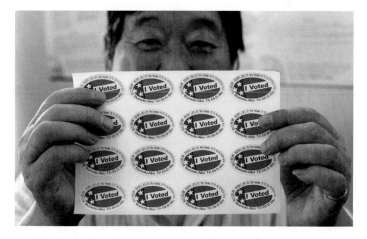

In 2009, Texas State Representative Betty Brown took an insensitive position that Asians in Texas should adopt names that were "easier for Americans to deal with."*

SOCIAL RESPONSIBILITY: **Are voters who are racial minorities better represented by members of their own race?**

Today Asians are the fastest-growing minority group in Texas. More than 50,000 immigrants from Asia arrived in Texas in 2013, double the number from 2005.[49] Although geographically contained in several larger cities, Asians are an emerging force in Texas politics and both parties court their votes. Like Hispanics, however, Asians are not a monolithic group—distinct ethnicities shape their voting behavior. As a group, however, they lean left with 60 to 70 percent supporting the Democratic Party in the 2016 elections.[50]

★ TEXAS TAKEAWAYS

4 What are some ways Texas has disenfranchised minority voters in the past?

5 What law that was passed in 1965 outlawed voter discrimination?

6 What percentage of African Americans support the Democratic Party?

🤠 VOTER TURNOUT IN TEXAS

4.3 Evaluate how different factors affect voter turnout.

Turnout shapes both election outcomes and which groups' political values elected officials will represent. Yet voter turnout in Texas is very low (see Table 4.1). In this section, we explore why turnout is low and what Texans have done to increase, or repress, voter turnout.

WHY TEXANS DON'T VOTE

Political scientists have identified several reasons why people decide not to vote in elections—some linked to rational choices while others emerge from the social environment and personal experiences.

The Rational Voter.   Many scholars believe that voters weigh the costs and benefits of voting. Voting doesn't cost money, but it does take the time to get informed about the candidates, find the polling station, wait in line, and fill out the ballot. Approximately 28 percent of Americans say that they don't vote because they are "too busy."[51]

There are others who don't vote because they don't see a benefit. They lack **political efficacy**—they don't believe that their vote will make a difference. Although a single vote does not usually make a major difference, several recent elections have been decided by small margins. Texas House District 144 (Pasadena area, east of Houston) was decided by 152 votes in 2014. A runoff election for Dallas City Council District 3 was decided by 186 votes in 2015. A Texas house district in Grand Prairie was decided by 64 votes in 2016.

political efficacy: the belief that your participation can influence the political system

| TABLE 4.1 | Most Texans Don't Vote, 2016 |

Voting Age Population: 20,832,609
Total Registered: 15,015,700
General Turnout: 8,878,152
Republican Primary Turnout: 2,836,488
Democratic Primary Turnout: 1,435,895

Source: Texas Secretary of State.

 COMMUNICATION:

What is voter turnout like in Texas?

- Most Texans don't vote, even in a presidential election year. Only 59 percent of registered voters turned out to vote in 2016. That is only 43 percent of adults eligible to vote.

- Only 2.8 million voted in the Republican primary, but this was significantly higher than the 1.4 million that voted in the Democratic primary.

 CRITICAL THINKING:

Why are there significant differences between the parties?

- Turnout in presidential election years is higher than other elections because competition is higher. In Texas, however, the Republican candidate is likely to win and the general election is not usually competitive.

- Republican primary turnout was higher because the election contest was ongoing and competitive and US Senator Ted Cruz of Texas was on the ballot.

Some people abstain from voting because they don't see any differences between the parties or candidates. Political scientist Anthony Downs called this the "expected vote differential"—voters judge the past success of the current party in power and compare this to the other party. If voters believe that one party is more successful, they vote for that party. If they perceive no difference between the parties, they abstain from voting.

Some elections—like the 2016 presidential election—have a greater "wow" factor than others because they stir up controversy or feature candidates who are more entertaining to watch. Elections can be similar to horse races or sporting events, with the media supplying daily updates on opinion polls and analyses of what candidates have said or done. Competitive elections bring out more voters. Non-presidential elections, such as midterm elections, special elections, and municipal elections, are critical to democracy, but voter turnout drops by about 20 percent.

SOCIAL PRESSURE AND POLITICAL SOCIALIZATION

Of course, a voter's sense of civic duty plays a role as well. If Texans feel a responsibility to participate in democratic governance or feel a sense of pride, they will show up at the polls. Social pressure also enhances civic duty. In political science experiments, individuals who were informed about their neighbors' voting participation were more likely to vote because of the shame they would feel for not participating.[52] But where does this sense of civic duty spring from?

Political socialization is the process by which individuals acquire political values and behaviors that have a strong influence on future voting behavior. Family, friends, media, religion, region, and other sources of political socialization impact not only whether someone will vote but also how they will vote. Family is often pointed to as the primary influence in the development of a young person's political orientation. These bonds are tight but do not always last forever. Texas Senator John Tower, who upset the Democrat's stranglehold on Texas in 1961 by winning a special election, described how he switched parties: "I decided in 1951 that being a Democrat because Granddaddy was a Democrat was foolish."[53]

School is another major agent of political socialization, part of the reason that Texas seventh graders, high school students, and college students are required to take courses in civics and Texas government. Race and ethnicity also factor in—for example, experiences with local government, the role of democracy, and lack of English proficiency all contribute to a lower turnout for Hispanic foreign-born voters and their children.[54] All these factors combine to give Texas a lower voter turnout than most other states (see Figure 4.5).

political socialization:
the process in which individuals acquire political values and behaviors that have a strong influence on future voting behavior

HOW CAN VOTER TURNOUT BE INCREASED?

Texas is a large, diverse, young, and mobile state long-dominated by one party—today, the Republicans. These attributes produce poor turnout among registered voters. What might be done to increase turnout?

For Convenience Sake.   "Convenience" voting—same-day registration, no-excuse absentee voting, and statewide voting by mail—has been shown to lift voter turnout between 2 to 10 percent in states that initiate these practices.[55] Texas has none of these. Adopting one or more of these measures could increase turnout.

Why Tuesday?   Elections in the United States have by law and tradition been on a Tuesday, but because this is a weekday, getting off work or taking time away from life is difficult. Texas does have laws requiring employers to allow voters to have two paid hours off to vote. However the vast majority of countries hold Election Day on a weekend or make the day a holiday from work. Such a change could increase turnout by 5–6 percent.[56]

Voter Targeting.   Actively reminding and encouraging voters to vote spurs turnout. Even in local municipal elections, research shows that effective local campaigns push voters to the polls.[57] Reminder phone calls and campaign mailers written in the language of the potential voter have been shown to successfully mobilize Asian Americas.[58]

IS IT BIGGER IN TEXAS?

FIGURE 4.5   **Voter Turnout by State, 2016**

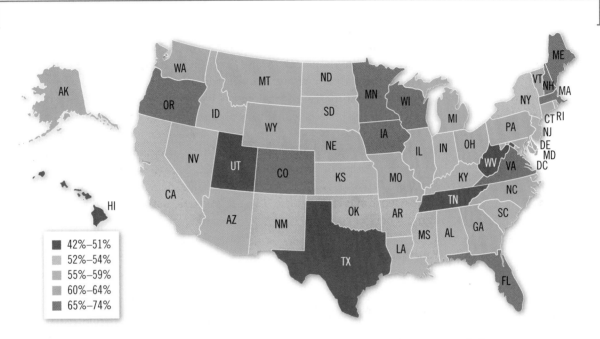

42%–51%
52%–54%
55%–59%
60%–64%
65%–74%

Source: US Elections Project. Percent voting estimates in each state out of total eligible voting population.

 COMMUNICATION:

Which states have the highest percent of voter turnout?

- Minnesota and New Hampshire led the nation with more than 70 percent of voting age population voting.

- Texas is in the bottom five of turnout, with just over 50 percent of the voter-eligible population voting. Below Texas and rounding out the bottom four are West Virginia, Tennessee, Utah, and Hawaii.

 CRITICAL THINKING:

Why do some states' citizens vote at higher rates?

- There are several factors that increase voter turnout. Some states make voting easier. Oregon allows voters to mail in their ballots. Some states make registering to vote easier. Minnesotans and Mainers can register and vote the same day.

- Texas, New Mexico, and California all have significant foreign-born populations and new emigrants to the states from other states—a recently arrived population may take time to register to vote and then turn out. These states also have significant Hispanic populations who find barriers or choose not to register.

We're All in This Together.   A sense of shared interests spurs voter turnout. For Latinos in California and Texas, appeals to ethnic group interests (called solidarity) can be especially effective for those who are less assimilated into the broader American culture or who more strongly identify with their Latino identity.[59]

I'm Asking for Your Vote.   Research also shows that well-organized get-out-the-vote efforts by parties or organizations are effective if they rely on door-to-door visits or on phone calls from a volunteer. Repeated phone calls (at least two) are especially effective and in-person persuasion produced major gains of up to 40 percent increased turnout.[60] Live volunteer calling is critical because prerecorded "robo-calls" can annoy potential voters and reduce turnout.

Thanks for Voting.   Political scientists have also shown that thanking individuals for voting in previous elections is effective in spurring turnout in the current election by about 3 percent.[61] Because social pressure works to activate voters' sense of civic duty, the "I voted" stickers may also be effective in encouraging others to vote.

Your Ballot is Safe with Me.   For first-time voters or those voters with lower awareness, voting can be intimidating. Scholars have shown that reminders from official sources (like the secretary of state) that the vote a voter casts is kept secret helps to increase turnout.[62]

Viva Votación.   Political science scholars have found that Spanish language messages in a variety of mediums, including text messages, e-mails, mailed reminders, and radio advertisements, are effective in motivating Latinos to vote. The content of the message mattered less than the language. The results are strongest on low-propensity voters and those whose primary language is Spanish.[63]

VOTER ID

In recent years, Texans waged a war in the legislature and the courts over whether to institute a voter ID requirement that might suppress voter turnout while reducing voter fraud. Voter fraud has a long tradition in Texas. Lyndon Johnson is believed to have stolen the 1948 Democratic primary runoff for US Senate when "Box 13" was "discovered" in an uncounted precinct.[64] In Texas today, many Republican politicians have expressed concerns about voter fraud. As attorney general, Greg Abbott identified 50 voter fraud cases and declared that they were just the "tip of the iceberg." The Texas Attorney General's office opened a massive investigation into a vote-harvesting scheme in which individuals collected the mail-in ballots of other voters. These involve as many as 20,000 ballots in Tarrant County. Others argue, however, that voter fraud is extremely rare in Texas today.[65] In one case, the conservative Heritage

Foundation identified only a dozen convictions in Texas between 2006 and 2015 for schemes ranging from vote buying to voter impersonation to falsely registering to vote without citizenship.[66] Another study found a "trickle not a flood" with only three cases of fraud for every one million votes cast.[67]

Whatever the true extent of the problem, the state legislature in 2011 passed a bill (SB 14) that required voters who vote in person in Texas show an official, government-issued photo identification (including a driver's license, an election identification certificate, or a passport). The law created immediate controversy and provoked a lawsuit. Opponents claim that the law would disproportionately prevent African American, Hispanic, and older Texans from voting because these groups are less likely to have identification. A federal appeals court agreed and in 2016 ruled that Texas's voter ID law is racially discriminatory and unconstitutional. The court ordered that Texas allow those without a picture identification to show they were citizens by other means, and the state must advertise this to voters before the election. Despite the legal controversy, 75 percent strongly or somewhat supported the photo ID requirement.[68]

Critics of the voter ID law argue that these measures unfairly target individuals who are new to the process, unfamiliar with voting, and those who are less likely to have identification (individuals who are poor or racial minorities).

PERSONAL RESPONSIBILITY: **How would you design a voting system that protected the security of the ballot but also promoted fairness and access?**

TEXAS TAKEAWAYS

7 Why do some Texans not vote?

8 How can voter turnout be increased?

HOW TO CAMPAIGN, TEXAS STYLE

Before launching his 1968 gubernatorial campaign, wealthy businessman and rancher Dolph Briscoe invited a dozen political players from around the state to his South Texas ranch for a weekend of hunting and fishing. Some committed right away to Briscoe's candidacy; others did not. Fort Worth businessman Jack Bean was one of the undecided. In the afternoon, a group including Bean went out to fish on the property. About the time the group started back to the house, the jeep suddenly quit. "Well, it's 20 miles back to the house," one of Briscoe's aides quipped with a straight face. "Do you want to sign up for Dolph—or walk back?" "I'll sign, I'll sign," panted Bean "amid gales of laughter."[69] In the 1930s and 1940s, Texas politics was largely run by oil millionaires and other "Big

4.4 Describe how candidates campaign in Texas.

Rich." Today, a candidate needs to run a good campaign to connect with voters in addition to securing strong backing from political elites to win. In this section, we examine successful campaign strategies.

BUILDING CAMPAIGN INFRASTRUCTURE

Campaign staff are the engine that runs the machine of a campaign: political consultants who craft strategy, a campaign manager who executes the strategy, a fundraising director who raises funds from individuals and political action committees (PACs), a field (voter) director who coordinates the voter contact program, and volunteers who walk door to door to talk to voters. The main goal of the campaign is to get the candidate's message out to voters. Driving the strategy are two key components: persuading independents ("swing voters") and mobilizing the candidate's partisan base. Campaigns use **public opinion polling** to obtain information about what issues respondents support, what attributes of a candidate they like, and what factors would change their vote.

public opinion polling: a battery of survey questions asked of a representative sample of individuals

name identification: familiarity with a candidate's name

incumbents: candidates who are also the current officeholder

IMAGE, LIMELIGHT, AND THE MEDIA

A candidate's **name identification** (or name ID) is a benefit, as voters unfamiliar with the background of every candidate tend to pick those whose names they have heard. This is one great advantage of **incumbents**. In one campaign, to stoke his name identification, Governor John Connally (1963–1969) had his staff call around to airports in the state and have him urgently paged to make sure voters were thinking of him.[70] Today candidates carefully craft their image by using the media to highlight their position, record, and biography.

A candidate's actions may hurt them politically in the long run. In the 2014 governor's race, Republican supporters exploited Wendy Davis's main claim to fame, a senate filibuster of a bill restricting abortion, to paint her as a flaming liberal. Ads derogatively referred to her as "abortion Barbie."[71] As a result, the Davis campaign was unable to persuade swing voters that she was more than a single-issue candidate.

Candidates can pay for advertising via direct mail, radio, television, or the Internet. They can also access free media by staging an event, like a visit or a speech, and making themselves available for interviews. Dan Patrick visits the Texas border near McAllen in 2016.

SOCIAL RESPONSIBILITY: **Do these staged events take the place of real leadership on issues? Do they overshadow real problems?**

NEGATIVE CAMPAIGNING

Politics can be a blood sport—full of mudslinging. When progressive columnist Jim Hightower learned that conservative gubernatorial candidate Bill Clements was learning Spanish, he replied, "Oh good. Now he'll be bi-ignorant."[72] Quips like these are plentiful in Texas. But to get real traction with voters, candidates need to create a negative image of an opposing candidate that hits and sticks, an effective strategy called **negative campaigning** that can at times backfire. During the 2014 Republican primary race for lieutenant governor, Land Commissioner Jerry Patterson leaked documents that revealed that Republican candidate Dan Patrick had spent time in a mental health facility for depression and anxiety and had attempted suicide in 1984. In response, Texans rallied behind the candidate. Patrick reported, "I have received a flood of new support and encouragement—much from those Texans who have suffered from depression or had it touch their families or loved ones."[73] Patrick won the primary runoff election by 30 percent.

Wendy Davis "Wheelchair" Ad. A 2014 ad accused Republican nominee for governor, Greg Abbott, who was paralyzed after a tree fell on him in 1986, of profiting from his settlement while opposing large damage awards to other accident victims.

PERSONAL RESPONSIBILITY: **Should personal attacks be off-limits in campaign advertising?**

Voters claim to dislike negative advertising, but it often works. Why? Political scientists have shown that overall negative advertising does not necessarily win votes, but rather demobilizes the electorate by decreasing political efficacy and reducing support for the candidate who is the target of the negativity.[74] The rise of external groups who fund campaigns and the rise of political polarization have increased the amount of negative campaigning.[75]

negative campaigning: a campaign that highlights the negative of their opponent over the positive of their own candidate

COURTING THE BASE

Lieutenant Governor Bill Hobby recalls that when he was running in the 1970s in about 20 counties in Texas, getting votes was a "one-stop shop" up to "the man." "The man" was usually a party boss who controlled the votes of a political party in a local area. Hobby recalled "if 'the man' was for you, you would get about 75 percent of the vote." In Fayette County, that man was Sheriff Jim Flournoy, featured in the *Best Little Whorehouse in Texas*, who had the ladies (prostitutes) of the famous Texas Chicken Ranch addressing postcards for Hobby's election.[76] Courting the base, by whatever methods, has long been key to electoral success.

In Texas politics today, candidates find it difficult to persuade members of the opposition party to side with them on policy matters. The electorate is too polarized to cross party boundaries, so campaigns spend more time courting those voters most likely to vote for them.[77] This practice is especially prominent during early voting where candidates' **"get out the vote"** (**GOTV**) operations are designed to get friendly voters to the polls.[78] Both parties seek ways to

"get out the vote" (GOTV): a tactic to get friendly voters to the polls

maintain and widen their base. The Democrats have been losing Anglo voters, especially males, while the Republicans have been losing Hispanics.

MICROTARGETING

microtargeting: identifying potential subgroups of supporters for customizable messages; also known as narrow casting

Political campaigns also try to court new voters through **microtargeting** to identify potential supporters online and in the real world. Your viewing, shopping, and eating habits tell campaigns much about you politically. Political marketers want to know whether you watch Fox News or read *The New York Times*. Do you shop at Neiman Marcus or hunt for bargains on eBay?[79] Based upon this type of data, campaigns can figure out how to persuade you to vote for their candidate. Online advertisers track your Internet search history and browser cookies to determine your personal preferences as well as your racial, gender, and regional characteristics. Campaigns pay these online advertisers to display customized messages to target those voters who are most likely to support their candidates. In the field, campaigns use neighborhood demographic characteristics along with household consumer behavior and past voting behavior to target individuals for door-to-door campaigning.

SURFING NATIONAL TRENDS

National-level trends drive much of the state-level political changes we see in Texas. The popularity of the party in control of US Congress or the occupant of the White House can shift voter sentiment in faraway Texas. Dissatisfaction with the presidential administration of Jimmy Carter drew record conservatives to the polls in the historic 1978 election that brought Republican Bill Clements into the governor's seat. Donald Trump's inflammatory rhetoric on immigration in the 2016 presidential race increased turnout among Latino and Asian Democrats in Texas.

FUNDING ELECTIONS

A major component of getting the party's message out is fundraising. Money is often called the "mother's milk" of politics because it is essential to paying for a professional campaign staff, media, marketing, and research. Record amounts of money are raised and spent nationally in elections, especially in recent years. According to the Center for Responsive Politics, more than $6.8 billion was spent on the 2016 presidential campaign, making it the most expensive election in history.[80]

The same patterns hold in Texas. Candidates for all offices in the state (both federal and state) raised over $330 million in 2014. This was up from $280 million in 2012 and $273 million in 2010. As campaigns become more contested, especially in the primary, the cost of campaigns rises. Therefore, races in which there is no incumbent tend to be the most expensive (see Table 4.2).

TABLE 4.2 **Campaign Funds Raised for State and Federal Texas Offices, 2014**

FUNDS RAISED BY PARTY OF CANDIDATE	
Party	**Total Funds Raised**
Republican	$263,781,225
Democratic	$62,998,098
Third Parties	$164,608
Funds Raised by Incumbency Status of Candidate	
Open	$155,231,988
Incumbent	$148,853,628
Challenger	$22,853,391

Source: National Institute on Money in State Politics.

 COMMUNICATION:

What type of candidate gets more funds?

- Republican candidates tend to dominate Democrats in raising money by a margin of just over four to one.
- By incumbency status, candidates for open seats raised the most. Incumbents (mostly Republicans) were close behind.

 CRITICAL THINKING:

What explains a plump war chest for some candidates?

- There are more Republican than Democrat incumbents in Texas, giving them the fundraising edge because of resources and connections.
- Incumbents generally raise more money because they have an established donor base and ties to groups looking to donate to those in power.
- Open seats are the most competitive type of election and historically draw a crowded and quality field. Fundraising spikes in these races as the campaigns battle for the seat.

These funds were driven by contributions to two high-profile statewide races for governor and lieutenant governor. The governor's race between Wendy Davis and Greg Abbott collectively raised $51 million.[81] The nasty lieutenant governor's primary race between four Republicans and then the general election contest between Leticia Van De Putte and Dan Patrick altogether raised $43 million. These high figures still fall short of the record spending in the 2002 election, which cost $95 million, where wealthy Democrat Tony Sanchez spent $67 million to Rick Perry's $28 million.[82]

Donate and I'll Shoot. Candidates often find unusual ways to raise money. Governor Greg Abbott's 2014 campaign hosted a contest where anyone who donated $25 could win a Texas-made shotgun. The campaign was quick to point out that the winner must be eligible to purchase the shotgun through a licensed gun dealer.**

SOCIAL RESPONSIBILITY: **What limits should there be on how candidates raise funds?**

political action committees (PACs): an organization that collects donations from donors and uses these funds to donate to candidates, parties, or other political causes

super PACs: independent expenditure committees that are legally permitted to raise and spend unlimited funds from individuals, corporations, unions, or other groups to advocate on behalf of their causes but are not permitted to give to candidates directly

PACS and Super PACs. Most candidates raise money from individuals, hosting events where donors are wined and dined, calling them on the phone (called "dialing for dollars") or soliciting donors through e-mail or social media. Corporations, unions, and interest groups are barred from contributing directly to candidates for federal offices, but may form **political action committees** (**PACs**) to contribute to campaigns.

Some candidates themselves may also form PACs. High-profile incumbents or party leaders may form "leadership PACs" to donate funds to other like-minded candidates or causes. Texas House Speaker Joe Straus's PAC contributed almost $1 million in 2014 to allies. PACs are regulated by state or federal law.

In *Citizens United v. Federal Election Commission* (2010), the Supreme Court triggered a political earthquake when it ruled that it is unconstitutional to ban independent political spending by corporations and unions. **Super PACs** are independent expenditure committees that are legally permitted to raise and spend unlimited funds from individuals, corporations, unions, or other groups to advocate on behalf of their causes but are not permitted to give to candidates directly. The Supreme Court ruling opened the door to massive spending from wealthy organizations in both parties and tied most major candidates, especially presidential candidates but also state and local candidates, to a super PAC with whom they could not coordinate on strategy. Super PACs have prompted an explosion of money into electoral races.

Rules and Limits. Federal election funding is regulated by the Federal Election Campaign Act, which requires candidates, party committees, and PACs to disclose the amount of campaign funds they raise and spend. Federal regulations on campaigns were originally designed to limit the lopsided influence of wealthy individuals and interest groups in federal elections. Individual candidates can accept $2,700 per person per election cycle (primary and general). PACs can accept $5,000 per person per election cycle and can donate $5,000 to candidates and other PACs and $15,000 to a political party. The national party committee for the Republicans or Democrats can accept up to $33,400 per person per cycle. Campaigns must identify the PACs that donate funds and any individual who contributes over $200.

State election funding for statewide and local candidates is regulated by the Texas Ethics Commission. Unlike federal rules that tightly limit campaign donations, there are few restrictions on Texas political giving. Texas has no contribution limits, except on judicial candidates (see Chapter 10), which make it unique among the states. By contrast, the national average limit on donations in governors' races is $5,600 and in state legislative races it is about $2,500.

Do these limits even out the playing field? Does money make a difference in elections? We'll explore these questions in the next section.

★ TEXAS TAKEAWAYS

9 What does negative advertising do to voters?

10 Why are there limits on campaign funding?

🤠 WHO WINS AND WHY

Hoping to appeal to conservative voters in his district, an East Texas state representative had a cousin shoot him in the arm and falsely blamed it on a satanic and communistic cult "out to get him" because of his pro-family and pro-American stands in the legislature.[83] The ploy didn't work and the candidate wound up in jail, but candidates in Texas do try to game the process to their advantage. Let's take a look at some of the factors they should keep in mind.

4.5 Analyze factors that influence election outcomes in Texas.

MONEY AND ELECTION OUTCOMES

In Texas, as elsewhere, candidates need money to hire campaign staff, activate their base, and, most importantly, advertise. Not surprisingly, winning candidates raise more funds. In 2014, winners outraised losers by 2.7 to 1. However, money is not always the most significant factor in winning elections. In many races, Texas judicial elections, in particular where there are strict limits on funds raised, party trumps fundraising as the key determinant of electoral success.[84] Why is this the case? To answer this question, we need to look at who contributes and how they contribute.

Who Contributes.   A wide range of individuals and causes donate to candidates. Some donors have broad ideological agendas while others have very targeted, narrow objectives to donating. Campaign funds are often more targeted when issues of concern to a group arise (see Figure 4.6). For instance,

FIGURE 4.6   **Contributions by Group, 2014 Texas State Election**

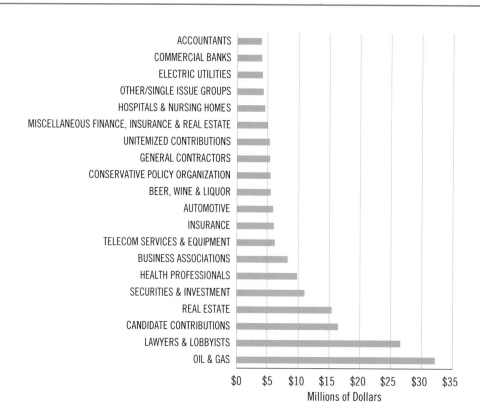

Source: National Institute on Money in State Politics.

COMMUNICATION:

Who gives in Texas political races?

- Three big industry groups dominate the funds contributed in Texas: oil and gas, lawyers, and real estate professionals.
- Oil- and gas-related industry donors are by far the most generous, providing almost $23 million in 2014.
- Candidates themselves donated $11 million to their colleagues, shoring up support from within the party (or on occasion across parties).

CRITICAL THINKING:

Why do some groups dominate political donations?

- The state has the most regulatory control over the locating, refining, and production of oil and gas, making state politicians a good target for access.
- Major legislation on local bans on fracking, property tax cuts, and a ban on real estate transactions taxes were on the agenda for the 2015 legislative session, making lobbyists and real estate donors particularly interested in election outcomes.

as the state ended a decade-long fight with Farmers Insurance Group, which Texas contended charged too much on homeowners' insurance rates for mold-damaged houses, the insurance group gave $50,000 in PAC funds to then Attorney General Greg Abbott's race for governor. Critics contended that as attorney general, Abbott gave Farmers a "sweetheart" deal, while Abbott's office argued that the deal was fair.[85]

Not surprisingly, wealthy individuals give at higher rates than poorer individuals and organizations with more resources give more than those with fewer resources. Scholars surveying the top 1 percent of earners have found that 68 percent of their respondents made a political contribution (averaging $4,633) and 21 percent had solicited or bundled contributions.[86] The political process, according to many observers, has evolved in ways that reinforce the advantages of wealth, especially as campaigns have become more expensive to run and organizations have raised spectacular amounts of campaign money.[87]

Who Donors Give To.   Some donors contributed only to candidates who align with their own economic interests or political ideologies. Several wealthy donors, such as oilman Tim Dunn of Midland and Farris Wilks of Cisco who have interests in natural gas, have given tens of millions of dollars to conservative candidates in the last few election cycles.[88] These individuals have business interests in the energy industry to protect in addition to political interests that match the conservative wing of the Republican Party. Steve and Amber Mostyn, two prominent attorneys who made a small fortune on hurricane-related litigation, have given more than $11 million to the Democratic Party. But on election night 2014, those funds seemed wasted. As early votes rolled in, Steve put is as bluntly as he could: "We're f&%ked."[89]

Does Money Buy Influence?   Do these donations have an effect on elected officials? Political science research finds that the more time a candidate spends fundraising, the greater the influence of that fundraising on their political decisions.[90] Scholars have shown that political donations do not necessarily "buy" votes (by influencing the outcome of legislation) but do buy access to an elected official's time.[91] Many interest groups and PACs donate funds to multiple candidates (even in the same race) in order to hedge their bets when it comes to access to whichever party wins. In short, a politician to whom you donate may listen to you make your case about an issue but not necessarily vote your way.

PARTIES AND STRAIGHT TICKET VOTING

Straight ticket voting helps both parties gain and maintain power, and parties exploit this advantage. In South Texas, where the Hispanic vote is often handled as a commodity by *politiqueras*, political workers who are paid to go door-to-door to get out the vote, target Democrats who are likely to vote straight

FIGURE 4.7   **Straight Ticket Voting in the Eight Largest Counties**

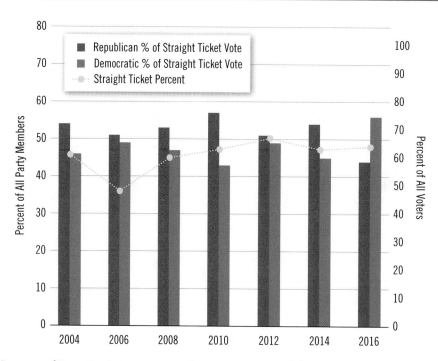

Source: Texas Secretary of State. Austin Community College Center for Public Policy and Political Studies. Total percent are straight ticket votes as a percentage of all ballots cast. Democratic and Republican figures are the percentage of the straight ticket vote (out of 100 percent).

 COMMUNICATION:

How has straight ticket voting changed over time?

- The percent of straight ticket voting statewide has increased from below 50 percent to above 60 percent in ten years.

- Republican straight ticket voting is generally higher than Democratic straight ticket voting, although that trend reversed in 2016.

 CRITICAL THINKING:

Why has straight ticket voting increased?

- As parties become more polarized ideologically, more Texans vote straight ticket.

- In conservative strongholds like the highly populated suburban areas, Republican unity is high, increasing the rate of straight ticket voting.

- In 2006, several strong candidates challenged Rick Perry in the governor's race. As a result, more Republicans split their ticket, voting for an Independent candidate rather than the Republican nominee. Since then Republican unity has been higher.

- In 2016, Donald Trump's fights with other Republican leaders led to less Republican straight ticket voting. Democratic reaction to the Trump nomination spurred Democratic straight ticket voting in Harris and El Paso counties.

ticket.[92] In major suburban counties, in contrast, Republicans benefit from this practice, receiving three out of four straight ticket votes.[93] Overall, this practice preserves the status quo.

Ten states (including Texas) allow for straight ticket voting, including Alabama, Indiana, Pennsylvania, South Carolina, and Utah.[94] The number of Texans voting straight ticket is rising steadily (see Figure 4.7). Some states have moved away from straight ticket voting. In 2016, the Supreme Court let a lower court decision stand and undid Michigan's ban on straight ticket voting, allowing the state to continue the practice.[95]

INCUMBENTS AND VOTER TURNOUT

Incumbency, the type of election, candidates, and voter turnout strongly influence who wins the election. Incumbents are more likely to win a general election with greater voter turnout because their name identification is higher, they are able to raise and spend more funds, and moderate voters participate more in these elections. This is known as the incumbent advantage. Challengers have a better chance of winning low-turnout primaries and runoffs—elections dominated by the most passionate voters.

When only 1.3 million primary voters vote, for example, a candidate backed by conservative Tea Party groups can win with as few as 650,000 votes. As a result, the Republican Party power center has shifted to the ideological right.[99]

GREAT TEXAS POLITICAL DEBATES
Straight Ticket Voting

A *Dallas Morning News* editorial opined that there are three types of Texans come election time: Republicans, Democrats, and Can't Be Bothered to Vote. The editorial continued, "dogs and cats will lie together long before the typical Texas Republican or Texas Democrat will cross over and vote for someone from 'the other side.'"[96] Straight ticket voting reinforces the two-party system by giving voters a direct way to vote for their party but does not encourage voters to think about candidates and issues.

SOCIAL RESPONSIBILITY: **Should Texas abolish straight ticket voting?**

NO: Voters are busy and look for convenient but meaningful ways to understand the positions of a candidate. Political parties serve as cues for a voter facing a long ballot. Political scientist

Richard Murray at the University of Houston argued that in Harris County, "We'll have about 100 races and hell, it would take 15 or 20 minutes to vote the ballot individually. But [with straight ticket voting] people get in and out in 30 seconds."[97]

YES: Lazy voters make for bad democracy. Texas Representative Ron Simmons pointed out that straight ticket voting "leads voters to elect candidates without any knowledge whatsoever of who they are."[98] Voters can still choose to vote for candidates of the same party if they wish, just not in a single vote.

MAYBE: Let voters straight ticket vote for statewide and federal elections, but not for judicial elections in which party affiliation doesn't serve as a good predictor of an official's behavior in office.

In the 2012 race for the US Senate, Lieutenant Governor David Dewhurst, who had served in statewide office for a decade in various offices, was the favorite and received 45 percent of the votes in the primary. The runoff was a different story. Passionate conservatives were "in the mood to drop anvils on establishment folks" and put their support behind a relatively obscure candidate named Ted Cruz. Cruz, who went on to win the runoff with 57 percent of the vote, serves in the US Senate, and subsequently made a bid for the presidency in 2016.[100]

THE ELECTORAL SYSTEM

at-large: an electoral unit where all citizens in a county can vote

The type of electoral system—how votes are counted—also impacts the outcome. Candidates who run locally are either elected from districts or **at-large** in a county, meaning that all citizens in a county can vote in the election. Federal court decisions in the early 1970s required Texas cities to have city council districts instead of at-large races because at-large districts dilute the power of minority voters.[101] Single-member districts, which are smaller, improve minority representation, as we will see in later chapters.

WILL TEXAS TURN BLUE?

The prospect of increasing voter turnout among low-turnout groups, as well as the growth of the Hispanics population, have prompted many to wonder whether Texas could turn from a solid Republican "red" to a Democratic "blue"—or at least to a state with a more robust two-party system. Texas is already a majority–minority state. If the trends continue, Hispanics and Anglos will each account for 41 percent of the state's population within the next decade. With more voter registration and robust turnout, Hispanics, who lean Democratic, could tilt the state Democratic "blue."

Texas an electoral battleground? Battleground Texas, a grassroots campaign organized to make Texas competitive for the Democratic Party, established roots in 2013. The impact was small in turnout or vote share for Wendy Davis in the 2014 election, but several thousand volunteers turned out to canvass voters and make millions of phone calls to voters.

PERSONAL RESPONSIBILITY: **If elections were more competitive, would you be more likely to vote?**

However, there are several reasons to doubt this claim. While the Hispanic share of voters in gubernatorial elections rose from 11 percent in 1990 to 17 percent in 2010 and in presidential elections from 20 percent in 2008 to 24 percent in 2016, the total number of Hispanic voters is still low in comparison to Anglo voters.[102] In 2012, 49 percent of the voting age population was Anglo, compared to 33.6 percent Hispanic, primarily because many Hispanics are not citizens.[103] Second, turnout among Hispanics lags significantly behind Anglos. This trend will change slowly as the Hispanic vote ages and organizations emerge to turn these voters out. Third, the migration to Texas from other states has come from other southern states where voters lean Republican.[104] Fourth, the Democratic Party has a larger deficit with Anglo voters than the Republicans have with Hispanic voters. As the demographics of the state continue to change, both parties will vie for the Hispanic vote. All this said, the potential for the state to change exists, as other states with increasing Hispanic populations, like California, Colorado, and Virginia, have transitioned from red to blue.

 ## TEXAS TAKEAWAYS

11 Which groups were the top two donors to state candidates?

12 Does straight ticket voting help or hurt incumbent parties?

THE INSIDER VIEW

Elites have always had a major say in the recruiting and funding of political candidates. Gone are the traditional "smoke filled" rooms in Texas, only to be replaced by newer hangouts for politicians like the Austin Club. However, today, Texas is no longer ruled by party bosses or one economic or demographic group. The road to voting rights has been long and difficult for women, African Americans, and Latinos, their struggle punctuated by demographic shifts, social changes, and favorable court rulings. The suffrage battles have given way to challenges in representation and opportunities to participate in parties and policymaking. Who runs and wins matters, but so do the tone of campaigns, the process of how Texans vote, and who votes—as they all shape the politics of the state. Change in Texas politics is slow, but it has and will result from battles over the electoral process and the collision of the political ideas of those who choose to vote.

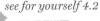

see for yourself 4.2

Watch Julian Castro discuss why he thinks Texas will turn blue.

TEXAS TAKEAWAYS

1 A Texas citizen must be registered to vote thirty days before an election.

2 Texas voters need a photo identification or provide a sworn statement of citizenship and non-photo proof of residency like a birth certificate, a utility bill, or a paystub or bank statement.

3 In an open primary, any qualified registered voter can vote in the primary for any party. In a closed primary, only voters registered with a party may vote in that party's primary.

4 The poll tax, the white primary, and voter intimidation by certain people or groups are ways that Texas has disenfranchised minority voters.

5 In 1965 Congress passed the Voting Rights Act, which prohibited discrimination against racial minorities.

6 Approximately 85 percent of African Americans support the Democratic Party.

7 There are some who don't vote because voting is time-consuming and difficult. There are others who don't vote because they don't see a benefit.

8 Voter turnout can be increased if the structure of voting is changed (having convenience voting), or with greater efforts to reach out to and educate voters.

9 Negative advertising often demobilizes the electorate by decreasing political efficacy and reducing support for the candidate who is the target of the negativity

10 Federal regulations on campaigns were originally designed to limit the lopsided influence of wealthy individuals and interest groups in federal elections.

11 The top group were oil- and gas-related donors. The second group were lawyers and lobbyists.

12 Straight ticket voting generally helps parties gain and maintain power.

KEY TERMS

at-large
closed primary
disenfranchise
early voting
Fifteenth Amendment
"get out the vote" (GOTV)
incumbent
microtargeting
motor voter law
name identification
negative campaigning
open primary
political action committees (PACs)
political efficacy
political socialization
poll tax
primary election
public opinion polling
register
runoff election
single-member district
special election
split ticket voting
straight ticket voting
super PACs
Voting Rights Act

PRACTICE QUIZ

1. The National Voter Registration Act of 1993, or the "Motor Voter Law," provided for the opportunity to
   a. Vote via "drive-thru" voting booths.
   b. Register to vote when applying for a driver's license.
   c. Register to vote when buying a car.
   d. Vote when registering a car with the State Vehicle Inspection Office.

2. Compared to all other states, Texas ranks _____ in the percentage of the state's registered voting turning out to vote.
   a. In the top five
   b. In the top half
   c. In the bottom half
   d. In the bottom five

3. The process where individuals acquire political values and behaviors, which have a strong influence on future voting, is called
   a. Political socialization
   b. Sociology
   c. Political pandering
   d. Straight ticket voting

4. Which of the following is/are **not** a type(s) of primary election?

   a. Open
   b. Closed
   c. Neither A nor B are primary elections.
   d. Both A and B are types of primary election.

5. In Texas, if no candidate wins (gets a majority of the vote in) the primary election, which of the following occurs?

   a. Special election
   b. General election
   c. Runoff election
   d. Plural election

6. For most counties in Texas that switched to vote centers, the impact on turnout was

   a. Positive
   b. Negative
   c. No change
   d. None of the above

7. Suffrage refers to passing the age threshold to be eligible to vote.

   a. True
   b. False

8. Jim Crow laws mandating segregation and voting restrictions marginalized African Americans politically for almost a century.

   a. True
   b. False

9. Most Texans do not vote, even in a presidential election year.

   a. True
   b. False

10. In *Citizens United v. Federal Election Commission* (2010), the Supreme Court ruled that it was constitutional to ban independent political spending by corporations and unions.

    a. True
    b. False

[Answers: B, D, A, D, C, B, B, A, A, B]

5

POLITICAL PARTIES: TEXAS IN BLUE AND RED

In the century after Reconstruction, Democrats dominated Texas politics. Most Texans identified as "yellow dog" Democrats, a group that got their name because they would rather vote for a yellow dog than a Republican. The Democratic Party was an odd mix of liberals and conservatives but always backed the Democratic ticket. The 1994 gubernatorial election, however, marked a turning point in Texas party politics.

The candidates, incumbent Democrat Ann Richards and political newcomer Republican George W. Bush, squared off in a televised debate. Ann Richards was no stranger to tough political fights—she had survived a brutal primary and general election battle in 1990. Fearing (or realizing) a rising conservative tide and resurgent Republican Party, Richards slung mud at Bush every which way. She challenged his business record and charged that he had skipped out on service during his National Guard duty in the 1970s.

The attacks didn't stick. In a fast-growing conservative state, Bush picked the right issues in the right moment. Texas had shifted politically to a suburban, middle class conservatism with strong ties to the Christian right.[1] In his opening statement that night in Dallas, he laid out his premise: "I'm the conservative candidate and she's the liberal."[2] That said it all. Richards was hardly a liberal, having ramped up law enforcement and supported the death penalty, but Richards had raised taxes and vetoed legislation to allow concealed carrying of firearms. She lost in November by 8 percent.

Ann Richards was not the first Democrat to lose a statewide office but her defeat demonstrated a fundamental shift within the state's party system. In offices at the top and bottom of the ballot,

LEARNING OBJECTIVES

5.1	Describe the function of political parties in Texas.
5.2	Explain the levels of organization of political parties and their roles.
5.3	Outline the changes in party dominance since the Civil War.
5.4	Analyze the factors that affect party competition.
5.5	Evaluate the impact third parties have had on Texas party politics and the challenges they face.

● Delegates at the 2016 Texas Republican Party ready for Governor Greg Abbott to speak.

Democrats began to lose their grip on Texas politics as voters migrated to the Republican Party. How do parties change? How do they rise and fall? What political struggles erupt within parties to drive these transformations?

The structure and function of different parties is often similar, but who makes up the parties, and the ideologies of their members, may shift dramatically over time. This chapter shows how individuals and factions within parties shape the electoral prospects for state parties as well as the ability of parties to govern. We also observe how the state party system shifted from one-party rule favoring the Democrats to one-party rule favoring the Republicans. The struggle over economic issues, growing concerns about federal intervention, and demographic changes ousted one dominant party—and may yet oust another.

THE FUNCTIONS OF PARTIES

5.1 Describe the function of political parties in Texas.

Nowhere does the US Constitution mention the word "party," but it is hard to imagine how government would run without them. When most of us think of political parties, we think of their role in elections: parties organize political interests, form a shared platform—or goals—and thus provide a way for citizens to choose candidates to represent them in government. But parties do much more than that.

Famous political scientist (Austin native and University of Texas graduate) V.O. Key suggested that parties engage in three basic functions: assisting voters (parties-in-the-electorate), facilitating party goals (parties-as-organizations), and organizing government by structuring and controlling government (parties-in-government). In this section, we look closely at each function.

SIMPLIFYING ELECTORAL CHOICES

Politics can be a confusing mash of personality and policy—along with a lot of noise. Voters, especially less politically involved voters, may need assistance to understand the political process. Shortcuts, such as the party identity of a candidate or a party platform, are easy and convenient ways to summarize a great deal of information into understandable bites.

conservative: a political philosophy that believes in limited government, free markets, and individual entrepreneurship

Party labels are often enough to tell people how they should vote. Voters can assume that Republican candidates in Texas are **conservative** and prefer a smaller role for government, including fewer taxes, more support for business, and an adherence to socially conservative values. Voters can also trust that

Democratic candidates in Texas will generally be **liberal**—favoring expanded government, working to improve economic equality and access to health care, and favoring the right to have an abortion. However, party labels are not perfect indicators of ideology, especially in a conservative state like Texas. Modern Democrats sometimes take conservative positions on fiscal and economic matters, and Republicans may take liberal positions on social issues.

liberal: a political philosophy that emphasizes social equality and a large role for government to protect liberties and alleviate social problems

RECRUITING CANDIDATES

Local and state party leaders evaluate potential candidates, often screening them for quality and party loyalty. Parties also recruit candidates to widen the appeal of the party. Starting with the election of Governor Bush, Republicans have made concerted efforts to recruit Hispanics to run for office in order to make inroads into socially conservative segments within Texas's growing Hispanic population.[3] In 2016, thirty-eight Hispanics ran as Republicans in local and statewide races.

How do parties recruit leaders and candidates for office? Until the early 1900s, party leaders at state conventions nominated candidates for state and local offices. Considerable power was centralized in the party elite and special interests. Abuse was rampant. Friends of certain candidates would visit roundups in cattle country in West and Central Texas, persuade cowboys and their foreman to constitute themselves as "local conventions," and carry away enough commitments to sway the outcome at the state convention.[4] The progressive movement in the early twentieth century led to reforms to fight government corruption. In 1905, Texas passed legislation to hold a public primary to nominate candidates directly. This change weakened the party leaderships' role in choosing candidates and opened up opportunities for attentive voters, large campaign donors, and interest groups to have a greater say in the electoral process.

However, parties still play a role in recruitment. Once a good candidate is identified, parties offer candidates support services such as issue and logistical expertise, data on voters, campaign materials, and assistance with digital media strategies. They also use their considerable funds to finance the campaigns of their recruits (see Figure 5.1).

MOBILIZING VOTERS

During elections, political parties fire up their turnout machines to get loyal voters to the polls to support party-endorsed candidates. Party activists often call other members to remind them to vote and even provide transportation to the polls. Turnout is critical to electoral victory. During the mayoral election in usually Democratic-leaning San Antonio in 2014, Leticia Van de Putte, who resigned her long-held senate seat to run, lost to Republican Ivy Taylor, the interim mayor, by 3,331 votes. An exasperated consultant commented: "At the end of the day, we needed 3,000 Democrats to get off their asses and go vote, and they didn't." Taylor became the city's first African American mayor.[5]

FIGURE 5.1   **Texas Party Political Spending**

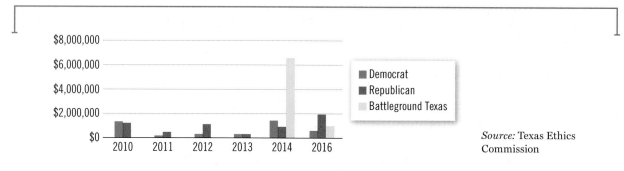

Source: Texas Ethics Commission

 COMMUNICATION:

How much do the parties spend?

- Both parties spend more money in election years (2010, 2013, 2014) than non-election years (2011, 2013).
- The Democratic and Republican Parties in Texas spend about the same overall but Republicans spend more in presidential election years.
- Battleground Texas, a group allied to the Democratic Party, spent more than both traditional parties in 2014, but less in 2016.

 CRITICAL THINKING:

Why are there differences?

- Since more races have a Republican incumbent, Democratic challengers require more money to help fund their elections.
- Faith that demographic change will favor Democrats in the future has prompted Democratic-leaning donors to give funds and more organizations to spend the funds (like Battleground Texas).

ARTICULATING INTERESTS

Parties represent groups of citizens with shared values. Political scientists Robert Y. Shapiro and Joe Bafumi found that since the 1980s, political ideology has become a stronger predictor of party identification.[6] Civil rights battles in Texas presented such an issue in the 1960s and 1970s—conservatives concerned with states' rights flocked to the Republican Party and liberals interested in pursuing voting rights and equal access to public facilities gravitated to the Democratic Party.

Parties also have an incentive to sharpen their differences: If voters perceive marked distinctions, parties can recruit candidates and passionate voters more effectively. These **partisans** tend to volunteer more of their time and money and are more likely to turn out to vote in party primaries and other elections. However, partisans do not necessarily represent Texan voters as a whole because they are typically more ideologically extreme.

Partisans play an oversized role in party politics by pushing the party to the extremes and exacerbating conflict.[7] Activists within a party may target a

partisans: strongly committed members of a party

lawmaker and threaten party stability when representatives fail to deliver on promises or satisfy expectations. One Texas conservative activist growled, "I'm going to be the skunk at the picnic," after Republican legislators failed to enact policies to his liking in 2015.[8]

ORGANIZING GOVERNMENT

Parties work to make sure that their candidates, once elected, toe the party line to deliver on electoral promises. Parties often organize legislators into forums where they work together to discuss and formulate policy. Party leaders then make sure that their members implement the party's plan. In this way, parties provide accountability to voters. This accountability is called responsible party government.

⬛ TEXAS TAKEAWAYS

1 Name the three functions of political parties.

2 How are partisans important to parties?

🤠 PARTY ORGANIZATION

The backbone of the party is the party organization: the group of individuals who volunteer or are paid minimally for positions at local and state levels. Parties are hierarchical, with authority flowing from the national to state to local levels. However, due to the **decentralization** of party structure in the United States, state and local activists wield considerable influence over the future of the party and often go to battle over policy and politics. Because these positions are influential, they are coveted and involve contentious elections.

5.2 Explain the levels of organization of political parties and their roles.

decentralization: the distribution of authority between national, state, and local party organizations so that each level exercises a degree of independent authority

PRECINCT CHAIRS

Counties are subdivided into smaller units called precincts. Precinct chairs are elected in the party's primary and serve for two years. As the most local party leaders, the precinct chairs recruit volunteers, coordinate campaign workers during elections, and participate in get-out-the-vote and voter registration drives.[9] Precinct chairs also serve their precinct on county executive committees where they choose state convention delegates and may be called on to replace a candidate on the ballot who resigns or otherwise can't stand for election. In 2016, Democratic precinct chairs worked overtime in Houston to replace a county commissioner who died, the state senator who took his place, and the state representative who took her place.

Robert Morrow, with a penchant for wearing a jester's hat, was elected Travis County Republican Chair despite making obscene comments about Texas politicians, advancing conspiracy theories, and posting pictures of naked women on his Twitter account. He was removed from his position after he filed to be a write-in candidate in the 2016 U.S. presidential election.

SOCIAL RESPONSIBILITY: **How might the party organization balance the need to include many voices with the need to maintain control and discipline of their message?**

Biennial elections for precinct chair positions are proxy wars for battles fought at the state level. In 2004, 62 of the 85 Republican precinct chair races in Montgomery County were contested. A party activist had recruited a slate of male challengers because, he claimed, the state platform called for "godly men" to represent the party. Republican women, silently protesting the effort, circled the parking lot outside the voting center dressed in black burkas that covered them from head to toe.[10] Most of the incumbents won.

COUNTY PARTY CHAIRS

County party chairs recruit candidates to run for local or regional offices, act as a spokesperson for local issues, manage the funds of the local party, and serve with precinct chairs on the county executive committee, which organizes party primaries and hosts county and senate district conventions.

Ideology rarely plays a role in these biennial elections but can sometimes become an issue. The 2014 race for Harris County Republican Chair was portrayed as a battle for the ideology of the Republican Party: fiscal conservatives versus social conservatives. Challenger Paul Simpson claimed incumbent Jared Woodfill spent too much time spearheading a lawsuit against Houston for providing benefits to same-sex partners of city employees and not enough time growing the party and winning local seats like sheriff and county attorney. High profile local and statewide officials took sides in the ideological faceoff.[11] Simpson won with 53 percent of the vote.

STATE PARTY CHAIR

The state party chair's primary responsibility is to develop and communicate the party's brand to the voters and to raise and manage political funds for the party at the state level. The race for party chair is largely conducted outside of the public eye. Party veterans communicate with each other to select a roster of candidates who then compete to obtain the support of some 14,000 delegates across Texas. The Republican Party holds a caucus by state senate district while the Democrats have an open vote for all delegates.[12] Both parties mandate that one man and one woman serve as chair and vice-chair.

Ideology does not always factor into the biennial elections for this office, primarily because candidates tend to be similarly situated ideologically. Rather, state chair campaigns zero in on management and leadership skills. In 2010, for example, the state Republican Party was half a million dollars in debt. During the heated battle for the Republican state chair, the two challengers attacked the incumbent state chair on the issue of fiscal responsibility, dear to the heart of Republican voters.[13] The incumbent lost his seat and party finances rebounded.

PARTY EXECUTIVE COMMITTEES

Executive committee members are the center of party power, as they govern the operations of the party and direct the overall message. Both the Republican and Democratic Party executive committees have 62 members (two members from each of 31 state senate districts), elected by the delegates to the party convention in each district. Democratic Party rules state that one man and one woman are selected from each district. Because these groups have so much authority to direct the ideological trajectory of the parties, their actions are often controversial. In 2015, the Republican Party Executive Committee rejected a resolution to poll Republican primary voters about whether Texas should secede from the Union if "the federal government continues to disregard the constitution."[14] Opponents felt the resolution was frivolous while supporters argued that it would show that the party was taking a strong stand against federal government intrusion into Texas.[15]

PARTY CONVENTIONS

Every two years, the party hosts conventions to decide how the party functions and to set the political agenda. Precinct conventions elect delegates to county conventions. County conventions elect delegates to the state convention but also may submit resolutions that may become part of the **party platform**. In presidential election years, state conventions select delegates for the national convention, and also elect the slate of presidential electors to cast ballots for Texas in the Electoral College if their nominee wins the White House.

STATE PARTY PLATFORMS

The planks of a party's platform range from providing concrete policy solutions to more general and ideological opinions (see Figure 5.2). For instance, the 2016 Texas Democratic platform called for specific recommendations to end overcrowding in public schools, reform high-stakes testing, and set a $15 minimum wage, as well as ideological statements against capitol punishment and border walls. The 2016 Republican platform called for the abolishment of multiple government agencies and the enactment of a law to require individuals to use locker rooms, bathrooms, and showers corresponding to their biological sex. The platform also contained a provision advocating strict adherence to the

see for yourself 5.1

Discover how the Republican and Democratic state party platforms are different.

party platform: a list of values, beliefs, and policy issues that are endorsed and supported by a political party

FIGURE 5.2 Word Clouds of Democratic and Republican Party Platforms, 2016

Democratic Platform

Republican Platform

Source: Republican Party of Texas and Texas Democratic Party

COMMUNICATION:

What are the most common words in each party platform?

- For Democrats, the most prominent words are state, health, public, and programs. Somewhat prominent words include education, communities, services, and believe.

- For Republicans, the most prominent words are oppose, united, and public. Somewhat prominent words include urge, federal, believe, law, and right.

CRITICAL THINKING:

Why are the party priorities different?

- The Democratic Party platform is issue-based but, without being in power, amplifies what they believe and emphasizes education and health programs.

- The Republican Party platform takes a more negative posture, emphasizing opposition to the federal government but also adherence to rights and laws.

US and Texas Constitutions. These state platforms can differ significantly from the national party platforms that have to appeal to a broader set of voters.[16]

Platforms are used as much for political marketing as they are as a guide to understanding party positions. Each state party's executive committee writes and revises the platform every two years (in even-numbered years when the convention meets). The convention delegates approve the platform at the convention. In contrast to assertions that political parties desire to moderate their views to attract more swing voters, studies show that the ideological distance between state party platforms of the two parties has been increasing.[17] State party competition also increases the ideological gap between the party platforms as each party attempts to shore up more ideologically extreme voters who are more likely to vote in primary elections.

★ TEXAS TAKEAWAYS

3 What does the state party chair do?

4 Why is the party platform is important to the party?

RISE AND FALL OF POLITICAL PARTIES IN TEXAS

For more than 130 years after the Civil War, Texas was dominated by the Democratic Party. The decline of the Democratic Party and the rise of the Republican Party is a story about shifting political power, the people who made it happen, and the events that shaped it.

> **5.3** Outline the changes in party dominance since the Civil War.

Texas has traditionally been a "weak party" state. Strong, cohesive parties are able to use partisan endorsements and funding to control nominations and present a unified front in elections.[18] Strong party states also discipline legislators to uphold a governor's program and maintain a party "brand" that voters can understand. Because Texas has been dominated by one political party or another since the Civil War, and most of the policy fights have been internal to the majority party, the party is not as closely tied to a set of core principles. As we will see, significant divisions within both the Democratic and Republican Parties during their years of governmental control have created a weaker party system.

DEMOCRATIC REIGN IN THE POSTBELLUM ERA

Republican representation in Texas was nearly uniform immediately following the Civil War, as it was the party of Abraham Lincoln that had waged the Civil War and spearheaded Reconstruction. But once the national government pulled its soldiers out of Texas, many Texans rallied against the Republican Party—associating it with the scarcity that followed the Civil War and unwanted military rule.[19] The elections of 1871, 1872, and 1873 broke the Republican stranglehold on state politics. Moderate Republicans and Democrats unified against the "carpetbagger" Union (Republican) government and in their dislike of Republican Governor Davis, and a "Taxpayer's Convention" that expressed frustration with increases in school taxes and wasted taxpayer funds pulled many voters into the Democratic Party. Democrats won all the Congressional seats in 1871, took majority control of the state legislature in 1872, and captured the governorship in 1873. The Democratic Party dominated Texas for the next hundred years.

THE DECLINE OF THE DEMOCRATS

New Deal: a federal economic recovery program in response to the Great Depression that stabilized the banking industry, created jobs, promoted fair labor standards, and created a social welfare network

In the 1930s, President Franklin Roosevelt pushed through the **New Deal**, which enabled Democrats to tie voters closer to party through patronage—participation in party politics meant contracts, jobs, and status. However, as is frequently the case, national politics also seeded a split between the liberal and conservative wings of the Democratic Party at the state level.

During President Roosevelt's first term, the Supreme Court declared much of the New Deal legislation unconstitutional. After a momentous re-election in 1936, Roosevelt pushed a plan in Congress to give the president the power to appoint a new justice to the Supreme Court whenever a justice reached 70 and failed to retire. In this way, Roosevelt could "pack" the court with his supporters. The vice president, John Nance "Cactus Jack" Garner, was a Texas Democrat but came from the conservative, rural wing of the party. He and other conservative Democrats, known as the "Texas Regulars," quietly and privately began to drum up opposition to the court packing plan. Meanwhile, Texan House members Lyndon Johnson and Sam Rayburn backed President Roosevelt. Publicly accused of "sticking his knife into the President's back,"[20] Garner tried to smooth the matter over, but Roosevelt's confidence could not be restored. The president replaced Garner on the 1940 presidential ticket, a decision that sent tremors down the foundation of the state party and produced the first crack between the wings of the party.

In the 1952 presidential election, the crack permanently damaged that wall. The state Democratic convention divided along ideological lines, with some supporting national Democratic welfare programs and some supporting a more conservative economic approach. On one side were the conservative to middle-of-the road Democrats—the "Shivercrats"—led by Texas Governor Allan Shivers. In the other camp stood the "Loyalists," a liberal wing of the party. Both factions claimed to represent the "true" Democratic Party. Conservatives won the day, holding more statewide offices and the party leadership structure, but a precedent was set: the factions held separate party conventions to support their preferred presidential candidates.[21] The Shivercrats favored Republican General Dwight Eisenhower,

WHICH TWIN IS THE PHONY?

Shivers was accused in 1954 of being a "Republican in Democratic clothing" by liberal wing affiliate Ralph Yarborough.* Many liberals in the Democratic Party hoped that the conservative Democrats leaving the party would allow them to take the party back. Instead, the shift strengthened the Republican Party.

CRITICAL THINKING: **How did the Shivercrats weaken the Democratic Party? Was this weakening inevitable?**

an ardent states' rights supporter, while the Loyalists favored the Democratic Illinois Governor Adlai Stevenson. Although no Republican had won political office in Texas since Reconstruction, the Shivercrats' work on behalf of the Republican nominee led to Eisenhower's narrow victory in the state. This began the process of ideological sorting—conservatives began to gravitate toward the Republican Party and liberals to the Democratic Party.

The 1970 primary for US Senate increased tensions between the liberal and conservative wings of the Democratic Party. Lloyd Bentsen, a conservative, wealthy Democrat from Hidalgo County, challenged a leading liberal in the Democratic Party, Ralph Yarborough. Bentsen, with masterful timing, attacked Yarborough for endorsing Vietnam War moratorium demonstrations, missing votes in the Senate on school busing, and opposing voluntary school prayer.[22] Yarborough lost the primary race.

The rise of conservative, pro-Ronald Reagan Democrats, who favored cutting taxes, increasing military spending, and reducing social services, also widened the fissures in the party. Many conservative Democrats—so called "blue dog Democrats"—supported Reagan. Liberal stalwart and Democratic state representative from Houston Mickey Leland sought to expel these traitorous "boll weevil" Democrats from the party in the 1980s.[23] This led to the further exodus of conservatives from the party.

Meanwhile, economic development and population growth weakened the Democratic Party. Upper-class whites moved to the Republican Party. As cities boomed, rural areas, which had traditionally been havens of Democratic power, lost influence. As migrants from other states poured into Texas to take jobs in rapidly expanding urban centers, the Democratic Party had trouble connecting with new voters unfamiliar with the customs and traditions of politics in the state. Texas voters had overlooked ideological differences and loyally voted the Democratic ticket. New voters often rejected Democrats no matter their ideology.[24] Support for the Democratic Party declined (see Figure 5.3).

How did the Democrats maintain power? The party leaders, mostly from the conservative wing of the party, served as gatekeepers for those seeking higher office. Taking advantage of rules called "cross filing" that allowed a Democrat to run as both a Republican and a Democrat in the primary (a practice no longer allowed), Texas conservatives stunted Republican Party ambitions and blocked liberals from securing party nominations.[25] Moderates were systemically purged from the Democratic Party and liberals found few friends.

The last hurrah for the Democrats occurred in 1982—the last election in which Democrats captured all statewide offices. But the party was hemorrhaging support, losing the vote of Anglos.[26] Observers point to December 2, 1997, as the day the Democratic Party in Texas collapsed, "not with a bang but a whimper" when Democratic Attorney General Dan Morales, the last statewide elected Democrat, announced he would retire from politics.[27] For the first time since Reconstruction, the Democrats held no statewide office.

FIGURE 5.3   **State Party Affiliation**

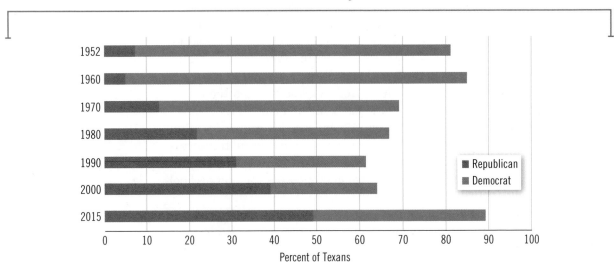

COMMUNICATION:

How has party affiliation changed?

- In 1952 and 1960, nearly 80 percent of Texans identified with the Democratic Party.
- More Texans today identify with the Republican Party (nearly 50 percent) than the Democratic Party. If "leaning" conservatives are added, those identifying with Republican Party politics gain clear majorities in the state.

CRITICAL THINKING:

Why has political party affiliation changed over time?

- Attachment to Presidents Kennedy and Johnson and their policies initially spiked support of the Democrats, but conservative rejection of civil rights policies reduced support for the Democratic Party.
- The sorting of the parties by ideology drove conservative Texans toward the Republican Party.

THE RISE OF THE REPUBLICANS

The Texas Republican Party was outflanked, dismissed, or outright ignored in electoral battles for the better part of a century. In some years, they hadn't even held primaries because they didn't have enough candidates to run.[28] To claim that the Democrats dominated state politics for much of the first half of the twentieth century would be an understatement. Future First Lady Barbara Bush recalled when she and the future president volunteered to work the Republican primary polls in Midland in 1958: "Exactly three people voted Republican that day. The two of us and a man who you could say was a little inebriated and wasn't sure what he was doing."[29]

Then Democratic Senator Lyndon Johnson vacated his seat in the US Senate to serve as vice president in the Kennedy Administration. Republican John Tower, a staunch conservative with a penchant for fancy suits, entered the special election in 1961 for the seat left open by Johnson's departure with little hopes of winning. The diminutive Tower, cool and often aloof, was an unlikely choice to lead the Republicans back to political relevance—as he often joked, "My name is Tower, but I don't."[30] Tower and the Republicans, however, took advantage of the disunity in the Democratic Party and campaigned effectively.[31] Local Republican operatives in Houston and Dallas began courting donors in industry, especially oil services.[32] Tower solicited grassroots support by vowing to protect constitutional and states' rights. The unthinkable happened: Tower became the first Republican to win statewide office since Reconstruction.

Tower's win established a bridgehead to legitimacy for other Republicans in the 1960s. Several future major Republican Party figures emerged in Texas at this time. A young George H.W. Bush won a position as Harris County Republican Party Chair in 1962, which he used as a springboard for a challenge to incumbent Democratic Senator Ralph Yarborough for the US Senate in 1964.[33] Bush took up the mantle of the rising conservatism in the state by campaigning against the Civil Rights Act, claiming states' rights should be paramount. The fortunes of Bush and the Republican Party were smashed the night that Democratic presidential candidate Lyndon Johnson, incredibly popular after the assassination of John F. Kennedy, carried Texas by an overwhelming margin.

Subsequent Republican takeover at the national level improved the fortunes of Texas Republicans. Presidents Nixon and Ford were able to bring home the "big rock candy mountain" of federal patronage, including jobs and funds for projects.[34] Nixon in particular made use of what he called the "southern strategy"—an emphasis on exposing divisions within the Democratic Party over racial integration and civil rights and in the general public on law and order issues. This approach was persuasive to the growing middle-class suburban electorate.[35] Republican strongholds in suburban and small town areas from 1978 to 1994 made the state more competitive and grew the number of elected Republican officials.

By 1978, a deeply divided Democratic Party and a well-financed Republican Party cut a trail to the election of Bill Clements as governor and the re-election of John Tower to the US Senate. As governor, Clements expanded the party's brand by putting a priority on reducing taxes and government bureaucracy and expanding appointments of Republicans. By the 1980 presidential election, headlined by a very popular Ronald Reagan and hometown Republican favorite son George H.W. Bush, the Republicans had elected more than 150 county officials to compliment substantial gains in the state legislature.[36] The 1998 state elections, a watershed for Republicans, saw the party sweep all statewide offices and win a majority on both supreme courts.[37]

As candidates began to see federal intervention as a primary cause of economic troubles in Texas during the 1970s and 1980s, more Republican candidates began to run for federal offices. Pathways to Washington opened up as well with gerrymandered districts favoring Republican candidates.

Texas fire ants may be responsible for Republican success in congressional elections during the 1980s. Tom DeLay, Republican of Sugar Land, was an exterminator and nondescript back bencher in the Texas House of Representatives when the federal government banned Mirex, the pesticide that was used to kill fire ants. The action radicalized DeLay, who decided that the Environmental Protection Agency (EPA) was an "evil empire" that had to be destroyed. He ran for the US House of Representatives in 1984 and won. Reelected ten times, Delay rose to the ranks of majority leader. A beleaguered EPA official, hearing the story, would later mutter, "Christ, we could have lived with Mirex."[38]

Other Republicans ran for the US House objecting to excessive regulation and wistful spending by the federal government. By 2002, the Republican Party of Texas not only boasted strong representatives in the US Congress, but also controlled every single statewide office and both chambers of the state legislature (see Figure 5.4).

TEA PARTY

The rise of the Republican Party led to the evolution of distinct wings in the party. Even in 1987, *Texas Monthly* observed that the party had moved "away from the genteel conservatism of John Tower toward the fierce ideological populism of Ronald Reagan."[39] One wing consisted of traditional business-minded conservatives who were often socially moderate, and the other of a far-right-wing faction who were rabid anti-Communists. These ultra-conservative Republicans were essential to the rise of the Republican Party in Texas and the South more broadly. They courted anxious, middle-class white suburban voters who embraced the values of individualism and "small government."[40]

The 2006 primary elections brought out a new breed of Republican voter to the polls, angry at the legislative session in 2005, which could not pass meaningful school voucher legislation, property tax relief, or budget restraints on local government. Influential donors, conservative activists, and leading political figures (like Governor Rick Perry) sought to purge the party of RINOs, Republicans in Name Only.[41] One journalist concluded that "having devoured the Democrats, the Republicans have turned on one another."[42]

The rise of the Tea Party in the mid-2000s deepened the fissure between economic conservatives and social conservatives. The Tea Party reached national prominence when it held a series of rallies in 2009 in response to the Obama Administration's economic recovery plans and the Affordable Care Act (or Obamacare).[43] A coalition of grassroots conservative organizations rather than a separate party, the Tea Party originally pursued primarily the goal

Ideological divisions have produced a civil war within the Republican Party to gain control of the party and government.

SOCIAL RESPONSIBILITY: **Are divisions within a party healthy or disruptive to democratic government?**

FIGURE 5.4 **Political Party Representation in the Texas Legislature**

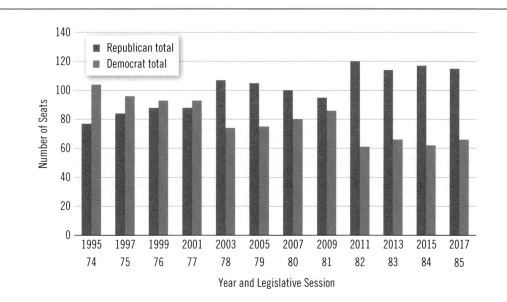

Source: Legislative Reference Library of Texas. Bars represent total party members for both House and Senate. Number below the year corresponds to legislative session.

 COMMUNICATION:

What are the trends in party membership?

- Democrats maintained control of the legislature through the 1990s.
- Republicans gained a majority of the Texas House in the 2003 session for the first time since after the Civil War.
- Republicans possess supermajorities in both the House and Senate in the most recent legislative session.

 CRITICAL THINKING:

Why did the number of Democrats decline?

- Redistricting (see below) shaped seats with an even number of party voters into seats with a majority of one or the other party. Formerly strong Democratic districts were turned into weaker ones and as Democrats switched parties to join the Republican Party, the advantage for Democrats began to shrink.
- Ideological changes pushed conservative Democrats out of the Democratic Party and into the Republican Party.

of the original Boston Tea Party activists from the time of the American Revolution: relief from taxation. However, over time, the Tea Party has adopted a wider agenda, embracing traditional family values, advocating for a smaller government that is more connected and accountable to the people, supporting gun rights, and opposing illegal immigration.

FIGURE 5.5   **Texas Tea Party Affiliation**

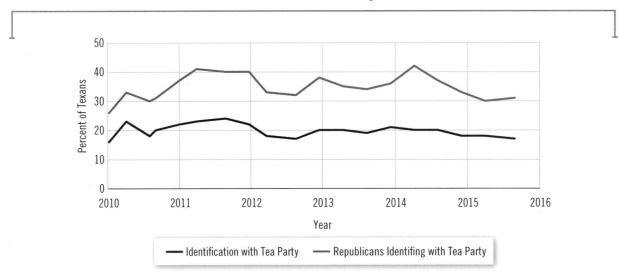

Source: Texas Politics Polling. Question asked: "Suppose the Tea Party movement organized itself as a political party. When thinking about the next election for Congress, would you vote for the Republican candidate from your district, the Democratic candidate from your district, or the Tea Party candidate from your district?"

 COMMUNICATION:

What percentage of the Texas electorate identifies with the Tea Party?

- Those identifying with the Tea Party have been around 20 percent of the electorate.
- Among Texas Republicans, on average between 30 and 40 percent of the public identify with the Tea Party.

 CRITICAL THINKING:

Why have these percentages changed?

- Tea Party-backed candidates express conservative policy views on issues that resonate with Republican primary voters and Tea Party activists rally support for these candidates.
- Support for the Tea Party spikes before primary elections (spring and summer) as candidates stoke the fire of conservative politics.

The movement has a national following but deep Texas roots, sprouting from an organization formed by US House Republican Texan Dick Armey.[44] Nationally, 17 percent of the public indicates support for the Tea Party.[45] The situation is different in conservative Texas. Texans' support for the Tea Party is higher than it is nationally, especially within the Republican Party (see Figure 5.5). Tea Party-backed candidates, such as Senator Ted Cruz and Lieutenant Governor Dan Patrick, have expanded their influence and local Tea Party activists continue to rally voters around conservative candidates.

The Tea Party sets the conservative litmus test for prospective nominees. Candidates who embrace the Tea Party in Republican primaries are often advantaged with a label that places them to the ideological right of their opponents and signals social conservatives, who make up a majority of the Republican primary electorate, to support them in the primary. A journalist noting these changes in Texas politics asked: "The question no longer is, 'Would Ann Richards be too liberal to be elected in Texas today?' but rather, 'Would George W. Bush?'"[46] This ideological party split makes it difficult to maintain party unity around legislative issues as more Tea Party-backed candidates are elected to the legislature.

FISSURES IN THE REPUBLICAN PARTY

The consequences of the rise of the Tea Party movement have been profound for Texas. The conflicts are unavoidable in a "big tent" party that seeks to continue to win elections and govern. Friction has developed between socially conservative voters who want their ideas of morality imposed on state policies and libertarians who want government out of just about everything. Skirmishes have also flared between fiscal conservatives who want a low-tax state with minimal spending on government services and business conservatives who see the need for increased spending on infrastructure, transportation, and education. Looking ahead, the growing political demands of the Tea Party may alienate moderate voters, causing them to leave the Republican Party.

LESSONS FROM TEXAS PARTY POLITICS

As with all party rises and falls, lessons can be learned from the events that preceded them. The power swings of party politics in the state demonstrate that history can repeat itself, and often does in Texas politics.

Develop New Party Blood. The Democratic Party was criticized for embracing a "wait your turn" system of elections, where talented younger elected officials waited in line behind more senior members to have a shot at higher office. This was argued to create "an ossified party rather than a dynamic one."[47] Candidates unwilling to wait either dropped out of politics or switched parties.

Offer A Bigger, Better Vision. Connecting with voters through issues that resonate with them is one of the most important ways that a party can win. While in office in the 1990s, Governor Ann Richards said that Democrats need to "bring them into a new decade that requires new thinking and new resolutions."[48]

Give Goodies. Governor Bill Clements, the first Republican elected governor since the Civil War, doled out dozens of appointments to Republicans, reshaping the landscape of the state's appointed officials. This tactic emphasizes both the governor's power of appointment as a tool of political power and the importance of these positions to government in Texas. Governor George W. Bush, elected in 1994, was able to take control of state agencies early in his term

Jared Woodfill, Former Harris County Republican Party Chair

How can majority parties attract new members?

If we want to continue to grow our [Republican] party, we must be responsive to our grassroots base. We must embrace the principles identified in the Republican Party of Texas platform. We must embrace these principles and be loud and proud of our positions on issues. We must continue to support conservative social and fiscal policies. We must take our winning message to communities that have not traditionally voted Republican. People are looking for a party that stands for something.

 PERSONAL RESPONSIBILITY: **What tactics would you use to bring together a divided party?**

because of legislation passed that allowed prior Governor Ann Richards to oust the prior governor's appointees.[49]

Co-opt Emerging Ideologies.   Incumbent party loyalists are often forced to adapt or reject new ideologies as they emerge from within a party. The rise of the Tea Party movement from within the Republican Party changed the dynamics of Texas politics. In the 2010 Republican primary, Rick Perry, running for reelection as governor, smartly inoculated himself from a more robust Tea Party challenge by adopting the Teary Party ideological platform early in the campaign and quelling any serious opposition.[50]

Build from the Bottom Up.   Republicans in the 1960s changed Texas from a one-party to a two-party state by running candidates in every local election possible. As the old saying goes: in Texas politics, if you control the county courthouse, you control the county. Following the momentum of Tower's 1961 victory and the party's first State Senate win since 1927 in 1966, the Republicans fielded a full slate of candidates in the 1968 elections. Most did not win, but the slow road to competitive politics began to take hold for the Republicans.

★▬ TEXAS TAKEAWAYS

5 When did the Democrats begin their domination of state politics? Approximately when did it end?

6 How did the Republican Party rise to prominence in Texas politics?

7 When and on what issue did the Tea Party emerge as a major force in Texas elections?

🤠 PARTY COMPETITION

Political parties at the state level have become better organized and more competitive. Political scientist Austin
Ranney developed a widely used measure of **party
competition** referred to as the Ranney Index based on the
percentage of votes for the governor's office, the percentage of legislative seats, and other measures. A higher score
indicates more competition. The most significant change across the past four
decades is the increase in the level of two-party competition in the South as the
dominant Democratic Party began to lose its grip on the region.

> **5.4** Analyze the factors that affect party competition.

party competition: electoral conflict that signals how successful one party is over another

This growing party competition may be explained by a number of factors.
A decline in traditional party loyalty means that more voters are willing to split
their tickets in national and state elections.[51] The rise of "candidate-centered"
campaigning channels voter loyalty toward the candidate rather than toward
the party. Candidates can thus be competitive no matter the partisan balance
in a state or district. Today, however, Texas is not fully competitive, but it is
more competitive than in the past (see Figure 5.6).

The change to Republican rule started in federal offices but gradually migrated to state offices as well. As the former Texas Republican state party chair
noted in his book *Red State*, Republican candidates were first able to compete
successfully in Texas federal elections, followed by gubernatorial elections,
and then state legislative elections.[52] The best indicator of the shift in party
power is in the legislature, which accumulates the partisan interests of the
state's voters. District elections did not witness much competition between
the two parties until the late twentieth century. Indeed, from 1900 to 1960,
there were never more than three members of the Texas House and one state
senator elected as a Republican.[53] Only later did Texas House and Senate districts become competitive. Today, Republicans have a supermajority in the
Texas House and a majority in the Senate. Republicans also hold all statewide elected positions and have majorities in both state supreme courts. Texas
is not alone in Republican-run government. Republicans across the country
have gained 913 state legislative seats since 2010 and control more than 30
state legislatures.[54]

What factors make one state more competitive than another? And is party
competition likely to increase once again in Texas? To begin to answer those
questions, we must look at apportionment, legislative redistricting, and party
switching.

REDISTRICTING AND PARTY COMPETITION

The US Constitution mandates that representation in the US House of Representatives be assigned based on state population after every census (which
takes place every decade). Following the last two censuses, Texas gained seats
in the US House of Representatives because Texas's population has been rising
more sharply than other states. This process is called **reapportionment**. Each

reapportionment: redistribution of representation based on decennial recounting of residents

IS IT BIGGER IN TEXAS?

FIGURE 5.6   **Party Competition, 1972–2015**

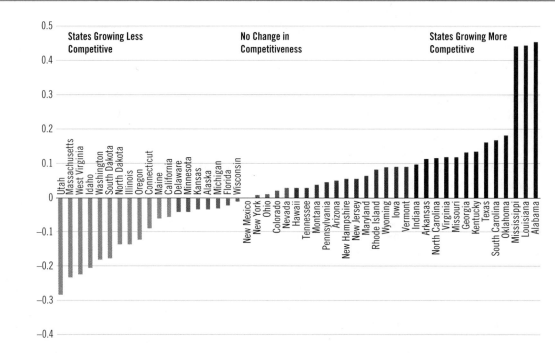

Source: Folded Ranney Index (represent a four-year moving average, with the last year being used to compute the average being the year in question). A score closer to .5 indicates party domination in a state (one party or the other). Higher scores mean more party competition.

 CRITICAL THINKING:

How competitive is Texas?

- Most states have seen increased electoral competition, especially southern states. Texas has grown more competitive but not as significantly as other southern states.

- Some states have seen decreased competition as the party in power their expands electoral influence, such as Oregon (Democrats), South Dakota (Republicans), Massachusetts (Democrats), and Utah (Republicans).

 CRITICAL THINKING:

What factors explain the change in party competition in Texas?

- Gubernatorial elections became more competitive as Republicans began to win elections in the 1980s.

- In more recent years, partisan gerrymandering has made seats safe for each party, providing a floor of party competition. Texas Democrats in particular have won districts drawn to favor them and several swing districts in some elections.

Congressional district has an estimated 700,000 residents. Texas House districts have approximately 167,000 residents while Senate districts have 811,000 residents.

State legislatures are responsible for redrawing the district lines to reflect population growth and to ensure that citizens have equal representation, making sure districts are of compact size, keeping communities together, and adhering to the geographical boundaries of local government. This redrawing process is called **redistricting**. Most states allow the state legislature to draw district lines but a few have an independent commission to set the boundaries. The Texas Constitution requires the state legislature to redraw the district boundaries in the first regular session after the federal census.

Agreeing on legislative boundaries, which largely determine who will or will not get elected, is difficult because most members have some skin in the game. How these lines are drawn directly influences who is elected. In 1951, the legislature developed a backup plan—a five-member board, called the **Legislative Redistricting Board** (LRB), would draw the district lines if it were the case that the legislature was not able to agree. The board is made up of most statewide elected officials: the lieutenant governor, the speaker of the house, the attorney general, the state comptroller, and the land commissioner.

Even if the Legislative Redistricting Board can agree on a set of electoral maps, these maps may

TEXAS 27TH
"Glock Pistol"

Districts often take odd shapes as the architects attempt to include or exclude certain communities, geographic regions, or groups. Texas 27th Congressional district resembles a gun pointed at a 45 degree angle. The gun's "handle" expanded to include more conservative areas in the 2010 redistricting, allowing a Republican to unseat a long-serving Democrat.

SOCIAL RESPONSIBILITY: **Would it be fair to the party affiliation of the population to be a factor in drawing district lines? What about race or ethnicity?**

still be deemed unconstitutional by the US Supreme Court. From the 1960s through the 1990s, the Supreme Court in a string of rulings laid down detailed guidelines that enforced the "one man, one vote" rule established in *Baker v. Carr* (1962), which prohibited congressional, state, and local districts from having a significantly greater population than another district.[55] This ruling altered the balance of power in Texas by forcing the state to draw district lines to equalize populations and thus reducing the number of rural districts, increasing the number of urban districts, and shifting the power to legislators in urban districts. Explaining the Court's reasoning, Chief Justice Warren wrote the famous line, "Legislators represent people, not trees or acres."[56]

A major point of legal contention has been the use of race to draw legislative lines. The Supreme Court ruled in 1960 in *Gomillion v. Lightfoot* that districts drawn to discriminate against racial minorities violated the Fifteenth Amendment and states could not draw districts to diminish the political power of minorities. As the Court found in *Shaw v. Reno* (1993), however, the state cannot **gerrymander** a district for race alone, a process of manipulating district

redistricting: the redrawing of the legislative districts to meet federal and state requirements

Legislative Redistricting Board: the group of officials who draw the district lines if it were the case that the legislature was not able to agree

gerrymander: a process of manipulating district boundaries to benefit a single group

Senate Democrats who took cover in New Mexico during a redistricting fight in 2003 hold a makeshift press conference from their Albuquerque hotel with the Texas flag behind them (see Angles of Power).

boundaries to benefit a single group, but can do so on the basis of a combined set of factors including community cohesion, political subdivisions, or to keep together neighborhoods historically in the same district.

Legislatures often draw seats with prospects for their party's electoral success in mind. This leads to districts that protect incumbent members or make a district held by the opposition party more vulnerable to challenge. However, legally, redistricting may not purposely draw district lines to advantage one party over another. District lines drawn in this way over time lead to "safe" seats where one party or the other dominates because a significant majority of the voters in the district are loyal to the dominant party.

Common gerrymandering tactics include "cracking" (spreading a population group across several districts to reduce influence), "packing" (stuffing a population group in a single district to reduce influence in neighboring districts), and "hijacking" (redrawing lines to pit two incumbents against each other). One legislator, who was unhappy about his district being redrawn in a way that included his house but excluded much of his core constituency, called his new district the "fickle finger" district because "it had a little finger that went down and got my house."[57]

see for yourself 5.2

Evaluate whether the twenty-third congressional district in Texas was redrawn to create a safe seat or make the Democratic candidates more vulnerable to challengers.

THE 2001 AND 2003 REDISTRICTING BATTLES: THE DRAMA BEGINS

Following the 2000 census, Texas was slated to receive two additional Congressional seats. Republican Governor Rick Perry controlled the governor's chair, but the Democrats controlled the state house and the senate was split between the two major parties. As a result, the Texas legislature was unable to agree on new district lines in the 2001 session because both parties attempted to draw new district lines that would favor their own party. The task for redistricting fell to the Legislative Redistricting Board. Since four of the five members of the LRB were Republican, the lines favored Republican candidates. The redistricting efforts shifted many "safe" Democratic districts to safe Republican districts. Not surprisingly, Republicans took a majority of the legislature in 2002 elections. With this new majority, Republicans, led by US House Majority Leader Tom DeLay, proposed the legislature draw new lines in the 2003 legislative session. This led to a contentious legislative session (see Angles of Power).

A legal challenge (*League of United Latin American Citizens v. Perry*) to the rare "mid-decade" redrawn lines ended in 2006 with the Supreme Court

ANGLES OF POWER
The 2003 Redistricting Battle and the Killer Ds

Fearing a redistricting plan would pass in the legislature that would greatly reduce the number of Democrats, fifty-two Democrats from the House and Senate fled Austin to a Holiday Inn in Ardmore, Oklahoma, for eleven days in 2003 to stall a vote. Without a sufficient number of senators to vote, a vote in the chamber could not be held. The Texas Rangers have the authority in Texas to escort lawmakers home but that jurisdiction ends at the state line. The Democrats were powerless as the minority party in the House, whose rules afford little options for lawmaking. Representative Jim Dunnam of Waco bragged to a cheering crowd upon the return of the "Killer Ds" (as they were called), "I went to Ardmore, Oklahoma, and all I got was this hat from Denny's."[58]

The regular session ended with no redistricting bill, but Governor Perry called a special session to finish the job. The Democrats bolted to Albuquerque, New Mexico, this time, but one Democrat, Senator John Whitmire of Houston and the longest-serving member of the Senate, broke ranks and returned to Austin to "preserve consensus in the state Senate instead of engaging in no-holds-barred partisan civil war."[59] For all of the delays, the redistricting bill eventually passed anyway.

SOCIAL RESPONSIBILITY: **Should parties use legislative majorities to engineer more electoral support for their party?**

upholding the redrawn districts (except for one district). Using these maps, Republicans dominated the 2004 elections, taking more than two-thirds of the open seats in the House (see Figure 5.7).

REDISTRICTING IN 2011: MAPS AND MORE MAPS

Texas's booming population registered in the 2010 census added four US House seats to the Lone Star State. The growth was fueled by individuals moving to Texas from out of state and the rapidly rising population of racial minorities.[60] The Republican supermajorities in the Texas House and Senate recrafted the lines in 2011, only to be challenged in court for not taking the growth of the state's minority population into account. A panel of three San Antonio federal judges redrew the lines for use in the 2012 elections, only to have the Supreme Court order them to draw new lines based more closely on the maps designed by the state legislature. The awkward timing of this process forced the state to delay the scheduled 2012 primary elections from March to May.

REDISTRICTING IN 2013: BACK TO COURT

Legislative redistricting in a special session in 2013 took place during the ongoing ping-pong match between the legislature, the US Justice Department, and the federal courts over the 2011 and 2012 maps. The legislature modestly doctored the maps used in the 2012 elections for the Texas house but left the Texas senate and US Congressional maps in place. The new boundaries again generally favored Republicans—eighty districts became

FIGURE 5.7   **Texas Representatives in the US House**

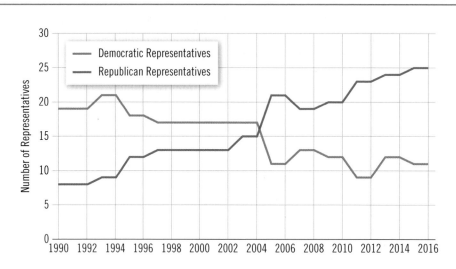

Source: Texas Legislative Reference Library

 CRITICAL THINKING:

How has the partisan composition of the legislature changed?

- The largest increase in legislative representation of US House Republicans in Washington came in the mid 2000s as the Texas delegation became a Republican majority.

 CRITICAL THINKING:

Why has it changed?

- Republican wins in the 1960s and 1970s spurred an investment in party organization that made running for office as a Republican easier. Recruitment efforts paid off in the 1990s.

- Redistricting in 2000, aided by Republicans hungry to elect more of their own, drew district lines that favored Republican House candidates.

more Republican-leaning. Democratic-held districts also solidified their advantage—sixty-five districts swung to a more liberal direction.[61] Latino organizations like the Texas Latino Redistricting Task Force proposed expanding the number of Latino seats and the Texas legislative Black Caucus asked for nondiscriminatory lines to be drawn. Ultimately Republicans in charge of redistricting strengthened some Democratic districts while weakening others. A federal judge allowed the state to hold elections using these maps in 2014, claiming the courts didn't have adequate time to settle the legal dispute before the elections took place.[62] The present maps are still under review for discriminatory intent, but a three-judge federal panel in San Antonio ruled in 2015 that in order to avoid delay or confusion, the state should use the 2013 redrawn maps for the 2016 election.

A separate legal challenge was brought arguing the boundaries were based on total population, not total voting population. The concern was that although most districts had a similar number of citizens, the number of voters was not equal because some racial groups, like Hispanics, are less likely to register to vote.[63] The Supreme Court ruled in 2015, in *Evenwel v. Abbott*, that the legislature was required to draw districts to equalize the total population of districts rather than the number of eligible voters. Using only registered voters, the court reasoned, runs against the "one-person, one-vote" principle. The case demonstrates the importance of adequate representation, reemphasizing the need to participate in the electoral system.

PARTY SWITCHING

One factor that reduces party competition within a district is party switching— when politicians of one party opt to switch to another, frequently to join the "winning team." National level factors, such as Republican Party success in Congress beginning in the 1980s, pushed several incumbent southern legislators to switch from the Democratic to Republican Parties.[64] Between 2008 and 2013 in Texas alone, more than 200 Democrats at all levels of elected government switched to the Republican Party as the Democratic Party swung to the left and conservative Democrats felt left behind.[65]

Party switchers were mostly "WD-40s"—white Democrats over 40 years of age—who held onto their seats while fellow Democrats fell to Republican challengers.[66] Other officials found themselves in redrawn districts that would not elect a candidate from their party, prompting a switch. Corpus Christi Representative J.M. Lozano took the path of self-preservation by switching from the Democratic to the Republican Party in 2012 as his coastal district was redrawn to favor Republicans.[67] Happy to have another possible member and a Hispanic lawmaker to boot, the Republican Party turned on the money spigot for Lozano, contributing more than $40,000 to his campaign.[68]

Does party switching change political voting habits? When Texas Representative Charlie Evans, who switched from the Democratic Party to the Republican Party in 1987, was asked about his party loyalty, he replied "I'll probably be about as good a Republican as I was a Democrat."[69] Party switching muddies the ability of a switched candidate to send a clear signal of values and political stances. To compensate, legislators often change their voting behavior to adhere to their new party's ideology, especially on votes on amendments and other procedural votes. Greater polarization increases pressure for members of a new party to toe the party line so highly that partisan periods cause more extreme changes in voting behavior of newly joined party members.[70] How does party switching impact electoral fortunes?

GREAT TEXAS POLITICAL DEBATES
Switching Parties

Switching parties, and the timing of it, can cause electoral problems but it also poses ethical problems. In 1983, Phil Gramm, a former economics professor at Texas A&M University and Democratic member of the US House, jumped from the donkey stables (Democrat) to the elephant pen (Republican). Observers noted Gramm, who grew more unhappy with the Democrats' economic plans, "didn't quietly walk away from the Democratic Party in 1983; he gave it a kick in its moldering ass and strutted into history." Gramm resigned his House seat and immediately re-filed to run as a Republican in the special election his resignation created.[72]

His high-profile exit opened the door to more. Future governor Rick Perry turned Republican in 1989 as his views grew more conservative. Texas House Representative Allan Ritter joined the Republicans when he saw his district change: "I try to be what my district is," he explained as he gave Republicans a supermajority in 2010.[73] Texas House member Aaron Pena switched parties immediately after his reelection in 2010, from the Democratic to the Republican Party, because he felt that the Democratic Party had grown too liberal and for political survival. Pena remarked, "Somebody once told me that if you don't have a seat at the table, you may be on the menu."[74] Texas House Representative Bernard Erickson, hoping to avoid a primary challenge, switched to the Democratic Party. Erickson lost his reelection bid by fifty-six votes.[75]

SOCIAL RESPONSIBILITY: Is it ethical to switch parties?

YES: Politicians with credible and heartfelt core reasons to switch parties may be more able to survive political challenges than opportunistic politicians. Many officials legitimately gravitate to new issues, change their opinions on issues, or, as many claim, "the party leaves them" behind by taking on new, more extreme issues.

NO: Voters elect candidates because of their party label. The party platform tells a voter what that party (and candidate) stand for. Switching parties confuses voters and breaks the contract that elected officials have with the public.

MAYBE: The nature and timing of the switch matters. Candidates who get elected by one party and switch to another party hoodwink voters and leave the public with a fundamentally different elected official. Party switchers who switch before elections give voters an opportunity to reassess that candidate's qualities and value.

Many of these party switchers do survive. Political scientists Christian Grose and Antoine Yoshinaka found that incumbents who switch parties receive less vote share in the general election than before they switched, but most switchers stay in office.[71]

TEXAS TAKEAWAYS

8 How do we define party competition?

9 What is the relationship between redistricting and party competition?

10 Since the 1980s, have more Democrats switched to the Republican Party or have more Republicans switched to the Democratic Party?

🤠 THIRD PARTIES AND INDEPENDENTS

Traditionally, the United States has had two major political parties. Why only two political parties? Political scientists suggest that the structure of the electoral system is a major reason: a **winner-take-all election** in which whatever candidate wins the most votes wins the seat. This is sometimes referred to as a "first past the post" system. In contrast, a proportional system elects several candidates—usually from a larger geographic area—based upon the proportion of the vote won. So, if voters backed three parties equally in a geographic area represented by three elected officials, each party would have a representative in the government. Political scientist Maurice Duverger argued that winner-take-all systems generally lead to a two party system because it encourages individuals and groups to band together to win that single seat. This is known as **Duverger's law**.

> **5.5** Evaluate the impact third parties have had on Texas party politics and the challenges they face.

winner-take-all election: whichever candidate wins the most votes wins the seat

Duverger's law: a winner-take-all electoral system generally leads to a two-party system

Several factors further obstruct the rise of independent and third-party candidates in Texas. Most voters are attached to the "name brand," or political platform, of one of the two major parties. The two major parties also have a significant head start on fundraising and can tap a deep bench of donors. Furthermore, state laws set requirements that serve as obstacles for third parties and independent candidates. A new third party must create a state executive committee and establish procedures for governing the party meetings and selection of candidates. A new third party must also file a list of party participants with the secretary of state —and the number of participants must equal 1 percent of the total votes received by all candidates for governor in the most recent gubernatorial election. That figure is currently 47,183. Once these requirements are met for the first time, a third party is guaranteed an automatic slot on the ballot if the party received at least 5 percent of the vote in any state-wide race.

Still, while rare in Texas, third parties have upended state politics on occasion. These parties bring to light issues, such as underrepresentation of a minority, that have later been co-opted by major parties. Let's explore a few.

LA RAZA UNIDA PARTY

Unsettling the Democrats' hold on party politics in the 1970s was a social movement that grew into a political party called La Raza Unida (The United Race). Reacting to a rule at Crystal City High School that mandated the homecoming queen be the daughter of a graduate (a transparent attempt to ensure the election of an Anglo), graduate student Jose Angel Gutierrez formed a group to protest. To capitalize on this organizational success, Gutierrez and allies formed La Raza Unida to break the Democrats' monopoly on local politics. The party gained control of the school board, the county court house, and the city council. As a separate political entity, La Raza Unida posed serious problems for Democrats as Mexican Americans began defecting from the party and voting for the new party.[76]

Ramsey Muñiz ran again for governor in 1974, but as La Raza Unida waned in influence, he drew only half the votes (94,000) that he did in his historic 1972 run. His 1972 campaign for governor accelerated the inclusion of Latinos into Texas politics.

PERSONAL RESPONSIBILITY: **What role does your own race, ethnicity, religion, gender, or sexual orientation play in influencing which political party you support?**

La Raza Unida candidate Ramsey Muñiz, received more than 200,000 votes in the 1972 gubernatorial election, dangerously reducing Democrat Dolph Briscoe's margin to just under 100,000 votes. Although the La Raza Unida Party as a political power was in decline by the mid-1970s, the Democratic Party still viewed it as a threat. Democrat John Hill as attorney general led several investigations into the group's finances. The political payback was swift. La Raza Unida and allied groups partnered in the 1978 gubernatorial election to back Republican Bill Clements instead of the Democratic nominee, La Raza Unida nemesis John Hill. Republican Bill Clements ended up winning that race and became Texas's first Republican governor in 100 years.

The Democratic Party learned its lesson. In 1982, the liberal Democratic faction successfully courted the Hispanic vote and elected Democrat Mark White governor. Inclusion of Mexican Americans into the Democratic Party did not occur on purpose—it unfolded through "trench warfare" as former La Raza Unida members (running as Democrats) broke the Anglo hold on several counties.[77]

Women were also a key part of the La Raza Unida's growth as a third party in the 1970s. Forming a caucus called Mujeres por La Raza Unida (Women for the People's Party), women served as organizers and often candidates when the men could not run for fear of retribution at work. Still, Latinas were excluded from the highest ranks of party leadership. At one meeting to express concern about the party's need to be inclusive of women's ideas, a young male shouted "why don't you go home to the dishes, where you belong?"[78] Over time, women like Virginia Muzquiz, who worked her way from county chair to state party chair, have demonstrated that women can advance in the party.

LIBERTARIAN PARTY OF TEXAS

The Libertarian Party of Texas emphasizes liberty as their main philosophy, encouraging freedom of choice and the importance of individual judgment. In practical terms, the party stands for a limited welfare state, free market economic principles, and small government—thus sharing the political values of fiscal conservatives within the Republican Party.

The Libertarian Party does not hold any state or federal offices at any level in Texas but does hold offices at the local level. Libertarians also peel off votes from other candidates, especially Republicans whose general philosophy they share. As a result, the Libertarian Party has played spoiler in swing districts.[79] In 2006, the impact of the Libertarian candidate was enough to swing a west Austin House seat to the Democrats.[80]

GREEN PARTY OF TEXAS

The Green Party of Texas emphasizes local control of communities, nonviolent resolution of disputes, and social justice. Specifically, the party supports public election financing in Texas, universal voter registration, universal health care, establishing corporate income taxes in Texas, expanding the use of medical marijuana, and abolishing the death penalty. The Green Party has consistently fallen below the 5 percent threshold that would allow them to gain a position on the ballot. As a result, the Democratic Party—the major party ideologically closest to the Green Party—has not been forced to adopt the main goals of its platform.[81]

INDEPENDENTS

A Texan can run as an independent if he or she files a declaration to run. An independent candidate must then get signatures of registered voters that equal either 1 percent or 5 percent (depending on the office) of the total vote received by all gubernatorial candidates in the recent past gubernatorial election in the district, county, or precinct sought. The signatures must also be from voters who did not vote in the primary of another party for that election cycle.

Independent candidates can sap electoral support away from a majority party frontrunner. The wild 2006 gubernatorial race featured two independents, Carole "Grandma" Strayhorn and Richard "Kinky" Friedman, in addition to Democrat Chris Bell and incumbent Republican Governor Rick Perry. Strayhorn, a Republican and the state's comptroller of public accounts, was seen as a moderate alternative to Perry and styled herself "one tough grandma." Friedman was a cigar-chomping musician and author who, fed up with politics as usual, mounted a quixotic bid to unseat Governor Perry. With the votes split between four main contenders, Perry ended up with only 39 percent of the electorate voting for him, the lowest percentage of the electorate since Democrat Dolph Briscoe's 48 percent in the 1972 election (which also featured a third-party challenger). These "kooky independents" revealed that populist candidates can pierce the one-party rule and even swing elections in some cases, often in local elections.[82]

★ TEXAS TAKEAWAYS

11 What is the biggest impact of a winner-take-all election?

12 What requirements do third parties have to meet in order to be on the ballot?

🤠 THE INSIDER VIEW

The transition in Texas from a one-party Democratic state to a one-party Republican state was a struggle over issues, ideology, and demographics. Future Majority Leader in the US House Republican Tom Delay recalled when he first ran for the Texas House in 1978, a farmer was taken aback when informed that candidate Delay was a Republican: "I want to tell you something, boy. It'll be a cold day in hell when a Republican wins this county."[83] And yet today Republicans dominate elected offices in the state. What happened? National politics first shook the state party as the New Deal alienated economic conservatives, demographic change provided a foothold for the Republican Party, and then ideological division within the Democratic Party sent conservatives into the arms of the Republican Party. The Republican Party is as fragmented in the present as the Democrats were in the past. Observers have argued that there are again three functional parties in Texas: the mainstream Republicans, the Democrats, and the Tea Party Republicans.

★— TEXAS TAKEAWAYS

1 Parties engage in three basic functions: assisting voters (parties-in-the-electorate), facilitating party goals (parties-as-organizations), and organizing government by structuring and controlling government (parties-in-government).

2 Partisans are the most strongly committed party loyalists and can be counted on to volunteer, donate money, and vote for the party candidates.

3 The state party chair's primary responsibility is to develop and communicate the party's brand to the voters and to raise and manage political funds for the party at the state level.

4 A party platform is a list of values, beliefs, and policy issues that are endorsed and supported by a political party. It serves as a roadmap for the party during elections and in agenda setting.

5 Democrats won all the Congressional seats in 1871, took majority control of the state legislature in 1872, and easily won the governorship in 1873. Observers point to December 2, 1997, as the day the Democratic Party in Texas collapsed.

6 The Democrats were divided along ideological grounds. Republicans began to see federal intervention as a primary cause of economic troubles. The growth of the suburbs gave rise to new conservatives. Residents arriving from other states did not have the same attachments to the Democratic Party as long-term Texans.

7 The Tea Party reached national prominence when it held a series of rallies in 2009 in response to the Obama Administration's economic recovery plans and the Affordable Care Act.

8 Party competition is defined as the relative electoral winning success between the parties.

9 Gerrymandered district lines drawn over time lead to "safe" seats where one party or the other dominates given the voters stacked into a district. It tends to reduce party competition.

10 More Democrats have switched to the Democratic Party since the 1980s.

11 One winner generally leads to a two-party system because individuals and groups band together to win that single available seat.

12 A third party must create a state executive committee, establish procedures for governing the party meetings and selection of candidates, and file a list of party participants with the secretary of state.

KEY TERMS

conservative
decentralization
Duverger's law
gerrymander
Legislative Redistricting Board
liberal
New Deal
partisans
party competition
party platform
reapportionment
redistricting
winner-take-all election

PRACTICE QUIZ

1. Strongly committed members of a political party are called

   a. Polarizers
   b. Blue Dog Democrats
   c. RINOs
   d. Partisans

2. Which of the following are not formal positions in the party organization?

   a. State Representatives
   b. Precinct Chairs
   c. State Party Chair
   d. Party Executive Committee Members

3. Between the years of 1952 and 2015, in what decade did the number of affiliated Republicans *first* surpass the number of affiliated Democrats in Texas?

   a. 1960
   b. 1980
   c. 1990
   d. 2010

4. On average, what percentage range of Texas Republicans identify with the Tea Party?

   a. 5–15 percent
   b. 30–40 percent
   c. 55–65 percent
   d. 80–90 percent

5. What percent of votes are third parties required to achieve on a statewide election for their candidates to continue to appear on ballots?

   a. 3 percent
   b. 5 percent
   c. 7 percent
   d. 10 percent

6. Which of the following factors did not contribute to the declining power of the Democratic Party?

   a. Party switching
   b. Suburban growth
   c. Newcomers to the state
   d. Growth of the Green Party

7. Political parties are organizations of individuals that aggregate political and policy interests for their members.

   a. True
   b. False

8. Texas Democrats currently dominate the Texas political landscape.

   a. True
   b. False

9. The term "WD-40" in the context of political party switchers refers to white Democrats over forty years of age.

   a. True
   b. False

10. Third parties have a strong presence in Texas politics.

    a. True
    b. False

[Answer Key: D, A, C, B, B, D, A, B, A, B]

6 | INTEREST GROUPS

In 1989, Governor Bill Clements called a special session of the Texas legislature on workers' compensation. At issue was legislation that would force workers to negotiate with employers prior to accessing their right to a jury trial. This change to worker's compensation would limit the number of cases that went to a jury and save business interests millions of dollars a year. The legislature was deadlocked. Early in the session, Lonnie "Bo" Pilgrim, a big Republican donor and founder and chairman of the Pilgrim's Pride Corporation based in Pittsburg, Texas, roamed the floor of the Texas Senate. His chicken empire was the largest poultry processing firm in the nation at the time and he had a keen interest in the outcome of the legislation. Worker claims had cost his business millions of dollars annually. Pilgrim sidled up to several legislators, handing out $10,000 checks and bluntly explaining, "We need some help." Pilgrim left the payee's name blank on checks he gave to nine members in the two days before the Senate's vote on the workers' compensation bill. Several legislators quickly returned the checks, one accepted the check because Pilgrim was a "longtime friend," one angrily refused and escorted Pilgrim out of his office, and several did not make up their minds.[1]

Word reached Lieutenant Governor Bill Hobby in his capitol office, who reported the incident to the Travis County district attorney. Calling the act "outrageous," the district attorney nevertheless indicated that "in Texas, it's almost impossible to bribe a public official as long as you report it." Pilgrim emphatically denied

LEARNING OBJECTIVES

6.1 Explain the theories that describe the role of interest groups in Texas.

6.2 Assess the incentives for individuals to join interest groups.

6.3 Identify the types of interest groups in Texas.

6.4 Describe the types of activities interest groups engage in to pursue their agendas.

6.5 Explain what lobbying is and how lobbyists serve the interests of those involved.

6.6 Illustrate the role of scandals in shaping interest group politics and reform efforts.

6.7 Outline the ways the state oversees the interactions of interest groups and state officials.

● Lobbyists at the state capitol spend much of the legislative session monitoring the progress of legislation, reviewing proposed agency rules, talking to legislative staff, and educating members on the pros and cons of legislation. Relationships are key to this communication, so lobbyists spend time wining and dining lawmakers as well.

the checks were bribes: they were standard lobby practice, he claimed.[2] The bill failed to pass, as Pilgrim had wanted, but the incident hurt the credibility of the business interests.

The episode spurred the legislature to pass a series of new campaign finance laws, including one that prohibits lawmakers from accepting campaign contributions while the legislature is in session and another that restricts accepting contributions inside the Capitol building.

The affair also highlights the role of **interest groups** in influencing the policy process. "For virtue," wrote journalist Molly Ivins, "try Minnesota."[3] Yet, interest groups do not always go unopposed in Texas. The scuffles between two or more interest groups shape both policy and the political process—as we just saw with the legislation that followed the Bo Pilgrim incident. Interest groups also serve important functions within Texas society and government. As a longtime Texas lobbyist once said, the negative attention on interest groups overshadows the positive role that they play in representing the public's interest—"if you're a florist, you think, 'thank goodness for the Texas State Florists' Association's lobbyist.'"[4]

interest group: any formal organization of individuals or groups that seeks to influence government to promote their common cause

Bust of Bo Pilgrim a few miles down the road from his massive estate, Cluckingham Palace. Although famous for his chicken empire, his legacy will live on in the reforms that followed his lobbying efforts.

CRITICAL THINKING: **How should Texas regulate the influx of money from business interests into the political system?**

Interest groups attempt to influence government for the benefit of their members through legislation, rules, or actions that are aligned with their cause. A successful interest group has both the ability to get things done and the ability to keep things from getting done. In this chapter, we explore the types of interest groups, the functions they serve, and the role they play in the policymaking process. We discover how interest groups sometimes become too influential, requiring oversight and regulation through various state agencies. Moments of crisis, as in the Bo Pilgrim example, reveal the ongoing struggle to police interest groups and ensure that they play a role that strengthens, rather than weakens, democracy in Texas.

INTEREST GROUPS IN THE POLITICAL PROCESS

Since the birth of this country, the founders had a vision for the role organized interests might play in the political process. In Federalist Paper 10, founder James Madison referred to the undue influence of powerful interest groups as the "mischief of factions," but argued that multiple competing interests would reduce this mischief. One group checks the influence of another. In practice, however, the imbalance of power may allow some groups to have greater influence. Political scientists have advanced several theories to explore the role of interest groups in American democracy today.

> **6.1** Explain the theories that describe the role of interest groups in Texas.

PLURALIST THEORY

Scholars writing in the 1950s and 1960s developed **pluralist theory,** which, similar to Madison's vision, viewed competition among many groups as keeping any one group from exercising too much control over policy.[5]

We can find examples of pluralism among the political struggles in Texas. The legislature created the Texas Windstorm Insurance Association (TWIA), a public–private agency, in 1971 to provide insurance for costal residents. TWIA was the only option for many coastal residents to get necessary insurance for their properties, especially after several major hurricanes. In 2011, two powerhouse interest groups, Texans for Lawsuit Reform and the Texas Trial Lawyers Association, went to war against each other when the Texas legislature tried to change the way that TWIA handled the claims process. The two groups battled over the number of permitted lawsuits filed against the agency, the cap on damages claimants could collect, and the ability of policyholders to sue to recover money.[6] When the dust settled, the law that passed made claimants' route to the courthouse more difficult by requiring more evidence to prove a claim. However, the outcome was not all bad for the Texas Trial Lawyers Association. The law also allowed for mediation or a full jury trial.[7] This compromise suggests that the pluralist theory can be applied to understand the role of interest groups in policymaking.

pluralist theory: competition keeps powerful interest groups in check and no single group dominates

ELITE THEORY

Not all scholars accept pluralist theory. Political scientist E.E. Schattschneider famously articulated that "the flaw in the pluralist heaven is that the heavenly chorus sings with a strong upper-class accent."[8] According to the **elite theory** that he and others advanced, groups that have greater resources are in a better position to accomplish their goals. Sociologist C. Wright Mills suggested that

elite theory: groups that have greater resources are in a better position to accomplish their goals

Large groups are thought to have the most sway but grassroots lobbying from smaller organizations, like the Farm & Ranch Alliance that advocates for independent farmers, ranchers, and livestock owners, can find legislative success on the right issues.

SOCIAL RESPONSIBILITY: **Do large or powerful interest groups have too much sway in Texas politics? What should be done to make sure the people have a voice in the democratic process?**

this power elite is drawn from high-ranking government officials and major corporate owners.

Examples of elite theory in Texas politics abound. In the 2011 legislative session, for instance, the legislature passed a bill requiring the disclosure of the names of chemicals used to extract natural gas from the ground (fracking), but lobbying from industry groups postponed the disclosure for two years and allowed certain operators not to disclose certain chemicals by declaring them trade secrets.[9] Was it in the best interests of the people of Texas to protect these trade secrets? Or was this undue influence by the oil and gas industry? Former member of the Texas House of Representatives Mike Martin put it this way, "there's the Texas Chemical Council; there's the oil and gas interests; there the electrical utility industry; there's the hazardous waste interests—that's four right there. The amount of money they have pumped into the legislature is phenomenal. And when those issues come up, straight up, those guys, the big guys, win all the time."[10]

TRANSACTIONAL THEORY

transactional theory: public policy is bought and sold like a commodity to the highest bidder

An extension of the power elite theory is a **transactional theory**. This theory proposes that public policy is bought and sold like a commodity to the highest bidder. For example, mega-donor Bob Perry of Perry Homes leaned on the Texas governor and legislature to create a state agency, the Texas Residential Construction Commission in 2003. The mission of the agency was to protect homeowners and improve construction, but the commission consistently favored builders when disputes arose. After years of homeowners' complaints, the agency was shut down in 2010.[11]

WHICH THEORY FITS TEXAS?

Which theory best explains how interest groups influence policy in Texas? Pluralist, elite, or transaction theory? Perhaps all three. It depends on the circumstances. For example, political scientists have found that transaction theory and elite theory might explain the policymaking process at the state level, where legislatures have significant authority and oversight is modest.[12] However, for cases in which two powerful interest groups vie for different policy outcomes or for cases that enjoy a high degree of public attention, pluralist theory might provide a better explanation.

★ TEXAS TAKEAWAYS

1 What do interest groups do?

2 Explain the differences between pluralist and elite theories.

3 What is transactional theory?

WHY JOIN INTEREST GROUPS

For our democracy to move toward the pluralist ideal envisioned by James Madison and others, individuals and groups must be motivated to join interest groups. **Private interest groups**, like the labor unions, advocate for the benefit of their members. **Public interest groups** in Texas benefit the public in general, all Gulf Coast residents, all Texans, or all Americans. However, interest groups, especially those devoted to solving shared problems, suffer from the **free rider problem**. Let's take a closer look at this problem and some solutions.

6.2 Assess the incentives for individuals to join interest groups.

private interest groups: groups that advocate for the benefit of their members

public interest groups: groups that benefit the public in general

free rider problem: a situation in which individuals benefit from a publicly provided good or service without paying for it and actively supporting its acquisition

THE FREE RIDER PROBLEM

Many interest groups work to solve collective action problems—problems that are shared by a large group of people. You want clean air, more efficient government, or expanded civil rights? There are dozens of organizations that are working to ensure this goal. Why should you join if they'll do the work without your help? Free riders are people who receive the benefits without paying the cost. For example, the group Texas Campaign for the Environment advocates for curbside composting, battery recycling, firmer enforcement of oil and gas regulations, and other environmental protections. Do you enjoy a good environment with clean air and water? If so—and if you are not a member of this interest group or a similar group that has worked for these policies—then you are a free rider.

The Texas National Rifle Association advocates for open carry laws, but it also provides members with discounts on car rentals, legal consultation, the opportunity to purchase rare firearms, and contributions to student scholarship funds.

PERSONAL RESPONSIBILITY: **What kinds of organizations have you joined because of the benefits you received? Would you have joined them without the offer of these benefits?**

selective benefits: private goods made available to people who organize for a collective good

Don't feel bad, you are not alone. Economist Mancur Olson famously argued in his book *The Logic of Collective Action* that it is rational for individuals to leave it to others to solve the problem and to reap the benefit without having paid the cost of participation. The end result, however, is that interest groups that pursue altruistic, public goals often have a harder time acquiring the resources to be successful than do interest groups that pursue narrower, more selfish goals. Interest groups thus provide incentives for participation that help overcome the free rider problem.

SELECTIVE BENEFITS

One way to solve the free rider problem is by providing **selective benefits** (or incentives) to people who organize for a collective good. They can be material, solidary, or purposive. Material benefits are tangible rewards, generally monetary, such as wages, fringe benefits, or patronage. The Texas Public Employees Association is a nonpartisan advocacy organization that advocates for higher wages and better health and retirement benefits for state employees. Members receive discounted tickets to Texas Rangers games and Six Flags Over Texas amusement park.[13]

Solidary benefits are intangible rewards from joining a group, such as social status or social interactions with like-minded people. Do you live in a big city and sometimes feel like you are stuck in a giant concrete jungle? The Dallas Downriver Club or the Adventure Club of San Antonio gives you the opportunity to enjoy outdoor activities and a chance to socialize with people who have similar interests.

Often Texans join an interest group to serve a cause. Groups like Texas Right to Life or Planned Parenthood Texas take opposing views of abortion, but both advance the cause their members care about. The satisfaction that members feel when working with a group to realize their political values is called a purposive benefit.

★ TEXAS TAKEAWAYS

4 How is the free rider problem associated with interest groups?

5 What kinds of benefits might interest groups offer to encourage people to join?

TYPES OF INTEREST GROUPS

Are you a member of an interest group? You might be and not even realize it. If you are part of a business group, trade association, professional organization, or labor union, you are a member of an economic interest group. You might also be a member of a noneconomic group, for example, a public interest group like the Sierra Club or a single-issue group like the San Antonio Humane Society. Let's take a closer look at some of your options.

6.3 Identify the types of interest groups in Texas.

BUSINESS GROUPS

If you are a small business owner, you might be a member of the Chamber of Commerce. Individual businesses and organizations representing many businesses often advocate on behalf of their own interests—and sometimes battle each other. For example, ahead of the 2015 legislative session, Tesla Motors, a maker of electric cars, unleashed a powerful group of lobbyists in Texas. Their goal: to persuade lawmakers to allow Tesla to bypass auto dealerships and sell electric cars in Texas directly to the public. Unlike other automakers, Tesla sells their cars directly to consumers, but is prohibited from doing so in Texas. A dealership can make between $400 to several thousand dollars per car sold at a dealership, and auto dealerships in Texas are organized into an interest group. In fact, the Texas Automobile Dealers Association has gained serious political influence over the decades, and deep-pocketed car franchise owners are also often big campaign contributors.[14] So, despite spending almost $1 million, Tesla failed. Governor Greg Abbott shut the garage door on Tesla, insisting that the state would not carve out a loophole to allow Tesla to sell cars directly to the public.[15]

Political scientists have found that business lobbies prevail mainly on issues that are important only to a single company or industry because these usually attract little media coverage.[16] These victories can often be hidden from public view or ignored because they may consist of a small regulatory change. Yet these changes may supply a significant financial benefit to industry groups.

TRADE ASSOCIATIONS AND PROFESSIONAL ORGANIZATIONS

You might also be a member of an interest group because of the job you have. Trade associations serve the interests of an industry, such as farmers, locksmiths, or realtors. Professional organizations are groups that represent a specific occupation. For example, among the most powerful groups in the state are the Texas Trial Lawyers Association, the Texas Medical Association, the Texas Association of Realtors, and the Texas State Teachers Association. These

IS IT BIGGER IN TEXAS?

FIGURE 6.1   **Rates of Union Membership**

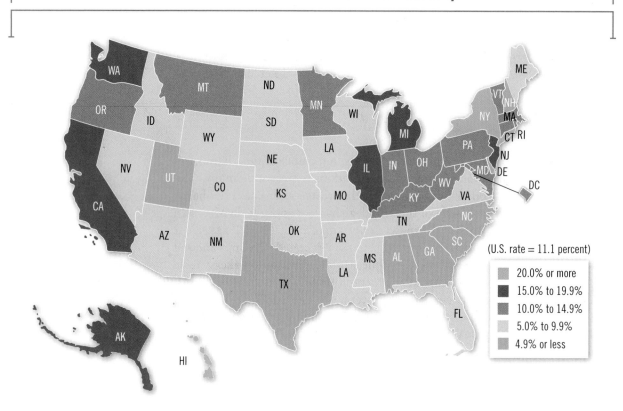

(U.S. rate = 11.1 percent)

	20.0% or more
	15.0% to 19.9%
	10.0% to 14.9%
	5.0% to 9.9%
	4.9% or less

Source: US Bureau of Labor Statistics, 2015 annual averages of union rates as a percentage of the employed population.

 COMMUNICATION:

Which states have more union members?

- Southern states, like Texas, Georgia, South Carolina, and North Carolina, have lower unionization rates than other states.
- States with stable agricultural economies, like California, Washington, and some of the upper plains states, have more union members.
- States whose economies rely on manufacturing, like Michigan, Ohio, and Pennsylvania, have more unionized workers.

 CRITICAL THINKING:

Why are some states union rates lower than other states?

- Texas, like other southern states, allows workers to choose to join a union, while other states like New York require union membership.
- Recent employment gains in construction and agriculture in states like California and Oregon have increased their union participation rates.
- Growth in hospitality and construction trades have boosted New York to the highest unionization rates in the country.

groups represent tens of thousands of industry professionals and millions of dollars in political contributions. Considering their strength, trade associations are frequently successful in the legislature.

LABOR UNIONS

Organized labor first entered Texas state politics in the early 1900s, as the oil and manufacturing boom drew new workers into the state. After World War II, organized labor emerged as a powerhouse, backing winning candidates in several Democratic primary races, including Senator Ralph Yarborough's successful races for the US Senate in the 1950s and 1960s. An endorsement by labor unions meant not only funding but also "boots on the ground" to walk neighborhoods to get out the vote.

However, labor's position has declined in the last few decades. Texas is a "right to work" state, which means an employee can decide whether or not to join a union. In other states, all employees in professions like electrician and construction are required to join unions when they get the job. Due to outsourcing, downsizing, and contracting out, union membership has tapered off. Fewer than 5 percent of workers in Texas are unionized today (see Figure 6.1).

Skilled labor is more organized than less-skilled labor. Why? Skilled labor, like electricians organized by the International Brotherhood of Electrical Workers, have a well-defined constituency and specific interests on a range of policy issues. Groups dedicated to lower-wage workers are not often organized by occupation, like janitors, cleaners, or fast-food workers.[17]

IDENTITY GROUPS

Identity groups represent the interests of specific groups based on such aspects as race, ethnicity, religion, age, sexual orientation, gender, or income. These identity groups form in part because they have been ill-served by the two major political parties or feel underrepresented by the electoral system.[18] National Council of La Raza, the Texas National Association for the Advancement of Colored People (NAACP), the Bangladesh Association of North Texas and other of these identity groups make up a small share of the total number of organized interest groups, but can be influential in state politics. The most pronounced success of these organizations comes in following up on the victories of a social movement through lobbying, litigation, or government monitoring.[19] Building on the fight for bilingual education during the civil rights movements of the 1960s and 1970s, Latino groups challenging the "No Spanish" in public schools rule successfully advocated for legislation at the federal and state level to improve education levels among native Spanish speakers. Student groups, the Mexican American Legal Defense Fund (MALDEF), and the League of United Latin American Citizens (LULAC) continue to pursue their agendas in the courts today.[20]

see for yourself 6.1

Listen to Michael Quinn Sullivan talk about the goals of conservative interest group Empower Texas.

Run out of a basement office in Austin by Craig McDonald, TPJ adopted a "no frills" approach that underscores their interest in good government and public disclosure of political financial information. Says McDonald of his office, which has three employees, one intern, and a budget of $250,000: "Once a year, I bring in cookies, but that's about it."*

SOCIAL RESPONSIBLY: **Should the work of "watchdog" be a government oversight responsibility or an independent group responsibility?**

PUBLIC INTEREST GROUPS

Public interest groups focus on providing quality collective goods, such as environmental protections, natural resource conservation, or consumer safety. Texans for Public Justice (TPJ) advocate for more efficient and transparent government. The group monitors and reports on campaign financing and has filed twenty-two legal actions with the Texas Ethics Commission. TPJ's complaints have led to indictments against former House Speaker Tom DeLay, Governor Rick Perry, and Attorney General Ken Paxton.[21]

SINGLE-ISSUE GROUPS

Are you a member of the NRA or an animal rights group? Single-issue groups like these are interest groups dedicated to one specific issue, often ideological. Texans for Education Reform spent more than $1 million to push for greater state use of vouchers and expanded charter schools in the state. These efforts almost paid off. In 2015, the senate passed legislation to provide $100 million in tax credits to businesses that donated scholarship money to public school students to pay tuition at private schools, but the bill did not pass the House due to conflicts over public funds being used to subsidize private schools.

GOVERNMENT INTERESTS

Local, state, or even national governments often seek the assistance of other governments to advance their goals. State government attempts to influence the federal government. Political scientist Kay Schlozman argues that because the national government often ties financial support to regulations, state, and local governments have an incentive to organize to express their collective interest.[22] Texas has both acted alone and banded together with other states to persuade the US Congress to enact policies, such as expanding transportation funding or easing regulations on carbon emissions. Local government also tries to influence the state government. The City of Houston, for example, has lobbied state officials to reform the city's pension obligations, which the state, not the city, controls.[23]

★ TEXAS TAKEAWAYS

6 Which type of interest group serves the interests of a group of specific industries?

7 What is the primary characteristic of single-issue groups?

8 Explain the differences between government interest groups and public interest groups.

WHAT INTEREST GROUPS DO

Interest groups have a range of resources and strategies that are available to them. Political scientist Amitai Etzioni calls interest groups that represent a broad base of individuals and address a wide range of issues constituency-representing organizations. Their size alone can make them a powerful player on the policymaking scene. Some interest groups are small but have access to significant funding. Interest groups access many resources—

6.4 Describe the types of activities interest groups engage in to pursue their agendas.

membership, funding, leadership, skills—to pursue a menu of tactics to achieve their goals. Political scientists Frank Baumgartner and Bryan Jones argue that interest groups engage in "venue shopping,"[24] looking for opportunities and tactics that will be most persuasive. In this section, we will examine many of these tactics.

EDUCATION

Ever pick up a voter information pamphlet at a laundromat or a coffee shop? You might have noticed a logo with the words, The League of Women Voters of Texas. The league provides details about current elections, researches issues important to Texans, and lets you know where candidates stand on issues—without endorsing a party or candidate. Interest groups often reach out and educate their members or the public at large. They also develop policy and research expertise that makes them useful partners in understanding specific issues.

CITIZEN CAMPAIGNS

When a student at the University of Texas at Austin tried to plan an event in which students "catch" other students wearing "illegal alien" pins around campus,[25] hundreds of students, led by a group called the University Leadership Initiative, protested.[26] Interest groups, like the University Leadership Initiative, often use people power to get their message across. **Grassroots lobbying** involves getting members of the general public who are interested in an issue to contact elected officials to persuade them on an issue. On most any day you visit the Texas capitol, you will see an individual or groups outside protesting a government decision or proclaiming their positions on a range of issues. Group members may also call, e-mail, or meet with members of the legislature. For example, if a funding issue jeopardizes a popular school program in a small town in the middle of the state, the Texas State Teacher's Association can have hundreds of activated residents, upon command, flood the legislature with angry letters or show up at lawmakers' offices in Austin.[27]

grassroots lobbying: getting members of the general public who are interested in an issue to contact elected officials to persuade them on an issue

Not all grass in the grassroots is real, however. Savvy public relations experts make issue advocacy appear as though it originated from the

AstroTurf lobbying: involves manufacturing public support and making it appear as though it was inspired organically by a swell of public opinion

bottom up, but in reality it masks corporate interests. This is referred to as **AstroTurf lobbying**, named after the artificial grass used in Houston's Astrodome. AstroTurf lobbying will often take the form of an "inspired" letter or social media campaign that is in fact manufactured by an organized interest. Texas Senator Lloyd Bentsen coined the term in response to an outpouring of similarly worded letters favoring the insurance industry. Bentsen noted: "a fellow from Texas can tell the difference between grass roots and AstroTurf."[28]

An AstroTurf lobbying campaign is only as effective as it is stealthy. In 1995 State Senator Jim Turner, a Democrat from Crockett and a proponent of House Bill 2766, which tightened regulations on managed care group health care plans, had his district office flooded with calls against the legislation. "Don't tax my health care," callers told the office manager who fielded calls ranging from matter-of-fact to highly abusive. Every time the staff hung up the phone, the red light on the desk phones blinked again. What seemed to be public pandemonium in this sleepy East Texas town was in fact a campaign facilitated by an organization called Citizens for a Sound Economy. The group called locals to persuade them the law was a bad idea and then patched them directly to the senator's office in Austin to flood his phone lines with outraged constituents. The senator angrily denounced the tactic. The head of Citizens for a Sound Economy, however, told reporters, "It's amazing to me that he doesn't want to hear from his constituents, especially if they disagree with him on an issue. If you can't stand the heat, get out of the senate"[29]

electioneering: advertising for or against issues or candidates (radio, mail, Internet, or television), granting endorsements, and raising funds

Austin-based lobbyist Mike Toomey served as a chief of staff to Governor Clements, a Republican legislator, as chief of staff to longtime friend Governor Rick Perry, and finally as a lobbyist for health care and lawsuit reform clients. One journalist noted, "His nickname, Mike the Knife, originally referred to his budget-cutting proposals as a legislator but now conveniently describes his propensity to carve up his enemies."**

ELECTIONEERING

Interest groups also promote their agenda through **electioneering**. Generally, electioneering involves advertising for or against issues or candidates (radio, mail, Internet, or television), granting endorsements, and raising funds. Endorsements from influential groups serve as a cue for voters about where candidates stand on issues (see Figure 6.2).

Interest groups often donate to a politician's campaign by hosting a fundraiser, bundling several contributions from individuals, or "buying a table" at a fundraising event where ticket purchases funnel into candidate fundraising accounts. Interest groups contribute funds by setting up Political Action Committees (or PACs). Interest groups also vet candidates to determine

FIGURE 6.2   **Endorsement Success in 2016 Republican Primaries**

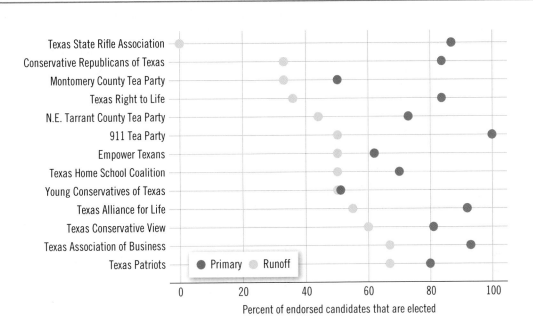

Source: Author compiled data.

 COMMUNICATION:

Which groups endorsed best?[30]

- In the primary, the groups with the highest rate of successful endorsements were the 911 Tea Party, the Texas Association of Business, and the Texas Alliance for Life.

- Some groups such as Empower Texans, the Texas State Rifle Association, and the N.E. Tarrant County Tea Party were effective in the primary (endorsing the winning candidate 60 percent of the time) but were less successful in the runoff.

 CRITICAL THINKING:

Why the variation in success rates?

- The most broadly conservative (religiously oriented and Tea Party-based) groups appear to have the most sway with Republican voters, endorsing the highest percentage of winning candidates in the primary. The signal of these groups to some Republican primary voters was sufficient to get the candidate enough recognition to get to a runoff.

- Groups with narrower political interests, such as Empower Texans, the Texas Home School Coalition, and Texas Right to Life, had fewer endorsement successes, especially in the runoffs, often choosing more extreme ideological candidates.

whether they support or oppose the issues of the group. As one veteran lobbyist representing the powerful Wholesale Beer Distributors of Texas explained, when someone becomes a candidate, he asks of that candidate, "Does he drink an occasional beer or is he high tenor in the Baptist Church choir who denounces demon rum every Sunday?"[31] However, interest groups frequently give funds to both candidates to "hedge their bets"—particularly in close electoral races.

Most scholars find mixed results with respect to spending by interest groups in campaigns, but the consensus is that electioneering can lead to positive outcomes under certain conditions. Campaign donations facilitate access for lobbyists to legislators.[32] However, as predicted by pluralist theory and as with any interest group tactic, electioneering becomes less effective when more interest groups with opposing interests become involved in the political process or when the private issues an interest group is concerned with attract public attention.

According to former Democratic House Speaker Bill Clayton, "If you give $100 to a candidate running for office and somebody else gives $50,000, who's going to have that open door policy a little better?"[33] Yet, this access does not always mean members of the legislature will vote the way of the special interest. Former Democratic Texas House Representative Robert Early noted that a lobbyist for "the Texas Chemical Council helped me when I first got elected, and later sent a message that I wasn't doing very well for him once I was in office. And I sent a message back that I couldn't care less. I found that to be kind of bold and brazen. S—t, I was going to do what I wanted."[34]

LOBBYING THE COURTS, THE LEGISLATURE, AND THE EXECUTIVE BRANCH

Interest groups directly lobby all three branches of government, including the courts, who are also part of the policymaking process. Is the Texas Alcoholic Beverage Commission (TABC) "stifling the Texas craft beer renaissance"? The Institute for Justice thinks so. Joined by three Texas craft brewers, they filed a suit against the TABC for prohibiting brewers from charging beer distributors a fee for the right to sell their beer.[35] Interest groups may file lawsuits or briefs to challenge policies that impact their members.

amicus curiae briefs: a legal filing with relevant opinions or information pertinent to a case that affects a group's interests, even if they are not directly part of the case

Interest groups also file **amicus curiae briefs**, literally "friend of the court" briefs, when they have relevant opinions or information pertinent to a case that affects their interests, even if they are not directly part of the case. The Supreme Court of Texas met in 2015 to consider whether or not the state's funding system for schools was constitutional.[36] Two organizations, the Association of Texas Professional Educators and Pastors for Texas Children, teamed up to file a brief against channeling state funds into private religious schools through a voucher system that diverts funds from public school districts.[37]

Interest groups can also hire lobbyists to communicate directly with the Texas legislature or the executive branch to influence policy. We discuss their strategy in-depth in the next section.

★ TEXAS TAKEAWAYS

9 What is AstroTurf lobbying?

10 What types of activities characterize electioneering?

LOBBYING: THE THIRD HOUSE

When Andrew Jackson, "the people's president," first took office, Americans who were not allowed in the House or Senate chambers poured into the lobby of the White House to ply the president with their requests, hence the term **lobbying**. Lobbyists in Texas are often called the "Third House," the other two being the house and senate. Legislation was considered in the 1930s to require lobbyists to wear uniforms so they could be easily spotted, but the measure was laughed down.[38]

6.5 Explain what lobbying is and how lobbyists serve the interests of those involved.

lobbying: direct communications with members of the legislative or executive branch of government to influence legislation or administrative action

THE ROLE OF LOBBYISTS

As the Texas economy grows and lawmakers deal with increasingly complicated and diverse issues, more and more lobbyists file into Austin to meet with government agencies, state senators and representatives, and their staff (see Figure 6.3). Houston Texans owner Bob McNair, who keeps an array of lobbyists on hand, provided free tickets and food valued up to $9,600 to host Houston lawmakers (including families and guests) who make rules on taxation, traffic, and alcohol sales. Attendees of these events claim the interactions are about building relationships: "We usually talk football," said Houston Representative Harold Dutton.[39]

Individual lobbyists or organizations that employ lobbyists (law firms or other interest groups) must file reports specifying the type of lobbying that they engage in. In 2015, more lobbyists lobbied on behalf of economic interests than on social issues (see Figure 6.4). To better understand the role lobbyists play in economic and social policymaking, we now look at what they do and how they work with government to influence policies.

WHAT LOBBYISTS DO

With the crack of the gavel convening the new legislative session, lobbyists begin the endless round of gratuities. They chat up the staff, offer to buy senators or representatives lunch or drinks, backslap those who respond to flattery, and keep

FIGURE 6.3   **The Number of Lobbyists in Texas**

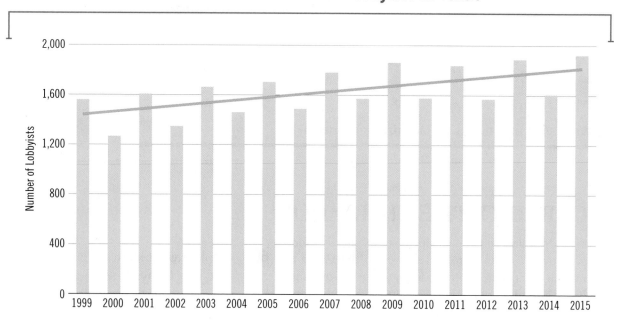

Source: Texas Ethics Commission annual reports. Line represents a predicted linear fit of the trend.

 COMMUNICATION:

How many lobbyists are there in Texas?

- The number of registered lobbyists has increased steadily over the past decade and a half.
- The number of lobbyists grew from 1,560 in 1999 to 1,922 in 2015.

 CRITICAL THINKING:

Why have these numbers increased?

- Years where the legislature is in session (every odd-numbered year) generate more lobbying and more lobbyists. The number of registered lobbyists is higher in years with sessions than in other years.
- The growth in the Texas economy, the expansion of the bureaucracy, and the regulation of industry in the state produce more issues on which groups may wish to lobby.

a respectful distance from fiercely independent legislators.[40] Lobbyists make themselves essential to legislators by seeing to their needs, whether it is to run messages, obtain legal expertise, or just tell a good joke on a gloomy morning.

Shape Legislation.   Lobbyists help shape legislation by bringing issues and possible solutions to the attention of legislators and by providing research,

FIGURE 6.4   **Number of Lobbyists Per Issue in 2015**

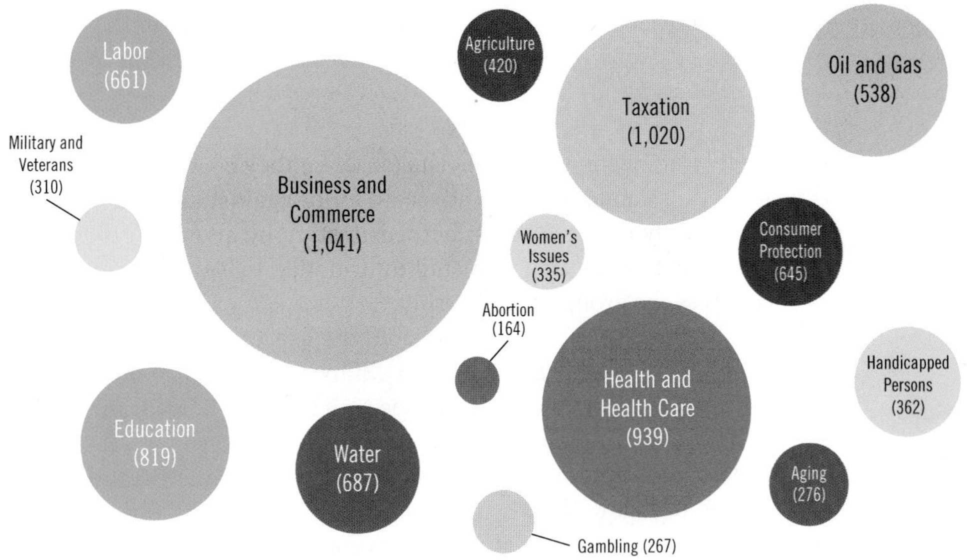

Labor
(661)

Agriculture
(420)

Oil and Gas
(538)

Military and
Veterans
(310)

Taxation
(1,020)

Business and
Commerce
(1,041)

Women's
Issues
(335)

Consumer
Protection
(645)

Abortion
(164)

Handicapped
Persons
(362)

Health and
Health Care
(939)

Education
(819)

Water
(687)

Aging
(276)

Gambling (267)

Source: Texas Ethics Commission annual reports.

 COMMUNICATION:

On what issues do lobbyists lobby?

- More than 2,000 lobbyists lobby on behalf of business, commerce, and taxes.
- Other industry groups also were frequent lobbyers, including agriculture, health and health care, oil and gas, and highways and roads.
- Social issues, like abortion and gambling, or issues involving handicapped persons were lobbied on less frequently than economic issues.

 CRITICAL THINKING:

Why are some issues lobbied on more than others?

- Issues where there is a financial outcome at stake are more likely to have more lobbyists on the payroll.
- Issues involving more technical know-how or specific (sometimes minor) regulations require more lobbyists to communicate with legislators.

technical knowledge, legal expertise, and ideas. The American Legislative Exchange Council, a conservative pro-business group, has contributed ideas to dozens of bill in Texas, such as voter ID laws and "loser pays" rules to put limits on frivolous lawsuits.[41] Lobbyists may also encourage legislators to water down enforcement mechanisms and design rules to favor the group's interests. Former Democratic legislator John Hirschi remembers reviewing a bill during a committee meeting in the Texas House attended by a tobacco lobbyist—who was a friend of the committee chairman. Hirschi recalls, "Well, I just happened to look up and see eye contact between the committee chairman and the lobbyist, who was shaking his head, and that was the end of that bill. It was pretty obvious where the power was—it wasn't in the legislature, it was in the lobby."[42]

Testify at Hearings.   Lobbyists (or those they coach) often testify at hearings on legislation as a way to advocate for or against an issue. Testimony at hearings rarely changes votes, but this testimony allows a group's position to attract media attention, transmit information to legislators, and—importantly—impress the group's membership.[43]

In the 2015 legislative session, the executive director of the Texas Coalition for Affordable Solutions, an alliance of insurance providers, testified in a House Transportation Committee on a texting-while-driving bill that "texting is the king of distraction" and that "it is time to change the culture that considers it acceptable to use electronic devices while behind the wheel."[44] The coalition followed up by introducing fatality figures and comparative data on state bans on distracted driving. The legislature, however, did not pass the bill because many members objected to what they felt was overregulation.

Educate Members.   Most members of the state legislature have general information about the many issues before them, but to write or form an opinion about a bill, they need to know the nitty-gritty details of legislation (such as the capacity of existing oil refineries) that is often beyond their expertise. Lobbyists are experts in their fields—or can access experts—and, although often tilted toward a specific outcome, they can provide statistics, legal language, and technical specifications. This process underscores the symbiosis of lobbying and legislating: members receive valued information and lobbyists have a chance to make their case.

Lobbyists, however, must earn legislators' trust. Former Democratic Representative Mike Martin remarked that lobbyists "who are trustworthy and who are good at communicating their position, as well as being fair in their communication about an issue" become valuable to legislators.[45] Austin lobbyists are keenly aware of the "one lie rule"—furnishing false information to or about a legislator will damage the lobbyists' credibility and they will not be trusted again. Lobbyists also never ask a legislator to vote for or against a bill; this is considered bad form. They explain their position on the bill, answer questions, and suggest how it might hurt or help the legislator back home in the next election.[46]

Comment on Rulemaking.   When the State Board for Educator Certification made a preliminary decision to change its rules and remove teaching experience as a requirement for serving as a school superintendent in 2015, lobbyist

Andrea McWilliams, co-founder of McWilliams Government Affairs Consultants

What makes some lobbyists more effective than others?

There are three key elements to successful lobbying: telling the truth, being present, and persevering despite the circumstances. In my business, your reputation determines your ability to be effective. Elected officials must know that you will tell them the truth about an issue, always. Without a reputation for honesty, it is extremely difficult to be effective. Given Texas's 140-day biennial session, decisions are made very quickly at the Capitol and at all times of the day and night. It is critical to always be "present" at the Capitol during session to ensure you do not miss a moment that could potentially impact your cause.

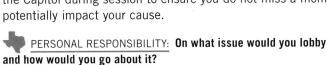 PERSONAL RESPONSIBILITY: **On what issue would you lobby and how would you go about it?**

Kate Kuhlmann made sure the public knew about it. Speaking to the press, she quoted a report that showed superintendents needed more teaching experience, not less. The state board shifted course and voted to keep the teaching requirements.[47] Agencies are required to publicly post proposed rule changes for public comment, and although most in the public don't notice these potential rule changes, lobbyists often do and they can press for or against it.

Build Coalitions.   Interest groups build coalitions to push their mutual agendas forward. When Texas voters were deciding on whether or not to vote to approve Proposition 2 in 2011, which authorized adding $6 billion in dedicated funding to construction and maintenance of the state's water infrastructure, the state's business heavyweights, including the Texas Farm Bureau, the Texas Association of Realtors, and the Texas Association of Builders, banded together to back the proposition. Opposing the measure were conservative elements in the Republican Party who were worried that the amount of bond-issued debt would increase future payments on that debt.[48] Successful coalition building can overcome the opposition by the ruling political party. The measure passed statewide by a small majority of 51 percent.

Monitor Programs.   After legislation is passed and a law is put into effect, interest groups then work with the bureaucracy to monitor the program for compliance and efficiency. The process, called program monitoring, is time-consuming and often requires significant technical skills or training. As the legislature is swamped with pressing work, interest groups often fill this oversight role.

IRON TRIANGLES IN TEXAS

iron triangle: the relationship that forms between interest groups, the legislature, and executive agency regulators in the policy formation and implementation process

issue network: a single-issue iron triangle

revolving door: when agency bureaucrats and legislators leave their jobs to become lobbyists, or vice versa

SOCIAL RESPONSIBILITY:
Is it ethical to have former members of the legislature lobby? What kinds of rules should be in place to restrict this, if any?

Like legislators, bureaucrats in state agencies also rely on lobbyists to provide the detailed information they need to implement their programs effectively. An **iron triangle** describes the cozy relationship that forms between interest groups (lobbyists), the legislature (staffers), and executive agency regulators in the policy formation and implementation process. When iron triangles develop around a single issue, the relationship is often called an **issue network**. These working relationships generally produce policy decisions that are mutually agreeable.

Critics complain that iron triangles and issue networks put public policy into the hands of corporate interests. In 2015, for example, Texas Railroad Commission (TRC) Chairman David Porter sent a letter to the Federal Communications Commission urging the federal agency to process applications for certain Texas pipeline companies. The letter, however, wasn't written by the chairman but by lawyers for Enbridge, one of the pipeline companies stuck in the application muck. A Houston-based government affairs specialist intervened, writing "if you guys could put your letterhead on it and sign it and return to me electronically, our DC guys can add it to the docket for you. Does this work?"[49]

Another cause for concern is the **revolving door**, which occurs regularly when bureaucrats and legislators leave their jobs to become lobbyists, or vice versa (see Table 6.1). Members of the Legislature who have funds in their campaign accounts left can use that money to donate to other politicians. Two of the legislators who retired in 2013 donated more than $500,000 to current members.

The legislature is the perfect training ground for lobbyists—former members have an intimate knowledge of the rules and procedures of the legislature, they have established relationships with key political figures, and they are known figures around the statehouse. About 5 percent of registered lobbyists include former Texas legislators.[50] Former US legislators or federal executive branch officials are banned from lobbying for one year after leaving office—termed the "cooling off period." No ban exists in Texas for former elected officials (see Figure 6.5). However, former agency heads

| TABLE 6.1 | Spinning and Spinning: 2013 Legislators Working in the 2015 Lobby |

HOUSE MEMBER	MAXIMUM VALUE OF LOBBYING CONTRACTS	NUMBER OF CLIENTS	UNUSED CAMPAIGN DONATIONS
Jim R. Pitts (R)	$335,000	9	$493,991
Craig Eland (D)	$250,000	3	$ 70,942
John Davis (R)	$ 90,000	6	$ 0
Lon Burnam (D)	Pro Bono	1	$ 0

Source: Texans for Public Justice. Former legislators may obtain many contracts as lobbyists. The table shows the value of each legislator's largest contract. Former legislators can also contribute unused campaign donations to other candidates making them even more powerful.

IS IT BIGGER IN TEXAS?

FIGURE 6.5   **Number of Years Elected Officials Must Wait Before Becoming Lobbyists**

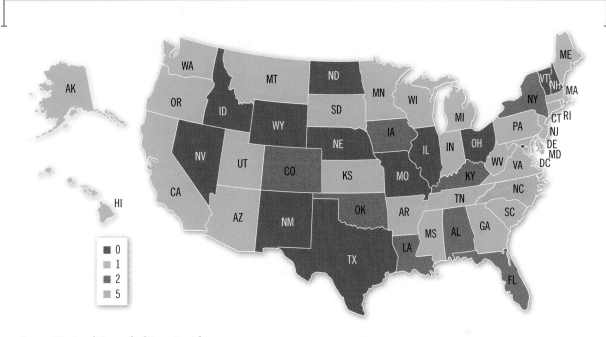

Legend:
- 0
- 1
- 2
- 5

Source: National Council of State Legislatures.

 COMMUNICATION:

Which states ban "revolving door" practices?

- Only a handful of states (twelve), including Texas, do not ban revolving door practices.
- Most states (thirty-seven) have between a one- and two-year ban on former state officials lobbying the state legislature.
- Attempts to pass laws to slow the revolving door in other states have failed recently—New Mexico, Washington, and Illinois all considered but did not pass legislation to ban postemployment lobbying for state officials.

 CRITICAL THINKING:

Why do some states have stricter laws?

- States with a history of prominent scandals involving former legislators or high-profile ethics issues prompt more laws banning lobbying after leaving office.
- Western states with a small government ethos or part-time legislatures are less likely to have bans.

are prohibited for two years to formally "communicate" with their former agency.[51] Similarly, Texas bars state employees who work on procurement or contract negotiations from working for that vendor for two years after leaving the agency.

Companies have also made it a habit to hire well-connected legislators—or their law firms—to work for them in the private sector. For instance, in 2002, two Republican lawmakers, State Senator Jeff Wentworth and Representative Rick Green, worked to persuade the state health department not to require prescriptions for taking Metabolife International's weight-loss products that include ephedrine, a stimulant linked to various medical issues, including addiction, strokes, and seizures.[52] Metabolife was a client of both representatives' law firm. The department ruled that the Metabolife supplement would not require prescription, only strong warning labels.[53]

Government agencies established to regulate an industry sometimes end up being "controlled" by the very industries that the agency was designed to regulate. Political scientists call this **agency capture**. The Texas Railroad Commission (TRC) is a classic example. The oil and gas industries pay serious attention to the work of the commission because the commission sets rules regarding the production of natural resources, well drilling, and physical conservation, and it referees ownership of petroleum.[54] Members of the TRC are elected rather than appointed to office. Oil and petroleum industry groups contributed more than $20 million to candidates for the TRC between 2007 and 2014, 31 percent of the total funds raised—providing a strong motivation to TRC commissioners to be attentive to industry needs.[55]

agency capture: Government agencies "controlled" by the industries that the agency was designed to regulate

★ TEXAS TAKEAWAYS

11 What is lobbying?

12 What type of activities do lobbyists generally do?

13 How is the concept of a revolving door related to agency capture?

SCANDALS AND REFORMS

6.6 Illustrate the role of scandals in shaping interest group politics and reform efforts.

Iron triangles, the revolving door, and agency capture reinforces the public's perception of collusion between government and industry groups, and diminishes confidence in government. But do these institutions necessarily lead to corruption and the undue influence of wealthy industries? The sordid history of ethics scandals in Texas has highlighted some high-profile wrongdoing but has also led to significant political reform. In this section, we examine several of those scandals and the resulting reforms.

SHARPSTOWN SCANDAL

In 1971, Houston businessman and bank owner Frank Sharp pressed powerful state legislators to pass new state bank deposit insurance legislation that would benefit his banks. However, the media leaked a major scandal: to convince Governor Preston Smith, House Speaker Gus Mutscher, Jr., and several legislators to support the legislation, Sharp had promised to grant loans of more than $600,000 from his Sharpstown State Bank to the state officials. The officials denied the charges, but Speaker Mutscher, Representative Shannon, and another staff member were tried in Abilene, convicted, and sentenced to five years' probation.

Some of the key players in the Sharpstown financial scandal that ripped through Texas politics in 1971 were well connected. Pictured here: Speaker of the Texas House Gus Mutscher, Governor Preston Smith, former President Lyndon Johnson, and Lieutenant Governor Ben Barnes.

The Sharpstown affair sparked a call for reform. A group of legislators originally called the "dirty thirty" by a lobbyist in the house gallery called for an internal investigation of Speaker Mutscher.[56] The dirty thirty brought legislation to a halt by voting "no" on any bill and then leaving for Scholz Beer Garden for a long lunch. The dirty thirty thus blocked all bills the chamber considered until ethics legislation was passed.[57] Key among the changes were disclosures of income of elected officials, public access to donor information, and regulation of lobbyists. Voters also backed a drive to "throw the rascals" out in the 1972 elections. The Sharpstown scandal was the first of its kind in Texas—but not the last—to lead to lasting political reform (see Table 6.2).

THE 1991 REFORMS

Two incidents provoked major changes to campaign finance in Texas: Bo Pilgrim passed out checks on the Senate floor, as described in the opening paragraphs of this chapter, and Speaker Gib Lewis, whom columnist Molly Ivins said had the "ethical sensitivity of a walnut," accepted illegal (and unreported) gifts from a law firm such as travel and payment of his tax bills.[58] Many in Texas government realized something had to change.

Indeed, when Lieutenant Governor Bob Bullock gaveled the ethics bill to passage in 1991, he did so with a golf club. The session produced impressive reforms, including a gift reporting law, restrictions on lobbying expenditures,

see for yourself 6.2

The media helps monitor corruption. Watch a report about the amount of money Texas senators have received from the energy industry whose leader these same lawmakers are responsible for interrogating during an investigation into rolling blackouts.

TABLE 6.2   Scandals and Effects

SCANDAL	YEAR	PERSONNEL	REFORM
Frank Sharp, in exchange for passage of favorable banking bills, helped politically connected friends get loans to buy stock in his insurance company for a quick profit.	1971	Governor Preston Smith, Speaker of the House Gus Mutscher, and several members of the legislature	Passage of freedom of information law, open meetings legislation, lobbyist registration, and financial disclosure statements
Speaker Billy Clayton was indicted but acquitted for taking a bribe on behalf of a company. The speaker claimed that he had planned to return the money left in a credenza at the Capitol.	1980	Speaker Billy Clayton	Legislation to limit cash donations to $100
Speaker Gibson "Gib" Lewis was accused of accepting an illegal gift (a lobbyist paid for delinquent property taxes) and not reporting it.	1990	Speaker Gib Lewis	Creation of Texas Ethics Commission, ban on donations inside Capitol, requirements for lawmakers to reveal business dealings
Texas Health and Human Services Department inappropriately awarded contract to Austin-based company with ties to agency staff.	2014	HHSC Commissioner Kyle Janek	Tightened requirements on local government contracting, disclosure requirements for agency personnel with financial interest in contracts

Source: Jay Root, "Long Haul Taking on a History of Scandal." *The New York Times,* January 31, 2013.

SOCIAL RESPONSIBILITY:
Is the legislative reaction to these scandals sufficient to keep interest groups responsible and hold government accountable?

and the establishment of the Texas Ethics Commission. Although the session was a success for ethics, Bullock used the opportunity to rib the ethics bill sponsor, Senator Bob Glasgow, who played golf with lobbyists. Some argued that the reason the gift limit was $50 was so that the golf greens fees would not exceed the $50.[59] Such is the trend in ethics reform: every step toward greater disclosure opens new holes and workarounds for those seeking to beat the new system.

"A SESSION OF ETHICS"

Concerns about "no bid" contracts given out by state agencies prompted Governor Abbott in his first State of the State address (2015) to call on legislators to "dedicate this session to ethics. I want to work with you to strengthen the faith and the trust Texans deserve from us."[60] However, there is an old saying in Texas politics that the only way you'll find bipartisanship in Austin is through unity against ethics reform. The governor managed to push through a few of his reforms but much of his agenda was stalled by disagreement in the legislature. One lawmaker, in an eleventh-hour maneuver, added a clause not requiring legislators to disclose spousal business interests over which the member had no "actual control."[61] This action killed the bill. The chair of the TEC commented that, "If there was any ethics reform, it was in reverse."[62]

Due to unwillingness from legislators and resistance from interest groups, the state still lags behind many others in responsible laws to provide answerability to the public. This places the ability of the system to check the influence of interest groups on shaky ground.

 TEXAS TAKEAWAYS

14 Why is ethics reform so difficult to pass?

OVERSIGHT OF INTEREST GROUPS

US constitutional architect James Madison noted that the best counterweight to the influence of a powerful interest group is other powerful interest groups. Yet, government oversight and laws supervising members of the legislature also have a role in regulating and overseeing the impact of interest groups.

6.7 Outline the ways the state oversees the interactions of interest groups and state officials.

TEXAS ETHICS COMMISSION

Since 1991, the Texas Ethics Commission (TEC) has served as the primary agency for regulating and enforcing laws related to interest group lobbying and campaign disclosure. The TEC has eight commissioners who are appointed by the governor, lieutenant governor, and speaker of the Texas House.

Among the TEC's primary duties are collecting and maintaining records related to political fundraising, campaign spending, political lobbying activity, and the personal financial disclosure statements by state elected officials and officers. In practice, anyone can consider themselves a lobbyist, but Texas law requires an individual who receives more than $1,000 in salary from an organization or who spends more than $500 in a calendar year for lobbying to register as a lobbyist. Lobbying expenditures include payments, loans, gifts, meals, awards, or other entertainment.

Lobbyists are also required to detail any expenditure on behalf of a state officer or employee, their spouses, and their children. If a lobbyist spends more than $114 for entertainment, food and beverages, lodging, or transportation, this information must be recorded.[63] Gifts are not to exceed $500 in a given year to any individual official and any gift with a value over $50 must be reported (see Table 6.3). The state punishes violators through criminal penalties or civil sanctions. Depending on the nature of the infraction, the fines range from $4,000 to $10,000 and the criminal punishments are either misdemeanors or

| TABLE 6.3 | Interesting Gifts to Legislators, 2011–2015 |

LEGISLATOR	GIFT
Dennis Paul	An International Space Station model
Jane Nelson	Battleship Texas Foundation commemorative poster
Brian Birdwell	Glass eagle head
Four Price	Helicopter model
Kelly Hancock	Model bulldozer
Jim Pitts	Framed and signed LIVESTRONG manifesto poster

Source: Texas Ethics Commission.

SOCIAL RESPONSIBILITY:
Should legislators be allowed to accept gifts? What limits, if any, should be placed on gifts to legislators?

second-degree felonies.[64] The TEC hears complaints related to these disclosure requirements and has the authority to issue fines for violations. The TEC also issues advisory rulings. These rulings do not have the force of law but are influential in future court proceedings (see Figure 6.6).

Despite the laws requiring full disclosure, lobbyists have found loopholes. One way this happens is by splitting restaurant checks. After a pricy steak dinner with cocktails and expensive wine, lobbyists may skirt disclosure requirements by splitting the ticket and staying under the dollar limit that would require naming the specific lawmaker wined and dined. In one instance, at the end of the 2013 legislative session, a $2,241 dinner for the House Calendars Committee at a famed Austin steakhouse was paid for by 65 different credit cards. The bill indicated that 121 people were in attendance but does not detail how many were lawmakers.[65] Legislation to require disclosure of the state official's name whose tab was picked up if it totaled over $50 died in committee in 2015.

You, as a member of the public, also have a role in ethics oversight. New technology has enabled citizens and activists to have access to campaign finance and lobbying records. The number of complaints in which the TEC reported a fine has increased in recent years. This is likely due to the fact that Texans now have online access to complaints through the Texas Ethics Commission website.

Because moving forward on an enforcement action is difficult for the TEC, observers of Texas government worry that the TEC is a toothless organization. Six of the eight members need to agree in order to fine or punish any individual thought to have violated the law. Because the members of the commission are appointed by the state's leading elected officials, these political interests have a significant say in how the rules are enforced.[66]

Even when the TEC fines an individual, the courts can reverse the decision. In response to a federal judge's dismissal of a fine against a lobbyist who had failed to register, TEC Commissioner Jim Clancy wrote to Paul Hobby, the chair of the TEC, to express his opinion that the agency must stop issuing

FIGURE 6.6   **Number of TEC Advisory Rulings**

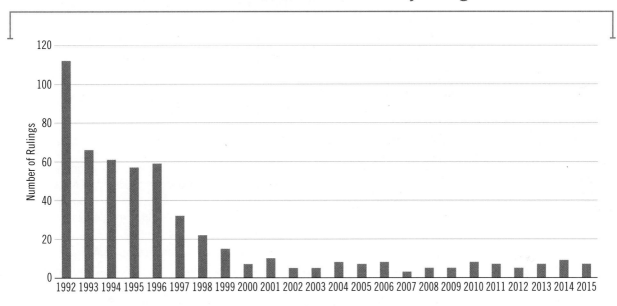

Source: Texas Ethics Commission.

 COMMUNICATION:

How many advisory rulings have been issued over time?

- Since the agency's inception in 1991, the number of rulings has decreased steadily.

- From a high of 112 in 1992 to a low of seven in 2015, the commissioners have ruled on fewer and fewer cases per year.

 CRITICAL THINKING:

Why has the number of opinions declined?

- Fewer rulings are likely due to previous settlement of legal questions or greater legislative oversight of ethics and attention to disclosure issues.

- Frustrated with their inability to enforce the rulings of the TEC, the commissioners may be issuing fewer rulings.[67]

orders if "those with extraordinary resources" can spend hundreds of thousands of dollars to challenge or delay paying a $10,000 fine.[68]

Yet, the courts also broker settlements between the TEC and the individuals it fines. When the TEC fined Texas Supreme Court Chief Justice Hecht for failing to disclose that he had reduced his legal fee while working for US Supreme Court nominee Harriet Miers, the courts eventually settled the case and forced Hecht to pay. However, while the TEC had fined him $29,000, the court-brokered settlement required the chief justice to pay only $1,000. Some argued

GREAT TEXAS POLITICAL DEBATES
Enforcing Ethics Violations

The chair of the Texas Ethics Commission came under intense fire in a hearing in 2016 over concern that the commission's actions were "haughty," "arrogant," and politically motivated. One point of contention was the 4½ year investigation of the conservative group Empower Texans and its President Michael Quinn Sullivan.[69] Several senators in the hearing expressed concern that the commission's authority was unchecked. "If you're untouchable, we've got a problem," charged Senator Brian Birdwell, Republican of Granbury. The chair, himself a former lawmaker, shot back that "the only guidepost we have is the law."[70] Other senators suggested the commission take a new direction by focusing less on penalizing state officials for paperwork errors and more on improving compliance. An attorney for the commission responded, "Y'all are going to have to decide whether you want these laws enforced or not. There

are enough liars in politics that we ought to know who's telling the lies."[71]

🔸 SOCIAL RESPONSIBILITY: **Should the TEC's authority be limited?**

YES: The TEC is wasting resources by nitpicking minor problems with ethics reports. Burdening members of the legislature and political organizations with unnecessary paperwork can cripple political actors with bureaucratic details and stifle free speech. The TEC has overstepped its mandate by injecting itself into the politics of the state.

NO: The bedrock of representative democracy is accountability. The TEC is the only government organization empowered to demand oversight of the actions of elected officials and political organizations. They need wider latitude, not narrower, to investigate and enforce ethics rules in Texas.

that the commission let Hecht "off the hook" and that the fine was coming years late and "$28,000 light."[72]

RECUSAL

State lawmakers are not prohibited from authoring or voting on legislation that may benefit them so long as it benefits all others in the same way. After all, it is difficult for legislators to avoid participating in issues in which they have some personal stake, sometimes on purpose and sometimes by accident. Representative Charlie Geren, Republican from Fort Worth, authored legislation aimed at lowering the renewal fees for bars and restaurants. Geren, owner of Fort Worth's Railhead Smokehouse barbeque restaurant, stated he was not sure whether the measure would have affected his restaurant (the measure passed but was vetoed by the governor).

recuse: decide not to participate in legislative activity as an elected official

Legislators, however, frequently **recuse** themselves—elect not to participate in decisions—from issues in which they have a personal stake. However, they are not required to recuse themselves if they have a conflict of interest. Those who argue against recusal suggest that legislators who have interests are uniquely situated to understand the ramifications of a particular policy issue and should be allowed to be directly involved.

DISCLOSURE

Texas has disclosure requirements for officials who have partial or total shares in a business entity. States are close to evenly divided on requirements for conflict of interest disclosures: twenty-nine states (including the District of Columbia) have it and twenty-two states do not. Although there may be some disagreement about recusal, Texans largely agree that **disclosure** of lawmakers' financial ties is critical for citizens to understand the possible financial conflicts of interest among legislators. Every year, lawmakers and appointed public officials are required to report details about their personal finances. Yet there are problems with the current disclosure laws. Texas does not require lawmakers' spouses to do the same. Some senators, led by Senator Joan Huffman, led the charge to exempt spouses from reporting requirements after a complaint filed with the TEC alleged that the senator filed "false" information by failing to list more than thirty-five nightclub businesses in which her husband had a stake.[73] Senator Huffman eventually voluntarily updated her disclosure forms to include her husband's businesses.

disclosure: the filing of a report that includes details about lawmakers' personal finances or business dealings

 TEXAS TAKEAWAYS

15 What is main function of the Texas Ethics Commission?

16 What is disclosure and what kinds of disclosures does Texas law require?

 THE INSIDER VIEW

An old Texas saying goes "if you can't drink their [interest groups'] liquor, take their money, and vote against them in the morning, you don't belong in Austin." Yet in a state as large and complex as Texas, interest groups with all sorts of political and policy interests battle one other. Small ideological groups take on larger industry groups. Large business associations take on other large business associations. These interactions are played out across all levels and points of government in Texas as powerful groups capture agencies and cajole lawmakers. In response, Texas has gone through several cycles of reform. Many of the most egregious problems have been addressed and practices are in place to provide limits to and disclosure of lobbying activities. Yet the struggle of reformers against those who would like to work around the system is likely to continue—although as Molly Ivins wrote, our elected representatives may continue to "dance with the special interests what brung'em."[74]

★▬ TEXAS TAKEAWAYS

1 Interest groups attempt to influence government for benefit of their members through legislation, rules, or actions that are aligned with their cause

2 In a pluralist theory, powerful groups are kept in check and no single group dominates. In elite theory, powerful groups with greater resources have more influence.

3 Transactional theory proposes that public policy is bought and sold like a commodity to the highest bidder

4 Free riders are people who obtain the benefits without paying the cost. Individuals who do not join groups still receive the benefits of groups that work for a collective good.

5 Selective benefits, such as material, solidarity, purposive benefits, encourage people to join interest groups.

6 Trade associations serve the interests of a specific industry.

7 Single interest groups are dedicated to addressing one specific issue, usually an ideological issue.

8 Public interest groups focus on providing quality collective goods, while government interest groups attempt to impact other local and state governments or the federal government.

9 AstroTurfing is advocacy that appears as though it originated from the bottom up, but in reality masks corporate interests.

10 Electioneering involves advertising for or against issues or candidates (radio, mail, Internet, or television), granting endorsements, and raising funds.

11 According to Texas law, lobbying consists of "direct communications" with members of the legislative or executive branch of government to influence legislation or administrative action.

12 Lobbyists shape legislation by testifying at hearings, educating members of the legislature, commenting on rule making, building coalitions for or against policies, monitoring enacted programs, and engaging in working with agencies.

13 A revolving door allows individuals to move between an agency and industry, leading to an agency being "controlled" by an industry.

14 Lawmakers dislike changing the rules of the game during the game.

15 The Texas Ethics Commission regulates and enforces laws related to interest group lobbying and campaign disclosure.

16 Disclosure is the filing of a report that includes details about lawmakers' personal finances or business dealings.

KEY TERMS

agency capture
amicus curiae briefs
AstroTurf lobbying
disclosure
electioneering
elite theory
free rider problem
grassroots lobbying
interest group

iron triangle
issue network
lobbying
pluralist theory
private interest groups
public interest groups
recuse
revolving door
selective incentives
transactional theory

PRACTICE QUIZ

1. The theory that holds that political power is distributed broadly among many organized interests who compete with each other for control of public policy, is called

   a. New institutionalism
   b. Separation of powers
   c. Pluralism
   d. Devolution

2. Individuals who obtain benefits from organized interests without paying the costs to get those benefits are called

   a. Partisans
   b. Lobbyists
   c. Smoke-screeners
   d. Free riders

3. All of the following are forms of selective benefits **except**

   a. Monetary
   b. Material
   c. Solidary
   d. Emotional

4. Which of the following is **not** a type of interest group?

   a. Trade associations
   b. The Presidential Cabinet
   c. Identity groups
   d. Public interest groups

5. As of 2015, there are how many lobbyists in Texas?

   a. 253
   b. 786
   c. 1389
   d. 1922

6. The "iron triangle" consists of all of the following, **except**

   a. Interest groups
   b. Legislators
   c. Political parties
   d. Agency regulators

7. Any formal organization or group that seeks to publically or privately promote a common cause is called an interest group.

   a. True
   b. False

8. Lobbyists must record gift expenditures over $50.

   a. True
   b. False

9. A good lobbyist knows when to ask a legislator to vote for or against a bill.

   a. True
   b. False

10. Members of the legislature are required to recuse themselves if legislation considered presents a conflict of interest.

    a. True
    b. False

[Answers: C, D, A, B, D, C, A, A, B, B]

7 THE LEGISLATURE

"You gave me your word!" shouted Republican Representative Jonathan Strickland into the face of fellow Republican lawmaker Byron Cook as Texas House security guards rushed to the scene and managed to separate the two. Strickland, furious that his abortion restriction bill did not make it into the 2015 House schedule, stormed off to confront the three House Republicans who had sided with Democrats. Cook claimed that he had only promised to get the bill out of committee.[1] The conflict between these legislators in 2015 was just the tip of the iceberg. In the past 100 years, the legislators have erupted into fistfights, waved around firearms (one shooting off blanks at the ceiling), and, bored by interminable debates, passed amusing resolutions such as one in 1973 requiring lawbreakers to give twenty-four hours' notice before committing a crime.[2]

But legislative politics is not all fun and fighting. The legislature passes laws that affect every part of the lives of Texans, from how much sales tax they pay to the quality of their schools to the condition of their roads. With a budget that tops $209 billion every two years, everyone has a stake in the game.

To examine the unusual but important world of the Texas legislature, we first analyze its function and the tasks legislators carry out. We examine the structure of the legislature and compare it to those in other states. We outline the legislative process, paying special attention to the scramble to beat the calendar and how political struggles are resolved within this framework. Finally, we examine the demographic mix of members and changes in recent years and how legislators cope with these changes.

LEARNING OBJECTIVES

7.1 Identify the functions of the legislature and legislators.

7.2 Compare the strength of the Texas legislature to other state legislatures.

7.3 Describe the organizational structure and leadership of the legislature.

7.4 Outline the legislative process.

7.5 Assess how legislative tools are used to speed up or slow down legislation.

7.6 Explain how legislators represent their constituents demographically.

● The swirl of the legislative session, called a "circus" by some observers, goes by in a 140-day blur but is essential to making laws for the state.

🤠 THE FUNCTIONS OF THE LEGISLATURE AND LEGISLATORS

7.1 Identify the functions of the legislature and legislators.

bicameral legislature: a legislative body with two houses or chambers

The grand wings of the enormous Texas Capitol—which appears pink because of its "Sunset Red" limestone color—house the 181 members of the Texas legislature every odd-numbered spring in Austin. Like Congress, the Texas legislature (called the "Lege" by observers) is a **bicameral legislature**, meaning it has two houses or chambers: the house of representatives and the senate. French political theorist Montesquieu first conceived of this division as a means of ensuring that no one chamber dominated the other. The "dissimilarity" of the chambers provided that the minority would have a voice not shouted down by the majority.

POWERS OF THE LEGISLATURE

general law: law where the bill potentially affects all Texans

local law: law that only affect units of government at the local level

special law: law that exempt businesses or individuals from state laws

resolutions: legislation that conveys the will of the chamber

The Texas legislature's chief responsibility is to create and pass legislation. Laws establish and reinforce economic interactions, resolve disputes between individuals or groups, and protect individual rights and liberties. The legislature's laws dictate everything from the sales tax you pay on cars, to the type of insurance you are required to carry, to how many hours of training your hairstylist needs to be certified.

The state legislature introduces bills on a wide variety of matters (see Table 7.1). Legislation considered by the legislature can be a **general law** if the bill potentially affects all Texans, a **local law** if it affects only units of government at the local level (often carried out by a legislator at the request of local government leaders), or a **special law** if it exempts businesses, organizations, or individuals from state laws. Three bills filed by El Paso Democratic Representative Mary Gonzales illustrate these different types: a general law filed to prevent discrimination against gender identity in public schools, a local bill to expand the jurisdiction of certain border county municipalities, and a special bill to exempt certain farm vehicles owned by farmers' cooperatives from registration fees.

In addition to bills that carry the force of law (after being signed into law), legislators debate and pass **resolutions** that convey the will of the chamber. These are distinct from bills but often follow similar procedures for passage.

- *Joint resolutions* are used to propose amendments to the Texas Constitution or to ratify proposed amendments to the US Constitution.

- *Concurrent resolutions* are passed separately but at the same time by both chambers and are used to give directions to state agencies on procedural issues such as legislative adjournment or special sessions initiation.

- *Simple resolutions* are passed by a single chamber and are used for adopting or changing rules of procedure or expressing congratulations

TABLE 7.1	**Odd Laws Proposed in the 84th Legislature**
HB 483	Create a Fort Knox-like repository for state gold bullion
SB 191	Prohibit ownership or control of management of the Alamo complex by a foreign entity, such as the United Nations
HB 92	Make Bowie knives legal to carry
HB 35	Make the cowboy hat the official hat of the state
HB 161	Allow authorities to house prisoners in tents
SB 1721	Add Alamo specialty license plates that include the word "Remember" at the bottom
HB 1751	Exempt Texas from federal laws that violate the state constitution

Source: Allan Turner and Brian Reynolds. 2015. "Texas Legislators Introduced Some Odd Bills." *Houston Chronicle,* March 16.

 CRITICAL THINKING:

HBs are house bills and SBs are senate bills. Where do the oddest bills originate? Is this what you would expect given the difference between the two chambers?

or condolences. Simple resolutions are also used ceremonially to highlight Texas's history or to promote local tourism, such as declaring the state dish (chili), the state fruit (red grapefruit), or the wedding capitol of Texas (Dripping Springs).

The legislature is also tasked with overseeing the implementation of the laws passed in previous sessions to ensure that the programs and policies are operating effectively. Oversight may include program evaluation for executive agencies, periodic audits of legislative spending, or regulation of the rules implemented by executive agencies. The legislature can hold hearings to investigate abuse, mismanagement, or abuse of power, typically of executive agencies.[3] Lawmakers lashed officials from the Department of Family and Protective Services in 2016 for an unexpected increase in reported cases of abuse and for a shortage of foster care beds.[4] Heads roll when investigations lead to the removal or impeachment of officials. With the governor's consent, two-thirds of the senate can remove an appointed official. The house can also initiate impeachment by bringing charges against an executive or judicial branch official, and the senate sits as the jury where a two-thirds majority is needed to convict.

TEXAS HOUSE V. SENATE

Although both chambers serve the same general function, they retain important differences. The larger number of members and the shorter length of term, in theory, make the Texas House of Representatives a more representative and responsive body than the Texas Senate. Like the US Constitution, the Texas Constitution designed the legislature with the idea that the house would be more accountable to popular will and the senate would be more deliberative.

House.   The Texas House is made up of 150 members, elected for two-year terms. The entire membership of the House is up for election every two years. The Texas Constitution requires members of the Texas House to be at least twenty-one years of age, a citizen of Texas for two years prior to election, and a resident of the district from which he or she is elected one year prior to election.

Senate.   By contrast, the Texas Senate has thirty-one members, elected for four-year terms from districts that carve up the state. One half of the membership of the senate is elected every two years, so the entire chamber is not up in any single election cycle. As outlined in the Texas Constitution, a senator must be twenty-six years of age, a citizen of Texas five years prior to being elected, and a resident of the district from which he or she is elected one year prior to the election.

Responsibilities.   Similar to the US Constitution, the Texas Constitution grants the house responsibilities that the framers believed belonged in the hands of the people, while the senate serves as the vehicle for protecting minority interests against the tyranny of the majority. So, for example, all revenue bills must originate in the house, so that the power of the purse (funding policies) remains in the hands of the people. The house and senate take turns originating the budget bill every other session.

The senate, by contrast, is granted responsibilities that require more deliberation, such as confirming or rejecting all of the governor's appointments to state boards and commissions. The senate confirms a nominee through a two-thirds vote. Hometown senators (senators from the hometown of the nominee) are given some authority to reject a nominee, but this is usually not necessary because an astute governor will clear the nominee with the hometown senator before submitting his or her nomination. Most nominations are confirmed because problems are smoothed out early as part of the senate's more deliberative process. Indeed, when one senator from Houston was going to "bust" (reject) a nominee because she was the daughter of the *Houston Chronicle*'s publisher who had not supported the senator's election, Lieutenant Governor Ramsey arranged a "come-to-Jesus" meeting with the senator to strongly persuade him to change his mind. After the meeting the senator changed his vote so that the nominee was confirmed.[5]

Texas Representative Jason Villalba speaks passionately during a house debate on abortion.

SOCIAL RESPONSIBILITY: **What makes a good legislator in your opinion? How might we judge legislator performance?**

CASEWORK

Legislators also have extra tasks outside the legislature that they must attend to if they are to succeed in future legislative sessions and win reelection. Between sessions, legislators and their staff spend time on **casework**, assisting constituents in their districts with specific requests, often acting as facilitators, go-betweens, or advocates. For instance, a constituent may request help applying for a state grant, locating a specific government benefit, or seeking relief from a state agency.[6] Legislators also meet with citizens, lobbyists, and organized groups to facilitate (or to stop) legislation of interest to the district. For example, early in the 2001 legislative session, Senator Van de Putte met with lobbyists representing teachers, prison guards demanding a pay raise, and leather-clad bikers who wanted to exempt alcohol carried in saddlebags from the state's open-container law.[7]

casework: legislators and their staff assist constituents in their districts with specific requests

POSITION TAKING

Legislators must engage in what political scientist David Mayhew identifies as position taking and credit claiming in order to win reelection. Position taking involves members proclaiming where they stand on certain issues or policies. Former Speaker of the Texas House Pete Laney would say "Members vote your districts" before every vote as a reminder not to forget why the legislators were in Austin in the first place. He commented after he left office: "Pay attention to the process, pay attention to your constituents, and do what you think is right for the State of Texas. Sometimes you've got to weigh that: what's right for your constituents and what's good for the whole population."[8]

Indeed, some legislators act as **trustees** of their constituency, voting in accordance with their interpretation of what their district would want. Other legislators act as **delegates**, where the member is simply a mouthpiece for the wishes of their constituency. Speaker Laney once noted, "The first time I ever voted in 1973 on a real controversial bill, I worried about it, and I finally said, 'This is not worth it. I'm going to vote for what I think is right for my constituents.' Thirty years later, I was still there. There's no way you can worry about getting reelected and do what's right."[9]

Legislators often craft an image to appeal to voters to gain their trust, which they then use to explain and justify decisions made in Austin. Political scientist Richard Fenno calls this development the "home style" of legislators. The way in which legislators are elected encourages a close relationship between the member and the citizens, fostering accountability. Members are elected through single-member districts that are shaped by legislative redistricting, often through gerrymandering (see Chapter 5).

see for yourself 7.1

Listen to past legislative leaders discuss their decision-making process while in office.

trustee: a legislator who votes in accordance with their interpretation of what his or her district would want

delegate: a legislator who is simply a mouthpiece for the wishes of his or her constituency

CREDIT CLAIMING

Credit claiming occurs when legislators point out the positive things they have done while in office. Most members produce newsletters for their constituents

FIGURE 7.1   **Issues Tweeted about in 84th Legislature Using #txlege Hashtag**

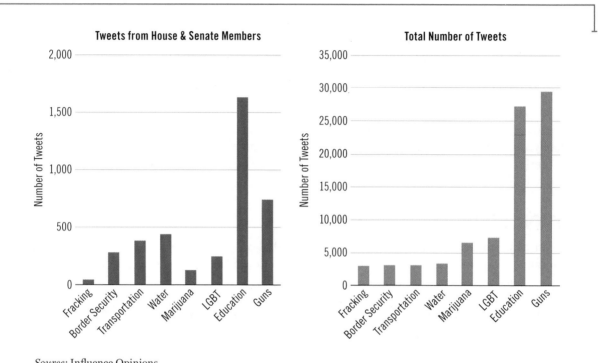

Source: Influence Opinions.

CRITICAL THINKING: **What issues were most Tweeted about in 2015? Why do some issues get more attention?**

and make frequent trips home for town hall-style meetings. This communication creates a pathway to accountability.

In recent years, legislators have begun utilizing social media to make sure their constituency follows their achievements. The #txlege hashtag has become a one-stop shop for breaking news and instant opinions from legislators and Capitol watchers, including journalists and lobbyists (see Figure 7.1).[10] Representative Wayne Christian notes "The reason I got involved in social media then is because, back home—and I lived 300 miles away—while I was up in Austin working a ten-month session, my opponent is saying 'Hey, where's your rep? He's not working for you,' so I started posting pictures of where I was and what I was doing, so I could prove I was working hard for them in that ten-month session we had."[11] The number of tweets from legislators rose 133 percent between the 2013 and 2015 legislative sessions.

★ TEXAS TAKEAWAYS

1 How many total individuals serve in the Texas legislature? How many in each chamber?

2 Explain the difference between a trustee and a delegate as a representative function?

🤠 THE TEXAS LEGISLATURE IN CONTEXT

Political scientists classify legislatures as "strong" or "weak" based upon whether they have access to adequate resources to address key issues. "Strong" legislatures consist of full-time, professional, well-paid legislators, year-round or annual sessions, plentiful legislative staff, and competitive elections. By many of these standards, Texas has a "weak" legislature—due to the length of its sessions, salary, staff, and boards that facilitate the legislative process.

7.2 Compare the strength of the Texas legislature to other state legislatures.

THE LEGISLATIVE SESSION

The Texas legislature meets biennially (every two years) in January of odd-numbered years. In this, Texas is unique among large states. Just three other smaller states have biennial legislative sessions. In the nineteenth century, when travel was more difficult and the public distrusted corrupt state legislatures, many states switched to a biennial system. However, between 1960 and 1970, as state budgets became larger and legislation more complicated, most legislatures switched back to annual sessions.[12]

Many watchers of Texas politics believe the state legislature should hold annual rather than biennial sessions. As the population has increased and the economy has diversified, the legislature must continually address a broader spectrum of issues. Indeed, the number of bills filed has risen sharply, and yet the percentage of bills passed has declined—suggesting that the legislature may not be able to keep up with all the issues the members wish to address (see Figure 7.2). Between 1945 and 1975, however, Texas voters—wary of powerful government—rejected five constitutional amendments calling for a switch to an annual session.

Each **regular session** of the Texas legislature meets for 140 days, longer than most states with set lengths (see Figure 7.3). In addition, the governor can call a **special session** on any issue he or she would like the legislature to address (see Chapter 8). Special sessions are limited to thirty days. These sessions

regular session: legislative session meeting for 140 days in January of odd-numbered years

special session: legislative session that can be called by the governor on any issue the governor decides requires attention

FIGURE 7.2 **Bills Passed by Session**

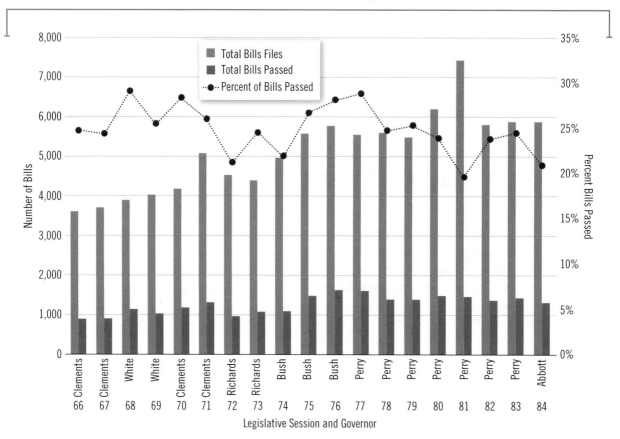

Source: Data taken from Legislative Reference Library. Bars represent total bills filed and passed by house and senate. Line represents percent passed of those filed.

 COMMUNICATION:

What are the trends in laws introduced and passed over time?

- The total bills filed has risen sharply since the 66th legislature to the present, from 3,500 to more than 6,000.

- This growth (more than 70 percent) has exceeded the growth in the state population during that time.

- The percent of bills passed (out of bills filed) is lower than a decade ago.

 CRITICAL THINKING:

Why the difference between legislation filed and legislation passed?

- More students in public schools and state universities, an expanding criminal justice system, booming populations, and a growing economy all give way to a rising need for new laws.

- Lower percentages of bills passed in the last few sessions reflect the increasing dominance of conservatives, who favor fewer laws and less regulation, in the legislature.

IS IT BIGGER IN TEXAS?

FIGURE 7.3   **Length of Legislative Session**

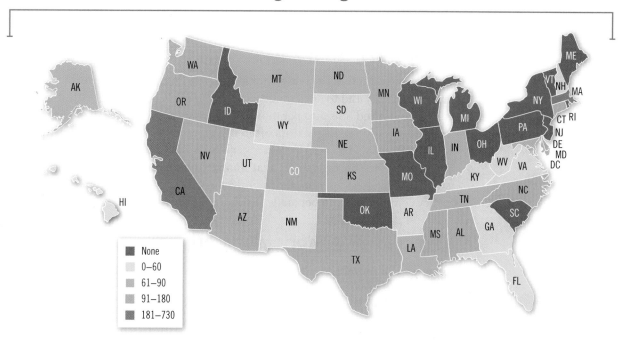

Source: National Council of State Legislatures. Number indicates the maximum number of legislative days or, if the session had different lengths for different years, the longer of the two session dates. "None" signals that the chamber decides how long the session lasts.

 COMMUNICATION:

How long do legislative sessions last?

- Most states' legislative sessions last less than 100 days, especially states with smaller populations.

- Texas has a long session compared to other states, but Texas only meets once every two years, while most states meet annually.

- Fourteen states have no limit on the length of the session—legislators in these states agree on the length of the session instead of having this set by law.

 CRITICAL THINKING:

Why is Texas an outlier?

- Texans decided long ago that a shorter legislative session every two years should produce a smaller government footprint.

- While other states can decide to extend their legislative sessions, the Texas Constitution limits the legislators' ability to run longer than the 140-day session.

are called roughly every other legislative session (as we will see in Chapter 9) and allow the legislature to address issues that were not addressed or settled in a regular session, emergencies, or legislative "bellyflops" on an important issue.[13] The end of the legislative session is called ***sine die***, Latin for "without day," during which the body adjourns, accompanied by much rejoicing of weary legislators and exhausted staffers.

sine die: the end of a legislative session

LEGISLATIVE STAFF

Critics complain that the budget for staff salaries is too low to hire an adequate number of staff and to keep quality staff from taking other opportunities. Senators are allotted $38,000 per month and house members $13,250 each month to run their offices. Legislators often use campaign funds to supplement staff salaries, but this too may indebt legislators to organized interests by forcing greater reliance on the groups that finance their campaign.[14] This insufficient staffing creates an opening for organized interest groups to step in to provide policy competency and persuade legislators to vote with them on legislation.

LEGISLATIVE BOARDS AND COUNCILS

Some of the powers of the legislature are siphoned off to several boards and councils, all of which serve important roles in the Texas legislature. The Legislative Budget Board (LBB) writes the first draft of the state budget, setting the stage for future debate. The lieutenant governor and speaker of the house co-chair the LBB. The remaining eight members are appointed by these two from their respective chambers. Because many legislators may not have the expertise necessary to draft bills, the Legislative Council assists in writing legislation, conducting research, and providing legal support services. The Legislative Council provides the technical nuts and bolts evaluations of policy options in state government to back up the substantive interest of the members of the executive and legislative branches. These boards are a way to compensate for a part-time legislature.

SALARY

Despite the size of its economy and population, Texans belief in small government keeps legislators' annual salary at $7,200—the lowest set legislative salary in the nation. Legislators also receive a $190 per diem for meals and travel, a total of $26,600 for daily expenses for a regular session. The per diem pay also is fixed to the amount lobbyists can spend on lawmakers before they have to submit a detailed expense report—that threshold is $114 (60 percent of the per diem). Legislators are expected to have other jobs because lawmaking in Texas is not designed to be a full-time occupation. Professionalized legislatures (full-time, year-round sessions) in other states tend to pay legislators more. Members can use campaign accounts to supplement their lifestyles but not to pay

GREAT TEXAS POLITICAL DEBATES
Should Texas Have Annual Legislative Sessions?

A vestige of Reconstruction era distrust of government, the Texas Constitution limits the length of the legislative session to minimize the scope of government. The state has grown immensely in the intervening 200 years. The population has exploded, the economy larger than all but twelve nations, and the needs of the state have diversified—all developments of a major modern state.

SOCIAL RESPONSIBILITY: **Should Texas switch to an annual legislative session?**

NO: There is an old saying in Texas politics: "no man, woman, child or their property are safe when the legislature is in session." With a limited window of time to meet and legislate, the legislature is less likely to expand government and intervene into the lives (and wallets) of Texans. Representative Donna Campbell argued, "It makes us look less like Washington [DC]."[15]

YES: In a massive, complex, and growing state like Texas, a biennial session for only four months is not a sufficient amount of time to craft, consider, and confer on important legislation. Legislation may be hastily written, poorly researched, or insufficiently debated. This leads to consistently unfinished business and no policy progress on a range of critical, longstanding issues like the structure of the tax system, education financing, or border security. More frequent opportunities to legislate would lessen the partisan friction caused by short sessions.

MAYBE: Texas could hold shorter annual sessions with the possibility of extension if necessary.

themselves a salary. Senator Trey Fraser spent more than $300,000 from his campaign account maintaining a personal airplane, paying country club fees, buying suits, and traveling to faraway locations like Hawaii and Buenos Aires.[16]

The relatively low pay makes serving as a legislator easier if she is wealthy enough to self-finance. But the vast majority of legislators hold day jobs. This can create conflicts of interest. Senator Rodney Ellis of Houston worked for or owned several firms that have underwritten billions of dollars in bonds in the state, serving as an intermediary between those issuing the bond (the state) and those selling the bonds to buyers.[17]

INCUMBENCY AND TURNOVER

Low salaries and a biennial session can potentially lead to high **turnover** rates among legislators. Too much turnover can be a problem, leading to a loss of **institutional memory**, an understanding of how a complex organization runs. Representative Garnet Coleman of Houston argued that "Your power comes from your knowledge of the subject matter. Ultimately, that's the thing with seniority: It's being around long enough to actually learn something."[18] The Texas legislature has strong continuity and institutional memory because most elections for Texas legislators are won by the incumbents (see Figure 7.4). In the 84th Legislative Session (2015), most legislators had between one and ten years of legislative experience, and sixteen members had served for more than

incumbent: an individual who currently holds a public office

turnover: when incumbents lose their seats or leave their seats, and new members (freshmen) are voted into office

institutional memory: a collective understanding of the way an organization works held by those who run it

FIGURE 7.4   **Incumbents Reelection Rate**

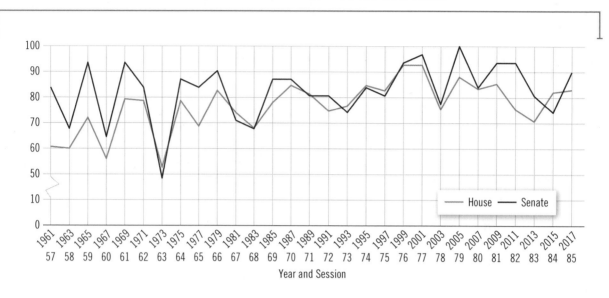

Source: Texas Legislature Online

 COMMUNICATION:

What percentage of the Texas legislature is returned to office each election?

- Generally, the incumbency advantage is high for legislators in Texas, although not as high as the 90 percent or higher for the US Congress.

- The Texas House and Senate have similar rates of incumbents returning to office.

 CRITICAL THINKING:

Despite the strong incumbency advantage, what accounts for periods of decline?

- Certain years saw fewer incumbents returned to office as a result of political scandals, such as the Sharpstown scandal in 1973.

- Turnover is also larger where one party made major political gains in unseating incumbents, like 2003 when Republicans made major gains over Democrats in the state. Redistricting in 2001 contributed by making seats held by incumbent Democrats vulnerable.

- The incumbency advantage also lowers when internal party fights lead to unseating incumbents. The incumbency rate fell to 70 percent in 2013 after several incumbent Republicans lost to conservative challengers in primary elections.

twenty-one years.[19] Lack of turnover, however, can mean that leadership positions are held by the same senior members and frustrated younger members who want a turn in management are frozen out.

CONSEQUENCES OF THE TEXAS LEGISLATIVE STRUCTURE

The consequences of the part-time legislature—columnist Molly Ivins called it a "sometimes government"—may hinder representation and cutting-edge public policy development.[20] Fewer resources, a shorter time span to meet, and lower salaries may put part-time Texas legislators at a disadvantage. Scholars of state politics have found that part-time legislators are less likely to have as much contact with their constituents, are less likely to be attentive to their concerns, and are more influenced by party leadership and the governor. In terms of public policy, part-time legislators are less willing to take on government reforms and enact the complex and innovative policies a state may need.[21]

 **TEXAS TAKEAWAYS**

3 Why is the Texas legislature considered a "weak" legislature?

4 What are the differences between the regular legislative session and a special session?

HOW THE LEGISLATURE IS ORGANIZED

The legislature isn't just a collection of individual legislators. The organization of the legislature shapes the ways that issues are introduced, legislation is debated, and laws are passed (or not).

7.3 Describe the organizational structure and leadership of the legislature.

THE COMMITTEE SYSTEM

Most of the work of the two chambers is carried out through **committees**, a small group of legislators who investigate, craft, assess, and take action on legislation before it is considered by the whole body on the house or senate floor. Each member of the legislature sits on at least one committee, but often more. Legislators specialize in policy topics and craft legislation that addresses a particular problem. Membership on committees is usually determined by a combination of seniority and policy expertise, but politics plays a role as well.

committee: a small group of legislators who investigate, craft, assess, and take action on legislation before it is considered by the whole chamber

standing committees:
permanent committees
that deal with a specific
issue or topic

select committee: a
committee that is
temporary and has a fixed
issue to investigate or
legislation to consider

seniority: having a
lengthier legislative service
than others

The 84th Legislature (the 2015 session) had thirty-eight committees, including fourteen standing committees.[22]

Standing committees are permanent committees that deal with a specific issue or topic. The Senate Affairs Committee is where most legislation important to the senate is handled. This committee is often a clearing house for the lieutenant governor's bills and the place where most controversial legislation is vetted. Important standing committees in the house are the appropriations committees (there are several, each devoted to a specific part of spending funds from the budget) and the House Ways and Means Committee, which monitors state revenue and taxes. All budget and funding items for the state flow through these powerful committees.

A **select committee** is a committee that is temporary and has a fixed issue to investigate or legislation to consider. In the 2011 session, for example, the House Select Committee on State and Federal Power and Responsibility was tasked with investigating the possible overreach of the federal government in Texas's affairs, a hot political topic.

Legislators compete to get onto the most influential committees and onto committees that consider policy issues that are especially relevant to the districts they represent. Legislators ultimately hope to serve as chairs of committees to be better able to direct and influence legislation. The leaders of each chamber, the speaker of the house, and the lieutenant governor in the Texas Senate, determine which legislators to reward with these more powerful positions.

SPEAKER OF THE HOUSE

The presiding officer in the Texas House, the speaker of the house, has several powers that make him the most influential member of the chamber (see Table 7.2). The speaker resolves all questions of process and procedure within the house. The speaker also decides which legislators become committee chairs. He assigns most of the committee members—those not determined by **seniority** which fixes half of committee positions in the House—and so can stack committees with allies. This is an especially important power when it comes to assigning the Calendar Committee that determines the order of bills considered. Because most action takes place in committees, positions on these committees are highly sought after. The speaker is elected by a simple majority of the house in a recorded vote at the beginning of every session. Members who aren't part of the speaker's "team" are often less influential in the session and may have a tougher time raising the funds and votes necessary to win reelection.

Speakers can use committee assignments to punish disloyalty. When Ben Barnes was a twenty-two-year-old legislative freshman in 1961, he privately admitted to the newly elected speaker of the house that he had campaigned against him and thus didn't deserve a committee assignment. The speaker asked Barnes which committees he didn't want to be on. Barnes answered the Liquor Regulation Committee because "I come from a mostly dry district with about 27 Baptist churches." The next week when the committee lists came out, Ben Barnes was at the top of the list for the Liquor Regulation Committee.[23]

TABLE 7.2	Recent Speakers' Successes and Political Problems

	Bill "Billy" Clayton, 1975–1983	Gib Lewis, 1983–1993	Pete Laney, 1993–2003	Tom Craddick, 2003–2009	Joe Straus, 2009–Present
Greatest success	Worked to modernize legislature operations.	Ushered through public education reform. Appointed record number of women, African Americans, and Hispanics to leadership positions.	Fostered bipartisanship by appointing Republicans to key committees and other means.	Handled a serious $10 billion state budget deficit.	Balanced budgets while investing in higher education and keeping taxes low.
Political struggle	Urban legislators complained about strong rural influence of "Billy's Boys" who had the ear of the speaker. Indicted on bribery allegations in 1980.	Pled guilty to campaign finance violations in 1983 and indicted in 1990 of skirting disclosure laws.	Failed to approve redistricting plan favored by Democrats in 2001, and reduced his party's seats.	Ran the house in autocratic way, which led to a revolt from his fellow Republicans against him.	Persistent calls that he isn't conservative enough from his own party prompt frequent attempts to unseat him.

Committee Assignments and the Craddick Ds. After taking over in 2003 as the first Republican speaker since Reconstruction, Tom Craddick had to contend with modest Republican support in the house. He doled out committee assignments that punished political foes and rewarded political friends, particularly Democrats who were willing to cross party lines and support Republican initiatives—a group that became known as the "Craddick D's."[24]

Speaker Craddick, however, eventually got his comeuppance. The speaker is elected every two years (at the beginning of the legislative session) by a majority of house members. Craddick's autocratic style even rubbed Republicans the wrong way. Eleven Republican members of the House—called the Polo Road Gang because they met at Representative Byron Cook's house on Polo Road in Austin—decided to join with House Democrats to back Republican Joe Straus as speaker over Craddick.[25] Craddick's overthrow sent a clear message to future speakers that house representatives would not be tyrannized by a speaker who abused his or her power. New Speaker Straus met with the committee chairs and told them that the pace of the session was up to them, to stop looking to the speaker's office for instructions on how to run their committees, and, if everyone followed the rules, he wouldn't call any fouls.[26]

Process and Procedures. Speakers decide all questions of process and procedure and so can indirectly influence the success or failure of specific legislation. For example, speakers assign legislation to committees. If a speaker sends a bill to a hostile committee, the committee can kill the bill. If they send it to a friendly committee, the committee can enhance its chance of success. A similar

PERSONAL
RESPONSIBILITY:
What lessons from the downfall of Texas speakers would you give to the next speaker?

recognition: the power to call on a legislator to allow him or her to speak during debates

procedural tool is the power of **recognition.** Speakers call on house members to allow them to speak during the discussion of a bill. Seemingly unimportant, the power of recognition allows speakers to lengthen discussion or to end debate. Speaker Mutscher, in the 1971 session, presided over a house that was split between "wets," who, like Mutscher, favored the sale of alcohol, and "drys" who did not. At one point during the debate, the speaker looked up, saw that there were 100 (out of 150) legislators who stood in favor of the measure, enough to pass the motion. He quickly announced that "the gavel is coming down aye" to end the debate and had the sergeant at arms lock the door to the chamber so those legislators present couldn't leave and change their minds.[27]

THE LIEUTENANT GOVERNOR

As we shall see in Chapter 9, the lieutenant governor (often referred to as the "lite" governor) is one of the most powerful elected officials in the state government. Although not a member of the senate, the lieutenant governor acts as the presiding officer of the senate and is officially called the president of the senate. Thus the lieutenant governor only casts a vote in the case of a tie. But he or she enjoys other more extensive powers. The lieutenant governor has full authority to appoint senators to committees and as committee chairs. Unlike the speaker of the house, the lieutenant governor is not limited by seniority in assignments. Informally, senior senators get first pick at committee assignments until one third of the committee is filled.

The lieutenant governor assigns legislation to specific committees, allowing him or her to influence the chances of a bill becoming law. For example, in 2015, Lieutenant Governor Dan Patrick sent a bill to ban in-state tuition for the children of undocumented immigrants to the Border Security Subcommittee instead of the Higher Education or Senate Committee on State Affairs. Patrick knew that the Border Security Subcommittee was more likely to be against the measure, and indeed the subcommittee killed the bill.[28]

★ TEXAS TAKEAWAYS

5 What is the function of committees?

6 Who are the leaders of the Texas house and Texas senate?

 THE LEGISLATIVE PROCESS

7.4 Outline the legislative process.

How a bill becomes a law in Texas echoes the federal legislative process in many ways: bills pass from the committees to the floor of each chamber and require coordination between the chambers (see Figure 7.5). Legislators work up bills, often inspired by residents in

FIGURE 7.5   **How a Bill Becomes a Law in Texas**

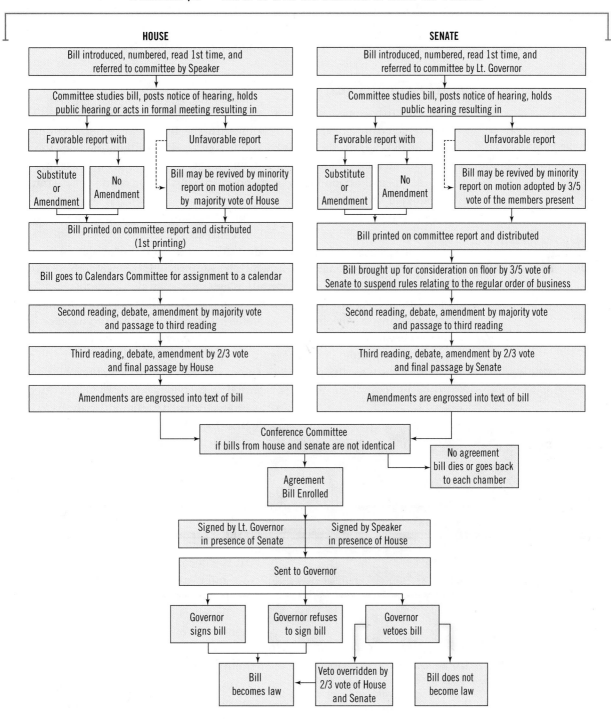

Source: Guide to Legislative Information (Revised). 2015. Texas Legislative Council for the 84th Legislature.

CRITICAL THINKING: **What role do the speaker, the lieutenant governor, committee chairs and members, interest groups, party leaders, the governor, and citizens play in each stage of the legislative process?**

the district, interest groups, or committee investigations, with the help of staff members and the Legislative Council. The multiple stages of the process and a short calendar, however, makes passage of legislation even more challenging and exacerbate the competition among parties as well as individual legislators.

IN COMMITTEE

first reading: legislation considered at the committee stage

For a bill to become law in Texas, each chamber has to hear it three times. These are referred to as the three readings. In the **first reading**—the committee stage—the clerk in the house or senate will read the bill on the floor to introduce it and then the speaker or lieutenant governor will refer it to a committee.

All formal action taken by a committee in the house and senate must be conducted in open meetings called hearings. Interested parties may not only attend but also testify at these hearings to shape or stop legislation. Most witnesses are lobbyists or concerned bureaucrats.

amend: the process of bill

markup: where legislators add, subtract, or replace part of the original legislation so that it meets the preferences of the committee

The representatives in the committee may **amend** the legislation, in a process known as bill **markup**, in which legislators add, subtract, or replace part of the original legislation. Committee members may also amend legislation by substituting the bill with another version of the bill. This process saves time of amending the original bill and offers a smooth transition to passage in the other chamber.

second reading: legislation considered at the floor stage

The committee can approve a bill, sending it to the full chamber, or do nothing with the bill, letting it wither and die for lack of attention. Most bills end up dying in committee. For bills reported favorably, meaning the committee approves the bill, the committee drafts a report that includes recommendations regarding the placement on the calendar, the text of the bill, a bill analysis, and a fiscal note (reflecting the potential economic impact and the consequences of balancing the budget).

Witnesses testify about a proposed $150 million cut to Medicaid payments for disabled children's therapy. While generally testimony is professional and orderly, witnesses—and legislators—can become so wrapped up in the politics that they violate etiquette and have to be removed.

PERSONAL RESPONSIBILITY: **Is there an issue that riles you up enough to interrupt a legislative hearing in protest?**

ON THE FLOOR

In the **second reading**—the floor stage—the full chamber debates the measure and amends it as desired (with a simple majority backing). Effective legislators do their homework on the bills, cut the deals, hustle for votes, and navigate the floor debate so nothing goes wrong when legislation they favor or dislike comes up for discussion.[29] Most deals on legislation are made away from the floor.

During the second reading stage, members publically debate the legislation being considered. In the senate, the senators speak from their desks using a portable microphone. In the house chamber, much larger by comparison, the representatives speak either from the front microphone (where the defender of the bill speaks) or the back microphone (where members ask questions of those on the front microphone). Representatives have taken it upon themselves to use unusual measures to limit debate. In 2015, one representative dangled a cookie on a string in front of another to lure him away from the back microphone so he would stop asking questions and the chamber could move on to other legislation.[30]

The **third reading** is the final stage—the voting stage (called engrossment in the house). After the third reading, amendments can be offered, but a two-thirds majority is needed for approval. This high voting hurdle makes amendments at this point infrequent. A simple majority is required to finally pass the legislation. The constitution requires bills to be read on three separate days, but the legislature can suspend the law with a four-fifths vote and conduct the second and third readings on the same day to speed things along.[31]

third reading: the voting stage of legislation

HOUSE AND SENATE AGREEMENT

Separated by an opulent tiled walkway under the tall, pink dome in Austin, both chambers have to agree on legislation in order for it to arrive at the governor's desk. However, political agendas don't always match up. In the 2003 session, the state was looking for additional tax revenue but the house and senate disagreed about how to get it. The senate considered legalizing limited gambling, such as a lottery at the gas pump where you could buy lottery tickets along with your gas and car wash. The house vehemently opposed this or any form of gambling. The house further rejected a statewide property tax to support local school districts. The senate put a state property tax on the table anyway.[32] The session ended with no action taken on the matter.

When the two chambers are in agreement about a policy goal but have disagreements about specific aspects of the legislation, there are a few ways to reconcile house and senate bills. When a bill is still in committee in one of the chambers, a house bill can be amended by substituting it with a senate bill and vice versa, which can save time because ultimately the legislature must reconcile house and senate bills to get them passed into law. If this swap does not occur and the house and senate versions of the bill differ, the bills are sent to a conference committee made up of lawmakers from both chambers.

see for yourself 7.2

Watch former Lieutenant Governor Bill Hobby and his chief of staff discuss the challenges in pushing through legislation.

IN CONFERENCE COMMITTEE

The speaker and lieutenant governor each appoint five members from their respective chambers to serve on the committee. Senate rules require that at least two of the conferees be members of the original committee that first heard the bill. The conference committee limits itself to only the points of disagreement—it cannot add text or address areas of agreement.[33]

If the conference committee members hammer out differences and agree on a final version, a committee report is produced to summarize the changes. The house and senate must again vote to finalize the same version of the legislation. The report cannot be amended by either chamber but must be accepted or rejected in its entirety. If no agreement is reached, the bill returns to the originating chamber. After the same version of the bill is agreed upon, it is sent to the governor for signature. The governor has ten days (excluding Sundays) to sign or veto the bill or the bill automatically becomes law. Alternately, the governor can veto the bill. If the legislature feels strongly enough to reconsider the legislation, two-thirds of the members of both houses of the legislature can override the veto.

Once legislation is passed by both chambers and signed by the governor, the legislation takes effect as specified by the text of the passed legislation. If a bill does not specify an "effective date," or a date when it is to take effect, the act becomes effective on the ninety-first day after the date of final adjournment of the legislature.

This process makes who gets on the conference committee important. The speaker and lieutenant governor want smooth passage, so they tend not to appoint members who have voted against a budget bill to the budget conference committee so that they can assure that the bill passes. This often leaves the minority party without a seat at the table.

THE REAL ENEMY: THE CALENDAR

The rules of the house and senate allow for bills to be "pre-filed" from the Monday following the general election in November or filed in the first 60 days of a regular legislative session. "The first 60 days is like two-a-days for legislators," said Republican Representative Cecil Bell of Magnolia, referring to grueling twice daily practices for football teams.[34]

Lawmakers confer and jockey for attention to their issues, pressured by the calendar, their party, interest groups, and voters.

SOCIAL RESPONSIBILITY: **Should legislators prioritize the needs of their districts, their party, or the state as a whole?**

After this 60-day deadline, only local bills (bills that deal with a fixed local entity), emergency appropriations, or emergency matters formally submitted by the governor can be considered. The 60-day deadline can also be waived if four-fifths of members present vote to do so. After a certain point in the calendar, time runs short and the political will to battle subsides. One member referred to these days as "bloody days" as many bills die.[35]

Two calendars' committees in the house, the Committee on Local and Consent Calendars and the Calendars Committee, set the priorities and make the schedule for the legislative session. The Local and Consent

Calendars Committee sets uncontested or local legislation on the agenda—legislation concerning fees of a local water district, for example. The Calendars Committee prepares the daily calendar for all bills, and, most importantly, determines the importance of a bill by prioritizing some over others. In the senate, the secretary of the senate schedules most bills for floor debate, while the Senate Committee on Administration schedules noncontroversial legislation.

Given the short time for the full session, fixed chamber deadlines by which legislation must pass, and thousands of bills to sift through, any delay or distraction can lead to bills being killed. In 2011, puppies temporarily bottle-necked legislation in the house. Long-time and much respected Representative Senfronia Thompson, Democrat of Houston and chair of the committee that sets the local and consent calendar, introduced legislation to regulate "puppy mills." Freshman lawmaker David Simpson opposed it and knocked the bill off the calendar. She put it back on again. He bumped it back off. The house eventually passed the bill but it ate up significant legislative time in the process.[36] Similarly, important bills were stalled in 2005 when the legislature considered the "cheerleader booty bill," a measure regulating "overly sexual dance moves by school cheerleaders at sporting events."[37]

RULES RULE THE CHAMBERS

The house and senate have both formal and informal rules that govern the chambers (see Table 7.3). When ethics legislation was voted on just before midnight the day the session was to end in 1991, most members had not even read the bill. Determined that this wouldn't happen again, Speaker Pete Laney pushed through new rules, setting deadlines by which bills are to clear committees, be passed by the full house and senate, and cleaned up. These rules compacted timelines and—in the words of columnist Dave McNeely—turned "a stock car race in the mud into a parade of septuagenarians showing off their walkers."[38]

The senate also has rules that govern when and if a bill can be brought to debate on the floor. By tradition, the senate considers bills in numerical order. So, bills with lower numbers are brought up first. Bills can, and frequently

TABLE 7.3	"Unwritten" Rules for Members of the Legislature
Always applaud when a fellow legislator recognizes constituents in the balcony.	
Never launch a filibuster without informing the lieutenant governor and bill sponsor.	
Don't knock bills off the uncontested calendar without first informing the author.	
Never waste the chamber's time—especially applies to freshmen.	
Never act as though you know more than another member.	

Source: Adapted from Pittman's "The Third House"

ANGLES OF POWER
Politics Sometimes Makes Unlikely Bedfellows

Testy debates about the right of Texans to openly brandish firearms in public (called "open carry") dominated much of the 2015 legislative session. The Texas House passed legislation allowing individuals who possessed a proper concealed handgun license to openly carry a firearm in public. Senator Don Huffines, a Republican conservative Tea Party-backed candidate from Dallas, and Royce West, a liberal Democrat from Dallas, joined forces to offer an amendment banning police from asking individuals openly carrying weapons whether or not they had a license. These two unusual allies objected to possible unlawful intrusion by police officers who could profile a gun carrier for racial or other reasons, thus violating gun owners' civil rights. Conservative Democrats balked at the change, and numerous police and law enforcement organizations opposed the bill altogether. Conservative Republicans also detested the amendment, calling it a "poison pill" designed to kill the legislation.[42] The amendment was added, and the legislation passed primarily to appease mainstream Republican voters. In the last few sessions, however, divisions within the political parties have encouraged unusual alliances, such as socially liberal Republicans siding with Democrats on abortion issues and Democrats backing fiscally oriented Republicans to increase education funding.

SOCIAL RESPONSIBILITY: **What kinds of issues or events encourage legislators to work together?**

are, taken out of order but three-fifths of the membership must agree to do so.[39] To counter the power of the lieutenant governor who has absolute power to bring up legislation, senators pass a "blocker bill" each day the senate is in session. It ensures that no other bill can be passed unless three-fifths of the senators agree to "suspend the regular order of business" and skip over the blocker bill.[40] This rule empowers the minority party who could halt discussion on an issue with enough votes.

The three-fifths requirement is a recent development; until 2015, only two-thirds of Texas senators were required to agree to bring a measure up for debate. The rule still requires senators to build bridges to those in the other party. Even on hot button political issues like gun control, school choice, and education accountability, Senator Kevin Eltife, Republican of Tyler, noted, "You don't know how hard the sponsor of that bill would have worked to turn votes. If the rule was 21 and I was stuck at 19, I'm going to work my tail off to find two more and turn them."[41]

⭐ TEXAS TAKEAWAYS

7 Identify what each of the three "readings" of a law entails.

8 What is the purpose of the conference committee?

🤠 WORKING TOGETHER

Each chamber has unique rules and traditions that contribute to the passage (or more than often stoppage) of legislation. Similar to the US Congress, the process is designed purposely to slow down the passage of legislation to restrict the number of laws that can be passed. However, with a short session and partisan politics at play, tension increases during the lawmaking process, making it difficult to accomplish important legislative goals.

> **7.5** Assess how legislative tools are used to speed up or slow down legislation.

Maintaining relationships and building bridges is more than professional courtesy—it is necessary for legislation to pass. In the 2001 legislative session, Senators Leticia Van de Putte and Royce West were debating legislation introduced by Van de Putte in committee that would stiffen penalties for grabbing a police officer's firearm. Longtime colleagues and allies, the two talked back and forth about the merits of the legislation, with West unsure the legislation was needed considering there are already fines for assaulting or killing police officers. As the questions became more damag-

logrolling: trading favors, votes, or influence for legislative actions

ing to her bill, Senator Van de Putte discreetly passed West a note, placing a kiss with her red lipstick at the bottom. West received the note, smiled, and stopped asking questions. When asked later what she wrote, Van de Putte responded that she had asked him to "knock it off—in unprintable language."[43]

Some legislators use **logrolling** (or favor trading) to get things accomplished and get their preferred legislation passed or action taken. Lieutenant Governor Ben Barnes, one of two people elected as both house speaker and lieutenant governor, turned making (and keeping) allies into a "political crusade"—everyone got a chance to bend his ear, "Baptist or boozer, labor or management, bigot or black."[44]

Tiffs, however, are common. For the third time in as many legislative sessions, a bill to ban texting while driving was introduced in the house in the 2015 session by longtime advocate, and former Speaker of the House, Tom Craddick. The bill easily passed the house, but Senator Konni Burton successfully led a group of conservative Republicans to block the bill from being heard.[45] Blocking the bill came at a political cost—several bills by Burton and her allies never came up for a

Republican Representative Jonathan Stickland changed the nameplate on his office door to "Representative Jonathan Stickland, FORMER FETUS, District 92, E1.402" to greet visitors on the day Planned Parenthood lobbied the Texas Capitol. The house's chief rule-enforcer promptly removed the sign, saying the State Preservation Board prohibits such displays. Underlying the skirmish was the presence of a growing lack of civility among the members of the chamber.[1]

🌟 PERSONAL RESPONSIBILITY: **How do civility and camaraderie (or lack thereof) influence the legislative process?**

Ellic Sahualla, Chief of Staff and General Counsel to Representative Joe Moody

What is the most important source of power in the legislature?

Numbers, positions, and rules matter in Austin just as much as in Washington, but here, personalities play an outsized role on top of that. Legislators quickly build reputations—everyone knows who can be trusted on a particular topic and who's full of hot air. Professional respect crosses party lines so powerfully that who's talking usually determines who's listening. On top of that, relationships matter a great deal. An ideological opponent might still be a buddy whose toes you won't step on if you can possibly help it, whereas someone disagreeable might find themselves an outsider in their own party.

SOCIAL RESPONSIBILITY: **What sort of temperament is most effective in a legislator? How can voters determine this before election?**

---

vote in the house, in an "apparent act of political retaliation."[46] In these power struggles, legislators have access to an array of weapons that can slow down or speed up legislation.

SLOWING IT DOWN

Delay, distract, disrupt—these are all ways in which members of the legislature can interrupt or slow down the legislative process. This is an especially powerful tool when a party is in the minority and has less political muscle to force the chamber to a particular decision. The enemy of the majority is the clock, as delay is often the same as defeat. The following are a few effective tactics.

"Taking a walk."   A legislator will leave the chamber so there are not enough legislators present to bring up a bill—a minimum number of legislators being required by the rules to proceed. Slowing down the senate was a specialty of the Killer Bees, a group of determined Democrats who opposed Lieutenant Governor Bill Hobby in 1979. Hobby started calling them the Killer Bees because "no one knew when they would strike next." In one fateful episode, legislation came up that would split the date of the Texas primaries for the two major political parties. The Killer Bees feared that this would benefit former Governor John Connally who was running for president in the Republican primary in 1980—as a former Democrat. The Killer Bees anticipated that Connally could get support from conservative Democrats who could vote in the Republican presidential primary and in the Democratic primary for other races. In protest, twelve Killer Bees fled the Capitol to break the quorum, the minimum number needed to hold a vote. Texas Rangers were dispatched to round up the senators. Noting that the senators would have a "S.O." (State Official) tag on their license plates, one senator rhymed: "The Texas Rangers hunt for them; Bill Hobby issues pleas, And says that on their license plates, It shows that they're S.O. Bees."[47]

The event was a fiasco. Lieutenant Governor Hobby lamented that bringing up the bill was a mistake and the attempt to catch the Killer Bees was a failure. In one episode, a senator left the "hive" to see his granddaughter. A ranger came to her door only to arrest the senator's brother instead. The senator meanwhile jumped over the back fence and remained at large.

After the Killer Bees incident, the group reunited to celebrate their anniversary at Scholz Beer Garten in Austin. Lieutenant Governor Hobby sent the Texas Rangers to bring the group to a reception in the Capitol. Clad in a beekeeper's hat, he jokingly greeted them from the dais.

PERSONAL RESPONSIBILITY: **If you were a legislator, would you compromise on your principles to work together with fellow legislators to pass an important bill? On what issues?**

Point of Order.   A **point of order** (POO) is a technical objection to an error in a bill. Once declared, a point of order takes precedent on the floor and the presiding officer (the speaker or the lieutenant governor or whomever is presiding in their place) must address the argument. A POO can hold up the consideration of the legislation, send it back to the committee of origin for clarification, or kill it entirely (if it is missing a critical part of the bill like an enacting clause).

point of order: a technical objection to an error in a bill

For instance, in the 2015 legislative session, guns and gun control were a hot topic. Legislation that allowed individuals to carry a concealed firearm on college campuses was a top Republican priority. Not surprisingly, most Democrats objected. Democratic Senator Kirk Watson of Austin noted that the witness list on the bill was inaccurate—some of the witnesses listed as speaking "for" the legislation were only speaking "on" the legislation, making it subject to a point of order on the technicality.[48]

Sometimes a point of order can derail multiple bills. In the Democrat-controlled house in the 1997 session, Republican Representative Arlene Wohlgemuth called a POO that struck fifty-two bills from the house schedule in an episode that became known as "the Memorial Day Massacre."[49]

Trey Martinez Fischer, Democrat of San Antonio, made his name in part with his frequent use of the point of order. Texas Monthly crowned him the "prince of POO" in 2013.[2]

Stuffing the Box. Thousands of bills are filed each legislative session, making competition for attention and action significant. Opponents of a controversial bill may seek to debate noncontroversial bills to soak up time that would otherwise be spent on controversial bills. For instance, in the 2015 legislative session, the house was discussing an uncontroversial bill relating to limiting the fees for the Velaso Drainage District. Debate on this modest issue was delaying debate of the major issue of a provision of "open carry" of firearms. When fellow legislators called to end debate of the drainage bill, Democrat Terry Canalas coyly remarked, "Why, do we need to move the bill?" to laughter in the chamber.

Talk it to Death. For legislation on the local and consent calendar in the house that is not expected to provoke disagreement, a representative can kill a bill simply by talking about it for ten minutes in session and so stall a vote. House members can also hog the microphone in the chamber (from the "back mic," where members ask questions) for ten minutes at a time.[50]

Party of Five. In the house, five representatives can kill a bill on the local and consent calendar just by signaling their opposition to it.

Filibuster. Because debate is unlimited in the senate, a senator who objects to a bill or simply wants to slow the process down can hold the floor and talk until they are physically unable to do so. This is called a **filibuster**. During a filibuster, a senator who holds the floor cannot talk about issues not related to the legislation, eat or drink, leave the floor to use the bathroom, or lean on anything for physical support. Senators are allowed three warnings before the chamber can vote to end the filibuster by using a point of order to point out a rules violation. If the point of order is sustained by the chair, the senator must yield the floor.

filibuster: when a senator holds the floor and restrains the chamber from moving forward on legislation

Donning her pink tennis shoes in the 2013 legislative session, Senator Wendy Davis took to the floor of the Texas State Senate at 11:18 am on June 26 with the hopes of holding the floor long enough to run out the clock on the legislature's special session that ended at midnight. At issue was Senate Bill 5, which would institute a ban on abortions after twenty weeks of pregnancy, require clinics performing abortions to meet the same standards that other surgical clinics met, and force doctors performing abortions to have admitting privileges at a nearby hospital. Senator Davis got her first warning at 5:30 pm for talking about funding cuts to women's health services. Her second strike came from a colleague providing her with a back brace. Her third strike came when she mentioned Texas's mandatory pre-abortion ultrasound law, ruled to be off topic of the legislation. The jockeying about the rules on the third strike between legislative staff, the members, and the presiding officers, in addition to the rising crowd noise in the packed gallery, advanced the clock past the midnight deadline and ended the bill. The chaos surrounding the normally staid Capitol complex fell at the feet of the lieutenant governor. Leaving the dais after a ruling that time had expired, Lieutenant Governor Dewhurst said, "It's been fun, but, um, see ya soon." Accusing Dewhurst of a "lack of leadership," Republican Dan Patrick succeeded in unseating Dewhurst in the subsequent 2014 election.

The record for the longest filibuster in Texas history is held by Senator Bill Meier, Democrat from Hurst, who talked for forty-three hours in 1977 against a bill that eventually passed anyway. He sipped water, ate lemon slices, and relieved himself in an "astronaut bag" attached to his leg under his pants.[51] Most filibusters, however, last about an hour or so and are either used to make a political point or to draw attention to an issue.[52]

The lieutenant governor can use his power of recognition to block a filibuster. Late in a legislative session, Senator Oscar Mauzy of Dallas filibustered a school finance appropriation, prompting a special session. Thereafter, Lieutenant Governor Hobby kept a reminder on his desk that read "Do not recognize Mauzy on the last day for ANY reason!"[53]

In one of the most noteworthy filibusters in Texas history, Senator Wendy Davis held the senate floor to delay a vote on a controversial abortion bill.

PERSONAL RESPONSIBILITY: **Thousands of citizens rallied behind Senator Davis in the Capitol during her filibuster of abortion legislation—so much that the building literally shook. Critics complained about the lack of decorum. Do you agree or disagree? Why?**

"Chubbing."   Chubbing is a generic term for delay, usually involving a combination of procedural tactics, such as raising technical questions, and lengthy floor speeches all designed to eat up more time. Late in the 2015 legislative session, the house Democrats were looking for ways to prevent discussion of legislation that would allow for Texans to openly carry handguns in public. Democrats kept delaying, even by proposing 120 amendments on the campus carry legislation. Republicans complained. Reporters and other observers cracked jokes. One legislative intern tweeted a photo of a movie poster for the fictional film "Shakespeare in Chub."[54]

"Tagging."   In the house and senate, a lawmaker can "tag" a bill, informally putting it on hold for twenty-four hours. This is an effective tactic late in the session when deadlines for passing legislation are looming. Those who control the calendars are at their most powerful at this point. Senator Van de Putte, once fed up with her legislation being restrained in this way, joked to her fellow senators that she was running a two-for-one special—she would tag two of their house bills for every one of her bills that got tagged. By the end of the day, she won almost every house bill she carried in the senate.[55]

SPEEDING IT UP

The party in the majority knows full well that the party in the minority wants to slow the process down, so they attempt to counter these maneuvers with procedures of their own to speed the process up.

Suspending Twenty-Four-Hour Waiting Period. By the chamber rules, twenty-four hours must pass between readings of a bill. The chamber can suspend this rule with agreement of two-thirds of the members. On legislation concerning "campus carry," Republicans in the senate suspended the twenty-four-hour waiting period, holding the vote on a Saturday, and thus avoiding a Democratic filibuster.[56]

Discharge Petition. In 2005, proponents of the bill to limit third-party issue ads in primary and general elections appealed to House Speaker Tom Craddick. The bill had been bottled up in the Elections Committee for weeks. Proponents asked Craddick to pull out a "dusty" house discharge rule that allowed the full house to vote to yank a bill out of committee to the full chamber for consideration. The effort wasn't needed because legislators quickly killed the bill in committee before the full house could vote.[57]

Suspending Normal Business. The senate, on one occasion, while debating windstorm insurance, introduced a novel tactic. As the hands of the antique clock above the senate entry door approached midnight, the senate sergeant at arms, under orders from Lieutenant Governor David Dewhurst, opened a panel on the back of the clock, flipped a switch and "froze" time at 11:58. Senators continued to debate, and indeed actively played along with the charade of time. When asked what time it was about forty minutes later, Senator Kel Seliger responded, "It's nighttime. Has been for several hours and will be several hours more."[58]

INCREASING PARTISANSHIP

One obstacle to cooperation within the state legislature is rising partisanship. The growing gap between liberals and conservatives has come to define politics nationally but also in Texas (see Figure 7.6). As we saw in Chapter 5, the rise the Republican Party precipitated an ideological split between conservatives and liberals. As individual voters' opinions on policy become more tightly linked to their identification with a political party, **political polarization** increased. As Stanford political scientist Moris Fiorina wrote, "issues and ideology used to cross-cut the partisan distribution, now they reinforce it."[59]

Polarization has profound consequences for governing the Lone Star State. Former Democratic Senator Pete Gallego, who went on to serve in the US House

political polarization: voters' opinions on policy and political matters become more strictly defined by their identification with a political party

FIGURE 7.6 **Increasing Polarization in the Texas Legislature**

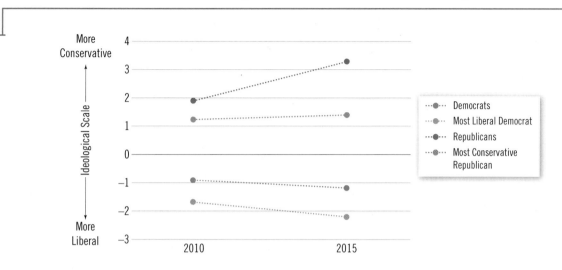

Source: State Ideologies Project, Boris Shor. Positive numbers designate conservative ideologies for median voter; negative numbers designate more liberal ideologies median voter.

 COMMUNICATION:

How polarized is the Texas House?

- The average ideology of the Republican Party has become more conservative from 2010 to 2015 and the average ideology of the Democratic Party has become more liberal.

- The Republican Party has become, on average, more conservative than the Democratic Party has become liberal.

- The most extreme liberal and conservative member of each party became more liberal and conservative from 2010 to 2015.

 CRITICAL THINKING:

Why has polarization increased?

- Longtime Austin-watchers claim that the extension of the Capitol in 1993 allowed members to spread out instead of being physically close together. The physical distance decreased personal contacts and hurt working relationships.

- The rise of social media allowed members to communicate directly to constituents, often in partisan ways.

- Partisan activists on both sides have become more partisan.

- Too few voters vote in primary elections, allowing the most active (and extreme) ideological voters to have an outsized say in who is elected.

of Representatives, said of politics in Austin: "In the old way of doing business, it was fine to disagree and then go to dinner. Now it's personal and more partisan, and a disagreement on one issue leads to a disagreement on another issue. As the polarization in D.C. spreads, the people willing to come to the middle find less and less acceptance."[60] As partisanship has increased, cooperation in both chambers has declined. For many decades, the majority party in the house voted as a bloc time after time. The senate, with a longstanding history of bipartisanship, deliberated and worked across party lines. Today, the senate acts more like the house, quashing any minority party input into the process.[61] These partisan conflicts limit the ability of the legislature to address many of the big problems the state faces and forces the two chambers to focus instead on temporary, incremental solutions.

★ TEXAS TAKEAWAYS

9 What is a filibuster?

10 What is chubbing?

DEMOGRAPHIC REPRESENTATION

7.6 Explain how legislators represent their constituents demographically.

Just as the composition of the state has changed over the last century, so have the demographics and characteristics of the legislators sent to Austin to represent its people. Political scientists find that there is both symbolic and substantive value to demographic representation. Political representation by ethnic or racial minorities produces legislative outcomes more congruent with the needs of the racial and ethnic groups represented, may foster increased civic engagement among those groups, and can reduce the perception of racial discrimination broadly.[62]

Texas legislators are a diverse group and are growing more diverse over time. However, some demographic groups are overrepresented and some are underrepresented. Although the legislature is still dominated by older white men, more women, African Americans, and Hispanics have been elected in the past two decades (see Figure 7.7). Let's take a closer look at some of these demographic trends.

WOMEN LEGISLATORS

Although women have made inroads in membership in both chambers, the perception that the legislature is a "boys club" persists in the behavior of some legislators. Before the civil rights movement in the 1960s, lobbyists would frequently hold "stag parties" and only invite male legislators, and legislative committees would meet in male-only clubs, excluding female members from attending.[63] The situation has improved from the 1990s, when then-Lieutenant

FIGURE 7.7 **Demographics of the Texas Legislature, 74th to 85th Sessions**

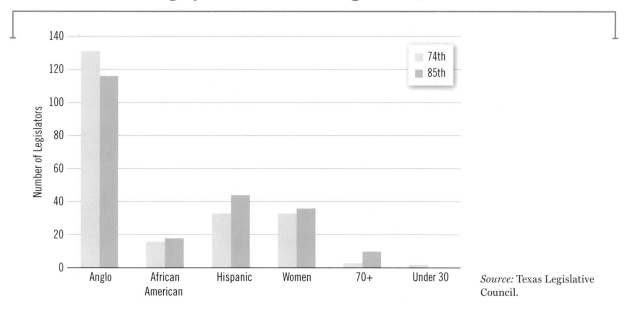

Source: Texas Legislative Council.

 COMMUNICATION:

How has the makeup of the legislature changed?

- The number of women has increased only slightly.
- The legislature has aged slightly, with more members in the seventy and over category and fewer in the thirty and under category.
- The number of African Americans has stayed relatively stable but the number of Hispanic representatives has increased.

 CRITICAL THINKING:

Why has the makeup of the legislature become more inclusive of racial minorities and women?

- Districts have been geographically created to favor racial minorities, increasing the number of districts where racial minorities may win office.
- More women have taken leadership roles in parties and organizations, creating more opportunities for moving into elected positions.

Governor Bullock famously said that if Senator Judith Zaffirini would "cut her skirt off about 6 inches and put on some high-heel shoes," she could pass whatever legislation she wanted. In 2011, however, when freshman Senator Wendy Davis raised a question about a male colleague's bill, she said he growled "don't talk to me like that, little lady."[64] Representative Jessica Farrar struck back at the "level of misogyny" she experienced in the 2015 session: "if one member can be disrespected, we all can be disrespected."[65]

AFRICAN AMERICANS

The pathway to inclusion of African Americans into the legislative process was a major battle in Texas politics. Legislatures drew district boundaries to carve up the African American population into several districts so that no black representative served in a legislative chamber anywhere in the South from 1906 to 1966. Even in cities with a significant black population, candidates were forced to run in citywide or countywide multimember districts where Anglo voters refused to vote for black candidates.

The fight over civil rights turned to electoral combat in the 1960s. Curtis Graves's election in 1966, the first African American elected to the Texas House since Reconstruction, highlights this remarkable accomplishment. Just a few years earlier, he had had to take a literacy test in order to be eligible to vote. Barbara Jordan was the first African American woman to be elected to the clubbish Texas Senate (1967). Eddie Bernice Johnson (1973) and Senfronia Thompson (1972) were the first African American women to serve in the Texas House.[66]

HISPANICS

Despite significant population numbers, Texas Hispanics' fight for inclusion came only recently. The 1971 reapportionment in Texas made it practically impossible for Hispanics to be represented, as Hispanic populations were carved up and spread thinly across districts. Only ten Hispanics served in the Texas House in 1971. But court-mandated redistricting plans in the 1970s and 1980s increased that figure dramatically. By 1999, Texas led all other states in the number of Latino representatives. Irma Rangel was the first Latina elected to the Texas State House of Representatives in history in 1976.[67] Judith Zaffirini was the first Latina elected to the Texas Senate in 1986. However, Latinas are still less represented in the Texas legislature than Latinos because traditional gender socialization may not encourage female participation in politics and women lack the support of party elites.[68]

RACE, RELIGION, AND OTHER FACTORS

When not at the Capitol in Austin, the 181 members of the Texas legislature are cotton farmers, lawyers, realtors, or pharmacists—representing a diverse set of occupations and backgrounds.[69] As a group, however, the legislators are highly educated: most hold bachelors or postgraduate degrees and most are alumni of the University of Texas (see Figure 7.8). In this sense, they do not "look like" the average voter. Most legislators consider themselves Christian, and in this sense, they do "look like" most Texans.

 TEXAS TAKEAWAYS

11 What are the benefits of demographic representation?

12 How do legislators differ from the average voter in terms of education?

FIGURE 7.8   **Education and College Attendance among Texas Legislators**

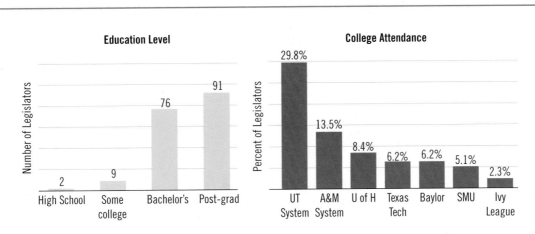

Source: Texas Tribune "84th Texas Legislature, by the Numbers."

 COMMUNICATION:

What is the education level of the members of the Texas legislature?

- Most members of the legislature are well educated, receiving most frequently a postgraduate degree (ninety-one) or at least a bachelor's degree (seventy-six).
- Many of those attending college attended the University of Texas, most at UT Austin.
- Texas A&M University and the University of Houston ranked behind UT as the institution of choice for most legislators.

 CRITICAL THINKING:

Why?

- Making laws and interpreting legislation requires a breadth of education, often specialized in law or business.
- Individuals who have worked in an industry with well-connected or wealthy colleagues may be more likely to undertake a run for office so that they will have an easier time fundraising.

THE INSIDER VIEW

Although it meets infrequently, the power of the Texas legislature is significant. The volume of laws passed even in a short window of time adds up over the years to affect nearly every aspect of the lives of Texans. Several pressure points in the Texas legislature determine whether or not legislation is passed—the short duration of the session, the desires of the speaker of the house and lieutenant governor, and partisan warfare. Colliding political rivalries shape the outcome of the legislative process, pitting the parties against each other with an arsenal of rules that speed up or slow down the process. Yet, crosscutting these ideological rivalries, personal relationships and the need to claim credit for accomplishments have allowed for legislators to work together for the good of the state, even if they don't always agree on what that is.

★ TEXAS TAKEAWAYS

1 One hundred and eighty-one members serve in the Texas legislature. One hundred and fifty in the house and thirty on in the senate.

2 Trustees vote in accordance with their interpretation of what their district would want. Delegates serve as a mouthpiece for the wishes of their constituency.

3 Short legislative sessions, part-time legislators, low salaries, few staff, and the power of external boards all demonstrate the "weak" qualities of the Texas legislature.

4 The regular legislative session is 140 days in every odd-numbered year; a special session is called by the governor and is limited to 30 days and specific issues.

5 Committees are a small group of legislators (and staff) that take action on legislation before the full chamber votes.

6 The leader of the Texas house is the speaker of the house and the leader of the Texas senate is the lieutenant governor.

7 The first "reading" is the committee stage. The second "reading" is the floor stage. The third "reading" is the final vote of the full chamber.

8 The conference committee's responsibility is to hammer out differences and agree on a final version; a committee report is produced to summarize the changes.

9 A filibuster is when a senator holds the floor and restrains the chamber from moving forward on legislation.

10 Chubbing is a generic term for delay, usually involving a combination of procedural tactics, such as raising technical questions, and lengthy floor speeches all designed to eat up more time.

11 Demographic representation may help government better meet the need of minorities, may foster increased civic engagement among minorities, and can reduce the perception of discrimination.

12 Legislators are more highly educated than the average voter.

KEY TERMS

amend
bicameral legislature
casework
committee
delegate
filibuster
first reading
general laws

incumbent
institutional memory
local laws
logrolling
markup
point of order
political polarization
recognition

regular session
resolutions
second reading
select committee
seniority
sine die
special laws
special session
standing committees
third reading
trustee
turnover

PRACTICE QUIZ

1. Areas with fixed geographical boundaries that elect legislators are referred to as

   a. Unitary actors
   b. Single member districts
   c. Legislative zones
   d. Multimember districts

2. What is casework?

   a. Legislators work with the Legislative Council to craft legislation
   b. Legislators hold hearings on specific legislation
   c. Legislators and their staff assist constituents in their districts with specific requests
   d. Legislators investigate claims by state agencies about fraud and waste

3. A special session can only be called by

   a. The speaker of the house
   b. The president of the senate
   c. The governor
   d. The chief justice of the supreme court

4. The Latin phrase for the end of the legislative session, which means "Without Day", is

   a. *Sine Die*
   b. *Ceteris Paribus*
   c. *Amicus Curiae*
   d. *Sic Semper Tyrannis*

5. The Texas Legislature is

   a. Unicameral
   b. Bicameral
   c. Neither unicameral nor bicameral
   d. Both unicameral and bicameral, depending on the election year

6. The final stage of a bill in the Texas Legislature is called _____.

   a. Final reading
   b. *Sine die*
   c. Third Reading
   d. Adjournment

7. If there are differences in legislation between the house and senate, the senate's version is always the version submitted to the governor.

   a. True
   b. False

8. The incumbency advantage is generally low for Texas legislators.

   a. True
   b. False

9. Resolutions convey the will of the chamber.

   a. True
   b. False

10. A POO stands for a "Point of Order," and is a technical objection to an error in a bill.

    a. True
    b. False

[Answers: B, C, C, A, B, C, B, B, A, A]

8 GOVERNORS OF TEXAS

On June 17, 2001, the Texas state legislature faced down the "Father's Day Massacre." Nothing like it had ever happened before. In a single day, Texas Governor Rick Perry axed 82 bills. The vetoed legislation spanned a wide gamut of issues. Some required racial and ethnic awareness training for state judges, equal access to public places for protected classes, and expansion of legal charitable bingo games. One banned the use of the death penalty for convicted killers with profound mental disabilities, another would have allowed undocumented immigrants to obtain driver's licenses, and still another would have created a low-interest loan program for building energy-efficient housing. The governor's reasons for issuing vetoes in these cases ranged widely. For some, he claimed that the laws were duplicative. For others, he argued that the laws overstepped the proper scope of government, intervening in areas where local authorities should have greater say. For many, he simply argued that the policy would be bad for Texas.

Why did Perry do it? The state legislature had spent valuable time and taxpayer money crafting the legislation, some of which passed with overwhelming support. Yes, the majority of the bills had Democrats as sponsors (56 out of the 82)—and Perry was Republican—but bills from Republicans were also terminated.[1] And many legislators didn't get courtesy calls that the governor was to veto their bill, which was a longstanding tradition. Charges of a power grab and political payback echoed through the state capitol.

Governor Perry's message was clear: Rick Perry would be a strong and active governor. He intended to invigorate the Republican Party at a time when Democrats and Republicans were vying for control of the legislature. Perry was determined to cement the development of a strong Texas governor—even though the Texas executive branch has

LEARNING OBJECTIVES

8.1 Identify the eligibility requirements, term, succession process, and removal process for Texas governors.

8.2 Analyze how governors use their formal powers.

8.3 Evaluate the governors' use of informal powers by the Texas governor to advance agendas

8.4 Assess the strength of the Texas governor and proposals to modify gubernatorial power.

● The longest-serving Governor in Texas history (by a large margin), Rick Perry established a precedent for a strong and active governor.

historically been weak and divided. The power of the governor is both independent from and connected to the larger executive branch (explored in Chapter 9), limiting the governor's overall power in many ways.

Governor Perry, like governors before and after him, battled both the legislature and other powerful members of the executive branch. These struggles are a legacy from the past. Fearful of unchecked executives following Texans' unpleasant experience with Reconstruction Governor Edmund Davis, every state constitution since that time has maintained a plural executive and limited the governor's power. And yet, through political will, party strength, and personal relationships, modern Texas governors are more powerful today than at any time in the state's history.

In this chapter, we take an in-depth look at the roles and powers of the Texas governor. We first outline the rules of the office, including the eligibility to serve, succession in office, lengths of terms, and removal from office. We then examine the formal powers of the governor, primarily as outlined in the Texas constitution. We next identify the informal powers of Texas governors: political and policy actions modern governors have taken to increase their political power. We end the chapter by distinguishing weak and strong governors and evaluating whether the Texas governor is weak or strong and the consequences for Texas government.

🤠 RULES OF THE OFFICE

8.1 Identify the eligibility requirements, term, succession process, and removal process for Texas governors

The Texas Constitution defines who can run for the governor's office, how long they can stay in office, and under what conditions they serve. These rules can also affect the power relationships between the governor and the rest of government in the Lone Star State. For example, the state legislature can use these rules to threaten the governor with impeachment. On the other hand, the length of the governor's term and the lack of term limits place a popular governor in a strong position relative to state legislators.

ELIGIBILITY

To serve as governor, an individual must be at least thirty years of age and a citizen of the United States and must have resided in Texas for at least five years immediately preceding his or her election. The governor cannot hold any other office (civil, military, or corporate) during their time in office and cannot accept any salary, reward, or compensation (or the promise of these) for any service rendered or preformed while governor. Interestingly, the governor need not be an eligible voter. Governor W. Lee "Pappy" O'Daniel was a registered voter but had not paid his poll tax (when a fee was required to vote) and could not even vote for himself in the 1938 election.

INFORMAL QUALIFICATIONS

The formal qualifications for governor are minimal, but informal qualifications such as race, gender, profession, political experience, social network, and charm and charisma also factor in. A 1962 *Houston Chronicle* editorial submitted that an ideal person for the office of governor needs "brilliance of mind," legal knowledge, political experience, and "sound knowledge of business and industry."[2] And almost all Texan governors have been white, protestant men with previous political experience. Texans have elected lawyers, bankers, baseball team owners, ranchers, and even a flour manufacturer to the highest office in Texas. But the political environment has changed since 1962, as the media and online social networking have made politics more accessible. In 2006, Jewish country singer and satirist Kinky Friedman challenged Rick Perry for the governor's seat and received almost 13% of the vote. His campaign slogan was "how hard could it be?"

In 2006, Kinky Friedman presented himself as a singing cowboy but also as a political outsider with a unique take on the power of the governor.

SOCIAL RESPONSIBILITY: **Should Texans take these kinds of candidates seriously?**

TERMS

Originally suspicious of executive power after their break with Mexico, the delegates at the constitutional convention of 1876 limited the governor's term to two years. In 1972, however, voters amended the constitution to extend the term to four years to reduce the frequency of election and allow the governor to focus on governing.

This expansion of time in office allows Texas governors to amass more power by leading the state for longer. Longer terms mean more opportunities for appointments, more favors granted, and a more significant say on two (rather than one) legislative sessions. There are no **term limits**, so an individual can run for governor as often as they wish. Most governors traditionally served only one term, so the average length of term since 1846 is about 3.5 years. But Governor Rick Perry broke that mold by serving as governor for more than twice as long as the 40 previous governors (see Figure 8.1).

term limits: legal restrictions on the number of terms that an elected official can serve in a specific office

FIGURE 8.1   **Longest Serving Governors**

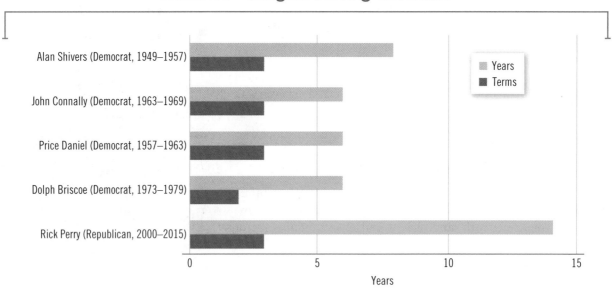

Source: Texas State Library and Archives

 COMMUNICATION:

Which governors have served longest?

- After Allan Shivers broke the longstanding Texas tradition by being elected for a third term; for much of the 1970s to 2000, no governor won more than two terms in office.
- Governor Perry is tied with Allan Shivers (1949-1957), Price Daniel (1957-1963), and John Connally (1963-1969) for three consecutive elected terms in office, but Governor Perry alone holds the record for years served as governor (14).

 CRITICAL THINKING:

Why do some governors serve longer than others?

- Longer serving governors cemented their powerful positions in their party, giving them incentives to serve longer in office.
- As the state became larger and the economy grew, the opportunity to leave a mark on state government required staying in office longer.

impeachment: the legal process in which the legislative branch has the authority to indict and remove a public official

REMOVAL FROM OFFICE

Impeachment is a legal process in which the legislative branch has the authority to indict and remove a public official. The state legislature can impeach both elected and non-elected officials. It carries out this process in two stages. First, the Texas House of Representatives must cast a majority vote in favor of impeachment. Second, the Texas Senate sits as a jury, hearing and evaluating the evidence in a trial setting. To convict an individual who has been impeached by the house and remove them from office, two-thirds of the senate must agree. Once removed, an individual is disqualified from holding "any office of honor, trust or profit" in the state (article 15, Section 4).

Unlike the US Constitution, the Texas Constitution provides no specific grounds for impeachment. The charges are generally criminal in origin, but on occasion they involve the misuse of public office. For instance, State District Judge O. P. Carrillo was impeached in 1976 for misuse of county funds for which he later spent three years in prison for tax fraud.

"Now sing us a little song"

"Ma" was accused of being a puppet for her husband's ideas. However, she showed some independence in her political appointments and executive branch reorganization.

Only one governor, James E. "Pa" Ferguson, has been impeached in Texas's history. After an unremarkable first term, Governor Ferguson raised the ire of the legislature when he vetoed the appropriation for the University of Texas because the University Board of Regents refused to remove certain faculty members whom the governor found objectionable. The governor was indicted on nine criminal charges, including misapplication of public funds and embezzlement, non-enforcement of state banking laws, and receipt of a mysterious $156,500 (the source of which the Governor refused to identify). The Texas House impeached the governor on twenty-one articles and the Texas Senate convicted the governor on ten of them.

Calling the process a "Kangaroo court," Governor Ferguson submitted his resignation one day before the Senate rendered its final judgment.[3] When he ran again for governor in 1918, he argued that he could still hold the office, despite the impeachment, because he was never convicted. He was easily defeated by William P. Hobby in the Democratic Party primary. Then in 1924, "Pa" Ferguson helped to elect his wife, Miriam A. "Ma" Ferguson to the governor's office. The 1924 slogan went "Me for Ma, and I Ain't Got a Durned Thing Against Pa."

SUCCESSION

If the governor resigns, is removed, or dies in office, the lieutenant governor becomes the governor in what is called **political succession**. The lieutenant governor also serves as the acting governor when the governor is out of the state. Lieutenant Governor Preston Smith served as Governor for 277 days during the term of John Connally, including during Connally's five week African safari.[4]

political succession: the sequential passing of authority from one person to another as the previous people are unable to serve

IS IT BIGGER IN TEXAS?

FIGURE 8.2   **Governor Staff Size**

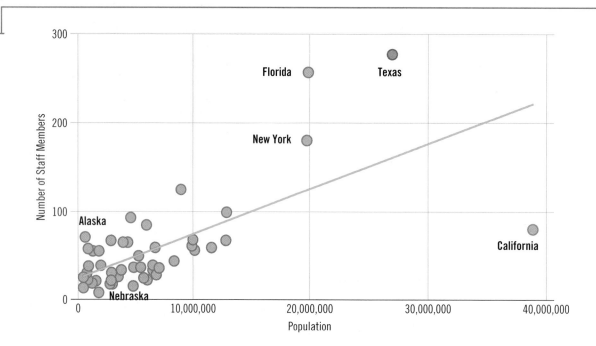

Source: Book of the States. Bureau of the Census. Figures represent executive staff and gubernatorial staff mapped with the population of the state. The line is a fitted prediction line—points above the line are above average in staff size, while those below are below average.

 COMMUNICATION:

How does Texas compare on gubernatorial staff size?

• Texas leads the nation in the size of the executive staff. Other large states like New York and Florida have large staffs. California is the exception to this trend.

• States with smaller populations tend to have a modest staff size.

 CRITICAL THINKING:

Why do some states have more staff?

• Larger states tend to have larger executive staff size and often also have a larger budget to grow staff size. California is the exception—budget cuts drove the number of staff members down.

• The power of the governor in states with larger staff is greater, as governors seek a political advantage to establish their policies and communicate their messages.

• New York, Florida, and Texas are largely dominated by one party, so the legislatures in each state may allocate more funds to allow the governor's office to grow in size.

SALARY AND STAFF

The current salary of the Governor is $150,000 annually. This salary puts Texas governors in the middle of the income spectrum for governors nationally. In practice, many modern governors of Texas are wealthy before they entered office, primarily in real estate or ranching, or having worked as an attorney. Because security is necessarily attached to a governors' travel, the taxpayers must pay the tab for this when governors travel for political events. At the height of his run for the White House in 2011, for instance, Governor Rick Perry was spending as much as $400,000 per month in security, some of which came out of taxpayer money.

The Texas governor's office employs almost 300 staff members with a diverse set of functions, including press relations, legal advice, scheduling and advance work, human resources, and expert policy advice (especially on the budget). These staffs work closely with the Governor to create, sharpen, and support the governor's priorities, protect the governor's image, and govern the executive branch. The Texas governor has a large staff in comparison to his counterparts (see Figure 8.2).

 TEXAS TAKEAWAYS

1 What requirements must candidates meet to run for governor in Texas?

2 How long do governors usually serve?

3 How can the Texas legislature impeach a governor?

FORMAL POWERS OF TEXAS GOVERNORS

The Texas Constitution outlines the formal powers granted to the governor. Governors use these formal powers to implement laws, manage the executive branch, push policies through the state legislature, check the judicial system, and protect Texans, particularly in the aftermath of natural disasters.

> **8.2** Analyze how governors use their formal powers.

EXECUTION OF LAWS

Like the US Constitution, the Texas Constitution charges that the Governor, as the state's chief executive, "cause the laws to be faithfully executed." Although the 1876 Texas Constitution is vague with respect to carrying out this responsibility, governors over time have expanded their executive authority through executive orders and proclamations. Today, governors have wide latitude in controlling the operations of the state, especially state agencies.

FIGURE 8.3   **Unilateral Orders by Governor per Year**

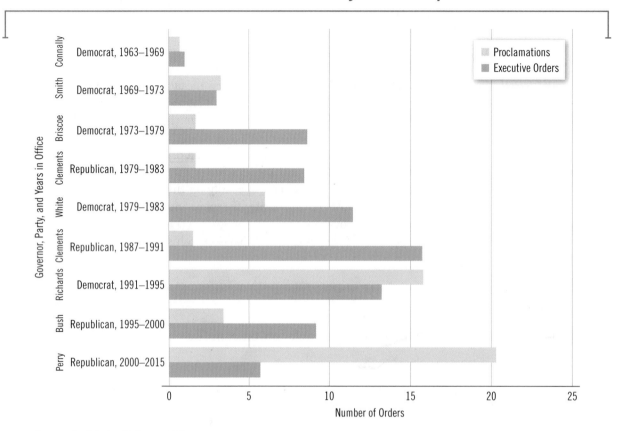

Source: Legislative Reference Library.

 COMMUNICATION:

How has the number of executive orders and proclamations changed over time?

- With a few exceptions, the number of executive orders and proclamations has increased over time, although the use of proclamations has increased more consistently.

 CRITICAL THINKING:

What explains the increases and decreases?

- The executive's power to act unilaterally expanded over this time as the legislature allowed the governor to do more by executive decree.
- Governors who serve when the opposition controls the state legislature, like Clements who confronted a Democratic legislative majority, have issued more orders than governors who enjoy majority support in the legislature. Richards also dealt with a growing Republican tide in the legislature.
- Governors Richards and Perry used proclamations to appeal to groups inside and outside of their party: Richards to maintain a party losing support and Perry to grow support.

Governors often issue unilateral **executive orders** to execute laws (see Figure 8.3). These orders have the force of law and often make use of powers granted to the governor by the legislature. Governors use executive orders for several purposes: to create task forces to assist with policy development, to respond to natural disasters and other emergencies, to fill interim political appointments, to call special sessions of the legislature, to issue "emergency" items for legislative consideration, and to hold special elections. For example, in 1978, Governor Dolph Briscoe established a task force to investigate and report on speedy criminal trials; and in 1996, Governor Bush ordered a ban on fireworks in Andrews County (just before the Fourth of July) due to extreme drought conditions.

Governors also use these orders to manage executive agencies and to push their political agenda, especially if they are up against opposition in the legislature (see Figure 8.4). To battle a rising state deficit, Republican Governor Bill Clements, who faced a majority Democratic legislature, directed each agency with an operating budget over $10 million to conduct an internal audit to find ways to save money.

Proclamations are similar to executive orders but are used to make factual determinations (such as a state of emergency) to trigger other available powers (such as the ability to ask for disaster relief funds). In 2011, when the state was in the throes of a terrible drought and vicious wildfires, Governor Perry issued a proclamation that designated three days as official days of prayer for rain. These orders often serve purely ceremonial purposes, allowing the governor to play a public role in the political culture of the state. In one of his first actions as Governor, Greg Abbott proclaimed February 2, 2015, as Chris Kyle Day in honor of Chief Petty Officer Chris Kyle, a native Texan and Navy SEAL who served four tours in Iraq and has been recognized as the most lethal sniper in United States military history, made famous by his book and movie *American Sniper.*

The use of unilateral power has been met with legislative backlash. In 2005, Governor Perry issued Executive Order 47, ordering the commissioner of education to establish a requirement that at least 65 percent of school districts' revenue be used for classroom instruction. In 2007, the Governor issued an executive order mandating that all eleven- and twelve-year-old girls get an HPV (human papillomavirus) vaccine, which protects women and teens against a sexually transmitted disease that causes cervical cancer. In both instances, the legislature overturned the actions.

APPOINTMENT POWERS

Another way in which the governor manages the executive branch and implements laws is through the power of appointment. In all, a governor can make appointments to more than 3,000 positions in executive agencies, boards, and commissions (all non-legislative offices). Most governors have the opportunity to fill about one-third of these positions in a four-year term. Because of the political power these appointees have and because appointments require senate approval, the selection

executive orders: legally binding orders from the governor that are used to direct government, especially state agencies, in the execution of law

proclamations: gubernatorial orders that are used to make factual determinations to trigger other available powers

IS IT BIGGER IN TEXAS?

FIGURE 8.4   **Unilateral Executive Orders by Governor in Select States**

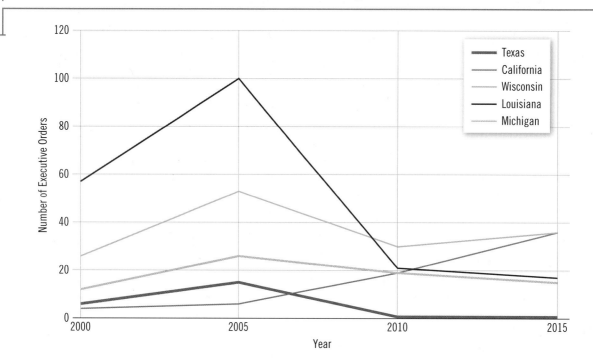

Source: Office of the Governor in each state.

 COMMUNICATION:

Where does Texas stack up with other states governors' use of executive orders?

- In recent years, Texas governors have used fewer executive orders, many fewer than many states such as Wisconsin and California.

- Of the states listed, Texas is the only one with a session every two years rather than every year. It is still the lowest of the group listed, despite the idea that less frequent legislative sessions might encourage the governor to issue more orders.

 CRITICAL THINKING:

What explains this trend?

- The biggest driver of more orders issued is when a state's government is divided: where the legislature is controlled by one party and the executive by the other.

- In recent times, Texas governors have been Republican and faced Republican legislatures, minimizing the need for more orders because the governor could count on legislation to his or her liking.

- States with conservative governors during this time who embraced small government, such as Texas and Louisiana from 2010 on, have fewer executive orders.

is often contentious. Governor Connally once joked, "if you want to talk about real infighting, try making an appointment to the Board of Cosmetology."[5]

Appointments can be political in function and appearance. During her single term as governor, Ann Richards made good on her campaign promise to make the government in Texas look like the people of Texas: 48 percent of her first 650 appointments were female, 12 percent were black, and 25 percent were Hispanic. This diversification did not sit particularly well with all segments of Texas, which were used to being run by conservative, white, Anglo men. On one occasion, Richards appointed Democratic State Representative Guerrero to a vacancy left on the Texas Railroad Commission while John Sharp was serving as comptroller. On the day of the appointment, Sharp received a phone call from an angry oilman who demanded to know, "Who the hell is Leonard Guerrero?" Sharp answered, "It's worse than you think; it's *Lena* Guerrero."[6]

see for yourself 8.1

Listen to Ann Richards describe her political ambitions and how she used the power appointment to help achieve them.

After Republicans won legislative majorities in the 2002 election, the legislature surrendered much of its power to appoint and oversee boards and commissions to Republican Governor Perry. The arguments against these expansive powers are that the governor has an outsized role in government, his or her appointees are responsive only to the governor and not necessarily to other agents in government, and the potential for cronyism is more pronounced as governors appoint influential political allies to government positions.

In one famous case, Governor John Connally entered his second term stinging after legislative losses at the hands of his nemesis conservative Speaker of the Texas House Byron Tunnell. Four days before the start of the 1965 legislative session, a vacancy opened up on the Railroad Commission. Seeing an opportunity to get rid of a powerful enemy, Connally nominated Speaker Tunnell to serve on the Railroad Commission and facilitated the election of his loyal ally Ben Barnes as Speaker of the Texas House.[7]

The governor's appointment powers are not absolute, however. Their appointment power is shared with the state Senate, which must approve of any appointee with a two-thirds majority. If the Senate is in recess, the governor's appointee stays in office until the state senate votes on the nominee during the first ten days in session. The legislature can also limit the term to be served by a person appointed by the governor should they wish to do so. Some boards and commissions also require by law that the representation be balanced by geography or professional background, limiting the governor's discretion.

About one in four of Governor Abbott's appointments in his first year in office were campaign contributors. In 2015, Governor Greg Abbott appointed Donna Bahorich as the new chair of the State Board of Education. Bahorich was criticized for being a vocal conservative voice for curriculum standards and a home school advocate.

PERSONAL RESPONSIBILITY: **Is it ethical to appoint political allies to important government posts? Why or why not?**

"I have a huge stack of bills to sign or veto. Decisions. Decisions." Greg Abbott wrote and posted this picture on his personal Twitter account.

LEGISLATIVE POWERS

A major function of the governor is to work with the legislature. An effective governor focuses on two or three key goals to push through a sometimes friendly but typically hostile legislature.[8] The Texas political system splits policymaking power between the legislative and executive branches of government, making for tense political interactions. Policy agendas, election promises, different constituency demands, and divergent ideological approaches frame the skirmishes between the branches. Let's take a look at the powers governors employ during these skirmishes.

Recommending Legislation.   By constitutional mandate, governors are allowed to "recommend to the Legislature such measures he may deem expedient." In other words, governors have the ability to suggest legislation to the legislature. Many governors take a direct role in the legislative arena. Governor Dolph Briscoe pledged to legislators that "the most persistent lobbyist you will see this session is the governor of Texas." Indeed, the introverted Briscoe successfully pushed through property protection laws, a streamlined penal code, and ethics reform legislation.[9]

Legislative "Emergencies."   During the first sixty days of each legislative session, lawmakers are barred from passing legislation. Instead, they focus time organizing each chamber, holding hearings on legislation, and debating issues. Only the governor can break through this line. The constitution allows the governor to declare an "emergency" item and have it be prioritized in the first sixty days. These "emergencies" enable the governor to highlight their pet issues and advance their political agenda. Governors often prioritize controversial matters to ensure that the legislature hears the issue before other issues.

At the outset of the 2011 legislative session, just before the 2012 elections in which Governor Perry was to run for president, the governor asked the legislature for two emergency items: to require a doctor to perform an ultrasound on a pregnant woman before an abortion was performed and to require voters to present photo IDs before voting. Both issues were raw "red meat" to the conservative Republican base across the country where he hoped to win points for his candidacy.[10] Newly elected Governor Greg Abbott declared "emergencies" in 2015 that would make good on his campaign promises—increased funding for transportation, pre-kindergarten education, and border security initiatives. These three items passed, but some of this other emergency items did not.

FIGURE 8.5 **Bills Introduced and Passed During Special Sessions**

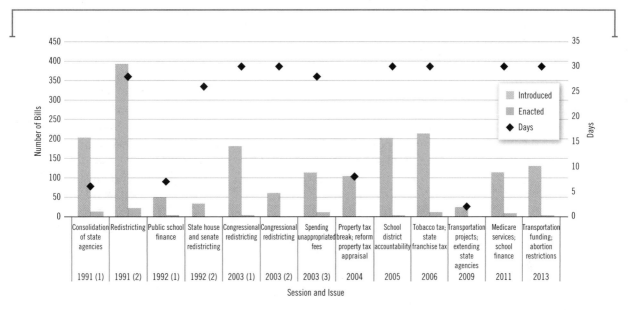

Source: Book of the States

 COMMUNICATION:

What topics have special sessions addressed?

- The issues that most frequently called for special session include education, redistricting electoral lines, and tax reforms.

 CRITICAL THINKING:

Is there a correlation between the length of a session and the number of bills enacted?

- Longer sessions tend to have more legislation enacted, while shorter sessions tend to have little legislation enacted at all.
- Yet longer sessions on contentious issues (such as redrawing the lines of the legislative seats in 2003) can often produce little legislation.

Special Sessions After the biennial 140-day session is over, the governor has the power to call the legislature into special session that can last up to 30 days. The governor sets the specific agenda for the session and can call as many as they desire. For this reason, these sessions are often called the "governor's session." The legislature can only consider legislation related to that issue; no other issues can be discussed. The governor's ability to call the session does not extend to issues that are executive or judicial in character, such as appointments or impeachments.[11] Recent governors have been more targeted in their calls, directing the legislature clearly on what issues they should discuss (see Figure 8.5). Historically, special sessions are more likely in times of war, depression, and financial crisis.[12] In modern Texas, special sessions are more likely to be called when the legislature is gridlocked over a specific issue, or when an issue is politically challenging and cannot be solved in the regular 140-day legislative session.

These sessions have ranged in timing from thirty seconds to thirty days. On the short end, Governor Neff vetoed the appropriations bill sent to him by the legislature and called a special session for the day after the adjournment of the regular session. Incensed by the governor's tactics and frustrated that they not return home to receive their mileage allowance, the legislature adjourned the special session without conducting any business.[13]

Governors can call a special session for any reason and at any time (outside of the biennial 140-day session). The governor's "call" (by executive proclamation) lets the legislature know what's on the menu for the session. Special sessions are politically risky for governors. They promise great ability to focus on the governor's agenda, but there is also blame if things go wrong. A failed session can hurt a governor politically and make them appear weak. Governor Mark White lost control of his special session in 1984 on education reform. Ann Richards's special session on education in 1993 failed to produce meaningful reform. Perceptions of ineffective leadership hurt both in their reelection efforts (neither of which was successful).

Veto Powers.   All constitutions in Texas have given the governor (or president under the Republic) the power of the **veto**. It is often called the "governor's gift" because it is such a valuable bargaining tool. A governors' veto includes a set of reasons for objection, which are sent to the chamber that introduced the original bill.

veto: formal, constitutional decisions to formally reject a resolution or bill made by the legislature

The veto is the governor's strongest constitutional power in his or her struggle with the state legislature to direct policy (see Figure 8.6). The governor has ten days (excluding Sundays) to sign or veto the bill or the bill automatically becomes law. If the legislature feels strongly enough about the legislation to reconsider it, two-thirds of the members of both houses of the legislature can override the veto. If the legislature adjourns after submitting a bill to the governor but before the normal ten-day period would have expired, the governor has twenty days from receipt of it to veto the legislation or the bill becomes law. During these periods when the legislature is adjourned, the governor can veto legislation without the threat of an override by the legislature.

Governors often veto to bring state policy in line with their political philosophy. Governor Ross Sterling, a businessman who lacked political experience and who took a view that limited government was best, vetoed the fewest. Miserly with the state's finances, Governor Dan Moody became a strong proponent of the use of executive authority to limit state spending. Governor Moody vetoed 76 pieces of legislation and 4 specific budget items in 1929. He went so far as to veto legislation that would have authorized funds

FIGURE 8.6 **Number of Vetoed Bills 1979–Present**

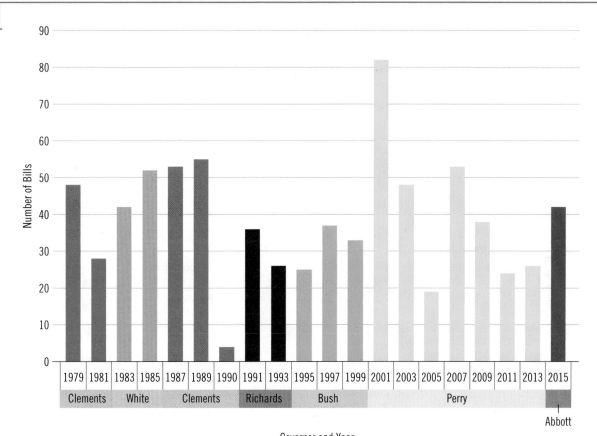

Source: Texas Reference Library.

 COMMUNICATION:

How frequently do governors use the veto?

- Since 1979, governors veto average approximately 30 pieces of legislation per session.
- Governor Clements vetoed more than those who preceded him in both of his terms of office, but Governor Perry vetoed the most legislation in a single session and overall.

 CRITICAL THINKING:

Why more vetoes in some years than others?

- Greater political disagreement within a party (such as conservative and liberal factions fighting) or when the legislature is of a different party than the governor increases the use of the veto. This was true especially for Governor Clements, who faced significant opposition in the Democratic legislature as the first Republican-elected governor since the Civil War.
- Governor Perry, who sought to strengthen the office of the governor, frequently used the veto stamp to express his authority.

FIGURE 8.7   **First Term Governor Line Item Veto Cuts**

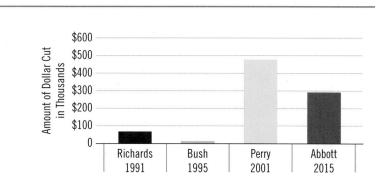

Source: Texas Reference Library

 COMMUNICATION:

How much do first-term governors cut from the budget using their line item strategy?

- First-term governors since 2001 have made significant use of the line item veto to cut funds from the budget.

- Governors Richards and Bush made modest use of the line item veto in their first years in office, cutting less than $100,000 combined, whereas Governors Perry and Abbott made more significant use.

 CRITICAL THINKING:

Why did some governors cut more than others?

- New governors with larger party majorities in the legislature, like Perry and Abbott, may be more willing to cut budgets with less fear of repercussions. Governors with smaller support in their majority party, like Richards and Bush, may be more reluctant to anger the legislature by cutting funds.

- Growing political pressure for slower state spending contributed to more recent governors reducing budgets unilaterally.

line item veto: a veto that allows the governor to reject a specific provision in a bill without rejecting the whole bill

for members of the Texas legislature to travel to Washington, DC, to lobby for a new veteran's hospital.

Unlike the president of the United States, Texas governors have a particularly effective defensive tool: the line item veto (see Figure 8.7). A **line item veto** allows the governor to reject a specific provision in a bill without rejecting the whole bill. The public (and to some degree the legislature) expect the governor to use the line item veto to hem in state spending. For instance, Governor Pat Neff line item vetoed items amounting to more than $39 million. He used his veto to kill the proposed West Texas A&M College, stating that the appropriation was against the will of the state Democratic Party convention. Governor James V. Allred line item vetoed an $817,000 appropriation in 1937 for a hospital, noting the state was already building one other hospital and didn't need a second.[14]

Vetoes are a potent power for Texas's chief executive, as they are rarely overridden—partly due to the fact that the legislature is often out of session by the time governors veto bills. From the 1876 to 1968, only 25 vetoes were overridden (out of 936 vetoes). Only one veto has been overridden since the 1960s. In 1979, Governor Clements vetoed legislation to limit the ability of county governments to prohibit hunters from killing female deer. The governor claimed that a central authority like the Texas Parks and Wildlife Department should be in charge of this initiative, not local governments. The legislature bristled, in part due to Governor Clements's approach to governing—he had declared that he was going to run Texas like a business, and "I'm the chief executive officer, and y'all can take it or leave it!"[15] The state legislature decided to leave it and rejected Clements' bid for centralization of power. As with many executive–legislative interactions, greater communication can resolve potential problems.

Because of the difficulty in overturning a veto, even the threat of a veto from the governor is a highly effective weapon. Governors threaten to veto legislation on matters where they are certain they can coerce the legislature to alter proposed legislation to their liking. In 2015, riding high off of impressive electoral victory, Governor Greg Abbott vowed to "reject any budget that is sent to my desk that does not include lower taxes for businesses."[16] Despite warnings from two prominent senate budget writers (one Democrat and one Republican) that major tax cuts would not be prudent, citing the uncertainty in oil prices and obligations the state has to public schools, pension funds, and transportation, Abbott's veto threat proved effective, and the legislature passed a 25 percent cut to the state business tax, a total of more than $2 billion.

MILITARY POWERS

As the president is the commander-in-chief of the US military, the Texas governor serves as commander-in-chief of the Texas military forces (except when they are called into service of the United States). In practice, this means that the governor is in charge of the National Guard, appointing the adjutant general of the Guard, and directing the guard to protect lives and property. The Guard is most often used during natural disasters, such as Hurricane Katrina, the north Texas wildfire, or the Marble Falls flooding.

However, the National Guard also protects the state in times of crisis. In 2014, Governor Rick Perry dispatched the National Guard to the border. Perry argued that he was forced to act because of a string of failures by the federal government in stemming the tide of illegal migration across the border, including drug smugglers and unaccompanied minors from Central America. More than 52,000 unaccompanied minors, mostly from Guatemala, Honduras, and El Salvador, illegally crossed the Texas border in 2014, more than four times the number just two years earlier.[17] Approximately 1,000 strong and dubbed "Operation Strong Safety," the deployment cost $18 million per month in an effort to boost the law enforcement presence near the border.[18] Governor Perry maintained that the presence of the Guard had served as an effective deterrent

ANGLES OF POWER

Governor Perry's Veto of Corruption Unit Funds

Using the line item veto can get a governor in legal hot water. In 2013, the Travis County (Austin) district attorney, Rosemary Lehmberg, was caught driving under the influence of alcohol and was caught on tape in a lengthy and embarrassing interaction with the police in which she was hostile and belligerent and eventually needed to be restrained. Following her arrest, Governor Perry publicly indicated that the office had "lost the public's confidence" and demanded she step aside. He threatened to line item veto $7.5 million in state funding for the public corruption unit, which is housed in the district attorney's office in Travis County, unless Lehmberg resigned. The long-simmering conflict between elected politicians (especially Republicans) and the Public Integrity Unit (PIU) spans multiple decades, as the PIU

targeted notable politicians such as Tom Delay (member of the US House of Representatives and the Republican Majority Leader). The governor followed through on his threat and used his line item veto to remove the funds.

On August 15, 2014, Governor Perry was indicted on two charges by a Travis County grand jury operating under the supervision of a special prosecutor. The allegations specified that the governor had abused his authority in using the veto to coerce the district attorney to step down. The law states that a public servant who knowingly inflicts harm or misuses government property is guilty. Governor Perry and his legal team decried that the "baseless political charges" were "partisan." Governor Perry asserted that it was his First Amendment right to speak out against the District Attorney. Perry's legal team asserted that there are no restrictions on how a governor can use a veto. The Court of Criminal Appeals agreed in 2016 and held that the governor had rightfully used his veto power.

SOCIAL RESPONSIBILITY: **Should the governor be given more powers to control the executive branch?**

---

when apprehensions of illegal migrants at the border dropped by 74 percent.[19] Opponents claimed the governor overreacted and wildly spent funds that could be better used elsewhere.

JUDICIAL POWERS: PARDON AND CLEMENCY

clemency: the power to reduce or delay punishment for a crime

pardon: the power to forgive a crime

In criminal cases except treason and impeachment, the governor has the power to grant reprieves and commutations of punishment, remit any fines and forfeitures, and issue **clemency** (reduction or delay of a sentence) or **pardons** (forgiveness for a crime) with the written support of the majority of the Texas Prisons Board. In capital murder cases, the governor can grant a temporary "jailhouse reprieve" for thirty days on his own, without Board approval. In a 1925 case, for example, Governor Pat Neff pardoned the famous bluesman Huddie William Ledbetter, better known as "Lead Belly," incarcerated in a Sugar Land prison for murder. Modern governors rarely use clemency or pardon powers, generally to appear tough on crime for political reasons.

The governor's ability to pardon is not absolute. Governor James E. "Pa" Ferguson exercised the power of the pardon so frequently he was said to have an "open door policy" at the Texas Penitentiary. Ferguson issued 2,253 pardons in just two years, a state record! In one instance, coming to the office to discuss clemency, a man placed several bills in Governor Ferguson's palm when he shook hands. Governor Miriam "Ma" Ferguson (1925–1927, 1933–35), wife to "Pa," was also criticized for abusing the pardon system, which led to legislative reforms. In two years, she granted 1,161 pardons, and rumors began to pop up that pardons were being sold. Approaches were made to "practically all members of the Ferguson family" including a blatant offer to the Ferguson's daughter of $5,000 to use her influence to secure a pardon.[21] The legislature passed a law to ensure that the governor must first receive majority support from the appointees of the Boards of Pardons and Paroles before granting clemency or pardons or remitting fines.

★ TEXAS TAKEAWAYS

4 What formal tools do governors have to executive the laws in Texas?

5 When can governors call special sessions?

6 How frequently do Texas governors veto legislation?

7 How often are vetoes overturned?

🤠 INFORMAL POWERS OF TEXAS GOVERNORS

The Texas Constitution gives governors a modestly sized toolbox of formal powers with which to work. Governors, however, have **informal powers** that derive from their experience, their natural ability to negotiate and lead, their popularity, and their relationship with the media. The prowess of each governor to exploit their informal powers largely defines their legacy, enabling skillful governors to effectively bargain with the legislature, set the policy agenda, and serve as an economic cheerleader for the state.

8.3 Evaluate the governors' use of informal powers by the Texas governor to advance agendas.

informal powers: actions governors might take that are not formally written but are exercised through the activities of the governor

LEGISLATIVE BARGAINING

Governors are granted the formal power to recommend legislation, but they have to work well with members of the legislature to ensure passage of their agenda. Governors work with allies and enemies in the legislature to iron out policy differences. A savvy governor works both within the Capitol (through

Former Democratic Governor Mark White

Who are the governor's greatest allies while in office?

Think of it like a kaleidoscope—a combination of allies depending on the issues. As an example, I called a special session for education in 1984, not having great success on the issue. Working together with schoolteachers, highway contractors, and business leaders, we got it done. Working just with schoolteachers, we would not have had adequate ability to change.

SOCIAL RESPONSIBILITY: **In attempting to solve a complex problem facing the state, whom or what groups would you reach out to first? Why?**

direct negotiation with members) and outside the pink dome (through indirect negotiation with the media).

Meals and Midnight Visits.   Being available and cordial can go a long way in legislative relations. On one occasion, Governor Price Daniel was called near midnight to the Capitol to break an impasse over the sales tax rate. The governor was already tucked in for the evening but arose, dressed, and sped across the street to the Capitol. Working into the early morning hours, the committee adopted a compromise sales tax bill with the governor's aid.

In contrast to the inaccessibility of Ann Richards and the imperial style of Bill Clements, George Bush would invite legislators late to his office with music playing, clad in a ball cap and no shoes. The governor and legislators hammered out many pieces of legislation over steaks and spirits, frequently at one of Austin's many locations frequented by the political elite, like Austin Land & Cattle or the Cloak Room.

Endorsements.   A governor can lend their personal prestige to candidates for office with the presumption of reciprocal support. The 1980 elections saw huge gains for Republican candidates across the nation, with newly elected President Ronald Reagan leading the charge. Republican Governor Bill Clements came into the 1981 session riding high in the saddle after backing several winning Republican candidates in the 1980 election. These new Republican members of the Texas Legislature, although outnumbered by Democrats at the time, owed their seats to Clements and returned the favor by supporting his proposed programs.

Working the Floor.   The governor and his or her staff also coordinate and communicate with members of the legislature while the session is ongoing—"working the floor." A longtime political observer from the *Dallas Morning News* likened the procedure in the Governor Shivers era to "a well trained army moving in."[22] Communication is key in making legislative deals, and staff with an eye toward legislative bargaining and the ear of the governor serve a vital role in a governor's success.

Going Public.   Just as presidents take their case to the American people, Texas governors frequently speak directly to the citizens of Texas. This persuasion technique is called "going public." No more colorful a character than radio personality and flour salesman Governor W. Lee O'Daniel made extensive use of his buoyant personality on the radio every Sunday from the "front room" of the executive mansion to discuss the business of Texas. A political showman with little political experience, he had acquired the nickname "Pappy" from a song his band played, "Please Pass the Biscuits, Pappy." On one occasion, however, his tactics backfired. The governor bitterly attacked the legislature, who opposed his proposed sales tax amendment. He read a list of the specific senators who had supported his program, labeling this group the "honor roll" and threatening to "take the stump" to oppose the reelection of those who worked against his program. Called a "Sabbath Caesar" for his coercive methods, O'Daniel failed to get his program to pass the Texas House.[23]

Dealing with the Media.   The most dangerous place in Austin is the space between the governor and a television camera, or so goes an old saying about the importance of the media to modern governors. Governors have used the media platform to press their agenda; negotiate publicly with the legislature; brag about economic growth; and, most prominently, run for reelection. For instance, back in the 1940s, Governor Coke Stevenson used the Capitol press corps as his "kitchen cabinet" where he would solicit the advice of these reporters. Governor Mark White was often called "Media Mark" for his affinity for talking with reporters about his administration's policies.

see for yourself 8.2

Watch Governor Briscoe respond to media queries about "The Best Little Whorehouse in Texas." Does the buck stop with the governor?

AGENDA SETTING

Because of constitutional limitations, the power of the governor is only as strong as the governor makes it. Governor George Bush campaigned and then governed on four themes he constantly refrained to anyone who would listen: education reform, welfare reform, tort reform, and juvenile justice reform. When pressed for elaboration, he added a fifth item: "pass the first four things." This insistent attitude allowed the governor to overcome the traditional weakness of the office and led to an unusually impressive winning streak on his legislative items.

   Agenda setting can often backfire if governors fail to communicate effectively with key legislators. In 1997, Texas was fat with a sizeable $3 billion surplus. Governor Bush laid claim to some of that money, announcing he wanted $1 billion of that surplus to go to reducing local school taxes. This proposition was a surprise to Lieutenant Governor Bob Bullock and Speaker Pete Laney,

agenda setting: an informal power of the governor to use his public platform to set the state's political and policy agenda

GREAT TEXAS POLITICAL DEBATES
Personal Relations Between Governors and Lieutenant Governors

As we see in Chapter 9, the lieutenant governor, who presides over the Texas Senate, is one of the most powerful figures in the state and a major part of the executive branch. The relationship between the lieutenant governor and governor is critical to the passage of legislation. Both have tremendous authority in shaping the state budget and legislation. Ann Richards was characteristically dismissive of the old political guard of "good old boys" in the Democratic Party and their behavior. After a full gubernatorial term (two legislative sessions) of Ann Richard's trusting but hands-off leadership in the Texas legislature, volatile Lieutenant Governor Bob Bullock found a more active partner in newly elected Governor George W. Bush. Bullock and Bush met frequently, with Bush passionately absorbing all the political wisdom Bullock had gained in 50 years in Texas politics. As a result, Governor Bush compromised and was more successful in getting his preferred legislation passed than Governor Richards. Other executives, like the lieutenant governor, are elected separate from the governor, giving the governor less influence over their actions.

SOCIAL RESPONSIBILITY: **Should the governor be given more powers to control the executive branch?**

NO: The framers of the Texas Constitution originally reduced the governor's power because of fear of government abusing power and interfering in their lives. The spreading out of powers across multiple executive offices requires that the individuals work together, and no one interest dominates.

YES: The Texas Constitution is outdated when it comes to efficient allocation of power to the governor's office. The Texas governor is the most prominent figure in state government and citizens rightly hold the governor accountable for policies. Therefore, the governor should have significantly more power than the lieutenant governor and other members of the executive branch.

A LITTLE: Expanded authority to hire and fire members of the executive branch would give the governor just enough more power to run the executive branch efficiently but not violate the separation of powers in the Texas Constitution.

who were central to passing Bush's agenda in the 1995 session. The three generally had good relations, but taking action without building consensus doomed the initiative. Speaker Laney told the governor to "stop listening to your political advisers and start listening to your legislative advisers,"[24] advice Bush then followed (see Great Texas Political Debates feature).

Citizen Advisory Group.   Governors can formally or informally assemble a citizens' advisory group that studies policy issues and recommends actions. Prominent individuals on these committees help the governor or lieutenant governor understand the needs of the state, prioritize problems, and come up with innovative solutions. Governor White, who made public education a priority in his term in office, appointed Dallas billionaire H. Ross Perot to chair the Select Committee on Public Education, which held hearings around the state on matters of school finance, teacher compensation, and secondary curriculum. Their fact-finding report led to the passage of House Bill 72 in 1984, which raised teacher salaries, but tied them to teacher performance; instituted teacher certification programs; set strict attendance rules; and introduced "no-pass, no-play," prohibiting students who were failing courses from participating in sports and extracurricular activities for six months.

Budget. The governor is required to submit a budget to the legislature but may also use their public voice to shape the content of the budget. Governors "recommend" a budget to the legislature which the legislature is free to ignore. Governors have historically only had a seat at the "kids table" on budget issues, yet this is changing as recent governors have been more likely to veto legislation to shape the budget. The Texas budget is required to include a list of appropriations for the current year and the amount requested by executive agencies for the two-year budget.

The governor, along with the Legislative Budget Board (LBB), does take the first step in the budget process—the preparation of a "mission statement" for the state in the fall before a legislative session—which sets out a framework for the development of strategic plans and constructs goals and principles to guide decision-making. This document serves as an agenda setter and promises strategic planning for the state. The Governor's Office of Budget, Planning and Policy and the LBB issue instructions for developing agency-specific strategic plans to be reviewed and submitted.

Republican Governor George W. Bush learned quickly that cooperation with Democratic Lieutenant Governor Bob Bullock was crucial to advancing his political agenda.

In his first proposed budget as Governor, Greg Abbott outlined a "something for everyone" agenda, emphasizing modest growth in funds for education and transportation. The legislature met his priorities by funding both agenda items.

As the chief executive in Texas, governors also have the authority, shared with the LBB, to administer the budget. When necessary, the governor and the LBB have joint authority to transfer funds between programs within an agency or between agencies. This process is known as **budget execution**. Budget execution allows changes to appropriations during the period in which the legislature is not in session. This power provides the governor with some flexibility to allocate budget funds to meet state goals. The public has some say too—any such transfers require a public hearing to be held and input to be received from citizens.

budget execution: the governor's implementation of the budget when the legislature is not in session

When Governor Perry unleashed "Operation Strong Safety," a surge of border patrol and guard troops along the border, some questioned his use of funds. He had three payment options: use an emergency rider, tap the governor's disaster funds, or utilize a traditional "budget execution" authority of the Legislative Budget Board. Governor Perry's office decided to redirect $38 million in unused Department of Public Safety funding for emergency radio communications to go toward the National Guard.[25] This action drew the scrutiny of lawmakers who claimed that the use of disaster funds would have made for a more transparent process.

Inaugural Speech. The **inaugural speech** is not constitutionally required but is traditionally delivered with much pomp and circumstance at the beginning of a new gubernatorial term. These speeches are more inclusive than partisan.

inaugural speech: an address that is not constitutionally required but is conventionally delivered at the beginning of a new gubernatorial term

The speech provides governors, especially new governors, a major platform from which to offer a strategic vision for the state.

Governor Greg Abbott's inaugural speech in 2015 was a departure from some of his fiery rhetoric during his 2014 campaign for governor. His remarks on a sunny Tuesday in Austin played up the commonality of Texans and the importance of thinking about the future needs of the state (see Figure 8.8).

State of the State Address:
address used by governors to set a policy agenda

State of the State Address.   Following the inaugural address, governors use the **State of the State Address** to set a policy agenda. The Texas Constitution requires the governor to "give to the Legislature information, by message, of the condition of the State." This message is usually an outline of the governor's legislative priorities and policy agenda. Before the 1960s, it was common for governors to submit their messages to the legislature in writing instead of in person. Recent governors have generally been successful at getting the initiatives that they lay out in their State of the State Address passed in the legislature, especially when the legislature and the governor's mansion are controlled by members of the same party (see Figure 8.9).

Party Leader.   The governor is often the most visible member of his or her party, making them the natural choice to serve as ambassador of the party's message. Governor Bill Clements, the first Republican governor (first elected in 1978, then again in 1986) since Reconstruction, is often referred to as the father of the modern day Texas Republican Party for establishing a foothold for Republicans in the state. Early in office, he vowed to turn Texas, run exclusively by Democrats at the time, into a "two-party state." The fate of the Republican Party, it was claimed, rested on his shoulders. He didn't disappoint. His first budget called for reducing taxes, shrinking the bureaucracy, and improving education. Clements recruited new appointees, making them pledge to run in the future as Republicans. Clements provided a new generation of young Republicans opportunities in state politics they would not have gotten in the Democratic-dominated state. Modern governors must balance the ideological wings of their party. Republican Governor Greg Abbott's party has both moderate and conservative members, necessitating a careful calibration of a policy agenda.

Personal Outreach.   Candidates who are successful are often the most personable; and when in office, Texas governors use these skills to court the electorate and develop powerful and important networks in state government. After her husband James "Pa" Ferguson was impeached, the charming Miriam "Ma" Ferguson ran and won the gubernatorial election in 1924 and was elected again in 1932. Both Fergusons created a well-crafted image of being simple farmers and built their campaign around appealing to a rural constituency. One aide to Governor Ferguson recalled that the reception room at the governor's mansion was continuously jammed with constituents waiting to see "one of the governors," referencing "Ma" and "Pa" Ferguson's campaign promise to elect "two governors for the price of one."[26] Similarly, Governor Preston Smith

FIGURE 8.8   **Word Cloud of Governor Abbott's Inaugural Address**

Source: Website of Governor Greg Abbott.

 COMMUNICATION:

What are the most commonly used words in the governor's speech?

- The words "Texas" and "Texans" are the most commonly used terms from the Governor's address. These are closely followed by words such as "great" and "state."

 CRITICAL THINKING:

What do the most commonly used words imply about the governor's agenda or his approach to governing?

- Emphasizing the importance and immediacy of his agenda, Governor Abbott used the terms "must" and "dreams" several times.
- Reflecting on his faith personally and politically, the governor also used the word "God" and "grace" several times during his speech.
- Governor Abbott also sought to unify Texans behind his agenda, using words such as "one," "today," and "opportunity."

had breakfast every morning at the Driskill Hotel a few blocks away from the Governor's Mansion and would welcome members of the public to join him.

The primacy of personality can be a boom or a bust for governors. In the clubby world of Texas politics, sometimes personality outranks policy. Two political rivals who ran against each other two different times for governor had

FIGURE 8.9   **Governor Legislative Success Rate**

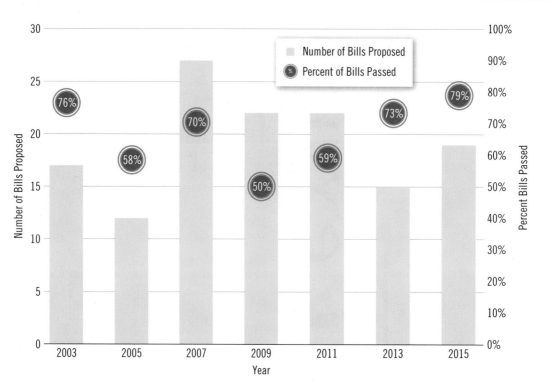

The bars represent the total requests in the governors' state of the state addresses: Governor Perry from 2003 to 2013 and Governor Abbott for 2015. The circles display the percent passed (out of the total number of requests).

Source: State of the State Speeches. Legislative Reference Library.

 COMMUNICATION:

How successful are governors at pushing through their agenda items?

- The size of the governors agenda (based on the number of requests) has decreased since 2007.

- Governors were successful in achieving more than 50% of their agenda items from the State of the State address, and in recent sessions that percentage has increased to 80%.

 CRITICAL THINKING:

Why have recent governors had more success?

- Governors use the increasing number of tools at their disposal (described in this chapter) to enhance their ability to enact their political agenda. This is especially true of Governor Perry beginning in 2001.

- The percentage of governor's initiatives passed has risen steadily since 2009 because of the growing number of Republican legislators in agreement with Republican governors.

problems resulting from their personality: Bill Clements and Mark White. Bill Clements was the model of a long series of wealthy oil men who entered Texas politics. He had a history of making mean-spirited remarks and was abrupt with friends and foes alike. This complicated his relationship with the legislature, particularly because it was controlled by the opposing party. He openly remarked that the legislature was full of a "bunch of idiots," referring to members of the Texas Senate as "prairie chickens" and state employees as "parasitic bureaucrats." Mark White was said to have good intentions, good ideas, and a good record but little ability to inspire loyalty. Slavishly listening to public opinion polls, washing back and forth between issue positions, and appearing weak on several positions, he lost his bid for reelection in 1986.

Governor Ann Richards on election night, 1990. Governors often use their big personalities to get elected and press their political agendas. Governor Richards once quipped, "I get a lot of cracks about my hair, mostly from men who don't have any."

Economic Cheerleader.   Recent Texas governors have spent a great deal of time on the road trying to lure jobs to the state. Governor Rick Perry spent months away from Austin recruiting companies to move to

PERSONAL RESPONSIBILITY: **How able are you to separate your personal feelings about a governor from your feelings about their legislative priorities? Do you think you tend to support candidates you "like" or candidates that align with your legislative goals?**

Texas, attracting Apple, Caterpillar, Facebook, and Toyota.[27] Governor Greg Abbott suggested that being the leader of the "Texas Chamber of Commerce" was one of the major responsibilities of the governor.[28] He spent several weeks out of the country in the summer of 2015 focusing on industries "ripe for a Texas pitch."[29] Texas led the nation in job growth during the economic downturn in the early 2000s, but the use of state funds to lure additional jobs to the state have produced decidedly mixed outcomes, with several high-profile projects delivering less than promised.[30] Critics have complained that these economic incentives are little more than corporate welfare that provide little in return.

★ TEXAS TAKEAWAYS

1 What informal powers do governors use to pursue their agenda?

2 How successful are governors at enacting their agenda?

3 How are the governor's annual State of the State Speech and their inaugural address similar?

🤠 WEAK AND STRONG GOVERNOR

8.4 Assess the strength of the Texas governor and proposals to modify gubernatorial power.

The Texas governor is a "weak" governor on paper. The framers of the sections on gubernatorial power were so wary when they created the Constitution in 1876 and the rule of former Governor Davis was so despised that there were no serious debates about the role of the chief executive. The framers of the 1876 constitution divided the powers of the executive branch into multiple agencies to weaken the power of the governor—as one framer of the constitution put it, "power is dangerous," and the only way to disarm the governor was to divide the powers.[31]

The effect was a discombobulated, decentralized position with short terms of office and low pay. The strength of a governor's office depends on the extent to which the governor appoints other important members of the executive branch, oversees administrative functions of the bureaucracy, can veto legislation and the budget, and can remove officials from office. The Texas governor has few of these powers. In addition, the legislative branch significantly checks the authority of the governor on appointment matters; and the branches share power on several other functions.

Texas ranks comparatively low on a scale of gubernatorial power (see Figure 8.10). However, if used properly, the governor's powers allow for significant expansion of executive authority. The example from Governor Perry's record-breaking number of vetoes in his first term in office makes this clear. Governors can use their power in ways that makes them powerful, if they use it properly. Consider a few ways Governor Perry left the office stronger than he found it.

SHEER LENGTH OF TERM

The position of governor is full-time. The legislature is part-time—they meet once every two years. This overlap of time gives the governor a natural advantage when it comes to policy expertise and political stamina. Governor Perry, as the longest-serving governor in state history at fourteen years, was able to make his mark on the politics of the state simply by holding the reins of government for so long.

APPOINTEES

By virtue of serving as governor for so long, Governor Perry was able to appoint nearly every member of every state committee, commission, or panel. He served long enough to go through the entire cycle of six-year executive appointments—twice. Perry appointed more than 8,000 individuals to head agencies, boards, and commissions during his terms as governor. Many of these are former staffers, aides, and allies.

IS IT BIGGER IN TEXAS?

FIGURE 8.10 **Map of Gubernatorial Power**

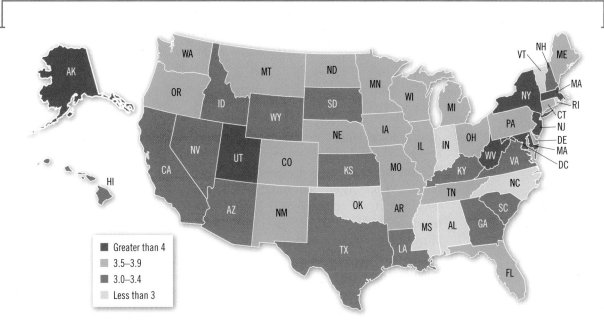

Legend:
- Greater than 4
- 3.5–3.9
- 3.0–3.4
- Less than 3

Rankings are based on appointment powers, veto powers, term length and limits, and budgetary control.

Source: Governor Institutional Power Index (updated measures, based on Beyle 1983).

 COMMUNICATION:

How does Texas compare to other states on executive power?

- Most states with large economies and significant industrial and manufacturing bases, such as New York, Pennsylvania, and Michigan, have strong governors.
- Even compared to smaller states with less robust economies, the Texas governor scores very low, practically near the bottom.

 CRITICAL THINKING:

What factors explain this trend?

- Many of the states in the original colonies (Massachusetts, New York, Maryland) had strong governors that were holdovers from an era of strong executives.
- The framers of the 1876 Texas Constitution made sure that the governor had minimal powers, at least on paper.
- Many southern states limited executive power following their experiences with overbearing governors during Reconstruction.

PARTY POWER

The resurgence of the Republican Party didn't occur overnight. Whereas other Republican governors before him opened the door to Republican Party rule, Perry took the door off the hinges. Governor Perry started off as a Democrat and switched parties, as many conservative Democrats did in the 1980s. Governor Perry topped the ticket in 2002 when Republicans made historic gains at all levels, including a sweep of all statewide offices. The governor took positions on social and cultural issues that have fueled the Republican Party's conservative shift in recent years.

CRITICISMS AND REFORMS

Although individual governors have expanded the power of the office, not all governors have been able to assert the institutional power that those few did. The Texas governor was designed to be a minimally powerful leader, but not an ineffective one. If efficiency and expedience of action is important in modern government, reformers point to several formal powers that should be expanded to ensure a more effective chief executive. Most of these reforms would require amending the Constitution.

Appointment Powers

Problem: Governors have limited influence over other key executive decision makers because of Texas's plural executive system. Governors have no appointment powers over important executive offices such as the state comptroller or attorney general. All of these offices are elected separately.

Context: One primary criticism in the 1960s was that after Governor Price Daniel's three terms in office, the bureaucracy in Texas, which was supposed to be independent of the executive, would be completely staffed by his loyalists. Opponents of Governor Daniel, who was eventually defeated after seeking an unprecedented fourth term, charged him with attempting to "control" the major agencies.[32]

Solution: Expand the appointment powers of the executive to other executive offices in state government.

Cronyism

Problem: Because there are no term limits for governors, no restrictions on whom a governor can appoint to an office, and there are few limits on political contributions, political appointments to the state's many important positions are often used as political patronage.

Context: One-fourth of Governor Rick Perry's nominees were donors to his campaign. For example, Peter Holt and Thomas Friedkin each donated more than half a million dollars to Perry between 2001 and 2010, according to one report. Chairman Holt, who heads the largest US Caterpillar dealership, is principle owner of the NBA's San Antonio Spurs. Vice Chairman Friedkin, a Toyota distributor, is an active wildlife conservationist.[33]They were appointed to the state Parks and Wildlife Commission.

Solution: Have the legislature submit a list of individuals the governor could consider to nominate. Increase the vetting process. Reduce the duration of time in office for appointees.

Removal Powers

Problem: The governor cannot remove an appointed official even if their performance declines or their support of the governor's program falters.

Context: With no formal removal powers, governors are forced to use alternative, often informal, means to coerce public officials to step down. In one instance, Governor Ferguson threatened to make public an inappropriate relationship between an appointee and his subordinate if the appointee did not step down. The appointee quickly signed the letter of resignation.

Solution: Expand the governor's removal powers so that the governor, similar to the president, has the power to replace appointees.

Budget Powers

Problem: The governor is charged with setting the state's financial agenda and executing the budget (spending the money), but the governor is at the mercy of the legislature and other groups for the budget.

Context: Although past Texas constitutions required the governor to submit a budget, similar to the president, the current process requires agencies to report requests to the governor and the governor reports these. The governor's budget power is also shared with the LBB.

Solution: Extend the governor's budgetary responsibility to require the governor to submit a budget and require the legislature to formally accept or reject it. Because the legislature's first order of business is to pass a budget, the constitution could be altered to require a governor to propose and the legislature to pass a budget in the first 60 days of a session.

★ TEXAS TAKEAWAYS

11 Is the Texas governor weak or strong? Explain.

12 How does the power of the Texas governor compare to other states' governors?

13 How have Texas's governors expanded their political powers?

⬤ THE INSIDER VIEW

Although the creators of the Texas Constitution intended to establish a weak governor, Texas governors have expanded their power through aggressive use of the veto power, the appointment power, and calling special sessions. Governors can also be highly effective when using their informal powers effectively. Ann Richards once said, "I'm not afraid to shake up the system, and government needs more shaking up than any other system I know." Like other governors, Richards attempted to leverage the "bully pulpit" and her standing with the legislature to set her political agenda. Still, governors need the legislature on their side to get things done—and in the absence of legislative success, governors become electorally vulnerable. Asked once what she might have done differently had she known she was going to be a one-term governor, Richards grinned, "Oh, I would probably have raised more hell."[34]

⬤ TEXAS TAKEAWAYS

1 To run for governor in Texas, a candidate must be at least 30 years of age and a citizen of the United States and must have resided in Texas for at least five years immediately preceding his or her election.

2 Governors serve three and one-half years, on average.

3 The Texas legislature impeaches a governor in a two-stage process. First, the Texas House of Representatives investigates charges and must cast a majority vote in favor of impeachment. Second, the Texas Senate sits as a jury, hearing and evaluating the evidence in a trial setting. To convict an individual who has been impeached by the house and remove them from office, two-thirds of the senate must agree.

4 Governors routinely use executive orders, proclamations, political appointments, vetoes, line item vetoes, pardon powers, and military powers to run the executive branch. The governor also has his or her hand in the legislative side of things. Governors recommend legislation, declare legislative emergencies, call special sessions, and bargain with legislators.

5 The governor has the power to call the legislature into special session on any issue they choose, and sessions can last up to 30 days after the biennial 140-day session is over.

6 Governors veto approximately thirty pieces of legislation per legislative session.

7 Vetoes are almost never overturned. Only one has been recorded in Texas history.

8 The Governors' informal powers are chief legislative bargainers, agenda setters and budget negotiators, party leaders, and economic cheerleaders.

9 Governors succeed more than 50 percent of the time on their agenda issues, although this is higher when governors are first elected to office or when political forces align.

10 The governor's annual State of the State Speech and their inaugural address are both used to set the governor's political and legislative agenda.

11 The powers of the Texas governor are weak on paper but strong in practice. Stronger governors exercise their powers more vigorously.

12 Texas ranks comparatively low on an index of power; but in practice, Texas governors have used the powers of the office to make themselves politically stronger.

13 Texas governors have expanded their political powers through aggressive use of appointment powers, the veto, party building, and staying longer in office.

KEY TERMS

agenda setting
budget execution
clemency
executive orders
impeachment
inaugural speech
informal powers
line item veto
pardon
political succession
proclamations
State of the State Address
term limits
veto

PRACTICE QUIZ

1. Who was the only Texas governor to be impeached?

   a. Allan Shivers
   b. James E. "Pa" Ferguson
   c. Mark White
   d. George W. Bush

2. Texas governor's enjoy all of the following power EXCEPT ONE of the following:

   a. Dispatch the National Guard
   b. Grant pardons
   c. Recommend legislation
   d. Submit a budget

3. What place is Texas ranked on the Governor Power Index?

   a. 1st
   b. 9th
   c. 32nd
   d. 41st

4. To serve as Texas governor, he or she must be at least how old (in years)?

   a. 30
   b. 35
   c. 37
   d. 40

5. The 1962 *Houston Chronicle* editorial submitted that an ideal person for the office of governor needs all of the "informal qualifications," EXCEPT which of the following?

   a. Brilliance of mind
   b. Legal knowledge
   c. Exceptional staffing
   d. Knowledge of business and industry

6. Texas governors use executive orders for several purposes, EXCEPT which of the following?

   a. To create task forces to assist with policy development
   b. To appoint legislative committee chairs
   c. To respond to natural disasters and other emergencies
   d. To fill interim appointments

7. Which governor, since the 1960s, issued the greatest number of executive orders and proclamations combined?

   a. Perry
   b. Bush
   c. White
   d. Smith

8. Governors can call a special session . . .

   a. Twelve days after the regular legislative session
   b. One month prior to the start of a legislative session
   c. Only during the summer, or the "off months"
   d. Any time outside of the biennial 140-day session

9. Which governor vetoed the fewest amount of bills?

   a. Abbott
   b. White
   c. Sterling
   d. Clements

10. What tactic is often employed by governors in the face of an obstinate legislature or to address an issue of special importance to the governor?

    a. "Going Public"
    b. "Grandstanding"
    c. "Ignoring Legislators"
    d. "Legislative Debating"

[Answers: B, D, D, A, C, B, A, D, C, A]

9 THE PLURAL EXECUTIVE AND THE BUREAUCRACY

In the 2006 gubernatorial elections, two longtime political rivals squared off against each other: Texas Comptroller Carole Keeton Strayhorn challenged sitting Governor Rick Perry. The race was a culmination of a bitter five-year duel over state authority. The apparent motive was a backroom dispute over funding for Strayhorn's pet project to provide a free community college education to high school graduates and Perry's decision to sign legislation that stripped the Comptroller's office of two popular programs.[1] The Texas comptroller audited the governor's office no less than seven times between 2002 and 2004. Perry responded by asking the State Auditor's Office to audit the Comptroller's Office to ensure state tax settlements were properly handled. "The mean-spirited vendetta continues today," Strayhorn said as she responded with more audits of the executive branch.[2] Perry beat Strayhorn and other candidates in the 2006 election, but he garnered less than 50 percent of the popular vote—a blow to the electoral punch governors need to push their agendas through the legislature.

Infighting weakens an already weak executive branch, but it is an inevitable result of the **plural executive**. The Texas Constitution fragments political power and policy management on purpose, so no single individual, group, or agency has the power to control government. The people elect the most powerful officers of the executive branch, including the lieutenant governor, the attorney general, the comptroller of public accounts, the land commissioner, and positions in dozens of boards and commissions that shape the policy direction of the state. The governor does not appoint many of them and has no direct authority over them.

LEARNING OBJECTIVES

9.1 Describe the roles, functions, and structure of the bureaucracy in Texas.

9.2 Explain the roles of the elected members of the executive branch.

9.3 Identify the functions of important governor-appointed, single-head agencies.

9.4 Describe the purposes important multimember agencies serve.

9.5 Differentiate between multimember elected commissions and hybrid agencies.

9.6 Assess how the plural executive influences policy and the methods of holding the bureaucracy in check.

plural executive: the diffusion of authority and power throughout several entities in the executive branch and the bureaucracy

● Former Lieutenant David Dewhurst shows off his roping skills. Like effective rodeo tie-down roping, navigating the Texas bureaucracy is a delicate art.

This structure creates an opportunity for friction within the executive branch itself because of the potential for internal disagreement and multiple executives running the show. Designed to prevent any one individual in the executive branch from acquiring too much power, the plural executive system can not only lead to slow, inefficient government but also to outright wastefulness, as officials use their power to engage in infighting. How serious a problem is this? Is there a solution?

To answer these questions, we must learn more about the executive branch, the plural executive, and the bureaucracy—the thousands of unelected individuals (bureaucrats) whom they oversee and who establish and enforce rules. In the sections that follow, we identify what a bureaucracy is, what it does, and how it is held accountable. The roles of the plural executive and bureaucracy have changed as the state has grown, and we chart the political implications of this expansion.

🤠 BUREAUCRACY IN TEXAS

9.1	Describe the roles, functions, and structure of the bureaucracy in Texas.

The largest but often most obscure level of the executive branch in Texas is the agencies and individuals who make and enforce the rules that govern us all. Yet this is the branch of government that directly touches everyone's life, whether they know it or not. Take student financial aid: more than 850,000 Texas college and university students are on financial aid, and they received more than $9 billion in 2014 alone.[3] The Texas Higher Education Coordinating Board, part of the Texas bureaucracy, sets rules for financial aid; and the Texas Education Agency, also part of the bureaucracy, collaborates with other agencies to use financial aid to increase enrollments, help students succeed, and achieve equality of opportunity. Even when you graduate, the Texas bureaucracy continues to touch your life. Did you graduate from a hairstyling school? Texas regulates health and safety standards for barber shops and establishes who can be certified to cut or shampoo hair, or own a salon.

The state agencies that administer financial assistance to college students and regulate standards of the state's hair, nail, and beauty salons are all part of the **bureaucracy**. Bureaucracies set up a hierarchical chain of command: employees at each level report to a single boss. The legislature or governor assigns each agency its own specialized mission, such as dispensing financial aid or regulating cosmetology standards. As a result, bureaucrats in these agencies have knowledge of or experience in a single issue or topic needed to carry out their mission.

bureaucracy: a government organization that implements laws and provides services to individuals

THE SIZE OF THE TEXAS BUREAUCRACY

Bureaucracies need staff to operate. Because of the size of the land mass, the number of businesses, the number of people, and the enormity of the economy, the executive bureaucracy in Texas is necessarily huge. However, when compared to other states, Texas has fewer bureaucrats per person—approximately 1 bureaucrat for every 3,500 Texas residents (see Figure 9.1). Still, over 7,800 people work for the Texas executive agencies, boards, and commissions that conduct most of the work in state government.[4]

Although it is comparatively smaller per person than most other states, why is the Texas bureaucracy as large as it is? The bureaucracy in the Lone Star State has expanded greatly since the early days of statehood. A growing population means more taxpayers, more driver's licenses, and more public school students. The bureaucracy administers to a growing population and must keep up with it. Likewise, Texas's economy has grown more diverse and larger—there are more agricultural products, more types of energy production, more technology firms, and hundreds more industries. The bureaucracy keeps track of these industries and oversees compliance with rules and regulations. So, although Texans generally dislike big government, the size of the bureaucracy reflects the services required by a diverse, modern economy.

WHAT THE TEXAS BUREAUCRACY DOES

The bureaucracy often gets a bad rap. Politicians engage in "bureaucracy bashing" as a foil for their inability to make government work to their liking. Reporters often highlight the worst abuses, such as the denial of workers' compensation claims, to hold the government responsible, but these events may be isolated incidents. Texans complain about "red tape," hassles of simple procedures such as renewing a driver's license or obtaining vehicle inspections. In reality, the bureaucracy in Texas, while imperfect, performs a wide variety of vital tasks.

implementation: the execution by the bureaucracy of laws and decisions made by the legislative, executive, or judicial branch

rules: regulations designed to control government or the conduct of people and industries

Policy Implementation.   Bureaucrats engage in **implementation** when they carry out laws and decisions made by the legislative, executive, or judicial branch. For instance, a 2001 Texas law required students in public elementary schools to participate in "physical activity" in a coordinated school health program but did not set a specific duration for the activity. The Texas Education Agency interpreted the new law to mean that each elementary student should exercise 30 minutes per day.

Rule-making.   The legislature or the governor may establish a broad policy with broad goals, but bureaucrats create **rules** to make

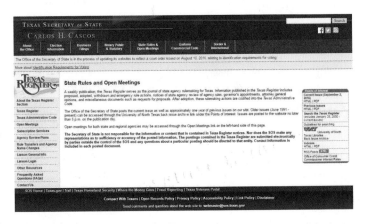

Where Can I Find All These Rules? The Texas Register, the journal of state agency rulemaking in Texas, keeps a record of rules proposed, adopted, and withdrawn. It can be accessed online.

IS IT BIGGER IN TEXAS?

FIGURE 9.1   State Employees Per 10,000 Residents, 2015

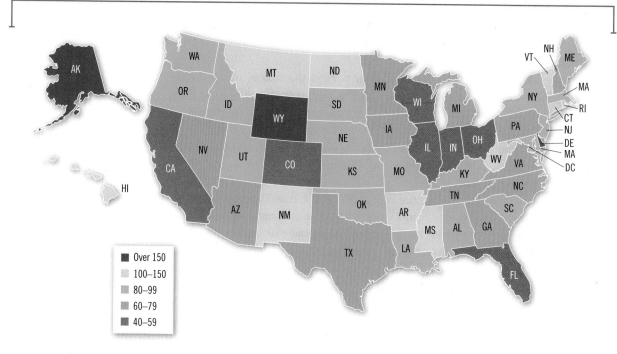

Legend:
- Over 150
- 100–150
- 80–99
- 60–79
- 40–59

Source: US Census Bureau. Total includes non-education (primary, secondary, or higher) employees per 10,000 in 2012 estimated population.

 COMMUNICATION:

Which states have larger bureaucracies?

- Smaller states such as Alaska, Delaware, and Wyoming have more employees per 10,000 residents. Texas falls toward the bottom of the list.
- States with smaller populations tend to have a modest staff size.

 CRITICAL THINKING:

Why do some states have more employees per 10,000 residents than others?

- Even for small states, a certain minimum number of employees is necessary to run the government.
- States in fiscal trouble tend to reduce the number of employees. Fiscal troubles in Illinois and Wisconsin caused employee reductions between 2014 and 2015.
- Conservative states, which prefer small government, like Texas, attempt to keep the number of bureaucrats low. The same is true of other large southern states such as Florida, Georgia, and Tennessee.

sure that specific targets are met. For example, the Texas Racing Commission (TRC) created its own rules when it tried to expand "historic racing" in Texas. "Historic racing" used video of past races with the dates and names removed and allowed individuals to gamble on the results. The TRC established rules that equated this racing with live horse racing, allowing the racing industry to make money from the practice. The ruling did not sit well with socially conservative Texans who oppose gambling. The legislature, led by prominent social conservatives Lieutenant Governor Dan Patrick and Senator Jane Nelson, objected that only the legislature could decide what was technically gambling. Under pressure from the legislature that included threatening to kill the agency's budget, the TRC voted to repeal the rule.

The Texas bureaucracy regulates and licenses animal breeders. Here 500 dogs and cats are rescued from a puppy mill in Kaufman County.

PERSONAL RESPONSIBILITY: **Should citizens only engage in business with licensed and regulated businesses? In what circumstances might you feel it acceptable to work with an unlicensed business or vendor? Why might you do so?**

Regulation. Bureaucrats regulate industry, business, individuals, and other parts of government. **Regulations** are often used to protect people, such as environmental regulations, which the Texas Commission on Environmental Quality (TCEQ) uses to minimize air pollution. They also extend to projects that enrich communities, such as the guidelines for preservation of statewide historic sites issued by the Texas Historical Commission.

Licensing. **Licensing** gives a company, an individual, or an organization permission to carry out a specific task. For instance, if you wanted to sell gasoline, market a Texas-made item, sell plants, or cut flowers in the state of Texas, you'll need a license from the Texas Department of Agriculture. If you want to become a teacher in one of the more than 8,000 public schools in the state, the Texas Education Agency sets out a criterion to become a certified educator. Opponents of big government argue that licensing leads to overregulation. In 2015, Governor Abbott signed legislation to lift regulations requiring a license to braid hair.

Enforcement. The power of **enforcement** of rules falls to bureaucratic entities in the state. If rules are broken, the bureaucratic agents can investigate, issue warnings, levy fines, or even refer criminal activity to the court system. In 2015, the Texas legislature passed a law that allowed properly licensed individuals to openly carry firearms in public. Religious institutions, courthouses, schools, and other institutions were allowed to ban openly displayed weapons with proper public notice. The Dallas and Houston Zoos, citing the large number of visitors that are families with small children, banned guns in their parks. Gun rights advocates objected, but the attorney general ruled in favor of the zoos, enforcing the ban.

regulations: standards that are established for the function and management of industry, business, individuals, and other parts of government

licensing: the authorization process that gives a company, an individual, or an organization permission to carry out a specific task

enforcement: the carrying out of rules by an agency or commission within the bureaucracy

FIGURE 9.2   **Scale of Governor Influence**

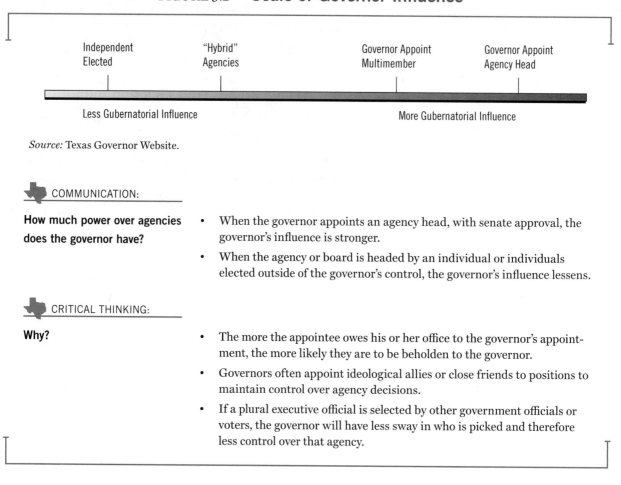

Source: Texas Governor Website.

COMMUNICATION:

How much power over agencies does the governor have?

- When the governor appoints an agency head, with senate approval, the governor's influence is stronger.
- When the agency or board is headed by an individual or individuals elected outside of the governor's control, the governor's influence lessens.

CRITICAL THINKING:

Why?

- The more the appointee owes his or her office to the governor's appointment, the more likely they are to be beholden to the governor.
- Governors often appoint ideological allies or close friends to positions to maintain control over agency decisions.
- If a plural executive official is selected by other government officials or voters, the governor will have less sway in who is picked and therefore less control over that agency.

THE STRUCTURE OF THE TEXAS BUREAUCRACY

There are four broad types of bureaucracies in Texas. All of these entities perform similar types of functions, but each is unique in how the key personnel are selected. These organizations provide the governor and the other players in the state's plural executive a way to control (or not control) the actions of these bureaucratic organizations. These types of agencies include the following:

- Agencies headed by officials appointed by the governor
- Agencies headed by officials independently elected by the people, outside of the governor's control
- Boards and commissions headed by a multimember, governor-appointed board or commission
- Hybrid agencies where there is a mix of elected and appointed boards and commissions headed by a multimember appointed board or commission

The plural executive limits the influence the governor has over the bureaucracy (see Figure 9.2). The governor appoints some employees within the bureaucracy, particularly upper-level management, but most of them are hired by management and perform administrative roles. Do governors influence agency action? Undoubtedly, some governors require strict loyalty as repayment for appointment. Other governors are more hands off, like Governor Price Daniel (1957–1963), who, after watching the swearing in of the members of the State Board of Insurance, told the members "you're on your own."[5]

The governor has the least influence over independently elected officers, and so we turn our discussion to these rivals for political power.

★ TEXAS TAKEAWAYS

1 What functions do bureaucracies perform?

2 Why has the Texas bureaucracy grown?

3 What kinds of offices are more influenced by governors?

🤠 INDEPENDENTLY ELECTED OFFICERS

Every four years the citizens of Texas elect a range of important executive branch officials. The most powerful of these officers is the lieutenant governor, whose influence rivals the governor's. But neither the comptroller, attorney general, nor the commissioners of agriculture and the General Land Office is beholden to the governor for their position, so they have a sizeable degree of autonomy and an ability to stir up trouble—like an armadillo in a garden, if they so desire.

> **9.2** Explain the roles of the elected members of the executive branch.

LIEUTENANT GOVERNOR

Unlike lieutenant governors in other states, and unlike the US vice president, the Texas lieutenant governor plays a formidable role within both the executive and legislative branches. The lieutenant governor's duties are primarily managerial, but this responsibility makes him the most powerful force in state government on paper. When Governor Bush, a Republican, asked one of his consultants why he had a "Bob Bullock for lieutenant governor" bumper sticker on his car instead of a "Bush for governor" sticker, the consultant noted, "you don't understand Governor, everyone in Texas works for Bullock."

TABLE 9.1 Lieutenant Governors, Major Achievements/Controversies

LIEUTENANT GOVERNOR (PARTY)	CONTROVERSY
Ben Barnes (1969–1973)	Tainted by Sharpstown stock fraud scandal, eventually leading to him losing bid for reelection.
William "Bill" Hobby, Jr. (1973–1991)	Ordered the arrest of a dozen senators who were purposely not attending floor debates to block the passage of legislation.
Bob Bullock (1991–1999)	Hands-on management style and abusive behavior rubbed many the wrong way.
Bill Ratliff (2000–2003)	Broke from his party in joining Democratic state senators opposing redistricting proposals. Refused to bring the matter to the Senate floor.
David Dewhurst (2003–2015)	Embarrassing phone call made to Allen, Texas police, regarding jailed relative who was incarcerated during 2012 election.
Dan Patrick (2015–present)	Tweeted "a man reaps what he sows" hours after 50 people were killed at an LGBT night club in Miami. Patrick responded that the tweet was prescheduled and was removed.

Source: Information is from the *Texas Almanac.* Beginning in 1974, the electoral term changed from two to four years

PERSONAL RESPONSIBILITY:

Do Texas voters have the right to expect their elected officials to act in accordance with their moral values?

presiding officer: a role of the lieutenant governor who is in charge of the administrative and procedural duties of the Texas Senate

Since the end of the Second World War, the lieutenant governor has had a significant say in the administration of the state and lawmaking in Texas (see Table 9.1). The lieutenant governor serves as the **presiding officer** of the Texas Senate, meaning that he or she is in charge of the administrative and procedural duties of the chamber.

The lieutenant governor must be at least thirty years old, a US citizen, and a Texas resident for more than five years prior to the election. Because it is such an insider's position, candidates for lieutenant governor tend to be politically connected and experienced. One exception was William Hobby, Sr., who was elected in 1915. On being asked to run, a surprised Hobby—who had no political experience—replied, "Why, I can't tie a string cravat. I don't even own a swallow-tailed coat. And my hair just won't seem to grow down the back of my neck!"[6] Hobby would go on to be elected governor, his son would go on to serve as lieutenant governor, and his grandson would serve as a member of the Texas Ethics Commission.

Lieutenant governors serve for four-year terms with no term limits and tend to stay longer in office by comparison to other elected officers. Since 1894, most lieutenant governors have served more than one term. Ben Ramsey holds the record at six consecutive terms.

A closer look at the duties of the lieutenant governor shows how the lieutenant governor has a foot in both the legislative and executive camps. The lieutenant governor has a role in both making and executing the laws. This combination is why the position is so powerful.

ANGLES OF POWER
The Power of the Lieutenant Governor Beyond Politics

The influence of the lieutenant governor can extend beyond leiglsative politics—even to the gridiron. In 1995, athletic conferences were negotiating directly with universities over television rights and revenue sharing. The Big 8 Conference was looking to expand to ten teams, and the University of Texas and Texas A&M University were being courted. This move would leave the Southwest Conference, once a powerhouse football conference, without two major schools; and TCU, Houston, Rice, SMU, Texas Tech, and Baylor would find themselves in a much weakened conference.

Lieutenant governor Bob Bullock, a graduate of both Texas Tech and Baylor, wanted his teams to join the expanding conference. Bullock summoned the presidents of UT and A&M and, glaring at the two, said, "You're taking Tech and Baylor, or you're not taking anything. I'll cut your money off, and you can join privately if you want, but you won't get another nickel of state money." Calling his bluff, the presidents attempted to negotiate. "If you want to try me, go ahead." Observers reported that "at that moment, for all practical purpsoes, the Big 8 became the Big 12."[11] Although not a policy over which he had direct control, the lieutenant governor was able to exert political pressure to get his way.

PERSONAL RESPONSIBILITY: **Can a public official overstep his or her job description? In what circumstances do you think this is justified?**

Working with the Governor.   As we saw in the previous chapter, governors often must rely on lieutenant governors to advance their agendas. Republican Governor George W. Bush made friends with the normally prickly Democratic Lieutenant Governor Bob Bullock, known to be as tough on subordinates as on fellow politicians. Bush's fondness for nicknames extended to the lieutenant governor, whom he called "Bully." In his first year as governor, and on his signature issue of tort reform, Bush looked to Bullock to govern over a fragile coalition of Democrats in the Senate. Lobbyists tried to convince Bush to lower the ceiling on damages, but Bush stood by the compromise position to which he had worked with Bullock. The governor could have threatened a veto, but he wisely chose not to turn his back on a key ally. When working together, jocular Bush would sometimes ask of Bullock, "You gonna get mad at me today, Bully?"

Before the beginning of the eighty-fourth legislative session, Governor-elect Greg Abbott, Lieutenant Governor-elect Dan Patrick, and Speaker of the Texas House Joe Strauss convened a breakfast meeting, as is customary before the session starts, to talk about the session to come and outline priorities. The breakfast turned tense when Patrick declared he was tired of the other two "picking on him" because Patrick's informal advisers had challenged the governor's proposed pre-kindergarten program, which they said would force students into "a Godless environment."[7]

Managing the Senate.   As the leader of the Texas Senate, the lieutenant governor uses his discretion in following the chamber's rules on proper parliamentary procedures, such as deciding when a bill will come up for a vote, when

Bill Hobby, Former Democratic Lieutenant Governor of Texas

How do all the power players balance competing interests in a tight budget?

I scrubbed [balanced] the budget nine times during the 18 years I was in office. There is nothing happening on that front now that didn't happen many times in the past and won't many times in the future. Only the names are different. So, when you hear someone talk about scrubbing the budget, ask them how many teachers they want to cut, how many children they want to let go without health care, and how many prison guards they want to cut? How many universities or community colleges does the thrifty legislator want to close in his district?[13]

CRITICAL THINKING: **Is the Lieutenant Governor's approach to budget-cutting appropriate? Should legislators think about their own districts or the needs of the state?**

to allow a senator on the floor to speak, or how to deal with points of order (objections made to a bill).

One concern for the lieutenant governor is that contentious bills, with dozens of potential amendments, will stall Senate business and eat up too much precious time in a legislative session that lasts only 140 days, potentially killing many important but noncontroversial bills. Freshman Senator David Sibley attended a session in which Lieutenant Governor Bullock was "machine-gun" gaveling one bill after another to passage to move the process along. The senator asked to be recognized to complain that the Senate had not had a chance to study or debate the legislation being approved. After several such attempts, Bullock resentfully relented: "The chair recognizes the crybaby from Waco," he bellowed.[8]

Lieutenant governors adopt different management styles. Bob Bullock represented the firm-hand method, using rewards, old-fashioned threats, and sometimes name-calling to get the job done. On the other hand, Bill Hobby embodied the light touch method, pushing for nondramatic consensus on legislation.

Directing the Flow of Legislation.   As the presiding officer in the senate, the lieutenant governor has primary responsibility for where legislation goes, referring bills to one of the standing committees. In effect, he is the traffic cop for moving legislation within and through the Texas Senate. Knowing which committees might favor or disfavor a certain kind of legislation, the lieutenant governor can promote or kill specific legislation by manipulating which committee takes first crack at a bill.

Lieutenant Governor Ben Ramsey (1951–1961) had an encyclopedic memory for senate rules and a deep sense of tradition in the chamber. Ramsey would often tell his chief aide to "lose a bill" if the lieutenant governor opposed the legislation. When it came time for a senator's bill to be addressed, the bill would be missing (on purpose). In other instances, Ramsey referred a bill to the "Committee on S—it" by tossing into his desk drawer, effectively killing the bill's chances to be heard.[9]

Tiebreaking Vote in the Senate.   Similar to the vice president, the lieutenant governor has the tiebreaking vote in the state senate if the chamber is evenly divided on a vote. In a close vote on the Tort Claim Act in 1969, waiving immunity for the government in civil lawsuits, the senate tied 15–15 (with one member skipping the vote). Lieutenant Governor Ben Barnes, a member of the moderate-conservative wing of the Democratic Party, unexpectedly voted for the act, shocking those in the senate gallery—including a lobbyist for the Texas Municipal League who, mouth wide open, dropped the pipe he was smoking onto the Senate floor below, burning a hole in the carpet.

Appointments to Senate Committees.   The lieutenant governor is charged with appointing the legislative chairpersons and members of standing committees in the Texas Senate. This power, combined with the authority to dictate the flow of legislation, is a potent weapon in agenda control. Most lieutenant governors appoint sympathetic partisans to promote their party's agenda. However, Lieutenant Governor Ben Barnes, a bridge-builder across the liberal and conservative wings of the Democratic Party in the 1960s, did something no lieutenant governor had done before: he appointed a senator from the opposite wing of his party to serve on the powerful Senate Finance Committee. Conservative Democrats howled, "what the devil are you doing?," but the play was strategic. The appointed senator reported being "too busy" to make trouble.[10]

Efforts at political retaliation can backfire. The pugnacious Bob Bullock, first elected in 1990, resolved to show the teeth of the Democratic Party and declined to appoint any Republicans to lead legislative committees in the 1991–1992 session. He regretted it almost immediately. The Republicans used their legislative savvy to enforce minor rules and "knotted up things," halting legislation in the senate. Realizing this mistake, Bullock made peace with the ringleader, Senator O. H. "Ike" Harris (a Republican from Dallas) and made him the chairman of the Senate Committee on Jurisprudence.

When necessary, the lieutenant governor can also set up a new standing committee or special committee to investigate or review issues or policies.

Membership on Key Legislative Boards.   The lieutenant governor serves as chair of or as a member of several key boards that govern the state, including the Legislative Budget Board, the Legislative Council, and the Legislative Redistricting Board. The lieutenant governor shares appointment power with the governor on most of these boards, making cooperation essential to efficient government.

Involving Texans in the Law-Making Process.   Like governors, lieutenant governors also form policy networks to help develop legislation. Newly elected Lieutenant Governor Dan Patrick created six citizen committees (including fifty-five Texas business leaders) to advise him on legislation and policy matters affecting taxes, transportation, water, energy, and the economy. Some of the members are nationally known entrepreneurs and business executives, including oilman T. Boone Pickens and Woody Hunt, Chairman of the Hunt Companies.[12] Many critics complained that the advisory groups were dominated by conservative Republicans. Lieutenant Governor Patrick responded that he had picked the best people for the job.

ATTORNEY GENERAL

The attorney general (AG) is the state's lawyer, defending the laws and constitution of the State of Texas by representing the state in court. The attorney general provides legal services to the governor, state agencies, and local and state government entities. The AG's actions and opinions can actively shape state policies. When requested, the AG's office will file suit on behalf of state agencies in court (see Figure 9.3). The Texas Constitution does not specify that the attorney general be a licensed attorney, only that they "represent the state" in various legal capacities.

For instance, in the 1970s, Texans found themselves vulnerable to every manner of consumer fraud: negligent nursing home owners, con artists selling phony oil investments, and retailers advertising everyday prices as "sale prices." After a series of banking scandals swept the state, Attorney General John Hill sat down with his staff at a Tex Mex restaurant in Austin and came up with a bill that would give legal recourse to swindled Texans with small dollar claims. As they scribbled guidelines for how to deal with deceptive practices, they spilled chile con queso and salsa picante onto their papers.[14] That "queso-stained plea for help for Texas's consumers" formed the basis of legislation that empowered consumers with courthouse access.[15]

The office's legal duties have spread into other areas as well. The AG's office enforces health, safety, and consumer regulations and protects the rights of the elderly and disabled. The AG's office investigates deceptive business practices, including car repair fraud, telemarketing scams, identity theft, "diploma mills," health care fraud, price gauging, and other consumer-related complaints. The AG is also responsible for enforcement of child support payments, including locating absent parents, establishing paternity, reviewing and adjusting child support payments, and collecting and distributing child support payments. The AG's office can also punish parents behind on their child support payments by blocking car registration renewal, revoking a license, or stripping someone of a professional license. From 2015 to 2016, the office collected more than $3.86 billion in child support.[16]

IS IT BIGGER IN TEXAS?

FIGURE 9.3   **State Attorneys General Cases Filed, 1980–2013**

Source: Paul Nolette. 2015. *Federalism on Trial: State Attorneys General and National Policymaking in Contemporary America.* Lawrence, KS: University Press of Kansas.

 COMMUNICATION:

How often is the Texas AG involved in lawsuits in comparison to other states?

- The most highly populated states appear in the top ten most frequent litigants, such as New York and California.
- Texas is a frequent litigant. Texas is a leader among all states in cases filed (ranked six out of fifty) in litigating these issues.

 CRITICAL THINKING:

Why do some states' AGs file more suits?

- Federal policies often have a significant impact on larger states.
- States with more industry—either natural resources (Texas), pharmaceutical (New York), health care (California), or banking (Connecticut)—have more cases where the states challenge federal government regulations.

As a result of their constitutional role, lawyers from the AG's office spend a lot of time in court (see Figure 9.4). These cases fall into three categories: antitrust, consumer protection, and environmental. In one 2011 antitrust case, for example, the AG stopped a regional health care system in Wichita Falls from gaining a local monopoly on emergency and outpatient services. Cases are often filed *against* the federal government to challenge or provoke review of specific federal laws or regulations.

Another important function of the AG's office is to issue legal opinions to the governor, heads of state agencies, lawmakers, and local officials (see Figure 9.4). The courts view these opinions as so highly persuasive that the AG in effect makes policy by interpreting a statute, rule, or law that may serve as a basis for

FIGURE 9.4   **Attorney General Advisory Opinions**

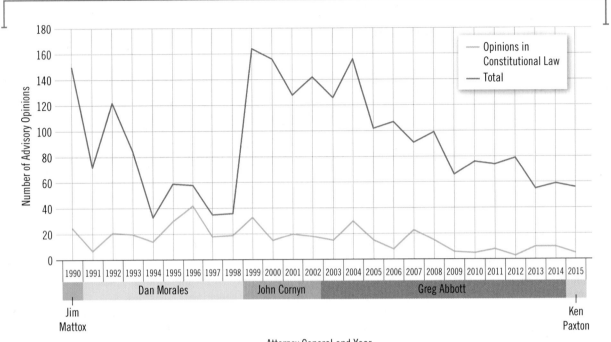

Source: Attorney General's Office

 COMMUNICATION:

How has the number of advisory opinions changed over time?

- The total number of advisory opinions decreased from 1999 to 2015, from 160 to around 60.
- The largest increase in advisory opinions was when John Cornyn (a Republican) took over as attorney general from Dan Morales (a Democrat).

 CRITICAL THINKING:

What factors have caused the attorney general to weigh in on a case?

- A change in the party controlling the office from Democrat to Republican may have prompted more legal inquiries from the new AG. Republicans had captured control of both the legislature and the governor's office at the time, and government entities were looking for the AG to provide favorable rulings for them.
- The AG is also asked to rule on more constitutional cases when major issues are being considered by the legislature, such as changes to tax policy or public school funding.

TABLE 9.2	Key Attorney General Opinions

YEAR	ATTORNEY GENERAL	OPINION
1990	Democrat Jim Mattox	Both "excused" and "unexcused" school absences count as absences for attendance counts.
1992	Democrat Dan Morales	Bingo games with monetary prizes authorized only if conducted for charity.
1994	Democrat Dan Morales	School district sponsored extracurricular activities may not take place at an athletic club that discriminates.
2001	Republican John Cornyn	Government body cannot prohibit holder of concealed handgun onto government property unless public notification is given.
2006	Republican Greg Abbott	State can deny driver's license renewal for failure to appear in municipal court or pay fines.

Source: Attorney General's Office.

 CRITICAL THINKING:

How do AGs shape public policy? Does the political party of the AG influence his or her decisions?

- Conservative Republicans tend to be tougher on crime and lawbreakers, such as Greg Abbott's decision to deny driver's license renewals for failure to pay fines.

- Democrats tend to fall in line with their party's ideology. For example, Dan Morales held that school extracurricular programs may not discriminate.

- Republicans also play to party loyalty, such as John Cornyn's finding that government organizations cannot prohibit concealed handguns without providing notification.

future legislative action (see Table 9.2). The power of the AG to interpret the constitution is second only to the Texas Supreme Court.

Consider, for example, the funding of education for veterans. The Hazelwood Act is a state law that covers the cost of tuition for military veterans and dates back to 1923, when the Texas Legislature directed state universities to cover college tuition costs for World War I veterans, nurses, and their children. In January 2015, a US District Court judge ordered universities not to exclude a veteran from the benefits solely because he or she enlisted in the army while living outside of Texas. Senator Jane Nelson, as head of the Senate Finance Committee, questioned this ruling in February 2015 by requesting an AG opinion about this section of the Hazelwood Act. The attorney general advised that it would be constitutional to include only those veterans who were Texas residents when they signed up for military service. The legislature,

In 2015, the attorney general was asked whether daily fantasy sports leagues, where players assemble teams online that are advertised with big payoffs, legally constitutes gambling. Like attorney generals in other states, AG Ken Paxton held that because the "house" takes a cut of the pot, it is gambling, and likely illegal under Texas law.

PERSONAL RESPONSIBILITY: **If you were attorney general, how would you rule in this fantasy sports leagues case?**

however, was unable to agree to program changes and let the program stand as it was. An appeals court upheld a requirement that veterans be Texas residents when enlisting in order to receive benefits in 2016.

The AG often wades in tenuous, swampy water between the solid shore of legal representation and the murky marsh of politics. Journalists accused Republican Attorney General John Cornyn of being too cozy with industries he was litigating against and of allowing politics to influence his legal decisions. Two years into Cornyn's tenure, journalist Paul Burka accused Cornyn of settling for less than expected on a water pollution suit against a pipeline company and of endorsing favorable settlements to health care providers.[17]

Because it is one of the most important and high-profile offices in the state, it has proven to be a good stepping stone to political advancement in recent years. The office has promoted Mark White (governor), John Cornyn (US Senator), and Greg Abbott (governor).

COMPTROLLER OF PUBLIC ACCOUNTS

Sometimes referred to as the "tooth fairy of public accounts" for his or her silent but authoritative approach to budgeting, the state comptroller is a powerful figure in Texas politics. The comptroller's role is to estimate revenue, certify budget funds, and chart state economic growth. The state's budget operates on a **pay-as-you-go system**: state funds spent must equal state funds received. The legislature must craft a budget that is only as big as the comptroller says it is allowed to be. The constitution requires that all appropriations bills (bills to allow spending) from the legislature be approved by the comptroller's office.

pay-as-you-go system: state funds spend must equal state funds received

Bob Bullock reinvented the comptroller's office when he was first elected in 1975. When he arrived in the office, "everything creaked: the procedures, the equipment, the employees."[18] Bullock established the comptrollers' office as central in matters of taxes, schools' finance, and agency funding. He also jealously guarded state funds. One day, he walked into the store of a delinquent liquor distributor in San Antonio and confronted him: "I'm Bob Bullock. You owe me $236,000." The dealer said, "Say again?" And Bullock said, "I'm the state comptroller, and you owe the people of Texas $236,000 in sales taxes you haven't paid and I'm here to collect it." The dealer laughed and said he didn't have that kind of money. Bullock retorted, "I think you've got that kind of whiskey." And he turned to one of his employees and ordered, "Start hauling this shit out of here." Bullock carried off two eighteen-wheelers full of whiskey. The media called the trucks Bullock's Raiders.[19]

The comptroller has an early, primary say in the amount of money that Texas spends, giving them significant control over the pot of money the legislature has to work with. After submitting the budget, the comptroller can still give the legislature the go-ahead to spend extra money. The comptroller also certifies that Texas's budget books are balanced.

The fiscal power of the comptroller also may extend into the political arena. Independent-minded Republican Comptroller Carole Keeton Rylander was a fiscal thorn in the side of Governor George W. Bush. Rylander reduced the previously plump revenue estimate by $700 million in 1999, effectively jeopardizing the property tax cut that Governor Bush had promised voters. With the proposed reduction in state revenue at $5.6 billion and projected slower growth of the economy, there would not be enough money to cover essential public services and public school enrollment growth and to reimburse local school districts for property tax revenue lost to the tax relief.

Misestimating this revenue can have serious ramifications for both politics and policy. In 2011, Comptroller Susan Combs overestimated tax revenue by a whopping $11.3 billion, or 14 percent. Expecting economic bedlam, lawmakers cut more than $5 billion from public education, impacting the delivery of quality public education, laying off thousands of teachers, and prompting a constitutional challenge over educational quality in the state. Less disastrous errors are not uncommon (see Figure 9.5). Estimates are most frequently wrong due to unexpected recessions, overestimated tax collections, or precipitous declines in energy prices. Estimates are also required to project up to thirty-two months into the future, a difficult challenge for any economist.

see for yourself 9.1

Watch Comptroller Glenn Hegar talk about his assessment of the Texas economy.

COMMISSIONER OF THE GENERAL LAND OFFICE

The land commissioner, the oldest continuously elected position in Texas history, oversees state-owned land, including open beaches and submerged land off the coast of the Gulf of Mexico. When Texas agreed to enter the Union in 1845, it negotiated to keep its public debt but also its public lands. The land commissioner administers these lands by leasing lands and generating funds from oil and gas production.

The General Land Office (GLO) pursues new revenue opportunities for the state. The GLO is investigating developing renewable offshore wind, solar, or geothermal energy on state lands. The GLO also has two functions nominally related to land: the Permanent School Fund, primarily because the proceeds from the sale of state lands and revenue from resource extraction from state lands fund public schools, and the Veteran's Land Board, which makes low-interest loans available to veterans and oversees state veterans cemeteries and skilled-care facilities.

FIGURE 9.5   **Difference between Estimated and Actual Tax Collections**

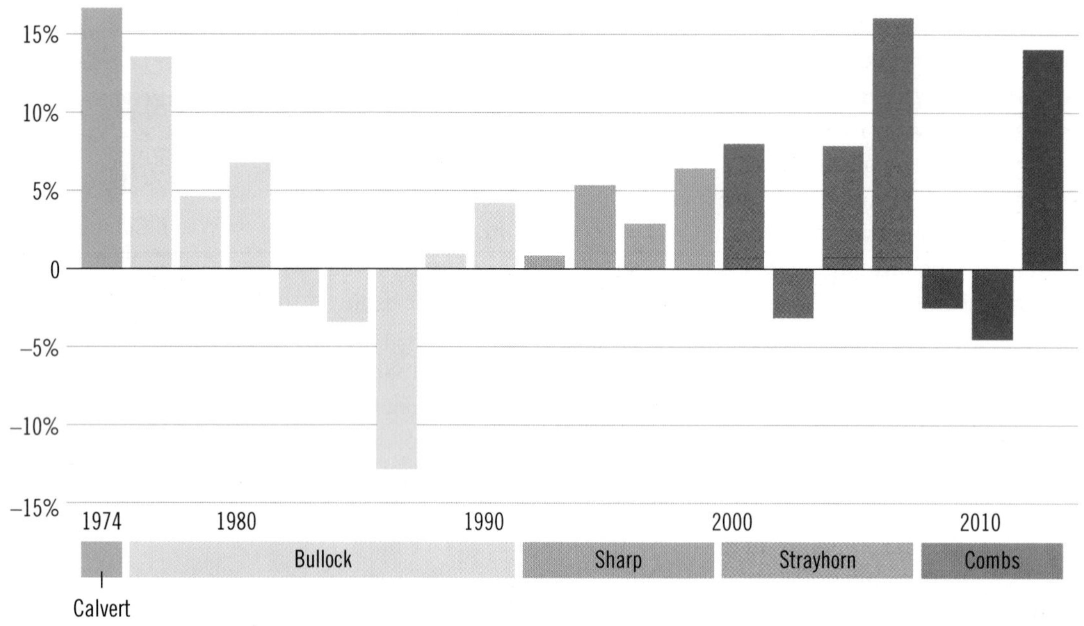

Source: Texas Comptroller's Office.

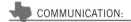 COMMUNICATION:

When have revenue estimates been incorrect?

- Sharp decreases in the price of oil consistently put revenue estimates off base. This occurred frequently in the late 1980s.

- Unpredicted population growth, such as in the late 1970s and late 2000s, increases sales tax revenue, driving revenue higher than expected.

 CRITICAL THINKING:

Why are some forecasts so wrong?

- Economic forecasts are based on assumptions. If these assumptions change, the forecasts change as well. Energy prices rise and fall, the housing market may be unpredictably weak in some areas of the state, or public spending (and therefore sales taxes) may slow down.

AGRICULTURE COMMISSIONER

The agriculture commissioner overseas the Department of Agriculture, which implements agricultural laws, promotes Texas's agriculture production and products, and administers school nutrition programs. The department also performs regulatory functions, such as protecting consumers from pesticides and certifying organic products. The simple acts of buying fruit at the grocery store or filling up your gas tank has you interacting with the Texas bureaucracy.

The Department of Agriculture certifies Texas-grown produce and inspects gas pumps for accuracy. Because one in every seven working Texans (14 percent) works in an agriculture-related job and the economic impact of agriculture-related production exceeds $150 billion annually, the role of the department in managing agriculture issues is critical to the economic welfare of the state.

Like all agencies, the department's regulatory role is limited by available funds. Agriculture Commissioner Sid Miller reported in 2015 that Texas consumers are "getting screwed" by unscrupulous businesses because the Department of Agriculture has not been able to perform many of its regulatory functions—such as checking gas pumps for accuracy, verifying grocery store scanners work properly, and inspecting taxicab meters to verify that people aren't being overcharged. Commissioner Miller briefed the legislature on the matter, requesting more funds to take care of the backlog. State Senator Paul Bettencourt, Republican of Houston, remarked that he discovered the problems with the oversight of gasoline sales firsthand: "I learned about this when I drove my car in and filled up 27 gallons on a 19-gallon tank."[20]

Agricultural Commissioner Sid Miller, in one of his first acts as agency head, granted full "amnesty" to cupcakes. Reminding Texans that the state had lifted the ban on selling cupcakes and other sugary treats, he delivered 181 cupcakes to the Capitol—enough for each member of the House and Senate.

SOCIAL RESPONSIBILITY: **Should the government be in the business of banning unhealthy foods? Why or why not?**

PLURAL EXECUTIVE FEUDS

Internal feuding within the Texas executive branch harkens back to the first days of the state's constitution. Governor O'Daniel once labeled the Board of Control and the Game and Fish and Oyster Commission "giant oligarchies and juicy play-pretties of the professional politicians." The governor lamented that he was unable to meet public demand for reform because his office had been "stripped" of the power that was given to the bureaucrats. Today, both agencies are defunct, but the complicated arrangement between the most powerful offices within the executive branch remains.[21]

The governor and lieutenant governor should see eye to eye, especially if they are of the same party, but relations are not always cordial, making for diverging strategies. In 2016, after five Dallas Police officers were killed by a lone gunman during a Black Lives Matter march, Lieutenant Governor Dan Patrick called protesters "hypocrites" while Governor Greg Abbott wrote an open letter to Texans saying that "our hearts are heavy" as he called for mourning and respect for the officers lost. Patrick took a more combative tone while Abbott attempted to invoke unity.[22]

Yet, despite the strength of the office, the lieutenant governor does not always win in internal fights with other executive officials. One heated exchange

see for yourself 9.2

Consider Agricultural Commissioner Sid Miller's view on cupcakes, fee increases, and the decline in rural population.

involved Attorney General Dan Morales's anger at Lieutenant Governor Bullock's office for hiring an outside attorney to consult on redistricting matters, a plum assignment because it involved the power to draw legislative district lines. Bullock became irritated by the attorney general's "incessant complaints" and physically challenged him by "bumping against him with his chest and lightly backhanding him."[23] The two were separated and the attorney general was eventually allowed to handle the redistricting issue.[24]

★ TEXAS TAKEAWAYS

4 What are the key roles of the lieutenant governor?

5 What are the consumer-based functions of the attorney general's office?

6 What are the chief powers of the state comptroller?

GOVERNOR-APPOINTED, SINGLE-HEAD AGENCIES

9.3 Identify the functions of important governor-appointed, single-head agencies.

The governor-appointed, single-head agencies are more likely to be influenced by the governor's agenda because the governor has a direct say in who gets appointed. Of course, the Texas Senate must approve the individuals the governor selects, so the control is not absolute. Moreover, these agencies often pursue their own prerogatives and incentives, occasionally—as we shall see later—with politically damaging results.

SECRETARY OF STATE

Can dead people vote in Texas? After 239 "dead" people did just that in the May 2012 primaries,[25] Secretary of State Hope Andrade decided to purge the voter registration records of Texans she believed to be deceased. Unfortunately, four voters presumed dead (but not) sued Andrade, the first Latina Secretary of State, for civil rights violations and for suppression of minority voters. Secretary Andrade suspended the purge.

More than a figurehead, the secretary of state serves as the chief elections administrator, the steward of all state records, and an ambassador of the state to other nations. First, the secretary assists county election officials, ensures the uniform application of election laws throughout the state, and maintains the voter registration records for more than 14 million voters and several voter education programs. Second, as the chief record keeper, the secretary publishes government rules and regulations and thus is often referred to as the "State's Filing Cabinet." Third, the secretary serves as the lead liaison on issues involving the Texas–Mexico border and Texas's relations with Mexico.

COMMISSIONER FOR HEALTH AND HUMAN SERVICES

The Health and Human Services Commission (HHSC), headed by a commissioner selected by the governor, is responsible for the health and welfare of many needy Texans. Because of wide-ranging responsibility, the HHSC is massive. HHSC oversees the operations of most health-related programs including the following:

- Medicaid
- Children's Health Insurance Program
- Texas Women's Health Program
- Temporary Assistance for Needy Families
- Supplemental Nutrition Assistance Program

HHSC is a mega agency with four different departments, 58,000 employees, and a $30 billion budget. The size and number of policies they implement make it one of the toughest to run in state government.

DEPARTMENT OF INSURANCE

Think you can get away with a fraudulent insurance claim about damage caused by the Memorial Day 2015 flooding? Think again. Insurance fraud costs millions of dollars to Texans and businesses annually, and the Fraud Unit of the Texas Department of Insurance (TDI) investigates more than 500 cases each year.

The TDI also regulates the insurance industry and provides consumer protection. In one recent case, the TDI caught a former insurance agent who convinced more than thirty elderly customers to liquidate insurance plans and hand over the funds to him.[26] Consumers can also comparison shop for various types of insurance through the TDI and register complaints against insurance companies, health maintenance organizations, insurance agents, or claims adjusters. TDI also oversees the allocation of workers' compensation benefits.

 TEXAS TAKEAWAYS

7 What does the Secretary of State do?

8 Why is the HHSC so difficult to manage?

GOVERNOR-APPOINTED, MULTIMEMBER AGENCIES

9.4 Describe the purposes important multimember agencies serve.

multimember agencies:
bureaucratic organizations staffed by a minimum of three individuals

Multimember agencies whose members are appointed by the governor are certainly influenced by the governor's agenda and ideology. This influence is lessened because there are many members of these organizations and the governor's reach may not grasp all of them all of the time. These groups operate largely independently of the other executive agencies but are accountable to the legislature through periodic review.

PUBLIC UTILITY COMMISSION

If you get an electricity bill that is alarmingly high, contact the Public Utility Commission (PUC). Created in 1975 to provide statewide regulation of the rates and services of electric and telecommunications utilities, the PUC offers Texans assistance in resolving consumer complains about electricity rates. Consumers can also use the "Power to Choose" website to compare company prices; and, if the consumer feels exploited, they can file a complaint for PUC to investigate.[27]

DEPARTMENT OF TRANSPORTATION

A large and diverse state provides many options for governors looking to add diversity to the executive branch in Texas. The growth of the Hispanic and Asian populations in Texas makes this more important. Many governors seek representatives from underrepresented groups to serve in Texas government.

SOCIAL RESPONSIBILITY: **Does diversity matter in gubernatorial appointments? In what way?**

Ever been stuck in traffic and wondered whom to blame? The Texas Department of Transportation (TxDOT), although not responsible for your immediate traffic delays, is in charge of operations and maintenance of the state's massive 80,000-mile highway system, in addition to overseeing aviation, railroads, and other public transportation systems in the state.

TxDOT also awards state contracts for the building and maintenance of highways. With urbanization and a growing population, Texas has an all-time high number of vehicles on its roads and number of miles traveled. The state's current infrastructure is aging, with tens of thousands of lane miles in need of reconstruction. As we've seen, the state is struggling to fund road construction. In 2014, Texas voters passed a constitutional amendment to divert half of the general oil and gas revenue to the State Highway Fund.

TEXAS PARKS AND WILDLIFE DEPARTMENT

If you've ever wetted a fishing line, hunted a buck, paddled a canoe, or popped a tent in Texas, chances are you've encountered the Texas Parks and Wildlife Department (TPWD). TPWD manages and protects wildlife and wildlife habitats and acquires and manages Texas's state parks and historic areas. Specifically, TPWD sells hunting, fishing, and boating licenses; issues fees for service (such as state park entrance fees); and creates and enforces regulations to protect wildlife and stock fish. TPWD's law enforcement, both game wardens and park police forces, make the department the second-largest statewide law enforcement agency!

TPWD is a traditionally rural agency that is attempting to serve an increasingly urban state. If an alligator shows up on your patio some summer afternoon, you can't simply shoot it. Getting an Alligator Nuisance Control Permit requires completing a course and passing two exams—one written exam and one "live alligator handling exam."[28] In 22 counties, hunters may secure a license but tag only one alligator per year and may only capture the creature with gigs and snares (although the alligator once caught can be "dispatched" with a firearm).

Hunting from a helicopter ("aerial management") requires more than finding a buddy with a chopper and a rifle. To participate, hunters must file the proper paperwork with Texas Parks and Wildlife Department. Aerial hunters must only hunt feral hogs and coyotes. It is otherwise illegal to sport hunt from aircraft.

PERSONAL RESPONSIBILITY: **Would you fish or hunt without a license? How much should the state regulate hunting?**

TEXAS COMMISSION ON ENVIRONMENTAL QUALITY

The TCEQ protects public health, preserves the natural resources of the state, maintains clean air and water, and assures the safe management of waste. The TCEQ is also responsible for licensing certain duties that have an environmental impact (such as wastewater operations), issuing permits to industry groups, and creating and enforcing environmental rules. TCEQ issues rules about responding to natural disasters, sets fees for environmental cleanups as necessary, and more tightly or loosely applies rules to industries.

The state clashes with both local and national actors on environmental protection, and not just for stringent pollution controls. Governor Abbott has consistently argued against tightening national emissions limits on smog-forming pollution on the grounds that these changes would hurt the Texas economy. Yes, Governor Abbott also recently sided with TCEQ in challenging a city ordinance in Houston that required pollution-emitting entities to register with the city and pay a fee. The governor argued that city rules are preempted by state law and that the ordinance undermines TCEQ's "efforts to achieve voluntary remediation and compliance." He called the decision to impose criminal fines on polluters "a clumsy approach to a complex problem."[29] Governor Abbott sought looser controls and state superiority in environmental regulations over both local and national concerns.

TEXAS TAKEAWAYS

9 Distinguish between governor-appointed agencies run by a single head or by more than one person.

10 Name three responsibilities of the Texas Commission on Environmental Quality.

MULTIMEMBER ELECTED COMMISSIONS AND HYBRID AGENCIES

9.5 Differentiate between multimember elected commissions and hybrid agencies.

In some cases, voters themselves elect the members of a commission, giving the public a more direct say in the regulatory process. Elections to these multimember commissions are held either at the district or statewide level. In addition, some **hybrid agencies** comprise both elected and appointed officials.

hybrid agencies: bureaucratic organizations whose leaders are selected by a mixture of appointments and elections

TEXAS RAILROAD COMMISSION

Ironically, the Texas Railroad Commission (TRC) has almost no authority over railroads in Texas! Originally created in 1891 to regulate corruption and monopolies in the railroad industry, TRC is Texas's oldest regulatory agency. In the late 1880s, to entice railroads to run their tracks through sparsely populated Texas, the legislature granted more than 24 million acres (38,000 square miles) to the railroads—an area larger than the state of Indiana—without oversight. The result was mayhem, fraud, and corruption. Public outcry and leadership from railroad-buster Governor James Hogg precipitated the creation of a regulatory agency to adopt necessary rates, correct abuses, and enforce penalties.

Decades after its creation, the TRC's book of responsibility has expanded significantly. Currently, the TRC's primary functions are the regulation of the oil and gas industry. The TRC issues permits for drilling for or extracting natural resources, inspects oil and gas facilities, licenses waste haulers, assesses fees for environmental damage in oil fields, and ensures that oil and natural gas pipelines run safely. These dealings can place TRC in the center of a controversy. In 2014, citizens of Denton County voted to ban the practice of hydraulic fracturing (fracking), a practice regulated by the TRC. The legislature rejected local control of fracking and reaffirmed the TRC's central role in the commercial development of land. Local officials and other critics maintain that the TRC is protecting the industries it is supposed to regulate and local control is needed to protect the health and safety of citizens.

TEXAS ETHICS COMMISSION

Which organizations are backing your elected officials? How much money do politicians spend to get reelected? How much money does the beer industry spend on lobbyists to persuade legislators to support a bill? The Texas Ethics Commission (TEC) keeps track of these figures by overseeing campaign contributions and regulating and enforcing lobbying activities. In terms of enforcement, the TEC hears complaints related to filing violations and can fine individuals.

STATE BOARD OF EDUCATION

How much should teachers in Texas focus on Thomas Jefferson's faith as part of his political beliefs? Should the study of important confederate leaders be expanded on in the coverage of the Civil War in US history classes? These questions are principally decided by the State Board of Education (SBOE). The SBOE is responsible for the oversight of public primary and secondary education, setting curriculum standards, and establishing graduation requirements.

Because they have control over the curriculum taught in public schools in the state, SBOE is no stranger to controversy. Curriculum decisions—especially concerning the role of religion, the coverage of political figures, and the treatment of race—have sparked national debate. In 2010, the SBOE, led by conservative members, reduced the coverage of US Senator Ted Kennedy, elevated the prominence of President Ronald Reagan, and removed hip-hop music from a list of influential cultural music because of complaints about inappropriate lyrics.[30] In 2014, the SBOE approved of new history texts that, critics charge, exaggerate the influence of Moses in American democracy.[31] Partisan politics plays a formidable role in these decisions. On a 10-to-5 vote, Republican appointees all supported the changes and the Democrats all opposed. Although the governor appoints the Commission of Education and the head of the board, the people elect all officials to the 15-member SBOE. So Texas voters can have a say in these controversial decisions.

★ TEXAS TAKEAWAYS

11 Name the primary functions of the Texas Railroad Commission.

12 What is the main goal of the Texas Ethics Commission?

13 Identify the primary responsibility of the State Board of Education.

🤠 CONTROLLING THE BUREAUCRACY

9.6 Assess how the plural executive influences policy and the methods of holding the bureaucracy in check.

Is the Texas bureaucracy too closely aligned with business interests at the expense of ordinary Texas citizens? Does the structure of the plural executive contribute to sluggish policy innovation and slow responses to state problems? Does the diffusion of power among the governor, the lieutenant governor, the comptroller, and the other executive officers, agencies, and commissions mean that the people cannot hold the Texas government accountable? And has the weak structure of the executive, established to prevent the government from stamping out individual freedom, become too inefficient to meet the needs of a modernizing Texas? To begin to answer these questions, we need to take a look at how the selection of bureaucracy impacts policy, how the plural executive impacts efficiency, and what mechanism state representatives and the people can use to reform the bureaucracy.

SELECTION OF THE BUREAUCRACY

How the bureaucracy is selected influences public policy in many ways. Texas voters influence public policy when they elect members of the bureaucracy. Governor appointees often shape policy in line with the governor's preferences, but the state legislature often sets requirements for appointments. Governor Abbott appointed Josh McGee, an advocate for pension reform that may limit benefits, to head the Pension Review Board. One observer compared the choice to "appointing Godzilla to guard Tokyo."[32] Although the Commissioner has limited power to change pensions, he has an influential voice in making changes to the pensions of state workers.

Often the legislature introduces requirements for appointments that limit the governor. For example, although the nine individuals who head the Texas Parks and Wildlife Department are appointed by the governor (with senate approval), the governor is obligated by law to attempt to include persons with expertise in diverse fields, such as historical preservation, conservation, and outdoor recreation. This limits—but does not remove—the influence of outside agents and improves the ability of an agency to act in the best interests of the people of Texas. Game wardens from the TPWD even filed state charges against Senate Majority Leader Lyndon Johnson in 1956 for shooting more than the legal limit of birds. The warden's charges were dismissed by a local justice of the peace who was politically friendly to Johnson.

Some agencies have appointees representing multiple interests across Texas government, attempting to balance the interests of all. The TEC's eight members are selected by three different officials: the governor appoints four members, the lieutenant governor appoints two members, and the speaker of the house appoints two members. As a result, no single part of government has full authority to staff the TEC with its associates. Given that the tasks of the

TEC are to serve as an enforcement agency on state ethics laws, this dispersion of power is important so that the commission is not beholden to any one individual. Governor Rick Perry himself was fined $1,500 for failing to report income from a rental house.

Voters also have a hand in selection, especially to agencies that make important policy decisions, such as the SBOE and the TRC. When voters don't like the policy created, they can vote office holders out of these agencies. The SBOE's rewriting of history standards (referenced previously), including limiting discussion about race and gender issues and emphasizing gun rights and free markets, reflected the political values at the time of the Texans who voted for the SBOE members.[33] With only the voters to hold these agency representatives accountable, they have a great deal of autonomy to influence policy. Voters rejected these pitched partisan battles in 2014 when they elected more moderates to the board to replace several controversial board members.[34] The board toned down the rhetoric and looked to make more reasonable standards for textbooks.

Sometimes agency officials are selected from industry groups that are regulated by that agency—even when voters elect these officials. These candidates have an advantage in that they have expertise in the field and often considerable campaign funds. The TRC provides a good example of how this can influence policy. Critics of the TRC suggest that the agency is too close to the industry it regulates and the TRC's dual role of regulating industry and environmental stewardship creates conflicts of interest. In late 2013 and early 2014, a series of mysterious earthquakes rattled north Texas along the Barnett Shale, home to gas-rich fields. Regulators worried that oil- and gas-related activities contributed to the seismic activities, as suggested by reports carried out by energy experts and seismologists at Southern Methodist University. The TRC cleared two oil field companies of responsibility, arguing that the study was preliminary and that the link between extraction efforts and earthquakes is inconclusive. Environmental activists accused the TRC of siding with the industry and insisted that further investigations were warranted.

SLUGGISH POLICYMAKING

Much of the weakness in Texas government is due to the plural executive's diffusion of power and to bureaucratic policies that contribute to sluggish policy innovation and slow responses to state problems. Rules and regulations from a large bureaucracy choke government's ability to be agile. Proposed rules changes must be advertised for a specific period of time, open for public comment, and often face administrative delays. The legislature may use this formal rule-making process to slow down bureaucratic rule-making. Instead of fixing serious policy problems, the bureaucracy is often a victim of its own rules.

For example, the foster care system in Texas has let down the state's most vulnerable kids—highlighted by the number of delinquent cases, which rose

TABLE 9.3	Sunset Agency Review Process

SUNSET STAFF EVALUATION	SUNSET COMMISSION STAFF
Sunset staff performs extensive research and analysis to evaluate the need for, performance of, and improvements to the agency under review.	• Reviews agency's Self-Evaluation Report • Receives input from interested parties • Evaluates agency and identifies problems • Develops recommendations • Publishes staff report

SUNSET PUBLISHES STAFF REPORT	

SUNSET COMMISSION DELIBERATION	PUBLIC HEARINGS
The Sunset Commission conducts a public hearing to take testimony on the staff report and the agency overall. Later, the Commission meets again to vote on which changes to recommend to the full Legislature.	• Sunset staff presents its report and recommendations • Agency presents its response • Sunset Commission hears public testimony • Staff compiles all testimony for Commission consideration • Sunset Commission meets again to consider and vote on recommendations

SUNSET COMMISSION RECOMMENDS ACTION	

LEGISLATIVE ACTION	TEXAS LEGISLATURE
The full legislature considers Sunset recommendations and makes final determinations.	• Sunset bill on an agency is drafted and filed • Sunset bills go through normal bill processes • The Senate and the House conduct committee hearings and debate the bill • Bill passes or fails adoption • Governor signs, vetoes, or allows bill to become law without signature

Agency continues with improvements. OR Agency is abolished but may continue business for up to one year.

Source: Texas Sunset Advisory Commission.

 COMMUNICATION:

How does the Sunset Advisory Commission review agencies?

The review process follows a simple three-step action:

- First, the staff of the commission works with each agency to collect information, performing extensive research to analyze and review the agency's required self-evaluation. Outside parties, including the public, weigh in at this stage as well. This first stage ends with a report with details about the efficiency of the agency, the success in achieving their mission, and the compliance with open government laws.

- In the second stage, the commission holds hearings on the preliminary report, receives a response from the agency, and votes on final recommendations to the legislature.

- The third stage involves the legislature, which turns the recommendations of the Commission into legislation to be sent through the normal legislative process, including a full vote of the House and Senate and the governor's signature.

17 percent. In addition, the Department of Family and Protective Services has overlooked dozens of cases of abuse, including one in which a young girl was killed by her foster family. Because of complex rules, the amount of paperwork, deadlines, and family visits creates a pressure-filled environment that pushes away experienced employees. The Commissioner of the Department of Family and Protective Services says part of the problem is that there are too many policies and rules, making it "impossible for people to know what the policies are."[35]

OVERSIGHT AND CHANGE

An accountable bureaucracy is the key to ensuring government is working properly and efficiently. With so many agency heads, staff, rules, and procedures, keeping tabs on the function of the bureaucracy in Texas is a massive task. Several players in government are in charge of reviewing agencies, monitoring their progress, evaluating their effectiveness, and altering or eliminating them.

Sunset Process. The Sunset Advisory Commission is a twelve-member commission established in 1977 whose responsibility is to review more than 130 state agencies on a twelve-year cycle. The Sunset process of agency review was set up to provide an ongoing evaluation of government efficiency and effectiveness. In the words of longtime journalist Paul Burka, "Sunset is not designed to change the world. It is designed to give government a periodic scrubbing."[36] Texas is one of only a few states that has this process (the federal government does not either).

The Sunset Commission asks a simple question: does an agency's function continue to be needed by the state? For each state agency, the legislature sets a date for its abolishment on a twelve-year calendar. The agency is set to be abolished unless legislation is passed to allow that agency to continue to function. The commission reviews agencies set to be "sunsetted" prior to that date, and the legislature decides whether to amend or abolish the agency. This process creates a unique opportunity for the legislature to establish rules and goals for agencies and to hold the bureaucracy accountable (see Table 9.3). Some boards or commissions are scheduled for periodic review, but not elimination, such as the Board of Pardons and Paroles. Between twenty and thirty agencies are reviewed every legislative session.

The good news for state agencies is that they are rarely given the death sentence (see Figure 9.6). Rather, specific functions are often transferred to another agency. For instance, Sunset recommendations for the Texas Higher Education Coordinating Board refocused the agency on coordination rather than regulation of higher education. The Sunset legislation removed significant pieces of the agency's authority to consolidate or eliminate low-producing academic programs and their ability to approve capital projects at state colleges and universities.

FIGURE 9.6   **Agencies Continued or Abolished**

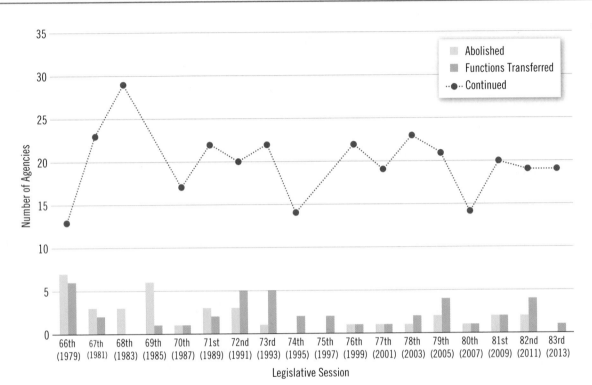

Source: Texas Sunset Advisory Commission.

 COMMUNICATION:

When are agencies continued, abolished, or transferred?

- Most agencies are continued after Sunset review, generally between fifteen and thirty per year.

- Agencies are not very likely to be abolished. Abolishment was more likely to occur in the early days of the Sunset Commission's work—in 1979, 1981, and 1985.

- The Sunset recommendations are more likely to transfer functions to another agency than abolish an agency. Beginning in the 1991 session, more agencies were asked to transfer functions rather than dissolve.

 CRITICAL THINKING:

Why are most agencies continued?

- Most agencies function well and efficiently, especially because Sunset regulations establish guidelines and benchmarks for success for agencies in years they are not reviewed.

- The process of shutting down an agency is difficult and is often enough to encourage agency officials and lawmakers to work together to reform a struggling agency.

Agencies that are abolished continue their function for one year as they transition into obscurity. Since 1977, seventy-nine agencies have been abolished or absorbed into other agencies. For example, in 2013, the Sunset recommendations abolished the Office of Fire Fighters' Pension Commissioner and put the Pension Review Board in charge of overseeing local firefighter pensions. The Commission estimates that it has generated almost one billion dollars since 1982 in savings or increased revenue; and for every dollar spent on the Commission, the state gets a return of approximately $23.[37]

The legislature has the authority to place some bodies that function like agencies under review, such as local transit agencies, the Port of Houston Authority, and the University Interscholastic League—important because it sets rules for and administers Friday Night Football in the state, along with other athletic, music, and academic contests.

Legislative Oversight.   The legislature is tasked with overseeing agency compliance with legislative polices. Standing and special committees in the legislature investigate matters involving agency compliance. In 2015, the State Senate investigated how state agencies develop and manage contracts with outside organizations for services. The Senate Finance Committee

GREAT TEXAS POLITICAL DEBATES
Sunset Sunset?

At the close of the 2009 legislative session, Representative Carl Isett rose to give a personal privilege speech with dire warning: the state's Sunset system is broken and needs repair. Just before the House adjourned on a pivotal day in the legislature, the Lubbock Republican, who served as the outgoing chairman of the Sunset Advisory Commission, leveled that the system was "adulterated." He continued to say that instead of being used for realistic reform efforts, Sunset bills are seen by lobbyists, special interests, and legislators as "targets of opportunity" to eliminate provisions they disliked. Representative Isett concluded by saying that it was "time to sunset the Sunset process."[38] Despite the Sunset Advisory Commission's noble cause, the process has been compromised. Increasingly, interest group participation has shaped the Sunset process. In a review of the Department of Transportation, Speaker Joe Strauss, commenting

on the 250 amendments in front of him, said that he "couldn't even see the parliamentarian" and that the lobbyists have taken control of the process.[39]

SOCIAL RESPONSIBILITY: **Should the state reform the Sunset laws?**

NO: Periodic review of individual agencies provides careful planning and oversight and most agency reviews run smoothly. Any flaws are minor in comparison to achieving efficiency of government and mandatory review.

YES: With increasing power from lobbying interests in Austin and less oversight for the Sunset process, more transparency is needed with respect to participation in the process. Sunset Commission members should disclose potential conflicts of interest. Legislative rules must be changed to not allow Sunset bills to be delayed or to have other legislation attached to them.

looked into questions about possible abuses in state contracting and found that even basic information about the state's current contracts was unavailable for more than twenty state agencies. "We're not even letting the horses run out of the barn," said State Senator Paul Bettencourt, Republican from Houston. "They don't even know where the barn is."[40] The committee recommended legislation to require a central contract management database and a public vendor tracking system that state agencies would have to use to grade vendors. The legislature can also transfer administration of a program to another agency, stripping a problematic agency or agency personnel out of the process.

Gubernatorial Oversight.   The governor has several ways to oversee and manage agencies. The Governor's Office of Budget and Planning prepares biennial budget recommendations for the legislature to consider and regularly monitors state appropriations and operations between formal Sunset reviews. The governor also has the power to direct state agencies to implement specific rules. In the aftermath of a 2015 scandal involving improper contracts being awarded to close business associates of an agency head, Governor Greg Abbott issued several rules designed to hold agency contracting accountable. These rules require agencies to publicly disclose no-bid contracts, justify these contracts, and ensure that agency employees involved in the contract disclose any possible conflicts of interest. If all else fails, the governor ask the agency head to resign (but not force them to).

Other Agencies with Oversight.   Other state agencies also provide oversight. The State Auditor reviews fiscal and management responsibilities and evaluates the efficiency, effectiveness, and legal compliance of state agencies. The State Auditor may also monitor an agency's implementation of legislative or Sunset committee management recommendations. The Legislative Budget Board prepares biennial appropriations bills, assesses performance reports from agencies, and reviews agency strategic plans. All job openings must be listed with the Texas Employment Agency, which screens applicants.

★ TEXAS TAKEAWAYS

14 Describe the mission of the Sunset Commission.

15 What are some measures taken by Texas to hold its bureaucracy accountable?

✪ THE INSIDER VIEW

The dispersal of authority across several individuals, elected agency heads, and thousands of individual bureaucrats across state government often makes the bureaucracy feel remote from public interest. Yet these organizations are the cornerstone of the institutional power that runs Texas from the small (operating nursery floral businesses) to the large (regulating environmental outcomes). Past internal conflicts, friction within the executive branch, and serious efforts to make government accountable have established checks on the actions of the plural executive and bureaucratic organizations in the state. These barriers do not allow any one person, branch of government, or agency to become too powerful and allow for government to stay limited in scope. However, the way the bureaucracy is selected plays a part in its power—some agencies (such as the Railroad Commission) have close ties to the organizations they work with, whereas others (the Texas Ethics Commission) do not. Officials, like the Lieutenant Governor, have significant sway in state policymaking. However, public policies are—at times—a product of the struggles between officers and agencies within the plural executive. The public has several ways to intervene, including tracking what government does and participating in reforms.

✪ TEXAS TAKEAWAYS

1 Bureaucracies administer rules, make rules, enforce laws, and provide services to individuals.

2 The Texas bureaucracy has grown due to a combination of population growth and economic expansion.

3 Agencies with more appointees from the governor are more indebted to the governor. Agencies that are elected independently are less likely to cater to the governor's will.

4 The lieutenant governor serves as the presiding officer of the Texas Senate, casts tiebreaking votes, and serves and appoints officials to key state boards and commissions.

5 The AG office's consumer functions involve enforcement of health, safety, and consumer regulations and protection of the rights of the elderly and disabled. The attorney general is also responsible for enforcement of child support payments, including locating absent parents, establishing paternity, reviewing and adjusting child support payments, and collecting and distributing child support payments.

6 The comptroller sets the revenue estimate and audits the budget.

7 The Secretary of State is the chief elections administrator, the steward of all state records, and an ambassador of the state to other nations.

8 The HHSC is so difficult to manage because it is a large agency and has many policies that it must implement.

9 In a governor-appointed, singled-headed agency, the appointee is often closer to the governor. Where there are more appointees on a larger commission, the governor may have less influence.

10 The Texas Commission on Environmental Quality deals with natural resources, maintains clean air and water, and protects the environment, among others.

—

11 The TRC's primary functions are the regulation of the oil and gas industry and environmental protection.

12 The main goal of the Texas Ethics Commission is to oversee, regulate, and enforce campaign finance and lobbying activities.

13 The State Board of Education oversees the curriculum standards for primary and secondary education.

14 The mission of the Sunset Commission is to periodically review the function and efficiency of agencies. An agency is set to be abolished unless legislation is passed to allow that agency to continue to function.

15 The state can hold the bureaucracy accountable in several ways, including the Sunset process and legislative, gubernatorial, and agency oversight.

KEY TERMS

bureaucracy
enforcement
hybrid agencies
implementation
licensing
multimember agencies
pay-as-you-go system
plural executive
presiding officer
regulations
rules

PRACTICE QUIZ

1. The diffusion of power and authority throughout several entities in the executive branch is called
   a. Delegation
   b. Reappraisal of Agencies
   c. Reorganization Planning
   d. Plural Executive

2. Regarding power and political role, the Lieutenant Governor in Texas is
   a. Strong
   b. Weak
   c. Non-existent
   d. None of the above

3. _____ is when a government agency gives a company, an individual, or an organization permission to carry out a specific task.
   a. Regulation
   b. Licensing
   c. Enforcement
   d. Rule-making

4. If the Senate is evenly split on a vote, which individual is responsible for being the "tiebreaking" vote?
   a. Governor
   b. Secretary of State
   c. Lieutenant Governor
   d. Senate Majority Leader

5. What is the name of the complex, professional organization that administers government actions through routine tasks?
   a. The Legislature
   b. The Vote Centers
   c. The Office of the Governor
   d. The Bureaucracy

6. What is the name of the organization that periodically reviews executive agencies for efficiency?
   a. The Attorney General
   b. Sunset Commission
   c. Department of Licensing and Regulations
   d. Texas Legislative Council

7. The Lieutenant Governor is the presiding officer of the Texas Senate.

   a. True
   b. False

8. The TRC's authority is limited to regulating railroads.

   a. True
   b. False

9. The Sunset Process is one of several ways that the state can hold the bureaucracy accountable.

   a. True
   b. False

10. The bureaucracy in Texas is made up of both independent agencies and agencies staffed by gubernatorial appointments.

    a. True
    b. False

[Answers: D, A, B, C, D, B, A, B, A, A]

10 THE TEXAS JUDICIARY

In December 1992, Pamela Jean Johnson collapsed in tears as a Texas jury awarded her $25 million after her breast implant burst and forced her to endure a partial mastectomy. This vast sum was the largest award against a producer of silicone implants to date, and served as a sign of things to come.[1] Over the next decade, Texas courts granted blockbuster damage awards, including the first multi-billion dollar settlement in Texas history.

Some Texans cried out for tort reform—laws that would limit damages granted for negligence. The battle pitched the powerful trial lawyers associations against Texas business interests and their Republican supporters. Republicans claimed that outrageously large awards led to skyrocketing Texas medical malpractice insurance rates, and that this was the reason Texas suffered from a shortage of physicians and medical specialists. The U.S. Chamber of Commerce had ranked Texas as among the five worst litigation states and that several counties were "judicial hell holes" where "normal rules of balance and fair play under the law don't exist."[2] Houston-based mega-lawyer Joe Jamail, who made so many millions defending clients that he was dubbed the "King of Torts," deemed reform initiatives as "tort deform, not tort reform."[3] Jamail and others argued that individuals who are harmed by companies or poor medical practices must be compensated properly. Coming off major electoral victories in 2002, Republicans secured the passage of the 2003 Texas tort reform law with bipartisan support.

The legislature's tort reform package profoundly impacted the legal process in state courts. It reduced the number of cases the

LEARNING OBJECTIVES

10.1	Outline the structure and functions of the Texas courts.
10.2	Describe the function of each of the trial courts in Texas.
10.3	Describe the function of the appellate courts in Texas.
10.4	Evaluate the quality of justice in Texas.
10.5	Identify problems associated with different methods of judicial selection.
10.6	Analyze the changes in the court's demographics.
10.7	Evaluate proposals for reforming the selection of the judiciary.

● Judicial decisions in Texas affects and is shaped by the political culture and shapes Texas's values. Since the Republic was formed, Texas courts have ruled on murder and death penalty issues, the legality of pool halls, and the ownership of surface water.

courts had to handle and helped unclog the system. In the decade after Texas implemented tort reform, medical malpractice lawsuits plummeted 64 percent[4] and civil lawsuits overall dropped by 17 percent.[5] As these events make clear, the judicial system crowns winners and losers. In theory, all Texans are equal before the law and judiciary. In practice, the fear is that the system is strongly influenced by the powerful because they have greater resources. The most obvious culprit is that judges are elected in Texas. Does this allow the people the ability to hold them accountable or does it give wealthy contributors to judicial campaigns an edge over others?

The power struggle between political, business, and public interests all collide in the elections of judges and rulings in the Texas courts. In this chapter, we explore the function, development, and impact of the judiciary in Texas. We examine how the power of the judiciary is constrained by the legislature, higher courts, and voters. Finally, we assess reform efforts that have followed political scandals and dysfunction within the courts.

THE ROLE OF THE COURT

10.1 Outline the structure and functions of the Texas courts.

The judicial system's role is to interpret Texas laws in matters ranging from minor criminal offenses to interpreting the Texas Constitution. Texans expect to have equal access to an efficient system that applies the law fairly and objectively and that protects their interests. Yet, is this task even possible? Interests often conflict and can be weighted in favor of one group over another. And while Texans might expect impartiality from judges, political struggles make their way into the courtroom in many ways. In this section, we begin to evaluate the Texas judiciary by exploring its basic structure and function.

DISPENSING JUSTICE

Texans did not always have ready access to the courts. Before the Texas revolution, justice was a scarce commodity. The Mexican constitutions of 1824 and 1827 established state and local courts. However, ordinary Texans, in practice, could not appeal local decisions because higher courts were located several hundred miles away in the state's capital.[6] After Reconstruction, resentment of central government swelled and Texans reacted against the "interests" (corporations) and demanded accountability to the people. The current Texas Constitution's Article 5 divides the judiciary in Texas into many types of courts allowing for both local access and appeal to higher courts. The legislature subsequently established additional courts to allow the state to handle a rising caseload as the economy and the population boomed after Reconstruction. As a result, the Texas judicial system has the greatest number of courts in the nation (see Figure 10.1). More courts means, in principle, more access to justice for Texans. In practice, however, multiple layers of courts may increase the cost of a legal verdict for many Texans.

Judicial Hierarchy. The structure of the court system is hierarchical, meaning that cases start at the lowest level and funnel to the courts above as appropriate. The hierarchical nature of the court also allows for higher courts to check bad decisions or incorrect rulings by lower courts. This is one way in which the court balances competing interests and provides access to all groups.

Legal Jurisdiction. The legislature helps the courts set **jurisdiction,** the official territory and types of cases over which a court exercises authority. Trial courts often have **original jurisdiction**—they are the court in which the case is first heard. If one is not satisfied with the outcome and the case meets the criteria for an appeal, it may advance to an appellate court. Higher courts generally have discretion about which cases they choose to take from lower courts, making the appeals process something of a gamble. Higher courts with **appellate jurisdiction** review decisions of lower courts. This appeals process can be lengthy, depending on the nature of the case and the efficiency of the court system.

Cases can be either criminal or civil in nature. In **criminal cases,** the government brings charges against a person (the defendant) who is accused of breaking a law, such as in cases of murder, robbery, larceny, or bribery. The government must prove the defendant is guilty beyond a reasonable doubt. **Civil cases** involve conflict between two parties (litigants), whether individuals, corporations, or the government. The standard of proof is lower in civil cases. The plaintiff, the party who is bringing suit against a defendant, the party being sued, must prove that the harm was done to them beyond a "preponderance of evidence." This standard emphasizes the convincing quality of the evidence rather than the amount—for instance, a witness with clearer details about an event rather than several with hazier recollections.

Texas has many types of trial courts. How do you figure out which court hears a case? In civil cases, the amount of monetary damages helps determine which court will hear a case. The major factor that determines which court will

jurisdiction: the official territory and types of cases over which a court exercises authority

original jurisdiction: the court in which the case is first heard

appellate jurisdiction: the authority of a court to review a case first heard by a lower court

criminal cases: cases in which the government brings suit against the defendant for violating the law and in which the defendant is guilty beyond a reasonable doubt

civil cases: cases in which individuals, corporations, or the government bring suit against another party and must prove that the harm was done to them beyond a "preponderance of evidence"

IS IT BIGGER IN TEXAS?

FIGURE 10.1   **Total Trial Courts**

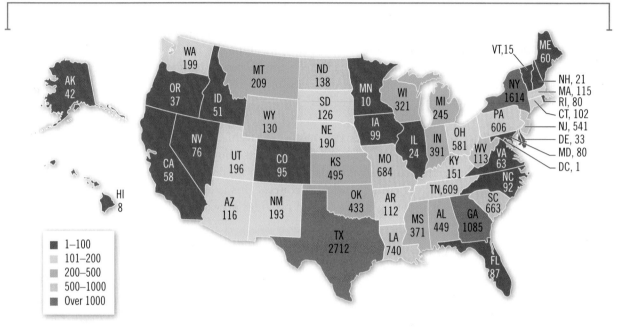

Source: Center for State Courts. Figures include all trial courts.

 COMMUNICATION:

Where does Texas rank on the number of trial courts?

- Texas ranks #1 in the total number of trial courts (2712).

 CRITICAL THINKING:

Why so many courts?

- The Texas Constitution divides judicial power locally to prevent centralized power, increasing the number of courts.

- Southern states, such as Georgia and Louisiana, tend to have more courts than other states, as they have been historically distrustful of judicial oversight from the days of Reconstruction following the Civil War.

- Large states tend to have a greater number of courts, such as New York and Pennsylvania. These states not only have large economies but also large populations, necessitating more courts to handle legal matters like divorce, contracts, and crime.

hear a criminal case is the severity of the transgression. A **felony** is the highest stage of crime under state or federal law. These offenses are more severe in character than **misdemeanors,** which are minor wrongdoings. The judiciary classifies the severity of a crime based on factors like the use of a weapon and whether the crime involved violence.

felony: the highest criminal offense under state or federal law

misdemeanors: a class of criminal offenses which are minor wrongdoings

common law: law that is established when judges apply past decisions by courts—called legal precedents—to the facts of a new case before them

INTERPRETING THE LAW

Texas courts interpret law by relying on legal traditions—the Texas Constitution, legislation, and **common law**. These decisions then become binding as future courts consider similar cases. In making these decisions, the judicial branch not only delivers justice, but it also acts as a check on the legislative and executive branches. Let's take a closer look at how this occurs.

Clarifying Laws. In their haste to make new laws and revise old laws in 140 days, the legislature often writes laws that are unclear, vague, misleading or, on occasion, unconstitutional. The Texas Supreme Court sorts out contradictions or clarifies legislative meaning. In his 2015 state of the judiciary address, Chief Justice Nathan Hecht remarked, "Ascertaining what is meant by what is said can be difficult. Try it with your spouse. Even when a statement is in writing, and has been carefully considered, its application in an unforeseen situation can be unclear."[7]

These clarifications are often minor but meaningful. For example, the court clarified the term *impounded* in 2016 when it ruled that the owner of a missing dog picked up by a private animal control shelter does not give up ownership rights to the shelter or foster family.

Checking the Legislature. The courts often take on political roles, acting to check or maintain legislative decisions by determining whether legislation is constitutional. For example, in 1995, the Texas legislature faced a crisis in school funding and passed a controversial law that distributed "excess wealth" from some

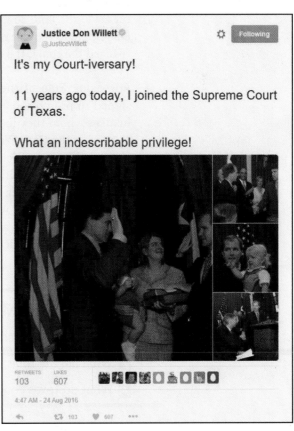

Despite the perception of justices as out of touch and humorless, Justice Don Willett tweets at least 10 times daily. "I'm the most avid judicial tweeter in America, which is like being the tallest Munchkin in Oz," said Willett, aka @JusticeWillett.*

🤠 SOCIAL RESPONSIBILITY: **Should a judge's ideology and personality influence the way in which he or she interprets the law?**

school districts to poorer districts. Several school districts challenged the law, but Texas Supreme Court Justice John Cornyn (who would go on to represent Texas in the U.S. Senate) saved the session by upholding it. A similar decision in 2016 reaffirmed the school funding system and ensured that the state legislature would not be legally required to pour tens of millions of dollars into the public school system.

Defining State Interests.   When state interests clash with business or citizens' interests, the court's job is often to sort out competing claims. For example, in the late nineteenth century, Texas transitioned from an open frontier to land ownership. In 1888, famed cattle rancher Charles Goodnight fenced in large tracts of state land, much of which he did not actually own. The state had set aside the land to generate revenue for the public school system and sued Goodnight to remove the fences from state land. When the "Grass Lease Fight" reached the court, the court ruled that the fences had to come down.[8]

Advancing Rule of the People.   The courts in Texas are not expressly designed to promote popular sovereignty. However, Texans have chucked out justices whom they feel don't represent their values. In a classic example, in 1874 after the Civil War, Texans who hoped to restore antebellum practices elected Governor Richard Coke, who obliged his supporters by appointing Confederate sympathizers to the Texas Supreme Court in what came to be called the "Redeemer Court." Although the issues and cases were different, over a century later when conservatives abandoned the Democratic Party and the Democrats ran more liberal judges, Texans swept in a new cast of conservative Republican judges to mirror the ideology of the voters.[9]

★ TEXAS TAKEAWAYS

1 Why is the Texas court system so fragmented?

2 What are the roles of trial versus appellate courts?

3 What do Texas courts do?

 TRIAL COURTS

10.2	Describe the function of each of the trial courts in Texas.

Trial courts hear both criminal and civil cases. In these lowest level courts, witnesses are heard, evidence is presented in the form of exhibits, testimony is taken, and ultimately a verdict is passed down. There are several levels of trial courts in Texas: local, county, and state trial courts. Each type of trial and appellate court hears different types of cases (see Figure 10.2).

LOCAL COURTS

Municipal Courts.   If you dump something in violation of city ordinances or if you are caught with alcohol as a minor, you'll end up in this court. Municipal courts in Texas have original and exclusive jurisdiction over violations of city ordinances and over Class C misdemeanors, the lowest level of punishment severity of all misdemeanors.

The punishment upon conviction is generally small. For example, if you steal property worth less than $50, speed, run a red light, engage in disorderly conduct, or are found in possession of alcohol when you are underage, you'll receive a fine that is $500 or less.

The Texas legislature has the power to create municipal courts to provide Texans with better access to justice. Larger cities generally have more municipal courts than smaller cities. For instance, in Houston (Harris County, population 4.3 million), there are twenty-eight courts. In Hill County, population 34,823, there are six.

Municipal courts handle the largest volume of cases of all courts. This makes sense given the nature of the cases these courts deal with—red light runners, parking tickets, abandoned motor vehicles, city code violations, possession of drug paraphernalia (like a bong with no drug), or a minor in possession of tobacco products. Most of the cases (33 percent) end up uncontested with the defendant paying a fine or submitting a guilty plea without a court appearance.[10]

Justice Courts.   "Justice" courts are a specific type of local trial court. Contrary to popular belief, justices of the peace who administer these courts do not just issue marriage licenses. In reality, they hear cases that involve small claims, civil actions of $10,000 or less, and criminal offences punishable by fine but not prison sentences. If your landlord refused to return your security deposit, you might appear before a justice of the peace to try to get your deposit back. Justices of the peace also serve as coroners in many small counties and as magistrate judges with authority to hold hearings to determine if there is probable cause to hold a criminal defendant in jail.

Like municipal courts, justice of the peace courts also handle a significant number of cases, 2.3 million in 2015, and most cases were uncontested (43 percent) or dismissed (more than 50 percent).

We think of courts as arbiters of justice, but they are also revenue-generating agencies, putting funds back into the budget. Increasing certain fines or imposing new criminal violations has an impact on state revenue. The justice of the peace courts collected more than $300 million in court costs, fees, and fines in 2015.

FIGURE 10.2   **The Structure of Texas Courts**

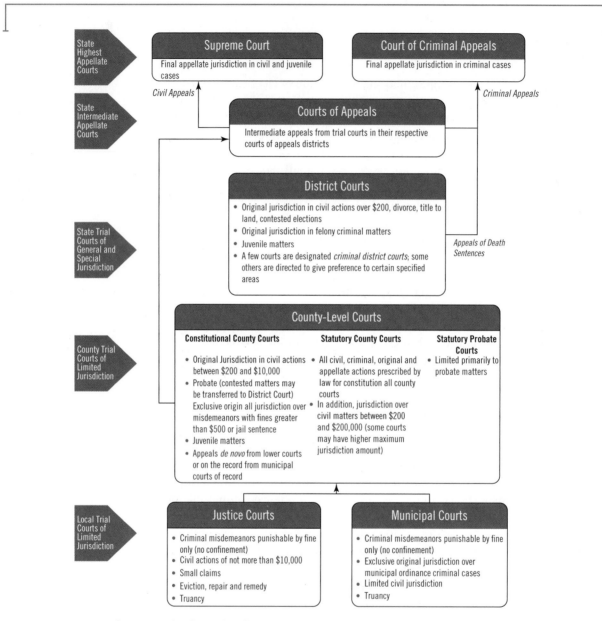

Source: The Texas Judicial Branch website.

SOCIAL RESPONSIBILITY: **There are many levels and types of Texas courts—do all these judicial layers slow justice or promote efficient justice?**

COUNTY TRIAL COURTS

Constitutional County Courts.   Although constitutional county courts do not always deal with legal matters, they are part of the judicial structure. The Texas Constitution vests broad judicial and administrative powers in county judges who also oversee a five-member commissioner's court. This court has budgetary and administrative authority over county government operations. County judges also have wide authority over several administrative matters, including hearings for beer and wine license applications, admittance to state hospitals for the mentally ill, juvenile work permits, and temporary guardianships.[11]

County Courts at Law (Statutory).   If you sue your roommate for ruining your laptop in justice court and she appeals the case, the case will end up in county court at law. These courts have original jurisdiction on civil matters between $200 and $200,000. County courts at law also have appellate jurisdiction in cases appealed from other local trial courts. In criminal appeals involving fines of $100 or less, the decision of the county courts at law is final.

Texas lawmakers cut $350 million from Medicaid in 2015, especially affecting in-home speech, physical, and occupational therapy providers and the families of children who receive these services. The Texas Supreme Court declined to hear a lawsuit seeking to block the cuts, which let the lower court decisions stand.

SOCIAL RESPONSIBILITY: **The Texas courts are designed to protect and promote justice and equality under the law. Do you think the courts do this? Why or why not?**

The Texas Constitution limits each county to a single constitutional county court, so the legislature established the first county court at law in 1907 to relieve the county judge of some or all of the judicial duties of the office. Today, there are over 240 of these courts.

Probate Courts.   Probate courts, where they are created, hear primarily matters of **probate**, the official recognition and registration of the validity of the last will and testament of a person. These courts only exist in the state's largest counties (18 total in 10 counties). If you don't live in these areas, you will need to settle these estates at a county court or district court.

probate: the process by which there is official recognition and registration of the validity of the last will and testimate of a person

STATE DISTRICT COURTS

District courts are trial courts that handle most major criminal and civil cases, including murder, drug trafficking, contested elections, and civil cases involving high amounts of monetary damages—any amount over $200. The district courts are often the first rung on the ladder of the criminal justice system, so many criminal cases begin here. Most criminal cases were drug offenses in

2015. The district courts also have original jurisdiction in all divorce cases, land title cases, and any cases that do not fall under the jurisdiction of other courts. Most cases the courts deal with are family related (38 percent), followed by criminal (33 percent), civil cases (26 percent), and juvenile and other cases (3 percent). A growing population leads to more family cases—more divorces, more child custody issues, paternity issues, child support orders, and adoptions.

Texans charged with crimes heard by district courts can choose between a **bench trial**, in which a single judge presides and decides guilt or innocence and punishment, and a **jury trial,** in which a group of individuals picked at random decides on guilt or innocence. The advantages of one versus the other depend on the details of the case (see Figure 10.3). In general, a defendant in Texas is convicted in more than half the cases, especially for felonies like driving while intoxicated (85 percent) and murder (68 percent).

However, prosecutors dismiss many cases (21 percent) for lack of evidence or other reasons. In civil cases, about a third of plaintiffs agree to dismiss their cases while a little over 10 percent end in a mutually agreeable settlement. So, only about half of cases filed actually go to trial.

bench trial: a single judge presides and decides guilt or innocence and punishment

jury trial: a group of individuals picked at random decides on guilt or innocence

TEXAS TAKEAWAYS

4 What do trial courts do?

5 What is the lowest level of trial court? The highest?

APPELLATE COURTS

10.3 Describe the function of the appellate courts in Texas.

What do appeals courts do different from lower level courts? **Appellate courts** do not hold trials, but only review legal issues of cases decided by lower courts. An appellant (or petitioner) first files a notice of appeal and then submits a written set of arguments containing the appellant's view of the facts and the law (called a brief).

appellate courts: courts that review legal issues of cases decided by lower courts

The justices in appellate courts may decide the case based upon the brief alone or they may hear oral arguments, during which attorneys for both sides present their cases in person to the justices.[12] *Amicus curiae* briefs (literally "friend of the court" in Latin) can be filed by interested parties that are not directly involved in the case, providing an avenue for outside groups to have a say in the judicial process. Interestingly, dissenting opinions also correlate to interest group participation. Amicus briefs allow interest groups to interject themselves into a case. They sometimes influence new judges but have little effect on veteran judges.[13]

FIGURE 10.3   **Aquittals and Convictions at State District Court (Criminal Cases)**

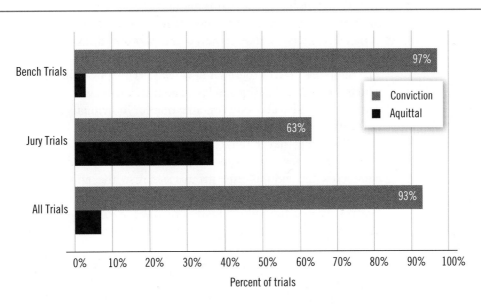

Source: Annual Statistical Report for the Texas Judiciary, 2015.

COMMUNICATION:

What was the outcome for cases at the district court level by type of trial?

- For criminal jury trials, the defendant was convicted 63 percent of the time.
- For bench trials, the defendant was convicted 97 percent of the time.

CRITICAL THINKING:

Why the differences in outcomes?

- Elected judges may be concerned about being perceived as "soft on crime" and may convict defendants more than juries.
- A jury of individuals may find a defendant sympathetic, and may be more likely to consider extenuating circumstances and less likely to convict.

After making a decision, the justices can either write an **opinion** to explain their reasoning or not. Justices often disagree on ideological or legal matters. In one recent case, the Texas Supreme Court limited the public's right to know about private groups that get government funds—three justices dissented.[14]

opinion: a document that can express the view of the judges and often takes the form of a majority opinion, when written by a justice representing the majority, but may also be a concurring or dissenting opinion

If the appeals court affirms the lower court's judgment, the case ends (unless a higher court can be appealed to). If the lower court's judgment is reversed, the higher court can remand (send) the case back to the lower court for further action (such as a new trial).[15] In 2014, the Texas Supreme Court reversed a decision that required Kia Motors to award $4.4 million to the family of a driver killed in a head-on collision when the airbag didn't deploy. The Supreme Court ordered a new trial.[16] This power hierarchy allows higher courts to check the actions of lower courts in the case of errors or other issues. These "redos" also allow for organizations or individuals to have a second strike at the case, in this case a powerful business (Kia).

Most cases never make it to the appellate level—less than 10 percent reach the highest appellate courts. Often only the most wealthy and well-connected individuals and groups can use the appellate system to their advantage given the time and expertise needed to successfully win cases here. A Texans for Public Justice report found that contributors to judges and justices were between seven and ten times more likely to have their case taken than noncontributors.[17]

The appellate courts in Texas are divided into two types: intermediate appellate courts and appellate courts of last resort. The creation of this tiered system reflects the suspicion of central authority stemming all the way back to the pre-Republic days but is designed to promote the legal access and options available to Texans.

INTERMEDIATE APPELLATE COURTS

The first (lowest) level of appeals courts are the courts of appeals organized into fourteen districts (see Figure 10.4). These courts agreed to review only 10 percent of appealed cases in 2015.[18] However, many of the courts of appeals cases involve mandatory review, primarily felony convictions in cases without the death penalty.

Each court of appeals has a chief justice and at least two other justices. When cases are heard, three justices hear the case, unless an **en banc** hearing is ordered where all of the justices of the court hear and consider the case. In each case, a determination is made by a majority of the justices.

en banc: where all of the justices of the court hear and consider the case

APPELLATE COURTS OF LAST RESORT

Sitting atop the appellate court structure are two supreme courts. Why two supreme courts? Appellants have one court for criminal matters and one court for civil matters. This creates a **dual structure** where cases are sorted by the type of issue. The dual structure was designed for efficiency but is also based on mistrust. The framers of the Texas Constitution were suspicious of centralizing universal power of legal decision-making in any one court.

dual structure: Texas's two supreme court system

FIGURE 10.4 **Court of Appeals Districts**

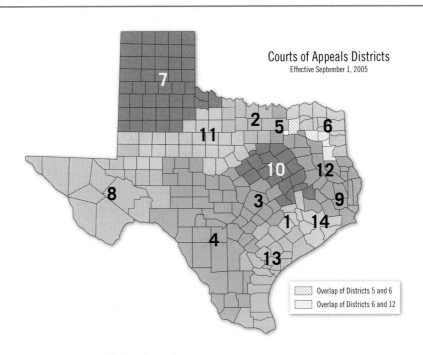

Source: Texas Legislative Council

 COMMUNICATION:

What are the geographical regions of the courts of appeals?

- The courts of appeals are organized into 14 geographical areas.
- More densely populated areas have a smaller geographical footprint for their district.

 CRITICAL THINKING:

Why are the districts carved like this?

- Districts reflect local political views and also help to distribute the caseload fairly.
- As regional populations grow, the legislature increases the number of justices in districts that serve those counties. For instance, in 1977, the First Court of Appeals (serving the Houston region) increased the size of the court to nine justices.

Texas Court of Criminal Appeals. The Texas Court of Criminal Appeals makes final determinations in all criminal matters, including applying (or not) the death penalty. The Texas Court of Criminal Appeals is comprised of nine justices: eight justices and a presiding judge. If four or more justices favor hearing a particular case, the case is scheduled for argument. However,

mandatory review: cases required to be heard by a specific court

most of the caseload of the Texas Court of Criminal Appeals—about 80 percent of its cases—consists of **mandatory review** of sentencing and direct death penalty appeals. The Texas legislature determines which sentences must be reviewed, giving the legislative branch a significant degree of control over the judicial branch. Most death penalty judgments are upheld by the court. Of the twelve direct appeal cases on the death penalty filed in 2014, ten were affirmed.

Texas Supreme Court. The Texas Supreme Court deals primarily with civil matters and juvenile justice. The Texas Supreme Court can either order monetary or equitable relief (directing the losing party do to something or not do something). The Supreme Court reversed about half of the intermediate courts decisions in 2015 and an even higher proportion of lower court cases.

The Supreme Court is comprised of nine justices: eight justices and a chief justice. Like the Court of Criminal Appeals, if four or more justices favor hearing a particular case, the case is scheduled for argument. The likelihood of the Supreme Court hearing a case is low. In most years, the Supreme Court is selective about the cases it takes, as most appellate courts are. In 2015 the Court only granted review in 10 percent of the cases filed, down from 15 percent in 2007. The system is designed to let lower courts handle much of the work—those cases that float up to the Supreme Court are of statewide importance.

★ TEXAS TAKEAWAYS

6 How likely is it that your case will make it to a higher court on appeal?

7 How many Supreme Courts does Texas have? Why?

QUALITY OF JUSTICE IN TEXAS

10.4 Evaluate the quality of justice in Texas.

Chief Justice Pope came before the state legislature in 1983 to make an important request. The judiciary is inexpensive to run, he noted. Yet, the courts are so overloaded that Texans had to wait months and even years to settle cases. If the legislature granted every judicial budget request, "it would be less than the utility and maintenance bill of the University of Texas at Austin."[22] The legislature agreed to appropriate more funds for the judiciary. But his plea illustrates two points: the judiciary is dependent on the legislature for funding and this funding is one factor that determines the quality of justice in Texas. Let's take a look at how well the judicial system is performing today.

ANGLES OF POWER
Two Supreme Courts?

By the time of the 1875 Constitutional Convention, the Texas Supreme Court had become overburdened with cases. To remedy this, "dual" Supreme Courts were proposed "so that when appeals in criminal charges come before them from criminal courts there should be a speedy response, so that the party might be either punished or released."[19] The two sets of supreme court justices would also be able to specialize in the law their courts heard. However, Texas and Oklahoma are currently the only two states with divided civil and criminal jurisdictions.

In 2013, a bill was introduced to merge the supreme courts. Representative Richard Pena Raymond, Democrat of Laredo, said "The model is there for most of the country."[20] Those in favor also like the efficiency of a single administration and cost savings with fewer judges. Others disagreed. Efforts to merge the courts failed six times since 1974. When Governor Clements publically announced support for the merger in 1987, Supreme Court Justice James P. Wallace huffed, "There's only 24 hours in a day, and we deserve some sleep like everyone else."[21] Political parties also opposed the change because more courts give them more opportunity to influence the legal system.

SOCIAL RESPONSIBILITY: **Should Texas merge its two Supreme Courts into one? What are the pros and cons of doing so?**

CASELOAD: OVERWORKED JUDGES?

Caseloads serve as an indicator of the efficiency of the judicial system and the speed of justice. Judges rushing to complete cases may make mistakes or be may be inconsistent. As case delays increase, witnesses' memories fade, those involved in cases may become financially bankrupt, companies may continue to lose revenue, and plaintiffs remain in harmful situations. In 2015, Texas's 3,200 judges disposed of over ten million cases, from not cleaning up dog poop on the sidewalk to traffic violations to capital murders. A case is **disposed** of when it is taken off the court's docket, generally when it is heard or dismissed.

caseload: the workload (in cases) of the judiciary

dispose: take a case off the court's docket generally by being heard or dismissed

Even so, over the last several decades, the court has become more efficient at handling the cases before it. For example, in 1984, the eighty justices on the courts of appeals disposed of 8,000 cases, while in 2015, with the same number of judges, the courts disposed of over 11,000 cases.[23] Generally, the Texas courts are efficient at disposing of cases. The number of filings in 2015 went down at the Texas Supreme Court and Texas Court of Criminal Appeals as compared to 2006, allowing the justices to handle fewer cases and dispose of them more quickly.

LENGTH OF COURT CASES

The saying goes, "justice delayed is justice denied." The length of time an individual's case takes to work through the system is another measure of the efficiency of the judiciary system. Overall, except for death penalty cases, the number of days until a final verdict decreased in 2015 (see Figure 10.5).

FIGURE 10.5   **Average Number of Days between Filing and Disposition**

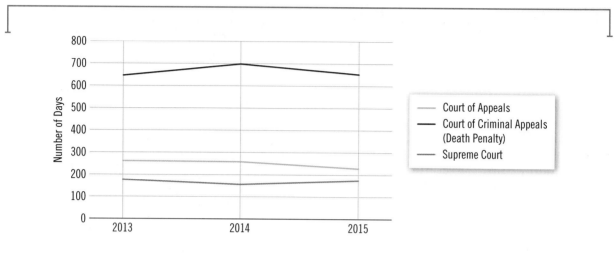

Source: Annual Statistical Report of the Texas Judiciary, 2015.

 COMMUNICATION:

How many days does it take for each Texas court to finish a case?

- Except for the Supreme Court, the appellate courts in Texas have reduced the total days for a final verdict.

- The Supreme Court was the quickest of the Texas appellate courts in 2015, at 173 days. This number is slightly lower than it was in 2013.

- Death penalty cases at the Court of Criminal Appeals take longer from start to finish (almost 700 days) than other types of cases.

 CRITICAL THINKING:

Why the longer wait for some courts than others?

- Supreme Court cases involve matters of legal interpretation, allowing the cases to be decided more quickly.

- Criminal cases often take longer because the rules are more expansive, making the number of possible delays greater in those courts. Criminal cases take more lawyers, more experts, and therefore more time.

SALARY: UNDERPAID JUDGES?

Because most judges could make high salaries in private practice, the state must offer a reasonable salary to keep quality lawyers on the bench. In the Republic's early days, judges received low pay ($1,750 a year)—and when times were bad, sometimes the state didn't pay the justices at all.[24] Financial times are better for modern judges (see Figure 10.6) but judicial salaries in Texas still lag behind other large states. Chief Justice Wallace Jefferson cited having a child in college and two in high school as a reason he stepped down

IS IT BIGGER IN TEXAS?

FIGURE 10.6   **Salaries of Judges in the Five Most Populous States**

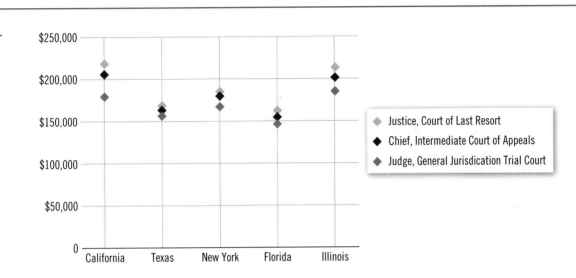

Source: 2015 Annual Texas Judicial Statistical Report. Average statewide salary, including supplements paid.

 COMMUNICATION:

How well are Texas justices paid?

- On average New York pays judges and justices $30,000 more, Illinois pays $40,000 more, and California pays $50,000 more.
- Of the five largest states, only Florida pays less on average than Texas. The Texas legislature considered raising judges pay by 21 percent in 2013, but ended up increasing it by only 12 percent.

 CRITICAL THINKING:

Why does Texas rank so low?

- Texas favors a lean government. Raising the pay to judges is not high on the list of funding priorities for the state.
- Texas generally pays elected officials low salaries, especially legislators who only received $7,200 per year.

from the bench in 2013.[25] These low salaries may impact the ability of the state to attract quality judges.

TURNOVER OF JUDGES

Because of the prestige, reasonable salary, job security, and a snappy wardrobe, judges generally stay in their positions. Stability in the tenure of judges is a welcome advantage for a system that must handle so many cases as quickly

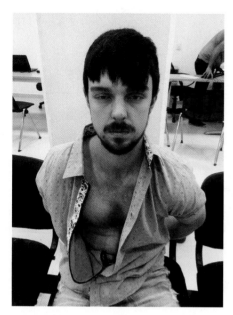

"Affluenza" teen Ethan Couch's case highlighted the role of wealth and personal responsibility in Texas courts.

SOCIAL RESPONSIBILITY: **Is justice blind to issues of wealth? Do those with wealth have better outcomes in the courts?**

as possible. Newer judges may have less experience and replacing justices who leave may take time. For those judges leaving the judiciary in 2015, several replied that the "judicial election" process was a major factor in their leaving and the same number replied that the low salary was a factor "to some extent."[26] Most judges choose to leave office before the mandatory retirement age. Although the prestige is high, the pay is comparatively lower than the judge would make in the private sector. Furthermore, the process of running for office can be taxing, costing significant time and money.

ACCESS TO JUSTICE

Many argue that the wealthy are at an advantage in the court system. Ethan Couch, a teenager from North Texas who drove drunk, killed four people, and injured two, was able to avoid jail time purportedly because of "affluenza," a legal defense in which the defense argues that the defendant's upbringing was so wealthy and pampered that he cannot understand the ramifications of his actions. Fearing that the terms of his ten-year probation might change once he turned nineteen, Couch fled to Mexico, was returned to Texas, and is currently serving time behind bars.[27]

Wealthy groups and individuals do have significantly better access to the legal system than others. This "justice gap" acutely affects the lower and middle class, the elderly, and veterans.[28] In 2015, a third-generation Army veteran escaped with her two young children from an abusive home. She sought help from a legal clinic, who got her and her boys court protection so they could get back on their feet.[29] This veteran was one of the lucky ones. While more than 5.6 million Texans qualify for legal aid, just 20 percent can access it.[30]

The Texas Access to Justice Commission has identified several ways to increase Texans' access to the justice system, including removing the cost barriers to the court system, ensuring legal aid providers have the resources to meet the needs of low income individuals seeking legal representation, and increasing pro bono services in the legal community. The Texas legislature allocated $17 million in state revenue in 2015 for civil legal aid.[31]

★ TEXAS TAKEAWAYS

8 What are some of the problems that limit the quality of justice in Texas?

9 For what reasons do judges in Texas typically leave the bench?

🤠 JUDICIAL SELECTION AND REMOVAL

One way to mitigate the influence of wealth on judicial outcome is to change the way judges are selected. In this section, we will take a look at different methods of judicial selection and their advantages and disadvantages. Judges may be appointed or elected to office. In some states, governors or legislatures appoint judges. Many states, however, have a **merit selection** system, in which a nonpartisan committee vets qualified candidates based upon their qualifications and offers these selections to the governor. After selection, judges typically stand for reappointment ("retention") by voters. Merit selection has been found to reduce the partisanship of judicial candidates and promote diversity on the bench. Judges can also be selected through partisan elections in which the party of the judge is listed on the ballot, or through nonpartisan elections in which the party is not listed.

Judicial selection methods often reflect a state's political culture (see Figure 10.7). In states that are more concerned about access to justice and popular control over judicial matters, judges are more likely to be elected. A handful of states have partisan elections. States more concerned with establishing an independent judiciary shielded from public opinion tend to appoint judges, often using a merit system.

> **10.5** Identify problems associated with different methods of judicial selection.

merit selection: a nonpartisan way to select judges in which a commission selected by state officials sends recommendations to the governor and the governor selects the nominees from that list

JUDICIAL SELECTION IN TEXAS

During Texas's long judicial history, the state has tried different methods of selecting judges: election of judges by the legislature, appointment by the executive branch, and election by the people. The election of judges gained popularity in the 1820s with the emergence of egalitarian democratic ideals and the belief that justices, like other public officials, should be accountable to the voting public.[32]

Today, there are two ways to become a judge or justice in Texas: appointment or partisan election. Election to office is the standard way that judges and justices are selected, and most obtain their seats in this manner. However, if there is an unexpected vacancy on a court at the district court level or higher, the Texas Constitution allows the governor to make a temporary judicial appointment until the next general election, in which that individual would have to run as a candidate.

The justices (courts of appeals, Texas Court of Criminal Appeals, and Texas Supreme Court) are elected statewide to six-year terms, which are staggered so that not all of the justices are up for reelection at the same time. Judges to lower-level trial courts are elected to four-year terms (or two for some municipal courts). The frequency of the election of trial court judges holds them strongly accountable to the public to whom they must justify their legal rulings to get reelected.

Clearly, politics is part of the process as judges must campaign to win votes. However, they campaign under a more specific code of conduct than other want-to-be-elected officials. The Texas Code of Judicial Conduct warns judicial candidates to refrain from inappropriate political activity and prohibits them

IS IT BIGGER IN TEXAS?

FIGURE 10.7   **Primary Judicial Selection Process by State**

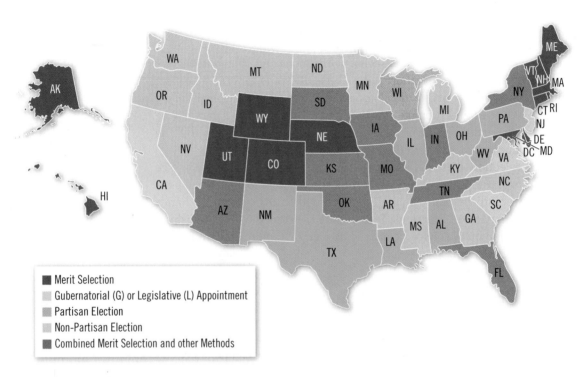

- Merit Selection
- Gubernatorial (G) or Legislative (L) Appointment
- Partisan Election
- Non-Partisan Election
- Combined Merit Selection and other Methods

Source: American Judicature Society

 COMMUNICATION:

How do states select their judges?

- Most states (twenty-two) still use the popular election method to select judges.
- Only eight states, including Texas, use the *partisan* method while the others use nonpartisan elections.
- In thirty-three states, the governor appoints the judges, usually based upon recommendations from a nonpartisan commission.

 CRITICAL THINKING:

Why is there so much variation by state?

- States that have elections (either partisan or nonpartisan) desire voters to have the final say in judicial selection to maintain the democratic value of the judiciary.
- This reflects Texas's political culture, which emphasizes a hierarchical political structure that meets the needs of the electorate.

from making pledges or promises about pending cases or knowingly misrepresenting the identity, qualifications, or position of an opponent.[33] To violate this code of conduct is to risk sanction by the court, fines, or possible disbarment by the Texas Bar Association, the organization that authorizes an attorney to practice law. Candidates for judicial office are also subject to the same campaign finance reporting requirements as other elected officials. Politics and ethics clash in elections for judges—judicial candidates must walk a fine line between not violating the ethics of their position but still communicating a partisan message to voters. In one instance, for example, a judge was warned for campaign ads that noted "I'm very tough on crimes where the victims have been physically harmed. . . . I have no feelings for the criminal." Observers fear that judges who make such promises are put in an ethical bind: they promise to dole out harsh sentences and yet they must be impartial.[34]

Campaign signs outside polling location.

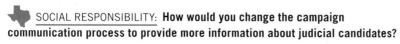 PERSONAL RESPONSIBILITY: **What kinds of promises might you make if you ran for judge? What would you avoid discussing? Why?**

INSIDER INTERVIEW

Former Chief Justice Tom Philips

Do you like running for election?

Yes and no. I don't like raising money. I don't like asking for it or getting it. . . . But I like the strategy of, or perhaps the discipline of, deciding how to communicate how you intend to perform in a very complex job with a number of duties to the voters in simple phrases and words. Specifically, the 30-second television commercial has about 130 syllables in it. That's the amount of communication time you have to reach the vast majority of voters in the state. If they're going to cast an informed vote in your race, they've either got to very closely read the back pages of the newspapers, or you've got to give them some information in a 130-syllable advertisement.[35]

Some people have told me that they are not willing to stand for judge because they don't want to be labeled a Democrat or a Republican or they don't want their children to see an ad accusing them of untoward conduct. But we still have a number of highly qualified people who do want to be a judge and are willing to run the possible risk of those bad consequences.

SOCIAL RESPONSIBILITY: **How would you change the campaign communication process to provide more information about judicial candidates?**

CENSURE AND REMOVAL FROM OFFICE

Judges who violate the standards of conduct described above face discipline, censure, or removal from office. Judges and justices can be removed in three primary ways in Texas: by the State Commission on Judicial Conduct (by recommendation of removal), by the Texas Supreme Court (by recommendation of removal), and by the legislature (by impeachment). These avenues provide multiple ways to limit unethical or illegal behavior by judges, giving power to the legislature and fellow justices to check the integrity of the judiciary.

State Commission on Judicial Conduct.   The SCJC, which is made up of thirteen commission members who include judges, attorneys, and citizens appointed by the governor, can investigate and prosecute allegations of misconduct by Texas judges. Justices can be removed from office for incompetence, for violation of the official Code of Judicial Conduct, or for conduct that is clearly inconsistent with the proper performance of judicial duties. The penalties include warning or reprimand, such as in the case of a judge who consumed too much alcohol at a social gathering and urinated into a garbage receptacle in sight of guests, or additional education, such as in the case of a justice of the peace who asked another judge hearing a case involving his son to let the son take a driving safety course in lieu of a fine.[36]

Recommendation of Removal by the Supreme Court.   The judiciary has to protect its own reputation, and this recommendation of removal provision allows the Texas Supreme Court to police the lower courts. The supreme court may sanction or recommend removal of district court judges, although it rarely does so.

Legislative Impeachment.   The other branches of government have considerable say in the removal of judges. The Texas legislature can, but rarely does, impeach judges (at the district court and above) "for willful neglect of duty, incompetency, habitual drunkenness, oppression in office, or other reasonable cause."[37] District Judge O.P. Carillo was impeached and removed from office in 1976 for fraud and spent three years in prison.

JUDICIAL QUALIFICATIONS

Each level of court specifies unique qualifications for being elected as a judge (see Table 10.1). Lower-level courts have shorter terms in office, allow younger attorneys to run for office, and have less restrictive residency or legal practice requirements. City governments determine the requirements for municipal court judges. The only legal qualification for county judges is that they "shall be well informed in the law of the State." A Texan whose knowledge of the judiciary is based only on watching reruns of *Walker Texas Ranger* can serve. As a result, justices of the peace are significantly less likely to hold law degrees than

TABLE 10.1 — Judicial Qualifications

COURT	AGE	LEGAL PRACTICE
County Court at Law	25 or older	A practicing lawyer or judge, or both, for at least 4 years.
District Court	25 to 74	A practicing lawyer or judge, or both, for at least 4 years.
Appellate and Supreme Courts	35 to 74	A practicing lawyer or judge, or both, for at least 10 years

Source: Texas Constitution.

SOCIAL RESPONSIBILITY: **Given their responsibility, are the age and work requirements sufficient?**

other justices. In 2015, only 34 percent graduated from college and only 8 percent were licensed to practice law. These judges, however, have enormous responsibility as they oversee county government operations, manage responses to emergency management, and hear criminal trials for misdemeanors that are punishable by a year in jail. Of course, as elected officials they are pressed by the public and businesses to do a good job keeping the streets safe and the roads in good shape.

The highest-level courts alter the age and experience requirements for justices. Justices for the appellate and two supreme courts must be over thirty-five but are forced to retire at seventy-four. Justices on these courts must also have ten years of legal experience instead of four for lower courts.

PROBLEMS WITH PARTISAN ELECTIONS

In a state that is most often dominated by one party (the Democrats until the 1980s, then the Republicans through the present), judicial contests are often one-sided and the primary is where the real battle for the office takes place. Party labels provide some basic information about the attitudes and values of judges and hints at the way they may decide matters of public policy. However, party labels become crutches for voters who have little information about the judicial candidates and often scant knowledge about the judiciary or the issues at stake. Furthermore, judicial partisan elections in Texas suffer from low turnout, low interest, and conflicts of interest that arise when judicial candidates must rely on individuals and groups for campaign contributions.

Low Turnout.   Voters are often less well informed about judicial races, which are often perceived to be less important and so are not as frequently discussed in the media. In fact, many voters simply do not complete their ballots all the way to the end where the judicial candidates are generally listed. The number

TABLE 10.2	"Undervote" for Judicial Elections, 2012		
COUNTY	TOTAL VOTES	SUPREME COURT	COUNTY COURT
Harris	688,018	670,979	484,249
Dallas	410,529	398,226	397,385
El Paso	82,588	79,198	54,206
Bexar	303,971	294,087	294,778
Cameron	40,439	37,864	39,313

Source: Texas Secretary of State.

COMMUNICATION:

What is the "undervote" for county judicial elections?

- Most counties in Texas had an undervote in the 2012 elections, some larger than others.
- The two counties with the biggest differences between the total vote and vote for county court positions were Harris (203,769) and El Paso (28,382).
- Most other large and small counties had relatively equal numbers of total votes and votes for judicial positions.

CRITICAL THINKING:

Why is there a drop off?

- There are a large number of positions to vote for (up to forty in some locations), the positions are generally at the end of a long ballot, and most in the public are unaware of what the court at each level does.
- The number of total judicial positions may affect the vote drop-off—Harris has many, Cameron has fewer.

of drop-off votes (called "undervotes") for the judicial electoral races is high (see Table 10.2).

Reliance on Name Recognition.   In low interest and low turnout judicial elections, voters often rely on name recognition to decide which candidate to select. As a result of mistakes in name identification, voters can elect a candidate they may not have intended to support.

In 1976, Don B. Yarbrough, an unknown Republican with modest legal experience, drew on the name recognition of the famous Yarborough family in Texas. Donald H. *Yarborough* had been a three-time candidate for governor (without winning) and Ralph *Yarborough* had served as a U.S. Senator. The lesser-known Yarbrough emphasized his youth and religiosity, running against the establishment "good-ole boys" from the big law firms and pledging to decide cases based upon the laws of God, not man. After winning the primary, Yarbrough admitted that there were eleven lawsuits pending against

GREAT TEXAS POLITICAL DEBATES
The First Negative Judicial Race

Livid about losing a case before the Supreme Court in 1942, Angus Wynne, former president of the Texas State Bar, vowed to run a candidate against Justice Richard Critz, who had written an opinion against him. Wynne recruited a former state representative and president of the State Bar, Gordon Simpson, to run for Justice Critz's seat. Oddly, Simpson was serving in the US army in Italy at the time but agreed to allow a campaign to be run on his behalf. Wynne unleashed a storm of attacks warning Texas voters that the Texas Supreme Court could choose any case they wanted, which he argued was undemocratic. Wynne also deliberately mispronounced Justice Critz's name to rhyme with "fritz," which was American slang for a German soldier, thus associating him with Nazi Germany. Simpson, still serving overseas, was said to be disparaged by Critz "behind his back and while he can't say one word in his own defense." Turnout in the runoff election was low, especially as voters were reluctant to use their rationed gasoline and rubber to drive to a polling station for a "mere judicial election."[38] Simpson won the seat by 1,097 votes.[39]

SOCIAL RESPONSIBILITY: Should the state regulate what can and can't be said in a judicial race?

YES: Judicial races are not like other elections. Judges and attorneys are held to high professional standards and should be restricted from discussing possible cases or issues on which they will be asked to make a legal ruling before the case facts are known. Those in the legal profession have a special responsibility for the quality of justice. Public confidence in the legal system is vital to its survival.

NO: Candidates especially must be allowed to exercise their free speech rights to advocate for their own electoral merits or against their opponent as they see fit. Just like any other election, voters are asked to make a choice based upon all the information they can access. Parties and the media help voters vet judicial candidates. However, more information from candidates is better for voters.

him for fraud and negligence in his legal practice, illegal stock selling, dealing in unauthorized loans, and other offenses. The legal community mounted a write-in campaign against the now-indicted Yarbrough, making every effort to inform voters what they were getting into. It was to no avail. With voter confusion as the likely cause, Justice Yarbrough won the election and took his seat on January 2, 1977. Six months later, Justice Yarbrough was indicted for forging a car title and lying in court. Facing legislative proceedings to impeach him, he resigned from the court.

The disinterest in and low turnout for judicial elections weakens the ability of Texans to hold judges accountable to the people, with random factors like a candidate's name—or the support of an interest group—factoring into who takes office.

Conflicts of Interest.   Because candidates for judicial office must raise money to campaign, and donors may become the litigants in court, some people have argued that justice is "for sale" in Texas. In 1983, Justice C.L. Ray ruled in favor of attorney Pat Maloney, Sr., and millionaire plaintiff Clinton Manges, who were accused of mismanaging mineral leases—both were major contributors to the judge's election campaign.[40] The media also reported that Judge Ray had told another major donor (and litigant in front of the court) that his case was a "tough one" and that if the millionaire didn't "win this one, he would win the next."[41] Shining the national spotlight on the case, a *New York Times* editorial decried Texas courts as dispensing "what passes for justice in small countries run by colonels in mirrored sunglasses."[42]

The Republican Party used such conflict of interest claims to launch a "Clean Slate in '88" effort, going into districts held by Democrats to convince them to support Republican candidates who embraced reform and appeared to be, according to architect Karl Rove, "champions of the little man and not the big boys."[43] The strategy worked: Republican candidates won five of the six vacant Texas Supreme Courts seats.

Compromising Judicial Experience.   In partisan elections, studies show candidate quality matters less than party affiliation.[44] Straight ticket voting contributes to this as voters choose party over individual justices. In 2010, Republicans won every judicial office in Bexar County. In 2012, Democrats won every judicial office in Bexar County. This lurching from party to party and the resulting chaos of staffing the judiciary leads to frequent turnover and courts staffed by individuals with little or no judicial experience.

The Influence of Money.   With billions of dollars at stake in the outcomes of judicial matters, interest groups from all political and financial angles pour millions of dollars into judicial races across Texas. Spending on state judicial races is increasing nationally. National interest groups and their affiliates spent an estimated $4.8 million on state Supreme Court races in 2014.[45] Candidates need on average more than $1.5 million to win election to the Texas Supreme Court or Court of Criminal Appeals. In total, Texas ranked third out of states with elected judges in total funds spent in 2014 (over $3.5 million).[46] Much of these funds come from trial lawyers and law firms, most of whom do business in front of the courts. On average, almost 50 cents of every dollar raised for the highest courts in Texas comes from these groups (see Figure 10.8).[47]

When major initiatives like tort reform gain momentum, big spending floods the political system. For example, when the legislature tried to limit the funds from the Texas Windstorm Insurance Association that could be awarded to Texans suffering after storms, Steve Mostyn, trial lawyer, major donor to Democrats, gave $10 million to unseat Republicans who voted in favor of the measure.[48]

Those opposed to judicial fundraising are concerned that a judge who takes money from a donor will rule in that donor's favor. One academic study found that campaign contributions to a state supreme court were correlated with judges' decisions.[49] The media have exposed instances in which this has happened, although it certainly does not happen all the time. Still, public

FIGURE 10.8 **Donations to Judicial Candidates from Lawyers**

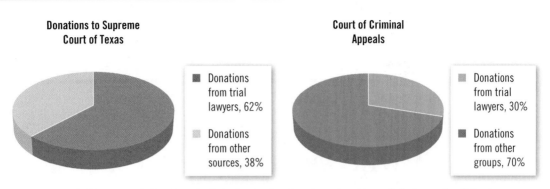

Donations to Supreme
Court of Texas

Court of Criminal
Appeals

■ Donations
from trial
lawyers, 62%

▨ Donations
from other
sources, 38%

▨ Donations
from trial
lawyers, 30%

■ Donations
from other
groups, 70%

Source: Texas Ethics Commission. Data include the April to October reporting period of 2014 for all justices. Includes both lawyers as individual donors (under occupation) and law firm PACs.

 COMMUNICATION:

From what sources do judicial campaign funds come?

- Most of the funds for the Supreme Court come from lawyers and law firms (62 percent).
- In contrast, most funds for candidates for the Court of Criminal Appeals come from sources other than lawyers or law firms (only 30 percent).

 CRITICAL THINKING:

Why the difference in donation patterns?

- The Supreme Court deals with civil matters that are often connected to large financial issues, making those justices the logical target of more funds from lawyers and law firms.
- Lawyers are the most attentive to these elections and have the greatest stake in the outcome of judicial elections. The ideology and ruling habits of justices may mean winning or losing (and how much) in court.

perception remains that justice is for sale. The gap between the high ideals of fairness and transparency set for the court and the practice of judicial politics in Texas seems to be widening.

Harsher Criminal Sentencing. Nonpartisan organizations have found that trial judges are more likely to sentence defendants convicted of serious felonies to longer sentences the closer they are to reelection. Judges in partisan elections were also less likely to reverse death sentences than judges selected by merit or by retention election.[50] These outcomes suggest that the partisan election system encourages a certain type of ruling and may compromise justice for Texans.

⭐ **TEXAS TAKEAWAYS**

10 How are judges selected in Texas?

11 How can justices be removed?

12 What are some of the problems with partisan elections?

🤠 WHO ARE THE JUSTICES?

> **10.6** Analyze the changes in the court's demographics.

In the first days of the Republic, many justices' careers were cut short. Some judges died from yellow fever, some were killed, and some dared outlaws to do their worst.[51] While we no longer face the challenges of the frontier in administering justice, the new challenge is to provide justice to a diverse and growing population in the state. The state has rapidly become more diverse both racially and ethnically. The justices on the bench need to reflect the population of Texas in order to develop trust in the legal system across racial groups. Greater judicial diversity can reduce racial resentment and enhance sensitivity to cultural issues in legal outcomes.[52] Increasingly, politicians, civil rights organizations, and the Texas Bar Association have taken notice and encouraged greater diversity in the judiciary (see Figure 10.9).

Justices on the Texas Court of Criminal Appeals. Although most judges on highest courts in Texas are Anglo men, the trend is changing.

 SOCIAL RESPONSIBILITY:
What does diversity in the Texas judicial system mean to legal outcomes for diverse groups and minorities?

FIGURE 10.9   **Demographics of Courts**

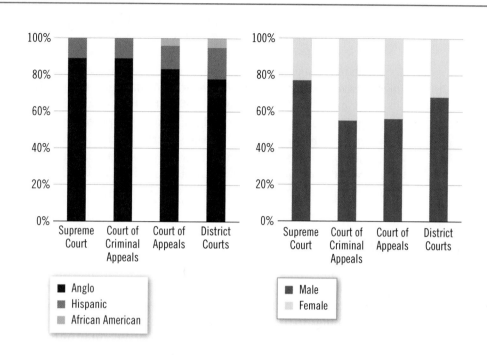

Source: 2015 Annual Texas Judicial Statistical Report. Party reports from court websites.

COMMUNICATION:

What are the demographics of Texas courts?

- Women make up about 38 percent of the judicial seats in Texas state courts.[53] The number varies from 23 percent on the Texas Supreme Court to 44 percent on the Court of Criminal Appeals.

- There are currently no African Americans on the highest appeals courts, and only 5 percent on the district courts and 4 percent on the courts of appeals.

- Hispanic jurists comprise 17 percent of district courts and 11 percent of the Supreme Court and Court of Criminal Appeals.

CRITICAL THINKING:

Why are some groups over (or under) represented?

- Recent governors have sought ways to diversify the bench as a way to improve racial tolerance of the judiciary and to present candidates more appealing to minority voters. This is especially true for Hispanic jurists.

- District courts are more diverse than other courts because the district lines are often drawn in a way that allows racial groups to form a larger voting block.

This diversity has come about through two ways. The first is by gubernatorial appointment of minority candidates. The second is through the centralization of racial and ethnic voters in geographic areas, which promotes voting for racial minorities to judicial offices. This electoral characteristic, however, limits the ascendency of racial and ethnic minorities to the bench in some districts. The federal courts considered the case of *United Latin American Citizens et al. v. Mattox* (1993) in which the plaintiffs argued that the countywide voting (instead of districts assembled from common geographic neighborhoods) for judges diluted the power of minority voting. No changes were made, but the issue spurred discussion about the importance of electoral rules in determining who wins elections, the value of minority representation on the bench, and the need to reform the Texas judiciary to make it more inclusive.

WOMEN

The first, and to date only, Texas Supreme Court made up entirely of women heard a case in 1925. All three male supreme court justices (the total at the time) had to recuse themselves on a case and Governor Pat Neff appointed three women to (temporarily) make up the bench. The first woman to serve on a district court in Texas was Sarah Hughes, appointed in 1935. It took another 50 years for the number of women on the bench to expand significantly. Women make up 30 percent of the State Bar and about 38 percent of the judicial seats in Texas state courts.[54] Today Texas is in the top ten states with the highest percentage of women judges.[55]

AFRICAN AMERICANS

African Americans make up 5 percent of the State Bar and approximately 4 percent of state courts. Chief Justice Wallace Jefferson was the first African American to be appointed, then elected and reelected, to the position. Governor Rick Perry appointed him in 2001, and he was reelected in 2006 by a large margin of the total vote (76 percent of the vote).

HISPANICS

Hispanics make up 6 percent of the State Bar and about 17 percent of state courts. Hispanics are the only racial or ethnic minority who hold a significantly higher percentage of judicial positions than the percentage of their representation of the State Bar. Raul A. Gonzales was the first Hispanic to join the Texas Supreme Court when he was appointed by Democratic Governor Mark White in 1984.

ASIANS

Asians make up 11 percent of the State Bar and less than 1 percent of the judicial positions on state courts. In percentage of judicial positions compared to percentage of bar members, they are the most underrepresented group in the judiciary.

TEXAS TAKEAWAYS

13 How would you summarize the racial makeup of the Texas courts?

14 Which groups are overrepresented (in terms of bar membership) on the Texas bench? Which underrepresented?

REFORMING THE SYSTEM

Concerns about the injection of partisan politics into the judiciary and the vast sums of money being spent on judicial elections have observers worried. In his 2015 State of the Judiciary, Chief Justice Nathan Hecht noted, "I have not spoken to the problems of judicial selection because I have no consensus solution." Indeed, advocates of reform of the judicial system in Texas have considered several imperfect options over the years.

10.7 Evaluate proposals for reforming the selection of the judiciary.

NONPARTISAN ELECTIONS

Some judicial advocates have recommended keeping the election of judges but removing the partisan label. Former Chief Justice Wallace Jefferson lamented the partisan process of elections. He commented, "It is an irrational way of selecting judges. Just because you have an 'R' or a 'D' by your name does not mean you are more qualified to be a judge."[56] Both political parties dislike nonpartisan elections because it reduces their influence in the system.

PUBLIC FINANCING OF ELECTIONS

Elections for the Texas high courts have become some of the costliest in the country, potentially allowing donors to have a larger say in who is elected. A pool of funds could be set aside (from taxpayer funds) to give each candidate a fixed sum with which to campaign. Representative Rafael Anchia of Dallas filed a bill in 2015 to start public financing of campaigns for appellate

PERSONAL
RESPONSIBILITY:
If you donated money to a
judicial candidate, would
you expect favorable
treatment in court?

TABLE 10.3	Funding Limits on Judicial Candidates		
Population of the judicial district	Less than 250,000	Between 250,000 to one million	Statewide judicial offices
Funding limit from each donor	$1,000	$2,500	$5,000

Source: Texas Ethics Commission, Campaign Finance Guide for Judicial Candidates and Officeholders.

judges in Texas. It was sent to the House Elections Committee and never heard from again.[57]

LIMITING FUNDRAISING TOTALS

In the wake of fundraising scandals, the state legislature passed the Judicial Campaign Finance Act in 1995, which capped contributions from each individual donor to judicial candidates. Contribution limits change depending on the type of judicial race and the population of the district (see Table 10.3). To ensure the integrity of the system, the state uses its authority to regulate these funds, making the process more transparent and less able to be influenced by campaign funds. This also allows potential challengers who may have a smaller fundraising base to compete with incumbent justices by limiting the amount of money that can be raised.

There are also limits on how much a law firm, the primary contributors to judicial candidates, can contribute to an individual candidate. The rules allow a maximum of a $30,000 contribution for a firm's associates for statewide courts, courts of appeals, and district courts. The legislature can decide to raise or lower these limits. If the Texas legislature wanted to take fundraising limits a step farther, the US Supreme Court ruled in 2015 that states can prohibit judicial candidates from personally asking supporters for campaign contributions.[58]

MERIT SELECTION

Often called the "Missouri Plan" (after Missouri's innovation of the plan in 1940), merit selection of judges is a nonpartisan way to select qualified judges from a vetted list of possible candidates. After being appointed to a fixed period of service (often a year), the judge must stand for reelection in a "retention" election. If a majority of voters vote against retention, the judge is removed and the process begins again. Texas has not tried merit selection.

★ TEXAS TAKEAWAYS

15 How much can a law firm legally donate to a judicial candidate?

16 What are some suggestions to reform the problems with the Texas judicial system?

🤠 THE INSIDER VIEW

Distrust of an overbearing centralized government put the Texas judiciary squarely in the hands of the people and designed an ordered system where judicial branch power checks but is also checked by the other branches. Yet, the participatory neglect of people in judicial elections and the injection of political parties and interest groups into the process foster the perception that justice can be purchased by the highest bidder. Reform efforts have minimized these potential problems by limiting the role of money in politics, expanding the size of the court, and ensuring continued public access to the courts for all Texans. Yet interest groups and political parties still play a leading role in judicial elections. As Texans look to improve the quality of justice in the state, they will look to greater legislative participation especially through funding, an internal check on judicial power by higher courts, and the will of the people through elections.

★ TEXAS TAKEAWAYS

1 The current Texas Constitution remedies the early frustrations with few outlets for the legal process by fragmenting the judiciary in Texas into many parts.

2 The court's roles at the trial court level are to introduce facts and make rulings. The court's roles at the appellate court level are to interpret legislative statute, sort out policy contradictions, and advance public opinion.

3 Texas courts clarify the laws, check the legislature's power, check the executive's power, and advance the rule of the people.

4 In these lowest-level courts, witnesses are heard, evidence is presented in the form of exhibits, testimony is taken, and ultimately a verdict is passed down.

5 Municipal courts are the lowest trial courts. District courts are the highest.

6 Most cases in Texas are handled at local levels. Very few cases end up making it to the appellate courts.

7 Texas has two Supreme Courts: one for criminal and one for civil matters. The dual structure allows for judicial specialization and, in principle, quicker case resolution.

8 Some of the problems that limit the quality of justice are overworked judges, delays in court cases, low judicial salaries, turnover of justices, and underfunded or nonaccessed legal aid.

9 Judges in Texas leave the bench to pursue more lucrative opportunities in private practice and to avoid having to run for reelection.

10 There are currently two ways to become a judge or justice in Texas: appointment or partisan election.

11 Judges and justices can be removed in three ways in Texas: by the State Commission on Judicial Conduct (by recommendation of removal), by the Texas Supreme Court (by removal), and by the legislature (by impeachment).

12 Judicial bias, low voter turnout, overreliance on name recognition, and straight ticket voting without regard to judicial quality are some of the problems with partisan elections.

13 The judges and justices who sit on the state's various courts are generally white males, but there are a growing number of females, African Americans, and Hispanics on the court.

14 White males are overrepresented. Asian Americans are the most underrepresented.

15 The rules allow a maximum of a $30,000 contribution for a firm's associates for statewide, courts of appeals, and district courts candidates.

16 Some of the proposals have included creating nonpartisan elections, public financing of elections, limiting fundraising, and moving to a merit selection system.

KEY TERMS

appellate courts
appellate jurisdiction
bench trial
caseload
civil cases
common law
criminal cases
dispose
dual structure

en banc
felony
jurisdiction
jury trial
mandatory review
merit selection
misdemeanors
opinion
original jurisdiction
probate

PRACTICE QUIZ

1. The standard of evidence in a civil case is:
   a. Beyond a reasonable doubt
   b. Within the range of reason
   c. A preponderance of the evidence
   d. Beyond the shadow of a doubt

2. Which court has budgetary and administrative authority over county government operations?
   a. Constitutional County Courts
   b. County Courts at Law
   c. Municipal Courts
   d. Probate Courts

3. Texas has _____ Court(s) of Last Resort (e.g. Supreme Court).
   a. 0
   b. 1
   c. 2
   d. 3

4. In comparison to past years regarding the handling of cases before it, the Texas courts of appeals are becoming...
   a. Less efficient
   b. More efficient
   c. About the same amount of efficiency
   d. There is not enough data to substantiate either way

5. Which Texas Supreme Court Justice is the "Tweeter Laureate of Texas"?

   a. Justice Sondock
   b. Chief Justice Hecht
   c. Justice Scalia
   d. Justice Willett

6. Voter turnout is often high in judicial races.

   a. True
   b. False

7. Most cases in Texas are handled at the most local levels.

   a. True
   b. False

8. Merit selection of judges is a partisan way to select judges.

   a. True
   b. False

9. A defendant in a criminal case is the individual who is bringing the suit against another individual.

   a. True
   b. False

10. Amicus curiae are briefs submitted by interest groups to appellate courts.

    a. True
    b. False

[Answers: C, A, C, B, D, B, A, B, B, A]

11 | CRIMINAL JUSTICE

Criminal justice in Texas occurs at the tense intersection of politics, personal freedom, and concerns about law and order. The authority granted to the state by the US Constitution to investigate criminal violations and punish those convicted places it in the center of controversy. Crime and punishment issues are often filtered through the lens of state politics as electoral candidates maneuver their positions around a Texas public hostile to criminals. However, pressure from advocates for change both within and outside the system has led Texas to be a leader in reforming the criminal justice system. Punishment in Texas, which prides itself on law and order, is often tempered with alternatives to incarceration and a public anxious for reform.

In this chapter, we examine the strain between the maintenance of law and order through law enforcement and punishment and the need to maintain a fair and bias-free approach to these issues. We start by exploring the norms and laws surrounding crime and punishment in Texas. We next paint a picture of the criminal justice process in Texas, incarceration and other types of punishment, and the obstacles felons face upon release from prison. In the final section, we examine reforms put into place to remedy flaws in the system.

TEXAN JUSTICE

Political columnist Molly Ivins remarked that a "favorite thing" of Texas politicians is to "git tuff" on crime.[9] It's a historical legacy that runs deep. The Texas Rangers, the state's oldest law enforcement agency, traces its roots back to Stephen F. Austin's call for a league to defend the Texas frontier against attacks by Native Americans in 1823. In the days of the Wild West, Judge Roy Bean, a saloonkeeper and justice of the peace in the dusty town of Langtry along the Rio Grande, was said to have fined a corpse $40 for carrying concealed weapons.[10]

Texans generally revere their law enforcement officers, believing them to be a critical front line of defense against crime. However, racial groups divide on opinions of law enforcement. Some racial groups are more likely than others to have a positive view of police, driven by personal interactions and

11.1 Identify the rights of the accused and of victims.

see for yourself 11.1

Learn about the Tulia drug bust that many believe violated the rights of many in the African American community.

Texans are allowed to use lethal force in their vehicles and workplaces in self-defense to stop specific crimes. Texas law also justifies killing to protect property. A 911 operator told a man whose neighbor's house was being robbed to remain inside rather than go after the burglars himself. The man ignored the advice: "You hear the shotgun clickin' and I'm goin'!" After a trial, he was acquitted.*

PERSONAL RESPONSIBILITY: Do you feel that a shooter should be allowed to use lethal force against a burglar leaving their property at night?

probable cause: the legal grounds law enforcement uses to make an arrest or conduct a search

search and seizure: where law enforcement agents search an accused's property and collect any evidence relevant to the alleged crime

exacerbated by high-profile incidents (see Figure 11.1). Texans also vary in their attitudes toward victims and those accused of crime, and so battle over victim rights and the rights of the accused.

RIGHTS OF THE ACCUSED

Sandra Bland protested during her arrest that her rights—as an accused—were being violated. Accused individuals are informed by law enforcement agents, just like in every television police show, that they have the right to remain silent, consult with an attorney, and have that attorney present when being questioned. Police officers are required to have **probable cause** to question a suspect. This assures the accused is protected from an unreasonable **search and seizure**. Most of these rights of the accused are guaranteed both by the US Constitution and the Texas Constitution.

VICTIM RIGHTS

The Texas Constitution guarantees several rights to crime victims and their families. Victims of crimes such as sexual assault, kidnapping, aggravated robbery or other criminal bodily harm are entitled to protection from law enforcement, the right to be informed about the progress of a case at various points, and the right to have the court take their safety into account on release of their attacker from a correctional facility. The legislature also created the Crime Victim's Compensation Act to provide funds to victims for loss of property, personal injury or death.

★ TEXAS TAKEAWAYS

1 What are the specific rights the US and Texas Constitutions grant the accused upon police interrogation?

2 What are the rights of victims in Texas?

FIGURE 11.1   **Attitudes toward Police by Race**

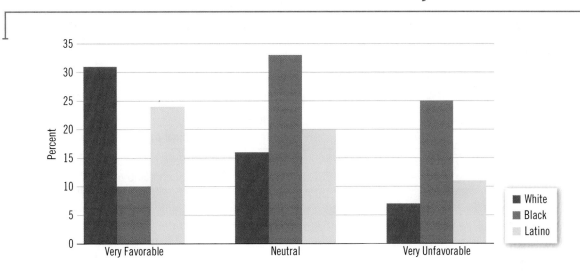

Source: Texas Tribune poll, February 2015.

 COMMUNICATION:

How do the major racial and ethnic groups feel about law enforcement?

- Anglo residents feel most favorable toward law enforcement, followed by Latinos.
- African Americans are less likely to have a very favorable opinion of law enforcement and are much more likely to have an unfavorable opinion than any other racial group.

 CRITICAL THINKING:

Why are there different responses across races and ethnicities?

- African Americans generally have a disproportionate amount of negative interactions with law enforcement, leading to diminished trust between the groups.
- Highly visible tragedies involving African Americans and law enforcement officers contribute to a widening gap in approval of law enforcement between African Americans and other racial groups in Texas.

🤠 TYPES OF CRIMES

As we saw in the previous chapter, felonies are more serious offences that elicit harsher punishments than misdemeanors. There are three classes of misdemeanors and five types of felonies in Texas, each associated with a range of penalties (see Table 11.1).

11.2 Distinguish the types of crimes and punishments in Texas criminal law.

TABLE 11.1	Misdemeanors and Felonies in Texas	
MISDEMEANORS		
Category	Punishment	Example
Class A	Up to one year in jail and/or a fine up to $4,000	Assault, harassment, burglary of a vehicle, theft/criminal mischief of $500 or more
Class B	Up to 180 days in county jail and/or a fine up to $2,000	Indecent exposure, disorderly conduct, DWI (first offense), theft/criminal mischief of $50 or more
Class C	Fine only, not to exceed $500	Possession of alcoholic beverage in motor vehicle, theft/criminal mischief of $50 or less
FELONY		
Capital	Death by lethal injection (only if 18 years or older) or life in prison without parole	Murder
First Degree	5 to 99 years or life in prison, and/or fine up to $10,000	Murder, aggravated sexual assault, injury to child, elderly or disabled individual, aggravated robbery, arson
Second Degree	2 to 20 years in prison, and/or fine up to $10,000	Murder (including sudden passion), manslaughter, indecency with a child, robbery, burglary of habitation
Third Degree	2 to 10 years in prison, and/or fine up to $10,000	Intoxication assault, kidnapping, stalking (first offense), DWI (with two prior convictions only), theft/criminal mischief of $20,000 or more
State Jail	180 days to 2 years in state jail, and/or fine up to $10,000	Criminally negligent homicide, burglary of a building, failure to pay child support, theft/criminal mischief of less than $1,500 to a habitation with a firearm, forgery

Source: State Bar of Texas, Criminal Justice Section.

SOCIAL RESPONSIBILITY:
Where would you draw the line between a misdemeanor and a felony? What kind of crimes and circumstances should shift the scale from minor to major?

MISDEMEANORS

As Table 11.1 illustrates, misdemeanors can range from Class A, the most severe, to Class C, the least. The most common Class C misdemeanor is a traffic offense (speeding). Other Class C misdemeanors are minor theft, usually shoplifting, a minor in possession of alcohol, or leaving a child unattended in a vehicle. In 2015, Houston Rockets point guard Patrick Beverley was arrested on a Class C misdemeanor warrant for an outstanding unpaid toll, which he attributed to an expired EZ-Tag account. He was taken to a police substation and paid the $321 fine on his warrant. Although late to practice, Beverley played in the game that evening.

Penalties increase for repeat offenders. For example, the most common misdemeanor in Texas is Driving While Intoxicated (DWI)—the first conviction is a Class B misdemeanor punishable by up to six months in jail or a $2,000 fine, and a second offense (or if the defendant's blood alcohol level is greater than .15) is considered a Class A misdemeanor.

FELONIES

Felonies in Texas range from failure to pay child support to murder and vary in punishment from short prison sentences to death by lethal injection. The circumstances of the crime also play a part in sentencing. If a defendant is convicted of a state jail-based felony, a judge can bump up the punishment to a third-degree felony if the defendant used or exhibited a deadly weapon during the crime or had been convicted of a felony in the past.

Although Texans have a reputation for being tougher than rawhide on crime and criminals, the criminal justice system—and the public—at times do have a soft spot for some offenders. Bernie Tiede, a thirty-eight-year-old mortician, befriended the gruff eighty-one-year-old wealthy widow Marjorie Nugent and the two became close companions, living, traveling, and shopping together. After Nugent's disappearance, Tiede continued to spend the widow's considerable fortune, giving much of it away as charitable contributions in the community. After months of questions about Nugent's whereabouts, police eventually discovered her body in a freezer in the garage, hidden under frozen food.[11] Although a cruel act, the town was sympathetic to the soft-spoken and well-liked Tiede. "From the day that deep freeze was opened, you haven't been able to find anyone in town saying, 'Poor Mrs. Nugent,'" said city councilman Olin Joffrion. "People here are saying, 'Poor Bernie.'"[12] Tiede was sentenced to life in prison in 2016.

DRUG CRIMES

Drug offenses are based on the type and amount of drug in question, how the drug was concealed, and whether the defendant manufactured, delivered, or possessed the drug. Since 1999, arrests for drug crimes have skyrocketed, although most arrests are for possession rather than distribution. Even trace amounts of drugs (1/100th the amount of a packet of Splenda) can lead to prosecution, often as a way to meet a political conviction goal for prosecutors.[13]

In a famous example, Willie Nelson was touring on Honeysuckle Rose, his tour bus, in Hudspeth County. The road was on a border checkpoint, and border patrol agents stopped the bus and searched it. The agents found enough marijuana to charge the Texas icon with a Class B misdemeanor. Hudspeth County Attorney C. R. "Kit" Bramblett joked that the legendary country artist play his 1975 hit "Blue Eyes Crying in the Rain" in the courtroom as community service.[14] The judge ultimately fined him $500.[15]

Willie Nelson, a notorious connoisseur of marijuana, pled guilty to lessened charges after his tour bus was stopped south of El Paso. Although it was reported that the bust was "not a holiday" for Nelson, the ordeal inspired a new song: "I'll Never Smoke Weed with Willie Again."**

SOCIAL RESPONSIBILITY: **Are punishments for drug crimes too harsh? What might be done alternatively to address drug problems in Texas?**

JUVENILE CRIME

The Texas Juvenile Justice Department is responsible for the supervising and rehabilitation of juveniles—aged ten to sixteen—in the criminal justice system. At seventeen, a defendant may be tried as an adult, and Texas is only one of nine states to do this. Juvenile justice is administered locally with the hearings, terms of detention, and probation determined at the county level. The state has established different procedures for police interrogations and confessions, and juveniles also have separate case managers, detention facilities, courts (for some offenses), and punishments. Juveniles may be designated to a "first offender" program as an alternative to jail or to programs for substance abuse, life skills, parenting, or animal therapy. A juvenile is not alone through this process: they are entitled to a lawyer and, if a parent or guardian cannot be located, a **guardian ad litem** is appointed.[16] However, once sentenced, these offenders are transferred to adult facilities at the age of nineteen. More than 2,000 are serving time in adult prisons for crimes committed as juveniles.

guardian ad litem: an appointed person to represent the best interests of a child if a parent will not or cannot fill the responsibility

---

★▄ TEXAS TAKEAWAYS

3 What is the maximum penalty for a misdemeanor? A felony?

4 What is the age range for a juvenile defendant?

🤠 CRIMINAL JUSTICE PROCESS IN TEXAS

11.3 Explain the stages of the criminal justice process in Texas.

Texans look to the state and municipal government to handle criminal justice, and the state has created a bureaucracy to administer justice. The judicial proceedings take two steps in Texas: pretrial and trial. Let's take a look at the specifics of each.

PRETRIAL

So you've been arrested on charges you violated the law—what's next? The first step is an appearance before a judge. Within forty-eight hours after an arrest, a suspect must have a hearing before a judge to inform the accused of the charges.[17] The judge must advise the accused that he or she can retain counsel, remain silent, and have an attorney present during interviews with law enforcement officers or attorneys representing the state.

If the accused would like to get out of jail, they need to post **bail**. Bail is a contract—the accused agrees to give something up (usually money) to ensure

bail: a contract where the accused is temporarily released from prison on the condition he or she pay a sum of money to guarantee an appearance in court that they will appear when the court orders them to do so. After a specific bail amount is set, a bond can be acquired to facilitate bail. A bond can be a cash bond in which the defendant pays the full amount of the bond immediately, a bail bond in which the defendant uses a bonding company to borrow the collateral, or "personal recognizance" where a defendant is not required to put up anything. When defendants use a bondsman to secure bail, they pay a fee—10 percent more than the set bail amount—and pledge collateral, usually property or automobiles, for the remaining amount. If the defendant doesn't show up for court, the bondsman must either pay the entire amount or produce the defendant.

If the accused is not in custody, the **prosecutor**—the state's lawyer who is responsible for bringing charges against accused lawbreakers—has up to two years from the date of the offense to file misdemeanor charges and between five and ten years to file felony charges.[18] Prosecutors have different titles, depending on where they work. Both district and county attorneys represent the state in criminal cases and work with law enforcement to investigate criminal cases in their jurisdiction. Once the charges are filed by the prosecutor the accused must make an initial appearance or **arraignment**. The charges will be read in open court and the defendant will enter a plea.

A **grand jury** determines, in conjunction with the prosecutor, whether there is sufficient evidence to bring criminal charges in serious cases against a defendant. The prosecutor presents evidence, in the form of physical items (such as an alleged murder weapon) and witnesses. These meetings are not public, and so protect the reputation of a defendant and allow witnesses to be speak freely without fear of retaliation. The Texas Constitution guarantees this right to a grand jury hearing, thought to be a wall against warrantless prosecution since a grand jury must agree to charge a defendant. Less serious felony charges can be brought in other ways, usually by a charging document.[19]

If the defendant wants to argue that law enforcement engaged in improper search, seizure, or statement, he or she engages in a suppression hearing to ask the judge to suppress the evidence, claiming it was collected illegally. Both sides in the case will also take discovery during this period, a process of collecting information. Texas does not have automatic discovery, so the defendant's lawyers must request the prosecution disclose specific items, such as witness statements, audio or video of the event, and physical objects like firearms or drugs. The accused may also plead guilty to reduced charges through a **plea bargain,** in which the defendant waives their right to a trial and the prosecutor recommends a punishment that the judge accepts or rejects. Almost all criminal cases are finalized with a plea bargain.[20]

TRIAL

If your case doesn't end in a plea, your case will likely go to trial. For jury trials, a jury must be selected through **voir dire**, from the French "to see to speak," where jurors are questioned by attorneys and judges in court to determine if

prosecutor: the state's lawyer who is responsible for bringing charges against accused lawbreakers

arraignment: the initial appearance of the accused in court

grand jury: a legal body charged with the task of conducting official proceedings to investigate potential criminal conduct

plea bargain: where the defendant agrees to a lesser set of charges than initially charged by the prosecutors

voir dire: jurors are questioned by attorneys and judges in court to determine if a potential juror is biased, cannot deal with the issues fairly, or knows a party to the case

Jury duty is often seen by most people as an important but cumbersome chore. Here, Senator Ted Cruz takes the juror oath in 2015. Most counties in Texas pay between $5 and $10 a day for jury duty, usually not enough to cover parking. Political science research shows that even increasing that pay shows no positive effect on compliance with a jury duty summons.[†]

PERSONAL RESPONSIBILITY: **Should payment be increased or is the civic responsibility important enough that the amount of pay is not important?**

a potential juror is biased, cannot deal with the issues fairly, or knows a party to the case. Some jurors may be dismissed for a legal reason (such as knowing the defendant). Other jurors may be dismissed by a "preemptory challenge" by one of the attorneys because of a perceived bias against the defendant, predispositions about the crime, or other reasons. For misdemeanor charges, each side may make three challenges. For felony charges, each side has ten challenges. These challenges can be used for any reason except those deemed discriminatory, such as gender or race.[21]

A defendant must enter a plea in response to the charges. The plea can be guilty, not guilty, or **no contest**, where a defendant does not admit guilt but is not contesting the underlying facts. No contest pleas allow the defendant to accept punishment from the court but avoid admitting guilt. If they do not plead to a charge against them, a defendant can request a jury trial with six jurors in misdemeanor cases and twelve jurors in felony trials.

If a defendant wants a trial but waives his or her right to a jury trial, and if the state agrees, the defendant can receive a bench trial. Misdemeanor defendants found guilty are usually sentenced by the judge immediately. In felony cases, judges consider factors such as the nature of the crime, remorse expressed by the defendant, the defendant's criminal history, personal circumstances, and the wishes of the victim. Sentencing could include jail, probation, fines, restitution, and community service.[22]

PUNISHMENT

In the 1840s, criminal justice apparatus in the Republic of Texas was ineffective by most any standard. Many residents of the early ramshackle Texas towns, now beaming silvery metropolises, were shiftless, rowdy, and sometimes vicious loafers who had to be corralled by corrupt sheriffs into poor jails. In 1842, the legislature, seeking some control over the system, voted to provide funds for the construction of a state penitentiary to improve local law and order. Over the years since then, the corrections system has adopted new solutions and has adapted to new trends, sparked by a mixture of state-based experimentation, evolving political values, and civil rights concerns.

no contest: a plea where a defendant does not admit guilt but is not contesting the underlying facts

ANGLES OF POWER
Race and Finances in the Texas Prison System

By 1911, the Texas prison system was low on funds. Prisoners who were supposed to be compensated for their grueling work in the fields were not. Wages were paltry, short-lived, and infrequently paid. Prison commissioners were forced to suspend pay (except Sunday overtime pay). Convict mutinies, called "bucks," broke out and convicts refused to work.

Governor Oscar Branch Colquitt—and the state legislature—passed reforms to invest more than $2 million in prison funding, but required a return to producing profitable "money crops" on prison plantations and closing other prison industries like iron works. Regulators required a strict separation of the races, with African Americans and Hispanics sent to the fields and Anglos sent to work in prison factories working on farm equipment.[23] The racial segregation perpetuated society's Jim Crow legal and race-based class distinctions as it provided job skills—that would be useful after release—to whites only and relegated the Latinos and African Americans to work in the fields.[24]

SOCIAL RESPONSIBILITY: **How would you create a race-blind punishment and incarceration policy?**

Physical Labor. Originally, prisons were largely expected to be self-sufficient by growing or manufacturing items to generate revenue.[25] They relied on the physical labor of convicts to generate revenue. Even the state capitol was built partially by 300 convicts from local prisons who earned 65 cents per day for the state breaking boulders of almost metallic density.[26] Prisoners produced millions of pounds of cast-iron works including the dome and ornamentation for the inside of the capitol building—much of which still stands today.[27] Today, young, first-time offenders are sometimes sentenced to a type of "boot camp" modeled after the military's basic training—a sentencing sometimes called "shock probation." In addition, in adult prisons, some of the convicted work on "hoe squads" where they plant and pick produce and carry rocks.[28]

IS IT BIGGER IN TEXAS?

FIGURE 11.2   **Comparing State Community Supervision Populations**

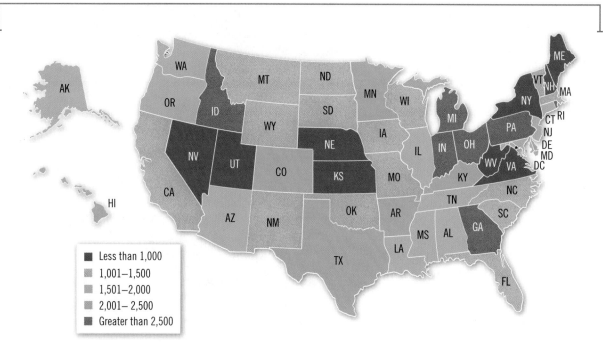

Legend:
- ■ Less than 1,000
- ▨ 1,001–1,500
- ▨ 1,501–2,000
- ▨ 2,001– 2,500
- ■ Greater than 2,500

Source: Bureau of Justice Statistics, 2014. Number on community service per 100,000 adult residents.

 COMMUNICATION:

How many defendants are on community supervision?

- Georgia leads the nation in community supervision population size.
- Texas ranks in the top ten but behind large states like Pennsylvania and Michigan.

 CRITICAL THINKING:

Why do some states have more individuals on community supervision?

- Community supervision is often less costly, so states experiencing economic downturns (such as Ohio and Pennsylvania) may turn to this approach to keep costs low.
- Tougher sentencing laws in states like Georgia and Idaho drive the size of the community supervision population.
- Texas has increased the use of community supervision as a way to reduce the jail population (which can be expensive to maintain).

Probation. **Community supervision,** or probation, is an alternative to incarceration that allows offenders to live and work outside of prison while they serve their sentence. The basic conditions require the defendant to commit no criminal offense while on probation, report to a supervision officer periodically, maintain employment to support dependents, and pay restitution to victims. Maximum periods are set for ten years for a felony conviction and two years in a misdemeanor case. The length of supervision depends on the offense, the use of a deadly weapon, and prior convictions. A judge can assign additional supervision for 10 years if the case involved indecency with a child, sexual assault, or aggravated assault.[29] Texas ranks comparatively high (number nine in 2014) nationwide on the number of defendants in community supervision (see Figure 11.2).

Other forms of community supervision allow flexibility in treating defendants. In **deferred adjudication** community supervision, a defendant pleads guilty and the judge delays a final verdict until the time the defendant successfully completes the supervision period. If the conditions are met, the judge dismisses the proceedings and discharges the defendant. If the defendant violates a condition, the defendant may not appeal and the punishment for the verdict will stand.

Community service can be a condition of probation and can range from picking up trash, to volunteering for the Society for the Prevention of Cruelty to Animals, to providing skilled labor at a construction site.[30]

community supervision: a defendant is released and allowed to live in the community under conditions set by the court

deferred adjudication: a defendant pleads guilty and the judge delays a final verdict until the time the defendant successfully completes the supervision period

INCARCERATION

Local, state, and federal governments maintain correctional facilities in Texas. Municipal (city) jails hold those arrested until either bail is made or they are transferred to county jails. County jails hold defendants awaiting trial or transfer to prison, community correctional facilities such as "boot camps," or substance abuse treatment facilities. The Texas Department of Criminal Justice oversees more than 100 state facilities of various types, including transfer facilities, state jail facilities, psychiatric units, and private prisons. Federal penitentiaries house convicts who have violated federal law. There are 112 correctional facilities in Texas, including federal correctional institutions, private correctional institutions, and residential reentry centers (halfway houses to provide assistance to inmates nearing release).[31]

Overcrowding. During the 1980s, Texas—and the nation as a whole—experienced a sharp spike in the crime rate. By 1991, Texas significantly outpaced the nation in crimes committed: murder 56 percent higher than the national average, rape 26 percent, aggravated assault 19 percent, and burglary 44 percent.[32] From the 1980s to the 1990s, dangerous youth crime nearly doubled while crimes committed by adults rose 25 percent.

Prison populations exploded in the 1980s as the US Congress and state legislatures began to pass "tough on crime" legislation to appeal to a growing conservative voter base and to stem rising crime rates (see Figure 11.3). This

IS IT BIGGER IN TEXAS?

FIGURE 11.3   **State and Federal Prisoners under Jurisdiction of Correctional Authorities**

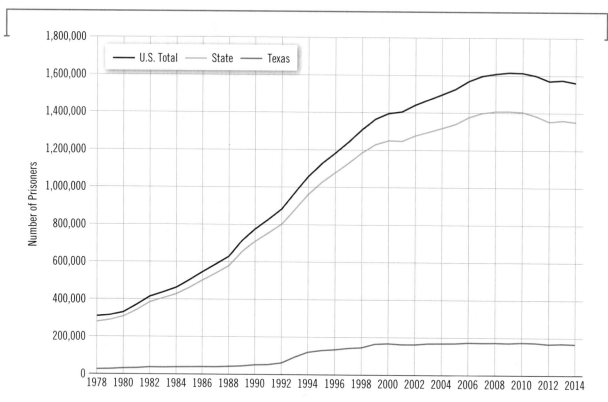

Source: Bureau of Justice Statistics, National Prisoner Statistics Program.

 COMMUNICATION:

How does the prison population in Texas compare to the rest of the states and the nation?

- State prison populations drove growth beginning in the 1980s.
- Texas's prison population rose in the 1990s and then plateaued, as other state prison populations continued to rise.
- Federal prison population rose too since the 1980s but gradually and only by about 200,000 prisoners.

 CRITICAL THINKING:

Why did the prison population increase, then level off?

- Much of the growth in prison population was escalated by states, especially southern states, who collectively doubled their prison population in the decade between 1990 and 2000.
- Conservative southern states are more likely to have more penalties and stricter enforcement of laws than other states.
- Texas's history of being tough on crime created incentives to fund more law enforcement and more prisons beginning in the 1990s. As the state sought to reduce the prison population after crime rates fell in the 2000s, the number incarcerated leveled off and then decreased.

overcrowding in Texas prisons instigated a seemingly unending series of law-suits involving Texas prisoners, the federal government, and the Texas Department of Corrections.

Following federal court mandates to end prison overcrowding and Texans' concerns about rising crime rates in the 1990s, the state nearly tripled the number of prison beds in the 1990s to 150,000.[33] One criminal justice observer noted that the ramping up was like "mobilizing for a world war."[34] However, rather than significantly reducing overcrowding, the incarceration rate shot up. Texas became an icon for states who wanted to get tough on crime. State court judges began handing out longer sentences for criminal defendants. State laws were passed that mandated that convicts serve a minimum of 50 percent of their sentences.[35] The prison population ballooned from 290 prisoners per 100,000 in 1990 to 704 prisoners in 1999. The average sentence served in prison tripled for violent crimes and burglary between 1991 and 1999. The number of prisoners paroled decreased by 60 percent during this time period. Punitive sentences targeted defendants who were disproportionately racial minorities (see Figure 11.4).

Several states copied elements of what prison experts called the "Texas Control Model"–which emphasized inmate obedience, discipline, work, and education, roughly in that order.[36] Politicians who believed longer sentences were best for rehabilitation took credit for getting tough on crime.[37]

Recent Fall in Crime Rate and Incarceration.   The prison population in Texas has slowly declined in the twenty-first century, partially driven by a falling crime rate, which fell just as quickly as it rose in the 1990s. Between 1994 and 2000, arrests for murder dropped 68 percent and arrests for robbery dropped 51 percent. Criminologists attribute the decline in crime to a strong economy, a shrinking market for drugs, new police strategies involving community policing, and efforts to keep guns out of the hands of juveniles.[38]

Drug Court Reform.   Funding was an issue as well. Republicans, while tough on crime, are also fiscally conservative. Prisons are expensive to maintain and run. Spending on incarceration increased by 205 percent during the 1990s.[39] Texas Republicans also responded by establishing drug courts to provide treatment for drug-addicted offenders rather than prison time. They also diverted funds from prison construction to alternative approaches. Governor Perry signed legislation to allow police officers to issue citations for misdemeanor possession of marijuana in place of arrests. He also supported legislation that mandated probation for first-time drug offenders who were caught with small amounts of drugs. The state poured significant funds into drug prevention programs and probation programs.[40] As a result, the state closed three prisons from 2000 to 2010.[41]

The public supports such reasonable measures that reduce incarceration rates. Polling from the Texas Public Policy Foundation, a conservative-leaning think tank in Austin, found that most Texas voters want to make penalties

FIGURE 11.4   **Demographic Makeup of Texas Prisons**

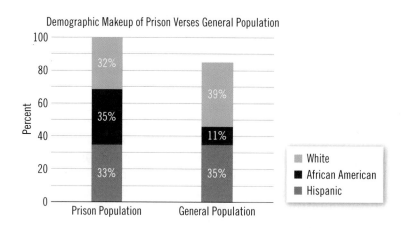

Demographic Makeup of Prison Verses General Population

Source: Texas Department of Criminal Justice, Statistical Report Fiscal Year 2014, Male and female prisoners both included. Figures rounded up. "Other" category = 0.5 percent. Population figures from the US Census Bureau.

 COMMUNICATION:

What is the racial makeup of prisons in Texas?

- The percentage of total prison population from each racial group is roughly equal at about one-third each. Although the percentage of the prison population is similar, the representation by each group in prison is not balanced.

- African Americans and Latinos, however, make up slightly more of the prison population than Anglos, and are disproportionately unrepresentative of their percentages in the population.

 CRITICAL THINKING:

Why the racial imbalance?

- Statewide figures may mask the degree to which certain groups are in prison for certain crimes (drug crimes versus property crimes versus murder). African Americans are more likely to be in prison on drug crimes than other racial groups, and these crimes have longer sentences than other crimes.

- Racial profiling, where racial minorities are targeted by police, may also be increasing arrest and conviction rates among African Americans and Latinos.

GREAT TEXAS POLITICAL DEBATES
Prison Conditions in Texas

The period of the 1950s to the 1970s was a particularly brutal time for convicts in Texas prisons. Prisoners who "bad eyed" a guard or picked "dirty cotton" in the field might be ordered to balance for three hours on an elevated two-by-four, called the Rail. He might be forced to stay up all night shelling peanuts. Abuse by guards was frequent—prisoners were whipped, beaten, or flogged with a curved wooden stick called the "bat." Prison officials used rudimentary solitary confinement, either in extreme heat or cold, to isolate and punish prisoners. Sexual abuse of prisoners was common.

Responding to these conditions in 1980, the appropriately named federal judge William Wayne Justice held that the prison conditions in Texas violated the Eighth Amendment of the US Constitution prohibiting "cruel and unusual punishment." In *Ruiz v. Estelle*, the courts prohibited the state from housing more than two prisoners per cell, ordered a 1:6 staffing ratio for guards to inmates and ordered the prison to reduce its population to 95 percent of capacity.[42] After the agreement went into effect, conditions improved— David Ruiz, who had handwritten the lawsuit himself,

commented, "It wasn't the Holiday Inn, but they started to treat us like human beings."[43]

SOCIAL RESPONSIBILITY: Should Texas take more stringent measures to protect prisoner rights?

NO: Prisoners have broken the social contract and have violated civil norms. Prison officials tasked with their care and possessing limited financial resources need to be given a wide variety of tools to manage the convicts. Basic care is all the state can afford and all prisoners have earned.

YES: Convicts are human beings who should be granted access to basic social services and who have the dignity of human rights. If the goal is to rehabilitate, not just punish, prisoners, they should be allowed to live as normal a life as possible.

MAYBE: Extending some privileges for good behavior at the discretion of the prison officials is a reasonable way to rehabilitate those in the prison population. Punishment for bad behavior while incarcerated should also be handled by prison official.

---

more proportionate to the crime. Sixty-one percent support drug treatment over prison, 57 percent support raising the standard for a drug felony, and 57 percent support community supervision over prison for some crimes.[44]

Privatization.   Privatization of prisons, where maintenance of a prison facility is outsourced to a private firm, saves money but also creates controversy. In 2015, some 2,800 inmates rioted by starting fires and took control of the privately owned Willacy County Correctional Center in Raymondville. Their purpose: protesting the rough conditions of the prison as imposed by the Utah-based company operating the facility, including insect infestation, exposure to raw sewage, substandard medical care, and excessive solitary confinement.[45] The US Bureau of Prisons cancelled the contract, the prison closed, and the inmates were transferred. Five private prison facilities currently in the state will be phased out due to a drop in the number of inmates and concerns about conditions at the prisons.[46]

DEATH PENALTY

death penalty: (capital punishment) the sentence of a convicted individual to death

Texas has a long history of issuing and implementing the **death penalty** for capitol offenses. Prior to 1923, individual counties were responsible for executing their own prisoners. After 1924, fears of overzealous sheriffs in conjunction with alleged abuse by county juries led the legislature to mandate that all prisoner execution be carried out by the state at the Walls Unit (named because of the tall walls surrounding the unit) in Huntsville.[47] From 1819 to 1923, execution was always by hanging. The state legislature allowed the use of the electric chair in 1923 and all executions between then and 1964 were carried out by electrocution. "Old Sparky," as the electric chair was familiarly known, was constructed by inmates out of an oak chair.[48] The chair was the means of executing 361 men between February 1924 and July 1964.[49] Texas temporarily stopped executing prisoners after the US Supreme Court banned capital punishment in the United States as a violation of the Eighth Amendment "cruel and unusual" prohibition in the case *Furman v. Georgia* (1972).

Once the death penalty was again permitted by the US Supreme Court in 1977, Texas adopted lethal injection for executing prisons, the first of which was executed in 1982.[50] Tough talking Governor Richards approved fifty executions in her term as governor. On the campaign trail in 1994, Richards, a Democrat, bragged about being as tough on crime as any Republican. George W. Bush responded that if elected, he promised to shorten the time spent on death-row appeals. The *Houston Chronicle* scolded them both in an editorial: "It is unseemly for political candidates to compete with one another over who would be the most enthusiastic and cheerful executioner."[51] After winning the election, Governor Bush signed off on 135 executions after signing legislation that expedited execution and limited capital appeals. "We're a death penalty state," he declared.[52] Governor Perry sanctioned more executions than any modern governor in US history and was stingy with pardons. He remarked in 2011, "If you come into our state and you kill one of our children, you kill a police officer, you're involved with another crime and you kill one of our citizens, you will face the ultimate justice in the state of Texas, and that is, you will be executed."

Despite talking tough, the governor supported legislation to allow juries in capital murder trial to consider life without parole instead of death, which has greatly decreased the number of people sentenced to death. The legislation—signed in 2005—dropped the number of executions from thirty-seven to nine in slightly more than a decade (see Figure 11.5).[53]

Almost every year, Texas leads all other states in the number of executions. Yet, Texas also leads the nation in reforming the criminal justice system. In recent years, judges have prodded lawmakers to change the law to allow Texans who had guilty verdicts based on potentially flawed science to challenge their convictions.

PERSONAL RESPONSIBILITY: **Does Texas's reputation for aggressive use of the death penalty hurt the image of the state?**

FIGURE 11.5   **Number of Prisoners Scheduled to be Executed and Executed**

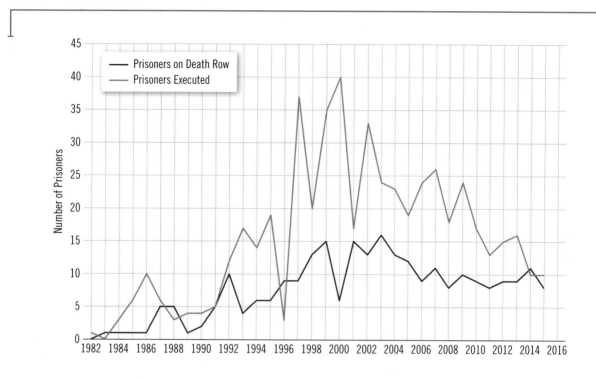

Source: Texas Department of Criminal Justice, 2015.

 COMMUNICATION:

How many prisoners are on death row or executed by year in Texas?

- The number of prisoners executed has declined from a high of thirty-three in 2002 to ten in 2014.
- The number of prisoners on death row has remained steady since the early 2000s but has fallen slightly from around fifteen to below ten.

 CRITICAL THINKING:

Why have the numbers executed or scheduled to be executed fallen?

- The homicide rate in the state has fallen during the 2000s, reducing the need to use the death penalty.
- Prosecutors in the state have more flexibility when pursuing the death penalty than in the past.[54] Problems with the fairness of the death penalty have reduced the likelihood of asking for it.
- Texans still support the death penalty but may be hesitant to use it unless the circumstances are extreme or the evidence in the case is very clear.

see for yourself 11.2

Judge Keller was accused of callously failing to leave her office open to hear a death penalty appeal. Listen to her explain the incident and her views on the death penalty in Texas.

Several crimes in Texas are eligible for the death penalty, including hiring someone to murder someone else, murdering a judge or correctional officer, and murdering during the act of specified felonies, such as kidnapping, burglary, and rape. When considering whether or not to apply a death sentence, a jury may weigh the circumstances of the crime and whether a defendant demonstrated remorse about the crime. Unanimous agreement that a defendant is likely to commit future criminal acts is required to sentence an offender to death.

Race is a significant factor in the application of the death penalty. For instance, between December 2004 and 2016, every death sentence handed down in Harris County was to an African American or Hispanic man. The current membership on death row is 44 percent African American, 27 percent Hispanic, and 27 percent Anglo. Concern over racial testimony about future criminal activity has slowed the rate of prosecutors asking for death penalty cases (Harris County had no sentences in 2015) and prompted the Supreme Court to review the practice of testimony discussing race as a factor in committing future crimes.

In 1999, death row was moved to a modern unit, called The Polunsky Unit, deep in the lonely, piney woods by Livingston, Texas. Today, Texas relies on lethal injection to carry out death sentences. Many lethal injection drugs, however, are in short supply, so the state relies on a single drug (pentobarbital, a drug used in animal euthanasia). The scarcity of the drug prompted more than 3,300 citizens to write to Governor Abbott between January and September 2015 to suggest alternative means to swiftly carry out the death penalty. The public's creative methods included blood draining, carbon monoxide poisoning, and a firing squad.[55]

Support for use of the death penalty for capital cases is high in Texas. In a 2015 survey, 72 percent of respondents favored the death penalty as a sentence in capital cases, compared to 21 percent who did not support it and 7 percent who were not sure. Nationally, only 49 percent support the use of the death penalty.[56] In Texas, however, even liberals, classically opposed, are split on the use of the death penalty but generally lean toward not supporting it (see Table 11.2).

★ TEXAS TAKEAWAYS

5 What kind of jury is responsible for bringing criminal charges against an individual?

6 What are some alternatives to incarceration?

7 What levels of government maintain prisons in Texas?

8 When did Texas prison populations increase significantly?

TABLE 11.2	Support for Death Penalty by Ideology	
IDEOLOGY	SUPPORT	NOT SUPPORT
Liberal	43%	51%
Moderate	70%	18%
Conservative	88%	10%

 COMMUNICATION:

How do Texans feel about the death penalty?

- Conservatives are overwhelmingly supportive of the use of the death penalty in capital crimes (88 percent) followed closely by moderates (70 percent).
- Liberals in Texas are generally opposed to the death penalty but by only a slim margin (51 percent opposed).

 CRITICAL THINKING:

Why the split in support among ideologies?

- Traditionalist political culture, dominant in Texas, holds that law and order is one of the main purposes of government. Most Texans, especially conservatives and moderates, embrace this function of government.
- Liberals disapprove more because of concerns about racial fairness of the penalty, denial of due process of law, and a belief that it is inhumane.

LIFE AFTER PRISON

After their release, persons with felony convictions may face **collateral consequences** by being banned from certain employment, access to benefits, and eligibility for specific programs.

11.4 Evaluate the consequences of postconviction punishment in Texas.

collateral consequences: additional civil punishments of criminal convictions

RESTRICTED LICENSING, EMPLOYMENT, AND ACCESS TO PROGRAMS

State law restricts felons from serving in many state positions, including as a railroad commissioner, a primary election judge, and several hospital district boards. Felons are also ineligible for food stamp benefits, selected Medicaid programs, and for higher education scholarships. Almost 200 certificates, permits, or specific types of employment are not available to felons. These include a license to sell alcoholic beverages, serve as director at a child care center, and obtain a charitable bingo license.[57]

VOTING RIGHTS

criminal disenfranchisement: the loss of voting rights for felons during incarceration and after they have served their sentence

Another significant collateral consequence is the loss of voting rights, called **criminal disenfranchisement**. More than 5.85 million Americans are unable to vote due to felony disenfranchisement policies.[58] States may suspend voting rights while the felon is in prison only, during parole and probation as well, or even for years after the sentence has been served (see Figure 11.6). There is a racial disparity in the voters who are disenfranchised. Nationally, one out of thirteen African Americans has lost their voting rights compared to one out of fifty-six non-African Americans.[59]

PAROLE

parole: a system in which a prisoner is released from prison prior to completing his or her full sentence

As the famous country musician Merle Haggard wrote in his hit song "Momma Tried," some Texans turn "21 in prison doing life without parole." A prisoner earns **parole** through good conduct while being locked up—these behaviors include effectively carrying out assignments, attempting to rehabilitate, and generally exhibiting good behavior (see Table 11.3). Except in cases where prisoners are not eligible for parole, such as those on death row, individuals are eligible for parole when their calendar time served plus good conduct time equals one-fourth of the maximum sentence or fifteen years—whichever is less.[60] Depending on the case, the standard for parole is higher. In certain capital offenses, the law requires a two-thirds vote of the parole board members to grant parole.

At the high point of parole granting in the 1980s, inmates served approximately twenty-two days for each year of their sentences.[61] Jail overcrowding spurred the state to release convicts like Kenneth McDuff, who served only twenty years for a violent triple homicide. While on parole, McDuff kidnapped and killed a Waco woman.[62] In response to this and other heinous crimes

TABLE 11.3   Risk Scores for Parole Justification

SCORE ASSIGNED RISK LEVEL (RISK LEVEL TO ASSIGNED INDIVIDUAL)	MALE POINTS	FEMALE POINTS
Low Risk	3 or less	3 or less
Moderate Risk	4–8	4–9
High Risk	9–15	10+
Highest Risk	16+	N/A

Source: Bureau of Pardons and Paroles.

SOCIAL RESPONSIBILITY: **Does the risk assessment rubric seem fair to you? Should there be different risk levels for male and female prisoners? Why?**

How does a prisoner get a good parole score? An offender can be assigned points on a range of factors. A low score is associated with low risk. The higher the score, the greater the risk the offender presents for successful parole.[63]

IS IT BIGGER IN TEXAS?

FIGURE 11.6   Restrictions on Voting Post Felony by State

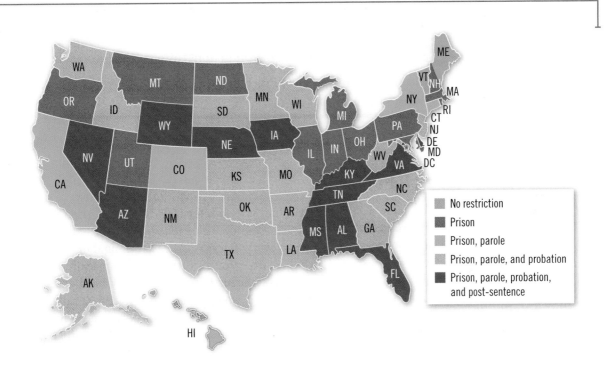

Source: The Sentencing Project.

 COMMUNICATION:

Which states restrict voting rights for prisoners or released felons?

- Most states have a ban on voting rights for the duration of a felon's prison sentence, while on probation, or on parole. Texas is in this category.

- Twelve states extend the voting restriction to after the offender has completed his or her sentence. Two of these states (Iowa and Florida) permanently ban felons from voting.

 CRITICAL THINKING:

Why are some states less likely to grant voting rights?

- The harshest postincarceration voting restrictions tend to be in the South (Florida, Mississippi, Alabama) likely due to a traditionalistic political culture that is tough on crime.

committed on parole, the state instituted minimum time-served requirements before parole could be granted. The parole rate came down dramatically from 80 percent in 1991 to 50 percent in 1992 and to 20 percent in 1994.[64] The parole approval rate for 2013 was 36 percent for the state overall.[65]

★ TEXAS TAKEAWAYS

9 What do we call the loss of voting rights after a felony conviction?

10 In capital offenses, how much of the parole board is required to agree to grant parole?

REFORMS

| **11.5** | Assess reforms to the Texas criminal justice process. |

Criminal justice reforms in Texas are often punitive in nature. One observer joked that when the legislature meets every two years, the first thing they do is increase the penalties for everything.[66] Historically, Democrats and Republicans have been equally hard on crime and criminals. Democratic Governor Dolph Briscoe (1973–1979) railed against "long-haired weirdoes," made vigorous enforcement of crime a major issue, and pushed a hulking anticrime package through the legislature.[67] Republican Governor George W. Bush (1995–2000) increased punishment for juvenile offenders and pushed "truth in sentencing" laws to limit parole options. The question is how to balance the generally tough on crime approach with the requirements for a just system. Add in the cost of the criminal justice system, especially to county jails, and it becomes clear that creative solutions are needed to reform the criminal justice system in Texas.

ALTERNATIVES TO INCARCERATION

On an average day, Texas county jails house about 65,000 individuals. Many of these incarcerated individuals are low-level, nonviolent offenders, especially those with mental illness or substance abuse problems. Both state and local governments have implemented strategies to provide alternative solutions for these specialized jail populations. One county sheriff rewarded positive inmate behavior with "good time" credits.[68] A legislative pilot program for offenders with mental health issues was initiated in 2013 to reduce repeat criminal behavior, limit time spent in jail, and expand clinical mental health and social support services through rehabilitation programs and residential housing opportunities.[69] However, overcrowding and inmate deaths have remained a problem.

BAIL REFORMS

Most prisoners in Texas and across the United States have not been convicted of any crime, but remain in jail because they cannot afford to pay bail. For instance, in Harris County, about three-quarters of the prisoners are only awaiting trial.[70] In 2001, 39 percent of inmates in Texas were pretrial detainees. It was 60 percent in 2015.[71] Each prisoner costs taxpayers about $45 a day. This is especially burdensome for low-income defendants who cannot go back to work, support their families, and aid in their own defense.[72]

Bail reform advocates also point to the Sandra Bland case (referenced at the beginning of this chapter). The judge set bail at $5,000. Bland would have had to pay a bondsman a nonrefundable $500 to post the full amount if she were unable to come up with the funds herself.[73] The rigid, predetermined bail schedule does not provide enough flexibility, reformers argue, to ensure that the bail is fair. Instead, reformers argue that the court system should improve the manner used to determine the risk of flight (which bail is supposed to reduce), rely less on financial bonds, and ensure that defendants have a bail hearing within 24 hours of their arrest.

ADDRESSING PRISON SUICIDES

Even as prison populations are falling, Texas prisons witnessed a 40 percent increase in suicides from 2008 to 2014. More than 980 inmates attempted suicide in 2014. Nearly one-third of the 134 suicides from January 2011 to September 2015 happened in cells designed for solitary confinement, yet this type of incarceration practice accounts for only 4 percent of the total prison population.[74] To address the issue, the Texas Department of Criminal Justice has increased training of prison officer cadets to spot a mental health crisis in a distressed inmate as one tool to prevent suicides. Criminal justice reform advocates also stress the need for access to services and more prison staff in general.

INSIDER INTERVIEW

Former Court of Criminal Appeals Judge Cathy Cochran

How is it that Texas, home to law and order, has enacted groundbreaking reforms to the death penalty?

I think that when you come right down to it, Texas is a pretty open-minded place. People listen and pay attention and acknowledge issues if you bring them to their attention in an appropriate sort of way. And all those DNA exonerations woke a lot of people up. I was as surprised as anybody.[75]

SOCIAL RESPONSIBILITY: **Is the criminal justice system fair?**
How would you design a system that protects the innocent, punishes the guilty, and upholds basic human rights?

GRAND JURY REFORM

Until 2015, a district judge would personally select citizens to be jury commissioners, and those commissioners then choose fifteen to twenty citizens to serve as the grand jury pool.[76] Critics believed this process encouraged the selection of grand jurors who were more likely to bring charges against a suspect. Indeed, one *Houston Chronicle* reporter uncovered an instance in which grand jurors actively collaborated with prosecutors to intimidate witnesses.[77] In 2015, Texas passed legislation to outlaw the "pick a pal" grand jury system. The new system institutes a random process for drawing jurors from a broader pool of potential applicants.[78]

DEATH PENALTY REFORM

While Texans overwhelmingly support the death penalty, 49 percent of Texans believe that people are wrongly convicted of the death penalty "occasionally" and 13 percent feel this happens "a great deal of the time."[79] This sentiment is backed by concrete evidence. The Innocence Project, a national organization dedicated to exonerating individuals wrongly convicted using DNA testing, report that fifty-two cases in Texas (and 330 nationally) have been exonerated as of 2015, more than any other state.

Kerry Max Cook's fight is one example. Arrested in 1977 for the rape, mutilation, and murder of a woman who lived in his apartment complex, Cook endured a forty-year ordeal including conviction for murder, three trials, two death sentences overturned, and freedom from death row in 1997. While in prison, he was repeatedly raped and stabbed—abuses that led him to attempt suicide twice.[80] In 1999, DNA tests revealed that none of the evidence collected at the scene of the gruesome murder belonged to Cook. The tests revealed that another man—the victim's lover, a married man—was linked to the evidence at the scene. Cook agreed to a plea deal that dropped the murder charges and allowed him to get out of jail but not be legally exonerated.[81] Even after four decades, Cook is still fighting to clear his name—winning could mean compensation of up to $2 million from the state including health and education benefits.

DNA testing of evidence in criminal trials holds great promise to identify persons responsible for crimes, yet it is not always reliable. The Texas Forensic Science Commission introduced new standards on

Pictured here is Kerry Max Cook. His saga resulted in three lengthy trials, a movie, and book. The case highlights important problems with the death penalty in Texas.

 PERSONAL RESPONSIBILITY: **Are you in favor or against the death penalty? Why?**

"mixed DNA" evidence (when more than one individual's DNA is found on evidence). These were adopted by the Texas Department of Public Safety, but questions remained.[82]

Other procedural safeguards can be employed to make the system fair and less fallible. Civil rights organizations have outlined dozens of recommendations to reform the death penalty in the states.[83] First, states should require review of credible claims of innocence even after conviction. Second, all evidence should be preserved for an extended time after a conviction and DNA databanks established to keep records, to which defendants should have access. Third, parameters should be established to ensure reliable testimony from eyewitnesses, including in jury instructions. Fourth, the state should create an independent authority to screen and train defense attorneys representing clients charged with capital crimes. Finally, because the death penalty is disproportionately applied to racial minorities, states are urged to pass legislation to ensure racial and ethnic diversity among the judges, lawyers, and jurors so that racial discrimination plays no role in capital punishment.

Although Texas is undeniably aggressive in using the death penalty as a sentence for capital crimes, the state has also led the nation in efforts to improve procedures in such cases passed relating to police practices, forensic evidence, and prosecutorial procedures. Legislation was passed to improve law enforcement lineups, require that any testimony of jailhouse informants be corroborated, guarantee a defendant's right to DNA testing after conviction, and increase compensation for those wrongfully convicted to $80,000 (through the 2009 Tim Cole Act).[84]

 TEXAS TAKEAWAYS

 What do prisoners cost taxpayers per day?

 How did Texas reform its grand jury system in 2015?

THE INSIDER VIEW

On a crisp September day in Austin outside the state capitol in 2015, two marches drew attention to the unnecessary violence against African Americans and police officers. The Black Lives Matter group chanted in rhythm with drums while a sea of blue-wearing individuals showed their support for Police Lives Matter.[85] State political officials, often responding to public outcry for retribution against criminals, have been punitive and harsh. These efforts have trickled into prison policy, sentencing policies, and punishment, but are often countered by voters who have grown weary of spending funds on prisoners.

In response, public officials have implemented reforms that have reduced the state's incarceration rate, dropped the state's crime rate to pre-1968 levels, and decreased the number of repeat offenders.[86] Many problems still remain to be solved, however, such as prison overcrowding, racial disparity in sentencing and incarceration, and treatment of prisoners.

★ TEXAS TAKEAWAYS

1 The accused has the right to remain silent, consult with an attorney, have an attorney present during questioning, and protection from unreasonable search and seizure.

2 Victims have the right to be informed about the progress of a case at various points and the right to have the court take their safety into account on release of their attacker from a correctional facility.

3 The maximum penalty for a misdemeanor is up to a year in jail and/or a $4,000 fine. The maximum penalty for a felony is death by lethal injection (the death penalty).

4 The age range for a juvenile in Texas is ten to sixteen years old; at age seventeen defendants can be tried as adults.

5 A grand jury is responsible for bringing criminal charges against an individual.

6 Probation and deferred adjudication are two alternatives to incarceration.

7 Local, state, and federal governments maintain correctional facilities in Texas.

8 Prison populations exploded in the 1980s as the US Congress and state legislatures began to pass "tough on crime" legislation.

9 Criminal disenfranchisement is the loss of voting rights after a conviction.

10 The law requires a two-thirds vote of the board members to grant parole for capital offenses.

11 Each prisoner costs Texas taxpayers about $45 a day

12 The old system allowed grand jury commissioners to pick the grand jury pool. The new system institutes a random process for drawing jurors from a broader pool of potential applicants.

KEY TERMS

arraignment
bail
collateral consequences
community supervision
criminal disenfranchisement
death penalty
deferred adjudication
grand jury
guardian ad litem
no contest
parole
plea bargain
probable cause
prosecutor
search and seizure
voir dire

PRACTICE QUIZ

1. The oldest law enforcement agency in the state of Texas is:

a. The Department of Public Safety
b. The Criminal Justice Division
c. The Texas Rangers
d. The Texas Lawmen

2. Which of the following is the **correct** order of the classification of penalties associated with the following felonies, ranked from most severe to least severe?

    a. State Jail, Capital, First Degree, Second Degree

    b. Capital, First Degree, Second Degree, Third Degree

    c. First Degree, Second Degree, Third Degree, Capital

    d. First Degree, Second Degree, Third Degree, State Jail

3. Which of the following is the **correct** order of the criminal justice process in Texas?

    a. Pretrial, Trial, Punishment

    b. Trial, Posttrial, Punishment

    c. Amicus Curiae, Trial, Punishment

    d. None of the above is correct

4. Where does Texas rank in relation to other states in terms of prison population?

    a. Lowest Prison Population

    b. Fourth in Prison Population

    c. Thirtieth in Prison Population

    d. Highest Prison Population

5. From 1819 to 1923, the means of execution in Texas was _____ until it switched to electrocution in 1923.

    a. Firing Squad

    b. Hanging

    c. Beheading

    d. Lethal Injection

6. The number of prisoners executed in 2014 was

    a. One

    b. Four

    c. Ten

    d. Thirty-five

7. Grand jury reforms in Texas now allow district judges and jury commissioners to select the individuals to serve on a grand jury.

    a. True

    b. False

8. Texas has a history of being "tough on crime."

    a. True

    b. False

9. Felony disenfranchisement (or criminal disenfranchisement) is the loss of voting rights for those currently incarcerated and also for felons who have been released.

    a. True

    b. False

10. The standard for parole is the same for all cases, no matter what crime the prisoner committed.

    a. True

    b. False

[Answers: C, B, A, D, B, C, B, A, B, A, A, B]

As natural gas extraction expanded in the land under Denton, Texas, residents of the North Texas town began to worry about the possible long-term environmental and public health damage of hydraulic fracturing (or "fracking"), a process that drills into bedrock and injects millions of gallons of high pressure, chemical-laced water into the earth to free up oil and gas. Reports revealed that there were more than 300 wells in the city limits, many very close to houses. The citizens responded by forming "Frack Free Denton."[1] The group rallied the city and 59 percent of the voters passed a local ordinance to ban the practice of fracking in 2014.

The Texas legislature reacted swiftly to Denton's ordinance. Claiming that Texas needs to avoid "a patchwork of local regulations" that threaten the ability of the state to govern, the legislature passed and Governor Abbott signed legislation in 2015 (the so-called "Denton Fracking Ban") that would preempt local government from regulating a wide variety of drilling activities.[2] The legislation drew a line defining just where local control ends and Texas state law begins.

Opponents derided the legislation as catering to oil and gas industry groups who sought fewer regulations on energy production. Environmentalists and local officials also worried that the legislation would erode the authority cities have long had to ensure local community health and safety. The legislation drew national attention with the media framing the initiative as a proxy fight between local environmental control and Big Oil.[3] Yet, the fight was broader than that—the debate over fracking exemplifies the longstanding power struggle between local and state governments. Railroad Commission Chair Christi Craddick summed it up: "Local control's great in a lot of respects. But I'm the expert on oil and gas. The city of Denton is not."[4] Fracking resumed in Denton in June of 2015.

LEARNING OBJECTIVES

12.1 Compare the functions and powers of local and state governments.

12.2 Outline the powers held by county government offices.

12.3 Explain the forms under which cities can incorporate.

12.4 Classify the types of city government.

12.5 Analyze the benefits and challenges of special districts.

12.6 Describe the process and challenges of local government elections.

12.7 Identify problems facing local government and possible solutions.

● "Frack Free Denton" supporters rally as state and local governments clash over fracking.

preemption: the supremacy of rules and laws handed down at the state level

Other legislation in the 2015 Texas legislative session aimed to roll back or limit local government's power to act—increasing the cost of challenging natural gas rates, capping local property tax hikes, nullifying ordinances that prohibit discrimination, and overruling ordinances banning plastic bags.[5] These **preemption** laws are becoming more common in statehouses across the country, especially as Republican legislatures attempt to control local municipal governments that are run by Democrats.[6] Preemption hinges on the supremacy of state laws that control the actions of local government and restrain flexibility. Not all of these efforts passed, but the long-fought feud between state and local leaders quickly turned into open warfare.[7]

A central struggle of modern government is the battle between state and local authorities over social policy and financial autonomy. Cities are given some autonomy to act but are still tethered to the laws of the state and dependent on state and federal funds to operate. In this chapter, we examine the powers and types of local government. Then we explore the role of smaller governments in local politics. Finally, we examine the problems facing local government. Pressure on city government to provide resources to residents and to promote economic growth may collide as modern cities confront tight fiscal times, minimal state aid, and a public that demands low taxes but robust services.

THE POWERS AND FUNCTIONS OF LOCAL GOVERNMENT

12.1 Compare the functions and powers of local and state governments.

Local government is often considered less powerful than state or national governments, and yet the actions taken by local governments have some of the most profound impacts on the daily lives of Texans. Local governments provide an extensive range of services, most often related to public safety (fire and police), sanitation, planning for future development, maintenance of roads, incentives for local economic development, and providing access to recreational facilities. Yet local governments struggle with state government, businesses, interest groups, and even their own citizens in providing these services.

DILLON'S RULE

Although the state and federal government share power across a range of policy issues, local government is often fenced in by state authority. The US Constitution does not mention local government. However, state leaders have interpreted

GREAT TEXAS POLITICAL DEBATES
Ban the Bag?

In 2016, fewer than a dozen Texas cities had ordinances that banned or charged a fee for plastic bags. The idea was to combat litter and improve the environment by encouraging the use of alternate bags. The state legislature in Austin considered legislation to outlaw these disposable bag ordinances. Governor Abbott expressed concern about local ordinances trumping state law but did not push for a ban on bags. Ultimately the bag ban legislation didn't make it out of committee and was left "dangling like a discarded plastic bag caught in a tree."[8] The Texas Fourth Court of Appeals found a ban on single-use bags in Laredo was illegal because it is preempted by state law regulating solid waste disposal.[9]

SOCIAL RESPONSIBILITY: **Should the state have broad control over city issues?**

YES: The state has an overarching obligation to look out for economic interests for the whole state. Unchecked overregulation by cities will stifle the state's ability to set priorities and encourage growth.

NO: If the city isn't violating any other laws or running afoul of the constitution, they should have the right to self-governance. Localities should have the ability to fit the rules and procedures to their local needs. City and county governments do a better job than state government on such issues.

MAYBE: Some issues are best handled from a statewide perspective while others are best handled locally. State oversight on all local issues creates a cumbersome bureaucracy but adequate controls and oversight are needed to ensure laws are not broken and local laws are not inconsistent with state priorities.

the Tenth Amendment to give states authority over local entities. In 1868, **Dillon's rule**, named after the Iowa justice whose legal rulings founded the principle, established that state governments can place restrictions on municipalities as long as these rules do not violate the state's constitution. Unless the state directly grants a local government a specific power, local governments must assume they do *not* have that power. Texas grants local governments the power to choose the form of government, the fiscal role of local government, and which offices can be filled by election or appointment. Local governments spend considerable time lobbying state governments for expanded power or fewer restrictions, and states have delegated more authority to cities in the last half century, but state power still rules the yard. Yet, power struggles do erupt when city and state needs periodically diverge.

Dillon's rule: a ruling that established that state governments can place restrictions on municipalities as long as these rules do not violate the state's constitution

LOCAL REGULATION

City government's "legislate" by using **ordinances**, the local law of a municipal area, passed by a city council. In providing services and dealing more directly with the people, local governments often grapple with policy issues that are not addressed at the state or national levels. With no state regulation of ride-on-demand services like Uber and Lyft, for example, cities are free to regulate companies selling rides. Houston and Austin passed ordinances requiring fingerprint background checks for drivers, treating Uber and Lyft more like traditional taxi companies. Uber hired twenty-three lobbyists and spent $700,000 in 2015 to press the state legislature to institute favorable laws that would override local ordinances (which

ordinances: the local law of a municipal area, passed by a city council

ANGLES OF POWER
Holding Out for a HERO

Some city ordinances intersect the legal, political, and policy dimensions of city government.

Houston's city council passed the Houston Equal Rights Ordinance ("HERO") in 2014, which prohibited discrimination on the basis of race, gender, religion, military status, disability, pregnancy, sexual orientation, and gender identity. Groups under the ordinance, except sexual orientation and gender identity, are protected by federal and state law, but the local ordinance would allow for a more rapid punishment. Within a few days of passage, a group of Houston-area pastors vowed to petition for its repeal. The petition was filed months later and initially certified as valid (the signatures were all properly collected), but the city attorney performed another review and found the signature count fell short by about 2,000 names.[13] The battle found its way to the courts. A Texas District Court ruled that the signatures were valid and ordered the council to repeal the ordinance or submit it to voters. The council decided to submit the ordinance to the voters.

Those in favor of HERO argued that discrimination is morally and legally wrong and should be checked by city power. Opponents argued that the ordinance went too far in protecting gender identity, as it would let men freely walk into women's bathrooms. Opponents ran ads that evoked fears of young girls being molested in bathrooms. When the voters finally had their say, they voted overwhelming against the ordinance, 61 percent to 39 percent.

Advertising against HERO featured a little girl being stalked in a women's restroom (left), which the opponents said would occur if the ordinance passed. Proponents of the ordinance argued this was a scare tactic—as suggested by the cartoon (right).

SOCIAL RESPONSIBILITY: **Should cities intervene in social issues, or should this be left to the state or federal government?**

the legislature did not do).[10] Uber and Lyft also spent more than $8.1 million in advertising to change the required fingerprint background check regulations in Austin in 2016.[11] However, voters rejected lifting mandatory background checks and Uber, making good on its promise, left the Austin market.

Regulations at the city level also raised a host of additional issues—can Uber or Lyft adjust fares based on demand and must they comply with other city regulations such as handicapped accessible vehicles and the number of vehicles allowed on the streets at any one time? Should a city enforce a fee structure per ride-hailing vehicle or require drivers to have insurance? Fighting against such measures in San Antonio, Uber closed up shop and left the city, creating a groundswell of public support for the city to relax regulations to allow the company to operate. Six months later, with pressure on Mayor Ivy Taylor and the city council, Uber signed an agreement with the city and resumed operations.[12]

★ TEXAS TAKEAWAYS

1 What functions do local governments fulfill?

🤠 COUNTY GOVERNMENT

Texas and much of the United States witnessed an explosion of local governments as rural expanses converted to urban centers during the nineteenth and twentieth century. The total number of local governments in the United States sum to just over 89,000, many in Texas (see Figure 12.1). The irony of a small government ethos in Texas is shattered by the sheer number and impact of local governments. Texas has several different types of local government—counties, cities, and special districts—that scramble to fulfill the growing needs of the people.

> **12.2** Outline the powers held by county government offices.

The state legislature approves the creation of new counties to tame and govern a geographic landmass as large as Texas. During the time of the Republic of Texas, the state had a modest twenty-three counties. When Texas became a state, that number increased to thirty-six. By 1931, and continuing to the present, the number is fixed at 254. The rise in the number of counties multiplied the number of elected officials and gave residents a more direct relationship with county officials.

Counties are the local arm of state government, carrying out state laws—since they cannot enact their own ordinances. Counties serve dual purposes: providing government services for residents and administrative services on behalf of the state.[14] Counties' responsibilities include public safety, property tax collection, jails, transportation and roads, elections, and environmental protection.

Some counties are small: Rockwall County, east of Dallas, is only 148 square miles. Some counties are huge: Brewster County, home to the Terlingua Chili Cook-off, is more than 6,000 square miles, three times the size of Delaware. Size impacts governance. In larger counties, for example, county government leaders play a larger role in the economic development of **unincorporated areas** of the county, regions that are administered as part of a county but not a city. Smaller counties may also be more restricted in other policy areas. For instance, 173 of Texas's 254 counties (those counties that do not have or are not adjacent to counties that have 250,000 or less residents) are not allowed by state law to have a fire code that would establish regulations on fire prevention and the storage of dangerous goods.

unincorporated area: a region that is administered as part of a county not a city

The legislature rigidly sets the structure of county governments, whether the county includes just over 100 people (Loving County) or over four million people (Harris County).[15] This structure is comprised of dozens of local officials

IS IT BIGGER IN TEXAS?

FIGURE 12.1   **Number of Local Governments**

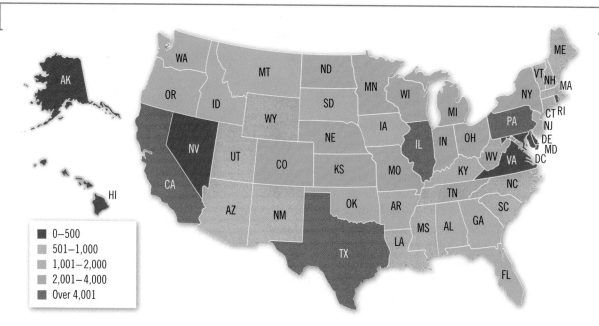

- 0–500
- 501–1,000
- 1,001–2,000
- 2,001–4,000
- Over 4,001

Source: US Census Bureau.

 COMMUNICATION:

Which states have the most local government entities?

- Illinois stands out with almost 7,000 localities, 2,000 more than Pennsylvania with the next most governments.
- Texas is in the top three with 4,856 total governments, behind Pennsylvania but ahead of California.

 CRITICAL THINKING:

Why do some states have more local governments?

- States with large populations have more local governments.
- In some states, like Illinois, localities increased the number of municipalities to thwart limits on debt and taxing.
- While some states, like California, grant authority to local government to handle water and other issues.
- In Texas responsibility for policy issues are shifted to local government entities. For instance, Nevada administers public libraries at the county level where Texas has smaller library districts.

who administer county government, elected by the county voters. Only the Texas legislature can—and sometimes does—authorize changes to county government structure.

COUNTY JUDGE AND COMMISSIONER'S COURT

At the top of county government are the county judge and commissioner's court. Each Texas county is run by a county judge and a commissioner's court made up of four county commissioners. These commissioners serve four-year terms and represent districts that must have equal populations, as decided by the US Supreme Court in *Avery v. Midland County* (1968).

County judges are frequently called on to manage crises that occur in their jurisdictions as they are responsible for homeland security and emergency management in their counties. County commissioners adopt a tax rate for the county, oversee a budget that they use to establish public works projects, and maintain county buildings and facilities. The largest expenditures are infrastructure (roads or bridges) and maintenance of the county jail.

Like cities, counties often engage in regulation. Travis County battled a private developer of an eleven million gallon, fourteen-acre "surf park" about whether or not the facility needed a swimming pool permit. Three days before surfers hit the waves, the Travis County Commissioner's Court voted to allow the lagoon to open as long as daily water quality reports are provided.

County commissioners often find consensus on how to allocate funds for projects or make strategic decisions for the county. For instance, to protect the farms and ranches that dotted the central Texas county, the Grimes County Commissioner's Court voted unanimously in 2016 to require the developers of a high-speed rail connecting Dallas and Houston to provide homeowner approval to build the line and maintain access to county roads.

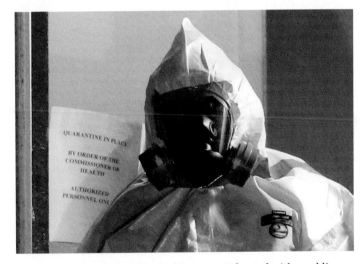

COUNTY SHERIFF

The county sheriff—part administrator, part politician, and full-time law enforcement officer—is often referred to as the "lord of the county line."[16] Sheriffs are charged with enforcing state laws, managing and operating the county jail, serving warrants and civil papers to residents, seizing property after court judgments, enforcing traffic laws on county roads, and providing security for the courts. In rural areas, the sheriff is often an all-around diplomat, troubleshooter, master of the county courthouse, and the last person

In Dallas, County Judge Clay Jenkins was confronted with a public health crisis: the first US case of a patient with the Ebola virus in 2014. Judge Jenkins led the efforts to contain the spread of the virus, working with the Dallas County Health Department, the Texas Department of State Health Services, and the US Centers for Disease Control and Prevention.*

teenagers want to see while drinking beer with their friends on remote county roads.[17] In larger urban areas, sheriffs and their many deputies carry out patrols on county roads and oversee the county jail. The number of inmates on any given month can reach several thousand. Careful management is critical because these jails functionally serve as the largest mental health facility in each county because some arrested and awaiting bail or trial often have such health issues.

COUNTY PROSECUTORS

see for yourself 12.1

Discover the history of Texas county governments.

The county attorney and district attorney are the chief prosecutors for criminal cases in Texas counties. The county attorney operates at the county court level and the district attorney handles the district court level. Although these positions are chiefly legal in nature, these officials often make policy. In a controversial move, Harris County District Attorney Devon Anderson announced in 2015 that her office would not arrest or prosecute first-time offenders caught with less than two ounces of marijuana.[18] The objective was to give nonviolent drug users a chance to avoid conviction, save space in the jail, and reserve court administrative resources. Opponents of the move challenged that the district attorney needed to get tougher, not more lenient, on drug abusers.

COUNTY ADMINISTRATORS

Several positions are purely administrative and have little influence on policy. A district clerk, if a county has one, is predominately a legal record keeper, processing passport applications, administrating child support payments, processing court fees, and recording all proceedings of the district courts. If you want to run a felony background check on your future spouse, the district clerk keeps these records. A county clerk maintains county records (like birth certificates), issues vital documents (like marriage licenses), and serves as the chief elections officer.

Although primarily administrators, clerks can find themselves in the middle of state or national political battles. Following the US Supreme Court's 2015 ruling that states could not restrict same-sex couples from marrying, Texas Attorney General Ken Paxton issued a statement encouraging clerks to follow their own religious beliefs

Rather than issue marriage licenses to gay couples, a clerk in Rusk County resigned. Some clerks who objected to gay marriage on religious grounds were simply reassigned or delegated the responsibility to other clerks.

SOCIAL RESPONSIBILITY: **Should local clerks have discretion about how and when they perform their duties? How should state and local government handle religious objections from government officials?**

and not issue marriage licenses to same-sex couples, but to expect lawsuits for violating the law. The attorney general's advice proved confusing to many clerks. Brewster County Clerk Berta Rios Martinez e-mailed colleagues: "I just had my first gay couple come in for a marriage license and I ran them off!! . . . Did I do right? HELP!!!"[19] Ultimately, clerks were required to issue licenses and those who were not were reassigned to a different job responsibility.

COUNTY FINANCE OFFICIALS

Several elected officials handle the county finances. The county tax assessor-collector collects revenue for both the state and the county. The county auditor oversees the distribution of county funds. The county treasurer receives, manages, and pays out county funds for both general revenue (through property taxes, controlled by the commissioner's court) and special revenue (from fees or other dedicated revenue, controlled by other governments such as special districts).

TEXAS TAKEAWAYS

2 How many county commissioners are there in Texas counties?

CITY GOVERNMENTS

From the end of the Republic in 1845 until 1858, the only way to incorporate a city was by special act of the state legislature.[20] In the early days of Texas, most cities were **general law cities** operating under laws created by the legislature. Today, as city populations and responsibilities have grown, most large cities are **home rule cities,** giving them greater autonomy. Texas has approximately 1,200 incorporated cities.

> **12.3** Explain the forms under which cities can incorporate.

general law city: a city that is only allowed to operate under laws the state provides

home rule city: city that is allowed self-governance independent of state law

GENERAL LAW CITIES

In the nineteenth century, the Texas legislature passed general laws that define the structure and powers of general law cities. If a general law city has not been specifically granted authority to act by the legislature, it may not undertake the action. General law cities, for example, may not add mandatory fees to utility bills without permission of the state.[21]

State law officials may also step in when local ordinances conflict with state laws. This happened in 2016 when a group called Texas Voices for Reason and Justice sent a letter to forty-five Texas general law cities demanding they

Because the state has failed to pass curbs on payday lenders, who may charge annual interest rates up to 300 percent, the Texas Municipal League worked with cities to pass ordinances to city charters to create a statewide standard.** Other local ordinances include banning specific dog breeds (like pit bulls), banning cell phones while driving, and restricting residency for registered sex offenders.

PERSONAL RESPONSIBILITY: **What sort of ordinance do you think your city should pass to address a substantive local problem? Is this better handled at the local or state level?**

repeal residency restrictions for sex offenders. The group argued that towns that passed these restrictions were in violation of the state constitution because the legislature had not granted them express permission to pass such laws.[22] The state agreed and the restrictions were lifted.

HOME RULE CITIES

By the early twentieth century, the state was growing rapidly enough to outstrip the legislature's ability to routinely deal with local matters. The number of cities grew by about ten per year.[23] By 1913, the state allowed municipalities to become home rule cities, giving them the authority to choose the structure of their government (such as size of and method used to elect the city council), annex land adjacent to the city, set property tax rates, create boards and commissions to handle city issues, and enact policies and rules for the city so long as they are not prohibited by state or federal law.[24] Unlike general law cities, home rule cities are permitted to do anything unless *prohibited* by state law. This is referred to as "inherent power" and has been sanctified by the Texas Supreme Court. Any city in Texas with more than 5,000 people can become a home rule city. Most large cities in Texas have home rule (only 19 of the 309 cities with more than 5,000 Texans do not have home rule status).

charter: a city's governing document

A home rule city **charter** serves as the municipality's organizational plan, similar to a state or national constitution. A city charter establishes the form of government, sets the rules for operation and amendment, and establishes procedures for taxing and spending city finances. City government may amend the charter as needed. Citizens can force lawmakers on the city council to call an election and amend a city charter by filling out a petition signed by 5 percent of qualified voters or 20,000 (whichever is less). Indeed, one of the main advantages of home rule cities over general law cities is the mechanisms of direct democracy.

Initiative, Referendum and Recall.   Citizens of home rule cities have the power to initiate policy issues or recall local public officials. What are these powers? An **initiative** is a process through which local voters can directly propose ordinances to city charters. If the proper number of signatures is obtained (the number is set by the city), the initiative is placed on the ballot in an election, and if a majority of voters agree, the initiative becomes law. For example, voters in

initiative: a process where local voters can directly propose ordinances to city charters

Texarkana used an initiative to approve beer and wine sales in 2014, allowing them to keep pace with alcohol-selling kin on the Arkansas side of the city.[25]

Referendum enables voters to repeal existing ordinances that a city council won't rescind. Once citizens gather a sufficient number of signatures, the ordinance is put before the city council to either repeal on their own or to put to all voters for repeal. College Station, for example, used a referendum to submit to voters a plan to ban the use of red light cameras, unmanned digital cameras that photograph a vehicle running a red light. College Station citizens then voted to remove red light cameras by a slim 51 percent.[26]

referendum: a procedure through which local voters can repeal existing ordinances that a city council won't rescind

Recall enables voters to oust sitting members of the city government before their terms are up. Most cities only allow recalls after a council member has served for a set period and limits the number of recall attempts of the same councilperson. In each case, these powers are designed to give citizens greater control over local government. The year 2011 saw 150 recall elections nationwide, prompting the US Conference of Mayors to produce a documentary called "Recall Fever" to educate the public and elected officials on the process. In Texas the number of recall elections has spiked—fifty-five since 2011. Although few were successful in removing the public officials in question, the cities in question had to front the cost of these elections.[27]

recall: a process through which voters can oust sitting members of the city government before their terms are up

Annexation. The strongest power of a home rule city is **annexation**, the joining of land into the boundary of an existing city. Annexation authority is how big Texas cities become gigantic Texas cities. A larger city cannot annex incorporated land—land that is unified as part of a city—but rather targets *unincorporated* areas, which are often developing or ripe for development.

annexation: the joining of unincorporated land into the boundary of an existing city

Local Activist Barry Klein, Texas Property Rights Association

How can citizens use the initiative and referendum process to make a difference?

"Micro-politics holds the prospect of genuine and ever-renewing reform in the American political system. Currently the U.S. has in excess of 5,400 home rule cities. Most are small enough that five-person teams of grassroots reformers can quickly gather sufficient signatures to put propositions on a city ballot that amend the local charter. This can occur hundreds of times a year across the country, creating new norms of governance that would inevitably shape the policy discussions at higher levels of government."

SOCIAL RESPONSIBILITY: **Some municipalities have attempted to increase the number of signatures required to amend a city charter to give government more control over policy. Should the public have more or less direct control over city policy? Why?**

Annexation has several advantages to a home rule city. First, annexation provides a larger tax base for a city, thus enabling cities to benefit from the financial growth of outlying, usually suburban, areas. These growing cities pull in more taxpayers and become wealthier. In fact, if San Antonio had the same boundaries today as in 1945, it would have the highest poverty and unemployment rate of any city in the nation. Annexation of more territory expanded the city's revenue. Second, a city can guide the development of the land surrounding the city. This may benefit unincorporated areas by facilitating development and projects there. However, annexation may not be met with open arms by the residents concerned over longer response times for police and emergency services, rising tax rates, and a change in municipal services like trash pickup.

An unincorporated area or city is generally powerless to stop a larger city from annexing it into their territory. Larger cities do not need the permission of the residents of an area to annex it. This unilateral home rule prerogative has caused significant friction. Beginning in 1994, the city of Houston announced plans to annex an affluent suburb called Kingwood with over 50,000 residents. Protestors showed up in busloads in Austin to ask the legislature to halt Houston's expansion with banners that read "Free Kingwood." Residents offered $4 million to the City of Houston in exchange for the community's independence. Kingwood residents also filed a lawsuit charging that the annexation laws amount to taxation without representation, a familiar rallying cry of the American Revolution. All efforts failed and Kingwood was absorbed into Houston's city limits.[28]

In 1999, responding to concerns from residents in surrounding cities in danger of being gobbled up by larger cities faster than brisket at a barbeque, the Texas legislature enacted a major revision of the municipal annexation laws. These reforms required cities to develop a three-year annexation plan for areas with more than 100 residential dwellings in order to give property owners and service providers proper prior notice. The state also required that cities negotiate with property owners regarding provision of services.

Many unincorporated areas have found a way around full annexation. Under the 1999 reforms, cities were allowed to create agreements with local utility districts to charge a 1 percent sales tax in locations outside the proper city limits.[29] With city budgets more difficult to balance and outlying areas wary of full annexation, this is a backdoor way to solve the annexation quagmire. Cities also use extraterritorial jurisdiction (ETJ) laws to control subdivision practices in unincorporated bordering territory.[30] Businesses or developers seeking to build in those areas are subject to city rules and regulations. ETJ laws enable cities to have some say in development in those extended areas.

★ TEXAS TAKEAWAYS

3 How are general law cities different from home rule cities?

4 Why is annexation unpopular in many communities?

🤠 TYPES OF CITY GOVERNMENT

Today cities govern themselves in different ways: a mayor-council form, a council-manager form, and a commission form. Let's look at each type.

> **12.4** Classify the types of city government.

MAYOR-COUNCIL SYSTEM

In a **mayor-council system**, a mayor acts as executive and a city council acts as a legislative body, enacting ordinances and adopting rules. There are strong and weak mayor-council systems. In a weak-mayor system, the mayor has no formal authority to act outside of the council. The mayor lacks veto power, and other important city officers, such as the treasurer or department heads, are elected by the people.

mayor-council system: a system of local government headed by an elected mayor and a city council

In strong-mayor systems, the mayor has legislative powers (voting on many matters and presiding over city council meetings) and executive powers are often exercised unilaterally. The mayor can often take a wide range of independent action, with little input from the council or the public.

What are the sources of the mayor's power in a strong mayor-council system? First, in mayor systems, there are less formal separations of powers—the mayor leads the executive branch but also presides over and votes on matters before the city council. The mayor also appoints the city judiciary, major boards and commissions, and department heads. One city council member who frequently clashed with the mayor of her city found out the hard way that crossing the mayor won't yield any favors, especially coveted positions—she recalls the mayor saying "You're not on the team. People who aren't on the team don't get chairmanships."[31] In a strong mayor-council system, the mayor also prepares the annual budget for the city. The city council must vote on the budget and the city controller usually has an important say, but the mayor is the first and last to act, as he or she also executes the budget. Perhaps most importantly, the mayor sets the agenda for city council meetings.

Irving mayor Beth Van Duyne sparked a controversy when she placed an item on the agenda to have the council back a bill in the state legislature that would forbid judges from using foreign law in their rulings. Several council members felt that the agenda item targeted a local Islamic Center that was using the Islamic code to settle disputes in a nonbinding way. The mayor argued that Islamic leaders were "bypassing Americans courts."[32] Several council members disputed the need for such a measure and argued that it only served to increase religious tension. However, the council passed the resolution by a five to four vote.

Mayors' power to implement their agenda is limited by the city council and their own budgets. The city council must approve the annual budget, sign off on appointments of department heads, and certify significant reallocations of budget funds during a year. The mayor must have a majority of support on the city council, in both the mayor-council system and other systems of local

FIGURE 12.2   Scale of Mayoral Influence

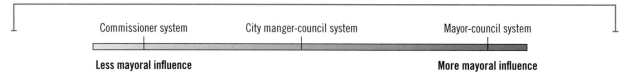

Commissioner system   City manger-council system   Mayor-council system

Less mayoral influence   **More mayoral influence**

 COMMUNICATION:

**How much influence does
a mayor have in the various
systems?**

- Mayors have the most influence in a mayor-council system, especially if it is a "strong" mayor system where the mayor is granted more executive power.
- Mayors have some but not great influence in a manager-council system and very little in a commissioner system.

CRITICAL THINKING:

**What distinguishes the types
of power mayors have?**

- In mayor-council systems, especially strong ones, mayors have legislative agenda control and executive ability to initiate policy or appoint officials.
- In council-manager systems and commissioner systems, mayors serve as figureheads, although their influence can be felt in political relationships and in marketing the city.

government (see Figure 12.2). Former City of Houston Mayor Bob Lanier found that by listening to the city council members, he could determine what policies would make the councilmembers popular in their home districts—goals he could help them secure. Perhaps because of this, Lanier lost as few as three council votes out of thousands during his tenure.[33]

Most mayors typically act in a nonpartisan fashion, often because they are elected as nonpartisans. Most city officials function as pragmatic problem solvers. One official noted that "a road is a road, and it doesn't care if you're a socialist or pro-life."[34] However, city officials often become ensnared in nonpartisan conflicts. City controllers (often called comptrollers) oversee and audit government finances, monitor compliance with laws, and serve vital efforts at transparency and credibility. In a high-profile instance, Houston city controller Ronald Green became concerned when a $1.5 billion expansion of Bush Intercontinental Airport planned to hire a firm that employed a sitting council member. In 2015, Green blocked the city council vote authorizing the project by not certifying city funds to fulfill the contracts.[35]

COMMISSION GOVERNMENT

A commission government is called the "Galveston Plan," as this form of government is a result of the catastrophic Galveston hurricane of 1900 that claimed more than 6,000 lives and caused millions of dollars in property damage. Community leaders feared the fragile island city might never recover its prosperity under the leadership of the city council at the time and persuaded the governor to appoint a commission during the rebuilding period. The commission served as the legislative and executive body for the city, handling taxation, appropriations, ordinances, and other functions.[36]

The commission form of government was popular in the early 1900s for its simplicity, nonpartisan approach, and merit selection. These features, however, also made it susceptible to corruption. Progressive reformers viewed the commission as a way to disenfranchise working class citizens and promote a business-friendly agenda by selecting commissioners cordial to industry. This government type was also highly influenced by political elites. The inefficient commission became steeped in patronage and ignored vital interests of the people, neglected basic city services, and was unresponsive to business concerns.[37] Today, no true commission form of government exists in Texas. Rather, most Texas cities, like San Antonio, that switched to a commission government early in the 1900s, changed to a more professional council-manager system later in the century.

COUNCIL-MANAGER SYSTEM

If you want to run a government like a corporation, a council-manager system is the best fit. In a **council-manager system**, the board of directors (the city council) acting on behalf of stockholders (the people) appoint a chief executive officer (city manager) to run city business. The **city manager** runs the day-to-day operations in the city, and serves as the chief administrator and budget officer for the city. The city manager's primary role is to enforce city regulations, supervise municipal employees and programs, execute the city budget, and prepare the agenda of the city council.

council-manager system: a system of local government in which the city council appoints a city manager to run city business

city manager: an administrator hired to run the day-to-day operations in a city

In a city manager system, the mayor and council members have no administrative duties. This does not mean they are unimportant. The city council sets all city policies, rules, and the budget. Mayors serve an important but largely symbolic role. They have only one vote and no veto power, but they can use their personality and popularity to push their agenda. Fort Worth Mayor Betsy Price rode her bicycle to "rolling town hall meetings" at different venues across the city to encourage other city residents to do the same—participate politically and stay fit at the same time.[38]

Dallas, the largest city to use the council-manager system of government, relies on its mayor as the chief salesperson for the business community, agenda setter for political issues, and advocate for the values of city residents. In 2016, for example, Mayor Mike Rawlings tried to prevent Exxxotica, a pornography exhibition, from appearing at the Kay Bailey Hutchinson Convention Center in downtown Dallas. The mayor requested the city attorney draft a resolution to direct the city manager not to enter into a contract with the organization to lease the space. The city's attorneys indicated such a move would be an

El Paso City Manager Tommy Gonzales was sanctioned for violating the city's ethics ordinance for his role in several city projects, including street repaving and other mobility projects.[†]

PERSONAL RESPONSIBILITY: **Should the standard for removal from office be the same for an elected official as for an unelected manager?**

unconstitutional violation of free speech.[39] So, the mayor put public pressure on the city council to ban the convention, which the city council did in an eight to seven vote. When challenged, a federal judge affirmed the decision.[40]

Studies show that growing cities often move from a mayor-council system to a council-manager arrangement.[41] This system is argued to provide a higher level of professionalism, continuity, and stability. In fact, about 90 percent of Texas home rule cities have a council-manager system.

One downside of the mayor-manager system is that it gives more power to the unelected officials than to the elected officials, allowing the city manager to set the agenda and enforce rules even over the objections of the elected city council. Cities, however, are at liberty to decrease the power of the city manager or fire him or her. As a result, many city council members prefer the manager system because it gives them greater control over city priorities and finances and avoids problems of mayors becoming too dictatorial.

Although the council-manager system is designed to get the politics out of government, it can invite corruption. One Dallas city manager approved a deal to sell land worth $1.7 million to major real estate developer Ray Hunt for $2,000. Hunt also did not want to pay property taxes on the land, so the city manager placed an item on the agenda to exempt the property from 90 percent of those taxes for ten years. The council approved by a vote of ten to five.[42]

Scholars have found failures to govern ethically may result in calls to move away from council-manager systems.[43] Larger cities outside of Texas frequently change to strong-mayor systems as a result. Dallas, however, overwhelmingly voted not to "take off the training wheels" and maintained its council-manager system.[44]

★ TEXAS TAKEAWAYS

5 What are the differences between a strong-mayor system and a weak-mayor system?

6 What is a disadvantage of council-manager government?

SPECIAL DISTRICTS

County and city government cover only a small fraction of the governments in Texas. **Special districts** make up the bulk of the local government in the state. These are single-purpose governments because they perform a specialized function, such as education, water supply, economic development, or hospital care.[45] These districts originated during the New Deal in the 1930s as a way to generate revenue and govern locally without having to sort through layers of state or local government. Special districts raise their funds from property taxes, giving way to concern about the rising tax burden from citizens. These governments operate in a set geographic area and are created because of an inability of other governments to provide a particular service. As Texas expands in population size and through urban growth, the battle to keep government small will be fought at the level of special districts, which is where government is growing rapidly.

> **12.5** Analyze the benefits and challenges of special districts.

special district: a single-purpose government that performs a specialized function

One advantage to these districts is that they specialize in a single issue or set of issues and allow residents' input into local decisions. Another advantage is that these districts do not require state funds, but rather can raise revenue on their own. A disadvantage is that they operate outside of the view of most citizens. These special districts are often referred to as "invisible governments" because they are less visible, but no less important, than city or county government.[46] Another disadvantage is possible inefficiency of overlapping services provided by city or county governments. Nationwide, there are more than 50,000 such districts. Texas relies heavily on these special districts (see Figure 12.3). Several types of special districts are highlighted below.

SCHOOL DISTRICTS

Texans interact most frequently with a special district we know as our local school district. There are 1,227 school districts in Texas. The number of school districts in Texas has declined as smaller, rural systems have been consolidated with larger ones. School boards of trustees oversee the school districts, managing schools and selecting superintendents. They make final decisions on district policies, personnel, textbooks, and budgets. Board members have exclusive power to govern and tax residents within the district and are elected usually to three to four year nonpartisan (candidates run without a political party affiliation) terms.

District authority extends to all aspects of education in the district, even naming schools. In a rash of reactions against Texas educational institutions named after Confederate military officers or segregationists, school districts tweaked their naming policies. In the Austin Independent School district, trustees voted unanimously to allow the school board to abolish controversial school names. Residents requested changing the names of several schools after confederate generals, like Robert E. Lee Elementary, most of which were named in the 1950s and 1960s when the district was forced to integrate its schools.[47]

IS IT BIGGER IN TEXAS?

FIGURE 12.3   **Special Purpose Districts Nationwide**

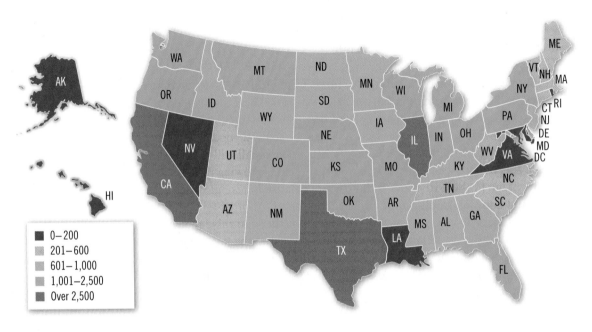

Legend:
- ■ 0–200
- ■ 201–600
- ■ 601–1,000
- ■ 1,001–2,500
- ■ Over 2,500

Source: US Census Bureau. Excludes school districts.

 COMMUNICATION:

How many special districts are there in each state?

- Texas is second only to Illinois and California in the number of special districts.
- Pennsylvania, Missouri, and Colorado follow Texas in the top six states with the most special districts.

 CRITICAL THINKING:

Why do some states have more special districts?

- Decentralized government allows for patronage at the local level, which is preferred by politicians in states with a larger urban population.
- Fast-growing states (especially with large suburban populations) with diverse local needs have expanded special districts for services like fire protection, sanitation, and public utilities.
- In Texas, local governments have taxing authority. As the state budget is less generous to local governments, special districts proliferate and raise money for local needs.

School districts also have exclusive control over what can be assigned to students within districts. In 2014, Highland Park Independent School District near Dallas, pressured by parents, banned seven books, including some Pulitzer Prize winners that depicted sexual intercourse, rape, abuse, and abortion. The board lifted the suspension within a week after national attention and criticism.[48]

SPECIAL IMPROVEMENT DISTRICTS

Special (or Public) Improvement Districts allow an area to levy and collect special assessments on properties for a limited range of services, including landscaping, construction, parking facilities, and improving streets and sidewalks. The Woodlands, Texas, north of Houston, has 110,000 residents. It is classified as a district, not a city, to the consternation of its residents. "It frustrates the hell out of me," said a board member complaining that these districts have "no power to do anything." Another resident expressed a desire for an incorporated city with a charter, "rather than a book of covenants that only tell you how far up the driveway your kid's in-ground basketball goal must be." However, state law was amended to allow the township board, which oversees city operations, to issue **municipal bonds** (like a bank loan paid back at a future date) and avoid annexation by Houston or Conroe until 2057.[49]

municipal bond: a debt security where a municipality takes out a loan to spend funds and agrees to pay the funds back, generally with interest

JUNIOR/COMMUNITY COLLEGE DISTRICTS

Texas has more than 50 locally governed community college or junior college districts (or boards) for institutions that offer vocational and academic courses for certification, continuing education, or associate degrees. The board sets district policy, the cost of tuition and fees, sets and modifies the budget, and creates the school calendar. A president or chancellor is hired by the board to govern day-to-day activities at the college.

LIBRARY DISTRICTS

The Texas Legislature in 1987 allowed the creation of districts to enhance community and economic development through various means. Library districts are designed to establish and maintain public libraries for public use. Like other special districts, library districts may request voter approval for a sales and use tax.

No one likes being bothered by the buzzing of mosquitoes. Mosquito control districts, an example of a special district, are permitted to tax residents to squish out mosquitoes.

SOCIAL RESPONSIBILITY: **Do the proliferation of districts to deal with smaller, targeted issues justify the considerable tax funds they are allowed to raise? Or should other larger government entities be responsible for these issues?**

MUNICIPAL UTILITY DISTRICTS (MUDS)

A MUD provides water, sewage, drainage, and other services within a fixed boundary. These districts deal primarily with the supply of water, including protection, conservation, and storage. A MUD can be created by the Texas Commission on Environmental Quality or by the legislature. These are distinct from water improvement districts or drainage districts, which are designed to provide for irrigation of land within the boundaries. Since a MUD district is the only government in many unincorporated areas, they have significant influence. MUD districts are popular among developers because MUDs can exclusively enter into cozy contracts with vendors or issue bonds related to district activities to cover the cost of development.[50] This may include solid waste disposal, parks, or swimming pools.

HOSPITAL DISTRICTS

Hospital districts provide for the creation, maintenance, and operation of hospitals. Districts have considerable financial power, including the ability to issue bonds, impose taxes (which cannot exceed 75 cents per $100 valuation on taxable property in the district). Hospital districts also have a considerable charge to implement and enforce state laws relating to access to health care, interpreting whether an individual qualifies for health care, and establishing mental health facilities.

HOMEOWNERS' ASSOCIATIONS

Although not technically a special district, homeowners' associations (HOAs) are one of the largest types of government in the state. Nearly five million people reside in HOAs statewide.[51] HOAs have government-like power to issue fines and foreclose on homes. Residents who live within the boundary of a HOA agree to a covenant of rules and pay a fee for community maintenance. Membership is not optional—if you live within the boundary, you play by their rules. HOAs are free to choose ancillary service companies and vendors, and are often strongly encouraged to use those partnered with the parent management company.[52]

State regulations control much of what homeowners' associations are allowed to govern. These interactions are often contentious, pitting homeowners against for-profit HOA contractors and their advocates, such as the Texas Community Association Advocates and the Community Associations Institute, who profit from HOA dues paid by residents. Industry officials have pushed back on residents of HOAs who have sought greater accountability and state oversight, and potential fines and prosecution of HOA board members who may develop cozy relationships with the management companies who run the HOAs.[53]

After several legislative sessions, sweeping changes to laws in 2012 now require HOAs to maintain open public records and hold meetings, post notices of board meetings, strengthen residents' voting rights, and allow greater public expression of opinion. Want to fly your Navy flag on Army–Navy football game day? Want to display your religious beliefs with symbols on your house? The law allows displaying of flags and religious displays. The legislation was changed partly in response to an incident where "a Jewish couple was threatened with a recurring fine for displaying a mezuzah, a parchment with Hebrew verses enclosed in a case affixed to the door post."[54] The new laws also established provisions to make sure deployed military don't unwittingly lose their homes while deployed, as happened in 2010 to an Army National Guard officer from Frisco.

TEXAS TAKEAWAYS

7 Why have "special districts" grown?

8 Which special districts deal with the supply of water, including protection, conservation, storage, irrigation, and drainage?

ELECTIONS

City and county elections can be either partisan or non-partisan elections. Voters tend to have little interest in these elections, and voter turnout is typically low—even though Texans interact closely with these governments. The outcome of these elections can vary widely as different electoral systems—countywide, citywide, or districtwide—have a significant effect on who gets elected and, in turn, who is represented.

12.6 Describe the process and challenges of local government elections.

COUNTY ELECTIONS

The county judge and commissioners are elected for four-year terms in partisan elections. Commissioners are elected to districts that divide the county into four geographic regions. County judges are elected countywide. Once county commissioners are elected, they often serve for a long period of time, being frequently reelected. Each county also elects a county sheriff every four years countywide. The positions of county attorney and district attorney are filled by partisan elections held every four years, as are positions for most administrative offices.

CITY ELECTIONS

Texas cities elect representatives in one of two ways. At-large members are elected citywide. These positions tend to be mayors, city comptrollers, and district attorneys. The **place system** elects council members from a citywide area

place system: an electoral system in which voters elect council members from a citywide area but that specifies a separate seat carved into districts

but specifies a separate seat carved into districts (referred to as "positions" or "places"). These elections are most often used for city council seats. Representation is largely determined by the electoral system. At-large elections tend to favor candidates who appeal to the majority of electors and who have the money to fund a citywide campaign. The place system tends to result in the election of representatives who are more concerned with voters' concerns in districts that council members represent.

MINORITY REPRESENTATION IN MUNICIPAL GOVERNMENTS

see for yourself 12.2

Watch Annise Parker talk about her journey to become the mayor of Houston.

Changing from one type of electoral system to another can create controversy. In 2014, Austin switched to a place system to elect the city council. Beginning in the 1970s, a "gentlemen's agreement" allotted two seats to racial minorities, but this arrangement did not yield a diversity that reflected the city's makeup. Half the city council and fifteen of the last seventeen mayors were elected from only four zip codes—out of seventy-eight total zip codes in the city.[55] The switch to a single member district place system increased the diversity of candidates and the diversity of those elected to the city council in terms of race and gender, and the public felt more involved in municipal government.

Other localities are moving from district representation to at-large representation, with much resistance. The city of Pasadena, east of Houston, former home to honky-tonk Gilley's of the movie *Urban Cowboy* fame, voted to replace two of its eight council seats with at-large seats. Hispanic leaders objected that the move would negate the clout of rising population numbers (the city is more than 60 percent Hispanic). Because Hispanic turnout is low in city elections, Anglos could outvote them in every election in a citywide race.[56]

cumulative voting: voters cast multiple votes (usually equal to the positions in an election)

Some localities have experimented with **cumulative voting** to help boost minority representation. Cumulative voting allows voters to cast as many votes as there are positions—so, if a board or commission had seven seats, voters would have seven ballots to cast. African American and Latino residents sued the city of Amarillo in 1995 claiming that the at-large system for electing school board and College Board members unfairly diluted minority influence. The groups settled out of court and agreed to implement a cumulative voting system which ultimately increased the minority representation on the boards. More recently, in 2016, Carrolton-Farmers Branch adopted cumulative voting in response to a legal challenge. Still, fewer than fifty municipalities conduct elections this way.

LOW TURNOUT IN MUNICIPAL ELECTIONS

Most Texans don't vote in general and even those that do vote regularly don't vote in local elections (see Figure 12.4). These elections are often held in May, separate from presidential and congressional elections that attract media attention. As a result, voters are often unfamiliar with the candidates and the issues and skip these elections altogether. Age makes a significant difference on

FIGURE 12.4 **Turnout in Local Elections in Selected Major Cities**

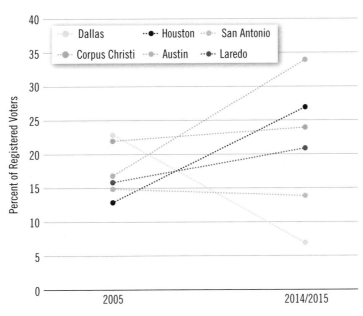

Source: County election websites. Turnout is percentage of registered voters.

 COMMUNICATION:

What percent of Texans turn out to vote in local elections?

- Turnout is generally low: fewer than a third, and usually no more than a quarter, of the electorate votes in local elections.
- Two cities had low or lower turnout in 2015 than 1995: Dallas and San Antonio.
- Houston and Austin both increased their turnout by more than 10 percent.

 CRITICAL THINKING:

Why is turnout in local elections so low?

- For Houston and Austin, election circumstances increased turnout: 2015 was a competitive mayoral race and featured a controversial ballot measure (see HERO above); 2014 was a presidential election year, likely driving up turnout in Austin and Laredo.
- Municipal elections often feature candidates who are more unfamiliar to voters than statewide or federal candidates.
- Local elections are often held in "off-year" elections (except Austin) so many voters don't show up to vote.

whether Texans vote in local elections. One study found that people over sixty-five were nineteen times more likely to vote in the primary elections and fourteen times more likely to vote in the general election than people ages eighteen to thirty-four.[57] Younger people are more transient, moving frequently, while older voters are more likely to live in their homes for longer, establishing roots. In many cases, only 10 to 15 percent of a city electorate is selecting leaders and voting on changes or creations of local laws. Low turnout can give those who do vote an outsized influence in local finances. In 2009, Allen, Texas, voters approved a major bond issue including $60 million for a massive new 14,000 seat football stadium by 1,000 votes out of 3,700 votes cast.

VOTING AND CORRUPTION

In 2016, all but one of the Crystal City, Texas, council members, including the mayor, city manager, city attorney, and mayor pro tem, were arrested on federal corruption charges alleging bribes to contractors wanting to do business with the city.[58] Referring to the self-made mess of city government, the executive of the Texas Municipal League said "there's no state agency that monitors this type of thing."[59]

Ultimately, voters are key players in keeping local government honest. In 2016, Denton County voters kicked out the incumbent sheriff, William B. Travis, after an investigation revealed that in the 1990s, as a Drug Enforcement Agency agent, Sheriff Travis fabricated evidence for a search warrant and had an affair with a high school-aged girl.[60]

 TEXAS TAKEAWAYS

9 Why don't Texans vote in local elections?

10 What is the difference between at-large elections and the place system?

ISSUES IN LOCAL GOVERNMENT

> **12.7** Identify problems facing local government and possible solutions.

Low turnout in local elections is one of many challenges facing local government in Texas. Let's explore a few more.

LOCAL GOVERNMENTS SHORT ON CASH

The size and functions of local government generally require them to have access to large budgets (see Figure 12.5). City and county operating budgets can run into the tens of millions of dollars to pay for all the services needed within their jurisdictions. Texas cities and counties can levy both property taxes and sales taxes. Most of that sales tax revenue goes to the state but about 1–2 percent is remitted to cities if they charge extra above the state's base tax rate. Home rule cities can also charge residents fees for various projects or businesses franchise fees.

FIGURE 12.5 **County Expenditures**

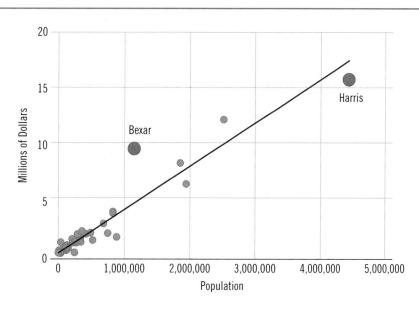

Source: Texas State Expenditures, Texas Comptroller of Public Accounts, 2014. The figure graphs expenditures and population. The fitted line is a linear representation of the two figures. Those counties above the line spent more than their population; those below spent less.

 COMMUNICATION:

Where do Texas counties rank on expenditures and population?

- Most counties are close to the line, showing a close correlation between expenditure and population. This means that they spend similar amounts per resident.
- Bexar County (San Antonio) and Harris County (Houston) are outliers.

 CRITICAL THINKING:

Why are some counties higher or lower than others?

- Bexar County spent considerable funds on public assistance (more than $2 billion), and so spends more per person.
- Harris County has budget restrictions in place that may limit city spending, keeping their spending below the mean.

Property taxes have long been a source of contention in Texas, especially because they are the single largest revenue generator in the state. Property tax receipts in 2015 were more than $50 billion from owners of everything from houses to commercial real estate. Special purpose districts had the fastest growing tax rate, increasing 74.3 percent over the past decade.[61] The state is not allowed to have a statewide property tax, or anything that resembles one. So some residents have argued that the high property tax rate charged by school districts amounts to an unconstitutional de facto state-mandated property tax, as we discuss in Chapter 13. Because of rising property taxes, some localities have placed a cap on property tax revenue. Moreover, during the 2015 session, the Texas legislature slashed billions of dollars from homeowners' taxes by increasing the exemption homeowners can claim (and the resulting taxes local government can collect).[62] This can create a squeeze of funds for local government.

Tax Increment Reinvestment Zones (TIRZs): special zones created to attract business and develop the economy within the geographic zone

One common way to generate additional revenue in city finances is **Tax Increment Reinvestment Zones** (or TIRZs). These are special zones created to attract business and develop the economy within the geographic zone. Taxes collected in these zones, however, are set aside to finance improvements within the boundaries of that zone, so the city may not collect a penny from the property tax revenue. As a result, these zones become private fiefdoms for trapping money for redevelopment in wealthy areas, often at the expense of poorer areas, and oversight is lax. Indeed, although the intent of the law was to help declining inner-city areas rehabilitate, TIRZs have quietly become a honeypot for developers to gain lucrative city subsidies.

RISING DEBT

In Texas, governments cannot spend more money than they receive in revenue, but they can accrue debt to fund activities. Texas cities and counties frequently issue debt for funding projects if they don't have the funds in the cookie jar. State and local governments that are short on cash can sell bonds to private investors with the promise to pay it back later with interest. Exploding population, the desire to keep taxes low, and the consequent tight budgets have caused local debt to skyrocket in recent years (see Figure 12.6). Bonds typically fund capital projects and long-term programs including highway construction, technology upgrades, water development, improvements to facilities, and even to service existing debt. Overall, in 2014, Texas local governments owed over $200 billion in debt.[63] The average debt per capita for Texans is about $600.[64]

Voters must approve of bond financing but do not always know what they are voting on. One solution is to require ballot propositions to include specific details about the project to be financed. An attentive public can halt more debt for undesirable projects. Indeed, this recently occurred in Montgomery County when voters rejected road bond proposals on two separate occasions (in 2014 and 2015). These proposals included a project that would have extended the Woodlands Parkway through undeveloped land, which would have worsened traffic conditions. Only after the bond proposal dropped the controversial parkway extension did it pass in late 2015.[65] City councils can also cap the total amount of debt available, although most

FIGURE 12.6 **Debt Per Capita by County**

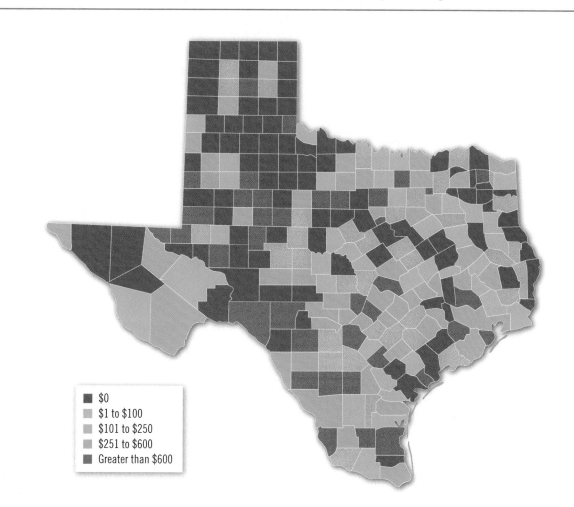

■ $0
■ $1 to $100
■ $101 to $250
■ $251 to $600
■ Greater than $600

Source: Texas Comptroller of Public Accounts. Debt statistics track per capita debt (including city, county, school districts, and community college districts).

 COMMUNICATION:

Which Texas counties have the most debt per capita?

- Loving County has the highest debt per capita ($215,465), but this is largely due to a small population (86 souls in 2014).

 CRITICAL THINKING:

Why do some counties have higher debt rates?

- Growing suburban counties (like Williamson, Hayes, Fort Bend, and Rockwall) have larger than average debt per capita.

- Counties with large capital investment projects (like Galveston or Bexar) also have a high amount of public debt.

TABLE 12.1	Debt in Major Texas Cities
CITY	PER CAPITA DEBT
Houston	$1,460
Dallas	$1,218
San Antonio	$1,040
El Paso	$1,541
Austin	$1,473
Fort Worth	$968
Arlington	$931
Corpus Christi	$1,384

Source: Texas Comptroller's Office.

COMMUNICATION:

Which cities have higher debt?

- El Paso ranks highest in public debt, followed by Austin and Houston.
- Although smaller than many large cities, Corpus Christi has a significant debt per capita rate.

CRITICAL THINKING:

Why do some cities have higher debts than others?

- El Paso has undertaken several "quality of life" improvements, financed by debts, including improving streets, building a children's hospital, and moving city hall to make room for a new baseball stadium.[66] Corpus Christi has also spent funds on infrastructure improvement projects.
- Austin's population has exploded in the past twenty years and debt is being used to finance construction of new roads and maintenance on old ones, renovation to libraries, and a new fire station.
- Houston has a massive pension debt that needs to be funded, a booming car population hungry for more roads, and strict limits on revenue receipts (from property taxes), requiring significant debt financing.

have not—it is difficult to curb politicians' appetite for bond-financed revenue (see Table 12.1).

Eventually, the state may be forced to pick up the tab for the interest on the debt, local government may have to raise taxes to pay for some debt, and cities may face a reduced credit rating for large debt financing making it harder to borrow funds in the future. "This is a pervasive problem at every single level," former State Comptroller Susan Combs insisted. "Nobody gets off scot-free on this."[67]

COOPERATION ACROSS GOVERNMENTS

Cooperation between local governments is challenging. The overlapping and interconnected elements of local governments may create duplicated efforts to address some needs or not enough attention to others as one government assumes another is handling the issue. Reform efforts or tackling major issues across boundaries may be more challenging because of this confusing web. These interactions are especially troublesome considering competing interests and the struggle for scarce budget resources. Conflict and poor communication may hinder planning efforts across these thousands of special districts, county governments, and city governments. For instance, the city of San Antonio pockets $40 million in annual revenue from energy fees in unincorporated city areas that it does not share with Bexar County.[68] The city benefits to the detriment of the county.

Cooperation does occur, but is often program specific rather than issue specific. The city of Houston and Harris County worked on a joint library project, a pauper's cemetery, a spaying and neutering program for stray dogs, and a voter approved city-county inmate processing center.[69] Teaming up to solve homelessness or access to health care facilities is less likely because of the cost and expansiveness of the problems.

One solution to this lack of coordination is **councils of governments (COGs)**. A COG is a regional planning commission made up of area-wide local governments. They are not like city government—they do not have the power to tax, collect fees, establish ordinances, or take on debt. Rather COGs work with local governments, the private sector, and state and federal agencies to address specific challenges, such as solid waste disposal, services for the elderly, specialized transit systems, regional 9-1-1 systems, as well as more general goals like economic development. Texas has twenty-four COGs, each covering a different region of the state.

councils of governments (COGs): a regional planning commission made up of area-wide local governments

SPRAWL

Thanks to permissive annexation laws, Texas cities are expanding rapidly. Suburban residents who have moved out of the immediate metropolitan area to escape the city are "clawed back into it—and often compelled to pay higher property taxes."[70] **Sprawl** creates several problems. It makes commuting difficult as people begin to live farther from the city center. More congestion on the roads leads to more cars and fossil fuel emissions. Growth of residential and commercial properties edges out nature, forcing wildlife to seek refuge in manicured yards and crawl spaces and tempting them with leftovers scrounged from trash cans. Habitat destruction has even shooed off bumblebees that are crucial to pollinating native and commercial plants, and so responsible for $15 billion in crop pollination.[71] Development reduces open green space and may contribute to flooding in some areas.

sprawl: rapid growth of urban and suburban areas spreading into the undeveloped land surrounding it

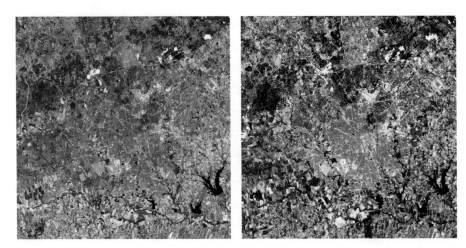

Sprawl in San Antonio has accompanied tremendous population growth, almost a million people in twenty years. Photo dates: June 16, 1991 and June 4, 2010.

SOCIAL RESPONSIBILITY: **Do cities and counties have a responsibility to manage sprawl? What is the proper balance between growth and management of the problems of sprawl?**

There has been pushback to creeping sprawl. Developers are finding older areas to develop closer to the city core. Cities are encouraging pedestrian-friendly developments closer to the city. Cities like Waco are creating plans to improve city infrastructure, revitalize its downtown area, and create a positive image for the city. Cities are turning to mass transit, even in car-loving Dallas and Houston.

TO ZONE OR NOT TO ZONE

City governments control and regulate the development of land through zoning. Zoning rules, for example, prohibit the erection of oil derricks next to multimillion dollar mansions—and massage parlors next to churches. Zoning regulations exist in every major Texas city except Houston. In a mix of vibrancy, can-do spirit, unbridled capitalism, and a distrust of government oversight, Houston is the only major city in Texas, and the United States, without a formal zoning code.[72] Proponents of no zoning argue that economic forces, rather than arbitrary rules, should govern development. Those opposed, including homeowners and many in the business community, argue that the ascetics of development require some government oversight. Houston instead relies on a mash of city regulations, "buffering" ordinances that restrict tall buildings next to major activity centers, and deed restrictions that create a net of control over development. Formal rules establishing zoning have been rejected by Houston voters three times.[73]

PENSIONS

One benefit to working for a local government is a pension when you retire. Local government employees such as police, firefighters, municipal workers, and teachers pay into a fund while employed by a city and receive benefits upon retirement. But with city budgets financially strapped, meeting obligations to pensions can be a challenge. Some pension plans are paying out more than they take in because those receiving pensions are living longer and extracting more funds.

Major Texas cities are in big financial trouble over pensions: Dallas has $5 billion in commitments that it doesn't have assets to pay, Houston has $5.6 billion, Fort Worth has $1.2 billion.[74] Cities are stuck: voters won't approve tax hikes to pay for pension costs, because paying more into pensions means less for police, fire, and road repair; beneficiaries currently in the funds don't want to make changes to their future benefits or pay more; and credit raters lambast city mayors for bad economic practice.

Complicating the problem is that cities don't have full control over the pensions—they share this power with the state legislature. In the previous four sessions, attempts by the Texas legislators to give more local control on pension issues was met with opposition. Individuals currently paying into the system object because they fear local governments would dramatically restructure the pensions to cost more and pay out less. The two major political parties are also split on this issue. Democrats, funded by the powerful unions who are the primary recipients, oppose local control while Republicans, looking for market solutions and to get a handle on spiraling costs, back local control.

How will Texas fix its pension problem? Current employees may be asked to pay more or have health benefits altered. Retirement ages may be raised. Retired employees may be asked to take less, especially in the form of lower cost of living adjustments.

 TEXAS TAKEAWAYS

 Why are local governments short on funds?

 How do local governments cooperate?

THE INSIDER VIEW

Local governments are "creatures" of state government as local government frequently grapples with restrictive state laws and oversight. The state has eased its domineering ways over local governments as home rule gives cities more authority, but the friction between state and local government remains. Beyond their clash with state government, local governments also confront other problems and are often handicapped by powerful forces beyond their control. Local governments are hemmed in by tight budgets, the public who disapproves of high taxes but demands quality services, interest groups (especially business groups), and the bureaucracy that enforces city rules. Local governments expand their authority as they seek to find new revenue sources as state funds shrivel and resident demands grow. The resulting issues, such as sprawl, annexation, and the growth of smaller subgovernments, manufacture more friction as cities battle rising demand for services and cries from taxpayers about the strain on their pocketbooks. Cities criticize the state for keeping their funding ability on a leash. Cooperation across cities, coordination between governments, and increasing voter participation all attempt to remedy the growing pains of the urban state Texas is rapidly becoming.

TEXAS TAKEAWAYS

1 Local governments provide an extensive range of services to the community spanning social, economic, environmental, recreational, and cultural. These usually relate to streets, sanitation, and safety.

2 Each Texas county is run by a county judge and a commissioner's court made up of four county commissioners.

3 General law cities have limited authority to make laws of their own, whereas home rule cities can largely govern themselves.

4 An unincorporated area or city is generally powerless to stop a larger city from annexing it into its territory. Annexation is occasionally done against the will of the community being annexed.

5 The mayor in a strong-mayor system can take a wide range of independent action, but in a weak-mayor system, the mayor has no formal authority to act outside of the council.

6 The council-manager system grants more power to the unelected officials than to the elected officials. The system can also invite corruption.

7 Special districts have grown because local government has passed off many of these functions to special districts and these districts are free to generate their own tax revenue.

8 Municipal Utilities Districts (MUDs) deal with the supply of water, including protection, conservation, storage, irrigation, and drainage.

9 Local elections often receive little media attention, include unfamiliar candidates or issues, and are held in years that are not presidential years.

10 Holders of at-large offices are elected by the voters in the whole territory. The place system elects individuals from separate seats carved into districts.

11 Local governments are short on funds because the state has reduced local property taxes and has not provided additional funds to make up these losses. Rising debt and pension payments are also eating up local government budgets.

12 Teaming up on specific projects and councils of governments are two ways that local governments may cooperate.

KEY TERMS

annexation
charter
city manager
council-manager system
councils of governments (COGs)
cumulative voting
Dillon's rule
general law city
home rule city
initiative
mayor-council system
municipal bond
ordinances
place system
preemption
recall
referendum
special district
sprawl
Tax Increment Reinvestment Zones
unincorporated area

PRACTICE QUIZ

1. Where does Texas rank regarding the number of local governments, compared to the other states?
   a. Lower than most
   b. About the same as most
   c. A little higher than most
   d. A lot higher than most

2. What are the two (2) administrative entities in each Texas county?
   a. County judge; commissioner's court
   b. Mayor; board of directors
   c. City councilors; town councilors
   d. Administrative judge; county judge

3. Which of the following is the city-level equivalent to a constitution?
   a. "Play Book"
   b. "Book of Local Laws and Ordinances"
   c. "City Constitution"
   d. "Charter"

4. What is the process called whereby a home rule city joins unincorporated land into the boundary of an existing city?
   a. Annexation
   b. Zoning
   c. Reconfiguring
   d. Redistricting

5. All of the following are exclusive powers of home rule cities, compared to general law cities, **except**
   a. Considering and passing initiatives
   b. Amending the state constitution
   c. Considering referenda
   d. Recalling city councilors

6. The system in which mayors have the least amount of influence is
   a. Council-manager system
   b. Mayor-council system
   c. Commissioner system
   d. None of the above

7. Special districts make up little of the local government in the state.
   a. True
   b. False

8. At-large city council members are elected citywide.
   a. True
   b. False

9. County sheriffs are elected.
   a. True
   b. False

10. For Texas, more local governments are created to deal with specific problems or issues.
    a. True
    b. False

[Answers: D, A, D, A, B, C, B, A, A, A]

Two weeks before the close of the 2015 legislative session, the heat was on to finalize the state budget. Governor Abbott had promised to reduce business taxes and Lieutenant Governor Dan Patrick had pledged to reduce property taxes. The Texas House insisted on cutting sales taxes. Some senators worried that Texas might underfund public employee pensions and critical transportation. Patrick also promised to dramatically build up border security—a move that would increase state spending.

Senate Finance Chair Jane Nelson, the senate's point person primarily responsible for writing the budget, along with her house counterpart John Otto worked day and night to resolve disagreements about how much to spend and where. When CEOs of large businesses plied Nelson with their budget concerns, she retorted, "Could you put together a $210 billion budget in six months?"[1] At the eleventh hour, Senator Kevin Eltife griped that the budget in committee left $15 to $20 billion in state funds unspent while public employee pensions were going underfunded. An irritated Senator Nelson snapped, "Well, have you filed a bill? . . . Go file a bill, senator."[2]

Why all the tension? It is because budgets matter—they determine the scope of taxes Texans pay and shape public policy. The battle over the budget is a war over policy priorities. The state legislature can pass any bill they want, but if the bill doesn't get signed by the governor or does not get funded, then the executive branch has no way to carry it out. According to journalist Paul Burka, the art of crafting a budget lies in "plucking the goose so as to get the most feathers with the least hissing."[3]

LEARNING OBJECTIVES

13.1	Distinguish the types of taxes and revenue sources.
13.2	Outline the state budget cycle.
13.3	Describe the social welfare programs Texas administers.
13.4	Analyze the role of the state in border issues and immigration.
13.5	Evaluate the challenges facing Texas's education system.
13.6	Assess Texas's transportation policy and future challenges.
13.7	Explain the state's environmental and energy policy.

● The complexities of budgets and policy in Texas often get sorted out on the floor of the state legislature, under the watchful eye of paintings of past Texas leaders.

In this chapter, we examine the nuts and bolts of state finance to uncover the political struggle involved in who, what, and how to tax—and how to spend the revenue collected from taxes and other sources. We then examine where Texans stand on health care, welfare, education, transportation, energy, and environmental policy. The confrontations on these issues divide along familiar battle fronts: partisanship, geography, and economic interests.

TAXES AND OTHER REVENUE SOURCES

13.1 Distinguish the types of taxes and revenue sources.

revenue: the income a state receives from taxes, fees, and other sources

Nobody likes paying taxes, especially Texans. Yet taxes are essential as they make up the funds the state and local governments use to operate. The state's **revenue** is primarily tax-funded, approximately 47 percent in 2015, although other funds are drawn from fees levied on the public, proceeds from the state lottery, and—as we saw in Chapter 3—receipts from the federal government.[4] Texas has hundreds of types of taxes, including unusual ones like a use tax for moving in a boat from another state and using it in Texas. Unlike many other states, Texas does not collect income tax. As a result, Texas is primarily a two-tax state (see Figure 13.1): property taxes and sales taxes. Property taxes are assessed locally and stay local for use by school boards, counties, and cities. Sales taxes are sent to the state government for use in the state budget, although cities are allowed to assess and keep additional sales tax revenue. These two major taxes, along with other assorted taxes and fees, form the state's tax base.

SALES TAX

Since 1967, the sales tax has served as the state's largest single source of tax income.[5] The state sets the rate at 6.25 percent and local government can add up to 2 percent to this (most of which do). These base funds are collected for use by the state, while the extra sales tax funds are returned to cities by the comptroller for city projects and programs. Some cities impose other dedicated sales taxes for specific purposes like mass transit, economic development, or building sports venues. Consumers pay most of these sales taxes (59 percent) while businesses pay the balance (41 percent).

regressive tax: a tax that exacts a larger percentage of the earnings of low-income than of high-income individuals

Sales tax is a **regressive tax**, because the tax rate is the same for everyone. This tax gobbles up a larger percent of the income of the poor and working

FIGURE 13.1 **Texas: A Two-Tax State: Property and Sales Taxes**

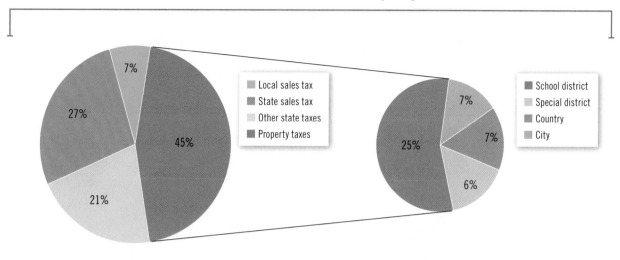

Source: Texas Comptroller of Public Accounts.

COMMUNICATION:

Where does tax revenue come from in Texas?

- Texas is a two-tax state: most revenue comes from property taxes (45 percent), which funds local governments, followed by sales taxes (27 percent) used by the state.

- Property taxes are collected primarily by school districts (25 percent) but cities, counties, and special districts also levy small amounts.

CRITICAL THINKING:

Why these sources?

- A tax on overall income is prohibited by the constitution and is politically unsavory to politicians in the current no-tax-increase climate.

- Property taxes have historically driven tax revenue for local governments. As the state's needs have expanded, the number and amount of these taxes has multiplied.

class than it does of the wealthiest Texans. Let's say you make $10,000 and spend $3 on sales tax at the grocery store. That $3 is going to be a larger portion of your total income ($10,000) than if you make $100,000. As a result, the poor and working class residents pay on average 12 percent of their income while the wealthiest pay just 3 percent. Texas relies more heavily on this regressive tax than most other states (see Figure 13.2).

Another downside to the sales tax is that collections fall when the economy takes a downturn. Falling oil prices reduced collections by 5 percent in 1983,

IS IT BIGGER IN TEXAS?

FIGURE 13.2   **State and Local Sales Taxes, 2016**

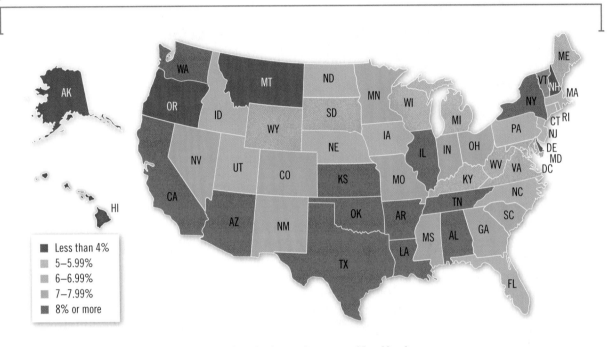

Less than 4%
5–5.99%
6–6.99%
7–7.99%
8% or more

Source: Tax Foundation. Figures represent combined sales tax for state and local levels.

 COMMUNICATION:

Where does Texas rank on sales tax rates?

- States with the largest sales tax include Texas, Illinois, California, New York, and Oklahoma.

 CRITICAL THINKING:

Why are some states higher and some lower?

- Texas has no income tax, so sales taxes are higher to generate revenue. This is also true for other states with no income tax like Tennessee and Washington.

- Sales taxes have gone up most in states where governors have made a push to reduce income taxes, such Arkansas.[6]

- States in economic distress have increased reliance on sales taxes, such as Illinois and California.

- Sales taxes are higher in states that rely more heavily on tourism, including Montana and Florida.

the economic slide in the wake of the terrorist attacks of September 11, 2001, reduced collections by 2 percent, and the national recession in 2009 dropped receipts by 3 percent.[7]

PROPERTY TAX

The battle over property tax is older than Texas dirt, going back to the days when the Mexican government's decision to eliminate property tax exemptions—previously used to attract Anglo settlers—sparked the Texas Revolution.[8] From the period of the Civil War to the Great Depression, properties were undervalued and tax collection was sporadic due to corruption among local tax collectors and inaccurate record keeping. Even so, property taxes have in the past supplied between 50 percent and 75 percent of tax revenue.

Property taxes (called *ad valorem*, meaning "according to value") are assessed based upon the value of the property the taxpayer owns. Although the state outlawed state-based property taxes in 1982, local governments use property tax revenue to fund schools, utility systems, fire and police protection, public libraries, parks, and other services. Most of the revenue from property taxes supports public schools and the state kicks in the rest. Property tax revenue is collected locally and—for the most part—stays local.

Property tax burdens are high today primarily because the state has no statewide income tax that could be shared with local governments, which consequently use the property tax revenue for projects and services. The largest jump in the source of revenue collected from taxpayers has been in the collection of property taxes—these increased from $15 billion (4.3 percent of revenue) in 1994 to $45 billion (45 percent of revenue) in 2013.[9] Why? A growing economy pushes up property values and the proliferation of special purpose districts means entities are allowed to tax residents (see Chapter 12).

The state constitution provides a **homestead exemption**, a portion of property value that home-owning Texans don't have to pay taxes on. Every Texan homeowner receives an exemption of $25,000 on their homes. Districts provide a $10,000 exemption for those over 65 and for veterans. Local governments may also offer an additional $3,000 (or more) exemption for disabled individuals.

homestead exemption: a portion of property value that Texans don't have to pay taxes on

Think your property taxes are too high? Protest it! Local governments appraise, or estimate, the value of property, whether it be a home, a commercial property, a ranch, or an oil refinery. Appraisal districts at the county level establish a review board that sets appraisal rates and hears property owner protests. The county tax assessor calculates the taxes, prepares the tax rolls, and generates bills, while the county tax collector facilitates payment. Every county has a process whereby taxpayers can challenge a property estimate, either online or in person. An appraiser will reassess and issue a new evaluation.

Property value is at the heart of rising property taxes. In Big Spring, Philip Dominguez bought an 800 square foot, run down old house for $6,000. In 2015, the county appraised the house at $25,000, a 316 percent jump in price and tripling the property taxes. An economic downturn in rural Texas

Big Spring homeowners protest against an appraisal hike on their homes which were of modest value.

SOCIAL RESPONSIBILITY: **Should there be limits on housing appraisals for individuals or groups who are less able to pay? The elderly? Veterans?**

kept wages down but taxes high. "If I could sell my home for what the property's valued at," said one Big Spring resident, "I'd get the hell out of here."[10] Across the state, low-income families and older Texans are worried about being taxed out of their homes.

The homestead exemption highlights the often tense relationship between local authority and state oversight. The legislature can only lower the homestead exemption and set limits for property value appraisal, but it cannot not appraise. This is politically frustrating for state representatives because efforts to reduce taxes require local counties to limit rising appraisals. In 2016, housing evaluations increased 11 to 15 percent in some areas of Texas. The state legislature took a big bite out of the local property taxpayers' bills, by increasing the homestead exemption from $15,000 to the current $25,000. But rising evaluations at the local level meant taxpayers saw only small tax cuts, between $125 and $150 on average. The cuts provided a windfall for homeowners in rural and South Texas but only mild relief to those with rapidly rising home values in suburban areas.[11]

FRANCHISE (BUSINESS) TAXES

The franchise tax (or "margins" tax) is the state's main business tax that flows to state coffers, amounting to about 9 percent of total tax receipts in 2015. Corporations, partnerships, business trusts, limited liability companies, and other businesses pay this tax of 0.5 percent to 1 percent of their total revenue. Most small businesses and nonprofits are not subject to this tax since the intent of the tax is to generate revenue from larger corporations. The legislature is constantly tinkering with this tax, often using it as a way to increase revenue to cut taxes paid by individuals or to balance budgets. In prosperous economic times, the state legislature often reduces the tax to keep Texas competitive. In 2015, the legislature cut the rate by a massive 25 percent.

OIL AND NATURAL GAS TAXES

Taxes on oil and natural gas (called "severance" taxes for the removal of oil from Texas land) come in two forms: oil regulation tax and oil production tax.[12] Together, these amounted to 5.6 percent of tax revenue and almost $3 billion in 2015. The state has kept the oil tax rate unchanged since 1951, a reflection of the friendly relationship between the oil and energy industries and Texas politicians.[13]

The amount of revenue Texas receives from severance taxes is connected to international events, technology, and natural occurrences. International events such as price spikes, threats from oil rich countries, or increasing demand cause price fluctuations. In 2005, Hurricane Katrina devastated the industry's pipelines, platforms, and other facilities, leading to significant production losses and less tax revenue. The technological innovation of hydraulic fracturing (or "fracking") increased production greatly in west Texas, increasing tax intake for the state.

CAR TAXES: MOTOR FUEL TAX ("GAS" TAX) AND MOTOR VEHICLE TAXES

The state imposes a gas tax on gasoline, diesel fuel, and liquefied gas. The more you drive, the more gas tax you pay. The state charges 20 cents per gallon. Five cents goes to public education, the rest goes to road-related projects. The gas tax has remained unchanged since 1991. During this time, however, construction materials (like pavement) and labor costs have increased (for building roads) while cars are more fuel efficient so Texans are buying less gas. Realistically, these taxes need to keep pace with the cost of building and maintaining roads, but as a former Republican state senator noted, "Nobody has the stomach to raise taxes."[14] In fact, in 2014, after Republican State Senator John Carona pushed to allow local governments to increase the tax, he lost his seat.

You also pay a motor vehicle tax that is levied when you buy a car, rent a car, or buy a manufactured (mobile) home. This amounted to about 9 percent of the state revenue in 2015.

"sin" taxes: taxes imposed on the sale of alcohol and tobacco and on some forms of gambling, and fees imposed on "sexually oriented" businesses

SIN TAXES

"Sin" taxes are imposed on the sale of alcohol and tobacco and on some forms of gambling, and fees are imposed on "sexually oriented" businesses (charging $5 for patrons of live nude shows). These taxes accounted for only 4.6 percent of total revenue in 2015, but are also levied as a deterrent to what lawmakers consider harmful behavior.[15] The cost is often factored into the cost of the liquor, beer, or cigarettes bought, so customers are not always aware they are paying the tax. State lawmakers see the "sin" tax as politically easier to swallow than other forms of taxes, especially in tough budget times. Since 2000, all states collectively increased taxes on cigarettes 125 times, alcohol 31 times, but sales taxes only 21 times.

Texas has taxed liquor since the Great Depression (1935), the only tax revenue that didn't decline in the economic calamity during that time. Today, the tax on liquor is 6.7%. The legislature repealed alcohol taxes for adult beverages sold on trains and airplanes.

SOCIAL RESPONSIBILITY: **Is it fair to levy taxes on certain products which a select few deem to be more harmful to society? Why?**

FEES AND FINES

fee: a payment for a
service rendered

Every time you turn around, you're paying a **fee** in Texas. The state has hundreds of fees—vehicle registration, state park admission, permission to sell fireworks, medical fees (like a facilities access fee, exam fees, and waste disposal fees), court costs, and even licensing fees for certain professions. The state also assessed fees for business, such as air pollution control fees, oil and gas regulation and cleanup fees, and waste treatment inspection fees. Fees are generally small but add up to big revenue. In fiscal year 2015, fees collected amounted to almost $10 billion, up from $4 billion in 1995. Fees go either to general revenue or to recoup the cost of a service provided by a program or agency.

fine: a financial
punishment for an offense

Fines also flow into the state's coffers. Fines Texans pay for violating certain traffic laws have swirled higher, especially for speeding, driving while intoxicated, or driving without a license. For instance, El Paso made $11 million each year between 2011 and 2014 on fines for traffic violations.[16] Some Texans just can't or won't pay. Of the $3.4 billion in fees that have been levied over the last decade, less than half has been collected. Nearly 1.3 million Texas drivers have an invalid license due to spiraling penalties from past infractions.[17] If these fees are not paid, the penalties get worse. In one well-publicized event, a 67-year-old woman paid nearly $25,000, spent four weeks in jail, and lost her driver's license because of a DWI in 2004.[18] The City of Amarillo has jailed people, including the elderly and disabled, for not paying city fines.[19] Bipartisan critics argue this is unfair to poor Texans.

THE RAINY DAY AND OTHER FUNDS

A small percentage of revenue is generated through several state funds. Ever sock away a little extra payday cash for the future? Texas does. In 1988, after Texas emerged from a major recession in 1983 that rocked the state's economy, the state established the Economic Stabilization Fund (ESF), almost always referred to as the "Rainy Day Fund." The fund is drawn from oil and natural gas production tax revenue. Leftover (surplus) unspent funds at the end of each year and interest on the balance of the fund are also pooled back into the Rainy Day Fund.[20] Currently, the fund is flush with north of $11 billion.

Spending the Rainy Day Fund has become a political hot spur. Hoarding the money in the Rainy Day Fund has become a badge of political honor and spending funds from the "sacred" fund may provoke an outcry from budget-conscious primary voters. Many argue the state has underfunded transportation and education in the name of fiscal conservatism and should use these funds to better address the fast-growing state's needs.[21] Legislators are reluctant to spend the money for fear of political retribution, but are comfortable asking voters to approve of changes to the distribution of funds. In 2015, voters approved a constitutional amendment diverting one-half of the funds that would normally go to the Rainy Day Fund to the State Highway Fund.

Other state funds include the State Highway Fund, the Texas Mobility Fund, the Property Tax Relief Fund, individual trust funds from past budget funds squirreled away, bond proceeds, interagency contracts, and certain revenue held in higher education accounts.[22]

WHY NO INCOME TAX?

When Democrats floated the idea of establishing an income tax in 1993, Lieutenant Governor Bob Bullock declared that Texas would get an income tax when a Russian submarine sailed up the Houston Ship Channel.[23] The concept of income tax runs against the grain of the individualistic political culture that most Texans embrace. It is a **progressive tax**: the more a person earns, the more a person pays. A progressive tax theoretically takes a larger percentage of income from someone earning more money than someone earning less money—this is based on a concept of "ability to pay." So, from one perspective, income taxes punish those who make more

The state lottery brought in $1.2 million in 2015 which goes to support public education and programs benefitting Texas veterans. Critics claim that it preys on financially vulnerable Texans or oppose it on religious grounds.

PERSONAL RESPONSIBILITY: **Should the state limit individual lottery purchases to protect people from themselves? What rules might it use?**

money. Others argue that an income tax is fairer to low salary earners since they would pay a lower tax rate on their comparatively smaller salaries. This would make the tax proportional to an individual's ability to pay. Polling suggests that the public is almost uniformly against a state income tax—94 percent oppose.[24]

progressive tax: a tax with a rate that increases as the amount that is taxed rises

    Fiscal conservatives also argue that avoiding a state income tax maintains the state's economic edge. Texas, however, is one of only seven states with no income tax. Income taxes provide a more stable funding source than sales taxes, particularly in sour economic times when consumers tighten their grip on their pocketbook.

DEBATES OVER TAXES

The ongoing mission to set low taxes and provide modest services butts up against legal constitutional requirements for state financing of education and persistent demands for governmental assistance on health care or social welfare programs. With sizable chunks of the population wanting to cut every type of tax (see Figure 13.3), deciding which taxes to cut creates political problems. In 2015, Lieutenant Governor Dan Patrick's "everybody's a winner" tax package increased the homestead exemptions, thus cutting property taxes for individual Texans.[25] But business interests bristled as the tax burden shifted slightly off individual Texans onto businesses paying franchise taxes.[26] After not a small amount of scuffling, Governor Abbott signed over $4 billion in property tax and franchise tax relief.

FIGURE 13.3   **Tax Attitudes in Texas**

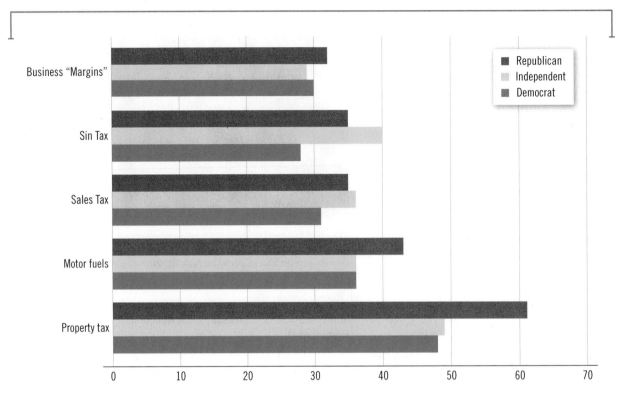

Source: Texas Politics Polling, February 2015.

 COMMUNICATION:

What taxes do Texans want cut?

- Property taxes are the tax most Texans across the ideological spectrum want cut.
- In general, Republicans are more likely to desire tax cuts than other groups. Democrats are less likely than Republicans or independents to desire to cut specific taxes.

 CRITICAL THINKING:

Why are property taxes the villain, especially for Republicans?

- Rising housing valuations and spiking property taxes grew to a fevered pitch in 2014 and 2015 and Texans looked for relief.
- Republicans believe in smaller government, so tax cuts fit naturally into that ideology. Republican political leaders have also made cutting taxes a major part of their appeal to voters, and Republicans in the state have followed.
- Texas Democrats look for ways for the state to invest in key services, like roads, education, and health care. They would rather pay more in taxes than see essential state services cut.

Some tax cuts have long-term budgetary effects that are not easily undone. For example, when Governor Bush made good on his pledge to cut property taxes in 1999, the state eventually had to balance out the loss of revenue by adding more items to the list of sales taxable goods and raising taxes on cigarettes, alcohol, and utilities.[27] Any reduction in revenue (through a tax cut) requires the legislature make up the funds elsewhere—which, as we are about to see—is not an easy task.

TEXAS TAKEAWAYS

1 What is a regressive tax?

2 What is the exempted portion of the property tax bill called?

3 In what year was the gas tax last changed?

 THE BUDGET

Most state tax revenues, fees, and other revenue are banked in **general revenue funds** that are channeled into the all-funds budget that also includes federal funding. Then the Texas legislature allocates—divvies up—the funds—which is not an easy job. Former Lieutenant Governor Bill Hobby famously stated that "the main business of the legislature is passing the budget; the rest is poetry."[28] The budget process is complicated, constrained by limits on spending, and rife with conflicts between groups, parties, and branches of government.

13.2 Outline the state budget cycle.

general revenue funds: state funds that include revenue from all sources (including federal funds)

BUDGET CYCLE

Each session, lawmakers pass a budget that is implemented in the following two fiscal years. Before 1942, budgets were approved for programs and departments without regard to the state's total biennial budget, leading to fiscal chaos.[29] Today, budget rules structure the budget process, but budgeting for two years is a challenge since the economy may tank, programs may fail, state priorities may change, or revenue may fall.

BUDGET LIMITATIONS

Although candidates for the state legislature may make lofty promises of reducing property taxes or drawing funds for underfunded public schools, once elected they are significantly constrained by the Texas Constitution and state laws.

"pay as you go": budget rule that Texas cannot spend more money than it receives in revenue

Pay As You Go.   Texas is constitutionally required to balance its budget. This is because Texas is a **"pay as you go"** state, meaning the government cannot spend more money than it receives in revenue. The Texas Constitution also sets limits on debt (capping it at 5 percent of the General Revenue Fund), welfare spending (which cannot exceed 1 percent of the budget), and total spending.[30] As the *Texas Tribune*'s Ross Ramsey puts it, the budget is "a dog already dragging four leashes."[31] The state comptroller must check the budget to make sure it meets these requirements.

The Spending Cap.   The most significant restraining rule is the spending cap, which restricts budget growth from the previous biennial budget to the estimated growth of Texas economy. The Legislative Budget Board (LBB) estimated the growth between 2014 and 2015 at 11.68 percent, giving legislators $94 billion to work with. The cap was a smaller 8% in the 2017–2018 budget. Texas legislators can bust the cap by a simple majority vote in both houses, but the political repercussions in a state that values small, efficient government are so high that this has only happened once (in 2006) in order to lower property taxes in school districts that had reached record highs.

expenditures: the total amount of funds that the state government can spend, as established by the spending cap

dual budgeting process: the legislative branch and executive branch coordinate to propose, shape, and pass a biennial budget

Dedicated and Nondedicated Revenue.   Legislators are further limited because they do not have discretion over all state **expenditures**. Almost one-fifth of the funds in the state budget are dedicated revenue, linked, either by constitution or by statute, to a specific purpose. For instance, revenue from hunting and fishing licenses is dedicated to conservation efforts, and a portion of marriage license fees are used to fund child abuse and neglect prevention programs.[32] Legislators do have discretion over how to spend general revenue funds, which in 2016–2017 amounted to only about 18 percent of state and federal funds (see Table 13.1).[33] Why is so much of the budget already fixed? Constitutional requirements, such as public education, and federal programs, such as Medicaid, siphon off significant amounts of the budget funds.

SOCIAL RESPONSIBILITY: **Should the state and federal governments require that so much of the budget be dedicated toward specific programs or purposes? Why?**

BUDGET PLAYERS AND PROCESS

Texas uses a **dual budgeting process**, in which the legislative branch and executive branch coordinate to propose, shape, and pass a biennial budget (see Figure 13.4). Although most every other state requires their governor to submit a budget, Texans' fear of a strong executive has driven the state to distribute the

TABLE 13.1	General Revenue Dedicated and Nondedicated Funds, 2016–2017	
TYPE OF REVENUE	PERCENT OF BUDGET (AMOUNT)	LARGEST EXPENDITURES
General Revenue (Nondedicated)	18 percent ($20.8 billion)	Public Safety and Criminal Justice ($8.4 billion)
General Revenue (Dedicated)	82 percent ($93.0 billion)	Public education, textbooks ($34 billion) Medicaid programs ($25 billion)

Source: Legislative Budget Board, Fiscal Size Up, May 2016.

FIGURE 13.4   **Roadmap of the Budget Process**

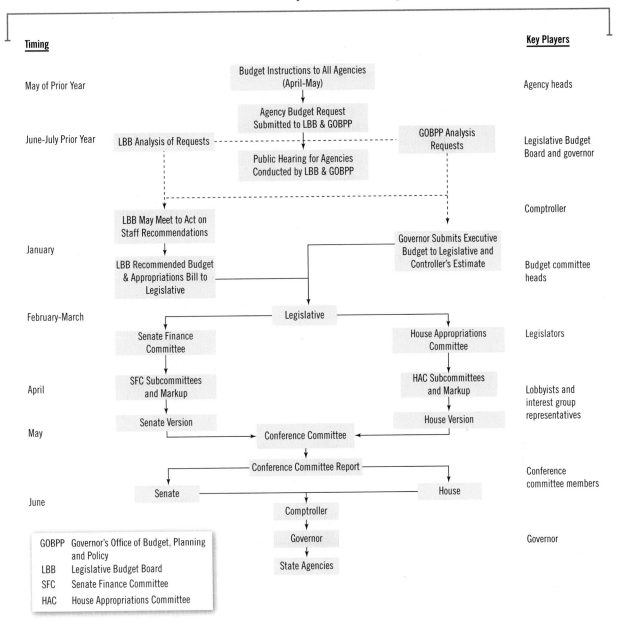

Source: Adapted from Senate Research Center, Budget 101: A Guide to the Budget Process in Texas, January 2011.

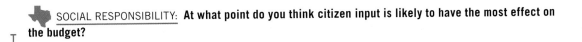

SOCIAL RESPONSIBILITY: **At what point do you think citizen input is likely to have the most effect on the budget?**

important task of budget making across the two branches. In this section, we explore the stages of this process.

Can We Afford This?   The state comptroller leads the parade by providing a biennial revenue estimate (or "BRE") at the beginning of each regular session. The BRE is used to make sure the state does not spend more money than it takes in. In addition, all bills submitted later during the legislative session must include a **fiscal note**, an overview of the estimated financial impact if the bill passes. The LBB adopts a constitutional spending limit in this early phase. The comptroller independently but concurrently prepares a statement about the financial condition of the state that estimates the revenue the state is to have in the upcoming biennium. The comptroller will also let the legislature know if there is any unspent money in the piggy bank. Before the 2015 legislative session, Comptroller Glenn Hegar reminded the legislature that there was more than $5 billion from the 2014–2015 budget that was unspent.

fiscal note: an overview of the estimated financial impact, including cost of the proposed changes, revenue generated, and staffing impacts to the bureaucracy resulting if the bill passes

What is Our Vision?   Since 1949, the LBB has been the most influential and active player in the budget, working with the governor to prepare a mission statement, set goals, adopt a spending limit, craft an **appropriation bill**, and review agency strategic plans. This early budget proposal is not binding but provides a starting point for negotiations. Conflicts frequently occur because of differences in opinion. In 1997, Governor Bush laid claim to some of that money, announcing he wanted $1 billion of a $3 billion budget surplus to go to reducing local school taxes,[34] and surprising the LBB who immediately threw up roadblocks. When Bush called Speaker of the House Laney to say, "I won't make that mistake again," Laney responded, "that's a good idea, governor."[35]

appropriation bill: legislation that specifies what spending the state will undertake

Who Has Input?   Executive branch agencies create long-term strategic plans and make budget requests. The LLB routinely—in boom or bust times—asks state agencies to provide evidence to justify their expenditures and to propose methods of cutting their budgets. If the revenue estimates go sour and don't show as much funds as expected, the state then already has a plan in place to make cuts. If the estimates show that the state has sufficient revenue, the cuts don't occur. In 2016, the LBB asked agencies to submit budget requests that would include a 10 percent reduction, what one observer called an "emergency warning signal test."[36]

How Are Requests Evaluated?   Because the state cannot spend more funds than it has, competition for budget menu items is fierce. Appropriation bills are submitted by the LBB to the House Appropriations Committee and the Senate Finance Committee. Both chambers' committees hold hearings, mark up legislation, and alter the budget bill with input from fellow legislators. The legislature often provides the governor with budget funds for their pet projects to smooth over any objections from the governor. According to one observer, the three "big lies" legislators often tell as they evaluate requests while writing up the package are: "We're already cut to the bone, Senator," "This program actually makes money for the state," and "This is one of the most important things the state does."[37]

Because the process has multiple points of access in this phase, interest groups have significant influence. Lobbyists are not allowed on the floor of the house or senate, but electronic devices can allow lobbyists to communicate with legislators on the floor without physically being there. During one twelve-hour budget debate later in the 2013 session, lawmakers were frantic to reconsider a vote that would have expanded the negotiating power of the state's chief health officer with the federal government on Medicaid. Why the sudden reversal? An e-mail "alert" sent from a conservative organization apparently prompted a change of heart for many lawmakers worried about political consequences.[38]

Representative Dennis Bonnen, Republican of Angleton, chairs the House Ways and Means Committee during budget hearings. The budget document is lengthy, complicated, and intimidating.

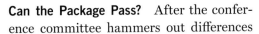 SOCIAL RESPONSIBILITY: **Beyond protecting the health and safety of Texans and promoting education, what responsibilities does the state have in the budget?**

Can the Package Pass?   After the conference committee hammers out differences between the house and senate budget bills, both chambers vote to agree to the final budget, and the governor signs the budget, vetoes it, or uses line item veto authority to trim it. A clash of budget titans put budget partners at odds in 2015. The legislature combined several items, including new state buildings in San Antonio and Austin, into one $1 billion line item for the Facilities Commission. The governor broke precedent and vetoed the funds for a few of the projects but not the full $1 billion line. Ursula Parks, the director of the LBB, wrote a letter of concern to Comptroller Glenn Hegar that the governor had misused the line item veto.[39] Until the Texas Supreme Court weighs in on the matter, the governor's interpretation of his budget veto authority holds.

Does the Budget Square with Available Funds?   "Is the sky falling in Texas?" State Senator Royce West asked Texas Comptroller Glenn Hegar, who had lowered his revenue projection by $2.6 billion because of slumping fossil fuel prices.[40] The state comptroller reviews the budget to **certify** that the anticipated revenue will be sufficient to cover the appropriations. The comptroller is essentially the budget enforcer.[41] This is usually a smooth process but in 2003, for the first time in Texas history, Comptroller Carole Keeton Strayhorn informed state lawmakers that they were close but no cigar—and the governor was forced to "cap the well" and use his veto powers to trim down the budget.

certify: the state controller stating that the state has enough money to cover the budget items

How Is the Budget Executed?   The governor and the LBB typically have joint authority to execute the budget—to prohibit or allow a state agency to spend budget funds, transfer budget funds, or to repurpose budget funds within an

FIGURE 13.5   **2016–2107 State Budget Highlights**

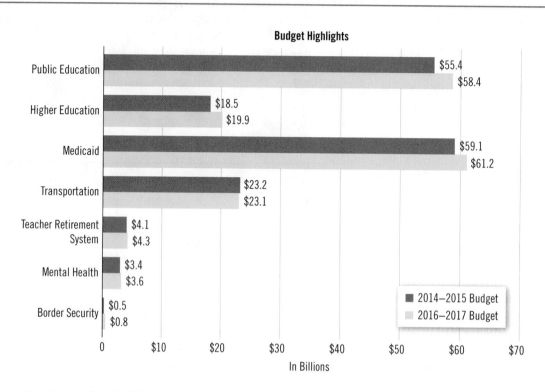

Budget Highlights

Category	2014–2015 Budget	2016–2017 Budget
Public Education	$55.4	$58.4
Higher Education	$18.5	$19.9
Medicaid	$59.1	$61.2
Transportation	$23.2	$23.1
Teacher Retirement System	$4.1	$4.3
Mental Health	$3.4	$3.6
Border Security	$0.5	$0.8

In Billions

Source: Texas Comptroller of Public Accounts.

 COMMUNICATION:

What does the Texas budget look like?

- The state's 2016–2017 budget increased spending for many of the big ticket items, including $3 billion for public education and $2 billion for Medicaid.
- Many Republican candidates also promised more spending for border security, which they did to the tune of about $800 million.

 CRITICAL THINKING:

Why modest spending increases for some programs but not for others?

- The state's Republican leadership promised small budgets and a minimal footprint of the state on local policy issues (like education).

agency for a different purpose than stated by the legislature. There are limitations on this authority: public hearings may be held on an issue, especially if the legislature objects to a decision; elected officials' salaries cannot be reduced or eliminated; and funds appropriated by the legislature for a specific purpose cannot be reduced or eliminated.

The LBB and the governor may do battle at this point of the budget process as well. In 2014, Governor Rick Perry declared a state of emergency so that he could bypass the legislature to deploy the National Guard to the US–Mexico border as more than 50,000 unaccompanied minors flooded across the border—primarily from Honduras, El Salvador, and Guatemala. The governor argued that the emergency situation justified tapping a budget rule that allowed him to use earmarked funds without going to the legislature. The LBB dug in their heels, arguing that the move would set a bad precedent: the governor could declare virtually any event an "emergency." The comptroller dove into the budget to find $38 million from another source to deploy the National Guard.[42]

POLICY PRIORITIES AND EXPENDITURE

Texas has a long history of being a "low tax, low service" state. Texas has no income tax, and Texas's support for social programs is generally low. Texas consistently spends less per capita—about $7,000 per person in 2013—than 45 out of 50 states.[43] Expenditures are an indicator of state priorities. The result of the pull and struggle of competing interests, however, produces a budget that reflects not only what Texans want to spend money on, but what Texans must spend money on (see Figure 13.5). Because the responsibilities of education and public safety are delegated to the state, Texas spends most of its revenue on those policies and programs. Texas also spends more on Medicaid than on any other program. However, most of the funds are provided by the federal government.

TEXAS TAKEAWAYS

4 What are some of the limitations on budget funding?

5 What is the dual budgeting process?

6 Who has authority to execute the budget?

HEALTH CARE AND WELFARE

Many Texans are just "one crisis away" from financial disaster. Nearly a quarter of Texas children live in poverty.[44] Poverty rates for African Americans and Hispanics are nearly three times higher than for Anglos or Asians. Geography matters as well: although poverty rates in North Texas have fallen 3 percent from 2014 to 2015, rates increased during the same period in South Texas (32 percent).[45] One in six Texas families is food "insecure," facing hunger or engaged in coping mechanisms to avoid it.[46] On health care issues, Texas has the biggest share of its population

13.3 Describe the social welfare programs Texas administers.

uninsured (19 percent) of any state in the union and has more people without health coverage than any other state, surpassing California, with more than 5 million residents without health coverage in 2015.[47]

redistributive policies: policies that transfer wealth from those who have more to those who have less

How does Texas address these issues? One path is **redistributive policies** that transfer wealth from those who have more to those who have less. Generally, social welfare programs pull taxes from working Texans to return them if and when they need assistance in the future. Like other Americans, Texans can receive health insurance as a benefit through their employer, purchase private plans, or qualify for government health care programs. These programs include Medicare, Medicaid, Social Security, Children's Health Insurance Program (CHIP), and other programs. These programs are jointly funded by the federal and state government, which allows each level to have input in determining the scope of the program—and illustrates how federalism, discussed in Chapter 3, works today.

MEDICARE

Medicare: a national social insurance program for older Americans funded by a payroll tax, premiums, and surtaxes and administered by the federal government

When you hit sixty-five, you'll be eligible for **Medicare**, a national social insurance program for older Americans aged sixty-five years and above funded by a payroll tax, premiums, and surtaxes and administered exclusively by the federal government. Medicare only partially covers health care expenses. As of 2015, more than 55 million Americans, about 3.5 million Texans, were beneficiaries of Medicare.[48] Although wholly a federal program, federal law does

---

INSIDER INTERVIEW

Eva DeLuna Castro, State Budget Analyst, Center for Public Policy Priorities

How does the budget process set priorities and impact Texas social welfare?

Because of the requirement that the general revenue part of the Texas state budget has to balance, legislators and interest groups wield the most power when they change the revenue side of the equation. Proposals to cut state taxes and other revenue that supports public and higher education, social services, and public safety sailed through the 2013 and 2015 legislative sessions. The 2015 session also saw a significant diversion of existing sales tax revenue from these areas of the budget to state highways, in what many Capitol observers have described as "robbing Peter to pay Paul." Most lobbyists and public interest groups focus their time and powers of persuasion on the appropriations bill drafts that move through the House and Senate, but proposals that affect state revenue merit just as much attention—if not more.

SOCIAL RESPONSIBILITY: **Should the state have a limit on lobbyist influence in the budget process? Why, or why not?**

require the state to pay deductibles and premiums for low-income Medicare beneficiaries.[49]

Critics charge that Medicare is inefficiently managed, gives inadequate access to medical providers, and is occasionally wrought with fraud. For instance, the largest Medicare fraud ring in history netted 300 people, including twenty-two Texans, charged with stealing more than $900 million in 2016.[50]

MEDICAID

Medicaid covers over three million Texans who have low income.[51] It was established in 1967 and is administered by the Texas Health and Human Services Commission. Medicaid is a basic health insurance program (acute care like visits to doctors) but also provides coverage for individuals in need of chronic care or long-term services. Federal law requires the state to cover certain population groups (such as the disabled, low-income families, children based on income levels) but gives the state the choice of whether to cover other population groups (such as coverage to pregnant women or infants up to 198 percent of the poverty level or providing mosquito repellant to pregnant mothers to prevent the Zika virus from infecting the child). This program increases the role of the national government in the states, especially Texas because of the state's large low-income population. The federal government determines specific eligibility rules and picks up the tab for most of the costs while the state must administer the program and can expand eligibility. Essentially, the federal government sets the table and cooks the meal but the states must serve it.

The number of Medicaid recipients is double today what it was in 2000 as the number of poor Texans expands. People enrolled in other low-income programs automatically qualify for coverage. The current Medicaid caseload for Texas is more than four million people, primarily comprised of females (55 percent of total clients) and 82 percent of those under twenty-one. Families with children make up 71 percent of the program participants. Texans with disabilities make up more than half of total Medicaid spending.[52] Statewide, 50 percent of Medicaid clients were Hispanic, 20 percent were Anglo, and 15 percent were African American.

Because the state has a large percentage of individuals in need of coverage and because federal and state laws do not limit those eligible, Medicaid in Texas is on an "unsustainable budget trajectory" as rising health care costs and growing enrollment consume an ever larger portion of the state budget.[53] The federal government funded almost 60 percent of the Medicaid program, but Texas was on the hook for the other 40 percent.[54] Texas's spending on Medicaid in the 2016–2017 budget—making up more than 25 percent of the budget—surpassed education spending for the first time in history. The state is allowed to add (but not subtract) individuals with specific needs to Medicaid, but this is less likely as the budget grows larger.

Medicaid: medical coverage for low-income Texans provided by the federal government

CHILDREN'S HEALTH INSURANCE PROGRAM (CHIP)

Children's Health Insurance Program (CHIP): a federal program that is run by the states to provide health coverage to children whose families who make too much to qualify for Medicaid but not enough to buy private insurance

Children can also get special health coverage through the Texas **Children's Health Insurance Program** (CHIP), a federal program that is run by the states to provide health (including dental) coverage to children whose families make too much to qualify for Medicaid but not enough to buy private insurance. Like Medicare, the federal and state government share costs for the program—the federal government picked up 71 percent in 2014 to the state's 29 percent.[55] The state has more than half a million children in CHIP. Medicaid, combined with CHIP, covers more than half of all children in the state and two-thirds of people in nursing homes.[56]

States have flexibility in designing their CHIP program. Texas's program expanded health coverage to children and families that earn up to 200 percent of the poverty line. Eligibility rules also require a child to be a Texas resident, under age nineteen, and uninsured for at least ninety days. Immigrant children were formerly ineligible for CHIP, but rules changes in 2010 enabled the state to receive matching funds from the federal government and Texas extended coverage to some of these children. The Affordable Care Act broadened federal funding for CHIP, prevented states from reducing certain eligibility standards, and required states to continue current levels of coverage.

THE AFFORDABLE CARE ACT

The Patient Protection and Affordable Care Act (PPACA), commonly referred to as the Affordable Care Act or "Obamacare" after President Barack Obama who championed the program, allows states to expand Medicaid coverage to families with incomes up to 133 percent of the federal poverty level and provides insurance subsidies for families with incomes between 100 percent and 400 percent of the federal poverty level. The catch is that every individual who was not covered by their employer's plan must buy insurance or pay a fine. After the PPACA was implemented, the national uninsured rate fell to 11 percent in 2015, the lowest of any time since 2008.[57] More than 85 percent of the Texans who enrolled receive subsidies averaging $244 per month to help pay for their premiums (see Figure 13.6).[58]

Approximately 1.5 million Texans could purchase subsidized policies under the ACA, Medicaid, or the Children's Health Insurance Program but aren't doing so. Many Texans don't understand that they are eligible, factors researchers chalk up to confusion to be solved by outreach and education. However, because the state did not expand Medicaid under Obamacare, the state has 766,000 adults who fall into a coverage "gap"—these "gappers" earn too much to qualify for Medicaid but not enough to qualify for marketplace tax credits.[59]

The struggle between the federal government and Texas continues over future health care funding. The federal government encouraged states to join the ACA but Texas has been reluctant to do so. The state was able to secure a waiver (called a Section 1115 waiver) until December 2017 to help Texas

IS IT BIGGER IN TEXAS?

FIGURE 13.6 **Health Care Sign Ups**

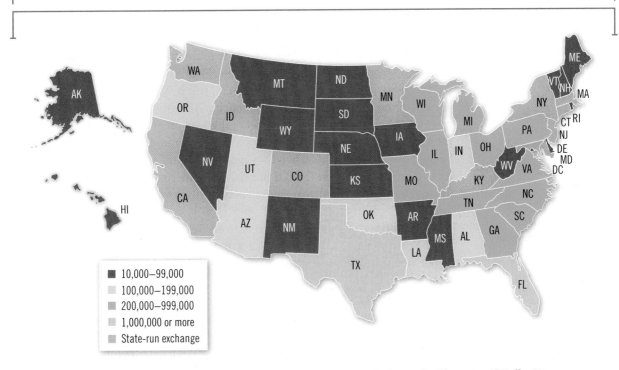

Legend:
- 10,000–99,000
- 100,000–199,000
- 200,000–999,000
- 1,000,000 or more
- State-run exchange

Source: Robert Garrett, "Why are so many more Floridians than Texans Signing up for Obamacare?" Dallas News, January 17, 2016.

 COMMUNICATION:

How many people signed up for health care through the ACA?

- Texas had more than 1.3 million individuals buy health insurance online through an exchange created under the Affordable Care Act through February 2016.[60]
- Florida led the nation with signups at 1.7 million people in the same period.

 CRITICAL THINKING:

Why is there so much variation by state?

- States with larger urban populations, and larger uninsured populations, had more sign ups. States with higher median ages also had more sign ups.
- In Texas, undocumented immigrants are not eligible for Medicaid and are barred from purchasing Obamacare, and legal immigrants are not allowed to apply for Medicaid.
- Texas has also been tightfisted about paying for public awareness campaigns and applications helpers (called "navigators"), although the Texas Hospital Association advertised to induce more people to sign up.

privatize its managed care health insurance system for Medicaid patients and tamp down the exploding cost of uncompensated care.[61] Texas agreed under the temporary waiver to develop a Medicaid expansion program.[62]

SOCIAL SECURITY

A rising urban population, the fragmentation of Americans' extended families, and an increase in life expectancy, combined with the crippling effects of the Great Depression, prompted President Franklin Roosevelt and Congress to enact the Social Security program in 1935, run by the federal government and administered through the Social Security Administration. Working Texans pay Social Security taxes and the federal government sets aside funds to help the blind and disabled and those with little income. In return, Texans receive Social Security payments when they reach the age of retirement (65) or Supplemental Security Income (SSI) if they become unemployed or disabled (and are 65 or older). The federal government sets eligibility caps, benefit rates, and determines eligibility.

Currently about one in seven retired Texas residents receives benefits from Social Security, about $1,202 a month.[63] Social Security is especially important to retired Hispanics. Almost three-fourths of Hispanic beneficiaries nationwide rely on payments from Social Security for at least half their retirement income—while Social Security payments make up only about one-third of retirement income for non-Hispanic Americans. This is because elderly Hispanics are more likely to live below the poverty line (average household income $16,020 in 2014) than other groups ($21,117).[64] Through SSI, blind, disabled or low income-aged Texans received $721 per month in 2014 to meet basic needs like food, clothes, and shelter.[65] Many states supplement SSI. Texas does not but allows for recipients to keep a larger share of income than other states that require a larger percentage of one's income to automatically go to their health care costs.

TEMPORARY ASSISTANCE TO NEEDY FAMILIES (TANF)

means-tested programs: income measured programs that provide aid to individuals and families with low incomes

Temporary Assistance to Needy Families (TANF): a program that provides financial and medical assistance to needy children and their parents or relatives

Several joint state and federal programs help Texans make ends meet. **Means-tested programs** are income measured programs that provide aid to Texans or communities with low incomes. The federal government pays for these welfare programs and any Texans who qualify can access them. These programs consumed $1 trillion of the federal budget in 2015.

The largest welfare program is **Temporary Assistance to Needy Families (TANF)**, a block grant to states. The federal government sets the basic rules, but the states develop the specifics of the programs, including eligibility limits and benefit levels. TANF provides financial and medical assistance to needy children and their parents or the relatives with whom they live. TANF also offers "one-time" assistance payments of $1,000 to families in need to help solve a short-term crisis. To be eligible in Texas, the head of the family must

GREAT TEXAS POLITICAL DEBATES
Drug Testing for Benefits

In 2015, the legislature passed a bill to subject people seeking cash assistance from TANF to drug tests—failure to screen clean would make the recipient ineligible for financial assistance temporarily or permanently, depending on the number of positive tests. Texas is not alone: twelve other states have instituted drug testing measures. Democrats and advocates for low-income families pushed back, arguing that the tests unnecessarily single out poor Texans and that such drug tests are not cost effective, and have even filed cases in court to determine if this measure is constitutional.[66]

SOCIAL RESPONSIBILITY: **Should a drug test be required to receive benefits?**

YES: If a recipient is receiving the public's money, they need to live drug-free and receive proper medical attention. Drug addicts are more likely to use cash assistance to purchase drugs. Moreover, individuals free of drugs are more likely to seek employment and be productive in their jobs.

NO: It is too costly to administer these tests to all welfare recipients, especially for minor violations. Furthermore, these tests that may lead to false positives. Drug testing also violates a beneficiary's right to privacy and subjects them to humiliation.

receive job training or seek employment, follow child support rules, not quit a job while receiving funds, not abuse alcohol or drugs, take parenting classes, and get vaccines for their child. The number of families receiving TANF in December of 2015 was 25,933, down from more than 50,000 in 2008.[67]

WORKERS' COMPENSATION

If you are injured on the job, you are likely entitled to paid medical care and you have the right to keep income and medical benefits. If you are killed on the job, your beneficiaries may be entitled to death and burial benefits.[68] These benefits are called workers' compensation. Texas leads the nation in worker fatalities: 531 in 2014, followed by California at 344.[69] The Texas Division of Workers' Compensation is responsible for the distribution of these benefits. However, the agency denies nearly half of all claims when they are first filed and, even when the claims are brought to trial, workers lose most of the time. "They throw these workers away like tissue paper. They're nothing more than a used Kleenex," said one employment attorney.[70] Although the state has fined businesses for failing to report injuries, the fines are generally small.[71]

TEXAS TAKEAWAYS

7 What is the difference between Medicare and Medicaid?

8 Who is covered under the Affordable Care Act?

♠ IMMIGRATION AND BORDER SECURITY

13.4 Analyze the role of the state in border issues and immigration.

Texas, settled by wave after wave of immigrants, shares a longer contiguous border with another country than any other state in the union. The first undocumented immigration to Texas was Anglo immigration from the United States into what was then Mexico. In 1830, a Mexican colonel encountered several immigrants, checked them for passports, and finding no proper documentation, ordered them to leave.[72]

Immigration is driving Texas's population growth, as more than 130,000 legal immigrants arrived in Texas in 2013, second only to California but ahead of Florida.[73] As of 2014, Texas had just over 4.5 million foreign-born residents, up from 2.9 million in 2000. Most (70 percent) were from Latin America, but a sizable group from Asia (20 percent) has driven much of the growth. One-third have become naturalized citizens.[74] Texas also has the second largest undocumented immigrant population—about 1.5 million—behind California. Most of these immigrants come from Mexico, followed by other Central American countries. Half of the incoming undocumented population are twenty-five to forty-five years old and more than half are male. Twenty percent speak English "very well," but more than half speak English "not well" or "not at all."[75] Difficulties with English may increase the cost of educating these students who need expanded translation assistance or instruction in English.

see for yourself 13.1

Take a deeper look at smuggling and undocumented immigration into Texas.

The effect of undocumented immigrants on the economy is a contentious point, but most agree that immigrants do displace workers for low-wage jobs while also creating new jobs by buying goods and services. According to the Federation for American Immigration Reform, undocumented immigrants cost Texas taxpayers $12.1 billion in 2013 in education, health care costs, and policing, but contributed $65 billion to economic output in wages, salary, and business earnings.[76] Estimates in a 2015 report claim undocumented immigrants pay $900 per person in property and sales taxes.[77]

Undocumented immigrants may also pay taxes for services they can never use (like Social Security or Medicare taxes). They often live in the shadows, often neglecting proper health care or educational opportunities, hoping not to get stopped by police or turned in by neighbors.[78] They may face abuse or exploitation as they are hired under the table for wages that are lower than those of other workers—especially in labor-intensive industries like construction. They may be forced to live in segregated, substandard housing because they do not want to risk obtaining official documentation for a bank loan. If you hire an undocumented immigrant, you face potential civil fines, although generally only businesses with multiple violations are fined. Children of undocumented immigrants cannot be denied access to public schools by federal law, regardless of the immigration status of the parents, as held by the US Supreme Court in *Plyler v. Doe* (1982).[79]

Texans have consistently ranked undocumented immigration and border security as the top two most important problems facing the state in the last several years. While legal immigrants are screened prior to entering the country, undocumented immigrants bypass federal screening—raising concerns that criminals may penetrate the long border. In 2005, Victor Reyes assaulted, shot, and killed a twenty-five-year-old Houston man at random who had stopped at a red light. Reyes was an undocumented immigrant who had been deported four times between 2003 and 2010 and had a criminal record that included burglary and illegal entry to the country. During a violent shootout, Reyes then killed two and wounded three before the sheriff's deputies shot him.[80] This senseless killing rallied Republicans who attempted but failed to pass legislation prohibiting local government from creating safe havens for undocumented immigrants known as sanctuary cities and ending in-state tuition for undocumented immigrants.[81]

The story of Texas is a story of immigration and two nations intertwined. Texas has always been a crucible for incorporating newcomers but struggles over equal education, voting rights, and poverty remain.

SOCIAL RESPONSIBILITY: **How can Texas balance a desire to welcome immigrants with the need for border security?**

Although immigration and border security issues fall under federal authority, aggressive politics and the practical need for solutions has led the state to step in frequently. Lawmakers, led by Republican Governor Greg Abbott, added $800 million to border security efforts, including new equipment, facilities, and law enforcement officers.[82] Critics claim the funds are a blank check for further increases in funds and the funds are not needed because they are an overreaction to the problems faced along the Texas border. Public pressure to act will spur politicians to act on immigration, no doubt fanning the flames of the tension between the state and federal government (see Chapter 3).

TEXAS TAKEAWAYS

9 What percentage of Texas's foreign-born population is from Latin America?

10 Approximately how many undocumented immigrants live in Texas?

🤠 EDUCATION

13.5 Evaluate the challenges facing Texas's education system.

The Texas constitution requires the state to provide for "efficient and adequate" funding for its public schools. However, school finance is the toughest political issue the state faces, because it historically has been the most expensive service the state provides.[83] Students, parents, and school districts have fought the battle over education through the state legislature, the courts, and bureaucratic agencies.

SOURCES OF K-12 FUNDING

permanent school fund:
the fund that contains the money from the state's long-term investment and that pays for public education

Schools are funded by a combination of state general revenue, local property taxes, and some federal taxes. The **permanent school fund** contains money from the long-term investment the state made in 1854. The state initiated the fund with a $2 million appropriation and set aside land whose proceeds go expressly for the funding of public schools. In addition, one-quarter of taxes on the production of fossil fuels and one-quarter of the gas, water, and electric utility tax are constitutionally dedicated to public education. Much of the proceeds from the state lottery are also earmarked for education. The state provides extra funds for students who need more support, such as students learning English, gifted and talented students, and students from low-income families. The **available school fund** is the pool of revenue schools are allocated annually for use from the permanent school fund and by one-quarter of the state's motor fuel tax revenue.

available school fund:
annual transfers from the permanent school fund to school districts

Individual schools receive money through a complicated formula that includes the number of students in class (attendance) plus extra funding for specific students like those with learning disabilities, gifted and talented students, low-income students, or those learning English.[84] Districts can also increase their pool of available funds locally by holding a bond election which, if approved, can fund the districts' construction projects, repairs, or technology upgrades. Critics of this system argue that it creates two districts: rich and poor.

SCHOOL FINANCE

Despite attempts to identify additional funds for increasing spending on public education, the issue of school finance is perpetually on the table. In the landmark US Supreme Court case *San Antonio Independent School District v. Rodriguez* (1973), the Court found that the school finance system relied too heavily on property taxes, which resulted in considerable inequities in state aid to education. But, as the fundamental right to a quality public education only existed in the Texas Constitution, not the US Constitution, the Court found no violation of federal law.

Since 1984, school districts have sued the state seven times over perceived inadequate funding.[85] Overreliance on property taxes to fund education and unequal distribution of education funds prompted the Texas Supreme Court

ANGLES OF POWER
School Finance

The debate over adequate school funding dates back to the debate over the 1876 Constitution. During the debates over ratification in 1876, political attitudes split on funding public education. Those in favor of significant education funding proposed spending one-fourth of general revenue on public schools. Opponents thought it "criminal to tax one man to help educate the children of another," many holding to beliefs from their southern roots of private, religious education or parental duty to educate.[86] Others felt the state only had an obligation to orphans and indigent children. Still others felt giving the state the power to prescribe the qualifications of teachers and the course of study "endangered religious liberty."

Modern debates about school finance center on how to equitably distribute the education funds and who should pay for it.

SOCIAL RESPONSIBILITY: **How would you design a system to meet Texas's constitutional standards for effective public education? What criteria and considerations would you use?**

to proclaim the state's school-finance system unconstitutional in 1989 in *Edge-wood Independent School District v. Kirby.* The court determined that the system "enabled rich districts to raise and spend far more money than poor districts."[87] Lawyers for the Mexican American Legal Defense Fund, representing Demitrio Rodriguez of San Antonio and his family, argued that there was a $500,000 difference in the property value taxed per student between the poorest and richest district. Lawmakers in 1991 created a new system they believed would fix the problem. First dubbed "recapture," then the "Fair Share Plan," then "Robin Hood," the current school finance structure redistributes tax money from wealthy school districts to poorer ones. The plan is the first constitutionally permissible school funding formula in thirty years. But the Robin Hood plan is disliked by many districts, especially the wealthier ones, who have to send extra funds to the state.

Equalizing spending across a giant state with wildly different local revenue, from rich suburbs to poor inner cities, is difficult. The state is forced to use some general revenue from sales taxes to pay for schools, making school funding subject to uncertain budgets and political infighting. A reform effort in 2003 (to replace the Robin Hood plan) which included a payroll tax, a restructuring of the franchise tax, and increased taxes on gambling failed when Republicans howled about higher taxes and Democrats complained about education being paid for with gambling, an unstable source of revenue.

Another court challenge by two-thirds of Texas state school districts was brought to Texas courts in 2014, charging again that the system was underfunded. The Texas Supreme Court in 2016 found that the state's school finance system was "imperfect" and with "immense room for improvement" but did meet constitutional requirements. The court urged the legislature to make transformational changes rather than just apply a temporary Band-Aid.[88]

FIGURE 13.7 **Top States Increasing and Decreasing Public Education Funding**

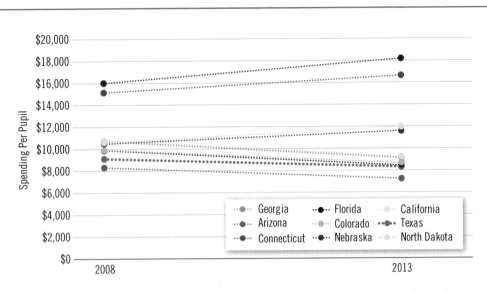

Source: US Census Bureau Annual Survey of School Systems. Calculations per pupil elementary and secondary spending on 2013 data.[89]

 COMMUNICATION:

How has public education changed since 2008?

- Several southern states, including Georgia and Florida, reduced spending per pupil by up to 15 percent. Western and southwestern states (California, Arizona, and Colorado) decreased spending by between 12 and 13 percent.

- Texas was on the high end of reduction, decreasing spending by about $800 per pupil.

- Nebraska, North Dakota, and Alaska all increased spending per pupil by more than 10 percent.

 CRITICAL THINKING:

Why does Texas rank so low?

- Budget crises in Texas, Arizona, and California caused budget rollbacks in those states. Education is often on the chopping block.

- Flush fiscal coffers in Nebraska, North Dakota, and Alaska from the energy boom of the early 2010s provided more funds for spending on public education.

Major spending cuts to education in 2011 totaled $5 billion, forcing cuts of up to 10 percent, which meant laying off teachers, increasing class sizes, and reducing other staff such as tutors and instructional specialists. State lawmakers returned much of that money in 2015. Although average state spending on education rose from 2008 to 2013, spending has dropped in Texas during that time (Figure 13.7).

TEACHER, STUDENT, AND SCHOOL PERFORMANCE

In 1984, the legislature passed a major reform bill that raised teacher salaries but tied them to teacher performance. The reforms also introduced more stringent teacher certifications, limited elementary school classrooms to twenty-two students, began competency testing for educators, initiated stricter attendance standards, and adopted a "no-pass, no play" rule that prohibited students with failing grades from participating in extracurricular activities.

Governor Mark White, who initiated the efforts with the help of Dallas billionaire Ross Perot, took the credit then the blame for the reforms. Anger was directed especially at the "no-pass, no play" restrictions, upheld by the Texas Supreme Court who ruled that students had no constitutional right to participate in sports. High school coaches were not the only ones upset—teachers were also angered over the competency provisions that required passage of the test to keep their jobs, even though the legislation included pay raises. Mock tests circulated at the time asked the following sample question: *"What comedy team had the greatest success in Texas since 1984?* (a) Laurel and Hardy, (b) Amos and Andy, (c) Tarzan and Cheeta, or (d) White and Perot"* and *"Which of the following best describes "an educational expert" in Texas?* [here only one answer is offered]: a billionaire with a burr in his ass."[90]

Lieutenant Governor Hobby became so irate that he called in the teachers groups to have it out with them—a senator who attended the meeting called it "like the Alamo, but without the blood." In the 1986 election, the Texas State Teachers Association lined up against the governor, despite the fact that 97 percent of teachers passed the competency provisions, which were, according to Texas Monthly, "so easy that only people who have trouble reading and understanding English are likely to fail."[91] Combined with a slumping economy and unpopular tax increases, the governor lost his reelection bid, but many of the reforms from 1984 are still in place.[92]

Parents are another major interest group in the education process. Reforms in 1995 cemented local control of schools by limiting the state's Texas Education Agency to broad education goal planning, managing the school fund accounts, and administering the accountability system. A decade later, beginning with the class of 2005, the state mandated that Texas students pass exit-level tests to meet graduation requirements, currently called the State of Texas Assessments of Academic Readiness tests, or STAAR. The percentage of students passing the test has remained flat, with between 64 percent and 78 percent of third through eighth graders statewide passing all subjects. Backlash over exit-level testing peaked in 2015 as parents complained that the state put too much emphasis on the test. The legislature softened the test requirement and allowed graduates who passed two of their five end-of-course exams to graduate.[93]

Rating schools is difficult because there are many ways to do so. Since 1993, Texas has rated its schools in one way or another. The most recent incarnation,

A group of teachers, parents and school administrators march up Congress Avenue toward the Capitol. These groups can exert significant pressure on legislators to reform education and can hold lawmakers accountable for their actions.

PERSONAL RESPONSIBILITY: **Think about your high school. Would the challenges facing your school be fixed with more money or greater teacher accountability?**

see for yourself 13.2

Consider how Texas educational standards are formed and influence the rest of the nation.

beginning in the 2017–2018 school year, assigns letter grades (A, B, C, D, or F) rather than the "met standard" or "improvement required" labels used before this system was established.

Nationally, Texas consistently ranks lower than most other states. *Education Week* gave Texas a C– overall, a C– for K-12 student achievement, a C for students' future success in life, and a D for school finance. This put Texas in forty-third place nationally. Texas was not alone in getting low grades—California, North Carolina, Michigan, and Missouri all scored a C– or worse.[94] Other reviews are more generous to the state but still put the state in the bottom third nationally, such as the National Education Association, which placed Texas thirty-eighth out of fifty states.[95] State law limits class size to twenty-two students, although more than 6,000 waivers were granted to allow school districts to exceed this amount.[96]

DIVERSITY IN PUBLIC EDUCATION

The makeup of state schools has grown increasingly diverse as the state matures and changes demographically. Texas schools are larger (now at 5.2 million public school kids), less white due to a rise in the state's Hispanic and Asian populations, and poorer in recent decades.[97] Many Texas public schools remain as segregated (either almost all Anglo, African American, or Hispanic) as they were in the 1970s when landmark legislation sought to end racial segregation in schools.[98] This presents challenges and opportunities.

Texas schools are allowed to file misdemeanor charges against students who skip school, and the fines can range up to $500 plus court costs.[99] But race may play a role in determining who gets charged. Ashley Brown, a sixteen-year-old African American sophomore from South Oak Cliff High School in Dallas, missed four days of school after her grandmother died of cancer. The school mistakenly charged her with more absences and she had to appear in court.[100] The court dismissed the charges, but Ashley's case is not uncommon in Texas. African Americans are more likely than Latinos or Anglos to be suspended from school—25 percent of black students in middle and high school in the Dallas Independent School District were suspended, compared to 6 percent of Anglo, and 9 percent of Latino students.

Another complication is the growing dropout rate among the state's poorer and Hispanic students. African Americans had the highest dropout rates

(9.5 percent), followed by Hispanics (7.7 percent), multiracial (4.3 percent), and Anglo students (3.4 percent).[101] Such problems put many students on the "school-to-prison" pipeline and contribute to an undereducated Texas.[102] Solutions applied include identifying "dropout factory" schools that graduate less than 60 percent of their students and intervening early for students at risk to drop out.[103] In recent years, because of these strategies, the performance gap between white students and black and Hispanic students has narrowed (see Table 13.2).

One reason Hispanic students have lagged behind is language issues. The state has been under legal scrutiny since the 1970s for failing to adequately fund English language learner education.[104] Texas public schools had almost one million English as a Second Language (ESL) students in 2015.[105] Some school districts have begun more rigorously tracking the amount of time ESL students spend learning English, using periodic testing to make sure students understand academic concepts in English, and furnishing a "Ferrari" of bilingual education programs where all students learn in both English and Spanish.

TABLE 13.2	Graduation Rates and Test Performance by Race			
	ANGLO 1995 / 2015	HISPANIC 1995 /2015	AFRICAN AMERICAN 1995 / 2015	ASIAN 1995 / 2015
Student population	47% / 30%	36% / 52%	14% / 13%	3% / 4%
Graduation rate[106]	91% / 94%	80% / 87%	80% / 85%	90% / 96%
TAAS / STARR "Satisfactory"	75% / 87%	46% / 72%	38% / 67%	78% / 93%

Source: TEA Snapshots of Public Schools. Including charter schools. TEA Completion Reports.

 COMMUNICATION:

What is the makeup and success of school kids in Texas?

- Overall, Texas's graduation rates are very high, outpaced only by Iowa in 2015.[107]
- Anglo and Asian students have the highest graduation rates and standardized test grades.
- Most gains between 1995 and 2015 have been among minority students.

 CRITICAL THINKING:

Why is there variation in dropout rates?

- One reason may be that the testing standards have produced more prepared students and make teachers accountable.
- The measurement may also be to blame: districts can avoid counting students who left for a variety of reasons, including taking the GED instead of graduating.[108] This may be artificially inflating the graduation rate.
- Poverty, racially segregated schools, and language issues may limit educational success for Hispanic and African American students.

VOUCHERS

vouchers: programs
to provide a student
with authorization for
government funding to be
used at a private school

One approach to public education is to make private schools more accessible through **vouchers** (or "school choice," or where the "dollars follow the child").[109] Voucher programs provide a student with authorization for government funding to be used at a private school. Opponents argue that vouchers divert funding from public schools and so hurt public schools to aid a small number of private school students. Proponents claim that vouchers make schools work harder to attract students. The legislature has attempted but failed on several occasions in the past few sessions to pass tax credits, a form of voucher, for Texans who send their children to private school to get a rebate.

HIGHER EDUCATION

Texas also funds and sets standards for higher education institutions. Mirabeau B. Lamar, often known as the "father of Texas education," is credited with the idea of establishing state support for higher education. In 1839 he outlined his vision for a public university system and professed, "a cultivated mind is the guardian genius of democracy."[110]

Funding.   The *Permanent University Fund* (PUF) was established in 1839, even before Texas had universities. The scrubland the state set aside wasn't worth much until oil was struck. Proceeds from natural resources (oil, gas, sulfur, water), mineral leases, and grazing rights generate income for the fund and for permanent members: campuses of the University of Texas and Texas A&M University. The fund was set in 1931 to provide two-thirds of the funds to the UT and one-third to A&M.[111] With a boom in oil revenue pumping $1 billion a year into the PUF, the universities are flush with funds and have seen their endowments grow by 70 percent.[112] The fund is currently worth more than $15 billion.

The substantial wealth benefiting some of the state's universities has the rest calling foul. "Texas is not just driven by UT and A&M," State Representative Sylvester Turner, Democrat of Houston, opined during a hearing of the House Committee on Appropriations. Representative Turner filed legislation to open up the PUF to other state schools, other than UT and A&M who routinely receive double or triple the amount of funding other schools receive. Opponents argue that the state established the PUF to fund the state's flagship universities only. This creates a system that advantages only two state universities, despite broad resources. Defenders of the current system argue that the state has expanded the institutions allowed to access the PUF (like additional UT campuses and A&M research centers) for the good of the state. Texas only has eight tier-one universities, four of them became tier one in 2016, compared to nine in California.

Tuition at public universities was set by the legislature until 2003 when a law was passed to allow individual universities to raise or lower tuition (called deregulation). As tuition has risen at all public schools, legislators have grumbled that they need to be regulated again. Yet, the rate of tuition increase in the years since deregulation was lower than the rate of increase in the decade before deregulation.[113]

Community Colleges. The most explosive growth in higher education has come from community colleges in Texas. Growth in these two-year institutions rose more than 102 percent since 1990, totaling 700,892 students in 2015. These colleges educate many students (47 percent of students enrolled in higher education are in a community college).[114] As discussed in Chapter 12, these institutions are funded by taxes from locally elected Community College Boards (about $1.65 billion in 2014) but are supplemented with funds from the legislature for operations and instructional programs (about $1.75 billion in the 2016–2017 biennium). A portion of the legislative funds are tied to "student success points" that assign point values for student-specific objectives, like passage of a math course the first time, degrees awarded in a critical field, and transfer to a four-year university.

Standards. With growing demand for a college-educated workforce and the sprouting of colleges and universities across the Lone Star State, the state created the Texas Commission on Higher Education in 1953 and followed this by establishing the Texas Higher Education Coordinating Board in 1965 to coordinate, develop, and evaluate Texas higher education. Primarily, the THECB approves construction of facilities, reviews and coordinates degree programs, and assists higher education institutions in student retention and success issues. Does the state need more nurses, veterinarians, or big data scientists? The THECB is responsible for assessing the need for additional programs and funneling students into the program.[115] Institutions, driven by local concerns and alumni, may have different objectives than state objectives, increasing enrollment or degrees for their own sake. Powerful university lobbyists often circumvent THECB by going to the legislature directly for funding help, increasing tensions between state resources, THECB, and institutions of higher education.

Affirmative Action. Abigail Fisher, a Sugar Land, Texas, student, dreamt of attending the University of Texas like her father and sister before her. Her high school grades, test scores, volunteer efforts, and cello playing were not enough, however, as the university rejected her application, she argues, because of the top 10 percent rule. The rule opens educational opportunities up by giving all racial and ethnic minority students who graduate in the top 10 percent at any Texas school, regardless of its rank or performance, automatic admission into a Texas public university. She sued the university arguing that her rejection was discriminatory based on race. The University of Texas, as well as other schools, have used **affirmative action**—a series of rules and procedures designed to give minorities a leg up by offering advantages in education or employment to specific groups to redress historic discrimination. The US Supreme Court upheld the university's affirmative action program in 2016, allowing UT to continue to consider a prospective student's race as one factor among many to ensure a diverse student body.

> **affirmative action:** a policy that provides additional benefits or opportunities to individuals who have suffered historically from discrimination

TEXAS TAKEAWAYS

11 How many times has the state been sued for inadequate funding since 1984?

12 What are vouchers?

TRANSPORTATION

13.6 Assess Texas's transportation policy and future challenges.

Tired of sitting in traffic? You're not alone. Road conditions and traffic issues affect all Texans in one way or another. Several Texas cities are ranked near the top for worst commutes. More than a million Texans living in and around major metropolitan cities commute annually.[116] Transportation is often cited as the number one issue of concern for Texans, especially in big cities. TxDOT argues that it needs an additional $5 billion annually to maintain the current roads. The main source of highway funds are from motor vehicle registration fees, federal highway funds from the national government, the sales tax on motor oils, and some part of the motor fuels (gas) taxes—these make up the State Highway Fund.

With a small appetite to spend funds on transportation, lawmakers use toll roads as a way to develop and maintain road projects. For large projects like the expansion of the LBJ Expressway in Dallas, toll revenue is critical to funding the completion. Texans want more funding for roads but don't want to pay for it with tolls. Opposition from fellow Republicans was enough to stop one of Governor Perry's 2001 solutions to the state's transportation woes: the Trans-Texas Corridor, a new 4,000 mile nexus of privately operated toll roads that would crisscross the state. The price tag was to be $175 billion.[117] A 2014 constitutional amendment kicks in $1.7 billion yearly, although this is subject to economic variability as these funds are related to taxes on oil and natural gas production. Until the funds kick in and congestion subsides, Texas drivers are going to be stuck behind the wheel in traffic.

TEXAS TAKEAWAYS

13 Where do state highway funds come from?

ENERGY AND THE ENVIRONMENT

13.7 Explain the state's environmental and energy policy.

The balance between concern over the environment and the promotion and regulation of energy sources reaches back generations. The political struggle between urban and rural interests also plays into regulating Texas's environment.

WATER

Since 2010, Texas has experienced drought conditions, draining reservoirs used for water, fueling wildfires and dust storms, and limiting water for

FIGURE 13.8   **A Thirsty Texas: Water Supply and Demand**

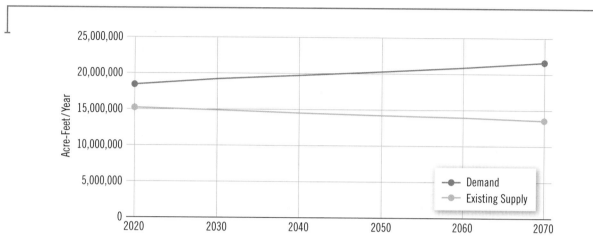

Source: The Texas Water Development Board.

 COMMUNICATION:

What are the trends in supply and demand in water?

- Demand for water is already outpacing supply, and the next fifty years will see demand rising much faster than supply.

 CRITICAL THINKING:

Why is demand rising but supply falling?

- A growing population, especially suburban areas, has the demand for water at historic highs.

- Irrigation need for agriculture, including cattle, is increasing. Manufacturing and steam electric power needs are also predicted to increase over time.

- The number of new water projects funded by the state are also not keeping up with the demand for more water.

agricultural use. At the height of the drought, cattle feed prices skyrocketed, rice farm output (using water to soak the crop) tumbled, corn output fell 40 percent, and peanut production dropped.[118] More than 1,000 areas in Texas enacted water restrictions.[119] Arlington banned watering between 10 a.m. and 6 p.m. year round and San Angelo reduced watering to once a week. The real danger facing Texas, however, lies not in the present but in the future as water demands surpass dwindling existing water supplies (see Figure 13.8).

The Texas Water Development Board.   In 1957, after a seven-year dry spell, the legislature founded an agency that would become the Texas Water Development Board (TWDB) to provide loans to local governments for water projects, administer water funds, and facilitate the transfer and sale of water and water rights throughout the state. The TWDB has promoted more efficient irrigation practices and the use of natural rainfall with the result that irrigation water demands are projected to fall by almost 18 percent between 2020 and 2070. Unfortunately, population growth is likely to increase the demand for municipal water, for drinking, bathing, and other purposes by 62 percent.[120]

Cities and suburbs are thirsty for more water. Parched rural agricultural land needs water for irrigation. It's no surprise then that instead of reflecting the polarized Republican versus Democrat politics, water politics divide over rural versus urban or suburban interests. Rural representatives worry that cities will pay more for water and leave rural areas dry.[121] Representative Drew Darby, arguing for rural Texas's fair share of the state's evaporating water supply, pointed out that "they don't grow cotton at Men's Wearhouse in San Antonio. They don't feed beef at the H-E-B in San Antonio. The food, the fiber, the natural resources are produced in rural Texas."[122]

The rain quells the water problem in more ways than one. In 2015, voters overwhelmingly approved allocating $2 billion from the state Rainy Day Fund to a water fund for projects approved by the TWDB. Twenty percent of the fund is earmarked for conservation projects and 10 percent was set aside for rural water projects.[123] The projects included building new reservoirs, fixing pipes, and pursuing groundwater development.

Water Control and Ownership.   A second battle front is the citizens versus the state over ownership of surface versus groundwater (the water beneath the surface). Surface water is subject to control and management by the state, but groundwater is owned by the landowner of the property above the groundwater, known as the right of **capture**. As the reach of the state grew and as water districts popped up around the thirsty state, landowners' use of this subsurface water was threatened. When local groundwater districts attempted to regulate how much water local property owners could pump, the cases ended up in court. The Texas Supreme Court in 2012 sided with landowners, certifying that the state could only issue rules that were "reasonable." The lack of clarity about what "reasonable" means vexes water politics to this day.

capture: groundwater is owned by the landowner of the property above the groundwater

ENERGY SOURCES

Texas is the largest electricity consumer of any state, using more than one-eighth of the total energy created in the United States. As the state's population has grown, electricity demand has grown. The need for air conditioning most of the year, a growing energy-intensive industrial sector, and longer commutes to work all contribute to significant consumption. How will Texas meet these needs?

Texas's power needs can be partially satisfied from homegrown natural sources. It is and has been a leading producer of energy, chiefly from crude oil,

TABLE 13.3	Innovations in Energy Production
1955	Half of energy generated in Texas comes from natural gas-fired power plants, while coal-fired power plants account for about one-third.
1988	Texas's two nuclear reactors account for 10 percent of the state's energy.
2014	Texas takes the lead nationally in wind-power generation, producing more than one-third of the nation's total.
2017	Texas is ranked number one in solar energy potential, but tenth in solar energy production.

Source: "The State Of Nuclear Energy In Texas," National Public Radio.

SOCIAL RESPONSIBILITY:
Should the Texas legislature provide incentives for energy companies to develop solar power? Why, or why not?

natural gas, and wind power (see Table 13.3).[124] In fact, Texas has its own electrical grid, which covers most of the state, unique because this is only one of three in the entire United States. The grid is run by the Electrical Reliability Council of Texas (ERCOT) and is separate, in part, to avoid interference from the federal government, which set rates for transmission service and wholesale power.[125]

Much of the state's energy independence has resulted from a boom in hydraulic fracturing (or "fracking") in 2012 and 2013. In 2005, the state legislature passed legislation requiring that 5 percent of the state's electricity quantity come from renewable sources by 2015. The state has exceeded these goals, with renewable sources accounting for about 10 percent in 2014, largely because of early investment in wind energy, the turbines from which dot the West Texas plains.

The role of tax incentives to encourage development of alternative energy is often hotly contested. In 2014, the state comptroller scratched up controversy when she said that the wind energy industry in the state "should stand on its own two feet."[126] Citing a job already completed, an unfair market advantage, and cheap natural gas, the comptroller advocated for stripping the state's role in boosting wind power. In 2015, the Texas legislature considered and rejected a bill to end subsidies for alternative energy and the creation of transmission lines to deliver the electricity generated by the turbines. Despite the state's reputation for oil and gas, Texas gets about 10 percent of its electricity needs from wind energy, one of only eleven other states with this high a percent, moving up to 37 percent by 2030.[127]

★ TEXAS TAKEAWAYS

14 What does the Texas Water Development Board do?

15 What is capture?

🤠 THE INSIDER VIEW

Former Governor Rick Perry spelled out his philosophy on Texas's budget and policy: low taxes, low regulation, tort reform, and "don't spend all the money."[128] This recipe has put the state in fiscal health, but the state's booming population, aging citizenry, booming diversity, and battles over natural resources mean that the economic fitness doesn't reach all Texans. The skirmishes over the budget, taxes, and public policy often center on party politics (Republicans versus Democrats) but just as often urban interests are pitted against rural interests and organized interests (environmental, health care) are pitted against industry interests. The balance of power of any one group at any one time determines the type of policy and often policy change. These changes are usually gradual but shift as the state adapts to new circumstances.

★ TEXAS TAKEAWAYS

1 A regressive tax, like the state's sales tax, is a tax rate that is the same for everyone.

2 The homestead exemption is part of a homeowner's property value on which Texans don't have to pay taxes.

3 The gas tax has remained unchanged since 1991.

4 Pay as you go, the spending caps on debt spending and total spending, and revenue already dedicated to a specific policy (dedicated revenue) are all budget limitations.

5 The dual budgeting process is where the legislative branch and executive branch coordinate to propose, shape, and pass a biennial budget.

6 The governor and the Legislative Budget Board (LBB) typically have joint authority to execute the budget.

7 Medicare is a national social insurance program for older Americans funded by a payroll tax, premiums, and surtaxes and administered by the federal government. Medicaid is medical coverage for low income Texans provided by the federal government.

8 The Affordable Care Act (ACA) (or "Obamacare") covers families with incomes up to 133 percent of the federal poverty level and provides insurance subsidies for families with incomes between 100 percent and 400 percent. But all individuals are required to have health insurance or pay a fine.

9 Seventy percent of Texas's foreign-born population are from Latin America.

10 Texas has approximately 1.5 million undocumented immigrants.

11 Since 1984, school districts have sued the state seven times over perceived inadequate funding.

12 Vouchers are programs that provide a student with authorization for government funding to be used at a private school.

13 The main source of highway funds are from motor vehicle registration fees, federal highway funds from the national government, the sales tax on motor oils, and some part of the motor fuels (gas) taxes.

14 The Texas Water Development Board (TWDB) provides loans to local governments for water projects, administers water funds, and facilitates the transfer and sale of water and water rights throughout the state

15 Capture is water above the ground that is owned by the landowner of the property.

KEY TERMS

affirmative action
appropriation bill
available school fund
capture
certify
Children's Health Insurance Program (CHIP)
dual budgeting process
expenditures
fee
fine
fiscal note
general revenue funds
homestead exemption
means-tested programs
Medicaid
Medicare
"pay as you go,"
permanent school fund
progressive tax
redistributive policies
regressive tax
revenue
"sin" taxes
Temporary Assistance to Needy Families (TANF)
vouchers

PRACTICE QUIZ

1. What is the current homestead exemption for most Texans?

   a. $5,000
   b. $10,000
   c. $25,000
   d. $35,000

2. What percent of total tax receipts were franchise (business) taxes?

   a. 5 percent
   b. 7 percent
   c. 9 percent
   d. 12 percent

3. On which of the following items does the state *not* include in a gas tax?

   a. Gasoline
   b. Propane

   c. Liquefied gas
   d. Diesel fuel

4. What is the duration of the state's budget?

   a. One year
   b. Two years
   c. Three years
   d. Four years

5. Which organization is responsible for preparing and executing the state's budget?

   a. Executive Finance Organization
   b. Legislative Redistricting Board
   c. Legislative Budget Board
   d. Texas Comptroller

6. What is another term for the state's "Robin Hood" plan?

   a. Redistributive
   b. Recapture
   c. Reorganization
   d. Restructuring

7. Dropout rates for Hispanic students is currently higher than for African Americans.

   a. True.
   b. False.

8. The state exceeded its self-imposed goal of 5 percent renewable energy earlier than anticipated.

   a True.
   b. False.

9. Only the Texas A&M University system and the University of Texas system schools are eligible for funds from the Permanent University Fund.

   a. True.
   b. False.

10. If you object to the appraisal of your house's value, you can appeal it.

    a. True
    b. False.

[Answers: C, C, B, B, C, B, B, A, A, A]

GLOSSARY

affirmative action: a policy that provides additional benefits or opportunities to individuals who have suffered historically from discrimination

agency capture: government agencies "controlled" by the industries that the agency was designed to regulate

agenda setting: an informal power of the governor to use his public platform to set the state's political and policy agenda

amend: the process of bill

amicus curiae briefs: a legal filing with relevant opinions or information pertinent to a case that affects a group's interests, even if they are not directly part of the case

annexation: the joining of unincorporated land into the boundary of an existing city

appellate courts: courts that review legal issues of cases decided by lower courts

appellate jurisdiction: the authority of a court to review a case first heard by a lower court

appropriation bill: legislation that specifies what spending the state will undertake

arraignment: the initial appearance of the accused in court

AstroTurf lobbying: involves manufacturing public support and making it appear as though it was inspired organically by a swell of public opinion

at-large: an electoral unit where all citizens in a county can vote

available school fund: annual transfers from the permanent school fund to school districts

bail: a contract where the accused is temporarily released from prison on the condition he or she pay a sum of money to guarantee an appearance in court

bench trial: a single judge presides and decides guilt or innocence and punishment

bicameral legislature: a legislative body with two houses or chambers

bill of rights: a formal declaration of the rights of the citizens within government

block grants: fixed funds that are transferred to states for the implementation of a policy or program

budget execution: the governor's implementation of the budget when the legislature is not in session

bureaucracy: a government organization that implements laws and provides services to individuals

capture: groundwater is owned by the landowner of the property above the groundwater

caseload: the workload (in cases) of the judiciary

casework: legislators and their staff assist constituents in their districts with specific requests

categorical grants: funds distributed to state or local governments for programs that require governments to meet conditions established by the federal government

certify: the state controller stating that the state has enough money to cover the budget items

charter: a city's governing document

CHIP: a federal program that is run by the states to provide health coverage to children whose families who make too much to qualify for Medicaid but not enough to buy private insurance

city manager: an administrator hired to run the day-to-day operations in a city

civil cases: cases in which individuals, corporations, or the government bring suit against another party and must prove that the harm was done to them beyond a "preponderance of evidence"

clemency: the power to reduce or delay punishment for a crime

closed primary: an election in which only voters registered with a party may vote for the party's candidates

coercive federalism: a system in which the federal government establishes guidelines for the states and may punish the states for not participating

collateral consequences: additional civil punishments of criminal convictions

commerce clause: the clause in the US Constitution that gives Congress the power to regulate commerce with foreign nations and among the states

committee: a small group of legislators who investigate, craft, assess, and take action on legislation before it is considered by the whole chamber

common law: law that is established when judges apply past decisions by courts—called legal precedents—to the facts of a new case before them

community supervision: a defendant is released and allowed to live in the community under conditions set by the court

concurrent powers: powers shared between the state and federal governments

confederal system: a power-sharing arrangement in which a central government's authority is granted by the individual political units

conservative: a political philosophy that believes in limited government, free markets, and individual entrepreneurship

constitution: a document that establishes principles, powers, and responsibilities of government

cooperative federalism: a federalist system in which each level of government has overlapping and intertwined authority over shared issues

council-manager system: a system of local government in which the city council appoints a city manager to run city business

councils of governments (COGs): a regional planning commission made up of area-wide local governments

criminal cases: cases in which the government brings suit against the defendant for violating the law and in which the defendant is guilty beyond a reasonable doubt

criminal disenfranchisement: the loss of voting rights for felons during incarceration and after they have served their sentence

cumulative voting: voters cast multiple votes (usually equal to the positions in an election)

death penalty: (capital punishment) the sentence of a convicted individual to death

decentralization: the distribution of authority between national, state, and local party organizations so that each level exercises a degree of independent authority

deferred adjudication: a defendant pleads guilty and the judge delays a final verdict until the time the defendant successfully completes the supervision period

delegate: where a legislator who is simply a mouthpiece for the wishes of his or her constituency

Dillon's rule: a ruling that established that state governments can place restrictions on municipalities as long as these rules do not violate the state's constitution

disclosure: the filing of a report that includes details about lawmakers' personal finances or business dealings

disenfranchise: deprive individuals of the right to vote

dispose: take a case off the court's docket generally by being heard or dismissed

dual budgeting process: the legislative branch and executive branch coordinate to propose, shape, and pass a biennial budget

dual federalism: a federalist system in which the federal, state, and local government each has exclusive powers that are reserved to it alone

dual structure: Texas's two supreme court system

Duverger's law: a winner-take-all electoral system generally leads to a two-party system

early voting: voters are able to cast a ballot in Texas two weeks before Election Day

electioneering: advertising for or against issues or candidates (radio, mail, Internet, or television), granting endorsements, and raising funds

elite theory: groups that have greater resources are in a better position to accomplish their goals

en banc: where all of the justices of the court hear and consider the case

enforcement: the carrying out of rules by an agency or commission within the bureaucracy

enumerated powers: powers that are expressly identified as powers that the federal government can take

executive orders: legally binding orders from the governor that are used to direct government, especially state agencies, in the execution of law

expenditures: the total amount of funds that the state government can spend, as established by the spending cap

federal system: a power-sharing arrangement between central governing authority and individual political units

fee: a payment for a service rendered

felony: the highest criminal offense under state or federal law

Fifteenth Amendment: the 1870 amendment to the US Constitution, which prohibited the denial of voting rights upon the basis of race

filibuster: when a senator holds the floor and restrains the chamber from moving forward on legislation

fine: a financial punishment for an offense

first reading: legislation considered at the committee stage

fiscal note: an overview of the estimated financial impact, including cost of the proposed changes, revenue generated, and staffing impacts to the bureaucracy resulting if the bill passes

free rider problem: a situation in which individuals benefit from a publicly provided good or service without paying for it and actively supporting its acquisition

full faith and credit clause: a Constitution clause that requires that each state respect the rights and proceedings of other states

general law city: a city that is only allowed to operate under laws the state provides

general laws: laws where the bill potentially affects all Texans

general revenue funds: state funds that include revenue from all sources (including federal funds)

gerrymander: a process of manipulating district boundaries to benefit a single group

get out the vote (GOTV): a tactic to get friendly voters to the polls

grand jury: a legal body charged with the task of conducting official proceedings to investigate potential criminal conduct

grassroots lobbying: getting members of the general public who are interested in an issue to contact elected officials to persuade them on an issue

guardian ad litem: an appointed person to represent the best interests of a child if a parent will not or cannot fill the responsibility

home rule city: city that is allowed self-governance independent of state law

homestead exemption: a portion of property value that Texans don't have to pay taxes on

homestead law: a law that prevents Texans from losing their homes in the event of bankruptcy or other financial problems

hybrid agencies: bureaucratic organizations whose leaders are selected by a mixture of appointments and elections

impeachment: the legal process in which the legislative branch has the authority to indict and remove a public official

implementation: the execution by the bureaucracy of laws and decisions made by the legislative, executive, or judicial branch

implied powers: powers that the federal government is not expressly granted but that it is assumed to possess so that Congress can carry out its duties

inaugural speech: an address that is not constitutionally required but is conventionally delivered at the beginning of a new gubernatorial term

incumbent: an individual who currently holds a public office

incumbents: candidates who are also the current officeholder

individualistic political culture: emphasizes personal achievement, individual freedoms, individual enterprise, and loyalty to self instead of others

informal powers: actions governors might take that are not formally written but are exercised through the activities of the governor

initiative: a process where local voters can directly propose ordinances to city charters

institutional memory: a collective understanding of the way an organization works held by those who run it

interest group: any formal organization of individuals or groups that seeks to influence government to promote their common cause

iron triangle: the relationship that forms between interest groups, the legislature, and executive agency regulators in the policy formation and implementation process

issue network: a single-issue iron triangle

jurisdiction: the official territory and types of cases over which a court exercises authority

jury trial: a group of individuals picked at random decides on guilt or innocence

law and order: a dimension of Texas political culture that demands a strict adherence to a fair and adequate criminal justice system and swift enforcement of laws

Legislative Redistricting Board: the group of officials who draw the district lines if it were the case that the legislature was not able to agree

liberal: a political philosophy that emphasizes social equality and a large role for government to protect liberties and alleviate social problems

licensing: the authorization process that gives a company, an individual, or an organization permission to carry out a specific task

limited government: a political system in which the government's functions and powers are restricted to protect individual liberty

line item veto: a veto that allows the governor to reject a specific provision in a bill without rejecting the whole bill

lobbying: direct communications with members of the legislative or executive branch of government to influence legislation or administrative action

local laws: laws that only affect units of government at the local level

logrolling: trading favors, votes, or influence for legislative actions

mandatory review: cases required to be heard by a specific court

markup: where legislators add, subtract, or replace part of the original legislation so that it meets the preferences of the committee

matching grants: funds the state adds to supplement specific federal government programs

mayor-council system: a system of local government headed by an elected mayor and a city council

means tested: income measured programs that provide aid to individuals and families with low incomes

Medicaid: medical coverage for low-income Texans provided by the federal government

Medicare: a national social insurance program for older Americans funded by a payroll tax, premiums, and surtaxes and administered by the federal government

merit selection: a nonpartisan way to select judges in which a commission selected by state officials sends recommendations to the governor and the governor selects the nominees from that list

microtargetting: identifying potential subgroups of supporters for customizable messages; also known as narrow casting

minimal government: a government that provides minimal services and interferes as little as possible in the transactions of individuals and institutions

misdemeanors: a class of criminal offenses which are minor wrongdoings

monarchy: a government run by a single individual, often a king or queen, until death or abdication

motor voter law: a statute mandating that state governments provide voter registration opportunities to individuals applying for or renewing their driver's license

multimember agencies: bureaucratic organizations staffed by a minimum of three individuals

municipal bond: a debt security where a municipality takes out a loan to spend funds and agrees to pay the funds back, generally with interest

name identification: familiarity with a candidate's name

necessary and proper clause: Article 1, Section 8 of the Constitution, which specifies that Congress is allowed to assume additional powers needed to carry out its function

negative campaigning: a campaign that highlights the negative of their opponent over the positive of their own candidate

New Deal: a federal economic recovery program in response to the Great Depression that stabilized the banking industry, created jobs, promoted fair labor standards, and created a social welfare network

new federalism: a federal system that returns greater responsibilities, duties, and funding to the states

no contest: a plea where a defendant does not admit guilt but is not contesting the underlying facts

open primary: an election in which any registered voter can vote for a party's candidates

opinion: a document that can express the view of the judges and often takes the form of a majority opinion, when written by a justice representing the majority, but may also be a concurring or dissenting opinion

ordinances: the local law of a municipal area, passed by a city council

original jurisdiction: the court in which the case is first heard

pardon: the power to forgive a crime

parole: a system in which a prisoner is released from prison prior to completing his or her full sentence

partisans: strongly committed members of a party

party competition: electoral conflict that signals how successful one party is over another

party platform: a list of values, beliefs, and policy issues that are endorsed and supported by a political party

pay as you go: budget rule that Texas cannot spend more money than it receives in revenue

pay-as-you-go system: state funds spend must equal state funds received

permanent school fund: the fund that contains the money from the state's long-term investment and that pays for public education

place system: an electoral system in which voters elect council members from a citywide area but that specifies a separate seat carved into districts

plea bargain: where the defendant agrees to a lesser set of charges than initially charged by the prosecutors

plural executive: diffusion of authority and power throughout several entities in the executive branch

plural executive: the diffusion of authority and power throughout several entities in the executive branch and the bureaucracy

pluralist theory: competition keeps powerful interest groups in check and no single group dominates

point of order: a technical objection to an error in a bill

political action committees (PACs): an organization that collects donations from donors and uses these funds to donate to candidates, parties, or other political causes

political culture: a set of shared values and practices held by people that informs their expectations of government and their vision of a just society

political efficacy: the belief that your participation can influence the political system

political polarization: voters' opinions on policy and political matters become more strictly defined by their identification with a political party

political socialization: the process in which individuals acquire political values and behaviors that have a strong influence on future voting behavior

political succession: the sequential passing of authority from one person to another as the previous people are unable to serve

poll tax: an unconstitutional tax that required those desiring to register to vote to pay a fee

popular sovereignty: rule by the people

preemption: the supremacy of rules and laws handed down at the state level

preemptions: when the federal government grants states permission and

funding to implement federal regulations in policy areas but only if the states comply with a host of conditions

presiding officer: a role of the lieutenant governor who is in charge of the administrative and procedural duties of the Texas Senate

primary election: an election in which each party selects its nominees for office

private interest groups: groups that advocate for the benefit of their members

probable cause: the legal grounds law enforcement uses to make an arrest or conduct a search

probate: the process by which there is official recognition and registration of the validity of the last will and testimate of a person

proclamations: gubernatorial orders that are used to make factual determinations to trigger other available powers

progressive tax: a tax with a rate that increases as the amount that is taxed rises

prosecutor: the state's lawyer who is responsible for bringing charges against accused lawbreakers

public interest groups: groups that benefit the public in general

public opinion polling: a battery of survey questions asked of a representative sample of individuals

reapportionment: redistribution of representation based on decennial recounting of residents

recall: a process through which voters can oust sitting members of the city government before their terms are up

recognition: the power to call on a legislator to allow him or her to speak during debates

recuse: decide not to participate in legislative activity as an elected official

redistributive policies: policies that transfer wealth from those who have more to those who have less

redistricting: the redrawing of the legislative districts to meet federal and state requirements

referendum: a procedure through which local voters can repeal existing ordinances that a city council won't rescind

register: sign up to vote in elections

regressive tax: a tax that exacts a larger percentage of the earnings of low-income than of high-income individuals

regular session: legislative session meeting for 140 days in January of odd-numbered years

regulations: standards that are established for the function and management of industry, business, individuals, and other parts of government

religiosity: the belief, practice, and activity of organized religion

republic: a form of government in which people rule indirectly through elected representatives

reserve clause: the Tenth Amendment to the US Constitution, which states that powers not delegated to the federal government are reserved for the states

resolutions: legislation that conveys the will of the chamber

revenue: the income a state receives from taxes, fees, and other sources

revolving door: when agency bureaucrats and legislators leave their jobs to become lobbyists, or vice versa

rules: regulations designed to control government or the conduct of people and industries

runoff election: an election where, if no candidate receives a majority of the votes, the two top vote getters run again

search and seizure: where law enforcement agents search an accused's property and collect any evidence relevant to the alleged crime

second reading: legislation considered at the floor stage

segregation: enforced or de facto separation of different racial groups

select committee: a committee that is temporary and has a fixed issue to investigate or legislation to consider

selective benefits: private goods made available to people who organize for a collective good

seniority: having a lengthier legislative service than others

separation of powers: a system that vests political, judicial, and policymaking authority across different branches of government

sin taxes: taxes imposed on the sale of alcohol and tobacco and on some forms of gambling, and fees imposed on "sexually oriented" businesses

sine die: the end of a legislative session

single-member districts: an electoral unit that elects only one member of a political body, such as a legislature, and through which smaller communities can gain representation on that bod

social contract: an agreement in which the governed give up freedoms in return for government protection

sovereignty: authority over a political entity, such as a province or a state

special district: a single-purpose government that performs a specialized function

special election: an election contest held as needed to fill vacancies created by death, resignation, or removal from office

special laws: laws that exempt businesses or individuals from state laws

special session: legislative session that can be called by the governor on any issue the governor decides requires attention

split ticket voting: choosing candidates from different parties for different offices

sprawl: rapid growth of urban and suburban areas spreading into the undeveloped land surrounding it

standing committees: permanent committees that deal with a specific issue or topic

State of the State Address: address used by governors to set a policy agenda

straight ticket voting: checking one box to vote for every candidate a specific party has on the ballot

suburbanization: population shifts from the urban and rural areas to suburban areas adjacent to major cities

suffrage: the right to participate in the electoral process by voting

super PACs: independent expenditure committees that are legally permitted to raise and spend unlimited funds from individuals, corporations, unions, or other groups to advocate on behalf of their causes but are not permitted to give to candidates directly

supremacy clause: Article VI, Section 2 of the Constitution that states that the US Constitution and federal laws "shall be the supreme law of the land"

TANF: a program that provides financial and medical assistance to needy children and their parents or relatives

Tax Increment Reinvestment Zones (TIRZs): special zones created to attract business and develop the economy within the geographic zone

Tejanos: Mexican Texans during the time of the Texas Revolution

term limits: legal restrictions on the number of terms that an elected official can serve in a specific office

Texas Miracle: economic good fortune the state experienced from 2001 to 2008

third reading: the voting stage of legislation

traditionalistic political culture: the goal of the political system is to maintain order and a hierarchical set of political elites largely determine public policy

transactional theory: public policy is bought and sold like a commodity to the highest bidder

trustee: a legislator who votes in accordance with their interpretation of what his or her district would want

turnover: when incumbents lose their seats or leave their seats, and new members (freshmen) are voted into office

unfunded mandates: federal or state legislation that requires the states to implement policies but does not supply funding necessary for implementation

unincorporated area: a region that is administered as part of a county not a city

unitary system: a central government that has complete authority over all levels of government

veto: formal, constitutional decisions to formally reject a resolution or bill made by the legislature

voir dire: jurors are questioned by attorneys and judges in court to determine if a potential juror is biased, cannot deal with the issues fairly, or knows a party to the case

Voting Rights Act: a landmark piece of federal legislation that outlawed racial discrimination in voting

vouchers: programs to provide a student with authorization for government funding to be used at a private school

winner-take-all election: whichever candidate wins the most votes wins the seat

NOTES

Chapter 1 The Struggle for Texas: Demographics, Culture, and Political Power

1. http://www.newswest9.com/story/29467476/83-year-old-pecos-man-killed-in-dog-attack
2. https://www.texastribune.org/2016/05/03/railroad-commission-vote-tiny-nordheim-loses-waste/
3. http://www.npr.org/2013/04/10/176677299/construction-booming-in-texas-but-many-workers-pay-dearly
4. Randolph B. Campbell. 2003. *Gone to Texas: A History of the Lone Star State*. Oxford University Press.
5. Robert Rickliss. 1996. *The Karankawa Indians of Texas*. Austin: University of Texas Press.
6. https://tshaonline.org/handbook/online/articles/bzi04
7. Marquis James. 1929. *The Raven: A Biography of Sam Houston*. Austin: University of Texas Press.
8. Robert A. Calvert, Arnoldo de Leon, and Gregg Cantrell. 2002. *The History of Texas*. Wheeling, IL: Harlan Davidson.
9. A. Ray Stephens. 2010. *Texas: A Historical Atlas*. Norman: University of Oklahoma Press.
10. Tejano Origins. http://www.tamu.edu/faculty/ccbn/dewitt/tejanoorigins.htm
11. Tejano Origins. http://www.tamu.edu/faculty/ccbn/dewitt/tejanoorigins.htm
12. Robert A. Calvert, Arnoldo de Leon, and Gregg Cantrell. 2002. *The History of Texas*. Wheeling, IL: Harlan Davidson.
13. https://tshaonline.org/handbook/online/articles/pkaan
14:. Sandy Sheehy. 1990. Texas Big Rich. New York: St. Martin's, 17.
15. http://www.beagsmart.org/a-look-at-texas-ag/crops/cotton
16. Robert A. Calvert, Arnoldo de Leon, and Gregg Cantrell. 2002. *The History of Texas*. Wheeling, IL: Harlan Davidson, 213.
17. https://tshaonline.org/handbook/online/articles/ama01
18. Judith Walker Linsley, Ellen Walker Rienstra, and Jo Ann Stiles. *Giant Under the Hill*. Austin: Texas State Historical Association, 89.
19. Randolph B. Campbell. 2003. *Gone to Texas: A History of the Lone Star State*. Oxford University Press, 363.
20. Office of the Governor, http://gov.texas.gov/files/ecodev/TXOil.pdf
21. Anne Dingus. 1984. "Texas Primer: Barbed Wire." *Texas Monthly*, March.
22. Texas Agriculture Stats, Texas Department of Agriculture. https://www.texasagriculture.gov/About/TexasAgStats.aspx
23. https://tshaonline.org/handbook/online/articles/npwnj
24. Sources: US Census Bureau, Texas Workforce Commission, Bureau of Economic Analysis, Bureau of Labor Statistics.
25. Randolph B. Campbell. 2003. *Gone to Texas: A History of the Lone Star State*. Oxford University Press, 401.
26. Sandy Sheehy. 1990. *Texas Big Rich*. New York: St. Martin's Paperbacks.
27. The Economic Impact of Travel on Texas, Prepared for Texas Tourism, Office of the Governor. http://travel.texas.gov/tti/media/PDFs/TX14pFinalrev.pdf
28. Erica Grieder. 2013. "Happy Trails." *Texas Monthly*, August.
29. Max Ehrenfreund. 2015. "The Facts about Rick Perry and the 'Texas Miracle'" *Washington Post* Wonkblog: http://www.washingtonpost.com/blogs/wonkblog/wp/2015/06/08/the-facts-about-rick-perry-and-the-texas-miracle/
30. Bureau of Economic Analysis, GDP changes classified by industry. Accessed 6/25/2015.
31. http://www.bloomberg.com/news/articles/2015-06-23/texas-has-a-great-and-most-unusual-economic-stimulus-package; https://www.houstonpublicmedia.org/articles/news/2016/01/26/135115/drop-in-oil-tax-revenue-not-going-to-be-pretty-for-texas/
32. http://kut.org/post/study-texas-income-inequality-could-affect-state-revenues
33. Erin Ailworth and Ben Leubsdorf. 2016. "Texas, Once a Star, Becomes a Drag on the US Economy." *The Wall Street Journal*, October 12.
34. Erica Greider. 2013. *Big, Hot, Cheap and Right: What America Can Learn from the Strange Genius of Texas*. PublicAffairs Books, 13.
35. Max Ehrenfreund. 2015. "The Facts about Rick Perry and the 'Texas Miracle'" *Washington Post* Wonkblog: http://www.washingtonpost.com/blogs/wonkblog/wp/2015/06/08/the-facts-about-rick-perry-and-the-texas-miracle/
36. Rice University, Baker Institute Center for Health and Biosciences, Characteristics of Uninsured Texans, March 2015.
37. http://www.star-telegram.com/news/state/texas/article3844307.html; http://dfw.cbslocal.com/2014/09/15/texas-fast-paced-growth-hasnt-reduced-inequality/
38. Randolph B. Campbell. 2003. *Gone to Texas: A History of the Lone Star State*. Oxford University Press, 327.
39. https://tshaonline.org/handbook/online/articles/hyunw
40. https://www.texastribune.org/2015/04/30/study-texas-rate-uninsured-dropped-31-percent/
41. http://www.pewhispanic.org/2013/08/29/ii-ranking-latino-populations-in-the-states/
42. Alexa Ura and Annie Daniel. 2015. "See Demographic Shift by Texas County." *The Texas Tribune*, June 25. http://www.texastribune.org/2015/06/25/see-demographic-shift-tx-counties-2010-2014/

43. http://www.npc.umich.edu/publications/policy_briefs/brief16/PolicyBrief16.pdf

44. http://www.sciencedaily.com/releases/2014/05/140509130038.htm

45. *tea.texas.gov/acctres/Enroll_2013-14.pdf*

46. David Montejano. 1987. *Anglos and Mexicans in the Making of Texas, 1836-1986.* Austin: University of Texas Press.

47. http://www.dallasnews.com/news/education/headlines/20130503-texas-leaders-educators-and-courts-grapple-with-segregated-public-schools.ece

48. http://www.governing.com/gov-data/education-data/state-high-school-graduation-rates-by-race-ethnicity.html

49. State of Student Aid and Higher Education in Texas, January 2015, TG Research Analytical Services. https://www.tgslc.org/pdf/SOSA.pdf, page 68.

50. http://www.slate.com/articles/news_and_politics/politics/2015/05/whites_prefer_to_live_with_whites_why_integrating_america_s_neighborhoods.html

51. Liz Crampton. 2015. "Supreme Court: Texas Reinforced Segregated Housing." *The Texas Tribune,* June 25. http://www.texastribune.org/2015/06/25/supreme-court-rules-dallas-fair-housing-case/

52. http://www.pewresearch.org/fact-tank/2015/06/29/in-greater-dallas-area-segregation-by-income-and-race/

53. Texas Department of Aging and Disability Services.

54. William A. Vega, Kyriakos S. Markides, Jacqueline L. Angel, and Fernando M. Torres, Editors. 2015. *Challenges of Latino Aging in the Americas.* New York: Springer.

55. http://www.mystatesman.com/news/news/appeals-court-tosses-lawsuit-blocking-texas-medica/nq8tC/

56. Lucian Pye. 1968. "Political Culture." *International Encyclopedia of the Social Sciences,* vol. 12. New York: Crowell, Collier and MacMillian. 218.

57. Daniel J. Elazar. 1984. *American Federalism: A View from the States,* 3rd Edition. New York: Harper and Row.

58. http://www.texastribune.org/2015/06/28/paxton-county-clerks-can-deny-same-sex-marriage-li/

59. Source: Texas Politics Project / University of Texas Poll, July 2008.

60. Source: Texas Politics Project / University of Texas Poll, July 2009. Question asked: "Some people think the country needs leaders who have experience and knowledge about how businesses, politics, and special interests work in the United States. Suppose these people are at one end of a 1-7 scale, at point 1. Others think things in government are so broken that we need to bring in people from outside politics who might be able to reform the way things are done. Suppose these people are at the other end of the scale, at point 7. People who are exactly in-between are at point 4, and of course other people have opinions at other points between 1 and 7. Where would you place yourself on this scale, or wouldn't you have any opinion about that?"

61. Ross Ramsey, "UT/TT Poll: Texans Distrust Big Institutions on Privacy." *The Texas Tribune,* November 8, 2013.

62. 2010 U.S. Religion Census, Church Membership Figures for Texas

63. Robert Wuthnow. 2014. *Rough Country: How Texas Became America's Most Powerful Bible Belt State.* Princeton: Princeton University Press, 442.

64. Mary Lasswell. 1958. *I'll Take Texas.* Boston: Houghton Mifflin.

Chapter 1 Photo Caption Notes

* http://kxan.com/2015/11/02/texas-home-schooling-case-where-do-religious-liberties-end/

Chapter 2 The Texas Constitution

1. BeaufordChambless. 1992. *The Birth of Texas: The Ad-Interim Government of The Republic of Texas March, 1836 - October, 1836.* Waco, TX: Printed by Author, 10.

2. Chambless, *Birth of Texas,* 16.

3. William C. Binkley. 1952. *The Texas Revolution.* Austin: Texas State Historical Association.

4. Manuel Mier y Teran's Letter to President Guadalupe Victoria, June 30, 1828. From AlleineHowren, "Causes and Origin of the Decree of April 6, 1830." *The Southwestern Historical Quarterly*16, no. 4 (April 1913): 395–398.

5. Ernest Wallace, David M. Vigness, and George B. Ward, eds. 1994. *Documents of Texas History.* Austin, TX: State House Press, 85.

6. From Eugene C. Barker, ed. 1927. *The Austin Papers,* vol. 3. Austin: University of Texas, 116–119.

7. Wallace, Vigness, and Ward, *Documents of Texas History,* 118.

8. Lewis W. Newton and Herbert P. Gambrell. 1949. *Texas: Yesterday and Today with the Constitution of State of Texas.* Dallas, TX: Turner Company, 144.

9. Wallace, Vigness, and Ward, *Documents of Texas History,* 149.

10. Frederic L. Paxson. "The Constitution of Texas, 1845." *The Southwestern Historical Quarterly* 18, no. 4 (1915): 386–398.

11. Richard Parker. "Sam Houston, We Have a Problem." *New York Times,* January 31, 2011. http://opinionator.blogs.nytimes.com/2011/01/31/sam-houston-we-have-a-problem/?_r=0

12. Parker, "Sam Houston."

13. "The Handbook of Texas: Reconstruction." Austin: Texas State Historical Association. https://tshaonline.org/handbook/online/articles/mzr01

14. Alwyn Barr. 1996. *Black Texans.* Norman: University of Oklahoma Press, 48.

15. "The Handbook of Texas."

16. Seth Shepard McKay, ed. 1930. *Debates in the Texas Constitutional Convention of 1875.* Austin: University of Texas Press, 40.

17. Barry A. Crouch and Donaly E. Brice. 2011. *The Governor's Hounds: The Texas State Police, 1870-1873.* Austin: University of Texas Press, 1.

18. Seth Shepard McKay. 1942. *Seven Decades of the Texas Constitution of 1876.* Lubbock, TX: Printed by Author, 31.

19. McKay, *Seven Decades,* 89.

20. Robert A. Calvert, Arnoldo De León, and Gregg Cantrell. 2013. *The History of Texas.* 5th ed. Chichester, West Sussex, UK: John Wiley & Sons, 175.

21. McKay, *Debates,* 147.

22. McKay, *Debates,* 177.

23. Harold H. Bruff. "Separation of Powers Under the Texas Constitution." *Texas Law Review* 68, no. 7 (1990): 1337–1367.

24. "Is a Confederate Flag License Plate Free Speech?" npr.org: LAW. March 23, 2015. http://www.npr.org/2015/03/23/394308609/is-a-confederate-flag-license-plate-free-speech

25. "Amendments to the Texas Constitution Since 1876: Current Through the November 3, 2015, Constitutional Amendment Election." Prepared by the Research Division of the Texas Legislative Council, February 2016. www.tlc.state.tx.us/docs/amendments/Constamend1876.pdf

26. University of Texas/Texas Tribune Poll, October 2014.

27. Frank M. Stewart and Joseph L. Clark. 1936. Rev. ed. *The Constitution and Government of Texas*. Boston: D.C. Heath and Company, 27.

28. McKay, *Debates*, 135.

29. McKay, *Debates*, 139.

30. Staff of the Office of Constitutional Research, Texas Legislative Council. *Constitutional Amendments Analyzed: Analysis of the Eight Proposed Amendments for Election—November 4, 1975.* http://www.lrl.state.tx.us/scanned/Constitutional_Amendments/amendments64_tlc_1975-11-04.pdf

Chapter 3 Federalism

1. "Greg Abbott Delivers 2015 Texas Inaugural Speech," Office of the Governor Greg Abbott: News, January 20, 2015, http://gov.texas.gov/news/speech/20415

2. Greg Korte and Melanie Eversley, "Judge Orders Halt to Obama Immigration Plan," *USA Today*, February 17, 2015.

3. JilianRayfield, "Texas AG Enjoys Suing the Federal Government," Salon.com, September 10, 2012, http://www.salon.com/2012/09/10/texas_ag_enjoys_suing_the_federal_government/

4. Brandi Grissom, "Dallas Sherriff Responds to Texas Governor: All ICE Detainers Honored this Year," Trail Blazers Blog, *The Dallas Morning News*, October 26, 2015, http://trailblazersblog.dallasnews.com/2015/10/gov-greg-abbott-wants-dallas-sheriff-to-honor-federal-immigration-detainers.html/

5. Morgan Smith, "Abbott: No Grants for Sheriffs who Don't Work

with ICE," *The Texas Tribune*, November 4, 2016, http://www.texastribune.org/2015/11/04/abbot-no-state-grants-sheriffs-who-dont-work-ice/

6. Sam Biddle, "'I DO NOT TRUST BARAK OBAMA': The Paranoid Emails of Jade Helm 15," Gawker.com, June 16, 2015, http://gawker.com/i-do-not-trust-barak-obama-the-paranoid-emails-of-ja-1711669400

7. Dylan Baddour, "Texans Organize 'Operation Counter Jade Helm' to Keep an Eye on the Federal Troops," updated Monday, July 13, 2015, http://www.chron.com/news/houston-texas/texas/article/Texans-organize-Operation-Counter-Jade-Helm-to-6378017.php?mc_cid=46356c6a06&mc_eid=101a099a60

8. Office of the Governor Greg Abbott: News. "Governor Abbott Directs Texas State Guard To Monitor Operation Jade Helm 15," April 28, 2015, http://gov.texas.gov/news/press-release/20805

9. Biddle, "Paranoid Emails."

10. Ross Ramsey, "UT/TT Poll: Texans Wary of Domestic Use of Military," *The Texas Tribune*, June 25, 2015.

11. Caitlin M. Dunklee and Rebecca A. Larsen, "Examining the Texas Prison Reform Model: How Texas is Maintaining Racial Disparity and Mass Incarceration," Institute for Urban Policy Research and Analysis, University of Texas at Austin, May 14, 2015, http://www.utexas.edu/cola/iupra/_files/Criminal%20Justice%20Brief%20Final%20final.pdf

12. U.S. Census Bureau. U.S. Department of Commerce Bureau of Economic Analysis.

13. Dan Mangan, "Don't Mess with Medicaid Expansion? A Lesson from Texas," CNBC.com, May 29, 2015, http://www.cnbc.com/2015/05/29/texas-pays-a-big-price-for-saying-no-to-medicaid-expansion.html

14. Paige Winfield Cunningham, "Texas Governor Rejects Medicaid Expansion in 'Obamacare,'" *The Washington Times*, July 9, 2012, http://www.washingtontimes.com/news/2012/jul/9/texas-governor-rejects-medicaid-expansion-in-obama/

15. "Legislative Budget Board Fiscal Size-Up: 2016–17 Biennium." Submitted to the 84th Texas Legislature, Prepared by Legislative Budget Board Staff, May 2016. http://www.lbb.state.tx.us/Documents/Publications/Fiscal_SizeUp/Fiscal_SizeUp.pdf

16. Andrew Reeves, "Political Disaster: Unilateral Powers, Electoral Incentives, and Presidential Disaster Declarations," *Journal of Politics* 73, no. 4 (2011): 1142–1151.

17. Fred Gantt Jr. 1964. *The Chief Executive in Texas: A Study in Gubernatorial Leadership.* Austin: University of Texas Press, 224.

18. Texas State Library and Archives Commission. "Texas Legislature, Joint Committee Investigating the Pink Bollworm Infestation in Texas: An Inventory of the Stenographic Report at the Texas State Archives, 1920." Austin: University of Texas Libraries. http://www.lib.utexas.edu/taro/tslac/50061/tsl-50061.html

19. Ben H. Procter, "Great Depression," *The Handbook of Texas Online*, Texas State Historical Association, uploaded on June 15, 2010, https://tshaonline.org/handbook/online/articles/npg01

20. CQ Researcher, "Reagan's 'New Federalism,'" cqpress.com, April 3, 1981, http://library.cqpress.com/cqresearcher/document.php?id=cqresrre1981040300

21. Republican Party of Texas, "Report of Permanent Committee on Platform and Resolutions as Amended and Adopted by the 2014 State Convention of the Republican Party of Texas," http://www.texasgop.org/wp-content/uploads/2014/06/2014-Platform-Final.pdf

22. Edgar Walters, "Feds Have New Leverage in Medicaid Showdown," *The Texas Tribune*, November 11, 2014, http://www.texastribune.org/2014/11/11/feds-consider-waiver-while-lawmakers-debate-medica/

23. Robert Pear, "Reagan Modifies 'New Federalism' Plan," Special to the *New York Times*, January 26, 1983, http://www.nytimes.com/1983/01/26/us/reagan-modifies-new-federalism-plan.html

24. Becca Aaronson, "Perry Directs HHSC to Pursue Medicaid Block Grant," *The Texas Tribune*, September 16, 2013, http://www.texastribune.org/2013/09/16/perry-directs-hhsc-pursue-medicaid-block-grant/

25. JohnKincaid, "From Cooperative to Coercive Federalism," *The Annals of the American Academy of Political and Social Science* 509 (1990): 139–152.

26. Jess Bravin and Louise Radnofsky, "Court Backs Obama on Health Law," *Wall Street Journal*, June 29, 2012, http://www.wsj.com/articles/SB10001424052702304898704577480371370927862

27. Will Weissert, "Could Texas Win Block Medicaid Grant from Feds?" *Dallas Morning News*, January 1, 2015, http://www.dallasnews.com/news/state/headlines/20150101-could-texas-win-block-medicaid-grant-from-feds.ece

28. Walters, "Feds Have New Leverage."

29. Report of Bipartisan Task Force on Unfunded Mandates to The Honorable Rick Perry, Governor of Texas, May 6, 2011, http://gov.texas.gov/files/press-office/5-6_Unfunded_Mandates_Narrative.pdf

30. Lucius Lomax, "Scoliosis Screenings Still Mandatory in Public Schools after Governor's Veto," *Newspapertree*: Health & Environment, September 13, 2013, http://newspapertree.com/articles/2013/09/13/scoliosis-screenings-still-mandatory-in-public-schools-after-governors-veto

31. NeenaSatija, "Texas May Refuse to Follow Climate Rules," *The Texas Tribune*, August 7, 2014, http://www.texastribune.org/2014/08/07/texas-may-refuse-follow-climate-rules/

32. Jennifer Hiller, "Texas Takes over Greenhouse Gas Permitting from EPA," *fuel fix* (blog), *Houston Chronicle*, November 25, 2014, http://fuelfix.com/blog/2014/11/25/texas-takes-over-greenhouse-gas-permitting-from-epa/

33. Price Daniel, "Tidelands Controversy," *The Handbook of Texas Online*, Texas State Historical Association, uploaded on June 15, 2010, https://tshaonline.org/handbook/online/articles/mgt02

34. Daniel, *Handbook of Texas*.

35. House of Representatives Judiciary Committee, Chairman Bob Goodlatte's Press Release December 1, 2014.

36. Brian M. Rosenthal and Patrick Svitek, "Judge Halts Obama's Executive Order on Immigration," *Houston Chronicle*, February 16, 2015, http://www.houstonchronicle.com/news/houston-texas/houston/article/Judge-halts-Obama-s-executive-order-on-immigration-6084556.php

37. Bobby Blanchard, "Abbott Takes Lead in Immigration Challenge," *The Texas Tribune*, December 3, 2014, http://www.texastribune.org/2014/12/03/greg-abbott-sues-over-executive-action-immigration/

38. Abby Livingston and Julian Aguilár, "Congress to Vote on Sanctuary Cities," *The Texas Tribune*, July 22, 2015, http://www.texastribune.org/2015/07/22/texas-congress-sanctuary-cities/

39. Julian Aguilár, "Day 24: Stringent Voter ID Law Means Changes at Texas Polls," *The Texas Tribune*, August 24, 2011, http://www.texastribune.org/2011/08/24/day-24-voter-id-law-means-changes-ballot-box/

40. Mitch Mitchell, "Fort Worth Woman Admits Guilt in Voter Fraud Case as National Debate Continues," *Fort Worth Star-Telegram*, June 7, 2015, www.star-telegram.com/news/local/community/fort-worth/article23415846.html#storylink=cpy

41. Wayne Slater, "Few Texas Voter-Fraud Cases Would Have Been Prevented by Photo ID Law, Review Shows," *Dallas Morning News*, September 8, 2013. http://www.dallasnews.com/news/politics/headlines/20130908-few-texas-voter-fraud-cases-would-have-been-prevented-by-photo-id-law-review-shows.ece

42. Jeffrey Weiss, "What Texans Need to Know about Common Core Education Standards," *Dallas Morning News*, June 24, 2014, http://www.dallasnews.com/news/education/headlines/20140623-what-texans-need-to-know-about-common-core-education-standards.ece

43. Andrew Ujifusa, "Days Apart, Two States Opt to Replace Common Core," *Education Week*, June 6, 2014, http://www.edweek.org/ew/articles/2014/06/06/35commonore.h33.html

44. "Inauguration Day Remarks by Lt. Gov. Dan Patrick," KSAT ABC 12 News, updated January 20, 2015, http://www.ksat.com/news/inauguration-day-remarks-by-lt-gov-dan-patrick

45. Texas Constitution, Article 1, Section 1. http://www.statutes.legis.state.tx.us/Docs/CN/htm/CN.1.htm

Chapter 4 Voting and Elections

1. http://www.expressnews.com/news/news_columnists/brian_chasnoff/article/Candidate-dressed-as-gay-Hitler-7217786.php

2. http://www.chron.com/news/politics/texas/article/Smith-Cain-legislative-race-turns-ugly-7850911.php

3. http://www.expressnews.com/news/news_columnists/gilbert_garcia/article/Madla-slings-mud-at-Uresti-with-new-ad-6807973.php; https://www.texastribune.org/2016/02/10/san-antonio-familiar-uresti-madla-ballot/

4. Jan E. Leighley and Jonathan Nagler. 2014. *Who Votes Now? Demographics, Issues, Inequality, and Turnout in the United States*. Princeton, NJ: Princeton University Press.

5. http://www.votetexas.gov/register-to-vote/

6. Stephen Knack and James Whit. 1998. "Did States' Motor Voter Programs Help the Democrats?" *American Politics Research* 26 (3): 344–65; Daniel P. Franklin and Eric E. Grier. 1997. "Effects of Motor Voter Legislation." *American Politics Research* 25 (1): 104–117.

7. Neiheisel, Jacob R. and Barry C. Burden. 2012. "The Impact of Election Day Registration on Voter Turnout and Election Outcomes." American Politics Research 40 (4): 636-664.

8. http://www.texastribune.org/2015/04/20/analysis-what-happens-when-texans-votes-matter/

9. http://www.eac.gov/assets/1/Page/Innovations%20in%20Election%20Administration%209.pdf, page 4.

10. http://www.texastribune.org/2015/08/28/new-law-aims-prevent-rolling-voting/

11. http://www.texastribune.org/2013/01/02/voting-mickey-mouse/

12. The National Conference of State Legislatures. "Vote Centers." http://www.ncsl.org/research/elections-and-campaigns/vote-centers.aspx

13. http://www.governing.com/topics/politics/States-Roll-Back-Early-Voting-Enforce-Voter-ID-Laws.html

14. Donald Strong. 1944. "American Government and Politics: The Poll Tax: The Case of Texas." *American Political Science Review* 38 (4): 693–709.

15. Arnoldo De Leon. 1999. *Mexican Americans in Texas: A Brief History.* Wheeling, IL: Harlan Davidson, 82.

16. https://tshaonline.org/handbook/online/articles/npg01

17. Conrey Bryson. 1993. *Dr. Lawrence A. Nixon and the White Primary.* El Paso: Texas Western Press.

18. Darlene Clark Hine. 1979. *Black Victory: The Rise and Fall of the White Primary in Texas.* Millwood, NY: KTO Press, 25.

19. Arnoldo De Leon. 1999. *Mexican Americans in Texas: A Brief History.* Wheeling, IL: Harlan Davidson, 82.

20. Darlene Clark Hine. 1979. *Black Victory: The Rise and Fall of the White Primary in Texas.* Millwood, NY: KTO Press, 25.

21. Arnoldo De Leon. 1999. *Mexican Americans in Texas: A Brief History.* Wheeling, IL: Harlan Davidson. 41.

22. Henry Flores. 2015. *Latinos and the Voting Rights Act: The Search for Purpose.* Lanham, MD: Lexington Books, 121.

23. http://www.texasmonthly.com/politics/el-gobernador/

24. http://www.nytimes.com/1990/02/11/us/how-johnson-won-election-he-d-lost.html

25. John E. Clark. 1995. *The Fall of the Duke of Duval.* Austin, TX: Eakin Press.

26. David Montejano. 1987. *Anglos and Mexicans in the Making of Texas, 1836–1986.* Austin: University of Texas Press, 278.

27. Ibid., 285.

28. http://www.nbcnews.com/news/latino/latinos-1965-voting-rights-act-impact-came-decade-later-n404936

29. http://articles.latimes.com/1988-06-16/news/mn-6570_1_latino-political-power

30. http://www.nytimes.com/1990/06/05/us/los-angeles-board-is-said-to-exercise-anti-hispanic-bias.html

31. Benjamin Marquez. 2014. *Democratizing Texas Politics: Race, Identity, and Mexican American Empowerment, 1945–2002.* Austin: University of Texas Press, 1.

32. http://www.texasmonthly.com/articles/swept-away/

33. Matt A. Bareto, Mario Villarreal, and Nathan D. Woods. 2005. "Metropolitian Latino Political Behavior: Voter Turnout and Candidate Preference in Los Angeles." *Journal of Urban Affairs* 27 (1): 71–91.

34. http://www.nytimes.com/2014/10/21/upshot/why-house-republicans-alienate-hispanics-they-dont-need-them.html?hp&action=click&pgtype=Homepage&version=HpSumSmallMediaHigh&module=second-column-region&region=top-news&WT.nav=top-news&_r=2&abt=0002&abg=0&mtrref=-undefined&assetType=nyt_now

35. Kenneth Bridges. 2008. Twilight of the Texas Democrats: The 1978 Governor's Race. College Station: Texas A&M University Press, 14.

36. The Establishment in Texas Politics: The Primitive Years. Norman: University of Oklahoma Press, 176

37. Alwin Barr. 1996. *Black Texans: A History of African Americans in Texas, 1528–1995.* Norman: University of Oklahoma Press, 178.

38. Ibid., 232.

39. https://www.washingtonpost.com/news/the-fix/wp/2015/07/07/when-did-black-americans-startvoting-so-heavily-democratic/

40. https://tshaonline.org/handbook/online/articles/viw01

41. Judith N. McArthur and Harold L. Smith. 2010. *Texas Through Women's Eyes.* Austin: University of Texas Press, 162.

42. Judith N. Macarthur and Harold L. Smith. Texas Through Women's Eyes. Austin: University of Texas Press, 2010.

43. Texas Politics Polling, February 2016.

44. http://www.people-press.org/2015/04/07/a-deep-dive-into-party-affiliation/

45. https://books.google.com/books?id=_qDQAgAAQBAJ&pg=PA135&lpg=PA135&dq=house-keeping"+chores+that+ "earned+male+praise+but+not+authority+in+the+party+hierarchy."&source=bl&ots=9hZ-j5ercql&sig=iLI_w7EcjvUZKew-4FYe6kXCaN0&hl=en&sa=X-&ved=0ahUKEwibyf_47bzQA-hWrj1QKHdOWASEQ6AEIG-zAA#v=onepage&q=housekeeping"%20chores%20that%20 "earned%20male%20praise%20 but%20not%20authority%20in%20 the%20party%20hierarchy."&f=false

46. http://www.texastribune.org/2016/03/11/texas-continues-dry-spell-among-congressional-wome/

47. Ronald Schmidt Sr., Yvette M. Alex-Assensoh, Andrew L. Aoki, and Rodney E. Hero. 2009. *Newcomers, Outsiders, and Insiders: Immigrants and American Racial Politics in the Early Twenty-First Century.* Ann Arbor: University of Michigan Press.

48. https://tshaonline.org/handbook/online/articles/pjc01

49. Office of the Texas State Demographer.

50. Janelle Wong, S. Karthick Ramakrishnan, Taeku Lee, Jane Junn. 2011. *Asian American Political Participation: Emerging Constituents and Their Political Identities.* New York: Russell Sage.

51. America Goes to the Polls, Nonprofit Vote. Based on Data from the Census Bureau's survey of 50,000 households. *www.nonprofitvote.org/.../america-goes-to-the-polls-2012-voter-participation-gaps-in...*

52. Alan S. Gerber, Donald P. Green, and Christopher W. Larimer. 2008. "Social Pressure and Voter Turnout: Evidence from a Large-Scale Field Experiment."*American Political Science Review* 102 (February): 33–48.

53. Jimmy Banks. 1971. *Money, Marbles, and Chalk.* Austin: Texas Publishing Company, 180.

54. Wendy K. Tam Cho. 1999. "Naturalization, Socialization, Participation: Immigrants and (Non-) Voting." *Journal of Politics* 61 (4): 1140–1155.

55. R. Michael Alvarez and J. Andrew Sinclair. 2011. "Making Voting Easier: Convenience Voting in the 2008 Presidential Election." *Political Research Quarterly* 65 (2): 248–262.

56. http://www.idea.int/publications/vt/
57. Thomas M. Holbrook and Aaron C. Weinschenk. 2014. "Campaigns, Mobilization, and Turnout in Mayoral Elections." *Political Research Quarterly* 67 (1): 42–55.
58. Melissa R. Michelson. 2014. "How to Increase Voter Turnout in Communities Where People Have Not Usually Participated in Elections." Scholars Strategy Network. See more at: http://journalistsresource.org/studies/politics/elections/increasing-voter-turnout-in-communities-where-people-have-not-usually-participated-in-elections#sthash.ywwlzgZQ.dpuf
59. Ibid.
60. Melissa R. Michelson and Lisa GarcisBedolla. 2012. *Mobilizing Inclusion: Redefining Citizenship Through Get-Out-The-Vote Campaigns.* New Haven, CT: Yale University Press.
61. CostasPanagopolous. 2011. "Thank You for Voting: Gratitude Expression and Voter Mobilization." *The Journal of Politics* 73 (3): 707–717.
62. Alan Gerber, Greg Huber, David Doherty, Conor Dowling, and Seth Hill. 2013. "Do Perceptions of Ballot Secrecy Influence Turnout? Results from a Field Experiment." *American Journal of Political Science* 57 (3): 537–551.
63. Marisa Abrajano and Costas Panagopoulos. 2011. "Does Language Matter? The Impact of Spanish versus English-Language GOTV Efforts on Latino Turnout." *American Politics Research* 39 (4): 643–663.
64. http://www.nytimes.com/1990/02/11/us/how-johnson-won-election-he-d-lost.html
65. http://www.dallasnews.com/news/politics/headlines/20130908-few-texas-voter-fraud-cases-would-have-been-prevented-by-photo-id-law-review-shows.ece
66. http://www.politifact.com/texas/statements/2016/mar/17/greg-abbott/light-match-greg-abbotts-claim-about-rampant-voter/
67. https://www.texastribune.org/2016/03/15/analysis-scant-evidence-abbott-rampant-voter-fraud/
68. Texas Tribune Polling, February 2011.
69. Jimmy Banks. 1971. *Money, Marbles, and Chalk.* Austin: Texas Publishing Company, 36.
70. H.C. Pittman. 1992. Inside the Third House. Austin, Texas: Eakin Press, 83.
71. http://time.com/132067/wendy-davis-texas-abortion-barbie/
72. https://books.google.com/books?id=ujpuujMJv-0C&pg=PA46&lpg=PA46&dq=Oh+good.+Now+he'll+be+-biignorant&source=bl&ots=2yo_vMsxyh&sig=Hihy1YjTL2BLmA-JLF1zArqJs-SA&hl=en&sa=X-&ved=0ahUKEwjV3PfA7rzQAhWmgFQKHSsmDToQ6AEILjAE#v=o-nepage&q=Oh%20good.%20Now%20he'll%20be%20bi-ignorant&f=false
73. http://abc13.com/politics/dan-patrick-mental-health-records-leaked-in-last-days-of-lt-govs-race/63863/
74. Richard R. Lau, Lee Sigelman, and Ivy Brown Rovner. 2007. "The Effects of Negative Political Campaigns: A Meta-Analytic Reassessment." *Journal of Politics* 69 (4): 1176–1209.
75. https://www.washingtonpost.com/politics/study-negative-campaign-ads-much-more-frequent-vicious-than-in-primaries-past/2012/02/14/gIQAR7ifPR_story.html
76. Bill Hobby. 2010. *How Things Really Work: Lessons from a Life in Politics.* Austin: University of Texas Press, 52.
77. Jeffrey E. Cohen. 2010. *Going Local: Presidential Leadership in the Post-Broadcast Age.* New York: Cambridge University Press.
78. http://www.dallasnews.com/news/politics/headlines/20141018-abbott-davis-launching-extensive-voter-turnout-efforts.ece
79. http://www.cnn.com/2012/11/05/politics/voters-microtargeting/
80. http://www.cbsnews.com/news/election-2016s-price-tag-6-8-billion/
81. http://www.texastribune.org/2014/07/30/texas-governors-race-analyzing-money/
82. http://blog.chron.com/texaspolitics/2014/10/abbott-davis-combine-to-spend-83-million-to-become-next-texasgovernor/
83. https://news.google.com/newspapers?id=MTNfAAAAIBAJ&sjid=VU8NAAAAIBAJ&pg=6718,4614285
84. Billy Monroe, Nathan K. Mitchell, and Lee Payne. 2016. "Texas Judicial Primary Elections: A Quantitative Analysis." *Journal of Political Science* 44.
85. http://www.governing.com/news/headlines/the-farmers-insurance-company-is-giving-a-lot-of-money-to-the-gops-greg-abbott.html
86. Benjamin I. Page, Larry M. Bartels, and Jason Seawright. 2013. "Democracy and the Policy Preferences of Wealthy Americans." *Perspectives on Politics* 11 (1): 51–73.
87. Larry M. Bartels. 2008. *Unequal Democracy: The Political Economy of the New Gilded Age.* Princeton, NJ: Princeton University Press.
88. http://www.dallasnews.com/news/politics/headlines/20140526-texas-gop-primaries-are-steeped-in-tea-party-agenda.ece
89. http://www.texasmonthly.com/politics/the-life-and-death-and-life-of-the-party/
90. Lynda W. Powell. 2012. *The Influence of Campaign Contributions in State Legislatures.* Ann Arbor: University of Michigan Press.
91. Stephen Ansolabehere, John M. De Figueiredo, and James M. Snyder. 2003. "Why Is There So Little Money in Politics?" *Economic Perspectives* 17 (1): 105–130.
92. http://www.texasmonthly.com/politics/minority-report/
93. Wayne Thorburn. 2014. *Red State: An Insider's Story of How the GOP Came to Dominate Texas Politics.* Austin: University of Texas Press, 164.
94. http://www.ncsl.org/research/elections-and-campaigns/straight-ticket-voting.aspx
95. http://www.nytimes.com/2016/09/10/us/politics/supreme-court-voting-michigan-straight-ticket.html
96. http://www.dallasnews.com/opinion/editorials/20130312-editorial-upgrade-texas-governing-by-ending-single-party-pull.ece
97. http://www.governing.com/topics/politics/Voting-the-Straight-Ticket-Sweep.html
98. http://www.tribtalk.org/2015/02/15/its-time-to-end-straight-ticket-voting-in-texas/
99. http://www.dallasnews.com/news/politics/headlines/20140526-texas-

gop-primaries-are-steeped-in-tea-party-agenda.ece

100. http://www.texastribune.org/2015/10/23/analysis-when-apathy-becomes-political-tactic/

101. Alwin Barr. 1996. *Black Texans: A History of African Americans in Texas, 1528-1995*. Norman: University of Oklahoma Press, 232.

102. http://www.star-telegram.com/news/politics-government/election/article113723174.html

103. http://www.pewhispanic.org/2012/11/14/an-awakened-giant-the-hispanic-electorate-is-likely-to-double-by-2030/

104. Nate Cohn. 2014. "Changing South Is at Intersection of Demographics and Politics." The Upshot, *The New York Times,* August 14. http://www.nytimes.com/2014/08/15/upshot/changing-south-is-at-intersection-of-demographics-and-politics.html?abt=0002&abg=0

Chapter 4 Photo Caption Notes
* http://blog.chron.com/intheloop/2013/02/is-texas-asian-american-political-voice-at-risk/
** http://www.star-telegram.com/news/politics-government/state-politics/politex-blog/article41247540.html

Chapter 5 Political Parties: Texas in Blue and Red
1. Lou Dubose and Jan Reid. 2004. *The Hammer: Tom Delay, God, Money, and the Rise of the Republican Congress*. New York: PublicAffairs Books, 25.
2. Jan Reid. 2012. *Let the People In: The Life and Times of Ann Richards*. Austin: University of Texas Press, 399.
3. Mary Beth Rogers. 2016. *Turning Texas Blue*. New York: St. Martin's Press, 143.
4. Fred Gantt, Jr. 1964. *The Chief Executive in Texas: A Study in Gubernatorial Leadership*. Austin: University of Texas Press.
5. http://www.texastribune.org/2015/06/14/taylors-triumph-new-day-or-another-fluke/
6. Joseph Bafumi and Robert Y. Shapiro. 2009. "A New Partisan Voter." *Journal of Politics* 71 (1): 1-24.
7. Geoffrey C. Layman, Thomas M. Carsey, John C. Green, Richard Hererra, and Rosalyn Cooperman. 2010. "Activists

and Conflict Extension in American Party Politics." *American Political Science Review* 104(2): 324–346. Michael A. Bailey, Jonathan Mummolo and Hans Noel. 2012. "Tea Party Influence: A Story of Activists and Elites." *American Politics Research* 40 (5): 769–804.

8. http://www.houstonchronicle.com/news/politics/texas/article/A-conservative-wave-swept-the-Texas-Legislature-6297070.php

9. http://tcgop.org/about-tcgop/precinct-chair-job-description/

10. http://www.yourhoustonnews.com/archives/local-gop-feud-fizzles-down-to-the-precinct-chairs/article_e1638d6e-36ff-5339-8c2a-a807b380745f.html

11. http://www.click2houston.com/news/harris-county-republicans-elect-new-county-chairman_20151123153109888

12. http://www.texastribune.org/2010/05/07/three-candidates-vying-to-lead-state-gop/

13. Ibid.

14. http://www.chron.com/news/houston-texas/texas/article/Texas-secession-resolution-passes-GOP-committee-6676280.php

15. http://www.texastribune.org/2015/12/05/texas-gop-votes-down-controversial-secession-propo/

16. Alan D. Monroe. 1983. "American Party Platforms and Public Opinion." *American Journal of Political Science* 27 (1): 27–42; Daniel J. Coffey. 2011. "More than a Dime's Worth: Using State Party Platforms to Assess the Degree of American Party Polarization." *PS: Political Science & Politics* 44 (2): 331–337.

17. Daniel J. Coffey. 2011. "More Than A Dime's Worth: Using State Party Platforms to Assess the Degree to American Party Polarization." *PS: Political Science and Politics* 44 (2): 331–337.

18. http://www.csg.org/knowledgecenter/docs/BOS2005-PoliticalParties.pdf

19. James R. Soukup, Clifton McCleskey, and Harry Holloway. 1964. *Party and Factional Division in Texas*. Austin: University of Texas Press, 22.

20. https://tshaonline.org/handbook/online/articles/fga24

21. Kenneth Bridges. 2008. *Twilight of the Texas Democrats: The 1978*

Governor's Race. College Station: Texas A&M University Press, 5.

22. Jimmy Banks. 1971. *Money, Marbles and Chalk*. Austin: Texas Publishing Company, Inc., 201.

23. Mickey Leland. Texas Observer, "The Tumor in the Texas Delegation." 207.

24. Kenneth Bridges. 2008. *Twilight of the Texas Democrats: The 1978 Governor's Race.* College Station: Texas A&M University Press, 15.

25. Texas Observer, "The Political Tumult." 151.

26. Mary Beth Rogers. 2016. *Turning Texas Blue*. New York: St. Martin's Press, 85.

27. http://www.texasmonthly.com/politics/who-killed-the-texas-democratic-party/

28. John R. Knaggs. 1986. *Two-Party Texas: The John Tower Era, 1961–1984.* Austin: Eakin Press.

29. Wayne Thornburn. 2014. *Red State: An Insider's Story of How the GOP Came to Dominate Texas Politics.* Austin: University of Texas Press, 68.

30. John R. Knaggs. 1986. Two-Party Texas: The John Tower Era, 1961–1984. Austin: Eakin Press, 13.

31. Ibid, 2.

32. Ibid, 5.

33. Jon Mecham. 2015. *Destiny and Power: The American Odyssey of George Herbert Walker Bush.* New York: Random House, 165.

34. John R. Knaggs. 1986. *Two-Party Texas: The John Tower Era, 1961–1984.* Austin: Eakin Press, 137.

35. Edward H. Miller. 2015. *Nut Country: Right-Wing Dallas and the Birth of the Southern Strategy.* Chicago: University of Chicago Press, 140.

36. John R. Knaggs. 1986. *Two-Party Texas: The John Tower Era, 1961–1984.* Austin: Eakin Press, 251.

37. Sam Kinch Jr. 2000. *Too Much Money Is Not Enough: Big Money and Political Power in Texas*. Austin: Campaign for People, 29.

38. Lou Dubose and Jan Reid. 2004. *The Hammer: Tom Delay, God, Money, and the Rise of the Republican Congress*. New York: PublicAffairs Books, 44.

39. http://www.texasmonthly.com/politics/power/

40. Edward H. Miller. 2015. *Nut Country: Right-Wing Dallas and the Birth of the Southern Strategy.* Chicago: University of Chicago Press.
41. http://www.texasmonthly.com/articles/the-elephants-in-the-room/
42. Ibid.
43. http://www.nytimes.com/2010/02/28/us/politics/28keli.html?login=email&mtrref=undefined
44. http://www.npr.org/templates/story/story.php?storyId=123229743
45. http://www.gallup.com/poll/186338/support-tea-party-drops-new-low.aspx
46. http://www.rollingstone.com/politics/news/lone-star-crazy-how-right-wing-extremists-took-over-texas-20140701?page=2
47. http://www.texasmonthly.com/politics/who-killed-the-texas-democratic-party/
48. Ibid.
49. http://www.texasmonthly.com/politics/more-power-to-him/
50. http://www.texasmonthly.com/politics/the-great-campaigner-2/
51. http://www.csg.org/knowledgecenter/docs/BOS2005-PoliticalParties.pdf
52. Wayne Thornburn. 2014. *Red State: An Insider's Story of How the GOP Came to Dominate Texas Politics.* Austin: University of Texas Press, ix.
53. Ibid, 51.
54. https://www.washingtonpost.com/news/the-fix/wp/2015/01/14/republicans-have-gained-more-than-900-state-legislative-seats-since-2010/
55. Victoria Loe. 1983. "The Deal That Didn't Work." *Texas Monthly,* August 1981.
56. http://www.redistrictinginamerica.org/reynolds/
57. http://www.texasmonthly.com/politics/the-agitator/
58. http://www.austinchronicle.com/news/2003-05-23/161001/
59. http://www.abqjournal.com/7348/remember-the-texas-eleven.html
60. https://www.texastribune.org/2013/08/17/legislators-volley-redistricting-back-courts/
61. Ibid.
62. https://www.texastribune.org/2013/09/06/2014-primaries-can-proceed-judges-rule/

63. https://www.brennancenter.org/blog/two-texas-cases-test-boundaries-redistricting-law
64. Seth C. McKee and Antoine Yoshinaka. 2015. "Late to the Parade: Party Switchers in Contemporary US Southern Legislatures." *Party Politics* 21 (6): 957–969.
65. http://www.texasgop.org/party-switchers-top-200/
66. http://www.texastribune.org/2009/11/06/hopson-switches-to-the-republicans/
67. http://www.texasobserver.org/portrait-of-a-party-switcher/
68. Ibid.
69. http://www.portasouthjetty.com/news/2009-12-03/Opinion/Cant_beat_em_Hopson_joins_em.html
70. Timothy P. Nokken. 2009. "Party Switching and the Procedural Party Agenda in the U.S. House of Representatives." In *Political Parties and Legislative Party Switching.* Edited by William Heller and Carol Mershon. New York: Palgrave MacMillian.
71. Christian R. Grose and Antoine Yoshinaka. 2003. "The Electoral Consequences of Party Switching by Incumbent Members of Congress, 1947–2000." *Legislative Studies Quarterly* 28 (1): 55–75.
72. Lou Dubose and Jan Reid. 2004. *The Hammer: Tom Delay, God, Money, and the Rise of the Republican Congress.* New York: PublicAffairs Books, 46.
73. https://www.texastribune.org/2010/12/11/allan-ritter-confirms-hes-switching-parties/
74. http://www.mysanantonio.com/news/politics/texas_legislature/article/Democratic-party-switchers-give-GOP-a-House-894784.php
75. http://www.lrl.state.tx.us/legeleaders/members/memberdisplay.cfm?memberID=292
76. David Montejano. 1987. *Anglos and Mexicans in the Making of Texas, 1836–1986.* Austin: University of Texas Press, 289.
77. Ibid, 292.
78. Judith N. McArthur and Harold L. Smith. 2010. Texas Through Women's Eyes. Austin: University of Texas Press, 208.
79. http://www.texastribune.org/2014/05/07/analysis-minor-parties-still-matter-even-if-they-l/

80. http://www.austinchronicle.com/daily/news/2013-12-12/libertarians-line-up-for-2014-election/
81. http://www.chron.com/news/politics/article/Third-parties-struggle-to-make-ballot-1985720.php
82. http://www.texasmonthly.com/politics/all-shook-up/
83. Lou Dubose and Jan Reid. 2004. *The Hammer: Tom Delay, God, Money, and the Rise of the Republican Congress.* New York: PublicAffairs Books, 36.

Chapter 5 Photo Caption Notes

* Texas Observer, "The Political Tumult." 151

Chapter 6 Interest Groups

1. Bill Hobby. 2010. *How Things Really Work: Lessons from a Life in Politics.* Austin: University of Texas Press.
2. http://www.nytimes.com/1989/07/09/us/texas-businessman-hands-out-10000-checks-in-state-senate.html
3. Quoted in http://www.texasmonthly.com/politics/the-private-sectors-influence-on-the-public-interests-of-texas/
4. http://www.texasmonthly.com/articles/lobbying/
5. Mark A. Smith. 2010. "The Mobilization and Influence of Business Interests." The Oxford Handbook of American Political Parties and Interest Groups. Oxford University Press.
6. Brandi Grissom. 2011. "Lawmakers: Get Lobbyists Out of Windstorm Fight." *Texas Tribune,* June 23.
7. http://www.texastribune.org/2011/08/14/storm-insurer-remade-vocal-critics-remain/
8. Quoted in Kay L. Schlozman. 2010. "Who Sings in the Heavenly Chorus? The Shape of the Organized Interest System." *The Oxford Handbook of American Political Parties and Interest Groups.* New York: Oxford University Press.
9. http://kut.org/post/texas-environmentalists-mostly-disappointed-legislative-session
10. Quoted in Sam Kinch Jr. 2000. *Too Much Money is Not Enough: Big Money and Political Power in Texas.* Austin: Campaigns for People, 81.

11. https://www.texasobserver.org/who-really-runs-texas/

12. Sam Best and Paul Teske. 2002. "Explaining State Internet Sales Taxation: New Economy, Old-Fashioned Interest Group Politics." *State Politics and Policy Quarterly*.

13. H.C. Pittman. 1992. *Inside the Third House: A Veteran Lobbyist Takes a 50-Year Frolic Through Texas Politics*. Austin: Eakin Press.

14. David Saleh Rauf and Neal Morton. 2014. "Austin Braces for Tesla Lobbying Blitz." *Houston Chronicle*, December 18.

15. http://www.texastribune.org/2015/07/14/abbott-tesla-dealership-model-works-just-fine/

16. Mark Smith. 2001. *American Business and Political Power: Public Opinion, Elections, and Democracy*. Chicago: University of Chicago Press.

17. Frank R. Baumbartner. 2010. "Interest Groups and Agendas." *The Oxford Handbook of American Political Parties and Interest Groups*. New York: Oxford University Press.

18. Dara Z. Strolovitch and M. David Forrest. 2010. "Social and Economic Justice Movements and Organizations." *The Oxford Handbook of American Political Parties and Interest Groups*. New York: Oxford University Press.

19. Ibid.

20. Guadalupe San Miguel, Jr. 1987. *"Let Them All Take Heed": Mexican Americans and the Campaign for Educational Equality in Texas, 1910–1981*. College Station: Texas A&M University Press.

21. Christy Hoppe. 2015. "Senate Panel Agrees to Change Corruption Investigations." *Dallas Morning News*, March 16.

22. Quoted in Kay L. Schlozman. 2010. "Who Sings in the Heavenly Chorus? The Shape of the Organized Interest System." *The Oxford Handbook of American Political Parties and Interest Groups*. New York:Oxford University Press.

23. https://www.houston.org/municipal-finance/pdf/Municipal%20Finance-FINAL.pdf

24. Baumgartner, Frank R. and Bryan D. Jones. 1993. *Agendas and Instability in American Politics*. Chicago: University of Chicago Press.

25. http://abcnews.go.com/blogs/politics/2013/11/texas-student-group-offers-25-reward-in-catch-an-illegal-immigrant-game/

26. http://www.mysanantonio.com/news/local/politics/article/Hundreds-protest-canceled-Catch-an-Illegal-game-4996381.php

27. Richard West. 1973. "Inside the Lobby." *Texas Monthly*, July.

28. http://www.nytimes.com/2009/08/19/opinion/19sager.html

29. George Anders. 1996. *Health Against Wealth: HMOs and the Breakdown of Medical Trust*. New York: Houghton Mifflin Harcourt, 213.

30. Taken from the website of each organization, usually in the form of a "voter guide," the average is calculated as the total number of successful (winning) candidates divided by the total number of endorsements. (although most of the endorsees were included on these lists, on occasion a group would endorse a candidate privately, in a newsletter (or listed elsewhere on their website), in a public event, or implicitly by saying good things about the candidate (for the analysis here, only the roster of endorsed candidates on each website was used since this is the most common way for voters to learn about the endorser preferences).

31. http://www.texasmonthly.com/the-culture/inside-the-lobby/#sthash.MgnytzkU.dpuf

32. Stratmann, Thomas. 1992. "Are Contributors Rational? Untangling Strategies of Political Action Committees." *Journal of Political Economy*, 100/3: 647–64.

33. Quoted in Sam Kinch Jr. 2000. *Too Much Money is Not Enough: Big Money and Political Power in Texas*. Austin: Campaigns for People, 43.

34. Ibid., 55.

35. https://www.texastribune.org/2014/12/10/state-sued-stifling-texas-craft-beer-renaissance/

36. http://www.teachthevote.org/news/2015/09/02/school-finance-case-atpe-attends-supreme-court-hearing/

37. Ibid.

38. Byron C. Utech. 1937. *The Legislature and the People*. San Antonio: The Naylor Company, 117.

39. http://www.expressnews.com/news/politics/texas_legislature/article/Free-tickets-just-part-of-game-for-legislators-4795420.php?t=a6cd9f8bb4

40. Richard West. 1973. "Inside the Lobby." *Texas Monthly*, July.

41. AmanBatheja. 2011. "Some Say Group Has Too Much Sway Over Legislation." *Fort Worth Star Telegram*, December 4.

42. Quoted in Sam Kinch Jr. 2000. *Too Much Money is Not Enough: Big Money and Political Power in Texas*. Austin: Campaigns for People, 75.

43. Alan Rosenthal. 2001. *The Third House: Lobbyists and Lobbying in the States*. Washington, DC: CQ Press.

44. Eva Hershaw. 2015. "'Texting is the King of Distraction,' Lobbyist Tells Panel." *Texas Tribune*, March 5.

45. Quoted in Sam Kinch Jr. 2000. *Too Much Money is Not Enough: Big Money and Political Power in Texas*. Austin: Campaigns for People, 79.

46. Richard West. 1973. "Inside the Lobby." *Texas Monthly*, July.

47. http://www.kcbd.com/story/29785294/state-could-allow-superintendents-without-teaching-experience

48. Kate Gailbraith. 2011. "Business Groups Back Texas Water Ballot Measure." *Texas Tribune*, October 5.

49. Jim Malewitz. 2015. "Pipeline Company Ghost-Wrote Texas Regulator's Letter." *Texas Tribune*, September 22.

50. Ross Ramsey. 2010. "Legislature Is a Training Ground for Lobbyists." *Texas Tribune*, June 10.

51. Texas Legislative Statutes. Sec. 572.054. Representation by Former Officer or Employee of Regulatory Agency Restricted; Criminal Offense.

52. AmanBatheja. 2013. "Despite Reforms, Some Elected Officials Still Lobby." *Texas Tribune*, February 8.

53. http://legacy.sandiegouniontribune.com/news/business/20020825-9999_1n25metabo.html

54. David Prindle. 1981. *Petroleum Political and the Texas Railroad Commission*. Austin: University of Texas Press.

55. http://www.followthemoney.org/research/blog/51-million-elected-utility-regulators-score-big-bucks/

56. Charles Deaton. 1973. *The Year They Threw the Rascals Out.* Austin: Shoal Creek Publishers.

57. H.C. Pittman. 1992. *Inside the Third House: A Veteran Lobbyist Takes a 50-Year Frolic Through Texas Politics.* Austin: Eakin Press, 202

58. Ibid., 102.

59. Ibid., 237.

60. http://kxan.com/2015/02/17/gov-greg-abbott-delivering-state-of-the-state-address/

61. http://www.houstonchronicle.com/news/houston-texas/houston/article/Ethics-gatekeeper-in-Texas-Senate-Huffman-6736830.php

62. http://www.texastribune.org/2015/06/11/ethics-commissioners-say-lawmakers-went-backward/

63. Texas Ethics Commission, A Guide to Texas Law. https://www.ethics.state.tx.us/main/guides.htm

64. Ibid.

65. Ross Ramsey. 2015. "Analysis: Lobbyists Can Split Tabs, Hide Names." *Texas Tribune,* February 2. http://www.texastribune.org/2015/02/02/analysis-splitting-tabs-and-hiding-names/

66. James Drew. 2015. "State Law Allows for Lobbying Deep in the Shadows of Texas." *Dallas Morning News,* September 9.

67. David Saleh Rauf. 2015. "Former Ethics Chief Says Agency Should Stop Enforcement Actions." San Antonio News Express. March 25. http://www.expressnews.com/news/politics/texas_legislature/article/

68. John Reynolds. 2015. "Clancy: Ethics Commission Should Stop Enforcing Law." *Texas Tribune,* March 24.

69. https://www.texastribune.org/2016/10/05/texas-senator-calls-ethics-commission-arrogant-and/

70. http://www.houstonchronicle.com/news/politics/texas/article/Top-ethics-officials-grilled-by-Republicans-9811157.php?t=807a619ffb438d9cbb&cm-pid=twitter-premium

71. https://www.texastribune.org/2016/10/05/texas-senator-calls-ethics-commission-arrogant-and/?utm_source=Texas+Tribune+Master&utm_campaign=1eaf99925b-trib-news-letters&utm_medium=email&utm_term=0_d9a68d8efc-1eaf99925b-101290241&mc_cid=1eaf99925b&mc_eid=101a099a60

72. http://www.expressnews.com/news/politics/texas_legislature/article/Texas-chief-justice-settles-ethics-fine-6591236.php?t=0c554511144b6b00f7&c-mpid=twitter-premium&mc_cid=6d7bff9970&mc_eid=101a099a60

73. https://www.texastribune.org/2015/06/20/abbott-vetoes-spous-al-loophole-davis-says/

74. H.C. Pittman. 1992. *Inside the Third House: A Veteran Lobbyist Takes a 50-Year Frolic Through Texas Politics.* Austin: Eakin Press, 234.

Chapter 6 Photo Caption Notes

* Manny Fernandez. 2015. "Texas Watchdog Group Calls Another Political Titan to Account." *The New York Times,* August 6.

** Patricia Hart. 2003. The Enforcer. *Texas Monthly,* May.

Chapter 7 The Legislature

1. http://www.houstonchronicle.com/news/houston-texas/houston/article/Senate-to-withdraw-proposal-to-require-Texans-to-6284479.php

2. Patricia L. Cox and Michael Philips. 2010. *The House Will Come to Order.* Austin: University of Texas Press, 118.

3. Douglas L. Kriner and Eric Schickler. 2016. Investigating the President. Princeton, NJ: Princeton University Press.

4. http://www.dallasnews.com/news/texas-legislature/2016/08/29/lawmakers-lash-texas-cps-offering-big-solutions-caseworker-turnover-foster-care-bed-shortages

5. Bill Hobby. 2010. *How Things Really Work.* Austin: University of Texas Press, 64.

6. https://www.fas.org/sgp/crs/misc/RL33209.pdf

7. Patricia Hart. 2001. "Session Player." *Texas Monthly,* July.

8. http://www.texasmonthly.com/politics/the-wise-men-pete-laney-and-bill-ratliff/

9. Ibid.

10. Joel Nihlean. 2014. "The History and Power of the Hashtag." *County,* December 16. http://county.org/magazine/features/Pages/2015Jan/The-History-and-Power-of-the-Hashtag.aspx

11. Ibid.

12. http://www.texastribune.org/2010/12/31/defying-national-trend-texas-clings-biennial-legis/

13. https://www.texastribune.org/2015/04/27/analysis-legislative-overtime-look-courts/

14. http://www.texastribune.org/2013/04/18/campaign-funds-prop-lawmakers-capitol-operations/

15. Will Weissert. 2015. "Texas' Every Two-Year Legislature Isn't So 'Part Time.'" *Dallas Morning News,* February 16.

16. http://www.texastribune.org/2013/04/14/exotic-trips-luxury-gifts-are-perks-elective-offic/

17. http://www.expressnews.com/news/local/article/Houston-senator-s-work-raises-questions-of-7225561.php

18. http://www.texastribune.org/2010/05/19/at-the-lege-age-mat-ters-seniority-may-not/

19. http://www.texastribune.org/2015/01/14/demographics-2015-texas-legislature/

20. Molly Ivins. 1991. *Molly Ivins Can't Say That Can She?* New York: Random House.

21. Harden, Jeffrey J. 2013. "Multidimensional Responsiveness: The Determinants of Legislators" Representational Priorities." *Legislative Studies Quarterly* 38 (2): 155–184; http://fivethirtyeight.com/features/how-much-should-state-leg-islators-get-paid/?ex_cid=538twitter

22. Guide to Legislative Information (Revised). 2015. Texas Legislative Council for the 84th Legislature.

23. Ben Barnes. 2006. *Barn Burning, Barn Building.* Albany, NY: Bright Sky Press, 46.

24. http://www.texastribune.org/2003/02/03/key-change-from-minor-to-major/

25. http://www.texastribune.org/2015/06/16/keffer-straus-lieuten-ant-wont-seek-reelection/

26. *Texas Tribune,* Texas Weekly, Volume 26, Issue 6. February 16, 2009.

27. Patricia L. Cox and Michael Philips. 2010. *The House Will Come to Order.* Austin: University of Texas Press, 97.

28. http://www.houstonchronicle.com/politics/texas-take/article/A-bloody-next-few-weeks-in-Austin-6171147.php

29. *Texas Monthly.* July 1983. "Ten Best and Worst Legislators."

30. https://www.texastribune.org/2015/05/03/stickland-and-texas-house/

31. https://www.texastribune.org/2011/04/27/texplainer-whats-a-third-reading/

32. *Texas Tribune,* Volume 20, Issue 46, May 17, 2004. https://www.texastribune.org/texas-weekly/vol-20/no-46/print/

33. Guide to Legislative Information (Revised). 2015. Texas Legislative Council for the 84th Legislature.

34. http://www.dallasnews.com/news/politics/state-politics/20150216-texas-every-two-year-legislature-isnt-so-part-time.ece

35. http://www.houstonchronicle.com/politics/texas-take/article/A-bloody-next-few-weeks-in-Austin-6171147.php

36. http://www.texastribune.org/2011/05/06/puppies-and-the-legislative-power-of-distraction/

37. Ibid.

38. Dave McNeely. 1999. "Rules Curtail Chaos." *Victoria Advocate,* May 16.

39. Bill Hobby. 2010. *How Things Really Work.* Austin: University of Texas Press, 133.

40. http://www.texastribune.org/2013/01/28/what-blocker-bill/

41. http://www.texastribune.org/2015/05/19/loss-two-thirds-rule-senate/

42. https://www.texastribune.org/2015/05/22/after-one-more-gun-fight-open-carry-passes-senate/; http://www.mystatesman.com/news/news/local/herman-open-carry-produces-strange-and-sad-day-in-/nmPCC/

43. Patricia Hart. 2001. "Session Player." *Texas Monthly,* July.

44. http://www.texasmonthly.com/politics/ben-barnes-is-still-running/

45. http://www.texastribune.org/2015/06/26/texting-bills-demise-victory-tea-party-freshmen/

46. http://www.texastribune.org/2015/06/26/texting-bills-demise-victory-tea-party-freshmen/

47. Carolyn Barta. 1996. *Bill Clements: Texian to his Toenails.* Austin: Eakin Press, 226.

48. http://www.chron.com/news/houston-texas/houston/article/Senate-to-debate-campus-carry-6138681.php

49. http://www.texastribune.org/2015/05/14/deadline-looming-democrats-drag-their-feet/

50. Ibid.

51. http://www.nytimes.com/2013/07/04/us/politics/you-call-that-a-filibuster-texas-still-claims-record.html?_r=0

52. Dave Montgomery. 2011. "Senate Gives up on Budget Deal; Special Session Looms." *Fort Worth Star Telegram,* May 20.

53. Bill Hobby. 2010. How Things Really Work. Austin: University of Texas Press, 64.

54. http://www.houstonchronicle.com/news/article/Democrats-run-out-the-clock-on-abortion-and-gun-6287927.php?t=c1188c8d824240fbdf&cmpid=twitter-premium&utm_source=WhatCountsEmail&utm_medium=newsmail_texastake&utm_campaign=newsmail_Texas%20Take%20Newsletter

55. http://www.texasmonthly.com/content/session-player?fullpage=1

56. http://www.chron.com/news/article/House-passage-is-final-hurdle-for-campus-carry-6296777.php

57. *Texas Tribune,* Texas Weekly, Volume 21, Issue 44, May 2, 2005.

58. http://www.statesman.com/news/news/state-regional-govt-politics/senate-stops-clock-to-finish-business-1/nRRX3/

59. https://www.washingtonpost.com/news/monkey-cage/wp/2014/06/23/americans-have-not-become-more-politically-polarized/

60. http://www.texastribune.org/2010/05/19/at-the-lege-age-matters-seniority-may-not/

61. Paul Burka. 2011. "Capitol Affair." *Texas Monthly,* July.

62. John D. Griffin. 2014. "When and Why Minority Legislators Matter." *Annual Review of Political Science* 17, May, 327–336.

63. Patrick L. Cox and Michael Phillips. 2010. *The House Will Come to Order: How the Texas Speaker Became a Power in State and National Politics.* Austin: University of Texas Press, 172, 174.

64. http://www.texastribune.org/2011/05/28/is-there-a-boys-club-under-the-pink-dome/

65. http://www.houstonpress.com/news/5-moments-of-misogyny-at-the-texas-legislature-8047015

66. Judith N. McArthur and Harold L. Smith. 2010. *Texas Through Women's Eyes.* Austin: University of Texas Press.

67. https://tshaonline.org/handbook/online/articles/fra85

68. Sonia R. Garcia, Valeria Martines-Ebers, Irasema Cornado, Sharon Navarro, and Patricia A. Jaramillo. 2008. *Politicias: Latina Public Officials in Texas.* Austin: University of Texas Press.

69. Patricia Hart. 2001. "Session Player." *Texas Monthly,* July.

Chapter 7 Photo Caption Notes

* Tim Eaton. 2015. "Does a Tiff over a Fetus Sign Portend Texas House Battles to Come?" Austin-American Statesman, March 11. http://www.mystatesman.com/news/news/does-a-tiff-over-a-fetus-sign-portend-texas-house-/nkTHT/#4a1a0824.3580657.735669
** http://www.houstonchronicle.com/news/politics/texas/article/Prince-of-POO-forces-delay-in-open-carry-6200056.php

Chapter 8 Governors of Texas

1. Katrina Trinko, "The Vetoes of Rick Perry," *The National Review Online,* September 6, 2011, http://www.nationalreview.com/article/276264/

2. Quoted in Fred Gantt Jr. 1964. *The Chief Executive in Texas: A Study in Gubernatorial Leadership.* Austin: University of Texas Press, 13.

3. Ralph W. Steen, "FERGUSON, JAMES EDWARD," *Handbook of Texas Online,* Texas State Historical Association, uploaded on June 12, 2010, accessed February 02, 2015, http://www.tshaonline.org/handbook/online/articles/ffe05

4. Brian McCall. 2009. *The Power of the Texas Governor: Connally to Bush.* Austin: University of Texas Press, 23.

5. James Reston Jr. 1989. *The Lone Star: The Life of John Connally.* New York: Harper and Row.

6. McCall, *Power of the Texas Governor,* 107.

7. Gantt, *Chief Executive*, 244.

8. McCall, *Power of the Texas Governor*, 5.

9. McCall, *Power of the Texas Governor*, 42–43.

10. Ross Ramsey, "Legislative Emergencies, Real Ones and The Governor's," *New York Times*, January 29, 2011, http://www.nytimes.com/2011/01/30/us/30ttramsey.html

11. Quoted in Gantt, *Chief Executive*, 211.

12. Gantt, *Chief Executive*, 234.

13. Gantt, *Chief Executive*, 222n9.

14. Quoted in Gantt, *Chief Executive*, 184.

15. McCall, *Power of the Texas Governor*, 52.

16. Robert T. Garrett, "Cut Business Taxes, Abbott Says, or I'll Veto the Budget," *Dallas Morning News*, February 3, 2015.

17. Rick Jervis, "Immigrant Moms Crossing Texas Border at Alarming Rate," *USA Today*, July 5, 2014.

18. Antonio Olivo, "Deployed by Governor Rick Perry, National Guard Adjusts to Its New Role on the Texas Border," *The Washington Post*, September 1, 2014.

19. D'Angelo Gore, "Fact Check: Rick Perry's Border Bragging," FactCheck.org, May 29, 2015, http://www.usatoday.com/story/news/politics/elections/2015/05/29/fact-check-rick-perry-border-apprehensions/28148725/

20. Manny Fernandez, "Governor Rick Perry of Texas Is Indicted on Charge of Abuse of Power," *The New York Times*, August 15, 2014.

21. Gantt, *Chief Executive*, 152.

22. Quoted in Gantt, *Chief Executive*, 248.

23. Quoted in Gantt, *Chief Executive*, 250.

24. Paul Burka, "The Honeymoon Is Over," *Texas Monthly*, January 1997.

25. Terri Langford and Jay Root. 2014. "Lawmakers Question Perry's Funding of National Guard." Texas Tribune, August 5, 2014. https://www.texastribune.org/2014/08/05/lawmakers-question-perrys-funding-guard-border/

26. Quoted in Gantt, *Chief Executive*, 86.

27. Aman Batheja, "'Deal Closer' Funds Draw Bipartisan Concerns," *The Texas Tribune*, December 28, 2014, http://apps.texastribune.org/perry-legacy/texas-enterprise-fund/

28. Brian Sweany, "The Abbott Interview," *Texas Monthly*, June 2015.

29. Peggy Fikac, "Abbott to Travel World to Lure Business," *Houston Chronicle*, June 3, 2015.

30. Batheja, "'Deal Closer' Funds."

31. Quoted in Gantt, *Chief Executive*, 25.

32. Quoted in Gantt, *Chief Executive*, 131.

33. Amy Bingham, "Rick Perry: One-Fourth of His Political Appointments Went to Campaign Donors," ABC News, August 17, 2011, http://abcnews.go.com/Politics/rick-perry-fourth-political-appointments-campaign-donors/story?id=14324227

34. "Quotes From Ann Richards," *New York Times*, September 14, 2006, http://www.nytimes.com/2006/09/14/us/richards_quotes.html?_r=0

Chapter 9 The Plural Executive and the Bureaucracy

1. "Strayhorn's Community College Plan Source of Feud with Perry," *Lubbock Avalanche-Journal*, August 6, 2004, http://lubbockonline.com/stories/080604/sta_080604080.shtml#.Vpl1MKbnaUk

2. "Strayhorn Claims Governor on Political Vendetta with State Audits," *Lubbock Avalanche-Journal*, June 25, 2004, http://lubbockonline.com/stories/062504/sta_062504071.shtml#.Vi6eJaYo6Ul

3. Texas Higher Education Coordinating Board, *Report on Student Financial Aid in Texas Higher Education for Fiscal Year 2014*, September 2015, thecb.state.tx.us, http://www.thecb.state.tx.us/reports/PDF/6613.PDF?CFID=41025589&CFTOKEN=37238257

4. This excludes those individuals working for university systems.

5. Fred Gantt Jr. 1964. *The Chief Executive in Texas: A Study in Gubernatorial Leadership*. Austin: University of Texas Press, 130.

6. James A. Clark and Weldon Hart. 1958. *The Tactful Texan: A Biography of Governor Will Hobby*. New York: Random House, 47.

7. R.G. Ratcliffe, "The Big Three Breakfast Blows Up," *Burkablog* (blog), *Texas Monthly*, April 22, 2015, http://www.texasmonthly.com/burka-blog/the-big-three-breakfast-blows-up/

8. Dave McNeely and Jim Henderson. 2008. *Bob Bullock: God Bless Texas*. Austin: University of Texas Press, 211.

9. Bill Hobby and Saralee Tiede. 2010. *How Things Really Work: Lessons from a Life in Politics*. Austin: University of Texas at Austin.

10. Ben Barnes. *Barn Burning Barn Building: Tales of a Political Life, from LBJ to George W. Bush and Beyond*. Albany, TX: Bright Sky Press. 2006.

11. McNeely and Henderson, *Bob Bullock*, 235.

12. Chuck Lindell, "Dan Patrick Taps Republicans, Donors for Advisory Boards," *Austin-American Statesman*, January 15, 2015.

13. Bill Hobby and Saralee Tiede. 2010 *How Things Really Work: Lessons from a Life in Politics*. Austin: University of Texas at Austin.

14. John L. Hill Jr. and Ernie Stromberger. 2008. *John Hill for the State of Texas: My Years as Attorney General*. College Station: Texas A&M University Press, 25.

15. Hill and Stromberger, *John Hill*, 33.

16. Madlin Mekelburg, "Texas to Tie Car Registration Renewal to Child Support," *Texas Tribune*, June 14, 2016, https://www.texastribune.org/2016/06/14/child-support-evaders-vehicle-registration-renewal/

17. Paul Burka, "The Case Against John Cornyn," *Texas Monthly*, June 2000.

18. McNeely and Henderson, *Bob Bullock*, 96.

19. Patricia Kilday Hart, "25 Stories about Bob Bullock," *Texas Monthly*, July 2003.

20. Jay Root and NeenaSatija, "Ag Commissioner Says Consumers Being 'Screwed,'" *Texas Tribune*, February 27, 2015.

21. Gantt, *Chief Executive*, 129.

22. Brandi Grissom, "Texas Lt. Gov. Dan Patrick Calls Dallas Protesters 'Hypocrites' for Running from Sniper's Bullets," Dallas Morning News, July 8, 2016. http://www.dallasnews.com/

news/crime/headlines/20160708-texas-lt.-gov.-dan-patrick-calls-dallas-protesters-hypocrites-for-running-from-sniper-s-bullets.ece

23. McNeely and Henderson, *Bob Bullock*, 214.

24. Lou Dubose, "So What's the Truth About Dan Morales and Tobacco?," *Texas Monthly*, March 2002, http://www.texasmonthly.com/politics/so-whats-the-truth-about-dan-morales-and-tobacco/

25. W. Gardner Selby, "Greg Abbott Says State Proved in Court that More than 200 Dead People Voted in the Latest Texas Elections," *POLITIFACT Texas*, July 24, 2012, http://www.politifact.com/texas/statements/2012/jul/24/greg-abbott/greg-abbott-dead-voters-Texas/

26. "Texas Investigated More than 550 Insurance Fraud Cases in 2013," *Insurance Journal*, April 28, 2014, http://www.insurancejournal.com/news/southcentral/2014/04/28/327471.htm

27. Jim Malewitz, "Report: Utility Regulators See Rise in Complaints," *The Texas Tribune*, October 14, 2014.

28. Casey Stinnett, "What Do You Do with a 'Nuisance Alligator'?," *Cleveland Advocate*, June 2, 2014, http://www.yourhoustonnews.com/cleveland/news/what-do-you-do-with-a-nuisance-alligator/article_83ea3f7c-9a93-5f03-ba5a-49e3ba0b9883.html

29. Jess Davis, "Texas Gov. Backs Industry Opposition To Houston Air Law," *Law360*, August 4, 2015, http://www.law360.com/articles/687356/texas-gov-backs-industry-opposition-to-houston-air-law

30. Terrence Stutz, "Texas State Board of Education Approves New Curriculum Standards," *The Dallas Morning News*, May 22, 2010, updated November 26, 2010, http://www.dallasnews.com/news/education/headlines/20100521-Texas-State-Board-of-Education-approves-9206.ece

31. The Associated Press, "Texas Approves Disputed History Texts for Schools," *The New York Times*, Nov. 22, 2014, http://www.nytimes.com/2014/11/23/us/texas-approves-disputed-history-texts-for-schools.html

32. Peggy Fikac, "Abbott Can Spark an Outcry with Appointments, by Design," *Houston Chronicle*, April 24, 2016, http://www.houstonchronicle.com/news/news_columnists/peggy_fikac/article/Abbott-can-spark-an-outcry-with-appointments-by-7306569.php?t=1d83695c94438d9cbb&cmpid=twitter-premium&utm_source=-WhatCountsEmail&utm_medium=newsmail_premium_texastake&utm_campaign=newsmail_Texas%20Take%20Newsletter

33. Brian Thevenot, "Social Conservatives Rewrite History Standards," *The Texas Tribune*, March 12, 2010, https://www.texastribune.org/2010/03/12/social-conservatives-rewrite-history-standards/

34. Lauren McGaughy, "Dems stay steady on State Board of Education: Panel's 15 Members Equally Divided into Dems, Far-Right GOP, Centrists," *Houston Chronicle*, November 8, 2014, updated November 8, 2014, http://www.houstonchronicle.com/news/politics/texas/article/Dems-stay-steady-on-State-Board-of-Education-5880898.php

35. Andrea Ball and Eric Dexheimer, "CPS Once Again Faces Overhaul, but Leaders Say This One Is Different," *Austin American-Statesman*, January 13, 2015, http://projects.statesman.com/news/cps-missed-signs/overhaul-strategy.html

36. Paul Burka, "Sunrise, Sunset," *Texas Monthly*, May 1993.

37. Texas Sunset Advisory Commission, "Frequently Asked Questions," https://www.sunset.texas.gov/about-us/frequently-asked-questions

38. Robert T. Garrett, "Taking Texas 'Sunset' Model Nationwide?," *Trail Blazers Blog* (blog), *The Dallas Morning News*, June 2, 2009, http://trailblazersblog.dallasnews.com/2009/06/taking-texas-sunset-model-nati.html/

39. Ross Ramsey, "Analysis: Texas Legislative Review Process Needs a Review," *The Texas Tribune*, April 25, 2016, https://www.texastribune.org/2016/04/25/analysis-texas-legislative-review-process-needs-re/

40. Aman Batheja, "Senators Worry State Contracting Is Too Decentralized," *Texas Tribune*, March 11, 2015.

Chapter 10 The Texas Judiciary

1. "Record $25 Million Awarded In Silicone-Gel Implants Case." *The New York Times*, December 24, 1992. http://www.nytimes.com/1992/12/24/us/record-25-million-awarded-in-silicone-gel-implants-case.html

2. Governor Rick Perry speech transcript, October 2003. http://www.manhattan-institute.org/html/clp10-8-03.htm

3. Evan Smith. 2003. "Joe Jamail." *Texas Monthly*, December; John Spong. 2015. "The Greatest Lawyer Who Ever Lived." *Texas Monthly*, January.

4. Brian Rosenthal. 2015. "How a Wayward Cow Could Change Texas' Tort Reform Law." *Houston Chronicle*, March 9.

5. Angela Morris. 2015. "Why Are Filings Falling? Civil Lawsuits Down 17 Percent in 10 Years." *Texas Lawyer*, March 9.

6. James L. Haley. 2013. *The Texas Supreme Court*. Austin: University of Texas Press.

7. The State of the Judiciary in Texas, Chief Justice Nathan L. Hecht. Presented to the 84th Legislature. February 18, 2015, Austin, Texas. http://www.txcourts.gov/media/857636/state-of-the-judiciary-2015.pdf

8. James L. Haley. 2013. *The Texas Supreme Court*. Austin: University of Texas Press, 123.

9. Ibid, 88.

10. Annual Statistical Report for the Texas Judiciary, 2015, page 46-7. Criminal and civil cases.

11. Texas Association of Counties, Description of Office, County Judge.

12. Oral Argument Information, Texas Supreme Court. http://www.txcourts.gov/supreme/practice-before-the-court/oral-argument-information.aspx

13. Rebe, Ryan. 2013. "Amicus Curiae and Dissenting Votes at the Texas Supreme Court." *Justice System Journal* 34 (2): 171–188.

14. http://www.houstonchronicle.com/news/houston-texas/houston/article/Texas-high-court-limits-open-government-law-GHP-6352311.php

15. "How Courts Work," American Bar Association, Division for Public Education.
16. http://www.law360.com/articles/522856/texas-high-court-gives-kia-new-trial-in-failed-airbag-suit
17. http://info.tpj.org/docs/pdf/paytoplay.pdf
18. Annual Statistical Report for the Texas Judiciary, 2015.
19. Michael Massengale. 2015. https://texconst.wordpress.com/2015/01/07/dual-texas-supreme-courts/, accessed January 19, 2016.
20. http://www.texastribune.org/2012/12/13/bill-merge-highest-courts-brings-back-old-debate/
21. Ibid.
22. James L. Haley. 2013. *The Texas Supreme Court*. Austin: University of Texas Press, 214.
23. The State of the Judiciary in Texas, Chief Justice Nathan L. Hecht. Presented to the 84th Legislature. February 18, 2015, Austin, Texas. http://www.txcourts.gov/media/857636/state-of-the-judiciary-2015.pdf
24. James L. Haley. 2013. *The Texas Supreme Court*. Austin: University of Texas Press, 32.
25. http://www.dallasnews.com/news/texas/2013/09/02/texas-chief-justice-wallace-jefferson-to-resign-oct.
26. 2014 Annual Texas Judicial Statistical Report. http://www.txcourts.gov/statistics/annual-statistical-reports/2014.aspx
27. http://www.cnn.com/2014/02/05/us/texas-affluenza-teen/
28. https://www.texastribune.org/2015/11/23/commission-will-address-justice-gap-working-class/
29. http://www.chron.com/opinion/outlook/article/Hecht-McRaven-Legal-aid-for-our-veterans-Now-6616182.php
30. http://www.dallasnews.com/opinion/editorials/20150503-editorial-texas-must-expand-funding-for-legal-aid.ece
31. http://www.teajf.org/news/releases/End%20of%2084th%20Session.aspx
32. The following ten states use merit plans only to fill midterm vacancies on some or all levels of court: Alabama, Georgia, Idaho, Kentucky, Minnesota, Montana, Nevada, New Mexico, North Dakota, and West Virginia.
33. Anthony Champagne and Kyle Cheek. 2001. "The Cycle of Judicial Elections: Texas as a Case Study." *Fordham Urban Law Journal* 29 (3).
34. Texas Code of Judicial Conduct, As Amended, 2002. http://www.scjc.state.tx.us/pdf/txcodeofjudicialconduct.pdf
35. Joanna Cohn Weiss. 2006. "Tough on Crime: How Campaigns for State Judiciary Violate Criminal Defendants' Due Process Rights." *New York University Law Review* 81 (June): 1101–1136.
36. *PBS Frontline, Justice for Sale*, Interview with Tom Phillips. http://www.pbs.org/wgbh/pages/frontline/shows/justice/interviews/phillips.html
37. http://www.scjc.state.tx.us/pdf/actions/SummariesofPrivateSanctions8-31-14.pdf
38. http://www.dallasnews.com/news/state/headlines/20100816-Texas-Supreme-Court-upholds-Judge-Sharon-4977.ece
39. Texas Constitution, Article 15, Section 8.
40. James L. Haley. 2013. *The Texas Supreme Court*. Austin: University of Texas Press, 178.
41. *Lubbock Avalanche-Journal*. August 27, 1944. Page 18.
42. Anthony Champagne and Kyle Cheek. 2001. "The Cycle of Judicial Elections: Texas as a Case Study." *Fordham Urban Law Journal* 29 (3): 912.
43. Ken Case. 1987. "Blind Justice." *Texas Monthly*, May.
44. Morgan Smith. 2010. "Can the Democrats Win a Supreme Court Race?" *The Texas Tribune*, April 12. http://www.texastribune.org/2010/04/12/ethical-lapses-become-focus-in-court-campaign/
45. Swansborough, Robert. 2008. *Test by Fire*. New York: Palgrave, 42.
46. http://scholar.harvard.edu/files/jsnyder/files/election_paper_jim_cl_feb2014_jle.pdf?m=1392404808
47. Bankrolling the Bench. The New Politics of Judicial Elections 2013–14. The Brennan Center and the National Institute for Money in State Politics, page 3.
48. Bankrolling the Bench. The New Politics of Judicial Elections 2013–14. The Brennan Center and the National Institute for Money in State Politics.
49. Anthony Champagne and Kyle Cheek. 2001. "The Cycle of Judicial Elections: Texas as a Case Study." *Fordham Urban Law Journal* 29 (3): 912. Texas for Public Justice report, "Interested Parties," October 2009. http://info.tpj.org/reports/supremes08/InterestedParties.oct09.pdf
50. http://www.texastribune.org/2011/07/06/perrys-twia-nemesis-promises-to-continue-his-fight/
51. Damon M. Cann. 2007. "Justice for Sale? Campaign Contributions and Judicial Decisionmaking." *State Politics & Policy Quarterly* 7 (3): 281–297.
52. https://www.brennancenter.org/publication/how-judicial-elections-impact-criminal-cases
53. James L. Haley. 2013. *The Texas Supreme Court*. Austin: University of Texas Press, 30.
54. Improving Judicial Diversity, Brennan Center for Justice Report. https://www.brennancenter.org/sites/default/files/legacy/Improving_Judicial_Diversity_2010.pdf
55. State Bar of Texas, Annual Report on the Status of Women and Racial/Ethnic Minorities in the State Bar. https://www.texasbar.com/AM/Template.cfm?Section=Facts_Stats_and_Reports&Template=/CM/ContentDisplay.cfm&ContentID=8876
56. http://www.judicialselection.us/uploads/documents/Racial_and_Gender_Diversity_on_Stat_8F60B84D96CC2.pdf
57. State Bar of Texas, Annual Report on the Status of Women and Racial/Ethnic Minorities in the State Bar. https://www.texasbar.com/AM/Template.cfm?Section=Facts_Stats_and_Reports&Template=/CM/ContentDisplay.cfm&ContentID=8876
58. Mark Curriden. 2013. "Texas Chief Justice Wallace Jefferson to Resign October 1." *Dallas Morning News*, September 3.
59. Ross Ramsey. 2015. "Analysis: Should Judges Exit Fundraising Business?" *Texas Tribune*, May 15. http://www.texastribune.org/2015/

05/15/analysis-distance-between-judges-and-politics/

60. Adam Liptak. 2015. "Supreme Court Upholds Limit on Judicial Fund-Raising." *The New York Times,* April 29.

Chapter 10 Photo Caption Notes

* Eva Ruth Moravec. 2015. "Meet the State Supreme Court Justice Who's Also Texas' 'Tweeter Laureate.' *Dallas Morning News,* June 5.

** http://www.chron.com/news/houston-texas/houston/article/Galveston-judge-who-pled-guilty-set-to-resign-4827842.php

Chapter 11 Criminal Justice

1. http://www.nytimes.com/interactive/2015/07/20/us/sandra-bland-arrest-death-videos-maps.html

2. http://www.huffingtonpost.com/entry/sandra-bland-arrest-transcript_55b03a88e4b0a9b94853b1f1

3. http://www.cnn.com/2015/07/23/us/sandra-bland-questions-remain-social-irpt/

4. http://www.texastribune.org/2015/09/14/sandra-bland-deputy-deaths-force-mental-health-age/

5. http://www.texastribune.org/2015/09/14/sandra-bland-deputy-deaths-force-mental-health-age/

6. http://www.nbcnews.com/news/us-news/texas-sheriffs-deputy-darren-h-goforth-killed-houston-gas-station-n418131

7. http://www.statesman.com/news/news/dan-patrick-texans-should-call-police-sir-and-maam/nnW8r/

8. http://www.nationaljournal.com/next-america/newsdesk/tearing-seams

9. Molly Ivins. 2000. *Shrub: The Short But Happy Political Life of George W. Bush.* New York: Vintage Books.

10. C.L. Sonnichen. 1991. *Roy Bean: Law West of the Pecos.* Lincoln: University of Nebraska Press, 5.

11. http://www.chron.com/news/houston-texas/article/Texas-killer-made-famous-by-Jack-Black-movie-goes-5456716.php

12. Skip Hollandsworth. 1998. "Midnight in the Garden of East Texas." *Texas Monthly,* January.

13. http://www.texasmonthly.com/politics/the-policy-and-politics-of-drug-sentencing/

14. http://www.cnn.com/2011/SHOWBIZ/celebrity.news.gossip/03/28/willie.nelson.pot.plea/

15. http://www.cnn.com/2011/SHOWBIZ/celebrity.news.gossip/06/07/willie.nelson.fine/

16. 2016 Juvenile Justice Handbook: A Practical Reference Guide Including Updates from the 84th Legislative Session, Texas Attorney General.

17. Criminal Law 101: Overview of the Texas Criminal Justice Process. Texas Young Lawyers Association and the State Bar of Texas. 2013. www.texaslawhelp.org

18. Ibid.

19. http://research.lawyers.com/texas/criminal-process-in-texas.html

20. Texas Criminal Justice Procedure: A Citizen's Guide. The State Bar of Texas Criminal Justice Section. Revised 2005. http://www.tombean.net/files/forms/the%20texas%20crimnal%20justic%20a%20citizens%20guide.pdf

21. http://www.criminaldefenselawyer.com/resources/criminal-defense/criminal-defense-case/jury-selection-texas.htm

22. http://research.lawyers.com/texas/criminal-process-in-texas.html

23. Robert Perkinson. 2010. *Texas Tough: The Rise of America's Prison Empire.* New York: Picador, 173.

24. Ibid., 172.

25. Ben M. Crouch and James W. Marquart. 1989. *An Appeal to Justice: Litigated Reform of Texas Prisons.* Austin: University of Texas Press, 13.

26. Gary Brown. 2001. *Singin' a Lonesome Song: Texas Prison Tales.* Plano: Republic of Texas Press, 39.

27. Ibid., 176.

28. http://interactives.dallasnews.com/2015/kids-or-criminals/part1.html

29. Criminal Justice Procedure: A Citizen's Guide. The State Bar of Texas Criminal Justice Section. Revised 2005. http://www.tombean.net/files/forms/the%20texas%20crimnal%20justic%20a%20citizens%20guide.pdf

30. http://www.spca.org/cacs

31. http://tdcj.state.tx.us/unit_directory/

32. http://www.ncpa.org/pub/st237?pg=2

33. https://www.brennancenter.org/publication/what-caused-crime-decline

34. Robert Perkinson. 2010. *Texas Tough: The Rise of America's Prison Empire.* New York: Picador, 7

35. http://www.ncpa.org/pdfs/st237.pdf

36. John J. Dilulio. 1987. *Governing Prisons.* New York: Macmillan, 105.

37. Robert Perkinson. 2010. *Texas Tough: The Rise of America's Prison Empire.* New York: Picador.

38. John Hubner. 2005. *Last Chance in Texas: The Redemption of Criminal Youth.* New York: Random House, xx.

39. https://www.brennancenter.org/publication/what-caused-crime-decline

40. https://www.washingtonpost.com/politics/prison-reform-advocates-press-states-to-shift-money-out-of-corrections-system/2011/04/04/AFeCXolC_story.html

41. http://www.texasmonthly.com/list/the-rick-perry-report-card/criminal-justice/

42. Robert Perkinson. 2010. *Texas Tough: The Rise of America's Prison Empire.* New York: Picador, 269.

43. Ibid., 358.

44. http://rightoncrime.com/2015/03/new-poll-shows-voters-strongly-support-new-justice-reforms-in-texas/

45. http://www.chron.com/news/houston-texas/article/Controversy-abounds-at-Texas-many-private-prisons-6101496.php

46. http://www.austinchronicle.com/news/2016-08-26/justice-department-begins-phase-out-of-private-prisons/

47. Gary Brown. 2001. *Singin' a Lonesome Song: Texas Prison Tales.* Plano: Republic of Texas Press.

48. Ibid., 15.

49. Ibid., 19.

50. https://www.tdcj.state.tx.us/death_row/dr_facts.html

51. http://www.rollingstone.com/politics/news/bush-the-texas-death-machine-20000803

52. Robert Perkinson. 2010. *Texas Tough: The Rise of America's Prison Empire.* New York: Picador, 341.

53. http://www.texasmonthly.com/list/the-rick-perry-report-card/criminal-justice/

54. http://www.economist.com/news/united-states/21601270-america-falling-out-love-needle-slow-death-death-penalty

55. Brandi Grissom 2015. "Firing Squad, Blood Draining Among Suggestions Sent to Gov. Greg Abbott to Continue Texas Death Penalty." *Dallas Morning News*, September 4. http://trailblazersblog. dallasnews.com/2015/09/firing-squad-blood-draining-among-suggestions-sent-to-gov-greg-abbott-to-continue-texas-death-penalty.html/

56. http://www.pewresearch.org/fact-tank/2016/09/29/support-for-death-penalty-lowest-in-more-than-four-decades/

57. http://www.abacollateralconsequences.org/search/?jurisdiction=45

58. Jeff Manza and Christopher Uggen. 2004. "Punishment and Democracy: Disenfranchisement of Nonincarcerated Felons in the United States." *Perspectives on Politics* (2): 491–505.

59. http://www.sentencingproject.org/issues/felony-disenfranchisement/

60. Texas Criminal Justice Procedure: A Citizen's Guide. The State Bar of Texas Criminal Justice Section. Revised 2005. http://www.tombean.net/files/forms/the%20texas%20crimnal%20justic%20a%20citizens%20guide.pdf

61. Ken Anderson. 2005. *Crime in Texas: Your Complete Guide to the Criminal Justice System*. Austin: University of Texas.

62. Ibid., 2.

63. http://www.tdcj.state.tx.us/bpp/parole_guidelines/parole_guidelines.html

64. Ibid., 4.

65. http://www.tdcj.state.tx.us/bpp/parole_increase.pdf

66. Robert Perkinson. 2010. *Texas Tough: The Rise of America's Prison Empire*. New York: Picador, 306.

67. Ibid.

68. Texas Criminal Justice Coalition, A Blueprint for Criminal Justice Policy Solutions in Harris County. January 2015.

69. Ibid.

70. Brian Rogers. 2015. "Harris County Being Eyed for Bail Reform." *Houston Chronicle*, June 26.

71. Ibid.

72. Ibid.

73. Leah Binkovitz. 2015. "Bail Reform Urged After Sandra Bland's Death." *Houston Chronicle*, August 19.

74. http://www.dallasnews.com/news/state/headlines/20151128-suicides-and-attempts-on-the-rise-in-texas-prisons.ece

75. Michael Hall. 2015. "The Reformer." *Texas Monthly*. February, 161.

76. https://tshaonline.org/handbook/online/articles/jlg01

77. http://www.texasmonthly.com/the-daily-post/is-the-grand-jury-system-in-texas-broken/

78. Patrick Svitek. 2015. "Abbott Signs Grand Jury Reform Legislation." *Texas Tribune*, June 19.

79. Texas Tribune Poll, February 2015.

80. Michael Hall. 2015. "Four Decades, Three Trials, Two Death Sentences, One Exoneree. Almost." *Texas Monthly*, September 14. http://www.texasmonthly.com/news/four-decades-three-trials-two-death-sentences-1-exoneree-almost/

81. Ibid.

82. Terri Langford. 2015. "Lawyers, Scientists Try to Unravel Thorny New DNA Standard." *Texas Tribune*, September 18. http://www.texastribune.org/2015/09/18/lawyers-scientists-try-unravel-thorny-new-dna-stan/

83. http://www.constitutionproject.org/issues/criminal-justice-reform/death-penalty/

84. http://www.texasmonthly.com/list/the-rick-perry-report-card/criminal-justice/

85. http://www.kvue.com/story/news/local/2015/09/19/rallies-converge-police-lives-matter-black-lives-matter/72473662/

86. http://www.hudson.org/research/12476-why-texas-criminal-justice-reforms-don-t-translate-to-the-federal-level

Chapter 11 Photo Caption Notes

*   Miles Graham, "When you can kill in Texas," Time, June 13, 2013, http://nation.time.com/2013/06/13/when-you-can-kill-in-texas/
**   http://www.cnn.com/2011/SHOWBIZ/celebrity.news.gossip/06/07/willie.nelson.fine/
†   Andrew J. Bloeser, Carl McCurley, and Jeffrey J. Mondak. 2012. "Jury Service as Civic Engagement." American Political Research 40 (2): 179–204.

Chapter 12 Local Government

1. http://www.politico.com/magazine/story/2014/12/texas-fracking-ban-113575#.VI-KaWTF9Xx

2. http://www.texastribune.org/2015/05/18/abbott-signs-denton-fracking-bill/

3. http://www.houstonchronicle.com/business/energy/article/As-fracking-vote-nears-a-city-divided-5862361.php

4. http://www.politico.com/magazine/story/2014/12/texas-fracking-ban-113575?o=2

5. http://www.texastribune.org/2015/05/12/amid-local-control-fight-gop-proposal-cities/; http://www.houstonchronicle.com/news/politics/texas/article/Big-city-mayors-to-Lege-Don-t-mess-with-taxes-6083909.php?t=4ea844c593b2e7d3f0&cmpid=email-premium

6. http://www.nytimes.com/2015/02/24/us/govern-yourselves-state-lawmakers-tell-cities-but-not-too-much.html?action=click&contentCollection=Health&region=Footer&module=TopNews&pgtype=Blogs&assetType=nyt_now&_r=0; http://planoblog.dallasnews.com/2015/03/bills-take-aim-at-lgbt-protections.html/

7. http://www.dallasnews.com/news/politics/state-politics/20150602-texas-legislators-mostly-kept-hands-off-local-control.ece?mc_cid=74cb229e8d&mc_eid=101a099a60

8. http://www.dallasnews.com/news/politics/state-politics/20150507-bills-that-would-sack-texas-bag-bans-left-hanging-in-committees.ece

9. http://www.governing.com/topics/transportation-infrastructure/tt-plastic-bag-ban-ruling-laredo.html

10. http://www.houstonchronicle.com/news/houston-texas/houston/article/Uber-fights-pushback-on-ride-service-with-politics-6109354.php?t=0230caa790b2e7d3f0&cmpid=email-premium

11. http://www.texastribune.org/2015/12/17/austin-city-council-approves-new-uber-regs-uber-th/

12. http://www.slate.com/articles/business/moneybox/2015/10/uber_returns_to_san_antonio_after_throwing_a_massive_tantrum_over_regulations.html

13. http://www.texasmonthly.com/the-daily-post/houstons-equal-rights-ordinance-explained/

14. Texas Municipal League, "Local Government in Texas." http://www.tml.org/Handbook-M&C/Chapter1.pdf

15. http://www.dallasnews.com/news/news/2013/05/25/texas-prohibits-nearly-70-percent-of-its-counties-from-having-a-fire-code

16. Thad Sitton. 2000. *The Texas Sherriff*. Norman: University of Oklahoma Press, xii.

17. Ibid.

18. http://www.chron.com/news/houston-texas/houston/article/DA-Marijuana-now-means-a-citation-not-a-ride-to-6613889.php

19. http://www.star-telegram.com/opinion/opn-columns-blogs/bud-kennedy/article25934896.html

20. http://www.tml.org/p/docs/typesofcities.pdf

21. Ibid.

22. David Warren. 2016. "More than 20 Texas Towns Repeal Sex Offender Residency Law." Associated Press, February 7.

23. Texas Municipal League, "Local Government in Texas." http://www.tml.org/Handbook-M&C/Chapter1.pdf

24. https://tshaonline.org/handbook/online/articles/mvhek

25. http://txktoday.com/news/texarkana-texas-voters-approve-beer-wine-sales/; http://www.ktbs.com/story/22312867/petition-circulates-for-texarkana-texas-alcohol-sales

26. http://www.star-telegram.com/news/local/community/arlington/article5553912.html

27. https://ballotpedia.org/Recall_campaigns_in_Texas

28. http://www.chron.com/neighborhood/humble-news/article/Annexed-Kingwood-split-on-effects-1868661.php

29. http://www.houstonchronicle.com/news/houston-texas/houston/article/Houston-plugs-budget-holes-with-suburban-sales-tax-6038195.php

30. Ann O'M. Bowman and Richard Kearney. 2013. *State and Local Government*. Boston: Wadsworth, 273.

31. http://www.texasmonthly.com/politics/how-i-learned-to-hate-the-media-and-love-politics-well-sort-of/

32. http://www.dallasnews.com/news/metro/20150319-dispute-on-islam-roils-irving.ece

33. Richard Murray. 2004. Governance in Houston: A Hamiltonian Model of Municipal Power in Action.

34. http://www.houstonchronicle.com/news/politics/houston/article/City-county-leaders-talk-up-possibility-for-6720378.php?t=421860299a&cmpid=email-premium

35. http://www.houstonchronicle.com/news/politics/texas/article/Controller-Green-holds-up-airport-contracts-6703744.php?t=26a0656293438d9cbb&cmpid=twitter-premium

36. https://tshaonline.org/handbook/online/articles/moc01

37. http://www.mysanantonio.com/opinion/commentary/article/Bumpy-road-to-city-s-current-form-of-government-6223668.php

38. http://www.foxbusiness.com/features/2015/07/07/how-fort-worths-bike-riding-mayor-steers-city.html

39. Robert Wilonsky. 2016. "Mayor Moves to Block Porn Expo." *Dallas Morning News*, February 7.

40. http://cityhallblog.dallasnews.com/2016/04/federal-judge-says-dallas-was-within-its-rights-to-ban-exxxotica-sex-expo-from-convention-center.html/

41. http://www.governing.com/blogs/by-the-numbers/government-mayor-council-manager-form-changes.html

42. http://www.texasmonthly.com/politics/how-i-learned-to-hate-the-media-and-love-politics-well-sort-of/

43. James H. Svara and Douglas J. Watson. 2010. *More Than Mayor or Manager: Campaigns to Change Form of Government in America's Large Cities*. Washington, DC: Georgetown University Press.

44. http://www.texasmonthly.com/articles/whats-the-matter-with-dallas/

45. Texas Municipal League, "Local Government in Texas." http://www.tml.org/Handbook-M&C/Chapter1.pdf

46. http://www.senate.state.tx.us/SRC/pdf/SL-SpPurposeDistricts.pdf

47. http://www.austinmonitor.com/stories/2015/11/aisd-changes-school-naming-policy-barely/

48. http://www.dallasnews.com/news/community-news/park-cities/headlines/20140929-highland-park-isd-reverses-book-suspensions-at-high-school.ece

49. http://www.houstonchronicle.com/neighborhood/woodlands/news/article/Woodlands-to-seek-legislative-OK-for-more-6044387.php

50. http://www.houstonchronicle.com/news/houston-texas/houston/article/Municipal-Utility-Districts-in-Texas-have-9175418.php

51. http://www.houstonchronicle.com/news/houston-texas/houston/article/Keys-to-unlocking-your-rights-with-HOA-4547900.php

52. http://www.texasmonthly.com/politics/growing-disillusioned-with-hoas/

53. http://www.texastribune.org/2013/04/09/hoa-accountability-bill-stirs-debate-capitol/

54. http://www.chron.com/business/article/HOA-changes-in-effect-3004723.php

55. http://leadershipaustin.org/wp-content/uploads/2015/11/Civic-Engagement-in-Austin-Report_November-2015.pdf

56. http://www.dallasnews.com/news/state/headlines/20150102-voting-rights-fight-looms-over-latino-clout-in-texas-city.ece

57. http://www.governing.com/gov-institute/voices/col-local-politics-voting-community-engagement-millennials.html

58. http://www.cnn.com/2016/02/05/us/crystal-city-texas-corruption/

59. https://www.texastribune.org/2016/02/13/crystal-city-left-alone-rebuild-troubled-governmen/

60. http://www.dallasobserver.com/news/denton-county-sheriff-william-travis-is-losing-endorsements-like-mad-8068237

61. http://www.texastribune.org/2015/10/15/analysis-shifting-numbers-your-property-tax-bill/

62. http://www.bloomberg.com/news/articles/2015-03-04/texas-tax-cut-plan-riles-cities-dealing-with-growth-muni-credit

63. http://www.texastribune.org/2015/03/05/rising-local-debt-draws-attention-legislature/

64. This excludes Loving County as an outlier.

65. http://www.houstonchronicle.com/politics/election/local/article/Road-bond-OK-d-on-3rd-try-6609206.php

66. http://www.elpasoinc.com/news/local_news/article_d9e0e61c-0b21-11e2-834c-0019bb30f31a.html

67. http://www.texastribune.org/2014/08/27/local-debt-soaring-across-texas/

68. http://www.mysanantonio.com/news/news_columnists/article/Helotes-vs-S-A-in-the-battle-for-ETJ-4432927.php

69. http://www.houstonchronicle.com/news/politics/houston/article/City-county-leaders-talk-up-possibility-for-6720378.php?t=421860299a&cmpid=email-premium

70. http://www.economist.com/news/united-states/21652342-texas-politicians-line-themselves-up-against-states-big-cities-texan-tug-war

71. http://www.star-telegram.com/news/local/education/article3864132.html

72. http://www.businessweek.com/the_thread/hotproperty/archives/2007/10/how_houston_gets_along_without_zoning.html

73. http://www.houstonchronicle.com/local/gray-matters/article/Houston-All-the-burdens-of-zoning-but-none-of-6493863.php?t=9da8de61db438d9cbb&cmpid=twitter-premium

74. http://www.dallasobserver.com/news/sizing-up-dallas-massive-pension-problem-7752330; http://www.fortworthbusiness.com/news/city-committee-to-tackle-pension-issues/article_a6816844-b660-11e5-b186-8befbbac14af.html

Chapter 12 Photo Caption Notes
* https://www.texastribune.org/2014/10/09/ebola-response-helps-jenkins-political-footing/
** http://trailblazersblog.dallasnews.com/2015/04/lawmakers-face-long-odds-in-effort-to- crackdown-on-predatory-lending.html/
† http://www.elpasotimes.com/story/news/2016/06/01/commission-city-manager-violated-ethics-policy/85269178/

Chapter 13 Budget, Finances, and Policy
1. https://www.texastribune.org/2015/05/18/brief/
2. http://www.dallasnews.com/news/state/headlines/20150326-senator-shame-on-budget-writers-if-pensions-roads-arent-funded.ece
3. http://www.texasmonthly.com/politics/for-an-income-tax/

4. http://www.texastransparency.org/State_Finance/Budget_Finance/Reports/Revenue_by_Source/
5. http://www.texastransparency.org/State_Finance/Revenue/Sources/2015/Sources_of_Revenue_2015.pdf
6. http://www.governing.com/topics/finance/gov-state-tax-collection-burden-shifts.html
7. Ibid.
8. http://comptroller.texas.gov/fiscalnotes/oct2015/proptax.php
9. http://www.texasmonthly.com/burka-blog/the-dark-lining-in-the-property-tax-cut-silver-cloud/
10. http://www.texasobserver.org/big-spring-exposes-texas-broken-property-tax-system/
11. http://www.texasmonthly.com/burka-blog/the-dark-lining-in-the-property-tax-cut-silver-cloud/
12. http://www.texastransparency.org/State_Finance/Revenue/Sources/2015/Sources_of_Revenue_2015.pdf
13. Ibid.
14. http://www.houstonchronicle.com/news/local/article/State-shuffles-other-sources-for-road-work-as-gas-6577475.php?mc_cid=d78c138ebc&mc_eid=101a099a60
15. http://comptroller.texas.gov/fiscalnotes/nov2015/sintax.php
16. http://www.texasmonthly.com/the-daily-post/texas-debtors-prisons-problem/
17. http://www.texasobserver.org/p-e-party-strikes-back-driver-responsibility-program/
18. http://trailblazersblog.dallasnews.com/2016/01/lawmakers-take-critical-look-at-driver-responsibility-program.html/
19. http://amarillo.com/news/crime-and-courts/2016-01-15/city-sued-over-municipal-fines-policy
20. http://www.texastransparency.org/State_Finance/Budget_Finance/Fiscal_Briefs/pdf/EconomicStabilizationFund.pdf
21. http://www.texasmonthly.com/burka-blog/budget-wizardry/
22. http://www.senate.state.tx.us/SRC/pdf/Budget_101-2011.pdf
23. Jan Reid. 2012. *Let the People In: The Life and Times of Ann Richards.* Austin: University of Texas Press, 386.

24. Texas Politics Polling, May 2011. Support for Revenue Increases: Implement a State Income Tax.
25. http://www.texasmonthly.com/burka-blog/budget-wizardry/
26. http://www.mystatesman.com/news/business/lawmakers-tax-cuts-for-business-may-be-divisive-an/njysM/?icmp=statesman_internal-link_invitationbox_apr2013_statesmanstubtomystatesmanpremium
27. http://www.washingtonpost.com/wp-srv/politics/campaigns/wh2000/stories/bush032199.htm
28. http://www.bizjournals.com/dallas/print-edition/2011/05/06/entertaining-lege-session-ends-this.html
29. Patricia L. Cox and Michael Phillips. 2010. *The House Will Come to Order.* Austin: University of Texas Press, 49.
30. http://www.lbb.state.tx.us/Documents/Publications/Presentation/1987_HACSpendingLimitandOverview.pdf
31. http://www.texastribune.org/2015/04/16/analysis-senate-trying-regulate-its-own-spending/
32. http://www.lbb.state.tx.us/Documents/Publications/Presentation/1987_HACSpendingLimitandOverview.pdf
33. Legislative Budget Board, Fiscal Size-Up, 2016–2017 Biennium, May 2016. Page 28.
34. Paul Burka. 1997. "The Honeymoon is Over." *Texas Monthly,* January.
35. Brian McCall. 2009. *The Power of the Texas Governor: Connally to Bush.* Austin: University of Texas Press, 125.
36. https://www.texastribune.org/2016/07/13/analysis-cutting-texas-budget-only-hypothetically/
37. http://www.texasmonthly.com/politics/the-bloody-billion/
38. http://www.houstonchronicle.com/news/kilday-hart/article/Electronic-lobbying-changes-influence-peddling-4432727.php
39. http://www.dallasnews.com/news/politics/state-politics/20150722-inside-the-dispute-about-gov.-greg-abbotts-budget-power.ece
40. http://lubbockonline.com/filed-online/2016-02-20/comptroller-oil-bust-does-not-have-sky-falling-texas#.WDtVi2bruUk

41. http://www.texasmonthly.com/politics/carole-keeton-strayhorn-has-guts-carole-keeton-strayhorn-is-nuts-discuss/

42. http://www.texastribune.org/2014/08/05/gov-office-defends-national-guard-deployment-fundi/

43. Kaiser Family Foundation. http://kff.org/other/state-indicator/per-capita-state-spending/?currentTimeframe=0

44. http://kxan.com/2016/04/13/report-nearly-a-quarter-of-texas-children-live-in-poverty/

45. http://tpr.org/post/fewer-texans-living-poverty-according-new-census-data#stream/0

46. https://www.news-journal.com/news/2016/sep/08/1-in-5-households-hungry-in-east-texas/

47. http://www.dallasnews.com/news/texas/2015/09/16/more-in-texas-lack-health-insurance-than-in-any-other-state

48. http://kff.org/medicare/state-indicator/total-medicare-beneficiaries/?currentTimeframe=0&sortModel=%7B%22colId%22:%22Location%22,%22sort%22:%22asc%22%7D

49. https://hhs.texas.gov/sites/hhs/files/documents/services/health/medicaid-chip/book/pink-book.pdf

50. http://www.houstonchronicle.com/news/houston-texas/houston/article/Largest-Medicare-fraud-takedown-in-history-nabs-8319743.php

51. Texas Health and Human Services Commission, Research and Statistics. Accessed February 2016.

52. https://www.texastribune.org/tribpedia/medicaid/about/

53. Texas Public Policy Foundation. 2015. Texas Medicaid Reform Model: A Market-Driven, Patient-Centered Approach.

54. https://hhs.texas.gov/sites/hhs/files/documents/services/health/medicaid-chip/book/pink-book.pdf

55. Ibid.

56. Ibid.

57. http://talkingpointsmemo.com/livewire/survey-uninsured-rate-record-low?utm_content=buffera5875&utm_medium=social&utm_source=twitter.com&utm_campaign=buffer

58. http://www.dallasnews.com/news/state/headlines/20150916-more-in-texas-lack-health-insurance-than-in-any-other-state.ece

59. http://trailblazersblog.dallasnews.com/2015/10/one-third-of-uninsured-texans-could-but-dont-accept-help-in-getting-covered.html/

60. http://trailblazersblog.dallasnews.com/2016/02/decent-bump-in-obamacare-signups-in-dfw-but-across-texas-not-so-much.html/

61. https://www.texastribune.org/2016/05/02/texas-feds-agree-short-term-medicaid-funds-renewal/

62. http://healthcare.dmagazine.com/2016/05/02/texas-receives-15-month-extension-on-its-29-billion-medicaid-1115-waiver/

63. American Association of Retired Persons, 2014. www.aarp.org/.../Social-Security-2014-Texas-Quick-Facts-AARP-res-gen.pdf

64. http://www.ncpssm.org/PublicPolicy/SocialSecurity/Documents/ArticleID/1590/Social-Security-is-Important-to-Hispanic-Americans

65. Social Security Administration, SSI Recipients by State and County, 2015. https://www.ssa.gov/policy/docs/statcomps/ssi_sc/; https://hhs.texas.gov/sites/hhs/files/documents/services/health/medicaid-chip/book/pink-book.pdf

66. http://www.texastribune.org/2015/02/05/drug-testing-welfare-benefits-back-table/; http://www.ncsl.org/research/human-services/drug-testing-and-public-assistance.aspx

67. Texas Health and Human Services Commission, Research and Statistics. Accessed February 2016.

68. http://www.oiec.texas.gov/documents/ierightsrespeng.pdf

69. http://www.bls.gov/iif/oshwc/cfoi/cfch0013.pdf

70. https://www.nytimes.com/2014/06/29/us/the-state-has-a-record-of-high-worker-fatalities-and-of-weak-benefits.html?_r=0

71. https://apps.texastribune.org/hurting-for-work/

72. https://www.texastribune.org/2012/12/14/back-when-americans-were-illegals/

73. Office of the State Demographer, "The Foreign Born Population in Texas: Sources of Growth," October 2015.

74. http://www.migrationpolicy.org/data/state-profiles/state/demographics/TX

75. http://www.migrationpolicy.org/data/unauthorized-immigrant-population/state/TX

76. http://archive.timesrecordnews.com/news/undocumented-immigrants-economic-impact-unclear-in-texas-ep-1242918902-332488592.html

77. http://www.texaspolicy.com/library/doclib/Immigration-s-Impact-on-the-Texas-Economy.pdf

78. http://www.nytimes.com/2014/06/09/us/for-illegal-immigrants-american-life-lived-in-shadows.html

79. http://www.texasmonthly.com/politics/everything-you-ever-wanted-to-know-about-illegal-immigration-but-didnt-know-who-to-ask/

80. http://www.texastribune.org/2016/01/31/houston-slayings-ignited-immigration-debate/

81. Enrique Rangel. 2015. "Immigration Debate Takes Center Stage." *Amarillo Globe News,* March 15.

82. http://www.pbs.org/newshour/rundown/texas-approves-800-million-border-security/

83. http://www.texasmonthly.com/politics/an-f-for-effort-2/

84. https://www.houstonpublicmedia.org/articles/news/2015/04/27/59742/learn-how-texas-funds-public-schools-in-7-easy-steps-2/

85. http://www.texastribune.org/2015/09/01/one-year-later-school-finance-appeal-back-court/

86. Seth Shepard McKay. 1942. *Seven Decades of the Texas Constitution of 1876.* Lubbock, TX: Privately published 98.

87. http://www.texasmonthly.com/politics/the-honeymoon-is-over/#st-hash.5Uuu7wKN.dpuf

88. https://www.texastribune.org/2016/05/13/texas-supreme-court-issues-school-finance-ruling/

89. http://www.governing.com/gov-data/education-data/state-education-spending-per-pupil-data.html

90. Paul Burka. "Degrading Teachers." *Texas Monthly.* June 1986, 216.

91. Paul Burka. "Degrading Teachers." *Texas Monthly.* June 1986.

92. Bill Hobby. 2010. *How Things Really Work: Lessons from a Life in Politics.* Austin: University of Texas Press, 107.

93. http://texasalmanac.com/topics/education/recent-changes-public-schools

94. http://www.houstonpublicmedia.org/articles/news/2016/01/07/133321/texas-ranked-43rd-in-nation-on-2016-education-quality-report/

95. http://www.dallasnews.com/news/education/headlines/20150830-texas-supreme-court-to-again-hear-that-state-is-shortchanging-schools.ece?mc_cid=5228fe3592&mc_eid=101a099a60

96. http://www.texastribune.org/2015/08/31/texas-schools-still-feeling-2011-budget-cuts/

97. http://www.texastribune.org/2015/12/09/new-schools-explorer-shows-changing-face-schools/

98. http://www.dallasnews.com/news/education/2013/05/03/texas-leaders-educators-and-courts-grapple-with-segregated-public-schools

99. http://www.texasappleseed.net/sites/default/files/TruancyReport_All_FINAL_SinglePages.pdf

100. https://www.propublica.org/article/federal-complaint-alleges-rampant-abuse-in-texas-truancy-program

101. Texas Education Agency, Secondary School Completion and Dropouts in Texas Public Schools, 2014–2015, August 2016.

102. http://www.dallasnews.com/news/education/2013/05/03/texas-leaders-educators-and-courts-grapple-with-segregated-public-schools

103. http://www.texastribune.org/2012/11/29/texas-high-school-graduation-rates-climb-why/

104. http://www.theatlantic.com/business/archive/2016/03/texas-experiments-with-teaching-english-language-learners/472401/

105. http://www.lbb.state.tx.us/Documents/Publications/GEER/Government_Effectiveness_and_Efficiency_Report_2015.pdf

106. 1996–1997 Report on High School Completion Rates (August 1999), TEA. Includes graduated, continued, or received GED. https://rptsvr1.tea.texas.gov/acctres/completion/2014/state_demo_4yr.html; Texas Education Agency, Secondary School Completion and Dropouts in Texas Public Schools, 2014–2015, August 2016.

107. http://www.texastribune.org/2015/02/20/texas-high-school-graduation-rate-behind-only-iowa/

108. http://www.texastribune.org/2012/11/29/texas-high-school-graduation-rates-climb-why/

109. http://www.statesman.com/news/news/state-regional-govt-politics/private-school-voucher-bills-face-backlash/nkf2q/

110. https://tshaonline.org/handbook/online/articles/fla15

111. https://www.tshaonline.org/handbook/online/articles/khp02

112. http://www.dallasnews.com/business/energy/20140531-oil-boom-sweeps-money-to-texas-universities.ece

113. https://www.texastribune.org/2015/03/17/deregulating-tuition-slowed-increase-universities-/

114. http://www.tacc.org/pages/data-and-info/community-college-enrollment

115. http://www.bovinevetonline.com/news/industry/does-texas-need-another-veterinary-school

116. http://www.texastribune.org/2015/08/27/where-suburban-texans-commute-work/

117. http://www.texastribune.org/2012/12/03/tolling-texans-impact-trans-texas-corridor-lingers/

118. https://stateimpact.npr.org/texas/tag/drought/

119. http://www.tceq.texas.gov/drinkingwater/trot/droughtw.html; http://www.nytimes.com/2013/03/24/us/in-texas-suburbs-water-restrictions-are-touchy-subject.html

120. https://2017.texasstatewaterplan.org/statewide

121. http://www.texastribune.org/2015/01/30/after-prop-6-water-politics-back-friday-night-foot/

122. Ibid.

123. https://stateimpact.npr.org/texas/tag/drought/

124. http://www.eia.gov/state/analysis.cfm?sid=TX&CFID=11103414&CFTOKEN=1a9f2eea7192e350-8E2301DF-5056-A727-59708466E4F1AFC-C&jsessionid=84308525203915367d-585e255711726d3731

125. https://www.texastribune.org/2011/02/08/texplainer-why-does-texas-have-its-own-power-grid/

126. http://www.texastribune.org/2014/10/20/big-tax-break-natural-gas-get-scrutiny/

127. http://lubbockonline.com/business/2016-03-05/wind-energy-technology-booms-increases-role-texas-electricity-power#

128. Erica Grieder. 2013. *Big, Hot, Cheap, and Right: What America Can Learn from the Strange Genius of Texas*. New York: Public Affairs Books, 23.

CREDITS

PHOTOS

Chapter 1

p. 2: The Lydia Hill Texas Collection of Photographs in Carol M. Highsmith's America Project, Library of Congress, Prints and Photographs Division; p. 7: The Lydia Hill Texas Collection of Photographs in Carol M. Highsmith's America Project, Library of Congress, Prints and Photographs Division; p. 14: © The Dallas Morning News, Inc.; p. 20: Russell Lee Photograph Collection, e_rl_14646_0038, The Dolph Briscoe Center for American History, the University of Texas at Austin; p. 29: Marjorie Kamys Cotera/Bob Daemmrich Photography/Alamy Stock Photo

Chapter 2

p. 32: Star of the Republic Museum; p. 35: Wilson Special Collections Library University of North Carolina at Chapel Hill; p. 36: Dolph Briscoe Center for American History; p. 39: AP Photo/Eric Gay; p. 46: Bob Daemmrich; p. 52: David Horsey

Chapter 3

p. 66: Office of Governor Greg Abbott; p. 69: © The Dallas Morning News, Inc; p. 73: dpa picture alliance/Alamy Stock Photo; p. 74: Jay Janner/Austin American-Stateman; Courtesy Dallas Historical Society. Used by permission; p. 87: AP Photo/Jacquelyn Martin

Chapter 4

p. 96: Michael Ciaglo/©Houston Chronicle. Used with permission; p. 111: FREDERIC J. BROWN/AFP/Getty Images; John Branch Editorial Cartoon used with the permission of John Branch, King Features Syndicate and the Cartoonist Group. All rights reserved. Marie D. De Jesus/© Houston Chronicle. Used with permission; p. 128: JENNIFER WHITNEY/The New York Times/Redux

Chapter 5

p. 132: From Fort Worth Star-Telegram, May 12, 2016 © 2016 McClatchy. All rights reserved. Used by permission and protected by the Copyright Laws of the United States. The printing, copying, redistribution, or retransmission of this content without express written permission is prohibited; p. 138: Photo by Dan Keshet; p. 142: Alan Shivers campaign flyer; p. 146: Nick Anderson Editorial Cartoon used with the permission of Nick Anderson, the Washington Post Writers Group and the Cartoonist Group. All rights reserved; p. 153: © 2012 The Atlantic Media Co., as first published in The Atlantic Magazine. All rights reserved. Distributed by Tribune Content Agency, LLC; p. 154: Photo by Rick Scibelli/Getty Images; p. 160: AP Photo/Fred Kaufman

Chapter 6

p. 164: © The Dallas Morning News, Inc.; p. 166: RoadsideAmerica.com; p. 168: Farm and Ranch Freedom Alliance; p. 170: Mark Elias/Bloomberg via Getty Images; p. 174: Ryan Poppe; p. 176: © Bob Daemmrich; p. 187: 1970/140-1, Current Events Photographic Documentation Program collection, Courtesy of Texas State Library and Archives Commission

Chapter 7

p. 196: AP Photo/Eric Gay, File; p. 200: REUTERS/Mike Stone; p. 214: MARJORIE KAMY COTERA/TEXAS TRIBUNE; p. 216: Bob Daemmrich for The Texas Tribune; p. 219: Rodolfo Gonzalez/Austin American-Stateman via AP; p. 221: Texas Senate Media Services; p. 222: Jay Janner/Austin American-Statesman via AP; p. 223: AP Photo/Eric Gay

Chapter 8

p. 232: AP Photo/Alice Keeney; p. 235: ZUMA Press, Inc./Alamy Stock Photo; p. 243: Juanito M. Garza/San Antonio Express-News; p. 252: Johnny Hanson/© Houston Chronicle. Used with permission; p. 255: Baylor Collections of Political Materials, W.R. Poage Legislative Library, Baylor University, Waco, Texas; p. 259: Dolph Briscoe Center for American History

Chapter 9

p. 266: Texas Senate Media Services; p. 271: Mark Greenberg/Humane Society; p. 276: Kerwin Plevka/© Houston Chronicle. Used with permission; p. 282: AP Photo/Stephen Savoia; p. 285: Marjorie Kamys Cotera/Daemmrich Photography; p. 288: AP Photo/Juan Carlos Llorca, File; p. 289: John Dumont/Helibacon

Chapter 10
p. 302: The Lydia Hill Texas Collection of Photographs in Carol M. Highsmith's America Project, Library of Congress, Prints and Photographs Division; p. 307: Rodolfo Gonzalez/Austin American-Statesman via AP; p. 320: Mexico's Jalisco state prosecutor's office via AP, File; p. 330: Texas Court of Criminal Appeals

Chapter 11
p. 338: Jon Shapley/© Houston Chronicle. Used with permission; p. 340: Waller County Sheriff's Department via AP, File; p. 342: Houston Chronicle, Nick Anderson; p. 345: Photo by Taylor Hill/Getty Images; p. 348: AP Photo/Houston Chronicle, Marya Beltran; p. 349: Courtesy of the Texas Department of Criminal Justice; p. 356: Nick Anderson Editorial Cartoon used with the permission of Nick Anderson, the Washington Post Writers Group and the Cartoonist Group. All rights reserved; p. 363: Jeff Wilson Photography; p. 364: © The Dallas Morning News

Chapter 12
p. 368: J. G. Domke/Alamy Stock Photo; p. 372: Nick Anderson, Houston Chronicle; p. 375: REUTERS/Jim Young; p. 376: Deborah Cannon/Austin American-Statesman via AP; p. 378: © The Dallas Morning News, Inc.; p. 384: Ruben R. Ramirez/El Paso Times; p. 387: AP Photo/Wilfredo Lee; p. 398: NASA, Images taken by the Thematic Mapper sensor aboard Landsat 5. Source: USGS Landsat Missions Gallery, "San Antonio, Texas 1991-2010," U.S. Department of the Interior / U.S. Geological Survey.

Chapter 13
p. 402: The Lydia Hill Texas Collection of Photographs in Carol M. Highsmith's America Project, Library of Congress, Prints and Photographs Division; p. 408: Patrick Michels/Texas Observer; p. 409: REX C. CURRY/The New York Times; p. 411: Patric Schneider Photo; p. 417: Jay Janner/Austin American-Statesman via AP; p. 427: Todd Heisler/The New York Times/Redux; p. 432: AP Photo/Eric Gay

FIGURES

Chapter 1
p. 5: University of Texas Libraries: http://www.mappery.com/map-of/Ethnolinguistic-Distribution-of-Native-Texas-Indians-from-1500-and-1776-Map; p. 10: iStock icons; p. 12: Texas Comptroller of Public Accounts; p. 16:U.S. Census Bureau; Population Projections; p. 21: Office of the State Demographer, Population Projections; p. 27: Texas Politics Project/University of Texas Polls; Texas Politics Project/University of Texas Poll, February 2014

Chapter 2
p. 43: Texas State Historical Association; p. 56: Source: Texas Legislative Council; p. 58: Source: Texas Secretary of State, Election returns; p. 60: Source: Book of States

Chapter 3
p. 76: Source: Texas Tribune Poll, February 2015; p. 77: Source: Texas Tribune Polling, February 2014; p. 79: Source: U.S. Census Bureau; p. 80: Source: Legislative Budget Board; p. 82: roccomontoya/iStockphoto

Chapter 4
p. 100: Source: Texas Secretary of State; p. 102: Source: Texas Secretary of State website; p. 108: Source: Texas Secretary of State; p. 110: Source: U.S. Census; p. 115: Source: U.S. Elections Project; p. 124: Source: National Institute on Money in State Politics; p. 126: Texas Secretary of State, Austin Community College Center for Public Policy and Political Studies

Chapter 5
p. 136: Source: Texas Ethics Commission; p. 140: Source: Republican Party of Texas and Texas Democratic Party; p. 147: Source: Legislative Reference Library of Texas; p. 148: Source: Texas Politics Polling; p. 152: Source: Folded Ranney Index; p. 156: Source: Texas Legislative Reference Library

Chapter 6
p. 172: Source: US Bureau of Labor Statistics, 2015 Annual Averages; p. 180: Source: Texas Ethics Commission annuals reports; p. 181: Source: Texas Ethics Commission annual reports; p. 185: Source: National Council of State Legislatures; p. 191: Source: Texas Ethics Commission

Chapter 7
p. 202: Source: Influence Opinions; p. 204: Source: Data taken from the Texas Legislative Library; p. 205: Source: National Council of State Legislatures; p. 208: Source: Texas Legislative Online; p. 213: Source: Guide to Legislative Information (revised) 2015, Texas Legislative Council for the 84th Legislature; p. 225: Source: State Ideologies Project; p. 227: Source: Texas Legislative Council; p. 229: Source: Texas Tribune "84th Texas Legislature, by the numbers."

Chapter 8
p. 236: Source: Texas State Library and Archives; p. 238: Source: Book of States, Bureau of the Census; p. 240: Source: Legislative Reference Library; p. 242: Source: Office of the Governor in each state; p. 245: Source: Book

of the States; p. 247: Source: Texas Reference Library; p. 248: Source: Texas Reference Library; p. 257: Source: Website of Governor Greg Abbott; p. 258: Source: State of the State Speeches, Legislative Reference Library; p. 261: Governor Institutional Power Index (updated measures, based on Beyle 1983)

Chapter 9

p. 270: Source: US Census Bureau; p. 272: Source: Texas Governor Website; p. 279: Source: Paul Nolette, 2015, *Federalism on Trial: State Attorney General and National Policymaking in Contemporary America.* Lawrence, KS: University of Kansas Press; p. 280: Source: Attorney General's Office; p. 284: Source: Texas Comptroller's Office; p. 296: Source: Texas Sunset Advisory Commission

Chapter 10

p. 306: Source: Center for State Courts; p. 310: Source: The Texas Judicial Branch; p. 313: Source: Annual Statistical Report for the Texas Judiciary, 2015; p. 315: Source: Texas Legislative Council; p. 318: Source: Annual Statistical Report of the Texas Judiciary, 2015; p. 319: Source: 2015 Annual Judicial Statistical Report; p. 322: Source: American Judicature Society; p. 329: Source: Texas Ethics Commission; p. 331: Source: 2015 Annual Texas Judicial Statistical Report

Chapter 11

p. 343: Source: Texas Tribune poll, February 2015; p. 350: Source: Bureau of Justice Statistics, 2014; p. 352: Source: Bureau of Justice Statistics, National Prisoner Statistics Program; p. 354: Source: Texas Department of Criminal Justice , Statistical Report Fiscal Year 2014; p. 357: Source Texas Department of Criminal Justice, 2015; p. 361: Source: The Sentencing Project

Chapter 12

p. 374: Source: US Census Bureau; p. 382: Author created; p. 386: Source: US Census Bureau; p. 391: Source: County Election Websites; p. 393: Source: Texas State Expenditures, Texas Comptroller of Public Accounts, 2014; p. 395: Source: Texas Comptroller of Public Accounts

Chapter 13

p. 405: Source: Texas Comptroller of Public Accounts; p. 406: Source: Tax Foundation; p. 412: Source: Texas Politics Polling, February 2015; p. 415: Source: Adapted from Senate Research Center, Budget 101: A Guide to the Budget Process in Texas, January 2011; p. 418: Source: Texas Comptroller of Public Accounts; p. 423: Source: http://www.dallasnews.com/news/local-news/20160117-texas-trailing-florida-in-obamacare-sign-ups.ece, 2014–2016; p. 430: Source: US Census Bureau Annual Survey of School Systems; p. 437: Source: https://2017.texasstatewaterplan.org/statewide

INDEX

Note: Page numbers followed by *f* and *t* indicate figures and tables, respectively.